THE WESTERN HERITAGE
since 1648

[FRONTISPIECE] The Dream of Reason Produces Monsters is from the series of paintings and prints called *Caprichos* by the Spanish artist Francisco Goya (1746–1828). The finished version shown here was completed about 1799; the Museo del Prado in Madrid has earlier sketches of it. The Dream of Reason has been variously interpreted, but critics generally emphasize Goya's apparent early recognition that reason is by no means the only, or even necessarily the ruling, force in the human personality. Goya's work with its alarming, threatening background, foreshadows awareness of the irrational, the unconscious, the "dark" dimensions of the mind—all of which played a large part in the Romantic movement and in the writings of many twentieth-century intellectuals. [Philadelphia Museum of Art, Philadelphia. (The Smith, Kline and French Laboratories Collection.)] Other Goya works will be found on page 630 and in the color album.

THE WESTERN HERITAGE

since 1648

DONALD KAGAN
STEVEN OZMENT
FRANK M. TURNER

Yale University

MACMILLAN PUBLISHING CO., INC.

New York

NOTE

The dates cited for monarchs and popes are generally the
years of their reigns rather than of their births and deaths.

MACMILLAN PUBLISHING CO., INC.
866 Third Avenue, New York, New York 10022

COLLIER MACMILLAN CANADA, LTD.

Library of Congress Cataloging in Publication Data

Kagan, Donald.
   The Western heritage, since 1648.

   Includes bibliographies and index.
   1. Civilization, Occidental. 2. Civilization,
Modern. I. Ozment, Steven E., joint author.
II. Turner, Frank Miller, joint author. III. Title.
CB245.K29 1979   909'.09'821   78-16642
ISBN 0-02-361860-4

Printing: 3 4 5 6 7 8   Year: 9 0 1 2 3 4 5

Preface

The Western Heritage recounts the experience of the peoples—primarily European—who shaped and in turn were formed by the civilization of the West. Although it owes much to earlier cultures, particularly those of the Near East, Western civilization proper began in ancient Greece and Rome. It received an infusion of new religious values and institutions from Christianity, and it devised new political and social systems during the European Middle Ages. The years of the Reformation witnessed a profound religious revolution and counterrevolution that has divided Western culture to the present day. Yet in the same era Western peoples settled the lands of North and South America and established commercial routes across the globe. The forces that made for an intellectual and artistic Renaissance brought further confidence to the West and paved the path for the Scientific Revolution and the Enlightenment. Since the seventeenth century the nations of the West have transformed their own societies and governments through industrialization, liberal democracy, and various models of socialism. Technological and military power allowed the nations of the West to dominate major portions of the rest of the world with immense consequences for both themselves and for the peoples they dominated. Even when societies outside the West have rejected the Western pattern, they have often used Western values, political ideologies, and technology to do so. Consequently, for better or worse the civilization of the West has become the most influential culture of the world.

For most people who live in the West, its society, values, and institutions seem normal, and those of other cultures appear peculiar. The opposite may in fact be true. Compared to other modes of life, the civilization that developed in Europe and spread abroad is unusual and even unique. In these pages, and within a fairly traditionally chronological framework, we describe some of that civilization's most important features and show how they evolved and molded the distinctive character of the West and in turn the nature of its impact on the rest of the world. We examine, for example, the special and complicated relationship between religion and the state. We trace the related theme of the growth of constitutional government and democracy, both of which stand as rare achievements in the human experience. The distinctive cultivation of rational thought is our third major concern. Through its influence on philosophy, natural science, and applied technology, such thought has produced unique ways of understanding and controlling physical nature. Finally, perhaps the most unusual feature of Western civilization, which, like the others mentioned here, should emerge from this account, is its cultivation of the faculty of criticism and the intensity with which the West has applied such criticism to its own experience. No other culture has committed itself so thoroughly to the Socratic proposition that the unexamined life is not worth living.

Because of these distinctive characteristics of its culture, Western civilization, unlike other civilizations, most notably that of ancient Egypt, did not reach a stable form early in its history and then stand still. On the contrary, religious turmoil, political conflict, a continuing struggle to master physical nature, the shifting balances of economic affairs, and the inclination toward self criticism produced in the West perhaps the most changeable and changing civilization in history. Another factor encouraging this cultural restlessness has been the habit of Western people to look to the past for guidance. Repeatedly when they have sought a better future, they have consulted their history and have found in it the source of diverse and often competitive ideals and models. In general, the people of the West have understood themselves to be heirs of a useful and instructive past. We hope to aid the reader in understanding the character and meaning of that heritage.

We do not write about Western civilization and its contacts with the rest of the world merely because it is our own. We think it impossible in the length of this work, a length determined by the time usually allotted for an introductory history survey, to do justice to all the world's civilizations and cultures. To render even incomplete justice to a single civilization is challenge enough. But we also believe that in recent years the study of the West has become relatively neglected in the worthy but perhaps vain attempt to provide within one work a comprehensive, balanced global outlook. The result has too frequently been an inadequate grasp not only of other cultures but of our own as well. Furthermore, in our time, the Western proclivity to self-criticism has led in some cases to a decline in the study of history itself. Some people apparently believe that the social and technological developments of this century—and the manifold problems in their wake—have forever separated the present from the past. We reject such an attitude. Men and women living in the West today are what they are, bearing their particular anxieties and holding their special hopes, because they possess a distinctive cultural and political heritage. We shall consider our task accomplished if the curious and serious reader leaves this work with a fuller appreciation of what it means to be such a Western person.

D. K.
S. O.
F. M. T.

New Haven, Connecticut

Contents

13

THE LATE MIDDLE AGES AND THE RENAISSANCE: DECLINE AND RENEWAL (1300–1527)

Contents **xi**

Contents **xiii**

32

EUROPE AND THE DEPRESSION OF THE 1930s

33

WORLD WAR II AND THE COLD WAR

34

EUROPE IN THE ERA OF THE SUPERPOWERS

Contents **XVii**

Documents

Illustrations in Color

Maps

by THEODORE R. MILLER

An Album of Illustrations in Color

[21] William Hogarth (1697–1764) did immensely popular paintings and etchings of scenes from the rich variety of English life in the eighteenth century. He was frequently satirical and witty, and his works make up a realistic survey of society from top to bottom. The dissolute party shown here is The Orgy, third in a series called The Rake's Progress. It dates from approximately 1734 and is in the Sir John Soane's Museum, London. [The Granger Collection.]

[22] Even when past the height of its medieval commercial power, Venice in the eighteenth century was a wealthy and unusually picturesque city. One of the numerous painters of its canals, festivals, and buildings was Giovanni Antonio Canaletto (1697–1768), represented here by his Stonemason's Yard, a behind-the-scenes picture of a humbler, seamier side of the city than that usually painted. Painted near 1740, it is in the National Gallery, London. [The Granger Collection.]

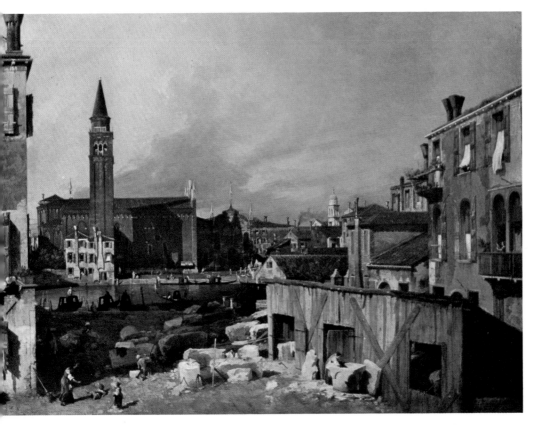

Color Album C17

[23] La Fontaine, by Jean Baptiste Siméon Chardin (1699–1779). Chardin was an important painter much admired by contemporaries such as Diderot for his pictures of quite ordinary people and situations in pre-Revolutionary France—a schoolmistress at work, a housewife returning from the market, and, shown here, the domestic scene of a woman drawing water and, probably, preparing to cook the meat hanging above her. The picture is in the National Gallery, London. [The Granger Collection.]

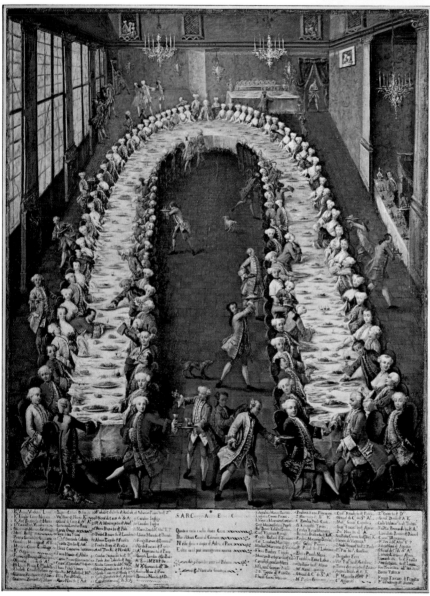

[24] In a painting attributed to Pietro Longhi (1702–1785), The Banquet at the Palazzo Nani, we see a self-conscious party of aristocratic Venetian ladies and gentlemen posing at a large formal dinner. The picture is in the Ca' Rezzonico in Venice. [SCALA/ Editorial Photocolor Archives.]

[25] A portion of the vast mid-eighteenth-century fresco that decorates the dining room of the bishop's residence, Würzburg, West Germany. The artist was Giambattista Tiepolo (1696–1770), and the building itself was designed by his contemporary, Balthasar Neumann (1687–1753). (See the illustration, page 575.) The scene is of the medieval ceremony of the royal investiture of a bishop (kneeling)—but with the principals portrayed in sixteenth-century dress. The overall fresco is one of the high points of Baroque decoration. [Adelmann/Editorial Photocolor Archives.]

[26] George Stubbs (1724–1806) was an artist with a special—even scientific—interest in animals, a concern that led him to dissect horses in order to get the creatures' anatomy just right. His works have been eagerly collected in this century. Lady and Gentleman in a Carriage (1787), seen here, is in the National Gallery, London. [The Granger Collection.]

[28 RIGHT] This handsome portrait (1788) of the eighteenth-century French chemist Antoine Lavoisier and his wife is by Jacques Louis David (1748–1825). Long owned by Rockefeller University, the picture was recently purchased by the Metropolitan Museum of Art, New York. Unlike Lavoisier, guillotined by the ungrateful French Revolutionists, the artist David lived to portray many events of the Revolution and the Napoleonic period. [The Granger Collection.]

[29 BELOW] The crucial naval battle of Trafalgar in 1805 between the English and the French fleets quickly caught the imagination of the English artist Joseph Mallard William Turner (1775–1851). He visited Nelson's ship immediately on its return to England with the admiral's body and in 1806 exhibited his first painting of the battle. The picture here (from the National Maritime Museum, London) is a later one (1820). Nelson's flagship, *Victory*, is in the center at the height of the battle. [The Granger Collection.]

[27 OPPOSITE, BELOW] Venice may have declined as a commercial power, but as a subject for its own artists and for those of other countries it was ever fascinating. In the generation following Canaletto, Francesco Guardi (1712–1793), as in this view of the Piazza San Marco, carried on the tradition of recording the city that was itself rapidly becoming a museum. The painting hangs in the National Gallery, London. [The Granger Collection.]

[31 OPPOSITE, TOP] The painter John Constable (1776–1837) failed to find wide popularity in his lifetime. He kept his attention on the peaceful English countryside that was destined to become the victim of industry, railways, and mines, and today we find his work an important record of a different world. This is his Haywain, painted in 1821. It hangs now in the National Gallery, London. [The Granger Collection.]

[32 OPPOSITE, BOTTOM] The hard, never-ending physical labor of the agricultural poor is the subject of The Gleaners by the Frenchman Jean François Millet (1814–1875). Millet is often thought over-sentimental, but this 1857 picture is a strong record of the necessary way of life of millions in the nineteenth century. It is in the Louvre, Paris. [The Granger Collection.]

[30] The work of the Spanish artist Francisco Goya (1746–1828), like David's, spanned Old Regime, Revolution, Napoleon, and Restoration. In 1814 he painted The Third of May 1808 in continuing revulsion and protest over the gunning down of Spanish hostages by French troops during the Napoleonic invasion of Spain. It remains a powerful indictment of human brutality and the horror of war. The painting is in the Prado, Madrid. [SCALA/Editorial Photocolor Archives.]

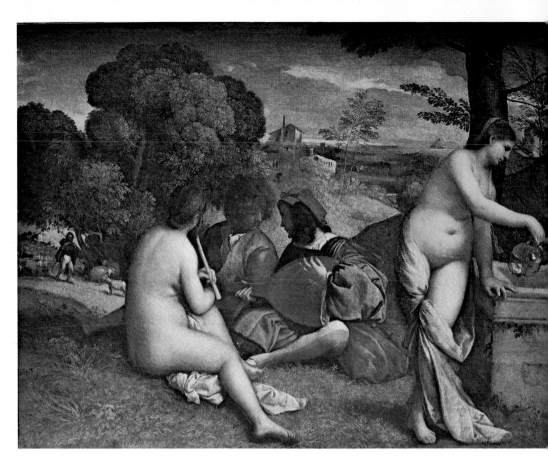

[33–34] Edouard Manet (1832–1883) created something of a scandal with his 1861 Luncheon on the Grass. The woman's undress was a shock to bourgeois attitudes, and official exhibition of the work was refused. Ironically, the arrangement of figures was almost identical with that of three undressed people in a famous Raphael drawing, and a similar grouping of clothed men and nude women by the Renaissance artist Giorgione (*ca.* 1476–1510), called Country Concert, had long hung quietly in the Louvre. Both the Giorgione [TOP] and the Manet [BOTTOM] are shown here, for they are both finally and happily displayed today in the Louvre. [SCALA/Editorial Photocolor Archives; The Granger Collection.]

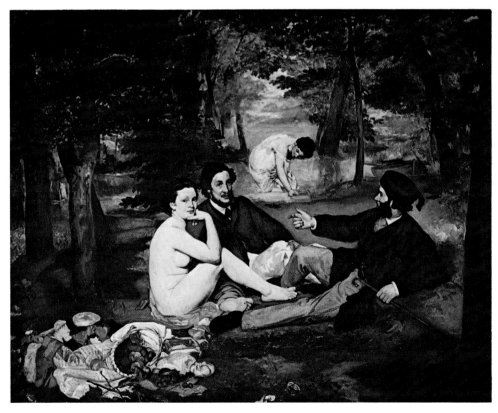

[35 OPPOSITE] Nineteenth-century Romanticism reached, literally, a reckless height in the castle of Neuschwanstein, ordered by the unstable King Ludwig II of the south German state of Bavaria. When the castle was built between 1858 and 1886, art and literature had taken on a character of realism; but architecture tended to remain elaborate and ornate—although Neuschwanstein in its spectacular setting was, of course, too extreme to be typical. [The Granger Collection.]

[36] The Third-Class Carriage (*ca.* 1860) is an example of the realism of the French artist Honoré Daumier (1808–1879). In addition to pictures with sharp political and social messages, Daumier produced such gentle, sympathetic works as this one of poor, almost defeated folk. It is in the Metropolitan Museum of Art, New York. [The Granger Collection.]

[37] The railway figures also in The Station at Penge (1871) by Camille Pissarro (1831–1903). Railroads caused a transportation revolution in the nineteenth century comparable to that of air travel in our own day, and artists were not long in creating a new kind of landscape that incorporated the new technological development. The machine, artists found, had esthetics of its own. This picture is in the Courtauld Institute, London. [The Granger Collection.]

[38] The Moulin de la Galette (1876) is by Pierre Auguste Renoir (1841–1919). One aspect of Parisian bourgeois leisure activity is illustrated in this painting of everyday friends of the artist enjoying the wine and the dancing at an outdoor café. The work is in the Louvre, Paris. [The Granger Collection.]

[39] This 1889 painting, The Starry Night by the Dutchman Vincent van Gogh (1853–1890), breaks out of earlier, more staid views of nature and the landscape. To van Gogh the heavens themselves are an exciting theater of colorful and continuing movement. [The Museum of Modern Art, New York.]

[40] Paul Cézanne (1839–1906) painted several pictures called The Card Players. Like the others, this one from about 1890 captures the personalities of its (probably) working-class subjects and is a realistic, unromanticized view of ordinary life. The painting is in the Jeu de Paume, Paris. [The Granger Collection.]

[41 BELOW, LEFT] Although the subject is too broad for such a narrow definition, "modern art" for many means abstract, nonrepresentational painting and sculpture. This aspect of modern painting is illustrated by the colorful Panel (3) by the Russian-French artist Wassily Kandinsky (1866–1944). Note that "modern" antedates World War I, for this work was painted in 1914. [The Museum of Modern Art, New York.]

[42 BELOW, RIGHT] Another popular Spanish artist—although he is taken less seriously by many critics—is Salvador Dali (born 1904). The odd, bleak landscape of his Persistence of Memory (1931) reminds some viewers of dreams and probably derives in part from the spread of Freud's ideas and general twentieth-century interest in the unconscious. [The Museum of Modern Art, New York.]

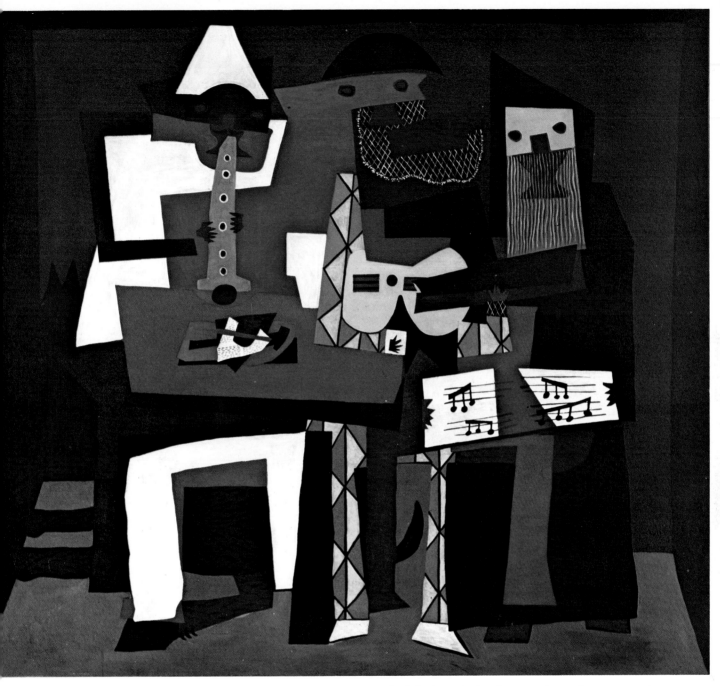

[43] Perhaps the best known painter of recent years is the Spaniard Pablo Picasso (1881–1973). His art went through a number of phases. The picture shown here, Three Musicians, comes from 1921 when he was interested in breaking his subjects down into planes, lines, and geometric bodies. [The Museum of Modern Art, New York.]

(Another Picasso painting in his later style is on page 898.)

[45 OPPOSITE] Family Group by the Englishman Henry Moore (born 1898) is a large bronze statue from the 1940s by one of the leading sculptors of the last few decades, most of whose pieces are effectively planned for outdoor display. This one is more clearly representational than others. [The Museum of Modern Art, New York.]

[44] The Holy Face by Georges Rouault (1871–1958) brings us back to a long-standing tradition of religious—specifically Christian—art. The 1933 painting of Christ, as well as other Rouault works, reveals the artist's earlier interest in stained glass, itself a largely religious art form, but with modern overtones. It is part of the collection of the Musée Nationale d'Art Moderne, Paris. [Editorial Photocolor Archives.]

[46–47] The Georges Pompidou National Center of Art and Culture in Paris, named for a recent president of France, was built in the 1970s to designs by an Italian-English team of architects, Renzo Piano and Richard Rogers. We spoke earlier of a Gothic structure's "skeleton" being, in a sense, external and visible. Here the designers have managed to make the building appear to be almost all skeleton and in the meantime have achieved a colorful display of its engineering and functional elements. [French Government Tourist Office, New York.]

THE WESTERN HERITAGE

LVDOVICVS XIIII DEI GRATIA FRANCIÆ
ET NAVARRÆ REX CHRISTIANISSIMVS.

W. Vaillant ad viuum faciebat cum Priuilegio Regis.   P. Vanschuppen Sculpebat 1660.

17
England and France in the Seventeenth Century

Constitutional Crisis and Settlement in Stuart England

BETWEEN 1603 and 1715 England experienced the most tumultuous years of its long history. In this period Puritan resistance to the Elizabethan religious settlement merged with fierce Parliamentary opposition to the aspirations to absolute monarchy of the Stuart kings. During these years no less than three foreigners occupied the English throne, and between 1649 and 1660 England was without a king altogether. Yet by the end of this century of crisis England was a model to Europe of limited monarchy, parliamentary government, and measured religious toleration.

James I

The first of England's foreign monarchs was James VI of Scotland, the son of Mary Stuart, queen of Scots, who in 1603 succeeded the childless Elizabeth as James I of England. This first Stuart king inherited not only the crown but also a royal debt of almost one-half million pounds, a fiercely divided church, and a Parliament already restive over the extent of his predecessor's claims to royal authority. Under James each of these problems worsened. The new king utterly lacked tact, was ignorant of English institutions, and strongly advocated the divine right of kings, a subject on which he had written a book in 1598 entitled *A Trew Law of Free Monarchies*. Both

King Louis XIV of France (1643–1715) at the age of twenty-two. Louis was the dominant European political figure in the second half of the seventeenth century, and the culture of his court was imitated throughout Europe. This rare 1660 portrait is by the engraver Van Schuppen after a painting by W. Vaillant. Its subject should be compared with the aged Louis shown on page 459. [Charles Farrell Collection.]

Parliament and the politically powerful Puritans were rapidly alienated.

The breach with Parliament was opened by James's seeming usurpation of the power of the purse. Royal debts and his own extravagance made it necessary for the king to be constantly in quest of additional revenues. These he sought to a large degree by levying—solely on the authority of an ill-defined royal prerogative—new custom duties known as tonnage and poundage. Parliament resented such independent efforts to raise revenues as an affront to its power, and the result was a long and divisive court struggle between the king and Parliament.

As the distance between the king and Parliament widened, the religious problems also worsened. The Puritans, who were prominent among the lesser landed gentry and within Parliament, had hoped that James's experience with the Scottish Presbyterian Church would incline him to favor their efforts to purify the Anglican Church. Since the days of Elizabeth the Puritans had sought to eliminate elaborate religious ceremonies and to replace the hierarchical episcopal system of church governance with a more representative presbyterian form like that of the Calvinist churches on the Continent. In January 1604 they had their first direct dealing with the new king. James responded in that month to a statement of Puritan grievances, the so-called Millenary Petition, at a special religious conference at Hampton Court. To the dismay of the Puritans the king firmly declared his intention to maintain and even enhance the episcopacy. "A Scottish presbytery," he snorted, "agreeth as well with monarchy as God and the devil." Nonconformists were clearly forewarned.

Both sides departed the conference with their worst suspicions of one another largely confirmed, and as the years passed the distrust between them only deepened. It was during James's reign in 1620 that Puritan separatists founded Plymouth Colony in Cape Cod Bay, preferring flight from England to Anglican conformity. The Hampton Court conference did, however, sow one fruitful seed. A commission was appointed to render a new

435

EUROPE IN 1648

SWEDISH DOMINIONS

BRANDENBURG-PRUSSIA

SPANISH MONARCHY

AUSTRIA HAPSBURGS

CHURCH LANDS

NORWAY

Bergen

Christiana

S W E D

FINLAND

Reva

ESTON

Stockholm

Stavanger

KINGDOM OF DENMARK AND NORWAY

LIVON

Riga

COURLAND

SCOTLAND

Edinburgh

NORTH SEA

DENMARK

Copenhagen

Memel

Danzig

EAS PRUSS

Belfast

SCHLESWIG

HOLSTEIN

BALTIC SEA

IRELAND

Dublin

York

ENGLAND

BOUNDARY OF THE EMPIRE

P

Cork

WALES

London

UNITED PROVINCES

Posen

Warsaw

ATLANTIC

Bristol

SPANISH NETH.

BRANDEN-BURG

Plymouth

Brussels

SAXONY

Breslau

SILESIA

Cracow

GA

Rouen

MINOR

HESSE

GERMAN

STATES

Prague

BOHEMIA

MORAVIA

HUNGARY

Reims

Paris

Orleans

Pressburg

OCEAN

Nantes

Tours

BAVARIA

AUSTRIA

Vienna

Budape

FRANCE

FRANCHE COMTÉ

SWITZ.

AUSTRIAN

HUNGA

Lyons

SAVOY

VENICE

CROATIA

SLAVONIA

SAVE

Bordeaux

PIED-MONT

MILAN

PAR.

Venice

BOSNIA

Belgrad

SERVI

Toulouse

LANGUEDOC

AVIGNON

MOD.

Genoa

LUCCA

Bologna

ADRIATIC SEA

Spalato

MONTE-NEGRO

Marseilles

TUSCANY

PAPAL STATES

Cattaro

León

NAVARRE

Burgos

CORSICA (GEN.)

ITALY

Rome

ALBANI

Oporto

Salamanca

Saragossa

CASTILE

ARAGON

Barcelona

Capua

Bari

PORTUGAL

Madrid

Naples

Lisbon

Toledo

SPAIN

BALEARIC IS.

SARDINIA (SP.)

KINGDOM OF THE TWO SICILIES

Cordova

MEDITER

Seville

Granada

Cadiz

SICILY

Tangier (PORT.)

Ceuta (SP.)

Algiers

ALGERIA

Tunis (OTT.)

RANEAN

FEZ & MOROCCO

436   *England and France in the Seventeenth Century*

James VI (of Scotland) and I (of England, 1603–1625), the first of the ill-fated Stuart line of England's monarchs. The artist is unknown. [The Granger Collection.]

OPPOSITE: At the end of the Thirty Years' War Spain still had extensive possessions, Austria and Brandenburg-Prussia were prominent, the independence of the United Provinces and Switzerland was recognized, and Sweden held important river mouths in north Germany.

translation of the Bible, a mission fulfilled in 1611 when the Authorized or King James Version of the Bible was published.

Though he inherited major political and religious difficulties, James also created special problems for himself. His court became a center of scandal and corruption. He governed by favorites, the most influential of whom was the duke of Buckingham, whom rumor made the king's homosexual lover. Buckingham controlled royal patronage and openly sold peerages and titles to the highest bidders—a practice that angered the nobility, who found that it cheapened their rank. James's pro-Spanish foreign policy also displeased Englishmen. In 1604 he concluded a much needed peace with Spain, England's chief adversary of the

Portrait of King Charles I of England hunting, by Anthony van Dyck (1599–1641). Charles was executed by order of Parliament in 1649 following the rise to power of Oliver Cromwell who, among other things, then sold the royal picture collection, so that this portrait is now in France. [Musée du Louvre, Paris. Cliché des Musées Nationaux.]

extra-Parliamentary measures. He levied new imposts, attempted to collect discontinued taxes, and even subjected the English people to a so-called forced loan (a tax theoretically to be repaid), imprisoning those who refused to pay. Troops in transit to war zones were quartered in private English homes.

When Parliament met in 1628, its members were furious. Taxes were being illegally collected for a war that was going badly for England and that now, through royal blundering, involved France as well as Spain. Parliament expressed its displeasure by making the king's request for new funds conditional upon his recognition of the Petition of Right. This major document of constitutional freedom declared that henceforth there should be no forced loans or taxation without the consent of Parliament, that no free man should be imprisoned without due cause, and that troops should not be billeted in private homes. Though Charles agreed to the petition, there was little confidence that he would keep his word.

In January 1629 Parliament further underscored its resolve to circumscribe royal prerogative. It declared religious innovations leading to "popery"—Charles's high-church policies were meant—and the levying of taxes without Parliamentary consent acts of treason. Perceiving that things were getting out of hand, Charles promptly dissolved Parliament and did not recall it again until 1640, when war with Scotland forced him to do so.

To conserve his limited resources, Charles made peace with France and Spain in 1629 and 1630, respectively. His finance minister, Thomas Wentworth, earl of Stafford, instituted a policy of "thorough," that is, strict efficiency and administrative centralization in government. This policy aimed at absolute royal control of England and required for its success the king's ability to operate independently of Parliament. Every legal fund-raising device was exploited to the full. Neglected laws suddenly came to be enforced, and existing taxes were extended into new areas. An example of the latter tactic was the inland collection of "ship money." This tax was normally levied only on coastal areas to pay for naval protection, but after

sixteenth century. His subjects viewed it as a sign of pro-Catholic sentiment on his part. Suspicions were further increased when James attempted unsuccessfully to relax the penal laws against Catholics. Englishmen had not forgotten the brutal reign of Mary Tudor and the acts of treason by Catholics during Elizabeth's reign. In 1618 James hesitated, not unwisely, to rush English troops to the aid of Protestants in Germany at the outbreak of the Thirty Years' War. This hesitation caused his loyalty to the Anglican Church to be openly questioned. In the king's last years, as his health failed and the reins of government were increasingly given over to his son Charles and Buckingham, Parliamentary power and Protestant sentiment combined to undo his pro-Spanish foreign policy. In 1624 England entered a continental war against Spain.

Charles I

Charles I (1625–1649) flew even more brazenly in the face of Parliament and the Puritans than did his father. Unable to receive adequate funds from Parliament to prosecute the Spanish war, Charles also resorted to

Parliament Attacks Charles I's Royal Abuses of His Subjects

The tension between King Charles I (1625–1649) and Parliament had very few causes that did not go back to earlier reigns. The Petition of Right can, therefore, be seen as a general catalogue of reasons for opposing arbitrary royal power. Specifically, angered by Charles and his levying of new taxes and other revenue-gathering devices, his coercion of freemen, and his quartering of troops in transit in private homes, Parliament refused to grant the king any funds until he rescinded such practices by recognizing the Petition of Right (June 7, 1628). Here is the Petition and the king's reply.

[*The Lords Spiritual and Temporal, and Commons in Parliament assembled*] *do humbly pray your Most Excellent Majesty, that no man hereafter be compelled to make or yield any gift, loan, benevolence, tax, or such like charge, without common consent by Act of Parliament; and that none be called to make answer, or take such oath, or to give attendance, or be confined, or otherwise molested or disquieted concerning the same, or for refusal thereof; and that no freeman, in any such manner as is before-mentioned, be imprisoned or detained; and that your Majesty will be pleased to remove the said soldiers and mariners* [*who have been quartered in private homes*]*, and that your people may not be so burdened in time to come; and that the foresaid commissions for proceeding by martial law, may be revoked and annulled; and that hereafter no commissions of like nature may issue forth to any person or persons whatsoever, to be executed as aforesaid, lest by colour of them any of your Majesty's subjects be destroyed or put to death, contrary to the laws and francise of the land.*

All which they most humbly pray of your Most Excellent Majesty, as their rights and liberties according to the laws and statutes of this realm.

[THE KING'S REPLY: *The King willeth that right be done according to the laws and customs of the realm; and that the statutes be put in due execution, that his subjects may have no cause to complain of any wrong or oppressions, contrary to their just rights and liberties, to the preservation whereof he holds himself as well obliged as of his prerogative.*]

The Constitutional Documents of the Puritan Revolution, ed. by Samuel R. Gardiner (Oxford, England: Clarendon Press, 1889), pp. 4–5.

1634 it was gradually applied to the whole of England, interior and coastal towns alike. A great landowner named John Hampden unsuccessfully challenged its extension in a close legal contest. Although the king prevailed, it was a costly victory, for it deepened the animosity toward him among the powerful landowners, who both elected Parliament and sat in Parliament.

Charles had neither the royal bureaucracy nor the standing army to rule as an absolute monarch. This became abundantly clear when he and his religious minister, William Laud (1573–1645; after 1633 the archbishop of Canterbury), provoked a war with Scotland. They tried to impose the English episcopal system and the Anglican prayer book upon the Scots as they had done throughout England. From his position within the Court of High Commission, Laud had already radicalized the Puritans by denying them the right to publish and preach.

When the Presbyterian Scots invaded England in 1640, Charles was forced to seek assistance from a Parliament that opposed his policies almost as much as the foreign invaders. Led by John Pym (1584–1643), Parliament refused even to consider funds for war until the king agreed to redress a long list of political and religious grievances. The result was the king's immediate dissolution of Parliament—hence its name, the Short Parliament (April–May 1640). But by November 1640 Charles was forced to reconvene Parliament, this time on the latter's terms and for what would be a long and most fateful duration.

THE LONG PARLIAMENT. The landowners and the merchant classes represented by Parliament had resented the king's financial measures and paternalistic rule for some time. To this resentment was added the fervent Puritan opposition. Hence the Long Parliament (1640–1660) acted with widespread support and general unanimity when it convened in November 1640. Disgraced and convicted by a Parliamentary bill of attainder, Charles's chief minister, Thomas Wentworth, was executed in 1641. Archbishop Laud was imprisoned and executed in 1645. The Court of Star Chamber and the

The House of Commons in session in 1648 toward the end of the Civil War, as seen in a contemporary engraving. [The Granger Collection.]

Court of High Commission, royal instruments of political and religious "thorough," respectively, were abolished. The levying of new taxes without consent of Parliament and the inland extension of ship money were declared illegal. Finally, it was resolved that no more than three years should elapse between meetings of Parliament and that Parliament could not be dissolved without its own consent.

There remained division within Parliament, however, over the precise direction of religious reform. Extremists—the Independents—wanted the complete abolition of the episcopal system and the *Book of Common Prayer*. The more moderate Puritan majority—the Presbyterians—wanted rather to reshape both along Calvinist State-Church lines. There were also a considerable number of conservatives in both houses who were determined to preserve the English church in its current form.

The division within Parliament was further intensified in October 1641, when a rebellion erupted in Ireland requiring an army to suppress it. Pym and his followers, loudly reminding the House of Commons of the king's past misdeeds, argued that Charles could not be trusted with an army and that Parliament should become the commander-in-chief of English armed forces. Parliamentary conservatives, who had winced once at Puritan religious reforms, winced thrice at this bold departure from English practice.

Charles saw the division within Parliament as a last chance to regain power. In January 1642 he invaded Parliament with his soldiers. He intended to arrest Pym and the other leaders, but they had been forewarned and managed to escape. Shocked by the king's action, a majority of the House of Commons thereafter passed the Militia Ordinance, a measure that gave Parliament control of the army.

The die was now cast. Charles assembled his forces at Nottingham, and in August the civil war began to determine whether England would be ruled by an absolute monarchy or by a parliamentary government and whether English religion would be conformist high Anglican and controlled by the king's bishops or tempered by a significant degree of decentralization and pluralism. Charles's supporters, known as *Cavaliers*, were located in the northwestern half of England. The Parliamentary opposition, known as *Roundheads*, had its stronghold in the southeastern half of the country. The nobility, identifying the power of their peerage with the preservation of the current form of the monarchy and the church, became prominent supporters of the king, whereas the townsmen were conspicuous in support of the Parliamentary army.

Oliver Cromwell and the Puritan Republic

Two factors led finally to Parliament's victory. The first was an alliance with Scotland in 1643 consummated when Pym signed the Solemn League and Covenant. The second was the reorganization of the Parliamentary army under Oliver Cromwell (1599–1658), a middle-aged country squire of iron discipline and strong Independent religious sentiment. Cromwell and his "godly men" favored neither the episcopal system of the king nor the presbyterian system of the Solemn League and Covenant.

Oliver Cromwell who, following the execution of Charles I, transformed England into a Puritan Republic and ruled as "Lord Protector" from 1553 until his death. The painting is by Samuel Cooper and is at Sidney Sussex College, Cambridge. [Bettmann Archive.]

The bleeding head of Charles I is exhibited to the crowd after his execution on a cold day in January 1649. The contemporary Dutch artist also professed to see the immediate ascension of Charles's soul to heaven. In fact, to many the king was seen as a martyr. [The Granger Collection.]

They wanted instead to let every congregation be its own master. The allies won the Battle of Marston Moor in 1644, the largest engagement of the war, and in June 1645 Cromwell's New Model Army, which fought with a disciplined fanaticism, decisively defeated the king at Naseby.

Though defeated militarily, Charles again took advantage of the deep divisions within Parliament, this time seeking to win the Presbyterians and the Scots over to the royalist side. But Cromwell's army firmly imposed its will. In December 1648 Colonel Pride physically barred the Presbyterians, who made up a majority of Parliament, from taking their seats. After "Pride's Purge," only a "rump" of less than fifty members remained. Though small in numbers, this Independent Rump Parliament had supreme military power within England. It did not hesitate to use this power. On January 30, 1649, after trial by a special court, it executed Charles as a public criminal and thereafter abolished the monarchy, the House of Lords, and the Anglican Church. The revolution was consummated.

From 1649 to 1660 England was officially a Puritan republic under Oliver Cromwell. Cromwell's army conquered Ireland and Scotland, creating the single political entity of Great Britain. Cromwell, however, was a military man and no politician. He was increasingly frustrated by what seemed to him to be pettiness and dawdling on the part of Parliament. When in 1653 the House of Commons entertained a motion to disband the expensive army of fifty thousand men, Cromwell responded by marching in and disbanding Parliament. He ruled thereafter as Lord Protector.

But his military dictatorship proved no more effective and became just as harsh and hated as Charles's rule had been. Cromwell's great army and foreign adventures inflated his budget to three times that of Charles's. Trade and commerce suffered throughout England, as near chaos reigned in many places. Puritan regulation of the moral life, which forbade such pastimes as theaters, dancing, and drunkenness, was resented. Cromwell's treatment of

---

The Regicides Deliver the Death Warrant of Charles I

This is the formal document, dated January 29, 1649, by which the court that convicted Charles I of England instructed that the sentence of death be carried out.

Whereas *Charles Stuart, King of England, is, and standeth convicted, attainted, and condemned of high treason, and other high crimes; and sentence upon Saturday last was pronounced against him by this Court, to be put to death by the severing of his head from his body; of which sentence, execution yet remaineth to be done; these are therefore to will and require you to see the said sentence executed in the open street before Whitehall, upon the morrow, being the thirtieth day of this instant month of January, between the hours of ten in the morning and five in the afternoon of the same day, with full effect. And for so doing this shall be your sufficient warrant. And these are to require all officers, soldiers, and others, the good people of this nation of England, to be assisting unto you in this service.*

To Col. Francis Hacker, Col. Huncks, and Lieut.-Col. Phayre, and to every one of them.

Given under our hands and seals.

John Branshaw.
Thomas Grey.
Oliver Cromwell.
Etc. Etc.

The Constitutional Documents of the Puritan Revolution 1628–1660, ed. by Samuel R. Gardiner (Oxford, England: Clarendon Press, 1889), p. 290.

Anglicans came to be just as intolerant as Charles's treatment of Puritans had been. And Cromwell was unable to get along even with the new Parliaments that were elected under the auspices of his army. By the time of his death in 1658, a majority of Englishmen were ready to end the Puritan experiment and return to the traditional institutions of government.

Charles II and Restoration of the Monarchy

The Stuart monarchy was restored in 1660 when Charles II (1660–1685) returned to England amid great rejoicing. A man of considerable charm and political skill, Charles set a refreshing new tone after eleven years of somber Puritanism. Politically and religiously his restoration returned England to the status quo of 1642.

Because of his secret Catholic sympathies the king favored a policy of religious toleration. He wanted to allow all persons outside the Church of England, Catholics as well as Puritans, to worship freely so long as they remained loyal to the throne. But the ultraroyalist Anglicans—the Tories—in Parliament decided otherwise. They did not believe patriotism and religion could be so disjointed. Between 1661 and 1665, through a series of laws known as the Clarendon Code, Parliament excluded Roman Catholics, Presbyterians, and Independents from the religious and political life of the nation. Penalties were imposed for attending non-Anglican worship services, strict adherence to the *Book of Common Prayer* and the Thirty-Nine Articles was required, and all who desired to serve in local government were made to swear oaths of allegiance to the Church of England. The Whigs in Parliament opposed this suppression of the Puritans, but they were not strong enough to override the Tory majority.

Under Charles II England also launched a bold new foreign policy, challenging the Dutch to become Europe's commercial and business center. Navigation Acts were passed that required all imports into England to be carried either in English ships or in ships registered to the same country as the imports they carried. Because the Dutch were original suppliers of hardly more than tulips and cheese, these laws struck directly at their lucrative role as Europe's commercial middlemen. A series of naval wars between England and Holland ensued. Charles also undertook at this time to subdue the rich English colonies in North America and the Caribbean that had been settled and developed by separatist Puritans and had broken away from English rule—a most enterprising move.

Although Parliament strongly supported the monarchy, Charles, following the habit of his predecessors, required greater revenues than Parliament appropriated. To fund his ventures fully, he became a secret client of the French king, Louis XIV. England and France formally allied against the Dutch in the Treaty of Dover in 1670. In a secret portion of this treaty Charles pledged to announce

Charles II of England in a portrait from an unknown hand. [The Granger Collection.]

his conversion to Catholicism as soon as conditions in England permitted. In exchange for this promise he received a French war chest that came to exceed 700,000 pounds.

In an attempt to unite the English people behind the war with Holland, and as a sign of good faith to Louis XIV, Charles issued a Declaration of Indulgence in 1672 suspending all laws against Roman Catholics and Protestant nonconformists. But again the Tory Parliament proved less generous than the king and refused to grant money for the war until Charles rescinded the measure. After Charles withdrew the declaration, Parliament passed the Test Act, which required all officials of the crown, civil and military, to swear an oath against the doctrine of transubstantiation—a requirement that no loyal Roman Catholic could honestly meet.

The Test Act was aimed in large measure at the king's brother, James, duke of York, who was heir to the throne and a recent, devout convert to Catholicism. A notorious liar named Titus Oates swore before a magistrate that Charles's Catholic wife was plotting with Jesuits to poison the king so that James could assume the throne. The matter was taken before Parliament, where it was believed. In the ensuing hysteria several people, including an Irish bishop, were tried and executed. In 1680–1681, riding the crest of anti-Catholic sentiment, Whig mem-

James II of England, the fourth Stuart, was painted about the time of his accession by Sir Godfrey Kneller (1646–1723). [The Granger Collection.]

bers of Parliament, led by the earl of Shaftsbury (1621–1683), made an impressive but unsuccessful effort to enact a bill excluding James from succession to the throne.

More suspicious than ever of Parliament, Charles II turned again to Louis XIV for extra income and was able to rule from 1681 to 1685 without recalling Parliament. In these years Charles suppressed much of his opposition, driving the earl of Shaftsbury into exile, executing several Whig leaders for treason, and bullying local corporations into electing members of Parliament submissive to the royal will. When Charles died in 1685 after a deathbed conversion to Catholicism, he left James the prospect of a Parliament filled with royal friends.

James II and Renewed Fears of a Catholic England

James II (1685–1688) did not know how to make the most of a good thing. He alienated Parliament by insisting upon the repeal of the Test Act. When Parliament balked, he dissolved it and proceeded openly to appoint known Catholics to high positions in both his court and the army. In 1687 James issued a Declaration of Indulgence, which suspended all religious tests and permitted free worship. Local candidates for Parliament who opposed the declaration were removed from their offices by the king's soldiers and were replaced by Catholics. In June 1688 James went so far as to imprison seven Anglican bishops who had refused to publicize his suspension of laws against Catholics.

Under the guise of a policy of enlightened toleration James was actually seeking to subject all English institutions to the power of the monarchy. His goal was absolutism, and even the Tories could not abide this. Englishmen had reason to fear that James planned to imitate the policy of Louis XIV, who in 1685 had revoked the Edict of Nantes (which had protected French Protestants for almost a century) and reconverted France to Catholicism by use of dragoons. A national consensus very quickly formed against the monarchy of James II.

The direct stimulus for Parliamentary action came when on June 20, 1688, James's second wife, a Catholic, gave birth to a son, a male Catholic heir to the English throne. Englishmen had hoped that James would die without a male heir and that the throne would revert to his Protestant eldest daughter, Mary. Mary was the wife of William III of Orange, *stadholder* of the Netherlands, great-grandson of William the Silent, and the leader of European opposition to Louis XIV's imperial designs. Within days of the birth of a Catholic male heir, Whig and Tory members of Parliament formed a coalition and invited Orange to invade England to preserve "traditional liberties," that is, the Anglican Church and parliamentary government.

The "Glorious Revolution."

In the face of sure defeat James fled to France and the protection of Louis XIV. When William of Orange arrived with his army in November 1688, he was received without opposition from the English people. With James gone, Parliament declared the throne vacant and on its own authority proclaimed William and Mary the new monarchs in 1689, completing a successful bloodless revolution. William and Mary in turn recognized a Bill of Rights that limited the powers of the monarchy and guaranteed the civil liberties of the English privileged classes. It also pointedly prohibited Roman Catholics from occupying the English throne. The Toleration Act of 1689 permitted worship by all Protestants and outlawed Roman Catholics and antitrinitarians.

The final measure closing the century of strife was the Act of Settlement in 1701. This bill provided for the English crown to go to the Protestant House of Hanover in Germany if Queen Anne (1702–1714), the second daughter of James II and the last of the Stuart monarchs, was not survived by her children. Consequently in 1715 the Elector of Hanover became King George I of England, the third foreign monarch to occupy the English throne in just over a century.

The "Glorious Revolution" of 1688 established a framework of government by and for the governed. It

With her husband already in exile and William and Mary about to be proclaimed sovereigns, the ex-queen, wife of James II, is pictured fleeing London in December 1688. [The Granger Collection.]

The bloodless revolution of 1688–1689 yielded the only instance of joint sovereigns in English history. Here are William III and Mary II as shown on a popular ballad sheet of 1689. [The Granger Collection.]

received classic philosophical justification in John Locke's *Second Treatise on Government* (1690), wherein Locke described the relationship of a king and his people in terms of a bilateral contract. If the king broke that contract, the people, by whom Locke meant the privileged and powerful, had the right to depose him. Although it was, neither in fact nor in theory, a popular revolution such as would occur in France and America a hundred years later, the Glorious Revolution did establish in England a permanent check on monarchical power by the classes represented in Parliament. Thereby it established a model for subsequent Western political history.

The joint monarchs' coronation medal, designed by George Bower. [The Granger Collection.]

Queen Anne was the last Stuart monarch of Great Britain. Because she outlived her numerous children, she was succeeded by George I of the new house of Hanover. This is a medal by John Croker. [The Granger Collection.]

England and France in the Seventeenth Century

Rise of Absolutism in France

Regional rights and a degree of religious diversity were recognized within the Holy Roman Empire, England, and the Netherlands during the seventeenth century. The assertion of local autonomy by the numerous member states and cities of the Holy Roman Empire made a strong central government there unthinkable. In England and the Netherlands centuries of parliamentary practice permitted regional freedoms to coexist with a strong central government.

Following the devastation of the Thirty Years War, the Peace of Westphalia (1648) reaffirmed religious pluralism within the Holy Roman Empire. A degree of religious diversity, long a Netherlands tradition, received final confirmation also in England after decades of dogged Puritan resistance, when the Toleration Act of 1689 granted rights of worship to protestant nonconformists.

Seventeenth-century France, in contrast to these developments, saw both representative government and religious pluralism crushed by the absolute monarchy and the closed Catholic state of Louis XIV (1643–1715). Louis XIV was determined to export abroad as well as to impose at home his motto of "One king, one law, one faith."

Henry IV and Sully

The foundation was well laid for Louis's grand reign by his predecessors and their exceptional ministers. It was Henry IV (1589–1610) who began in earnest the curtailment of the privileges of the French nobility necessary for the creation of a strong centralized state. His target was the provincial governors and the regional *parlements*,

In the English Civil War, 1645 was a crucial year; here the rapidly deteriorating Royalist position is shown. A bit later in France we see the territorial changes resulting from Louis XIV's first three major wars. The War of the Spanish Succession was yet to come.

especially the powerful *Parlement* of Paris, where the divisive feudal spirit still lived on. Here were to be found the old privileged groups, tax-exempt magnates whose sole preoccupation was to prevent royal laws from infringing upon their self-interests. During Louis XIV's reign their powers were completely usurped by royal civil servants known as *intendants,* who implemented the king's will in the provinces.

It was also during Henry IV's reign that a government-controlled economy emerged as part of the task of reconstruction after the long decades of religious and civil war. Henry and his finance minister, the duke of Sully (1560–1641), prepared the way for the later mercantilist policies of Louis XIV and his minister Colbert. They established government monopolies on gunpowder, mines, and salt. A canal system was begun to link the Atlantic and the Mediterranean by joining the Saône, the Loire, the Seine, and the Meuse rivers. An involuntary national labor force was created by the introduction of a royal *corvée,* and this drafting of workers provided the manpower to improve roads and the conditions of internal travel. Sully even dreamed of the political and commercial organization of the whole of Europe in a kind of common market.

Louis XIII and Richelieu

Henry IV was assassinated in 1610, and the following year Sully retired. Because Henry's successor, Louis XIII (1610–1643), was only nine years old when his father was assassinated, the task of governing fell to the queen mother, Marie de' Medici (d. 1642). Finding herself in a vulnerable position, she sought security abroad by signing a ten-year mutual defense pact with arch-rival Spain in the Treaty of Fontainebleau (1611), an alliance that also arranged for the later marriage of Louis XIII to the Spanish infanta as well as for the marriage of the queen's daughter Elizabeth to the heir to the Spanish throne. Internal security against the French nobility was obtained by the queen's promotion of the career of Cardinal Richelieu (1585–1642) as the king's chief adviser. Richelieu, loyal and shrewd, aspired to make France a supreme European power and more than any one person was the secret of French success in the first half of the seventeenth century.

Strongly Catholic in religion, Richelieu was just as strongly anti-Hapsburg in politics. On the one hand, he supported the Spanish alliance of the queen and Catholic religious unity within France; on the other, he was determined to contain Spanish power and influence, even when that meant aiding and abetting Protestant Europe. It is an indication both of Richelieu's awkward political situation and of his diplomatic agility that he could pledge funds to the Protestant army of Gustavus Adolphus in the Treaty of Barwälde, in 1631, while at the same time insisting on the condition that Catholic Bavaria be spared from attack and that Catholics in conquered countries be permitted to practice their religion.

At home Richelieu pursued his policies utterly without sentiment. Supported by the king, whose best decision was to let his chief minister make all the decisions of state, Richelieu stepped up the campaign against the separatist provincial governors and *parlements*. He made it clear to all that there was but one law, that of the king, and that none could stand above it. When disobedient noblemen defied his edicts, they were imprisoned and even executed. Louis XIV had Richelieu to thank for the fact that the French nobility became docile beggars at his court. Such treatment of the princes of the blood won Richelieu much enmity, even from the queen mother, who was not prepared to place the larger interests of the state above the pleasure of favorite princes. But the king let no criticism weaken his chief minister, not even that of his mother. The queen mother had largely ignored Louis during his youth—his education came mostly at the hands of his falconer—and they remained estranged and ill at ease in each other's presence. This was doubtless a factor in the king's firm support of Richelieu when his mother became Richelieu's accuser.

Richelieu began the campaign against the Huguenots that would end in 1685 with Louis XIV's shocking revocation of the Edict of Nantes. Royal armies conquered major Huguenot cities in 1629 and the subsequent Peace of Alais (1629) truncated the Edict of Nantes by denying Protestants the right to maintain garrisoned cities, separate political organizations, and independent law courts. Only Richelieu's foreign policy prevented the earlier implementation of the extreme intolerance of Louis XIV. In the same year that the independent status of Huguenots was rescinded, Richelieu also entered negotiations to make Gustavus Adolphus his counterweight to the expansion of Hapsburg power within the Holy Roman Empire. By 1635 the Catholic soldiers of France fought openly with Swedish Lutherans against the emperor's army in the final phase of the Thirty Years War.

In the best Machiavellian tradition Richelieu employed the arts and the printing press to defend his actions and to indoctrinate Frenchmen in the meaning of *raison de'état* ("reasons of state")—again setting a precedent for Louis XIV's elaborate use of royal propaganda and spectacle. It is one measure of Richelieu's success that France made substantial gains in land and political influence when hostilities were ended in the Holy Roman Empire by the Treaty of Westphalia (1648) and peace with Spain was sealed in the Treaty of the Pyrenees (1659).

Young Louis XIV and Mazarin

Richelieu's immediate legacy, however, was strong resentment of the monarchy on the part of the French aristocracy and the privileged bourgeoisie. He and Louis XIII died within months of one another in 1643.

During the minority of Louis XIV, who was only five years old at the time of Louis XIII's death, the queen mother, Anne of Austria (d. 1666), placed the reins of government in the hands of Cardinal Mazarin (1602–1661), who happened also to be her lover and, some report, her secret husband. Mazarin continued Richelieu's pitiless policy of centralization. During his regency the long-building backlash occurred, and France was shaken to its foundations by the Fronde (1649–1652).

Named after the slingshot used by street urchins to

Cardinal Mazarin, in whose hands lay the real power in France during the minority of Louis XIV. [The Granger Collection.]

strike the carriages of the rich, the Fronde was a series of widespread rebellions by segments of the French nobility and townsmen aimed at reversing the drift toward absolute monarchy—a last-ditch effort to preserve their local autonomy. These privileged groups saw their traditional position in French society thoroughly undermined by the crown's steady multiplication of royal offices, replacement of local with "state" agents, and reduction of the patronage they received.

The *Parlement* of Paris initiated the revolt in 1649 and the nobility at large soon followed. The latter were urged on by the influential wives of princes who had been imprisoned by Mazarin for treason. The many briefly triumphed over the one when Mazarin was forced to release the imprisoned princes in February 1651. He and Louis XIV thereafter entered a short exile and were unable to return to Paris until October 1652, when the inefficiency and near anarchy of government by the nobility made them very welcome. The period of the Fronde convinced a majority of Frenchmen that being left to the mercy of a strong king was preferable to being subjected to the competing claims of many regional magnates. After 1652 the French were ready to experiment in earnest with absolute rule.

The World of Louis XIV

UNITY AT HOME. Thanks to the forethought of Mazarin, Louis XIV was well prepared to rule France. The turbulent periods of his youth seem also to have made an indelible impression. Louis wrote in his memoires that the Fronde caused him to loathe "kings of straw" and made him determined never to become one. Indoctrinated with a strong sense of the grandeur of his crown, he never missed an opportunity to impress it upon the French people. When the dauphin was born in 1662, for example, Louis appeared for the celebration dressed as a Roman emperor. Although his rule became the prototype of the modern centralized state, its inspiration was a very narrow medieval ideal of personal glory.

KING BY DIVINE RIGHT. Reverence for the king and the personification of government in his person had been nurtured in France since Capetian times. It was a maxim of French law and popular opinion as early as the late Middle Ages that "The king of France is emperor in his realm," that the king's wish is the law of the land.

An important theorist for Louis's even grander concept of royal authority was the Jesuit tutor of the dauphin, Bishop Jacques-Bénigne Bossuet (1627–1704). An ardent champion of the Gallican Liberties—the traditional rights of the French king and church in matters of ecclesiastical appointments and taxation—Bossuet defended what he called the "divine right of kings." He cited the Old Testament example of rulers divinely appointed by and answerable only to God. Against the claims to power of princes and *parlements* Bossuet enunciated a secular version of an argument earlier used by medieval popes to secure their authority against the competitive claims of bishops and church councils. As medieval popes had insisted that only God could judge a pope, so Bossuet argued that none save God could sit in judgment on the king. Although kings remained duty-bound to reflect God's will in their rule—and in this sense Bossuet considered them always subject to a higher authority—as God's regents on earth they could not be bound to the dictates of mere princes and parliaments. Such were the assumptions that lay behind Louis XIV's alleged declaration: "L'état, c'est moi" ("I am the state").

VERSAILLES. The palace court at Versailles on the outskirts of Paris became Louis's permanent residence

[*Text continued on page 452*]

The sumptuous Salon de la Guerre in the Palace of Versailles. It was begun in 1678. Several rooms of the palace were badly damaged by a terrorist's bomb in June 1978. [French Embassy Press and Information Division, New York.]

A full view of Versailles as it appears today. Louis XIV vastly enlarged his father's hunting lodge into a palace estate beginning in 1661. It became not only the royal residence but the seat of the French government, a symbol of royal and national power, and the frequently imitated model for other seventeenth- and eighteenth-century monarchs. This photograph is from the opposite direction to Patel's painting; the coaches in his picture are arriving on the diagonal road at the top left of the photograph. [French Government Tourist Office, New York.]

after 1682 and was a true temple to royalty, architecturally designed and artistically decorated to proclaim the glory of the Sun King, as Louis was known. A spectacular estate with magnificent fountains and acres of orange groves, it became home to thousands of aristocrats, royal officials, and servants. Although its physical maintenance and new additions, which continued throughout Louis's lifetime, consumed over half his annual revenues—around five million livres a year—Versailles paid political dividends well worth the investment.

Life at court was organized around the king's daily routine.

His rising and dressing was a time of rare intimacy, when nobles, who entered their names on waiting lists to be in attendance, whispered their special requests in Louis's ear.

After the morning Mass, which Louis always observed, there followed long hours in council with the chief ministers, assemblies from which the nobility was carefully excluded. Louis's ministers and councillors were hand-picked townsmen, servants who owed everything they had to the king's favor and were for that reason inclined to serve faithfully and without question. There were three main councils: the Council of State, a small group of four or five who met thrice weekly to rule on all matters of state, but especially on foreign affairs and war policy; the Council of Despatches, which regularly assessed the reports from the *intendants* in the towns and provinces, a boring business that the king often left to his ministers; and finally, the Council of Finances, which handled matters of taxation and commerce.

The afternoons were spent hunting, riding, or strolling about the lush gardens. Evenings were given over to planned entertainment in the large salons (plays, concerts, gambling, and the like), followed by supper at 10:00 P.M.

Even the king's retirement was a part of the day's spectacle. Fortunate nobles were permitted briefly to hold his night candle as they accompanied him to his bed.

Although only five feet, four inches in height, the king

Bishop Bossuet Defends the Divine Right of Kings

The revolutions of the seventeenth century caused many to fear anarchy far more than tyranny, among them the influential French bishop, Jacques Bénigne Bossuet (1627–1704). Bossuet owed his rise to power as virtual leader of French Catholicism in the second half of the seventeenth century to his oratorical, literary, and historical skills. Louis XIV made him court preacher and tutor to his son, for whom Bossuet wrote a celebrated *Universal History*. Here he defends the divine right and absolute power of kings, who are depicted as embracing in their person the whole body of the state and the will of the people they govern and, as such, as being immune from judgment by any man.

THE *royal power is absolute. . . . The prince need render account of his acts to no one. "I counsel thee to keep the king's commandment, and that in regard of the oath of God. Be not hasty to go out of his sight; stand not on an evil thing for he doeth whatsoever pleaseth him. Where the word of a king is, there is power: and who may say unto him, What doest thou? Whoso keepeth the commandment shall feel no evil thing" [Eccles. 8:2–5]. Without this absolute authority the king could neither do good nor repress evil. It is necessary that his power be such that no one can hope to escape him, and finally, the only protection of individuals against the public authority should be their innocence. This confirms the teaching of St. Paul: "Wilt thou then not be afraid of the power? Do that which is good" [Rom. 13:3].*

God is infinite, God is all. The prince, as prince, is not regarded as a private person: he is a public personage, all the state is in him; the will of all the people is included in his. As all perfection and all strength are united in God, so all the power of individuals is united in the person of the prince. What grandeur that a single man should embody so much! . . .

Behold an immense people united in a single person; behold this holy power, paternal and absolute; behold the secret cause which governs the whole body of the state, contained in a single head: you see the image of God in the king, and you have the idea of royal majesty. God is holiness itself, goodness itself, and power itself. In these things lies the majesty of God. In the image of these things lies the majesty of the prince.

From *Politics Drawn from the Very Words of Holy Scripture*, in James Harvey Robinson, *Readings in European History*, Vol. 2 (Boston: Ginn and Co., 1906), pp. 275–276.

Bishop Cornelis Jansen (1585–1638) was the author of the intellectual and theological foundations of what came to be called Jansenism. Several of his key beliefs were eventually declared heretical by the Catholic Church. [The Granger Collection.]

The abbey of Port Royal near Paris in the seventeenth century, the main center of Jansenist theological activity. Its picture gives a good impression of the layout of a religious community of the time. [The Granger Collection.]

had presence and was always engaging in conversation. An unabashed ladies' man, he encouraged the belief at court that it was an honor to lie with the king. Louis was a bee who gathered nectar from many flowers. Married to the Spanish Infanta Marie Thérèse for political reasons in 1660, he kept many mistresses. After Marie's death in 1683 he settled down in secret marriage with one, Madame de Maintenon, and apparently became thereafter much less the philanderer.

All this ritual and play served the political purpose of keeping an impoverished nobility, barred by law from high government positions, busy and begging so that they had no time to plot revolt. The dress codes and the high-stakes gaming at court contributed to the indebtedness and dependency of noblemen on the king. Court life was a carefully planned and successfully executed domestication of the nobility.

Suppression of the Jansenists

Like Richelieu before him, Louis believed that political unity required religious conformity. To that end he suppressed two groups of religious dissenters: the Catholic Jansenists, who were opponents of the Jesuits, and the Protestant Huguenots.

Although the king and the French church had always jealously guarded their traditional independence from Rome, the years following the conversion of Henry IV to Catholicism saw a great influx of Catholic religious orders into France, prominent among which were the Jesuits. Because of their leadership at the Council of Trent and their close Spanish connections, Catherine de' Medici had earlier banned the Jesuits from France. Henry IV lifted the ban in 1603, with certain conditions: there was to be a limitation on the number of new colleges they could open; special licenses were required for activities outside their own buildings; and each member of the order was subjected to an oath of allegiance to the king. The Jesuits were not, however, easily harnessed. They rapidly monopolized the education of the upper classes, and their devout students promoted the religious reforms and doctrine of the Council of Trent throughout France. It is a measure of their success that Jesuits served as confessors to Henry IV, Louis XIII, and Louis XIV.

In the 1630s an intra-Catholic opposition to both the theology and the political influence of the Jesuits formed: the Jansenists. They were Catholics who adhered to the Augustinian tradition out of which many Protestant teachings had also come. Serious and uncompromising in their religious doctrine and practice, they were especially distinguished by belief in the utter bondage of man's will to sin without the special assistance of divine grace. Their namesake, Cornelis Jansen (d. 1638), a Flemish theologian and the bishop of Ypres, was the author of a posthumously published book entitled *Augustinus* (1640), which assailed Jesuit teaching on grace and salvation.

Jean du Vergier de Hauranne (1581–1643), the abbot of Saint-Cyran and Jansen's close friend, was instrumental in bringing into the Jansenist fold a Parisian family, the Arnaulds, who were prominent in the Gallican opposition to the Jesuits. The Arnauld family, like many other Frenchmen, believed that the Jesuits had been behind the assassination of Henry IV in 1610 and constantly suspected their intentions. Arnauld support added a strong political element to the Jansenists' theological opposition to the Jesuits. Jansenist communities in Port Royal and Paris were dominated by the Arnaulds during the 1640s. In 1643 Antoine Arnauld published a work entitled *On Frequent Communion* in which Jesuits were criticized for confessional practices that permitted easy redress of almost any sin. The Jesuits in turn condemned the Jansenists as "crypto-Calvinists" in their theology.

On May 31, 1653, Jansenism was declared a heresy. On that day five Jansenist theological propositions on grace and salvation, earlier condemned by the Sorbonne, were deemed heretical by Pope Innocent X. In 1656 the Pope banned Jansen's *Augustinus* and the Sorbonne censured Antoine Arnauld. It was in this same year that the latter's friend, Blaise Pascal (d. 1662), the most famous of Jansen's followers, published the first of his *Provincial Letters* in defense of Jansenism. A deeply religious man,

Louix XIV Revokes the Edict of Nantes

Believing that a country could not be under one king and one law unless it was also under one religious system, Louis XIV stunned Europe in October 1685 by revoking the Edict of Nantes, which had protected the religious freedoms and civil rights of French Reformed Protestants since 1598.

Aᴿᴛ. 1. *Know that we . . . with our certain knowledge, full power and royal authority, have by this present, perpetual and irrevocable edict, suppressed and revoked the edict of the aforesaid king our grandfather, given at Nantes in the month of April, 1598, in all its extent . . . together with all the concessions made by [this] and other edicts, declarations, and decrees, to the people of the so-called Reformed religion, of whatever nature they be . . . and in consequence we desire . . . that all the temples of the people of the aforesaid so-called Reformed religion situated in our kingdom . . . should be demolished forthwith.*

Art. 2. *We forbid our subjects of the so-called Reformed religion to assemble any more for public worship of the above-mentioned religion. . . .*

Art. 3. *We likewise forbid all lords, of whatever rank they may be, to carry out heretical services in houses and fiefs . . . the penalty for . . . the said worship being confiscation of their body and possessions.*

Art. 4. *We order all ministers of the aforesaid so-called Reformed religion who do not wish to be converted and to embrace the Catholic, Apostolic, and Roman religion, to depart from our kingdom and the lands subject to us within fifteen days from the publication of our present edict . . . on pain of the galleys.*

Art. 5. *We desire that those among the said [Reformed] ministers who shall be converted [to the Catholic religion] shall continue to enjoy during their life, and their wives shall enjoy after their death as long as they remain widows, the same exemptions from taxation and billeting of soldiers, which they enjoyed while they fulfilled the function of ministers. . . .*

. . . .

Art. 8. *With regard to children who shall be born to those of the aforesaid so-called Reformed religion, we desire that they be baptized by their parish priests. We command the fathers and mothers to send them to the churches for that purpose, on penalty of a fine of 500 livres or more if they fail to do so; and afterwards, the children shall be brought up in the Catholic, Apostolic, and Roman religion. . . .*

. . . .

Art. 10. *All our subjects of the so-called Reformed religion, with their wives and children, are to be strongly and repeatedly prohibited from leaving our aforesaid kingdom . . . or of taking out . . . their possessions and effects. . . .*

. . . .

The members of the so-called Reformed religion, while awaiting God's pleasure to enlighten them like the others, can live in the towns and districts of our kingdom . . . and continue their occupation there, and enjoy their possessions . . . on condition . . . that they do not make public profession of [their religion].

Church and State Through the Centuries: A Collection of Historic Documents, trans. and ed. by S. Z. Ehler and John B. Morrall (New York: Biblo and Tannen, 1967), pp. 209–213.

Pascal tried to reconcile the "reasons of the heart" with growing seventeenth-century reverence for the clear and distinct ideas of the mind. He found Jesuit moral theology to be not only lax and shallow, but also a rationalized approach to religion that did injustice to religious experience.

In 1660 Louis permitted the enforcement of the papal bull *Ad Sacram Sedem* (1656), which banned Jansenism, and he closed down the Port Royal community. Thereafter Jansenists either capitulated by signing retractions or went underground. At a later date (1710) the French king lent his support to a still more thorough Jesuit purge of Jansenist sentiment. With the fall of the Jansenists went any hope of a Catholicism broad enough to attract Huguenots.

Revocation of the Edict of Nantes

Since 1598, when the Edict of Nantes was proclaimed, a cold war had existed between the great Catholic majority (nine tenths of the French population remained Catholic) and the Protestant minority. Despite their respecta-ble numbers, about 1.75 million by the 1660s, the Huguenots were in decline in the second half of the seventeenth century. Government harrassment had forced the more influential members to withdraw their support. Officially the French Catholic Church had long denounced Calvinists as heretical and treasonous and had supported their persecution as both a pious and a patriotic act. Following the Peace of Nijmegen in 1678–1679, which halted for the moment Louis's aggression in Europe, a methodical government campaign was launched against French Huguenots as Louis became determined to unify France religiously. The Huguenots were hounded out of public life, banned from government office, and excluded from such professions as printing and medicine. Subsidies and selective taxation were used to encourage their conversion to Catholicism. In 1681 dragoons were quartered in Huguenot towns. The final stage of the persecution came in October 1685, when Louis revoked the Edict of Nantes. In practical terms the revocation meant the closing of Protestant churches and schools, the exile of Protestant ministers, the placement of nonconverting laymen in galleys as slaves, and the cere-monial baptism of Protestant children by Catholic priests.

The revocation of the Edict of Nantes was the major blunder of Louis's reign. Thereafter he was viewed throughout Europe as a new Philip II, intent on a Catho-lic reconquest of the whole of Europe, who must be resisted at all costs. Internally the revocation of the Edict of Nantes led to the voluntary emigration of over a quarter million Frenchmen, who formed new communi-ties and joined French resistance in England, Germany, Holland, and the New World. Thousands of French Huguenots served in the army of Louis's arch foe, Wil-liam III of the Netherlands, later King William III of England. Those who remained in France became an uncompromising guerrilla force. But despite the many domestic and foreign liabilities created for France by the revocation of the Edict of Nantes, Louis to his death considered it his most pious act, one that placed God in his debt.

Jean-Baptiste Colbert, the strongly nationalistic finance minister and sponsor of mercantilism under Louis XIV. His portrait is by Pierre Mignard. [The Granger Collection.]

War Abroad

War was the normal state for seventeenth-century rulers and for none more so than for Louis XIV, who confessed on his deathbed that he had "loved war too much." Periods of peace were viewed as opportunities for the discontented in town and countryside to plot against the king. By the 1660s France was the superior of any other nation in administrative bureaucracy, armed forces, and national unity. It had a population of nineteen million, prosperous farms, vigorous trade, and much taxable wealth. By every external measure Louis was in a position to dominate Europe.

LOUVOIS, VAUBAN, COLBERT. The great French war machine was the work of three ministers: Louvois, Vauban, and Colbert. The army, which maintained a strength of about a quarter of a million men, was the creation of Michel le Tellier and his more famous son, the marquis of Louvois (1641–1691). The latter was the supreme military tactician of the age before the emergence of the English duke of Marlborough. He served as Louis's war minister from 1677 to 1691.

Before Louvois the French army had been a medley of local recruits and mercenaries, uncoordinated groups whose loyalty could not always be counted upon. Louvois disciplined the French army and made it a respectable profession. He placed a limit on military commissions and introduced a system of promotion by merit, moves that brought dedicated fighting men into the ranks. Enlistment was for four years and was restricted to single men. The pay was good and regular. *Intendants,* those ubiquitous civil servants, carried out regular inspections, monitoring conduct at all levels and reporting to the king.

What Louvois was to military organization Sebastien Vauban (1633–1707) was to military engineering. He perfected the arts of fortifying and besieging towns. He also devised the system of trench warfare and developed the concept of defensive frontiers that remained basic military tactics through World War I.

War cannot be successful without financing, and here

Louis had the guidance of his most brilliant minister, Jean-Baptiste Colbert (1619–1683). Colbert centralized the French economy with the same rigor that Louis had centralized the French government. He put the nation to work under state supervision and carefully regulated the flow of imports and exports through tariffs. He created new national industries and organized factories around a tight regimen of work and ideology. Administrative bureaucracy was simplified, unnecessary positions abolished, and the number of tax-exempt nobles reduced. Colbert also increased the *taille* on the peasantry, the chief source of royal wealth. This close government control of the economy came to be known as *mercantilism.* Its aim was to maximize foreign exports and the internal reserves of bullion, the gold and silver necessary for war making. Modern scholars argue that Colbert overcontrolled the French economy and cite his paternalism as a major reason for French failures in the New World. Be that as it may, Colbert unquestionably transformed France into a major industrial and commercial power, with foreign bases in Africa, India, and the Americas from Canada to the Caribbean.

THE WAR OF DEVOLUTION. Louis's first great foreign adventure was the War of Devolution (1667–1668). It was fought, as still a later and greater war would be, over Louis's claim to a Spanish inheritance through his wife, Marie Thérèse (1638–1683). According to the terms of the Treaty of the Pyrenees (1659), Marie had renounced her claim to the Spanish succession on condition that a 500,000 crown dowry be paid to Louis within eighteen months of the marriage, a condition that was not met. When Philip IV of Spain died in September 1665, he left all his lands to his sickly four-year-old son by a second marriage, Charles II (1665–1700), and explicitly excluded his daughter Marie from any share. Louis had always harbored the hope of turning the marriage to territorial gain and argued even before Philip's death that Marie was entitled to a portion of the inheritance.

Louis had a legal argument on his side, which gave the

war its name. He maintained that because in certain regions of Brabant and Flanders, which were part of the Spanish inheritance, property "devolved" to the children of a first marriage rather than to those of a second, Marie had a higher claim than Charles II to these regions. The argument was not accepted—such regional laws could hardly bind the king of Spain—but Louis was not deterred from moving his armies, under vicomte de Turenne, into Flanders and the Franche-Comté in 1667. It was in response to this aggression that England, Sweden, and the United Provinces of Holland formed the Triple Alliance, a force sufficient to bring Louis to peace terms in the Treaty of Aix-la-Chapelle (1668).

INVASION OF THE NETHERLANDS. In 1670 England and France became allies against the Dutch by signing the Treaty of Dover, a move that set the Stuart monarchy of Charles II on a new international course. With the departure of the English from membership in it, the Triple Alliance crumbled. This left Louis in a stronger position to invade the Netherlands for a second time, which he did in 1672. This second invasion was aimed directly at Holland, the organizer of the Triple Alliance in 1667 and the country held accountable by Louis for foiling French designs in Flanders. Louis had been mightily offended by Dutch boasting after the Treaty of Aix-la-Chapelle; cartoons like one depicting the sun (Louis was the "Sun King") eclipsed by a great moon of Dutch cheese cut the French king to the quick. It was also clear that there could be no French acquisition of land in the Spanish Netherlands, nor European hegemony beyond that, until Holland was neutralized.

Louis's successful invasion of the United Provinces in 1672 brought the downfall of Jan and Cornelius De Witt, Dutch statesmen who were blamed for the French success. In their place came the twenty-seven-year-old William III, Prince of Orange (1650–1702), the great-grandson of William the Silent, who had successfully repulsed Philip II and dashed Spanish hopes of dominating the Netherlands in the sixteenth century.

After 1689 William III became King William III of England and proved more than any one man to be Louis's undoing. This unpretentious Calvinist, who was in almost every way Louis's opposite, galvanized the seven provinces into a fierce fighting unit that did not shrink from opening the dikes on French armies. In 1673 he united the Holy Roman Emperor, Spain, Lorraine, and Brandenburg in an alliance against Louis, who was now seen by his enemies to be "the Christian Turk," a menace to the whole of western Europe, Catholic and Protestant alike. Subsequent battles saw Louis lose his ablest generals, Turenne and Condé, in 1675, while the defeat of the Dutch fleet by Admiral Duquesne established French control of the Mediterranean in 1676. The Peace of Nimwegen, signed with different parties in successive years, ended the hostilities of this second war. In 1678 France entered agreements with Holland and Spain and in 1679 with the Holy Roman Emperor, Brandenburg, and Denmark. The settlements were not unfavorable to France—Spain, for example, surrendered the Franche-Comté—but France still fell far short of the European empire to which Louis aspired.

THE LEAGUE OF AUGSBURG. Between the Treaty of Nimwegen and the renewal of full-scale war in 1689, Louis restlessly probed his perimeters. The army was maintained at full strength. In 1681 it conquered the free city of Strasbourg, setting off the formation of new defensive coalitions against Louis. The League of Augsburg was created in 1686 to resist French expansion into Germany and grew by 1689 to include the Emperor Leopold, Spain, Sweden, the United Provinces, the electorates of Bavaria, Saxony, and the Palatinate, and the England of William and Mary. That year saw the beginning of the Nine Years' War (1689–1697) between France and the League. For the third time stalemate and exhaustion forced the combatants to an interim settlement. The Peace of Ryswick in September 1697 was a personal triumph for William, now William III of England, and the Emperor Leopold, as it secured Holland's borders and thwarted Louis's expansion into Germany. During this same period England and France fought for

The first duke of Marlborough (1650–1722) was the military genius of England and its allies in the War of the Spanish Succession. For him a grateful country built Blenheim Palace near Oxford, named for one of his famous battles, and still one of the grandest country estates of England. The portrait is by Sir Godfrey Kneller. [The Granger Collection.]

control of North America in what came to be known as King William's War (1689–1697).

WAR OF THE SPANISH SUCCESSION: TREATIES OF UTRECHT–RASTADT. After Ryswick, Louis, who seemed to thrive on partial success, made still a fourth attempt to realize his grand design of French European domination, this time assisted by an unforeseen turn of events. On November 1, 1700, Charles II of Spain, known as "the Sufferer" because of his genetic deformities and lingering illnesses, died. Both Louis and the Austrian Emperor Leopold had claims to the Spanish inheritance through their grandsons: Louis through his marriage to Maria Thérèse and Leopold through his marriage to her younger sister, Margaret Thérèse. Although the dauphin had the higher blood claim, it was assumed that the inheritance would go to the grandson of the emperor. The French painted the specter of a belligerent Hapsburg kingdom like that of Charles V in the sixteenth century should Spain come under the imperial crown. Maria Thérèse, however, had renounced any right to the Spanish inheritance in the Treaty of the Pyrenees (1659).

The nations of Europe were far more fearful of a union of the French and Spanish crowns than they were of a union of the imperial and Spanish crowns. Indeed, they were determined that the former alliance not occur. Hence, before Charles's death negotiations began to partition the inheritance in such a way that the current balance of power would be maintained.

Charles II upset all plans by leaving the entire Spanish inheritance to Philip of Anjou, Louis's grandson. At a stroke the Spanish inheritance had fallen to France. Although Louis had been party to the partition agreements in advance of Charles's death, he now saw God's hand in Charles's will and chose to enforce its terms fully rather than abide by those of the partition treaty. Philip of Anjou moved to Madrid and became Philip V of Spain, and Louis, in what was interpreted as naked French aggression, sent his troops once again into Flanders, this time to remove Dutch soldiers from Spanish territory in the name of the new French king of Spain.

In September 1701 the Grand Alliance of England, Holland, and the Holy Roman Emperor formed against Louis in The Hague. Its intent was to preserve the balance of power by once and for all securing Flanders as a neutral barrier between Holland and France and by gaining for the emperor his fair share of the Spanish inheritance. After the formation of the alliance, Louis increased the stakes of battle by recognizing the son of James II of England as James III, king of England.

Once again total war enveloped western Europe as the twelve-year War of the Spanish Succession (1702–1714) began. This time, and for the first time, France went to war with inadequate finances, a poorly equipped army, and mediocre military leadership. John Churchill, the duke of Marlborough, who succeeded William of Orange as leader of the alliance, bested Louis's soldiers in every major engagement. French armies were routed at Blenheim in August 1704 and on the plain of Ramillies in 1706—two decisive battles of the war. In 1708–1709 famine, revolts, and uncollectable taxes tore France apart internally. Despair pervaded the French court, and Louis

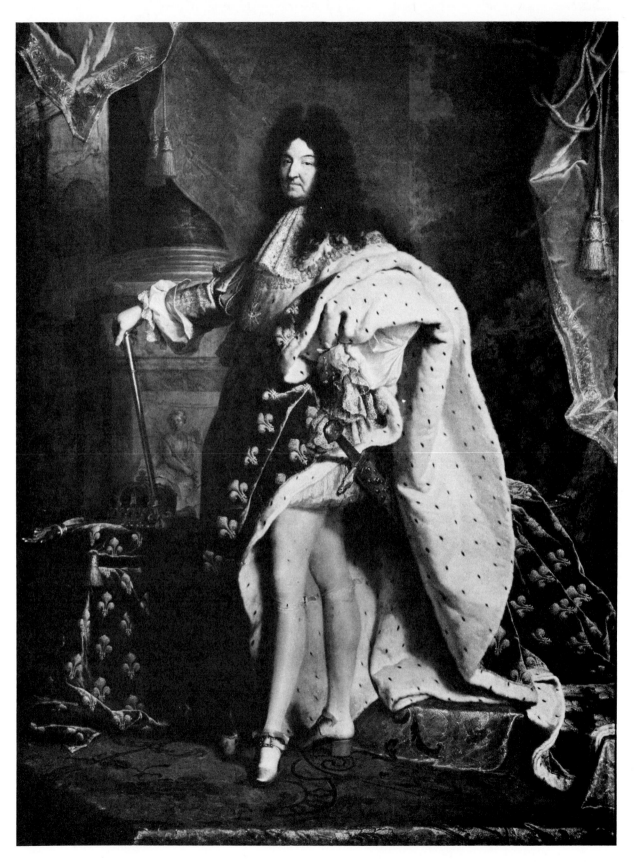

The World of Louis XIV 459

EUROPE IN 1714

The War of the Spanish Succession ended in the year before the death of the aged Louis XIV. By then France and Spain, although not united, were ruled by members of the Bourbon family, and Spain had lost her non-Iberian possessions. Austria had continued to grow.

plaquet (September 1709), which left carnage on the battlefield unsurpassed until modern times.

Under the English minister Bolingbroke the allies renewed peace talks in 1711. France signed an armistice with England at Utrecht in July 1712, and hostilities were concluded with Holland and the emperor in the treaty of Rastadt in March 1714. These agreements confirmed Philip V as king of Spain. They gave England Gibraltar, which made England thereafter a Mediterranean power, and won Louis's recognition of the House of Hanover's right of accession to the English throne.

wondered aloud how God could forsake one who had done so much for Him.

Though ready to make peace in 1709, Louis could not bring himself to accept the stiff terms of the alliance, which included the demand that he transfer all Spanish possessions to the emperor's grandson Charles and remove Philip V from Madrid. An immediate result of this failure to come to terms was a clash of forces at Mal-

Politically the eighteenth century would belong to England as the sixteenth had belonged to Spain and the seventeenth to France. The emperor received control of the Spanish Netherlands, which was established as a barrier between France and Holland, with Dutch troops stationed in key towns. France kept the cities of Strasbourg and Lille. Although France remained intact and quite strong, the realization of Louis XIV's ambition had to await the rise of Napoleon Bonaparte. On his deathbed on September 1, 1715, a dying Louis fittingly warned the dauphin not to imitate his love of buildings and his liking for war.

SUGGESTED READINGS

MAURICE ASHLEY, *The Greatness of Oliver Cromwell* (1966). Detailed biography.

TREVOR ASTON (Ed.), *Crisis in Europe 1560–1660* (1965). Essays by major scholars focused on social and economic forces.

WILLIAM F. CHURCH (Ed.), *The Greatness of Louis XIV: Myth or Reality?* (1959). Excerpts from the scholarly debate over Louis's reign.

C. H. FIRTH, *Oliver Cromwell and the Rule of the Puritans in England* (1900). Old but still very authoritative work.

WILLIAM HALLER, *The Rise of Puritanism* (1957). Interesting study based largely on Puritan sermons.

CHRISTOPHER HILL, *The Century of Revolution 1603–1714* (1961). Bold, imaginative synthesis by a controversial master.

W. H. LEWIS, *The Splended Century* (1953). Focuses on society, especially in the age of Louis XIV.

DAVID OGG, *Europe in the Seventeenth Century* (1925). Among the most authoritative syntheses.

SUART E. PRALL, *The Puritan Revolution: A Documentary History* (1968). Comprehensive document collection.

LAWRENCE STONE, *The Causes of the English Revolution 1529–1642* (1972). Brief survey stressing social history and ruminating over historians and historical method.

G. R. R. TREASURE, *Seventeenth Century France* (1966). Broad, detailed survey of entire century.

MICHAEL WALZER, *The Revolution of the Saints: A Study in the Origins of Radical Politics* (1965). Effort to relate ideas and politics that depicts Puritans as true revolutionaries.

C. V. WEDGWOOD, *Richelieu and the French Monarchy* (1950). Fine biography.

JOHN B. WOLF, *Louis XIV* (1968). Very detailed political biography.

net, in quo terram cum orbe lunari tanquam epicyclo contineri
diximus. Quinto loco Venus nono mense reducitur. Sextum
deniҩ locum Mercurius tenet, octuaginta dierum spacio circū
currens. In medio uero omnium residet Sol. Quis enim in hoc

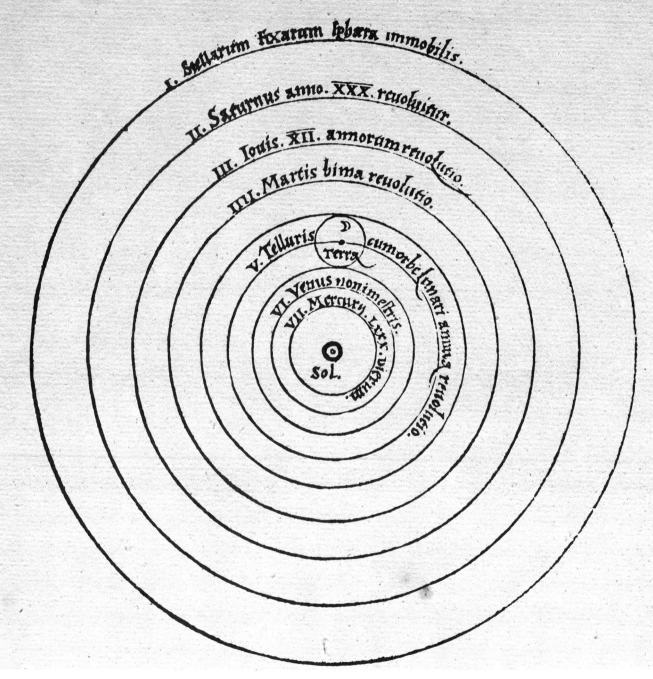

18

New Directions in Science and Thought in the Sixteenth and Seventeenth Centuries

The Scientific Revolution

New Departures

THE SIXTEENTH and seventeenth centuries witnessed a sweeping change in the scientific view of the universe. An earth-centered picture of the universe gave way to one in which the earth was only another planet orbiting about the sun. The sun itself became one of millions of stars. This transformation of humankind's perception of its place in the larger scheme of things led to a vast rethinking of moral and religious matters as well as scientific theory. At the same time the new scientific concepts and the methods of their construction became so impressive that subsequent knowledge in the Western world has been deemed correct only as it has approximated knowledge as defined by science. Perhaps no single intellectual development proved to be more significant for the future of European and Western civilization.

The process by which this new view of the universe and of scientific knowledge came to be established is normally termed the *Scientific Revolution*. However, care must be taken in the use of this metaphor. The word *revolution* normally denotes fairly rapid changes in the political world involving large numbers of people. The Scientific Revolution was not rapid, nor did it involve more than a few hundred human beings. It was a complex movement with many false starts and many brilliant people with wrong as well as useful ideas. It took place in the studies and the crude laboratories of thinkers in Po-

land, Italy, Bohemia, France, and Great Britain. It stemmed from two major tendencies. The first, as illustrated by Nicolaus Copernicus, was the imposition of important small changes on existing models of thought. The second, as embodied by Francis Bacon, was the desire to pose new kinds of questions and to use new methods of investigation. In both cases, scientific thought changed the current and traditional opinions in other fields.

Nicolaus Copernicus

Copernicus (1473–1543) was a Polish astronomer who enjoyed a very high reputation throughout his life. He was neither an obscure nor an unknown figure. He had been educated in Italy and corresponded with other astronomers throughout Europe. However, he had not been known for strikingly original or unorthodox thought. In 1543, the year of his death, Copernicus published *On the Revolutions of the Heavenly Spheres*. Because he died near the time of publication, the fortunes of his work are not the story of one person's crusade for progressive science. Copernicus's book was "a revolution-making rather than a revolutionary text."[1] What Copernicus did was to provide an intellectual springboard for a complete criticism of the then dominant view of the position of the earth in the universe.

At the time of Copernicus the standard explanation of the earth and the heavens was that associated with Ptolemy and his work entitled the *Almagest* (A.D. 150). There was not just one Ptolemaic system but rather several versions had been developed over the centuries by commentators on the original work. Most of these systems assumed that the earth was the center of the universe. Above the earth lay a series of crystalline spheres, one of which contained the moon, another the sun, and still others the planets and the stars. This was the astron-

Nicolaus Copernicus's view of the universe with the sun in the center. The basis of the scientific and intellectual revolution initiated by the Polish astronomer (1473–1543) is summarized in this diagram printed in his *De Revolutionibus Orbium Coelestium* (*On the Revolutions of Heavenly Bodies*) of 1543. [The British Library, London.]

---

1 Thomas S. Kuhn, *The Copernican Revolution: Planetary Astronomy in the Development of Western Thought* (New York: Vintage, 1959), p. 135.

Hypothetical reconstruction of the printing press
of Johannes Gutenberg of Mainz (in what is now West
Germany). Between about 1435 and 1455, Gutenberg
worked out the complete technology of making individual rectangular metal types, composing the type
into pages held together by pressure, and printing from
those on an adaptation of the wooden standing press
with ink of lampblack mixed with oil varnish. This
new technology for the first time made it possible
to manufacture numerous identical copies of written
works and was basic to the intellectual development
of the West. [Gutenberg-Museum, Mainz.]

omy found in such works as Dante's *Divine Comedy*. At
the outer regions of these spheres lay the realm of God
and the angels. Aristotelian physics provided the intellectual underpinnings of the Ptolemaic systems. The earth
had to be the center because of its heaviness. The stars and
the other heavenly bodies had to be enclosed in the
crystalline spheres so that they could move. Nothing
could move unless something was actually moving it. The
state of rest was natural; motion was the condition that
required explanation.

Numerous problems were associated with this system,
and these had long been recognized. The most important
was the observed motions of the planets. Planets could be
seen moving in noncircular patterns around the earth. At
certain times the planets actually appeared to be making
backward or retrograde motion. The Ptolemaic systems
explained these strange motions through *epicycles*. The

planets were said to make a second revolution in an orbit
tangent to their primary orbit around the earth. The
epicycle was compared to a jewel on a ring. Other intellectual but nonobservational difficulties related to the immense speed at which the spheres had to move around
the earth. To say the least, the Ptolemaic systems were
cluttered. However, they were effective explanations as
long as one assumed Aristotelian physics and the Christian belief that the earth rested at the center of the
created universe.

Copernicus's *On the Revolutions of the Heavenly
Spheres* challenged this picture in the most conservative
manner possible. It suggested that if the earth were
supposed to move about the sun in a circle, many of the
difficulties with the Ptolemaic systems would disappear or
become simpler. Although not wholly eliminated, the
number of epicycles would be somewhat fewer. The
motive behind this shift away from an earth-centered
universe was to find a solution to the problems of planetary motion. By allowing the earth to move around the
sun, Copernicus was able to construct a more mathematically elegant basis for astronomy. He had been discontented with the traditional system because it was mathematically clumsy and inconsistent. The primary appeal
of his new system was its mathematical aesthetics. He
wanted to put the sun at the center of the universe so that
mathematical astronomy would make more sense. A
change in the conception of the position of the earth
meant that the planets were actually moving in circular
orbits and only seemed to be doing otherwise because of
the position of the observers on earth.

Except for the modification in the position of the earth,
most of the other parts of Copernicus's book were Ptolemaic. The path of the planets remained circular. Genuine
epicycles still existed in the heavens. His system was no
more accurate than the existing ones for predicting the
location of the planets. He had employed no new evidence. The major impact of his work was to provide
another way of confronting some of the difficulties inherent in Ptolemaic astronomy. This work did not immedi-

View of the universe as described by Claudius Ptolemy, an astronomer of Alexandria, Egypt, in the second century. Ptolemy's view, which put the earth unmoving in the center with the other heavenly objects circling it (the sun being in the fourth circle), dominated astronomy until the sixteenth century. The illustration is from a book by Gregor Reisch, *Margarita Philosophica* (1515). [The British Library, London.]

ately replace the old astronomy, but it did allow other people who were also discontented with the Ptolemaic systems to think in new directions.

Copernicus's concern for mathematics provided an example of the single most important factor in the developing new science. Mathematics became the model to which the new emerging scientific thought would conform. However, from the late sixteenth century onward there was added to the mathematical bias a desire for scientific thought to conform to empirical observation. The major spokesman for this position was Francis Bacon.

Francis Bacon

Bacon (1561–1626) was an Englishman of almost universal accomplishment. He was a lawyer, a high royal official, and the author of histories, moral essays, and philosophical discourses. Traditionally he has been regarded as the Father of Empiricism and of the idea of experimentation in science. Much of this reputation is unearned. Nor was Bacon a scientist except in the most amateur fashion. His accomplishment was setting a tone and helping to create a climate in which other scientists worked. In books such as *The Advancement of Learning* (1605), the *Novum Organum* (1620), and the *New Atlantis* (1627), Bacon attacked Scholastic philosophy and reverence for intellectual authority in general. He believed that Scholastic thinkers paid too much attention to tradition and to knowledge achieved by the ancients. He urged contemporaries to strike out on their own in search of a new understanding of nature. He wanted seventeenth-century Europeans to have confidence in themselves and their own abilities rather than in the people and methods of the past. Bacon was one of the first major European writers to champion the desirability of innovation and change.

Bacon believed that human knowledge should produce useful results. In particular, knowledge of nature should be brought to the aid of the human condition. Those goals required the modification or abandonment of Scho-

Francis Bacon here muses in Trinity College Chapel, Cambridge University, as sculptured by Henry Weekes. [By courtesy of The Courtauld Institute of Art, London.]

flowers of the garden and of the field, but transforms and digests it by a power of its own. Not unlike this is the true business of philosophy.[3]

By directing scientists toward an examination of empirical evidence, Bacon hoped that they would achieve new knowledge and thus new capabilities for humankind.

Bacon compared himself to Columbus plotting a new route to intellectual discovery. The comparison is significant, because it displays the consciousness of a changing world that appears so often in writers of the late sixteenth and early seventeenth centuries. They were rejecting the past not from simple hatred but rather from a firm understanding that the world was much more complicated than their medieval forebears had thought.

Neither Europe nor European thought could remain self-contained. There were not only new worlds on the globe but also new worlds of the mind. Most of the people in Bacon's day, including intellectuals, thought that the best era of human history lay in the past. Bacon dissented vigorously from that point of view. He looked to a future of material improvement achieved through the empirical examination of nature. His own theory of induction from empirical evidence was quite faulty, but his insistence upon appeal to experience influenced others whose methods were more productive. His great achievement was to persuade increasing numbers of thinkers that scientific thought must conform to empirical experience.

Bacon gave science a progressionist bias: it was to have a practical purpose and the goal of human improvement. Some scientific investigation does possess this character. Much pure research does not. However, Bacon linked in the public mind the concepts of science and material progress. This was a powerful idea and has continued to influence Western civilization to the present day. It has made science and those who can appeal to the authority of science major forces for change and innovation. Thus,

lastic modes of learning and thinking. Bacon contended, "The [scholastic] logic now in use serves more to fix and give stability to the errors which have their foundation in commonly received notions than to help the search after truth."[2] Scholastic philosophers could not escape from their syllogisms to examine the foundations of their thought and intellectual presuppositions. Bacon urged that philosophers and investigators of nature examine the evidence of their senses before constructing logical speculations. In a famous passage he divided all philosophers into "men of experiment and men of dogmas." He observed;

The men of experiment are like the ant, they only collect and use; the reasoners resemble spiders, who make cobwebs out of their own substance. But the bee takes a middle course: it gathers its materials from the

2 Quoted in Franklin Baumer, *Main Currents of Western Thought*, 4th ed. (New Haven: Yale, 1978), p. 281.

3 Quoted in ibid., p. 288.

New Directions in Science and Thought in the Sixteenth and Seventeenth Centuries

though not making any major scientific contribution himself, Bacon directed investigators of nature to a new method and a new purpose.

Working Out a New Scientific World View

The key to the future development of the Copernican revolution lay in the fusion of mathematical astronomy with further empirical data and observation. Mathematics provided the foundation for the new scientific model; the new empirical evidence helped to persuade the learned public.

Tycho Brahe and Johannes Kepler

The next major step toward the conception of a sun-centered system was taken by Tycho Brahe (1546–1601). He actually spent most of his life opposing Copernicus and advocating a different kind of earth-centered system. He suggested that the moon and the sun revolved around the earth and that the other planets revolved around the sun. However, in attacking Copernicus he gave the latter's ideas more publicity. More important, this Danish astronomer's major weapon against Copernican astronomy was a series of new naked-eye astronomical observations. Brahe constructed the most accurate tables of observations that had been drawn up for centuries.

When Brahe died, these tables came into the possession of Johannes Kepler (1571–1630), a German astronomer. Kepler was a convinced Copernican, but his reasons for taking that position were not scientific. Kepler was deeply influenced by Renaissance Neoplatonism and its honoring of the sun. These Neoplatonists were also determined to discover mathematical harmonies in those numbers that would support a sun-centered universe. After much work Kepler discovered that to keep the sun at the center of things, he must abandon the Copernican concept of circular orbits. The mathematical relationships that emerged from consideration of Brahe's observations

Galileo Galilei, the Florentine whose observational work helped mightily to confirm Copernicus's theories. The Ptolemaic view of the universe was thus destroyed and the foundations of modern astronomy were laid. The portrait is from 1624. [Reproduced by courtesy of the Trustees of the British Museum.]

suggested that the orbits of the planets were elliptical. Kepler published his findings in 1609 in a book entitled *On the Motion of Mars*. He had solved the problem of planetary orbits by using Copernicus's sun-centered universe and Brahe's empirical data.

Galileo Galilei

From Copernicus to Brahe to Kepler there had been little new information about the heavens that might not have been known to Ptolemy. However, in the same year that Kepler published his volume on Mars, an Italian scientist named Galileo Galilei (1564–1642) first turned a telescope on the heavens. Through that recently invented instrument he saw stars where none had been known to exist, mountains on the moon, spots moving across the sun, and moons orbiting Jupiter. The heavens were far more complex than anyone had formerly suspected. None of these discoveries proved that the earth orbited the sun, but they did suggest the complete inade-

Galileo, working at first from others' suggestions, effectively invented the telescope. This is his 1609 instrument. His observations of the physical features on earth's moon and of the cyclical phases of the planet Venus and his discovery of the most prominent moons of the planet Jupiter were the first major astronomical observations since antiquity and had revolutionary intellectual and theological implications. [Istituto e Museo de Storia della Scienza, Florence.]

TVBVM OPTICVM VIDES GALILAEI INVENTVM ET OPVS, QVO SOLIS MACVLAS ET EXTIMOS LVNAE MONTES, ET IOVIS SATELLITES, ET NOVAM QVASI RERVM VNIVERSITATEM PRIMVS DISPEXIT A. MDCIX.

Spectacles were an earlier optical aid. They were known at least as early as the fourteenth century, and by the sixteenth they appear fairly frequently in portraits. Here the sixteenth-century German painter Hermann Tom Ring imagines the classical Roman author Vergil reading with spectacles. [Bettmann Archive.]

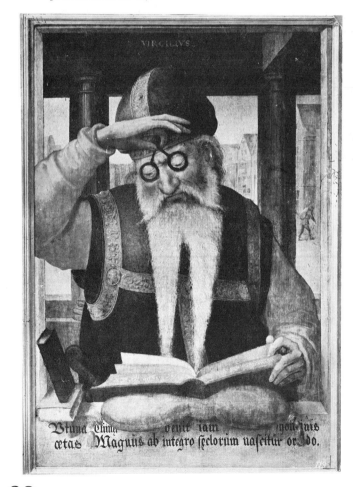

quacy of the Ptolemaic system. It simply could not accommodate itself to all of these new phenomena. Some of Galileo's colleagues at the university of Padua were so unnerved that they refused to look through the telescope. Galileo publicized his findings and arguments for the Copernican system in numerous works, the most famous of which was his *Dialogues on the Two Chief Systems of the World* (1632). This book brought down upon him the condemnation of the Roman Catholic Church. He was compelled to recant his opinions. However, he is reputed to have muttered after the recantation, "E pur si muove" ("It [the earth] still moves").

Galileo's discoveries and his popularization of the Copernican system were of secondary importance in his life

The microscope was the telescope's companion as a major optical invention of the seventeenth century. Several people, including Galileo, had a hand in its development, but the greatest progress—and the most amazing results—came from the Hollander Anton van Leeuwenhoek (1632–1723) who, using only primitive simple instruments made by himself, was the first person actually to see protozoa and bacteria, and the Englishman Robert Hooke (1635–1703). Hooke's fairly elaborate microscope is shown here. [Courtesy Bausch and Lomb, Inc.]

Robert Hooke carefully drew the startling results of his microscopic explorations. From his book *Micrographia* (1665) comes this rendering of the body louse; even such familiar small creatures had not been seen before in this detail.

work. His most important achievement was to articulate the concept of a universe totally subject to mathematical laws. More than any other writer of the century he argued that nature in its most minute details was mathematical. He once wrote;

Philosophy is written in that great book which ever lies before our eyes—I mean the universe—but we cannot understand it if we do not first learn the language and grasp the symbols in which it is written. This book is written in the mathematical language, and the symbols are triangles, circles, and other geometrical figures, without whose help it is impossible to comprehend a single word of it; without which one wanders through a dark labyrinth.[4]

4 Quoted in E. A. Burtt, *The Metaphysical Foundations of Modern Physical Science* (Garden City, N.Y.: Anchor-Doubleday, 1954), p. 75.

The universe was rational; however, its rationality was not that of Scholastic logic but of mathematics. Copernicus had thought that the heavens conformed to mathematical regularity; Galileo saw this regularity throughout physical nature. He believed that the smallest atom behaved with the same mathematical precision as the largest heavenly sphere.

Galileo's thought meant that a world of quantity was replacing one of qualities. Mathematical quantities and relationships would henceforth increasingly be used to describe nature. Color, beauty, taste, and the like would be reduced to numerical relationships. And eventually social relationships would be envisioned in a mathematical model. Nature was cold, rational, mathematical, and mechanistic. What was real and lasting in the world was what was mathematically measurable. Few intellectual shifts have wrought such momentous changes for Western civilization.

René Descartes

No writer of the seventeenth century more fully adopted the geometric spirit of contemporary mathematics than René Descartes (1596–1650). He was a gifted mathematician who invented analytic geometry, and he was the author of major works on numerous scientific topics. However, his most important contribution was to scientific method. Unlike Bacon he wanted to proceed by deduction rather than by empirical observation and induction.

René Descartes, the reputed father of modern philosophy. He was famed for his declaration, "Cogito, ergo sum" ("I think, therefore I am"), which was for Descartes the point of departure for all human knowledge. [Bettmann Archive.]

In 1637 Descartes published a *Discourse on Method* in which he attempted to provide a basis for all thinking based on a mathematical model. He published the work in French rather than in Latin because he wanted it to have wide circulation and application. He commenced by saying that he would doubt everything except those propositions about which he could have clear and distinct ideas. This approach rejected all forms of intellectual authority except the conviction of his own reason. He concluded that he could not doubt his own act of thinking and his own existence. From this base he proceeded to deduce the existence of God. The presence of God was important to Descartes because God was the guarantor of the correctness of clear and distinct ideas. Because God was not a deceiver, the ideas of God-given reason could not be false.

Descartes believed that this powerful human reason could fully comprehend the world. He divided existing things into mind and body. Thinking was the characteristic of the mind, extension of the body. Within the material world, mathematical laws reigned supreme. These could be grasped by the human reason. Because the laws were mathematical, they could be deduced from each other and constituted a complete system. The world of extension was the world of the scientist. The area of mind related to theology and philosophy. In the material world there was no room for spirits, divinity, or anything nonmaterial. Descartes had separated mind from body in order to banish the former from the realm of scientific speculation. He wanted to resurrect the speculative use of reason, but in a limited manner. It was to be applied only to the mechanical and mathematical realm of matter.

Descartes's emphasis on deduction and rational speculation exercised broad influence. Well into the eighteenth century European thinkers appealed to Descartes's method. However, it was eventually overcome by the force of Baconian induction. The chief reason for the demise of Descartes's influence was the association of the achievements of Sir Isaac Newton with the empirical method.

New Directions in Science and Thought in the Sixteenth and Seventeenth Centuries

Sir Isaac Newton, the Englishman who discovered the mathematical and physical laws governing the force of gravity in the universe. The portrait is by Sir Godfrey Kneller. [National Portrait Gallery, London.]

Isaac Newton

Isaac Newton (1642–1727) drew upon the work of his predecessors and his own brilliance to solve the major remaining problem of planetary motion and to establish a basis for physics that endured more than two centuries. The question that continued to perplex seventeenth-century scientists who accepted the theories of Copernicus, Kepler, and Galileo was how the planets and other heavenly bodies moved in an orderly fashion. The Ptolemaic and Aristotelian answer had been the crystalline spheres and a universe arranged in the order of the heaviness of its parts. Numerous unsatisfactory theories had been set forth to deal with the question.

In 1687 Newton published *The Mathematical Principles of Natural Philosophy*, better known by its Latin title of *Principia Mathematica*. Much of the research and thinking for this great work had taken place more than fifteen years earlier. Newton was heavily indebted to the work of Galileo and particularly to the latter's view that inertia could exist in either a state of motion or a state of rest. Galileo's mathematical bias permeated Newton's thought.

Newton reasoned that the planets and all other physical objects in the universe moved through mutual attraction. Every object in the universe affected every other object through gravity. The attraction of gravity explained why the planets moved in an orderly rather than in a chaotic manner. He had found that "the force of gravity towards the whole planet did arise from and was compounded of the forces of gravity towards all its parts, and towards every one part was in the inverse proportion of the squares of the distances from the part."[5] Newton demonstrated this relationship mathematically. He made no attempt to explain the nature of gravity itself.

Newton was a great mathematical genius, but he also upheld the importance of empirical data and observation. He believed, in good Baconian fashion, that one must observe phenomena before attempting to explain them. The final test of any theory or hypothesis for him was whether it described what could actually be observed. He was a great opponent of Descartes's rationalism, which he believed included insufficient guards against error. As Newton's own theory of universal gravitation became increasingly accepted, the Baconian bias also became more fully popularized.

With the work of Newton the natural universe became a realm of law and regularity. Spirits and divinities were no longer necessary to explain its operation. The Scientific Revolution in that manner liberated human beings from the fear of a chaotic or haphazard universe. Most of the scientists were very devout people. They saw the new picture of physical nature as suggesting a new picture of God. The Creator of this rational, lawful nature must also be rational. To study nature was to come to a better understanding of that Creator. Science and religious faith were not only compatible but mutually supporting. As Newton wrote, "The main Business of Natural Philosophy is to argue from Phaenomena without feigning Hypothesis, and to deduce Causes from

5 Quoted in A. Rupert Hall, *From Galileo to Newton, 1630–1720* (London: Fontana, 1970), p. 300.

New Directions in Science and Thought in the Sixteenth and Seventeenth Centuries

William Blake's *Newton* is, of course, not a portrait of an individual. Instead, it dramatizes and glorifies the detached, almost God-like scientist who can solve the mysteries of the universe and display the results with mathematical precision. [The Tate Gallery, London.]

Effects, till we come to the very first Cause, which certainly is not mechanical."[6]

This reconciliation of faith and science allowed the new physics and astronomy to spread rapidly. At the very time when Europeans were finally tiring of the wars of religion, the new science provided the basis for a view of God that might lead away from irrational disputes and wars over religious doctrine. Faith in a rational God encouraged faith in the rationality of human beings and in their capacity to improve their lot once liberated from the traditions of the past. The Scientific Revolution provided the great model for the desirability of change and of criticism of inherited views. Yet at the same time the new science caused some people to feel that the mystery had been driven from the universe and that the rational Creator was less loving and near to humankind than the God of earlier ages.

Writers and Philosophers

The end of the sixteenth century saw weariness with religious strife and incipient unbelief as many could no longer embrace either old Catholic or new Protestant absolutes. Intellectually as well as politically the seventeenth century was a period of transition. It was a transition already well prepared by the thinkers of the Renaissance, who had reacted strongly against medieval intellectual traditions, especially those informed by Aristotle and Scholasticism.

Even as they sought a purer culture behind the Middle

6 Quoted in Baumer, p. 323.

Ages in pagan and Christian antiquity, however, Humanists and Protestants continued to share much of the medieval vision of a unified Christendom. Few were prepared to embrace the secular values and preoccupations of the growing scientific movement, which found its models in mathematics and the natural sciences, not in the example and authority of antiquity. Some strongly condemned the work of Copernicus, Kepler, and Galileo, whose theories seemed to fly in the face of common-sense experience as well as to question hallowed tradition.

The thinkers of the Renaissance and the Reformation nonetheless prepared the way for the new science and philosophy both by their attacks on tradition and by their own failure to implement radical reforms. Humanist revival of interest in ancient skepticism proved an effective foundation for attacks on traditional views of authority and rationality in both religion and science. Already such thinkers as the Italian Pico della Mirandola (1463–1494), the German Agrippa of Nettisheim (1486–1535), and the Frenchman François Rabelais (1494–1553) had questioned the ability of reason to obtain certitude. Sebastian Castellio (1515–1563), Michel de Montaigne (1533–1592), and Pierre Charron (1541–1603) had been as much repulsed by the new Calvinist religion as John Calvin had been by medieval religion. It was in the wake of such criticism that Francis Bacon and René Descartes developed a more modest, yet surer, definition of rationality as the tool of the new scientific philosophy.

The writers and philosophers of the seventeenth century were aware that they lived in a period of transition. Some embraced the new science wholeheartedly (Hobbes and Locke), some tried to straddle the two ages (Cervantes, Shakespeare, and Milton), and still others ignored or opposed the new developments that seemed mortally to threaten traditional values (Pascal and Bunyan).

Miguel de Cervantes Saavedra (1547–1616)

Spanish literature of the sixteenth and seventeenth centuries was influenced by the peculiar religious and

Don Quixote's windmill was not a new invention. Instead, it was an important item of rural technology from at least as early as the twelfth century. The one shown here is equipped with an automatic winch to raise bags of grain for grinding. The mill itself is on a post that can be turned with the direction of the wind. This illustration is probably from the fifteenth century. [Bettmann Archive.]

political history of Spain in this period. Spain was dominated by the Catholic Church. Since the joint reign of Ferdinand and Isabella (1479–1504) the church had received the unqualified support of reigning political power. Although there was religious reform in Spain, there was never a Protestant Reformation, thanks largely to the abiding power of the church and the Inquisition.

The second influence was the aggressive piety of the Spanish rulers Charles I (who was also the Holy Roman Emperor Charles V) (1516–1556) and Philip II (1556–1598). The intertwining of Catholic piety and Spanish political power underlay the third major influence on Spanish literature: preoccupation with medieval chivalric virtues—in particular, questions of honor and loyalty. The novels and plays of the period almost invariably focus on a special decision involving a character's reputation as his honor or loyalty is tested. In this regard Spanish literature may be said to have remained more Catholic and medieval than that of England and France, both of which saw major Protestant movements. Two of the most important Spanish writers in this period became priests (Lope de Vega and Pedro Calderón de la Barca), and the one generally acknowledged to be the greatest Spanish writer of all time, Cervantes, was preoccupied in his work with the strengths and weaknesses of religious idealism.

Cervantes was born in Alcalá, the son of a nomadic physician. Having received only a smattering of formal education, he educated himself by insatiable reading in vernacular literature and immersion in the "school of life." As a young man he worked in Rome for a Spanish cardinal. In 1570 he became a soldier and was even decorated for gallantry in the Battle of Lepanto (1571), an engagement that also left one of his hands paralyzed for life. When he was returning to Spain in 1575, his ship was captured by pirates and Cervantes was forced to spend five years as a slave in Algiers. Upon his release and return to Spain he held many odd jobs, among them that of a tax collector. He was several times imprisoned for padding his accounts. *Don Quixote*, his most famous work, was conceived and begun in 1603, while he languished in prison.

The first part of *Don Quixote* appeared in 1605 and a second part followed in 1615. If, as many argue, the intent of this work was to satirize the chivalric romances so popular in Spain, Cervantes was nonetheless also unable to conceal his deep affection for the character he created as an object of ridicule, Don Quixote. The work is satire only on the surface and has remained as much an object of study by philosophers and theologians as by students of Spanish literature. Don Quixote, a none too stable middle-aged man, is presented by Cervantes as one driven mad by reading too many chivalric romances. He comes finally to believe that he is an aspirant to knighthood and must prove by brave deeds his worthiness of initiation into knightly rank. To this end he acquires a rusty suit of armor, mounts an aged steed (named Rozinante), and chooses for his inspiration a quite unworthy peasant girl, Dulcinea, whom he fancies to be a noble lady to whom he can, with honor, dedicate his life.

Don Quixote's foil in the story—Sancho Panza, a clever, worldly-wise peasant, who serves as Don Quixote's squire—is an equally fascinating character. Sancho

Panza watches with bemused skepticism, but also with genuine sympathy, as his lord does battle with a windmill (which he mistakes for a dragon) and repeatedly makes a fool of himself as he gallops across the countryside. The story ends tragically with Don Quixote's humiliating defeat by a well-meaning friend, who, disguised as a knight, bests Don Quixote in combat and forces him to renounce his quest for knighthood. The humiliated Don Quixote does not, however, come thereafter to his senses. He returns sadly to his village to die a shamed and broken-hearted old man.

Throughout *Don Quixote* Cervantes juxtaposed the down-to-earth realism of Sancho Panza with the old-fashioned religious idealism of Don Quixote. The reader perceives that Cervantes really admired the one as much as the other and meant to portray both as representing attitudes necessary for a happy life. Like his English counterpart William Shakespeare, Cervantes understood the complexity of human nature. He wanted his readers to remember that if they are to be truly happy, men and women need dreams, even impossible ones, just as much as they need a sense of reality.

The other major Spanish writers of the period had a far less universal vision than Cervantes. Lope Felix de Vega Carpio (1562–1635), the author of an incredible number of epics, romances, novels, lyrics, and plays, pandered to popular Spanish tastes and remained content to meet the contemporary demand for entertainment rather than venturing profound and lasting works. He never wanted for variety in his work, however, and almost singlehandedly created the Spanish national theater. Pedro Calderón de la Barca (1600–1681) wrote court dramas, comedies and highly sentimental "point of honor" plays that spoke to current national interests and became favorites among later Romantic writers.

William Shakespeare (1564–1616)

Shakespeare, to many the greatest playwright in the English language, was born in Stratford-on-Avon, where he lived almost all of his life. There is much less factual

The English dramatist and poet, William Shakespeare. This engraving by Martin Droeshout appears on the title page of the collected edition of his plays published in 1623 and is probably as close as we shall come to knowing what he looked like.

knowledge about him than one would expect of such an important figure. Shakespeare was married in 1582, at the early age of eighteen, and he and his wife, Anne Hathaway, had three children (two were twins) by 1585. He was apparently employed as a schoolteacher for a time and in this capacity acquired his broad knowledge of Renaissance learning and literature. The argument of

This 1596 sketch of the interior of the Swan Theater in London by Johannis de Witt, a Dutch visitor, is the only known contemporary view of an Elizabethan playhouse. In this kind of setting the plays of Marlowe, Shakespeare, Jonson, and their fellows were first seen. [The Granger Collection.]

some scholars that he was an untutored natural genius is highly questionable. His own learning and his enthusiasm for the education of his day are manifest in the many learned allusions that appear in such plays as *A Midsummer-Night's Dream* (1594–1595).

Shakespeare was a man of the country as well as of the town and manifestly enjoyed the life of a country gentleman. There is none of the Puritan distress over worldliness in his work. He took the new commercialism and the bawdy pleasures of the Elizabethan Age in stride and with amusement. The few allusions to the Puritans that exist in his works appear to be more critical than complementary. In matters of religion, as in those of politics, he was very much a man of his time and not inclined to offend his queen.

That Shakespeare was interested in politics is apparent from his history plays and the references, to contempo-

rary political events that fill all his plays. He seems to have viewed government simply, however, through the character of the individual ruler, whether Richard III or Elizabeth Tudor, not in terms of ideal systems. By modern standards he was a political conservative, accepting the social rankings and the power structure of his day and demonstrating unquestioned patriotism.

Shakespeare knew the theatre as one who participated in every phase of its life—as a playwright, an actor, and a part owner of a theater. He was a member and principal dramatist of a famous company of actors known as the King's Men. During the tenure of Edmund Tilney, who was the Master of Revels during the greater part of Shakespeare's active period (1590–1610), many of Shakespeare's plays were performed at court before the queen, who was a most enthusiastic patron of plays and pageants.

Elizabethan drama was already a distinctive form when Shakespeare began writing. Unlike French drama of the seventeenth century, which was dominated by the court and classical models, English drama developed in the sixteenth and seventeenth centuries as a blending of many extant forms, ranging from classical comedies and tragedies to contemporary Italian short stories. In Shakespeare's own library were to be found Holinshed's and other English chronicles; the works of Plutarch, Ovid, and Vergil, among other Latin authors; Arthurian romances and popular songs and fables; the writings of Montaigne and Rabelais; and the major English poets and prose writers.

Shakespeare's tragedies were especially influenced by the work of two of his contemporaries: Thomas Kyd and Christopher Marlowe. Kyd (1558–1594) was the author of the first dramatic version of *Hamlet* and a master at weaving together motive, plot, and tragic intensity. The tragedies of Marlowe (1564–1593) set a model for character, poetry, and style that only Shakespeare among the English playwrights of the period surpassed. Shakespeare's work is an original synthesis of the best past and current achievements.

Shakespeare mastered the psychology of human motivation and passion. He had a unique talent for psychological penetration, one rivalled only by the French Jansenist dramatist Jean Racine (1639–1699), who, however, remained confined to classical forms and rules. Later romantic writers claimed Shakespeare as one of their own and contrasted his work sharply with the neo-classicism of Pierre Corneille and Racine, who they found by comparison to be narrow and mechanical.

Shakespeare wrote histories, comedies, and tragedies. *Richard III* (1593), a very early play, stands out among the examples of the first genre, although historians have criticized as historically inaccurate his patriotic depiction of Richard, the foe of Henry Tudor, as an unprincipled villain. Shakespeare's comedies, while not attaining the heights of his tragedies, surpass in originality his history plays. Save for the *Tempest* (1611), his last play and his farewell to the stage, the comedies most familiar to modern readers were written between 1598–1602: *Much Ado About Nothing* (1598/99), *As You Like It* (1598–1600), and *Twelfth Night* (1602).

The tragedies are considered his unique achievement. Four of these were written within a three year period: *Hamlet* (1603), *Othello* (1604), *King Lear* (1605), and *Macbeth* (1606). The most original and independent of the tragedies, *Romeo and Juliet* (1597), transformed an old popular story into a moving drama of "star-cross'd lovers." Both Romeo and Juliet, denied a marriage by their factious families, die tragic deaths. Romeo, finding Juliet and thinking her dead after she had taken a sleeping potion, poisons himself. Juliet, awakening to find her Romeo dead, stabs herself to death with his dagger.

Throughout his lifetime and ever since Shakespeare has been immensely popular with both the play-goer and the play-reader. As Ben Jonson, a contemporary classical dramatist who created his own school of poets, aptly put it in a tribute affixed to the First Folio edition of Shakespeare's plays (1623): "He was not of an age, but for all time."

The English writer and poet John Milton in an engraving by William Faithorne—one of the few authentic contemporary likenesses of him.
[The Granger Collection.]

John Milton (1608–1674)

John Milton was the son of a devout Puritan father. Educated at St. Paul's School and Christ's College, Cambridge, he became a careful student of Christian and pagan classics. In 1638, he traveled to Italy, where he found the lingering Renaissance to be a very congenial intellectual atmosphere. The Phlegraean Fields near Naples, a volcanic region, later became the model for hell in *Paradise Lost*, and the Villa d'Este is suspected by some scholars to have provided the model for paradise in *Paradise Regained*. Milton remained throughout his life a man more at home in the Italian Renaissance, with its high ideals and universal vision, than in the strife-torn England of the seventeenth century.

Milton was a man of deep inner conviction and principle; standing a test of character was uppermost in his own personal life and in the subjects of his literary work. An early poem, *Lycidas*, was a pastoral elegy dealing with one who lived well but not long. Edward King, a close college friend who tragically drowned. In 1639 Milton joined the Puritan struggle against Charles I and Archbishop Laud. Employing his literary talents as a pamphleteer, he defended the presbyterian form of church government against the episcopacy and supported other Puritan reforms. After a month-long unsuccessful marriage in 1642 (a marriage later reconciled), he wrote several tracts in defense of the right to divorce. These writings became a factor in Parliament's passage of a censorship law in 1643, against which Milton wrote an eloquent defense of the freedom of the press, *Areopagitica* (1664).

Until the upheavals of the civil war moderated his views, Milton believed that government should have the least possible control over the private lives of individuals. When Parliament divided into Presbyterians and Independents, he took the side of the latter, who wanted to dissolve the national church altogether in favor of the local autonomy of individual congregations. He further defended the execution of Charles I in a tract on the *Tenure of Kings and Magistrates* and later served as secretary to the executive committee of Parliament during Cromwell's protectorate. It was after his intense labor on this tract that his eyesight failed. Milton wrote his acclaimed masterpieces as one totally blind.

Paradise Lost, Milton's masterpiece of English blank verse, was completed in 1665 and published in 1667. A study of the destructive qualities of pride and the redeeming possibilities of humility, it elaborates in traditional Christian language and concept the revolt of Satan in heaven and the fall of Adam on earth. Milton was throughout preoccupied with the motives of Satan and all who rebel against God. His proud but tragic Satan, one of the great figures of all literature, represents the absolute corruption of potential greatness.

In *Paradise Lost* Milton aspired to give England a lasting classic like that given Greece in Homer's *Iliad* and ancient Rome in Vergil's *Aeneid*. In choosing biblical subject matter, he revealed the influence of contemporary theology on his work. Milton tended to agree with the Arminians, who, unlike the extreme Calvinists, did not believe that all worldly events, including the Fall of Man, were immutably fixed in the eternal decree of God. Milton shared the Arminian belief that man must take responsibility for his fate and that human efforts to improve character could, with God's grace, bring man to salvation.

Perhaps his own blindness, joined with the hope of making the best out of a failed religious revolution, inclined Milton to sympathize with those who urged men to make the most of what they had, even in the face of seemingly sure defeat. That is a manifest concern of his last works, *Samson Agonistes*, which recounts the biblical story of Samson, and *Paradise Regained*, the story of Christ's temptation in the wilderness, both published in 1671.

John Bunyan (1628–1688)

Bunyan was the author of two classics of sectarian Puritan spirituality: *Grace Abounding* (1666) and *The Pilgrim's Progress* (1678). A Bedford tinker, his works speak especially for the seventeenth-century working man and popular religious culture. Bunyan received only the most basic education before taking up his father's craft. He was drafted into Oliver Cromwell's revolutionary army in 1644 and served for two years, although without seeing actual combat. The visionary fervor of the New Model Army and the imagery of warring abound in Bunyan's work.

After the restoration of the monarchy in 1660 Bunyan was arrested for his fiery preaching and remained in prison for twelve years. Had he been willing to agree to give up preaching, he might have been released much sooner. But Puritans considered the compromise of one's beliefs a tragic flaw and Bunyan steadfastly refused all such suggestions.

It was during this period of imprisonment that Bunyan wrote his famous autobiography, *Grace Abounding,* for his separated friends. It is both a very personal statement and a model for the faithful. Like *The Pilgrim's Progress,* Bunyan's later masterpiece, *Grace Abounding* expresses Puritan piety at its most fervent. Puritans believed that the individual could do absolutely nothing to save himself and this made them extremely restless and introspective. The individual believer could only trust that God had placed him among the elect and try each day to live a life that reflected such a favored status. So long as he struggled successfully against the flesh and the world, he had presumptive evidence that he was among God's elect. To falter or to become complacent in the face of temptation, was to cast doubt upon ones' faith and salvation and even raise the specter of eternal damnation.

This anxious questing for salvation came to classic expression in *The Pilgrim's Progress,* a work unique in its contribution to Western religious symbolism and imagery. The story of the journey of Christian and his friends Hopeful and Faithful to the Celestial City, it teaches that one must deny wife, children, and all earthly security and go in search of "Life, life, eternal life." During the long journey, the travelers must resist the temptations of Worldly-Wiseman and Vanity Fair, pass through the Slough of Despond, and endure a long dark night in Doubting Castle, their faith being tested at every turn. Bunyan later wrote a work tracing the progress of Christian's opposite, entitled *The Life and Death of Mr. Badman* (1680), the story of a man so addicted to the bad habits of Restoration society, of which Bunyan strongly disapproved, that he journeyed steadfastly not to heaven but to hell.

The loss of national unity during the Puritan struggle against the Stuart monarchy and the Anglican Church took its toll on English literature and drama during the seventeenth century. In 1642 the Puritans had closed the theaters of London. They were reopened after the Restoration of Charles II in 1660, and drama revived following the long Puritan interregnum.

Literary thought thereafter became less experimental and adopted proven classical forms as a new movement to subject reality to the strict rules of reason began. During the so-called Augustan Age, from John Dryden (1631–1700) to Alexander Pope (1688–1744), classicism was the literary rule. There was a preoccupation with the world of mundane facts, rather than with that of universal ideals, and a waning of the transcendental concerns of the Elizabethans and the Puritan divines. As in France, where the French comedy writer Molière (1622–1673) is the outstanding example, English writers tried to please the royal court and aristocracy by turning to more earthy and entertaining popular topics.

Blaise Pascal (1623–1662)

Pascal was a mathematician and a physical scientist widely acclaimed by his contemporaries. He was also a most devout man, who surrendered all his wealth so that he might more easily pursue an austere, self-disciplined life. Torn between the continuing dogmatism and the new skepticism of the seventeenth century, he aspired to write a work that would refute both the Jesuits, whose casuistry (i.e., confessional tactics designed to minimize and even excuse sinful acts) he considered a distortion of Christian teaching, and the skeptics of his age, who either denied religion altogether (atheists) or accepted it only as it conformed to reason (Deists). Such a definitive work was never realized, and his views on these matters exist only in piecemeal form. He wrote against the Jesuits in his *Provincial Letters* (1656–1657), and he left behind a provocative collection of reflections on man and religion that were published posthumously under the title *Pensées.*

Pascal was early influenced by the Jansenists, seventeenth-century Catholic opponents of the Jesuits. His sister was a member of the Jansenist community of Port Royal near Paris, and after 1654 Pascal himself was closely identified with this community. The Jansenists shared with the Calvinists St. Augustine's belief in man's total sinfulness, his eternal predestination by God, and his

The arithmetical machine invented in 1642 by Blaise Pascal, the French philosopher and mathematician. Its main feature was the automatic carry-forward. The wheels, each divided into nine sections, were connected in such a way that the complete rotation of one of them caused the wheel on the left of it to move forward by one digit. The foundations of adding machines and other mechanical calculators were thus laid by this device. [Culver Pictures.]

complete dependence on faith and grace for knowledge of God and salvation.

Pascal believed that reason and science, although attesting man's dignity, remained of no avail in matters of religion. Here only the reasons of the heart and a "leap of faith" could prevail. Pascal saw two essential truths in the Christian religion: that a loving God, worthy of man's attainment, exists, and that man, because he is corrupted in his nature, is utterly unworthy of God. Pascal believed that the atheists and the Deists of the age had spurned the lesson of reason. For him rational analysis of the human condition attested man's utter mortality and corruption and exposed the weakness of reason itself in resolving the problems of human nature and destiny. Reason should rather drive those who truly heed it to faith and dependence on divine grace.

Pascal made a famous wager with the skeptics. It is a better bet, he argued, to believe that God exists and to stake everything on his promised mercy than not to do so, because if God does exist everything will be gained by the believer, whereas the loss incurred by having believed in him should he prove not to exist is by comparison very slight.

Pascal was convinced that belief in God measurably improved man's present life psychologically and disciplined it morally, regardless of whether or not God proved in the end to exist; great danger lay in the surrender of traditional religious belief. Pascal urged his contemporaries to seek self-understanding by "learned ignorance" and to discover man's greatness by recognizing his

Even before Pascal's day, of course, there was a tradition of elaborate mechanical devices throughout Europe. For example, by 1500 there were public clocks in practically every town. One of the most famous is the astronomical clock of Strasbourg's cathedral in France, which presents a parade of allegorical figures every day at noon. [French Government Tourist Office, New York.]

OPPOSITE: The Glockenspiel, or clock performance, occurring hourly at the Munich city hall, is another ingenious time-keeping device. [German Information Center, New York.]

misery. Thereby Pascal hoped to counter what he believed to be the false optimism of the new rationalism and science.

Baruch Spinoza (1632–1677)

The most controversial thinker of the seventeenth century was Baruch Spinoza, the son of a Jewish merchant of Amsterdam. Spinoza's philosophy caused his excommunication by his own synagogue in 1656. In 1670 he published his *Treatise on Religious and Political Philosophy,* a work that criticized the dogmatism of Dutch Calvinists and championed freedom of thought. During his lifetime both Jews and Protestants attacked him as an atheist.

Spinoza's most influential writing, the *Ethics,* was published after his death in 1677. Religious leaders univer-

sally condemned it for its apparent espousal of pantheism. God and nature were so closely identified by Spinoza that little room seemed left either for divine revelation in Scripture or for the personal immortality of the soul, denials equally repugnant to Jews and Christians. The *Ethics* was a very complicated work, written in the spirit of the new science as a geometrical system of definitions, axioms, and propositions. It was divided into five parts, which dealt with God, the mind, emotions, human bondage, and human freedom.

The most controversial part of the *Ethics* dealt with the nature of substance and of God. According to Spinoza, there is but one substance, which is self-caused, free, and infinite, and God is that substance. From this definition it follows that everything that exists is in God and cannot even be conceived apart from him. Such a doctrine is not literally pantheistic because God is still seen to be more than the created world that he, as primal substance, embraces. It may perhaps best be described as *panentheism*: the teaching that all that is is within God, yet God remains more than and beyond the natural world. Nonetheless, in Spinoza's view, statements about the natural world are also statements about divine nature. Mind and matter are seen to be extensions of the infinite substance of God; what transpires in the world of man and nature is a necessary outpouring of the divine.

Such teaching clearly ran the danger of portraying the world as eternal and human actions as unfree and inevitable, the expression of a divine fatalism. Such points of view have been considered heresies by Jews and Christians because they deny the creation of the world by God in time and destroy any voluntary basis for personal reward and punishment.

Spinoza found enthusiastic supporters in the German philosopher Georg Wilhelm Friedrich Hegel and in romantic writers of the nineteenth century, especially Johann Wolfgang von Goethe and Percy Bysshe Shelley. Modern thinkers unable to accept traditional religious language and doctrines have continued to find in Spinoza a congenial rational religion.

Thomas Hobbes (1588–1679)

Thomas Hobbes is incontestably the most original political philosopher of the seventeenth century. The son of a clergyman, he was educated at Magdalen College, Oxford, during a period when Puritanism was dominant there. Although he never broke with the Church of England, he came to share basic Calvinist beliefs, especially the low view of human nature and the ideal of a commonwealth based on a covenant, both of which find eloquent expression in Hobbes's political philosophy.

Hobbes was an urbane and much-traveled man and one of the most enthusiastic supporters of the new scientific movement. He worked as tutor and secretary to three earls of Devonshire over a fifty-year period. During the 1630s he visited Paris, where he came to know Descartes, and after the outbreak of the Puritan Revolution in 1640, he lived as an exile in Paris until 1651. In 1646 Hobbes became the tutor of the Prince of Wales, the future Charles II, and remained on good terms with him after the restoration of the Stuart monarchy. Hobbes also spent time with Galileo in Italy and took a special interest in the works of William Harvey (1578–1657). Harvey was a physiologist famed for the discovery of how blood circulated through the body; his scientific writings influenced Hobbes own tracts on bodily motions. Hobbes became an expert in geometry and optics. Also highly trained in classical languages, his first published work was a translation of Thucydides' *History of the Peloponnesian War*, the first English translation of this work and one that is still reprinted today.

Hobbes was driven to the vocation of political philosopher by the English civil war. In 1651 his *Leviathan* appeared. Written as the concluding part of a broad philosophical system that analyzed physical bodies and human nature, the work established Hobbes as a major European thinker. Its subject was the political consequences of human passions and its originality lay in (1) its making natural law, rather than common law (i.e., custom or precedent), the basis of all positive law and (2) its

defense of a representative theory of absolute authority against the theory of the divine right of kings. Hobbes maintained that statute law found its justification only as an expression of the law of nature and that political authority came to rulers by way of the consent of the people.

Hobbes viewed man and society in a thoroughly materialistic and mechanical way. Man is defined as a collection of material particles in motion. All his psychological processes begin with and are derived from bare sensation, and all his motivations are egoistical, intended to increase his pleasure and minimize his pain. His power of reasoning, which Hobbes defined unspectacularly as a process of adding and substracting the consequences of agreed-upon general names of things, develops only after years of concentrated industry.

Despite this seemingly low estimate of man, Hobbes believed much could be accomplished by the reasoned use of science. All was contingent, however, on the correct use of that greatest of all human powers, one compounded of the powers of most men: the commonwealth, in which men are united by their consent in one all-powerful person.

The key to Hobbes's political philosophy is a brilliant myth of the original state of mankind. According to this myth, man in his natural state is absolutely insatiable; mankind is generally inclined to a "perpetual and restless desire of power after power that ceases only in death."[7] As all men desire and in the state of nature have a natural right to everything, their equality breeds enmity; competition, diffidence, and the desire for glory beget perpetual quarreling—"a war of every man against every man."[8] As Hobbes put it in a famous summary:

In such condition there is no place for industry, because the fruit thereof is uncertain; and consequently

---

7 *Leviathan Parts I and II,* ed. by H. W. Schneider (Indianapolis: Bobbs-Merrill, 1958), p. 86.
8 Ibid., p. 106.

The English philosopher Thomas Hobbes, author of *Leviathan*. Hobbes believed that once established in office rulers held an absolute power over their subjects, the alternative being the chaos of a brutish state of nature. The portrait is from a painting in The Royal Society, London. [Bettmann Archive.]

The famous title-page illustration for Hobbes's *Leviathan*. The ruler is pictured as absolute lord of his lands, but note that the ruler incorporates the mass of individuals whose self-interests are best served by their willing consent to accept him and cooperate with him.

Non est potestas Super Terram quæ Comparetur ei Iob. 4i. 24.

no culture of the earth; no navigation nor use of the commodities that may be imported by sea; no commodious building; no instruments of moving and removing such things as require much force; no knowledge of the face of the earth; no account of time; no arts; no letters; no society; and, which is worst of all, continual fear and danger of violent death; and the life of man solitary, poor, nasty, brutish, and short.9

Whereas earlier and later philosophers saw man's original state as a paradise from which he had fallen, Hobbes saw it as a corruption from which only society had delivered him. Contrary to the views of Aristotle and Christian thinkers like Thomas Aquinas, man in the view of Hobbes is not by nature a sociable, political animal; he is a self-centered beast, a law unto himself, utterly without a master unless one is imposed on him by force.

According to Hobbes, men escape the impossible state of nature only by entering a social contract that creates a commonwealth tightly ruled by law and order. They are driven to this solution by their fear of death and their desire for "commodious living." The social contract obliges every man, for the sake of peace and self-defense, to agree to set aside his right to all things and be content with as much liberty against others as he would allow others against himself. All agree to live according to a secularized version of the golden rule: "Do not that to another which you would not have done to yourself."10

Because words and promises are insufficient to guarantee this state, the social contract also establishes the coercive force necessary to compel compliance with the covenant. Hobbes believed that the dangers of anarchy were far greater than those of tyranny and conceived of the ruler as absolute and unlimited in his power, once established in office. There is no room in Hobbes's political philosophy for political protest in the name of individual conscience, nor for resistance to legitimate authority by private individuals—features of the *Leviathan* criticized by contemporary Catholics and Puritans alike. To his critics, who lamented the loss of their individual liberty in such a government, Hobbes pointed out the alternative:

> The greatest that in any form of government can possibly happen to the people in general is scarce sensible in respect of the miseries and horrible calamities that accompany a civil war or that dissolute condition of masterless men, without subjection to laws and a coercive power to tie their hands from rapine and revenge.11

It is puzzling why Hobbes believed that absolute rulers would be more benevolent and less egoistic than all other men. He simply placed the highest possible value on a strong, efficient ruler who could save men from the chaos attendant upon the state of nature. In the end it mattered little to Hobbes whether this ruler was Charles I, Oliver Cromwell, or Charles II, each of whom received Hobbes's enthusiastic support, once he was established in power.

John Locke (1632–1704)

Locke has proved to be the most influential political thinker of the seventeenth century. His political philosophy came to be embodied in the Glorious Revolution of 1688–1689. Although he was not as original as Hobbes, his political writings were a major source for the later Enlightenment criticism of absolutism, and they gave inspiration to both the American and the French revolutions. A direct line has been drawn between the political philosophy of Locke, whose works circulated in the American colonies in the eighteenth century, and that of Thomas Jefferson.

Locke was reared in a family whose sympathies lay with the Puritans and the Parliamentary forces that challenged the Stuart monarchy. His father fought with the

9 Ibid., p. 107.
10 Ibid., p. 130.

11 Ibid., p. 152.

The English philosopher John Locke, who influenced modern representative government by insisting that the people had inalienable rights of life, liberty, and property, which rulers overrode only at their peril. The portrait is from a painting at Christ Church, Oxford. [Bettmann Archive.]

Parliamentary army during the English civil war. Locke read deeply in the works of Francis Bacon, René Descartes, and Isaac Newton and was a close friend of the English physicist and chemist Robert Boyle (1627–1691). Some argue that Locke was the first philosopher to be successful in synthesizing the rationalism of Descartes and the experimental science of Bacon, Newton, and Boyle.

Locke was for a brief period strongly influenced by the conservative political views of Hobbes. This influence changed, however, after his association with Anthony Ashley Cooper, the earl of Shaftesbury. In 1667 Locke moved into Shaftesbury's London home, where he served as physician, secretary, and traveling companion. A zealous Protestant, Shaftesbury was considered by his contemporaries to be a radical in both religion (he is known as the father of Deism) and politics. He organized an unsuccessful rebellion against Charles II in 1682 in the hope of excluding Charles's Catholic brother, James, from the English throne and putting the king's bastard son, the earl of Monmouth, in James's place. Although Locke had no part in the plot, both he and Shaftesbury were forced to flee to Holland after its failure.

Locke's two most famous works were the *Essay on Human Understanding*, completed during his exile in Holland, and the *Two Treatises on Civil Government*. In the *Essay on Human Understanding* Locke stressed the creative function of the human mind. He believed that the mind at birth was a blank tablet. In Locke's view, contrary to that of much medieval philosophy, there are no innate ideas; all knowledge is derived from actual sensual experience. Human ideas are either simple (that is, passive receptions from daily experience) or complex (that is, products of sustained mental exercise). What people know is not the external world in itself but the results of the interaction of the mind with the outside world. Locke also denied the existence of innate moral norms. Moral ideals are the product of man's subjection of his self-love to his reason—a freely chosen self-disciplining of natural desires so that conflict in conscience may be avoided and

happiness attained. Locke also believed that the teachings of Christianity were identical with what uncorrupted reason taught about the good life. A rational man would therefore always live according to simple Christian precepts. Although Locke firmly denied toleration to Catholics and atheists—both were considered subversive in England—he otherwise sanctioned a variety of Protestant religious practice.

The *Two Treatises on Civil Government* was written during the reign of Charles II and was directed against the argument that rulers were absolute in their power. According to the preface of the published edition, which appeared after the Glorious Revolution, the treatises were written "to justify to the world the people of England, whose love of their just and natural rights, with their resolution to preserve them, saved the nation when it was on the brink of slavery and ruin."[12] Locke opposed particularly the views of Sir Robert Filmer and Thomas Hobbes.

Filmer had written a work entitled *Patriarcha, or the Natural Power of Kings* (published in 1680), in which the rights of kings over their subjects were compared to the rights of fathers over their children. Locke devoted the entire first treatise to a refutation of Filmer's argument,

12 *The Second Treatise of Government,* ed. T. P. Peardon (Indianapolis: Bobbs Merrill, 1952), preface.

maintaining that the analogy was not only inappropriate, but that even the right of a father over his children could not be construed as absolute but was subject to a higher natural law. Both fathers and rulers, Locke argued, remain bound to the law of nature, which is the voice of reason, teaching that "all mankind [are] equal and independent, [and] no one ought to harm another in his life, health, liberty, or possessions,"[13] inasmuch as all men are the images and property of God. According to Locke, men enter into social contracts, empowering legislatures and kings to "umpire" their disputes, precisely in order to preserve their natural rights, and not to give rulers an absolute power over them. Rulers are rather "entrusted" with the preservation of the law of nature and transgress it at their peril.

> Whenever that end [namely, the preservation of life, liberty, and property for which power is given to rulers by a commonwealth] is manifestly neglected or opposed, the trust must necessarily be forfeited and the power devolve into the hands of those that gave it, who may place it anew where they think best for their safety and security.[14]

From Locke's point of view absolute monarchy was "inconsistent" with civil society and could be "no form of civil government at all."

Locke's main differences with Hobbes stemmed from the latter's well-known views on the state of nature. Locke believed that man's natural state was one of perfect freedom and equality. Here the natural rights of life, liberty, and property were enjoyed, in unregulated fashion, by all. The only thing lacking in the state of nature was a single authority to judge among men when disputes inevitably arose because of the natural freedom and equality possessed by all. Contrary to Hobbes, men in their natural state were not creatures of monomaniacal passion but were possessed of extreme goodwill and rationality. They did not surrender their natural rights unconditionally when they entered the social contract; they rather established a means whereby these rights could be better preserved. The state of warfare that Hobbes believed characterized the state of nature emerged for Locke only when rulers failed in their responsibility to preserve the freedoms of the state of nature and attempted to enslave men by absolute rule, that is, to remove them from their "natural" condition. Only then was the peace, good-will, mutual assistance, and preservation in which men naturally live and socially ought to live undermined and a state of war created.

SUGGESTED READINGS

V. M. BRITTAIN, *Valiant Pilgrim: The Story of John Bunyan and Puritan England* (1950). Illustrated historical biography.

HERBERT BUTTERFIELD, *The Origins of Modern Science 1300–1800*, (1949). An authoritative survey.

JOHN CAIRD, *Spinoza* (1971). Intellectual biography by a philosopher.

NORMAN F. CANTOR (Ed.), *Seventeenth Century Rationalism: Bacon and Descartes* (1969).

CERVANTES, *The Portable Cervantes*, ed. and trans. by Samuel Putman (1969).

HARDIN CRAIG, *Shakespeare: A Historical and Critical Study With Annotated Texts of Twenty-one Plays* (1958).

MAURICE CRANSTON, *Locke* (1961). Brief biographical sketch.

MANUEL DURÁN, *Cervantes* (1974). Detailed biography.

GALILEO GALILEI, *Discoveries and Opinions of Galileo*, ed. and trans. by Stillman Drake (1957).

A. R. HALL, *The Scientific Revolution 1500–1800: The Formation of the Modern Scientific Attitude* (1966). Traces undermining of traditional science and rise of new sciences.

THOMAS HOBBES, *Leviathan. Parts I & II*, ed. by H. W. Schneider (1958).

T. E. JESSOP, *Thomas Hobbes* (1960), Brief biographical sketch.

H. KEARNEY, *Science and Change 1500–1700* (1971). Broad survey.

---

13 Ibid., Ch. 2, sects. 4-6, pp. 4-6.
14 Ibid., Ch. 13, sect. 149, p. 84.

ALEXANDER KOYRÉ, *From the Closed World to the Infinite Universe* (1957). Treated from perspective of the historian of ideas.

THOMAS S. KUHN, *The Copernican Revolution* (1957). A scholarly treatment.

JOHN LOCKE, *The Second Treatise of Government*, ed. by T. P. Peardon (1952).

JOHN D. NORTH, *Isaac Newton* (1967). Brief biography.

BLAISE PASCAL, *The Essential Pascal*, ed. by R. W. Gleason (1966).

E. M. W. TILLYARD, *Milton* (1952). Brief biographical sketch.

488

19
The Waxing and Waning of States (1686–1740)

THE LATE seventeenth and early eighteenth centuries witnessed significant shifts of power and influence among the states of Europe. Previously strong nations lost their status as significant military and economic units. Other countries that had in some cases figured only marginally in international relations came to the fore. Great Britain, France, Austria, Russia, and Prussia emerged during this period as the powers that would dominate Europe until at least World War I. The establishment of their political and economic dominance occurred at the expense of Spain, the United Netherlands, Poland, Sweden, and the Ottoman Empire. Equally essential to their rise was the weakness of the Holy Roman Empire after the Treaty of Westphalia (1648).

The successful competitors for international power were those states that in differing fashions created strong central political authorities. Farsighted observers in the late seventeenth century already understood that in the future those domains that would become or remain great powers must imitate the political and military organization of Louis XIV. Monarchy alone could impose unity of purpose on the state. The turmoil of seventeenth-century civil wars and aristocratic revolts had impressed people with the value of the monarch as a guarantor of minimum domestic tranquillity. Imitation of French absolutism involved other factors besides belief in strong monarchy. It usually required building a standing army, organizing an efficient tax structure to support the army, and establishing a bureaucracy to collect the taxes. Moreover the political classes of the country and especially the nobles had to be converted to a sense of duty and loyalty to the central government that was more intense than their

Peter the Great of Russia, through his centralization of tsarist power and his military exploits, epitomized the state-building monarchs of the late seventeenth and early eighteenth centuries. This portrait was painted in 1711 by I. Kupetsky. [The Granger Collection.]

loyalty to other competing political and social institutions.

The waning powers of Europe were those whose leaders failed to achieve such effective organization. They were unable to employ their political, economic, and human resources to foil external aggression or to overcome forces of domestic dissolution. The internal and external failures were closely related. If a state failed to maintain or establish a central political authority with sufficient power over the nobility, cities, guilds, and the church, it could not raise a strong army to defend its borders or its economic interests. More often than not the key element leading to success or failure was the character, personality, and energy of the monarch.

The Maritime Powers

In western Europe, Britain and France emerged as the dominant powers. This development represented a shift of influence against Spain and the United Netherlands. Both the latter countries had been quite strong and important during the sixteenth and seventeenth centuries, but they became negligible during the course of the eighteenth century. However, neither disappeared from the map. Both retained considerable economic vitality and influence. The difference was that France and Britain attained so much more power and economic strength.

Spain

Spanish power had depended on the influx of wealth from the Americas and on the capacity of Spanish monarchs to rule the still largely autonomous provinces of Spain. Within Castile, Aragon, Navarre, the Basque province, and other districts, there were strong noble and clerical estates without whose cooperation royal government was impossible. From the defeat of the Spanish Armada in 1588 to the Treaty of the Pyrenees in 1659, Spain had experienced a series of foreign policy reverses that harmed the prestige of the monarchy. Numerous treasure fleets from the New World were captured.

The reign of Charles II of Spain (1665–1700) saw the power of the crown greatly weaken. He was the last Hapsburg king of the country, for in him the line at last failed; deformed (the Hapsburg jaw carried to parody made it almost impossible for him to eat), dull, and impotent, he left no heir. Louis XIV's successful determination to have his grandson succeed Charles led to the War of the Spanish Succession. [The Granger Collection.]

Dutch shipbuilding remained important throughout the seventeenth and eighteenth centuries, although not as prosperous as in the sixteenth. Ships, such as this one being constructed at Amsterdam in 1694, were the sinews of trade during the period. The building in the background is the headquarters of the Dutch West Indies Company, which settled New Amsterdam (subsequently New York). [The Granger Collection.]

Between 1665 and 1700 the physically malformed, dull-witted, and sexually impotent Charles II was monarch. Throughout his reign the local provincial estates and the nobility increased their power. On his death the War of the Spanish Succession had seen the other powers of Europe contesting the issue of the next ruler of Spain.

The Treaty of Utrecht (1713) gave the Spanish crown to Philip V (1700–1746), who was a Bourbon and the grandson of Louis XIV. The new king should have attempted to consolidate his internal power and to protect Spanish overseas trade. However, his second wife, Elizabeth Farnese, wanted to use Spanish power to carve out interests for her sons on the Italian peninsula. Such machinations diverted government resources and allowed the nobility and the provinces to continue to assert their privileges against the authority of the monarchy. Not until the reign of Charles III (1759–1788) did Spain possess a monarch concerned with efficient administration and internal improvement. By the third quarter of the century the country was better governed, but it could no longer effectively compete in power politics.

The Netherlands

The demise of the United Netherlands occurred wholly within the eighteenth century. After the death of William III in 1702, the various local provinces successfully prevented the emergence of another strong *stadtholder.* Unified political leadership therefore vanished. During the earlier long wars of the Netherlands with Louis XIV and England, naval supremacy slowly but steadily had passed to the British. The fishing industry declined, and the Dutch lost their technological superiority in shipbuilding. Countries between which Dutch ships had once carried goods now came to trade directly with each other. For example, the British began to use more and more of their own vessels in the Baltic traffic with Russia. Similar stagnation overtook Dutch domestic industries, such as textile finishing, paper making, and glass blowing. The disunity of the provinces and the absence of vigorous leadership hastened this economic decline and

The Duke of Orleans was regent of France during the minority of Louis XV, years marked by financial scandal and weak administration. [The Granger Collection.]

prevented action that might have slowed or halted it. What saved the United Netherlands from becoming completely insignificant in European matters was their continued dominance of the financial community. Their banks continued well past the middle of the century to provide loans and financing for European trade.

France After Louis XIV

Despite its military losses in the War of the Spanish Succession, France remained a great power. It was less strong in 1715 than in 1680, but it still possessed a large population, an advanced if troubled economy, and the administrative structure bequeathed it by Louis XIV. Moreover, even if France and its resources had been badly drained by the last of Louis's wars, the other major states of Europe emerged from the conflict similarly debilitated. What the country required was a period of economic recovery and consolidation and better, wiser, and less ambitious political leadership. It enjoyed a period of recovery, but the quality of its leadership was at best indifferent. Louis XIV was succeeded by his five-year-old great-grandson Louis XV (1715–1774). Within two years the young boy's uncle, the duke of Orléans, had become regent and remained so until 1720. The regency further undermined the already faltering prestige of the monarchy.

The duke of Orléans was a gambler, and for a time he

John Law, a wily Scots speculator, became Controller General of Finances in France and was responsible for the Mississippi Company scandal (the Mississippi Bubble) that came to a head in 1719. [The Granger Collection.]

turned over the financial management of the kingdom to John Law (1671–1729), a fellow gambler and a Scottish mathematician. Law believed that an increase in the paper money supply would stimulate the postwar economic recovery of the country. With the permission of the regent he established a bank in Paris that issued paper money. Law then organized the Mississippi Company, which was to possess a monopoly on trading privileges with the French colony of Louisiana in North America.

The Mississippi Company also assumed the management of the French national debt. The company issued shares of its own stock in exchange for government bonds, which had greatly fallen in value. In order to redeem large quantities of bonds, Law encouraged speculation in Mississippi Company stock. In 1719 the price of the stock rose handsomely. However, smart investors took their profits by selling their stock in exchange for money from Law's bank. Then they sought to exchange the currency for gold. To make the second transaction they went to Law's bank, but that institution lacked sufficient gold to redeem all the money brought to it.

In February 1720 all gold payments were halted in France. Soon thereafter Law himself fled the country. The "Mississippi Bubble," as the affair was called, had burst. The fiasco brought disgrace upon the government that had made Law its controller general. The Mississippi Company was later reorganized and functioned quite profitably, but fear of paper money and speculation marked French economic life for the rest of the century.

The duke of Orléans made a second departure that also lessened the power of the monarchy. He attempted to draw the French nobility once again into the decision-making processes of the government. Louis XIV had downgraded the nobility and had filled his ministries and

Saint-Simon Shows the French Nobility's Incapacity to Govern

The regent under the young Louis XV hoped that the nobility of France might assume an active role in the government of the nation in place of the passive role assigned to them by Louis XIV. This plan involved displacing many non-noble bureaucrats. As described by the duke of Saint-Simon (1675–1755), the plan failed because the nobles proved unequal to their new duties.

THE *design was to begin to put the nobility into the ministry, with the dignity and authority befitting them, at the expense of the high civil servants and nobles of the robe, and by degree and according to events to guide affairs wisely so that little by little those commoners would lose all those administrative duties that are not purely judicial . . . in order to submit to the nobility all modes of administration. The difficulty was the ignorance, the frivolity, and the lack of diligence of the nobility who were accustomed to being good for nothing except getting killed, succeeding at war only by seniority, and romping around for the rest of the time in the most mortal uselessness. As a result they were devoted to idleness and disgusted with all knowledge outside war by their conditioned incapacity for being able to provide themselves with anything useful to do. It was impossible to make the first step in this direction without overturning the monster that had devoured the nobility, the controller general and the secretaries of state.*

Duc de Saint-Simon, *Memoires,* trans. by Frank M. Turner, cited in John Lough, *An Introduction to Eighteenth Century France* (New York: David MacKay Company, Inc., 1964), pp. 135–136.

bureaucracies with persons of nonnoble families. The regent was seeking to restore a balance. He adopted a system of councils on which the nobles were to serve along with the bureaucrats. However, the years of noble domestication at Versailles had worked too well, and the nobility seemed to lack both the talent and the desire to govern. The experiment failed.

The failure of the great French nobles to function as satisfactory councilors did not mean that they had surrendered their ancient ambition to assert their rights, privileges, and local power over those of the monarchy. The chief feature of French political life from this time until the French Revolution was the attempt of the nobility to impose its power on the monarchy. The most effective instrument in this process was the *parlements,* or

In 1722 the young great-grandson of Louis XIV was crowned the new King of France as Louis XV in the Cathedral of Rheims. He was then twelve years old and had already been king for seven years. This painting by J. B. Martin shows the moment in the darkened cathedral when the young king was anointed. It is now in the museum at Versailles. [Cliché des Musées Nationaux.]

courts dominated by the nobility of the robe. The most important of these was the Parlement of Paris. These bodies could refuse to recognize the legality of an act or law promulgated by the monarch. By long tradition their approval had been required to make a law valid. Louis XIV had often overridden stubborn, uncooperative *parlements*. However, the financial and moral weakness of the eighteenth-century monarchy allowed these judicial institutions to reassert their authority. One of the major blunders of the duke of Orléans had been to approve the reinstitution of the *parlements'* power to allow or disallow laws.

By 1726 the chief minister of the French court was Cardinal Fleury (1653–1743). He was the last of those great churchmen who had so loyally and effectively served the French monarchy. Like his seventeenth-century predecessors, Cardinals Richelieu and Mazarin, Fleury was a realist. He understood the political ambition and incapacity of the nobility and worked quietly to block their undue influence. Fleury was also aware of the precarious financial situation in which the wars of Louis XIV had left the royal treasury.

Madame de Pompadour (1721–1764) was the first official mistress of Louis XV and a person of beauty, cultivation, and ambition. After her death the king had an increasing number of mistresses, both unofficial and official, but none were as cultured as she, and inevitably, the increasingly low moral tone of the French court did much to undermine the loyalty of the general public for the throne. This lovely portrait of his patroness is by one of the eighteenth century's masters, François Boucher (1703–1770). It is now in the National Gallery of Scotland in Edinburgh. [The Granger Collection.]

The cardinal, who was seventy-three years old when he came to office, was determined to give the country a period of peace. He surrounded himself with generally able assistants who attempted to solve the financial problems. Part of the national debt was repudiated. New industries enjoying special privileges were established, and new roads and bridges were built. On the whole the nation prospered, but Fleury was never able to draw from the nobles or the church sufficient tax revenues to put the state on a stable financial footing.

Fleury died in 1743, having unsuccessfully attempted to prevent France from intervening in the war then raging between Austria and Prussia. All of his financial pruning and planning had come to nought. Another failure must also be credited to this elderly churchman. Despite his best efforts he had not trained Louis XV to become an effective monarch. Louis XV possessed most of the vices and almost none of the virtues of his grandfather. He wanted to hold on to absolute power but was unwilling to work the long hours required. He did not choose many wise advisers after Fleury. He was tossed about by the gossip and intrigues of the court nobles. His personal life was scandalous. His reign became more famous for his mistress, Madame de Pompadour, than for

anything else. Louis XV was not an evil person but a mediocre one. And in a monarch the latter fault was unfortunately often a greater failure than the former.

Despite this political drift France remained a great power. Its army remained at mid-century the largest and strongest military force on the Continent. Its commerce and production expanded. Its colonies produced wealth and spurred domestic industries. Its cities grew and prospered. The wealth of the nation waxed as the absolutism of the monarchy waned. France did not lack sources of power and strength, but it did lack political leadership that could organize, direct, and inspire its people.

George I of Great Britain was originally the Elector of Hanover in Germany. He succeeded to the British throne in 1714. The painting is from Godfrey Kneller's studio, and the medal is by John Croker. [The Granger Collection.]

Great Britain: The Age of Walpole

Britain in 1713 had emerged as a victor over Louis XIV, but the nation required a period of recovery. As an institution the British monarchy was not in the degraded state of the French monarchy, but its stability was not certain. In 1714 the Hanoverian dynasty came to the throne. Almost immediately George I (1714–1727) confronted a challenge to his new title. The Stuart pretender James Edward (1688–1766), the son of James II,

Sir Robert Walpole (1676–1745) brought political stability to eighteenth-century Britain by achieving the trust of the king and by using government patronage in a very skillful and sometimes ruthless manner. [Culver Pictures.]

landed in Scotland in December 1715. His forces marched southward but met defeat less than two months later.

Although militarily successful against the pretender, the new dynasty, designated by the Act of Settlement (1701), and its supporters saw the need for consolidation. During the seventeenth century England had been one of the most politically restive countries in Europe. The closing years of Queen Anne's reign (1702–1714) had seen sharp clashes between the political factions of Whigs and Tories over the coming Treaty of Utrecht. The Tories had urged a rapid peace settlement and after 1710 had opened negotiations with France. During the same period the Whigs were seeking favor from the Elector of Hanover, who would soon be their monarch. His concern for his domains in Hanover made him less than happy with the Tory peace policy. In the final months of Anne's reign some Tories, fearing loss of power under the waiting Hanoverian dynasty, opened channels of communication with the Stuart pretender; and a few even rallied to his losing cause.

Under these circumstances it was little wonder that George I, upon arrival in Britain, clearly favored the Whigs and proceeded with caution. Previously the differences between Whigs and Tories had been vaguely related to principle. The Tories emphasized a strong monarchy, low taxes for landowners, and firm support of the Anglican Church. The Whigs supported monarchy but wanted Parliament to retain final sovereignty. They tended to favor urban commercial interests as well as the prosperity of the landowners. They encouraged a policy of religious toleration toward the Protestant nonconformists in England. Socially both groups supported the *status quo*. Neither was organized in any way like a

This etching by William Hogarth is a satire of
the South Sea Bubble scandal in Great Britain in
1720. The Bubble was attended by the same kind of
frenzied financial speculation, corruption, and
crash that had gone on in the French Mississippi
scheme in 1719. [The Granger Collection.]

modern political party. However, after the Hanoverian accession and the Whig success in achieving the confidence of George I, the difference between Whig and Tory meant primarily that one group was in office and the other was out.

The political situation remained in a state of flux until Robert Walpole (1676–1745) took over the helm of government. This Norfolk squire had been active in the House of Commons since the reign of Queen Anne, and he had served as a cabinet minister. What gave him special prominence under the new dynasty was a British financial scandal similar to the French Mississippi Bubble.

Management of the British national debt had been assigned to the South Sea Company, which exchanged government bonds for company stock. As in the French case, the price of the stock flew high, only to crash in 1720 when prudent investors sold their holdings and took their speculative profits. Parliament intervened and under Walpole's leadership adopted measures to honor the national debt. To most contemporaries Walpole had saved the financial integrity of the country and in so doing had proved himself a person of immense administrative capacity and political ability.

George I gave Walpole his full confidence. For this reason Walpole has often been regarded as the first prime minister of Great Britain and the originator of the cabinet system of government. However, unlike a modern prime minister he was not chosen by the majority of the House of Commons. His power largely depended upon the good will of George I and later of George II (1727–1760). Walpole generally demanded that all of the ministers in the cabinet agree on policy, but this did not prevent frequent public differences on policy. The real source of Walpole's power was the combination of the personal support of the king, his ability to handle the House of Commons, and his iron-fisted control of government patronage. To oppose Walpole on either minor or more substantial matters was to risk the almost certain loss of government patronage for oneself, one's family, or one's friends. Through skillful patronage Walpole bought support for himself and his policies from people who wanted to receive jobs, appointments, favors, and government contracts. Such corruption supplied the glue of political loyalty. By 1730 to be a Whig meant essentially to be a supporter of Walpole.

Walpole's favorite slogan was *quieta non movere* ("let sleeping dogs lie"). To that end he pursued a policy of peace abroad and promotion of the *status quo* at home. In this regard he and Cardinal Fleury were much alike. The structure of the eighteenth-century British House of Commons aided Walpole in his pacific policies. It was neither a democratic nor a representative body. Each of the counties elected two members. But if the more powerful landed families in a county agreed on the candidates, there would be no election. Other members were elected from districts called *boroughs*, of which there were a considerable variety. A few were large enough for elections to be relatively democratic. However, most boroughs had a very small number of electors. For example, a local municipal corporation or council of only a dozen members might have the legal right to elect a member of Parliament. In Old Sarum, one of the most famous corrupt or "rotten" boroughs, the Pitt family for many years simply bought up those pieces of property to which a vote was attached and thus in effect owned a seat in the House of Commons. Through proper electoral management, which involved favors to the electors, the House of Commons could be controlled.

The structure of Parliament and the manner in which it was elected meant that the government of England was dominated by the owners of property and by especially wealthy nobles. They did not pretend to represent people and districts or to be responsive to what would later be called public opinion. They regarded themselves as representing various economic and social interests, such as the West Indian interest, the merchant interest, or the landed interest. These owners of property were suspicious of an administrative bureaucracy controlled by the crown or its ministers. For this reason they or their

William Hogarth's etching, Chairing the Member, after his own painting, illustrates the ritual of "chairing" the victorious candidate in an eighteenth-century English parliamentary election. These elections were frequently quite rowdy and involved much drinking and fighting; in this instance, the triumphal procession has run into opposition, with resulting loss of dignity for the newly elected member. In this role Hogarth portrayed an actual candidate named Bub Doddington. [Charles Farrell Collection.]

agents served as local government administrators, judges, militia commanders, and tax collectors. In this sense the British nobility and other substantial landowners actually did govern the nation. And because they regarded the Parliament as the political sovereign, there was no absence of central political authority and direction. Conse-

quently the supremacy of Parliament provided Britain with the kind of unity that elsewhere in Europe was sought through the institutions of absolutism.

There were limits in Britain to the power of Robert Walpole and to the unresponsiveness of Parliament. Newspapers and public debate flourished. Free speech was a reality, as was freedom of association. In 1733 Walpole presented to the House of Commons a scheme for an excise tax that would have raised revenue somewhat in the fashion of a modern sales tax. The public outcry in the press, on the public platform, and in the streets was so great that he eventually withdrew the measure. What the English regarded as their traditional political rights raised a real and potent barrier to the power of the government. Again, in 1739, public outcry over the Spanish treatment of British merchants in the Caribbean pushed Britain into the War of Jenkins's Ear, which Walpole opposed and deplored.

Walpole's ascendancy, which lasted until 1742, did little to raise the level of British political morality, but it brought the nation a kind of stability that it had not enjoyed for well over a century. Its foreign trade grew steadily and spread from New England to India. Agriculture improved its productivity. All forms of economic enterprise seemed to prosper. The navy became stronger. As a result of this political stability and economic growth, Great Britain became a European power of the first order and stood at the beginning of its era as a world power. Its government and economy during the next generation became a model for all progressive Europeans.

Central and Eastern Europe

The major factors in the shift of political influence among the maritime nations were naval strength, economic progress, foreign trade, and sound domestic administration. The conflicts among them occurred less in Europe than on the high seas and in their empires. Their nations already existed in well-defined geographical areas with established borders. Their populations generally accepted the authority of the central government.

The situation in central and eastern Europe was rather different. Except for the cities on the Baltic, the economy was agrarian. There were fewer cities and many more large estates populated by serfs. The states in this region did not possess overseas empires. Changes in the power structure normally involved changes in borders or at least in the prince who ruled a particular area. Their military conflicts took place at home rather than overseas. The political structure of this region, which lay largely east of the Elbe River, was very "soft." The almost constant warfare of the seventeenth century had led to a habit of temporary and shifting political loyalties. The princes and aristocracies of small states and principalities were unwilling to subordinate themselves voluntarily to a central monarchical authority. Consequently the political life of the region and the kind of states that emerged there were rather different from those of western Europe.

Beginning in the last half of the seventeenth century, eastern and central Europe began to assume the political and social contours that would characterize it for the next two hundred years. After the Peace of Westphalia, the Austrian Hapsburgs recognized the basic weakness of the title of Holy Roman Emperor and began a new consolidation of their power. At the same time the state of Prussia emerged as a factor in north German politics and as a major challenger to Hapsburg domination of Germany. Most importantly, Russia at the opening of the eighteenth century burst upon the eastern horizon as a military power of the first order. These three states achieved their new status largely as a result of the political

In this rather fanciful nineteenth-century engraving Charles XII of Sweden, in the upper right, leads his troops in battle even though he has himself been wounded. The Swedish king was known for such bravery, which most of his contemporaries considered simple foolhardiness. In 1718 he was finally killed in a battle. [Bildarchiv Preussischer Kulturbesitz.]

decay or military defeat of Sweden, Poland, and the Ottoman Empire.

Sweden: The Ambitions of Charles XII

Under Gustavus Adolphus II (1611–1632) Sweden had played an important role as a Protestant combatant in the Thirty Years' War. During the rest of the seventeenth century Sweden had consolidated its control of the Baltic, preventing Russian possession of a Baltic port and permitting Polish and German access to the sea only on Swedish terms. The Swedes also possessed one of the better armies in Europe. However, Sweden's economy, based primarily on export of iron, was not strong enough to ensure continued political success.

In 1697 Charles XII (1697–1718) came to the throne. He was headstrong, to say the least, and perhaps insane. In 1700 Russia began a drive to the west against Swedish territory. The Russian goal was a foothold on the Baltic. In the resulting Great Northern War (1700–1721), Charles XII led a vigorous and often brilliant campaign,

but one that eventually led to the defeat of Sweden. In 1700 he defeated the Russians at the battle of Narva, but then he turned south to invade Poland. The conflict dragged on, and the Russians were able to strengthen their forces. In 1708 the Swedish monarch began a major invasion of Russia but became bogged down in the harsh Russian winter. The next year his army was decisively defeated at the battle of Poltava. Thereafter the Swedes could maintain only a holding action. Charles himself sought refuge with the Ottoman army and then eventually returned to Sweden in 1714. He was shot four years later while fighting the Norwegians.

The Great Northern War came to a close in 1721. Sweden had exhausted its military and economic resources and had lost its monopoly on the Baltic coast. Russia had conquered a large section of the eastern Baltic, and Prussia had gained a portion of Pomerania. Internally, after the death of Charles XII, the Swedish nobles were determined to reassert their power over that of the monarchy. They did so but then fell into quarrels among themselves. Sweden played a very minor role in European affairs thereafter.

The Ottoman Empire

At the southeastern extreme of Europe, the Ottoman Empire lay as a barrier to the territorial ambitions of the Austrian Hapsburgs and of Poland and Russia. The empire in the late seventeenth century still controlled most of the Balkan peninsula and the entire coastline of the Black Sea. It was an aggressive power that had for two centuries attempted to press its control further westward in Europe. The Ottoman Empire had probably made its greatest military impression on Europe in 1683, when it laid siege to the city of Vienna.

However, the Ottomans had overextended themselves politically, economically, and militarily. The major domestic political groups resisted any substantial strengthening of the central government in Constantinople. Rivalries for power among army leaders and nobles weakened the effectiveness of the government. In the

A contemporary Dutch print views the 1683 Turkish siege of Vienna from a remarkably revealing position in the hills west of the city. We are fortunate to capture the scene on the point of the Turkish forces deciding to give up the summer-long attack; their commanders, the Ottoman Grand Vizier and the Pasha of Adrianople, lower left, are just beginning their flight back toward the Ottoman homelands. Polish and other Christian aid for the beleaguered Hapsburg forces had arrived, and the battle was clearly going against the Turks. Vienna was not captured, and never again did the progressively weakening Moslem Ottoman Empire penetrate so far west.

In the picture, note the Danube River toward the top, the elaborate zig-zag fortifications outside the walls, and bursts of artillery fire at several points. Most details inside the walled city are omitted, but the central cathedral and the imperial palace, toward the bottom, are shown. The walls themselves, when later torn down, made space for the Ring, the famous boulevard still encircling central Vienna.

One unforeseen lasting social result of the siege was the further boost given to coffee drinking by the Viennese discovery of the beverage in the deserted Turkish camps around the city. [The Granger Collection.]

THE AUSTRIAN HAPSBURG EMPIRE, 1521–1772

The Empire had three main units—Austria, Bohemia, Hungary. Expansion was mainly eastward: east Hungary from the Ottomans (17th century) and Galicia from Poland (1772). Meantime, Silesia was lost, but Hapsburgs retained German influence as Holy Roman Emperors.

outer provinces, such as Transylvania, Wallachia, and Moldavia (all parts of modern Romania), the empire depended upon the goodwill of local rulers, who never submitted themselves fully to the imperial power. The empire's economy was weak, and its exports were primarily raw materials. Moreover, the actual conduct of most of its trade had been turned over to representatives of other nations.

By the early eighteenth century the weakness of the Ottoman Empire meant that on the southeastern perimeter of Europe there existed an immense political vacuum. In 1699 the Turks concluded a treaty with their longtime Hapsburg enemy and surrendered all pretensions of control over Hungary, Transylvania, Croatia, and Slavonia. From this time onward Russia attempted to extend its territory and influence at the expense of the empire. For almost two hundred years the decay of the Ottoman Empire constituted a major factor in European international relations. The area always proved tempting to the major powers, but their distrust of each other and their conflicting rivalries as well as a considerable residual

strength on the part of the Turks prevented the dismemberment of the empire.

Poland

In no other part of Europe was the failure to maintain a competitive political position so complete as in Poland. In 1683 King John III Sobieski (1673–1696) had led a Polish army to rescue Vienna from the Turkish siege. But following that spectacular effort, Poland became little more than a byword for the dangers of aristocratic independence. In Poland as nowhere else on the Continent the nobility became the single most powerful political factor in the country. Unlike the British nobility and landowners, the Polish nobility would not even submit to a central authority of their own making. There was no effective central authority in the form of either a king or a parliament.

The Polish monarchy was elective, but the deep distrust and divisions among the nobility prevented their electing a king from among their own numbers. Sobieski was a notable exception. Most of the Polish monarchs came from outside the borders of the kingdom and were tools of foreign powers. The Polish nobles did have a central legislative body called the Diet. It included only the nobles and specifically excluded representatives from corporate bodies, such as the towns. In the Diet, however, there existed a practice known as the *liberum veto*, whereby the staunch opposition of any single member could require the body to disband. Such opposition was termed "exploding" the Diet.

Government as it was developing elsewhere in Europe simply was not tolerated in Poland. Localism reminiscent of the Middle Ages continued to hold sway as the nobles used all their energy to maintain their traditional "Polish liberties." There was no way to collect sufficient taxes to build up an army. The price of this noble liberty was eventually the disappearance of Poland from the map of Europe during the last half of the eighteenth century.

The Hapsburg Empire and the Pragmatic Sanction

The Hapsburgs in Austria came out of the Thirty Years' War much weaker than they had entered it. Their lands had been desolated by the conflict, and the Holy Roman Emperorship—the traditional base of Hapsburg political power—had been rendered a hollow title. The Treaty of Westphalia had recognized the political autonomy of the more than three hundred corporate entities of the empire. These included large political units, such as Saxony, Hanover, Bavaria, and Brandenburg, but they also included scores of small cities, bishoprics, principalities, and territories of independent knights. The role and power of the Holy Roman Emperor henceforth depended upon the cooperation he could elicit from these various political bodies. The Diet of the empire sat perpetually at Regensburg without new elections from 1663 until its dissolution in 1806. The Diet and the empire generally regulated the daily economic and political life of Germany. The post-Westphalian Holy Roman Empire in many ways resembled Poland with its lack of central authority. However, unlike its Polish neighbor, the Holy Roman Empire was reorganized from within as the Hapsburgs attempted to regain their authority and, as will be seen shortly, as Prussia set out on its course toward European power.

In addition to retaining the emperorship of the Holy Roman Empire, the Hapsburgs also held hereditary pos-

session of the kingdom of Bohemia (in modern Czechoslovakia), which included Silesia and Moravia, and the Crown of Saint Stephen, which ruled Hungary and Transylvania. They also possessed stretches of northern Italy and the Austrian Netherlands, which is present-day Belgium. They confronted immense problems in all these territories. In each they ruled by virtue of a different title and had to gain the cooperation of the local nobility. The most problematic province in this regard was Hungary, where the Magyar nobility seemed ever ready to rebel.

There was practically no common basis for political unity among peoples of such diverse languages, customs, and geography. Even the Hapsburg zeal for Roman Catholicism no longer proved a bond for unity when they confronted the equally zealous Calvinism of the Magyar nobles. The Hapsburgs established various central councils to chart common policies for their farflung domains. None of these proved effective because the dynasty repeatedly had to bargain with nobles in one part of Europe in order to maintain their position in another part of the Continent. Consequently, for all practical purposes, not until well into the nineteenth century did the Vienna government directly affect the lives of any social group below the nobility.

Despite all these internal difficulties Leopold I (1657–1705) rallied his domains to resist the advances of the Turks and to resist the aggression of Louis XIV. He achieved Ottoman recognition of his sovereignty over Hungary in 1699 and suppressed the long rebellion of his new Magyar subjects between 1703 and 1711. He also extended his territorial holdings over much of what is today Yugoslavia and western Romania. These eastward extensions allowed the Hapsburgs to hope to develop Mediterranean trade through the port of Trieste. The expansion at the cost of the Ottoman Empire also helped the Hapsburgs to compensate for their loss of domination over the Holy Roman Empire. Strength in the east gave them greater political leverage in Germany. Leopold was succeeded by Joseph I (1705–1711), who continued his policies.

Charles VI of Austria (Holy Roman Emperor) devoted most of his life to securing approval of the Pragmatic Sanction, which would guarantee the succession of his daughter Maria Theresa to the various Hapsburg domains. The portrait, of which this is a detail, is by Johann Gottfried Auerbach, and is in Vienna. [Bettmann Archive.]

Schönbrunn Palace of the Austrian Hapsburgs stands outside Vienna. Like many royal palaces of the eighteenth century, it was modeled after Louis XIV's palace of Versailles. [Austrian Information Service, New York.]

When Charles VI (1711–1740) succeeded Joseph he added a new problem to the old chronic one of territorial diversity. It was that he had no male heir, and there was only the weakest of precedents for a female ruler of the Hapsburg domains. Charles feared that upon his death the Austrian Hapsburg lands might fall prey to the surrounding powers as had those of the Spanish Hapsburgs in 1700. He was determined to prevent that disaster and to provide his domains with the semblance of legal unity. To those ends, he devoted most of his reign to seeking the approval of his family, the estates of his realms, and the major foreign powers for a curious document called the Pragmatic Sanction.

This instrument provided the legal basis for a single line of inheritance within the Hapsburg dynasty through Charles VI's daughter Maria Theresa (1740–1780). Other members of the Hapsburg family recognized her as the rightful heir. The nobles of the various domains did likewise after extracting various concessions from Charles. The major states of Europe followed a similar course. Consequently, when Charles VI died in October 1740, he believed he had secured legal unity for the Hapsburg Empire and a safe succession for his daughter. Less than two months after his death the fragility of such a paper agreement became all too apparent. In December 1740 Frederick II of Prussia invaded the Hapsburg province of Silesia. Maria Theresa would have to fight to defend her inheritance.

Prussia and the Hohenzollerns

The Hapsburg achievement was to draw together into an uncertain legal unity a collection of domains possessed by dint of separate feudal titles. The achievement of the Hohenzollerns of Brandenburg-Prussia was to acquire a similar collection of titular holdings and then to forge them into a centrally administered unit. In spite of the geographical separation of their territories and the paucity of their natural economic resources, they transformed feudal ties and structures into bureaucratic ones. They subordinated every social class and most economic

1417–1614

NIEMEN

ELBE

Berlin

KROSSEN, 1482

1462

RHINE

ODER

VISTULA

150 MI.

150 KM.

BEUTHEN 1603,07

▇ BRANDENBURG, 1417
▥ ACQUISITIONS, 1462–1614

1614–1688

FARTHER POMERANIA, 1648

EAST PRUSSIA, 1618

RAVENS-BURG, 1614

CLEVES, 1614

Berlin

MARK, 1614

MAGDE-BURG, 1648

ELBE

VISTULA

ODER

▇ BRANDENBURG, 1614
▥ BRANDENBURG-PRUSSIA, 1618

1688–1748

EAST FRIESLAND, 1744

Berlin

SILESIA, FROM AUSTRIA, 1740

ELBE

VISTULA

ODER

▇ PRUSSIA, 1688
▥ ACQUISITIONS, 1715–1748

1748–1807

WEST PRUSSIA, 1772

DANZIG, 1793

Berlin

NEW EAST PRUSSIA, 1795

MANSFELD, 1780

SOUTH PRUSSIA, 1793

ELBE

ODER

VISTULA

TRM

▇ PRUSSIA, 1748
▥ ACQUISITIONS, 1748–1772
⠿ TEMPORARY ACQUISITIONS, 1793–1795 TO 1807

EXPANSION OF BRANDENBURG-PRUSSIA

pursuits to the strengthening of the one institution that united their far-flung realms: the army. In so doing they made the term *Prussian* synonymous with administrative rigor and military discipline.

The rise of Prussia occurred within the German power vacuum created by the Peace of Westphalia. It is the story of the extraordinary Hohenzollern family, which had ruled the German territory of Brandenburg since 1417. Through inheritance the family had acquired the Duchy of Cleves and the counties of Mark and Ravensburg in 1609, the Duchy of East Prussia in 1618, and the Duchy of Pomerania in 1637. Except for Pomerania, none of these lands was contiguous with Brandenburg. East Prussia lay inside Poland and outside the authority of the Holy Roman Emperor. All of the territories lacked endowment of good natural resources, and many of them were devastated during the Thirty Years' War. At Westphalia the Hohenzollerns lost part of Pomerania to Sweden but were compensated by receiving three more bishoprics and the promise of the archbishopric of Magdeburg when it became vacant, as it did in 1680. By the late seventeenth century the scattered Hohenzollern holdings represented a block of territory within the Holy Roman Empire second in size only to that of the Hapsburgs.

Despite its size the Hohenzollern conglomerate was weak. The areas were geographically separate. There was no mutual sympathy or common concern among them. In each there existed some form of local noble estates that limited the power of the Hohenzollern prince. They were exposed to foreign aggression.

The person who began to forge these areas and nobles into a modern state was Frederick William (1640–1688), who became known as the Great Elector. He established

Seventeenth-century Brandenburg-Prussia expanded mainly by acquiring dynastic titles in geographically separated lands. Eighteenth-century expansion occurred through aggression to the east: Silesia seized in 1740 and various parts of Poland in 1772, 1793, and 1795.

Frederick William I of Prussia ruthlessly forged the Prussian army into a major instrument of state. But he also attempted to avoid committing his valuable troops to warfare. [The Granger Collection.]

himself and his successors as the central uniting power by breaking the estates, organizing a royal bureaucracy, and establishing a strong army.

Between 1655 and 1660 Sweden and Poland engaged in a war that endangered the Great Elector's holdings in Pomerania and East Prussia. Frederick William had neither an adequate army nor the tax revenues to confront this threat. In 1655 the Brandenburg estates refused to grant him new taxes; however, he proceeded to collect the required taxes by military force. In 1659 a different grant of taxes, originally made in 1653, elapsed; Frederick William continued to collect them as well as those he had imposed by his own authority. He used the money to build up an army, which allowed him to continue to enforce his will without the approval of the nobility. Similar processes of threats and coercion took place against the nobles in his other territories.

However, there was a political and social trade-off between the elector and his various nobles. These *Junkers*, or German noble landlords, were allowed almost complete control over the serfs on their estates. In exchange for their obedience to the Hohenzollerns the *Junkers* received the right to demand obedience from their serfs. Frederick William also tended to choose as the local administrators of the tax structure men who would normally have been members of the noble estates. In this fashion, he coopted potential opponents into his service. The taxes fell most heavily on the backs of the peasants and the urban classes. As the years passed, sons of *Junkers* increasingly dominated the army officer corps, and this practice became even more pronounced during the eighteenth century. All officials and army officers took an oath of loyalty directly to the elector. The army and the elector thus came to embody the otherwise absent unity of the state. The existence of the army made Prussia a valuable potential ally and a state with which other powers needed to curry favor.

Yet even with the considerable accomplishments of the Great Elector, the house of Hohenzollern did not possess a crown. The achievement of a royal title was one of the few state-building accomplishments of Frederick I (1688–1713). This son of the Great Elector was the least "Prussian" of his family during these crucial years. He built palaces, founded Halle University (1694), patronized the arts, and lived luxuriously. However, in 1700 at the outbreak of the War of the Spanish Succession he put his army at the disposal of the Hapsburg Holy Roman Emperor. In exchange for this loyal service, the emperor permitted Frederick to assume the title of "King in Prussia." Thereafter Frederick became Frederick I, and he passed the much-desired royal title to his son Frederick William I in 1713.

Frederick William I (1713–1740) was both the most eccentric personality to rule the Hohenzollern domains and one of its most effective monarchs. After giving his father a funeral that matched the luxury of his life, Frederick William I immediately imposed policies of strict austerity. In some cases jobs were abolished, and in others salaries were lowered. His political aims seem to have been nothing else than the consolidation of an obedient, compliant bureaucracy and the expansion of the army. He initiated a policy of *Kabinett* government, which meant that lower officials submitted all relevant documents to him in his office or *Kabinett*. Then he alone examined the papers, made his decision, and issued his orders. Frederick William I thus skirted the influence of ministers and ruled alone.

Frederick William organized the bureaucracy along the lines of military discipline. All departments were united under the *GeneraloberfinanzKriegsundDomainDirektorium*, which is more happily known to us as the General Directory. He imposed taxes on the nobility and changed most remaining feudal dues into money payments. He sought to transform feudal and administrative loyalties into a sense of duty to the monarch as a political institution rather than as a person. He once described the perfect royal servant as

an intelligent, assiduous, and alert person who after God values nothing higher than his king's pleasure and serves him out of love and for the sake of honor rather than money and who in his conduct solely seeks and constantly bears in mind his king's service and interests, who, moreover, abhors all intrigues and emotional deterrents.[1]

Service to the state and the monarch was to become impersonal, mechanical, and in effect unquestioning.

The discipline that Frederick William applied to the army was little less than fanatical. During his reign the size of the military force grew from about thirty-nine thousand in 1713 to over eighty thousand in 1740. It was the third or fourth largest army in Europe, whereas Prussia ranked thirteenth in size of population. Rather than using recruiters, the king made each canton responsible for supplying a certain number of soldiers.

After 1725 Frederick William always wore an officer's uniform. He built one regiment from the tallest soldiers he could find in Europe. Separate laws applied to the army and to civilians. Laws, customs, and royal attention made the officer corps the highest social class of the state. Military service attracted the sons of *Junkers*. In this fashion, the army, the *Junker* nobility, and the monarchy became forged into a single political entity. Militarism became a style of life and of governing. Military priorities and values dominated Prussian society and daily life as in no other state of Europe. It has often been said that whereas other nations possessed armies, the Prussian army possessed its nation.

Although Frederick William I built the best army in Europe, he followed a consistent policy of avoiding conflict. He wanted to drill his soldiers but not to order them into battle. Although Frederick William terrorized his family and associates and on occasion knocked out teeth with his walking stick, he was not a militarily aggressive person. The army for him was a symbol of Prussian power and unity, not an instrument to be used for foreign adventures or aggression. At his death in 1740 he passed to his son Frederick II (1740–1786; Frederick the Great) this superb military machine, but he could not pass to his son the wisdom to refrain from using it. Almost immediately upon coming to the throne, Frederick II upset the Pragmatic Sanction and invaded Silesia. He thus crystallized the Austrian–Prussian rivalry for control of Germany that would dominate central European affairs for over a century.

Russia and Peter the Great

Though ripe with consequences for the future, the rise of Prussia and the new consolidation of the Austrian Hapsburg domains seemed to many at the time only one more shift in the long-troubled German scene. However, the emergence of Russia as an active European power constituted a wholly new factor in European politics. Previously Russia had been considered a part of Europe only by courtesy. Geographically and politically it lay on the periphery of Europe. Hemmed in by Sweden on the Baltic and by the Ottoman Empire on the Black Sea, the country had no warm-water ports. Its chief outlet to the west was Archangel on the White Sea, which was open to ships during only part of the year. There was little trade. What Russia did possess was a vast reserve of largely undeveloped natural and human resources.

Religion also set off Russia from the rest of Europe. The Russian Orthodox Church was separated from Latin Christendom and was also frequently at odds with other sectors of the Eastern Orthodox communion. The church opposed the scientific as well as the theological thought of the West. In the mid-seventeenth century a sort of reformist movement led by Patriarch Nikon arose in the Russian church. In 1667 certain changes were made in the texts and the ritual of the church. These reforms caused great unrest because the Russian church had always claimed to be the great protector of true ritual. The Old Believers were a group of Russian Christians who strongly opposed these changes. They were condemned by the hierarchy, but they persisted in their opposition.

---

1 Quoted in Hans Rosenberg, *Bureaucracy, Aristocracy, and Autocracy* (Boston: Beacon Press 1958), p. 93.

Late in the century thousands of them committed suicide rather than submit to the new rituals. The Old Believers' movement represented a rejection of change and innovation; its presence discouraged the rest of the church hierarchy from making any further substantial moves toward modern thought.

The political structure of Russia had also contributed to its isolation. During the "time of troubles" in the early seventeenth century, it had experienced considerable conflict between the nobles, or *boyars,* and the tsar. In 1613, in hopes of resolving that tension, an assembly of nobles had elected a seventeen-year-old boy named Michael Romanov (1613–1645) to be tsar. Thus was established the dynasty that in spite of palace revolutions, military conspiracies, assassinations, and family strife ruled Russia until 1917. However, during the rest of the seventeenth century constant turmoil surrounded the tsars. The Moscow guards, or *streltsi,* made and unmade rulers; and the nobility fought to retain its privileges.

In 1682 another boy—ten years old at the time— ascended the fragile Russian throne as co-ruler with his half brother. His name was Peter (1682–1725), and Russia would never be the same after him. He and his ill half brother, Ivan V, had come to power on the shoulders of the *streltsi,* who expected rewards from the persons they favored. Much violence and bloodshed had surrounded the disputed succession. Matters became even more confused when their sister Sophia was named regent. Peter's followers overthrew her in 1689. From that date onward Peter ruled personally, although in theory he shared the crown with the unwell Ivan, who died in 1696. The dangers and turmoil of his youth convinced Peter of two things. First, the power of the tsar must be made secure from the jealousy of the *boyars* and the greed of the *streltsi.* Second, the military power of Russia must be increased.

Peter I, who became Peter the Great, was fascinated by western Europe. He particularly admired the military resources of those kingdoms. He was an imitator of the first order. The products and workmen from the West who had filtered into Russia impressed and intrigued him. In 1697 he made a famous visit in rather weak disguises throughout western Europe. There he dined and talked with the great and the powerful, who considered this almost seven-foot-tall ruler both crude and rude. However, his happiest moments on the trip were spent inspecting shipyards, docks, and the manufacture of military hardware. He returned to Moscow determined by whatever means necessary to copy what he had seen abroad, for he knew that warfare would be necessary to make Russia a great power. The tsar's drive toward westernization, though unsystematic, had four general areas of concern: taming the *boyars* and the *streltsi,*

After Peter the Great of Russia returned from his journey to western Europe, he personally cut off the traditional and highly prized long sleeves and beards of the Russian nobles. His action symbolized his desire to see Russia become more powerful and more modern. [SLEEVES: Culver Pictures; BEARDS: The Granger Collection.]

achieving secular control of the church, reorganizing internal administration, and developing the economy. Peter pursued each of these goals with violence and ruthlessness.

He made a sustained attack on the Russian *boyars*. In 1698, immediately upon his return from abroad, he personally shaved the long beards of the court *boyars* and sheared off the long sleeves of their shirts and coats, which had made them the butt of jokes throughout Europe. More important, he demanded that the nobles provide his state with their services. The *boyars* resisted these demands. Throughout Peter's reign that struggle continued. His strongest action to engage their service came in 1722. That year he published a Table of Ranks, which henceforth equated a person's social position and privileges with his rank in the bureaucracy or the army rather than with his position in the nobility. However, unlike the case in Prussia, the Russian nobility never became perfectly loyal to the state. They repeatedly sought to reassert their independence and control of the Russian imperial court.

The fate of the *streltsi* was less fortunate than that of the *boyars*. In 1698 they had rebelled while Peter was on his European tour. When he returned and put down the revolt of these Moscow troops, he directed massive violence and brutality against both leaders and followers. There were private tortures and public executions, in which Peter's own ministers took part. Almost twelve hundred of the rebels were put to death, and their corpses long remained on public display to discourage future disloyalty.

Peter dealt with the potential political independence of the Russian church with similar ruthlessness. The reformist theological policies that had created the Old Believers had also, of course, created a political problem for the tsar. Such was not to occur in the future. In 1721 Peter simply abolished the position of patriarch of the Russian church. In its place he established a synod to rule the church in accordance with secular requirements. The head of the synod was to be a layman. So far as changing a traditional institution was concerned, the policy toward the church was the most radical of Peter's reign. It produced further opposition from the Old Believers, who saw the tsar as leading the church into further heresy.

In his reorganization of domestic administration, Peter looked to institutions then used in Sweden. These were "colleges" or bureaus composed of several persons rather than departments headed by a single minister. These colleges, which he imposed on Russia, were to look after matters such as the collection of taxes, foreign affairs,

Peter the Great built St. Petersburg on the Gulf of Finland to prove his intention of maintaining recently conquered territory and to provide Russia with better contact with Western Europe. This is an eighteenth-century view of the city. [John R. Freeman.]

war, and economic matters. This new organization was an attempt to breathe life into the generally stagnant and inefficient administration of the country. In 1711 he created a central senate of nine members who were to direct the Moscow government when the tsar was away with the army. The purpose of these and other local administrative reforms was to establish a bureaucracy that could collect and spend tax revenues to support an efficient army.

The economic development advocated by Peter the Great was closely related to his military needs. He encouraged the establishment of an iron industry in the Ural Mountains, and by mid-century Russia was the largest iron producer in Europe. He sent prominent young Russians abroad to acquire technical and organizational skills. He attempted to attract west European craftsmen to live and work in Russia. Except for the striking growth of the iron industry, which later languished, all these efforts had only marginal success.

The purpose of these internal reforms and political departures was to support a policy of warfare. Peter was determined to secure warm-water ports that would allow Russia to trade with the West and to have a greater impact on European affairs. This policy led him into wars with the Ottoman Empire and with Sweden. His armies

commenced fighting the Turks in 1695 and captured Azov on the Black Sea in 1696. It was a temporary victory, for in 1711 he was compelled to return the port.

Peter was more successful against Sweden, where the inconsistency and irrationality of Charles XII were no small aid. In 1700 Russia moved against the Swedish territory on the Baltic. The Swedish king's failure to follow up his victory at Narva in 1700 allowed Peter the Great to regroup his forces and hoard his resources. In 1709, when Charles XII returned to fight Russia again, Peter was ready and the battle of Poltava sealed the fate of Sweden. In 1721, at the Peace of Nystad, which ended the Great Northern War, Russian conquest of Estonia, Livonia, and part of Finland was confirmed. Henceforth Russia possessed warm-water ports and a permanent influence on European affairs.

At one point the domestic and foreign policies of Peter the Great literally intersected. This was at the spot on the Gulf of Finland where Peter founded his new capital city of St. Petersburg (now Leningrad). There he built government structures and compelled his *boyars* to construct townhouses. In this fashion he imitated those west European monarchs who had copied Louis XIV by constructing smaller versions of Versailles. However, the founding of St. Petersburg went beyond the construction of a central court. It symbolized a new western orientation of Russia and Peter's determination to hold his position on the Baltic coast. He had commenced construction of the city and had moved the capital there in 1703, even before victory over Sweden was assured.

Despite the notable success on the Baltic, Peter's reign ended with a great question mark. He had long quarreled with his only son, Alexis. Peter was jealous of the young man and fearful that he might undertake sedition. In 1718 Peter had his son imprisoned, and during this imprisonment the presumed successor to the throne died mysteriously. Thereafter Peter claimed for himself the right of naming a successor, but he could never bring himself to designate the person orally or in writing. Consequently, when he died in 1725, there was no firmer policy on succession to the throne than when he had acceded to the title. For over thirty years, once again soldiers and nobles would determine who ruled Russia. Peter had laid the foundations of a modern Russia, but he had failed to lay the foundations of a stable state.

Eighteenth-Century European States

The major European powers by the second quarter of the eighteenth century were not yet nation-states. They were still monarchies in which the personality of the ruler and the personal relationships of the great noble families exercised considerable influence over public affairs. The monarchs had generally succeeded in making their power greater than the nobility's. However, the power of the aristocracy and its capacity to resist or obstruct the policies of the monarchs were not destroyed. In Britain, of course, the nobility had tamed the monarchy, but even

there tension between nobles and monarchs would continue through the rest of the century.

In foreign affairs the new arrangement of military and diplomatic power established during the early years of the century prepared the way for two long-term conflicts. The first was a commercial rivalry for trade and overseas empire between France and Great Britain. During the reign of Louis XIV these two nations had collided over the French bid for dominance in Europe. During the eighteenth century they dueled for control of commerce on other continents. The second arena of warfare was central Europe, where Austria and Prussia fought for the leadership of the states of Germany.

However, behind these international conflicts and the domestic rivalry of monarchs and nobles, the society of eighteenth-century Europe began to experience momentous change. The character and structures of the society over which the monarchs ruled were beginning to take on some features associated with the modern age. These economic and social developments would in the long run produce transformations in the life of Europe beside which the achievements of the early eighteenth-century state-building monarchs paled.

SUGGESTED READINGS

M. S. ANDERSON, *Europe in the Eighteenth Century, 1713–1783* (1961). The best one-volume introduction.

F. L. CARSTON, *The Origins of Prussia* (1954). Discusses the groundwork laid by the Great Elector in the seventeenth century.

A. COBBAN, *A History of Modern France*, Vol. 1, 2nd ed. (1961). A lively and opinionated survey.

R. R. ERGANG, *The Potsdam Führer* (1941). The biography of Frederick William I.

S. B. FAY AND K. EPSTEIN, *The Rise of Brandenburg-Prussia to 1786* (1937, rev. 1964). A brief outline.

M. T. FLORINSKY, *Russia: A History and an Interpretation*, 2 vols. (1953). A useful and far-ranging work.

G. P. GOOCH, *Maria Theresa and Other Studies* (1951). A sound introduction to the problems of the Hapsburgs.

G. P. GOOCH, *Louis XV, The Monarchy in Decline* (1956). A discussion of the problems of France after the death of Louis XIV.

H. HOLBORN, *A History of Modern Germany, 1648–1840* (1966). The best and most comprehensive survey in English.

V. K. KLYUCHEVSKY, *Peter the Great*, tr. by Liliana Archibald (1958). A standard biography.

DORTHY MARSHALL, *Eighteenth-Century England* (1962). Emphasizes social and economic background.

L. B. NAMIER AND J. BROOKE, *The History of Parliament: The House of Commons, 1754–1790*, 3 vols. (1964). A detailed examination of the unreformed British House of Commons and electoral system.

L. J. OLIVA (Ed.), *Russia and the West from Peter the Great to Khrushchev* (1965). An anthology of articles tracing an important and ambiguous subject.

J. H. PLUMB, *Sir Robert Walpole*, 2 vols. (1956, 1961). A masterful biography ranging across the sweep of European politics.

P. ROBERTS, *The Quest for Security, 1715–1740* (1947). Very good on the diplomatic problems of the period.

H. ROSENBERG, *Bureaucracy, Aristocracy, and Autocracy: the Prussian Experience, 1660–1815* (1960). Emphasizes the organization of Prussian administration.

B. H. SUMMER, *Peter the Great and the Emergence of Russia* (1950). A brief but well-organized discussion.

B. WILLIAMS, *The Whig Supremacy, 1714–1760* (1939). A general survey.

E. N. WILLIAMS, *The Ancien Regime in Europe* (1972). A state by state survey of very high quality.

A. M. WILSON, *French Foreign Policy During the Administration of Cardinal Fleury, 1726–1743* (1936). The standard account.

J. B. WOLF, *The Emergence of the Great Powers, 1685–1715* (1951). A comprehensive survey.

514

20
Society Under the Old Regime

Duʀɪɴɢ the French Revolution and the turmoil spawned by that upheaval it became customary to refer to the patterns of social, political, and economic relationships that had previously existed in France as the *ancien régime*, or the old regime. The term has come to be applied generally to the life and institutions of prerevolutionary Europe. Politically the term indicated the rule of theoretically absolute monarchies with growing bureaucracies and aristocratically led armies. Economically the old regime was characterized by scarcity of food, predominance of agriculture, slow transport, a low level of iron production, rather unsophisticated financial institutions, and in some cases competitive commercial overseas empires. Socially prerevolutionary Europe was based on aristocratic elites possessing a wide variety of inherited legal privileges, established Roman Catholic and Protestant churches intimately related to the state and the aristocracy, an urban labor force usually organized into guilds, and a rural peasantry subject to high taxes and feudal dues. However, it should be remembered that the men and women living during this period did not know it was the *old* regime. In most cases they earned their livelihoods and went through the various stages of life as their forebears had done for generations before them and as they expected their children to do after them.

Probably the most striking feature of the old regime was the marked contrasts in the lives and experiences of people in different social ranks, different countries, and even different regions of the same country. The bonds created by rapid transport and communication that have

Agriculture, basic to society, is illustrated in this plate from the mid-eighteenth-century French *Encyclopédie, ou Dictionnaire Raisonné des Sciences, des Arts et des Métiers* (hereafter the *Encyclopedia*). New machinery, such as the plows shown at the bottom, helped to increase yield from the land and thus the food supply for Europe.

today led to similar patterns of life throughout the Western world simply did not yet exist.

Within the major monarchies there was usually no single standard of uniform law, money, or weights and measures. Except in Britain there were internal tolls that hampered the passage of goods. The nobility of Great Britain lived in the most magnificent luxury the order had ever known. On the Continent some groups of nobles were also very wealthy, but other members of the continental nobility were little better off than wealthier peasants. So far as the peasantry was concerned, it tended to prosper in western Europe while reaching new depths of social and economic degradation east of the Elbe River.

In Britain, Holland, and parts of France there was a healthy and growing middle class, but such an order hardly existed in the German principalities, the Austrian Empire, or Russia. Finally, there was a stark contrast between the refinement of taste, fashion, and manners of the upper levels of society and the simultaneous presence of public whipping, torture, and executions inflicted upon the lower classes. Historians often point to the difficulties of life and the differences in wealth in our industrial society, but these were hardly lacking in the society of the old regime.

Eighteenth-century society was traditional. The past weighed more heavily on people's minds than did the future. Few persons outside the government bureaucracies and the writers of the Enlightenment considered innovation to be desirable. This was especially true of social relationships. Both nobles and peasants, for very different reasons, repeatedly called for the restoration of traditional or customary rights. The nobles asserted what they considered their ancient rights against the intrusion of the expanding monarchical bureaucracies. The peasants in petitions and revolts called for the revival or the maintenance of customary manorial rights that provided access to particular lands, courts, or grievance procedures.

With the exception of the early industrial development in Britain, the eighteenth-century economy was also quite traditional. The quality and quantity of the harvest re-

Castle Howard in Yorkshire, England, designed by the architect and playwright, Sir John Vanbrugh (1665–1726), was one of the grandest of the homes of the aristocracy from the time of its completion in 1714. From such great houses the aristocrats looked after their estates and their local political interests. [British Tourist Authority, New York.]

mained the single most important fact of life for the overwhelming majority of the population and the gravest concern of the governments.

Closely related to this traditional social and economic outlook was the hierarchical structure of the society. The medieval sense of rank and degree not only persisted but became more rigid in the course of the century. In several continental cities *sumptuary* laws regulating the dress of the different classes remained on the books. The hierarchy was enforced through the corporate nature of social relationships. Each state or society was considered a community of numerous smaller communities. People in eighteenth-century Europe did not enjoy what Americans consider to be individual rights. A person enjoyed such rights and privileges as were guaranteed to the particular communities or groups of which he was a part. The "community" might include the village, the municipality, the nobility, the church, the guild, or the parish. In turn each of these bodies enjoyed certain privileges, some of which were great and some small. The privileges might involve exemption from taxation or from some especially humiliating punishment, the right to practice a trade or craft, the right for one's children to pursue a particular occupation, or in the case of the church the right to collect the tithe.

Tradition, hierarchy, corporateness, and privilege were the chief social characteristics of the old regime. Yet it was by no means a static society. Factors of change and innovation were fermenting in its midst. There was a strong demand from the colonies in the Americas for European goods and manufactures. Merchants in seaports and other cities were expanding their businesses. By preparing their states for war, the various governments put new demands on the resources and the economic organizations of their nations. The spirit of rationality that had been so important to the Scientific Revolution of the seventeenth century continued to manifest itself in the economic life of the eighteenth century. Perhaps most important, the population of Europe grew rapidly. The old regime itself fostered the changes that eventually transformed it into a very different kind of society.

The Land and Its Tillers

Land constituted the economic basis of eighteenth-century life. Well over three fourths of all Europeans lived in the country, and few of these people ever traveled beyond a ten-mile radius of their birthplace. Male children tended to follow the occupation of their fathers.

At the opposite end of the social scale from Castle Howard is the mid-eighteenth-century rural laborer's hut far to the east in Austria. However proper a subject for the artist, Franz Edmund Weirotter (1730-1771), the scene is probably a realistic one of the wretched housing endured by many. [Charles Farrell Collection.]

Village families tended to intermarry; there were only occasional marriages between men and women from neighboring villages. The lot of women continued to be circumscribed by family duties, the family economy, and the burden of child bearing and rearing. With the exception of the nobility and the wealthier nonaristocratic landowners, the dwellers on the land were poor, and by any modern standard their lives were difficult. They lived in various modes of economic and social dependency, exploitation, and vulnerability.

Peasants and Serfs

The major forms of rural social dependency related directly to the land. Those who worked the land were subject to immense control from the landowners. This situation was true for free peasants, such as English tenants and most French cultivators, and for the serfs of Germany, Austria, and Russia, who were legally bound to a particular plot of land and a particular lord. In all cases the class who owned most of the land also controlled the local government and the courts. For example, in Great Britain all farmers and smaller tenants had the legal rights of English citizens. But the justices of the peace who presided over the county courts and who could call out the local militia were always substantial landowners, as were also the members of Parliament, who made the laws.

The intensity of landlord power increased as one moved from west to east. In France the situation differed somewhat from province to province. Most French peasants owned some land, but there were a few serfs. However, practically all peasants were subject to certain feudal dues, called *banalités*, that included required use for payment of the lord or seigneur's mill to grind grain and his oven to bake bread. The seigneur could also require a certain number of days each year from the peasant's labor. This practice was termed the *corvée*. Because even landowning French peasants rarely possessed enough land to support their families, they were also subject to feudal dues related to the plots of land they rented. In Prussia and Austria, despite attempts by the monarchies late in the century to improve the lot of serfs, the landlords continued to exercise almost complete control over them. In Austria law and custom required serfs to provide service or *robot* to the lords. Moreover, throughout continental Europe in addition to these feudal services, the burden of state taxation fell on the tillers of the soil. Through various legal privileges and the ability to demand further concessions from the monarchs, the

William Coxe Describes Serfdom in Eighteenth-Century Russia

William Coxe was an Englishman who travelled widely in eastern Europe. His description of Russian serfdom portrays the brutality of the institution. It also illustrates his amazement at the absence in Russia of civil liberties such as he and more humble citizens enjoyed in England.

PEASANTS *belonging to individuals are the private property of the landholders, as much as implements of agriculture, or herds of cattle; and the value of an estate is estimated, as in Poland, by the number of boors [serfs], and not by the number of acres. . . . If the Polish boor is oppressed, and he escapes to another master, the latter is liable to no pecuniary penalty for harbouring him; but in Russia the person who receives another's vassal is subject to an heavy fine. With respect to his own demands upon his peasants, the lord is restrained by no law, either in the exaction of any sum, or in the mode of employing them. He is absolute master of their time and labour: some he employs in agriculture: a few he makes his menial servants, and perhaps without wages; and from others he exacts an annual payment.*

Each vassal, therefore, is rated according to the arbitrary will of his master. Some contribute four or five shillings a year; others, who are engaged in traffic or trade, are assessed in proportion to their supposed profits. . . . . With regard to any capital which they may have acquired by their industry, it may be seized, and there can be no redress. . . .

[S]ome of the Russian nobility send their vassals to Moscow or Petersburg for the purpose of learning various handcraft trades: they either employ them on their own estates; let them out for hire; sell them at an advanced price; or receive from them an annual compensation for the permission of exercising trade for their own advantage.

William Coxe, *Travels into Poland, Russia, Sweden, and Denmark,* 4th ed. (London: T. Cadell 1972, first printed 1784), Vol. 3, pp. 174–181.

landlords escaped payment of numerous taxes. They also presided over the manorial courts.

The condition of serfs was worst in Russia. The contrast is best revealed by the Russian custom of enumerating the number of "souls," that is male serfs, owned rather than the acreage possessed. The serfs were merely economic commodities. Russian landlords could demand as much as six days a week of labor, and like Prussian and Austrian landlords they enjoyed the right to punish serfs. They could even exile a serf to Siberia on their own authority. The serfs had no legal recourse against the orders and whims of their lords. There was actually little difference between Russian serfdom and slavery.

The Russian monarchy itself contributed to the degradation of the serfs. Peter the Great gave whole villages to favored nobles. Later in the century Catherine the Great (1762–1796) granted nobles even more authority over their serfs in exchange for the political cooperation of the landowners. The situation in Russia led to considerable unrest. There were well over fifty peasant revolts between 1762 and 1769. These culminated between 1771 and 1775 in Pugachev's rebellion, during which all of southern Russia experienced intense unrest. Emelyan Pugachev (1726–1775) promised the serfs land of their own and freedom from their lords. The rebellion was brutally suppressed. Thereafter any thought of liberalizing or improving the condition of the serfs was set aside for a generation.

Pugachev's was the greatest rebellion in Russian history and the largest peasant uprising of the eighteenth century. Smaller peasant revolts or disturbances occurred elsewhere. Rebellions took place in Bohemia in 1775, in Transylvania in 1784, in Moravia in 1786, and in Austria in 1789. Revolts in western Europe were almost nonexistent, but England experienced numerous local enclosure riots. Rural rebellions were violent, but the peasants and serfs normally directed their wrath against property rather than persons. The rebels usually sought to reassert traditional or customary rights against practices they perceived as innovations. Their targets were carefully

OPPOSITE, TOP: Lunchtime on an eighteenth-century French farm. The softened style of drawing gives a somewhat romanticized cast to the scene, but farm workers did usually work in the kind of group shown here. [The Granger Collection.]

OPPOSITE: J. J. De Boissieu's 1780 etching of the interior of a French dairy barn associates the life of the land with the life of the family. [Charles Farrell Collection.]

Emelyan Pugachev (1726–1775) led the largest peasant revolt in Russian history. Here in a contemporary propaganda picture he is shown in chains. An inscription in Russian and German was printed below the picture discussing the evil of revolution and insurrection. [Bildarchiv Preussischer Kulturbesitz.]

Catherine the Great Issues a Proclamation Against Pugachev

Against a background of longstanding human degradation, and even increasing landowner authority, the greatest serf rebellion in Russian history was led by a Don Cossack named Emelyan Pugachev from 1773 to 1775. Empress Catherine the Great's proclamation of 1773 argues that he was alienating the serfs from their natural and proper allegiance to her and their masters.

B Y THE *grace of God, we Catherine II . . . make known to our faithful subjects, that we have learnt, with the utmost indignation and extreme affliction, that a certain Cossack, a deserter and fugitive from the Don, named Emelyan Pugachev, after having traversed Poland, has been collecting, for some time past, in the districts that border on the river Irghis, in the government of Orenburg, a troop of vagabonds like himself; that he continues to commit in those parts all kinds of excesses, by inhumanly depriving the inhabitants of their possessions, and even of their lives. . . .*

In a word, there is not a man deserving of the Russian name, who does not hold in abomination the odious and insolent lie by which Pugachev fancies himself able to seduce and to deceive persons of a simple and credulous disposition, by promising to free them from the bonds of submission, and obedience to their sovereign, as if the Creation of the universe had established human societies in such a manner as that they can subsist without an intermediate authority between the sovereign and the people.

Nevertheless, as the insolence of this vile refuse of the human race is attended with consequences pernicious to the provinces adjacent to that district; as the report of the flagrant enormities which he has committed, may affright those persons who are accustomed to imagine the misfortunes of others as ready to fall upon them, and as we watch with indefatigable care over the tranquillity of our faithful subjects, we inform them . . . that we have taken . . . such measures as are the best adapted to stifle the sedition. . . .

We trust . . . that every true son of the country will unremittedly fulfill his duty, of the contributing to the maintenance of good order and of public tranquillity, by preserving himself from the snares of seduction, and by discharging his obedience to his lawful sovereign.

William Tooke, *Life of Catherine II, Empress of Russia,* Fourth Edition (London: T. N. Longman and O. Rees, 1800), Vol. 2, pp. 460–461 (spelling modernized).

chosen and included unfair pricing, onerous new or increased feudal dues, changes in methods of payment or land use, unjust officials, or extraordinarily brutal overseers and landlords. In this respect the peasant revolts were quite conservative in nature.

The main goal of peasant society was stability that would ensure the local food supply. In western Europe most rural society was organized into villages. The owners of the individual plots or strips would decide communally what crops would be planted. In eastern Europe, with its great estates of hundreds or thousands of acres, the landlords decided how to use the land. But in either case the tillers resisted change that might endanger the sure supply of food that they believed to be promised by traditional cultivation. However, throughout the eighteenth century landlords across the Continent began to search for higher profits from their holdings. They embraced innovation in order to increase their own prosper-

ity. They commercialized agriculture and thereby challenged traditional peasant ways of production. Peasant
revolts and disturbances resulted. However, the governments of Europe, hungry for new taxes and dependent on
the goodwill of the nobility, used their armies and militias
to smash the peasants who defended the past.

The Revolution in Agriculture

Even more basic than the social dependency of peasants and small tenant farmers was their dependency upon
the productiveness of nature. The quantity and quality of
the annual grain harvest was the most fundamental fact
for their lives. On the Continent bread was the primary
component of the diet for the lower classes. The food
supply was never certain, and the farther east one traveled, the more uncertain it became. Failure of the harvest
meant not only hardship but actual death from either
outright starvation or protracted debility. Quite often
people living in the countryside encountered more difficulty finding food than did city dwellers, whose local
government usually stored reserve supplies of grain.

Poor harvests also played havoc with prices. Smaller
supplies or larger demand raised grain prices. Even small
increases in the cost of food could exert heavy pressure on
peasant or artisan families. If prices increased sharply,
many of those families would fall back on poor relief from
their local municipality or county or the church. What
made the situation of food supply and prices so difficult
was the peasants' sense of helplessness before the whims
of nature and the marketplace.

Over the course of the century, historians now believe,
there occurred a slow but steady inflation of bread prices
spurred largely by population growth. This inflation put
pressure on all of the poor. The prices rose faster than
urban wages and brought no appreciable advantage to the
very small peasant producer. On the other hand, the rise
in grain prices benefited landowners and those wealthier
peasants who had surplus grain to sell.

The increasing price of grain presented landlords with
the opportunity to improve their incomes and life style.
To those ends they began a series of innovations in farm
production that are known as the *agricultural revolution*.
This movement commenced in the Low Countries and
England but spread in varying degrees eastward.

The revolution in agriculture included new methods of
farming, new crops, and new modes of land holding, all

of which eventually led to greater productivity. This advance in food production was necessary for the development of industrial society. It assured food to people living in cities and freed agricultural labor for use in industrial production. The changing modes of agriculture sponsored by the landlords undermined the assumptions of traditional peasant production. Farming now took place not only for the local food supply but also to assure the landlord a handsome profit. The latter goal meant that the landlords began to exert new pressures on their tenants and serfs.

Landlords in Great Britain provided the most striking examples of the improving spirit. Jethro Tull (1674–1741) contributed a willingness to experiment and to finance the experiments of others. Many of his ideas, such as the refusal to use manure as fertilizer, were wrong. Others, however, such as using iron plows to overturn earth more deeply and planting wheat by a drill rather than by casting, were excellent. His methods permitted land to be cultivated for longer periods without having to be left fallow.

Charles "Turnip" Townsend (1674–1738) encouraged even more important innovations. He learned from the Dutch how to cultivate sandy soil with fertilizers. He also instituted crop rotation, using wheat, turnips, barley, and clover. This system abolished the fallow field and produced more food for both animals and human beings.

A third British agricultural improver was Robert Bakewell (1725–1795), who pioneered new methods of animal breeding that produced more and better animals and more milk and meat.

These and other innovations received widespread discussion in the works of Arthur Young (1741–1820), who edited the *Annals of Agriculture* and who in 1793 became secretary of the British Board of Agriculture. Young traveled widely across Europe, and his books are among the most important documents of life during the second half of the eighteenth century.

Many of these innovations, which were adopted only very slowly, were incompatible with the existing organization of the land in Britain. Most of the soil was still farmed by small cultivators who lived in village communities. Each farmer tilled an assortment of unconnected strips. The two- or three-field systems of rotation left large portions of land annually fallow and unproductive. Animals grazed on the common land in the summer and on the stubble of the harvest in the winter. Until at least the middle of the century the decisions as to what crops would be planted were made communally. The entire system discouraged improvement and favored the poorer farmers, who needed the common land and stubble fields for their animals. The village method provided little possibility for expanding pasture to raise more animals that would in turn produce more manure, which could be used for fertilizer. Thus, the methods of traditional production aimed at a steady but not a growing supply of food.

In 1700 approximately half the arable land in Britain was farmed by this open-field method. By the second half of the century the rising price of wheat encouraged landlords to consolidate or enclose their lands to increase production. The enclosures were intended to use land more rationally to achieve greater commercial profits. The process involved the fencing of common lands, the reclamation of previously untilled waste, and the transformation of strips into block fields. These procedures brought turmoil to the economic and social life of the countryside. Riots often ensued. Because many British farmers either owned their strips or rented them in a manner that amounted to ownership, the larger landlords had to resort to parliamentary acts to legalize the enclosure of the land, which they owned but rented to farmers. Because large landowners controlled Parliament, there was little difficulty in obtaining such measures. Between 1761 and 1792 almost 500,000 acres were enclosed through parliamentary act as compared with 75,000 acres between 1727 and 1760. In 1801 a general enclosure act streamlined the process.

The enclosures were at the time and have remained a very controversial topic. They permitted the extension of both farming and innovation. In that regard they increased food production on larger agricultural units. At the same time they disrupted small traditional communities. They forced off the land some independent farmers, who had needed the common pasturage, and very poor cottagers, who had lived on the reclaimed waste land. However, the enclosures did not depopulate the countryside. In some counties where the enclosures took place the population increased. New soil had come into production, and services subsidiary to farming also expanded.

The enclosures did not create the labor force for the British Industrial Revolution. What the enclosures most conspicuously display is the introduction of the entrepreneurial or capitalistic attitude of the urban merchant into the countryside. This commercialization of agriculture, which spread from Britain very slowly across the Continent during the next century, led to a breakdown of paternal relationships between the governing and governed classes. Previously the landlords had somewhat looked after the welfare of the lower orders through price controls or alleviation of rents during depressed periods. However, as the landlords became increasingly concerned about profits, they began to leave peasants to the mercy of the marketplace.

Improving agriculture tended to characterize farm production west of the Elbe. Dutch farming was quite efficient. In France, despite efforts of the government to improve agriculture, enclosures were restricted. Yet there was much discussion in France about improving methods. These new procedures benefited the ruling classes because better agriculture increased their incomes and assured a larger food supply, which tended to discourage social unrest.

In Russia, Prussia, Poland, and Austria only limited improvement took place. There the chief method of increasing production was to extend farming to previously untilled lands. The management of the farms was under the direction of the landlords or their agents rather than villages. By extending tillage, the great landlords sought to squeeze more labor from their serfs rather than

greater productivity from the soil. However, as in the West, the goal was increased profits.

Population Expansion

The assault on human dependence upon nature through improved farming was both a cause and a result of an immense expansion in the population of Europe. The population explosion with which the entire world must today contend seems to have had its origins in the eighteenth century. Prior to this time Europe's population had experienced dramatic increases, but plagues, wars, or harvest failures had in time decimated the increase. Beginning in the second quarter of the eighteenth century, the population began to grow without decimation.

Exact figures are lacking but the best estimates suggest that in 1700 Europe's population, excluding the European provinces of the Ottoman Empire, stood between 100 and 120 million people. By 1800 the figures had risen to almost 190 million, and by 1850 to 260 million. The population of England and Wales rose from 6 million in 1750 to 9 million in 1800. France grew from 18 million in 1715 to approximately 26 million in 1789. Russia's population increased from 19 million in 1722 to 29 million in 1766. Such extraordinary, sustained growth put new demands on all resources and considerable pressure on existing social organization.

The population expansion occurred across the Continent in both the country and the cities. There exists only a limited consensus of opinion about the causes of this growth. There was a clear decline in the death rate. There were fewer wars and somewhat fewer epidemics in the eighteenth century. Hygiene and sanitation also improved. Better medical knowledge and techniques were once thought to have contributed to the decline in deaths. This factor is now discounted because the more important medical advances came after the initial population explosion or would not have contributed directly to it. Rather, changes in the food supply itself may have provided the chief factor that allowed the population these pressures and demands continued to increase. The society and the social practices of the old regime literally outgrew their traditional bounds.

The Industrial Revolution of the Eighteenth Century

The second half of the eighteenth century witnessed the beginning of the industrialization of the European economy. The Industrial Revolution constituted the achievement of sustained economic growth. Previously production had been of a limited character. The economy of a province or a country might grow, but it soon reached a plateau. However, since the late eighteenth century the economy of Europe has managed to expand in a relatively uninterrupted manner. Depressions and recessions have been of a temporary nature, and even during such economic downturns the Western economy has continued to grow. Industrialism at considerable social cost made possible more goods and more services than ever before in human history. Industrialism in Europe eventually overcame the economy of scarcity. Whether that process has in our own day brought the West to a new confrontation with resource scarcity is a question and problem for the present generation.

NEW METHODS OF TEXTILE PRODUCTION. Although eighteenth-century society was primarily devoted to agriculture, manufacturing permeated the countryside. The same peasants who tilled the land in spring and summer often spun thread or wove textiles in the winter. Under what is termed the *domestic* or *putting-out system,* agents of urban textile merchants took wool or other unfinished fibers to the homes of peasants, who spun it into thread. The agent then transported the thread to other peasants, who wove it into the finished product. The merchant sold the wares. In literally thousands of peasant cottages from Ireland to Austria, there stood either a spinning wheel or a handloom. Sometimes the spinner or weaver owned his own equipment, but more often than not by the middle of the century the

growth to become sustained. The improved and expanding grain production made one contribution. Another and even more important modification was the cultivation of the potato. This tuber was a product of the New World and came into widespread European production during the eighteenth century. On a single acre a peasant could raise enough potatoes to feed his family for an entire year. With such an assured food supply more children could be reared, and more could survive.

The impact of the population explosion can hardly be underestimated. It created new demands for food, goods, jobs, and services. It provided a new pool of labor. Traditional modes of production and living had to be devised. More people came to live in the countryside than could find employment there. Migration increased. There were also more people to be socially and politically discontent. And because the population growth fed on itself, all of

La Rochefoucault-Liancourt Sees the Domestic System in France

In the domestic system of production different peasants were responsible for separate processes in the manufacture of cloth. Some spun and others wove, but all worked in their own homes. Merchants then sold the finished cloth all over Europe and the New World. The production of cloth was undertaken by peasants in addition to their farming. La Rochefoucault observed the system in France in the 1780s.

I THEN *saw the material called cotton check* [cotonnades]. *There are all sorts of cotton manufacture made up at Rouen and in the area 15 leagues around it. The peasant who returns to the plough to work his fields, sits at his cotton frame and makes either* siamoises [common cotton goods] *or ticking or even white, very fine, cotton cloth. One must admire the activity of the Normans. This activity does not interfere at all with their daily work. Land is very dear and consequently very well cultivated. The farmer works on the land during the day and it is in the evening by the light of the lamp that he starts his other task. His workers and his family have to help. When they have worked all week they come into the town with horses or carts piled up with material. Goods are sold in the Hall, which is all that remains of the palace of the former Dukes of Normandy, on Thursdays. It is truly a wonderful sight. It takes place at surprising speed. Almost 800,000 francs worth of business is transacted between 6:00 and 9:00 in the morning. Among those who do the buying there are many agents who buy for merchants and then the goods pass to America, Italy and Spain. The majority goes to America.*

Francois De La Rochefoucauld-Liancourt, *Voyages en France* (1781–1783), cited and trans. in S. Pollard and C. Holmes (Eds.), *Documents of European Economic History* (London: Edward Arnold, 1968), Vol. 1, p. 91.

merchant capitalist owned the machinery as well as the raw material.

What must be kept constantly in mind is the rather surprising fact that eighteenth-century industrial development took place within a rural setting. The peasant family living in a one- or two-room cottage was the basic unit of production rather than the factory. The family economy rather than the industrial factory economy characterized the century.

The small married farmer or peasant burdened by taxes and feudal dues could not support himself and his family by his own labor alone. It was necessary not merely for comfort but for economic survival that his wife spin or weave or knit and that his children be set to work as soon as they were physically able. The subsistence of these families depended upon their capacity to find makeshift ways of earning income beyond that from farming. Certain members of the family, including women, might migrate with the harvest. Children might ultimately go to the city to seek employment. If any of these sources of income failed, the entire family might fall into dependence on some form of charity or crime. As Olwen Hufton has written, it was a life in which "one lived daily from hand to mouth without provision for old age, sickness, incapacity to work, or disasters such as harvest failure or even the arrival of a baby."[1]

The domestic system of textile production was a basic feature of this family economy. However, by mid-century a series of production bottlenecks had developed within the domestic system. Demand for cotton textiles was growing more rapidly than production. This demand was felt particularly in Great Britain, where there existed a large domestic demand for cotton textiles from the growing population. There was a similar foreign demand upon British production from its colonies in North America. It was in response to this consumer demand for cotton textiles that the most famous inventions of the Industrial Revolution were devised.

Cotton textile weavers had the technical capacity to produce the quantity of fabric that was in demand. However, the spinners did not possess the equipment to produce as much thread as the weavers needed and could use. This imbalance had been created during the 1730s by James Kay's invention of the flying shuttle, which increased the productivity of the weavers. Thereafter various groups of manufacturers and merchants offered prizes for the invention of a machine to eliminate this bottleneck. About 1764 James Hargreaves (d. 1778)

1 Allan Mitchell and Istvan Deak (Eds.), *Everyman in Europe: Essays in Social History* (Englewood Cliffs, N.J.: Prentice-Hall, 1974), vol. 2, p. 82.

invented the spinning jenny. Initially this machine allowed 16 spindles of thread to be spun, but by the close of the century its capacity had been increased to as many as 120 spindles.

The spinning jenny broke the bottleneck between the productive capacity of spinners and weavers, but it was still a piece of machinery that was used in the cottage. The invention that took cotton textile manufacture out of the home and put it into the factory was Richard Arkwright's (1732–1792) water frame, patented in 1769. It was a water-powered device designed to permit production of a purely cotton fabric rather than a cotton fabric containing linen fiber for durability. Eventually Arkwright lost his patent rights, and other manufacturers were able to use his invention freely. As a result, numerous factories sprang up in the countryside near streams that provided the necessary water power. From the 1780s onward the cotton industry could meet an ever-expanding demand. In the last two decades of the century cotton output increased by 800 per cent over the production of 1780. By 1815 cotton composed 40 per cent of the value of British domestic exports, and by 1830 just over 50 per cent.

The Industrial Revolution had commenced in earnest by the 1780s, but the full economic and social ramifica-

tions of this unleashing of human productive capacity were not really felt until the early nineteenth century. The expansion of industry and the incorporation of new inventions often occurred rather slowly. For example, Edmund Cartwright (1743–1822) invented the power loom for machine weaving in the late 1780s. Yet not until the 1830s were there more power-loom weavers than hand-loom weavers in Britain. Nor did all of the social ramifications of industrialism appear immediately. The first cotton mills used water power, were located in the country, and rarely employed more than two dozen workers. Not until the late-century application of the steam engine, perfected by James Watt (1736–1819) in 1769, to the running of textile machinery could factories easily be located in or near existing urban centers. The steam engine not only vastly increased and regularized the available energy but also made possible the combination of urbanization and industrialization.

IRON PRODUCTION. Certain inventions and manufacturing improvements also had to await the next century for realization of their economic potential. The best example is that of the iron industry. Production of iron has been basic to modern industrial development. It constitutes the chief element for all heavy industry and has been the material out of which most productive machin-

OPPOSITE: This landscape painting by an unknown contemporary British artist portrays the pithead of an eighteenth-century coal mine in England. The machinery on the left included a steam engine that powered equipment either to bring the mined coal to the surface or to pump water from the mine. [Walker Art Gallery, Liverpool.]

ABOVE: Throughout most of the eighteenth century nearly all industrial manufacture took place in relatively small workshops such as the lead-casting shop illustrated in this print from the French *Encyclopedia*. Very large factories became established only quite late in the eighteenth century and early in the nineteenth.

ery itself has been manufactured. During the early eighteenth century British ironmongers produced somewhat less than twenty-five thousand tons annually. Three factors held back the production of the metal. Charcoal rather than coke was used to smelt the ore. Until the perfection of the steam engine, insufficient blasts could be achieved in the furnaces. Finally, the demand for iron was limited. The elimination of the first two problems eliminated the third.

In the course of the century British ironmongers began to use coke, and the steam engine provided new power for the blast furnaces. In 1784 Henry Cort (1740–1800) introduced a new puddling process that allowed more slag to be removed and a purer iron to be produced. These innovations achieved a better product at a lower cost. The demand for iron grew as its price became cheaper. By the early years of the nineteenth century British iron production amounted to over a million tons annually. The lower cost of iron in turn lowered the cost of steam engines and allowed them to be used more widely.

Industrial Leadership of Great Britain

Great Britain was the home of the Industrial Revolution and until the middle of the nineteenth century maintained the industrial leadership of Europe. Several factors

contributed to the early start in Britain. The nation constituted the single largest free-trade area in Europe. The British possessed good roads and waterways without internal tolls or internal trade barriers. The country was endowed with rich deposits of coal and iron ore. The political structure was stable, and property was absolutely secure. Taxation was not especially heavy. In addition to existing domestic consumer demand, the British economy was also influenced by demand from the colonies in North America.

Finally, British society was relatively mobile by the standards of the time. Assuming a person had money or could earn money, he could rise socially. The British aristocracy would receive into its midst people who had amassed very large fortunes. No one of these factors preordained the British advance toward industrialism. However, the combination of them plus the progressive state of British agriculture provided the nation with the marginal advantage in the creation of a new mode of economic production.

While this economic development was occurring, people did not call it a *revolution*. That term came to be applied to the British economic phenomena only after the French Revolution. Then continental writers observed that what had taken place in Britain was the economic equivalent of the political events in France; hence the concept of an *industrial* revolution. It was revolutionary less in its speed, which was on the whole rather slow, than in its implications for the future of European society.

The means of production demanded new kinds of skills, new discipline in work, and a large labor force. The goods produced both met immediate consumer demand and created new demands. In the long run, industrialism clearly raised the standard of living and overcame the poverty experienced by the overwhelming majority of Europeans who lived during the eighteenth century and earlier. Industrialization provided human beings greater control over the forces of nature than ever known before. The wealth produced by industrialism upset the political structures of the old regime and led to reforms. The economic elite of the emerging industrial society would eventually challenge the political dominance of the aristocracy.

The Aristocracy

Despite the emerging Industrial Revolution, the eighteenth century remained par excellence the age of the aristocracy. The nobility of every country was the single wealthiest sector of the population; possessed the widest degree of social, political, and economic power; and set the tone of polite society. Land continued to provide the aristocracy with its largest source of income, but the role of the aristocrat was not limited to his estate. The influence of aristocrats was felt in every area of life. To be an aristocrat was a matter of birth and legal privilege. This much they had in common across the Continent. In almost every other respect they differed markedly from country to country.

The smallest, wealthiest, best-defined, and most socially responsible aristocracy resided in Great Britain. It consisted of about four hundred families whose eldest male member sat in the House of Lords. Through the corruptions of the electoral system these families also controlled a large number of seats in the House of Com-

---

Josiah Tucker Praises the New Use of Machinery in England

The extensive use of recently invented machines made the Industrial Revolution possible in England. This passage from a 1757 travel guide illustrates how the application of machines in various manufacturing processes was regarded by contemporaries as new and exciting.

Few *countries are equal, perhaps none excel, the English in the number of contrivances of their Machines to abridge labour. Indeed the Dutch are superior to them in the use and application of Wind Mills for sawing Timber, expressing Oil, making Paper and the like. But in regard to Mines and Metals of all sorts, the English are uncommonly dexterous in their contrivance of the mechanic Powers; some being calculated for landing the Ores out of the Pits, such as Cranes and Horse Engines; others for draining off superfluous Water, such as Water Wheels and Steam Engines; others again for easing the Expense of Carriage such as Machines to run on inclined Planes or Roads downhill with wooden frames, in order to carry many Tons of Material at a Time. And to these must be added the various sorts of Levers used in different processes; also the Brass Battery works, the Slitting Mills, Plate and Flatting Mills, and those for making Wire of different Fineness. Yet all these, curious as they may seem, are little more than Preparations or Introductions for further Operations. Therefore, when we still consider that at Birmingham, Wolverhampton, Sheffield and other manufacturing Places, almost every Master Manufacturer hath a new Invention of his own, and is daily improving on those of others; we may aver with some confidence that those parts of England in which these things are seen exhibit a specimen of practical mechanics scarce to be paralleled in any part of the world.*

Josiah Tucker, *Instructions to Travellers* (London: Privately Printed, 1757), p. 20

---

mons. The estates of the British nobility ranged from a few thousand to fifty thousand acres, from which they received rents. The nobles owned approximately one fourth of all the arable land in the country. Increasingly the money of the aristocracy was being invested in commerce, canals, urban real estate, mines, and sometimes in industrial ventures. Because only the eldest son inherited the title and the land, younger sons moved into commerce, the army, the professions, and the church. The British aristocracy levied taxes in Parliament and also paid

This famous portrait painting, Robert Andrews and His Wife, by the British artist Thomas Gainsborough (1728–1788) illustrates the peaceful and prosperous life of an English landowner. As the gun and dog indicate, he enjoyed considerable leisure time for sports such as hunting. [Reproduced by courtesy of the Trustees, The National Gallery, London.]

taxes. It had practically no significant legal privileges, but its direct or indirect control of local government gave it immense political power and social influence. The aristocracy quite simply dominated the society and the politics of the English counties.

The situation of the continental nobilities was less clear-cut. In France the nobility was divided between nobles of the sword and those of the robe. The former families enjoyed privileges deriving from military service; the latter had either received their titles from serving in the bureaucracy or had purchased them. The two groups had frequently quarreled in the past but tended to cooperate during the eighteenth century to defend their common privileges.

The French nobility was also divided between those who held office or favor with the royal court at Versailles and those who did not. The court nobility reaped the immense wealth that could be gained from holding high offices. The noble hold on such offices intensified over the course of the century. By the late 1780s appointments to the church, the army, the bureaucracy, and other profitable positions tended to go to nobles already established in court circles. Whereas these well-connected aristocrats were quite rich, other nobles who lived in the provinces were often rather poor. These *hobereaux*, as the poverty-stricken nobles were called, were sometimes little or no better off than wealthy peasants.

Despite differences in rank, origin, and wealth, all French aristocrats enjoyed certain hereditary privileges that set them apart from the rest of society. They were exempt from many taxes. For example, most French nobles did not pay the *taille*, which was the basic tax of the old regime. The nobles were technically liable for payment of the *vingtième*, or the twentieth, which resembled an income tax. However, by virtue of protests and legal procedures, the nobility rarely felt the entire weight of this tax. The nobles were not liable for the royal *corvées*, or labor donations, which fell on the peasants. In addition to these exemptions, the approximately four hundred thousand French nobles could collect feudal dues from their tenants and enjoyed hunting and fishing privileges denied their tenants.

East of the Elbe River the character of the nobility became even more complicated and repressive. In Poland there were thousands of nobles, or *szlachta,* who after 1741 were entirely exempt from taxes. Until 1768 these Polish aristocrats possessed the right of life and death over their serfs. Most of the Polish nobility were relatively poor. The political power of the fragile Polish state resided in the few very rich nobles.

In Austria and Hungary the nobility continued to possess broad judicial powers over the peasantry through manorial courts.

In Prussia after the accession of Frederick the Great in

1740, the position of the *Junker* nobles became much stronger. Frederick's various wars required the support of his nobles. He drew his officers almost wholly from the *Junker* class. The bureaucracy was also increasingly composed of nobles. As in other parts of eastern Europe, the Prussian nobles enjoyed extensive judicial authority over the serfs.

In Russia the eighteenth century saw what amounted to the creation of the nobility. Peter the Great's linking of state service and noble social status through the Table of Ranks (1722) established among Russian nobles a self-conscious class identity that had not previously existed. Thereafter they stood united in their determination to resist compulsory state service. In 1736 Empress Ann reduced such service to a period of twenty-five years. In 1762 Peter III removed the liability for compulsory serv-

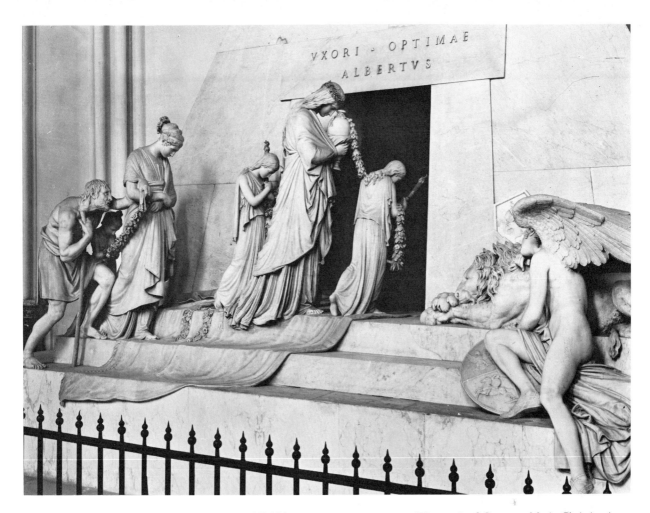

VXORI · OPTIMAE
ALBERTVS

OPPOSITE: The Scots brothers Adam dominated British decorative taste in the late eighteenth century. About 1770, Robert, the more important, planned this elegant drawing room for Home House in London. [The Courtauld Institute of Art and *Country Life*, London.]

ABOVE: The tomb of Countess Maria Christina in a church in Vienna by the Italian sculptor Antonio Canova (1757–1822). It represents the kind of artistic extravagance the European aristocracy could command in the late eighteenth century. [Eva Frodl-Kraft.]

ice entirely from the greatest nobles. In 1785, in the Charter of the Nobility, Catherine the Great granted an explicit legal definition of noble rights and privileges in exchange for assurances of voluntary state service from the nobility. The noble privileges included the right of transmitting noble status to one's wife and children, judicial protection of noble rights and property, considerable power over serfs, and exemption from personal taxes.

The Russian Charter of the Nobility constituted one aspect of the broader European-wide development termed the *aristocratic resurgence*. Throughout the century the various nobilities felt their social position and privileges threatened by the expanding power of the monarchies and the growing wealth of merchants, bankers, and other commercial groups. All nobilities attempted to preserve their exclusiveness by making entry into their ranks and institutions more difficult. They also pushed for exclusively noble appointments to the officer corps of the armies, the bureaucracies, government ministries, and the church. In that manner nobles hoped to control the power of the monarchies.

On a third level the nobles attempted to use the authority of existing aristocratically controlled institutions against the power of the monarchies. These institutions included the British Parliament and on the Continent the French courts or *parlements,* local aristocratic estates, and provincial diets. Economically the aristocratic resurgence took the form of pressing the peasantry for higher rents or collecting long-forgotten feudal dues. There was a general tendency for the nobility to shore up its position by various appeals to traditional and often ancient privileges that had lapsed over the course of time. To contem-

The Aristocracy 531

FORTITVDO

Fortitude, by the eighteenth-century Italian sculptor Giacomo Serpotta, is an allegorical statue in a church in Palermo, Sicily. It was intended to portray a particular value; the means of illustration was an aristocratic lady, and the statue was to be observed and appreciated primarily by the upper classes. [Alinari/SCALA.]

OPPOSITE: The great park in Edinburgh, Scotland, was created in the eighteenth century by draining a lake that had previously existed in its place. The mid-nineteenth-century building in the center of the picture is the National Gallery of Scotland. [British Tourist Authority, New York.]

poraries this aristocratic challenge to the monarchies and to the rising commercial classes constituted one of the most fundamental political facts of the day.

Cities

The Urban Setting

The influence of land and landed society extended to the cities of the old regime. The cities of the eighteenth century, like those of today, were dependent on the countryside for their food supply. The specter of famine or food shortages haunted cities. Their governments took great care to ensure adequate supplies of grain by building granaries and by paying careful attention to the fluctuation of bread prices. The nobility were not absent from the cities. They owned homes in the urban centers and often possessed large blocks of city real estate, which they developed as sources of new rents. Frequently no-

bles controlled the municipal government and sat as judges in municipal courts.

There also existed a two-way migration of people between the country and the city. In many cities, especially of central and eastern Europe, rural day laborers lived in the towns and traveled outward to find their work. Other cities witnessed what has become a common modern phenomenon—migration of people from the countryside into the town to find work, better wages, and possibly a more exciting life. Thousands of men and women born in the country moved to the city to become domestic servants or artisans.

Fernand Braudel has rightly described cities as "so many electric transformers," which "increase tension, accelerate the rhythm of exchange and ceaselessly stir up men's lives."[2] The eighteenth century witnessed a considerable growth of towns. The tumult of the day and the revolutions with which the century closed had no small relationship to that urban expansion. London grew from about 700,000 inhabitants in 1700 to almost a million in 1800. By the time of the French Revolution the population of Paris stood over a half million. Berlin's population tripled over the course of the century, reaching 170,000 in 1800. St. Petersburg, founded in 1703, numbered over a quarter million inhabitants a century later. In addition to the growth of these capitals, the number of smaller urban units of 20,000–50,000 people increased considerably. However, this urban growth must be kept in perspective. Even in France and Great Britain probably somewhat less than 20 per cent of the population lived in cities. And the town of 10,000 inhabitants was much more common than the giant urban center.

Practically all of these urban conglomerates were non-industrial cities. They grew and expanded for reasons other than the location of factories or other large manufacturing establishments. Only Manchester in England had experienced such industrial growth, and even its most spectacular expansion occurred after 1800.

2 Fernand Braudel, *Capitalism and Material Life, 1400–1800* (New York: Harper Torchbooks, 1973), p. 373.

Eighteenth-century cities fall into three broad and rather imperfect categories. The first and most common were market centers for the exchange of goods, most of which were produced locally. These relatively small provincial centers might also provide the location for local courts and state administration. The second category consisted of commercial, trading, shipping, and financial centers. These included the major sea and river ports. Finally, there were the great capital cities, which were also frequently commercial centers. In a sense both of the latter kind of cities were the creation of the expanding bureaucratic states. All of their rulers wished to see trade and commerce prosper. The great taxing power of those monarchies meant that vast wealth flowed into the capitals.

With the exception of St. Petersburg, the cities of the

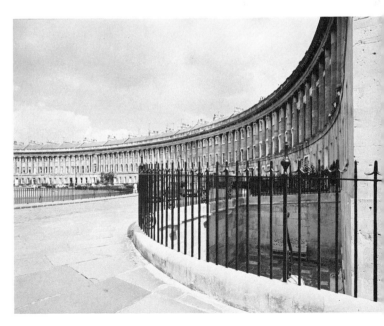

The Royal Crescent in Bath, England, is an example of fashionable eighteenth-century town planning. The elliptical crescent contained luxury housing for wealthy families who vacationed in Bath, which is on the site of a Roman town of the first century B.C. [British Tourist Authority, New York.]

eighteenth century were largely unplanned. A few urban developers might create elegant squares for the wealthy merchants or urban-dwelling aristocrats, but most cities simply expanded on the base of their medieval precursors. London had burned in 1666. Its reconstruction benefited from the planning and architecture of Sir Christopher Wren (1632–1723), but expansion was still quite haphazard. On the Continent many cities retained their medieval walls, within which and beyond which growth occurred. There was usually a central square with civic buildings or a cathedral or a fortress nearby. Quite often urban expansion pressed beyond the original city border and onto territory of non-urban landlords. The authority of the latter would then extend over that part of the city. Consequently some urban areas were governed by manorial courts and other institutions of the countryside.

There existed visible segregation between the urban rich and the urban poor. The former lived in fashionable townhouses, often constructed around newly laid-out green squares. The poorest town dwellers usually congregatated along the rivers. Small merchants and craftsmen lived above their shops. Whole families might live in a single room. Sanitary facilities such as now exist were still unknown. There was little pure water. Cattle, pigs, goats, and other animals walked the streets with the people. All reports on the cities of Europe during this period emphasize both the striking grace and beauty of the dwellings of the wealthy and the dirt, filth, and stench that filled the streets.

Despite the more obvious drawbacks, it was still in the cities that men and women from all walks and stations of life found entertainment and excitement. There were more modes of recreation in cities than in the countryside. The cities provided more opportunities for theater, gambling, womanizing, and husband hunting. The season of parties in London drew noble and upper-gentry families from all over England. Here marriages were sought, and friendships were renewed. The French nobility had learned to enjoy Paris after Louis XIV had initially forced them to come to his court at nearby Versailles. And many Russian nobles came to crave life in St. Petersburg after having first arrived under the compulsion of Peter the Great. The eighteenth-century townhouse as much as the country house provided the aristocracy with its public stage.

There was, however, another side to urban life. This was the lot of the poor, who often depended on charity in the city. Poverty was not a city problem; it was usually worse in the countryside. But in the city poverty more visibly manifested itself in terms of crime, prostitution, vagrancy, begging, and alchoholism. Many a young man or woman from the countryside migrated to the nearest city to seek a better life, only to discover poor housing, little food, disease, degradation, and finally death. It did not require the Industrial Revolution and the urban factory to make the cities into hellholes for the poor and the dispossessed. The full darkness of London life during the mid-century "gin age" when consumption of that liquor blinded and killed many poor people can be seen in the engravings of William Hogarth (1697–1764). Also contrasting with the serenity of the aristocratic and upper commercial-class life style were the public executions that took place all over Europe, the breaking of men and women on the wheel in Paris, and the public floggings in Russia. Brutality condoned and carried out by the ruling classes was quite simply a fact of everyday life.

Urban Classes

Social divisions were as marked in the cities of the eighteenth century as they were in the industrial centers of the nineteenth. At the top of the urban social structure was a generally small group of nobles, large merchants, bankers, financiers, clergy, and government officials. These men (and they were always men) controlled the political and economic affairs of the town. Normally they constituted a self-appointed and self-electing oligarchy who governed the city through its corporation or city council. These rights of self-government had normally been granted by some form of royal charter that gave the city corporation its authority and the power to select its

Design'd by W. Hogarth.

Gin cursed Fiend, with Fury fraught,
Makes human Race a Prey.
It enters by a deadly Draught,
And steals our Life away.

Virtue and Truth, driv'n to Despair,
It's Rage compells to fly,
But cherishes, with hellish Care,
Theft, Murder, Perjury.

Damn'd Cup! that on the Vitals preys,
That liquid Fire contains,
Which Madness to the Heart conveys,
And rolls it thro' the Veins.

Publish'd according to Act of Parliam.t Feb.y 1.1751.   Price i s.

In late eighteenth-century Vienna, apprehended prostitutes had to appear before courts, as in this print, where they were ordered to have their hair shorn and then sent out to sweep the streets. [Österreichische Nationalbibliothek, Vienna]

own members. In a few cities on the Continent, artisan guilds controlled the corporations, but more generally the councils were under the influence of the local nobility and the wealthiest commercial people.

THE MIDDLE CLASS. Another group in the city were the prosperous but not immensely wealthy merchants, tradesmen, bankers, and professional people. These were the most dynamic element of the urban population and constituted the persons traditionally regarded as the middle class or *bourgeoisie*. The concept of the middle class was much less clear-cut than that of the nobility. They had less wealth than most nobles but more than urban artisans. The middle-class people lived in the cities and towns, and their sources of income had little or nothing to do with the land. The middle class normally stood on the side of reform, change, and economic growth. The middle-class commercial figures—traders, bankers, manufacturers, and lawyers—often found their pursuit of both profit and prestige blocked by the privileges of the nobility and its social exclusiveness. The bourgeoisie also wanted more rational regulations for trade and commerce, as did some of the more progressive aristocrats.

During the eighteenth century the middle class and the aristocracy were on a collision course. The former often imitated the life style of the latter, and the nobles were increasingly embracing the commercial spirit of the middle class. The bourgeoisie was not rising to challenge the nobility; both were seeking to add new dimensions to their existing power and prestige. However, tradition and political connection gave the advantage to the nobility. Consequently, as the century passed, members of the middle class felt and voiced increasing resentment toward the aristocracy. That resentment became more bitter as the wealth and numbers of the *bourgeoisie* increased and the aristocratic control of political and ecclesiastical power became tighter. The growing influence of the nobility seemed to mean that the middle class would continue to be excluded from the political decisions of the day.

On the other hand, the middle class in the cities tended to fear the lower urban classes as much as they resented the nobility. The lower orders constituted a potentially violent element in the society, a potential threat to property, and in their poverty a drain on national resources. However, the lower orders were much more varied than either the city aristocracy or the middle class cared to admit.

Society Under the Old Regime

Several examples of non-agricultural working-class skills can be shown. Printing shops produced the flood of eighteenth-century publications. Type was set and presses operated by hand, and the workmen were among the most highly skilled urban craftsmen. The picture is from the *Encyclopedia*. [Charles Farrell Collection.]

ARTISANS. The segment of the urban population that suffered from both the grasping of the middle class and the oligarchy of the nobility was that made up of the shopkeepers, the artisans, and the wage earners. These people constituted the single largest group in any city. The lives and experience of this class were very diverse. They included grocers, butchers, fishmongers, carpenters, cabinetmakers, smiths, printers, hand-loom weavers, and tailors, to give but a few examples. They had their own culture, values, and institutions. Like the peasants of the countryside, they were in many respects very conservative. Their economic position was highly vulnerable. If a poor harvest raised the price of food, their own businesses suffered.

The entire life of these artisans and shopkeepers centered on their work. They usually lived near or at their place of employment. Most of them worked in shops with fewer than a half dozen other craftsmen. Their primary institution had historically been the guild. By the eighteenth century the guilds rarely possessed the influence of their predecessors in medieval or early modern Europe.

Nevertheless the guilds were not to be ignored. They played a conservative role. They did not seek economic growth or innovation. They attempted to preserve the jobs and the skills of their members. The guilds still were able in many countries to determine who might and might not pursue a particular craft. They attempted to prevent too many people from learning a particular skill. The guilds also provided a framework for social and economic advancement. A boy might at an early age become an apprentice to learn a craft or a trade. After several years he would be made a journeyman. Still later, if successful and sufficiently competent, he might become a master. The artisan could also receive certain social benefits from the guilds. These might include aid for his family during sickness or the promise of admission for his son. The guilds constituted the chief protection for artisans against the operation of the commercial market. They were particularly strong in central Europe.

The artisan class with its generally conservative outlook maintained a rather fine sense of social and economic justice. These ideals were based largely on traditional practice. If the collective sense of what was economically "just" became offended, artisans frequently manifested their displeasure through the instrument of the riot. The most sensitive area was the price of bread. If a baker or a grain merchant announced a price that was considered unjustly high, a bread riot might well ensue. Artisan leaders would confiscate the bread or grain and sell it for what the urban crowd considered a "just price." They would then give the money paid for the bread or grain to the baker or merchant. The possibility of bread riots acted as a restraint on the greed of merchants. Such disturbances represented a collective method of imposing the "just price" in place of the price set by the commercial marketplace. In other words, bread and food riots were not irrational acts of screaming hungry people but rather were highly ritualized social phenomena of the old regime and its economy of scarcity.

Other kinds of riots were also a basic characteristic of eighteenth-century society and politics. The riot was a way in which people excluded in every other way from the political processes could make their will known. Sometimes urban rioters were incited by religious bigotry. For example, in 1753 London Protestant mobs compelled the government ministry to withdraw an act for Jewish naturalization. In 1780 the same rabidly Protestant spirit manifested itself in the Gordon riots, named

[Text continued on page 542]

ABOVE: Barrel makers were included among the craftsmen of the eighteenth-century city. Jean Jacques De Boissieu of Lyons (1736–1810) made the etching. [Charles Farrell Collection.]

OPPOSITE: The skills of the blacksmith were required in both city and countryside. It is noteworthy that when Joseph Moxon, an English publisher and map-maker, wrote a series of *Mechanick Exercises: Or, the Doctrine of Handy-works*, published in parts between 1677 and 1683 and the first textbooks in any language on several of the major crafts, he began with the smith's trade because, as he said, "without the Invention of *Smithing* primarily, most other Mechanick Inventions would be at a stand: The Instruments or Tools that are used in them being either made of Iron, or of some other matter form'd by the help of Iron. But pray take notice, that by Iron I also mean Steel, it being originally Iron. . . . Some perhaps would have thought it more Policy to have introduced these *Exercises* with a more curious and less Vulgar Art than that of *Smithing*; but I am not of their opinion; for *Smithing* is (in all its parts) as curious a Handy-craft as any is . . ." This striking painting is by Joseph Wright of Derby (1734–1797). [Yale Center for British Art, New Haven.]

RIGHT: This etching from the *Encyclopedia* illustrates the foundry work involved in the casting of a bronze statue in the eighteenth century. Cannons would have been cast in a similar fashion, as suggested by the broken casts at the bottom of the illustration. For contrast, refer to the illustration on page 79 showing work in progress on a bronze statue in classical Greece about 2200 years earlier. [The Granger Collection.]

The fire and smoke in this contemporary drawing are billowing out of the furnace being used to produce sulphuric acid in an eighteenth-century Italian precursor of an industrial laboratory. The artist was Louis-Jacques Durambeau, and the original is in the Louvre. [Courtesy Charles Farrell.]

Bread was the single most important foodstuff in the eighteenth century, and its relative availability and price were constant social, economic, and political problems. This etching of an urban bakery from the *Encyclopedia* illustrates, from right to left, the kneading of the dough, the weighing of the loaves, the shaping of the loaves, and the baking of the bread. [The Granger Collection.]

Torture and public executions were still quite common during the eighteenth century. In some places, weights, as shown here, were used as a torture to extract information. Pressing was also a mode of execution for prisoners who refused to plead to the charges. [Bettmann Archive.]

The burning of Newgate Prison, London, in June 1780 during the anti-Catholic Gordon riots, which raged for several days. It is said that some three hundred prisoners were released and the unfortunate warden, Mr. Akerman, lost all his furniture in the fire. [The Granger Collection.]

after Lord George Gordon, who had raised the specter of an imaginary Catholic plot against England. In these riots and in food riots, violence was normally directed against property rather than against people. The rioters themselves were not "riffraff" but usually small shopkeepers, freeholders, craftsmen, and wage earners. They usually had no other purpose than to restore a traditional right or practice that seemed endangered. Nevertheless considerable turmoil and destruction could result from their actions.

During the last half of the century urban riots increasingly involved political ends. Though often simultaneous with economic disturbances, the political riot always had nonartisan leadership or instigators. In fact, the "crowd" of the eighteenth century was often the tool of the upper classes. In Paris the aristocratic Parlement often urged crowd action in their disputes with the monarchy. In Geneva middle-class citizens supported artisan riots against the local urban oligarchy. In Great Britain in 1792 the government turned out mobs to attack English sympathizers of the French Revolution. All of these and other various outbursts of popular unrest suggest that the crowd or mob did not first enter the European political and social arena during the Revolution in France.

A Society on the Edge of Modern Times

This chapter opened by describing eighteenth-century society as traditional, hierarchical, corporate, and privileged. These features had characterized Europe for hundreds of years. However, by the close of the eighteenth century each of these facets of European life had been undermined or challenged in a fundamental fashion from developments within the society itself. Europe stood on the brink of a new era in which the social, economic, and political relationships of centuries would be burst.

The society had remained traditional and corporate largely because of the economy of scarcity. The agricultural and industrial revolutions would eventually overcome most scarcity in Europe and the West generally. The commercial spirit and values of the marketplace clashed with the traditional values and practices of peasants and guilds. The desire to make money and accumulate profits was hardly new, but beginning in the eighteenth century, it was permitted fuller play than ever before in European history. The commercial spirit was a major vehicle of social change and by the early nineteenth century led increasingly to conceiving of human beings as individuals rather than as members of communities.

The expansion of population provided further stimulus for change and challenge to tradition, hierarchy, and corporateness. Economic and social organization had presupposed a stable or declining population. The additional numbers of people meant new ways had to be devised to solve old problems. More people also meant more labor, more energy, and more minds contributing to the creation and solution of social difficulties. The improvements in health and the longer life span may have given that larger population a new sense of confidence. The social hierarchy had to accommodate itself to more people. Corporate groups, such as the guilds, had to confront the existence of an expanded labor force. Moreover the products and industries rising from the Industrial Revolution made the society and the economy much more complicated. Class structure and social hierarchy remained, but the boundaries became blurred. New wealth meant that birth would eventually become less and less of a determining factor in social relationships except in regard to the social role assigned to the two sexes.

Finally, the conflicting political ambitions of the monarchs, the nobilities, and the middle class generated innovation. The monarchs wanted to make their nations rich enough to wage war. As will be seen, this goal led them to attempt to interfere further with the privileges of the nobles. In the name of ancient rights the nobles attempted to secure and expand their existing social privileges by achieving further political power in the state. By making their privileges so exclusive, they helped to undermine the principle of privilege itself. The middle class in all of its diversity was growing wealthier from trade, commerce, and the practice of the professions. They wanted social prestige and political influence equal to their wealth. And they wanted the government to function in an efficient and businesslike manner. They resented privileges, frowned at hierarchy, and rejected tradition.

All of these factors meant that the society of the eighteenth century stood at the close of one era in European history and at the opening of another. What began to make contemporaries aware of that fact were the great wars of mid-century, the revolt of the British colonies in North America, and the intellectual currents of the Enlightenment.

SUGGESTED READINGS

C. B. A. BEHRENS, *The Ancien Régime* (1967). A brief account of life in France with excellent illustrations.

J. BLUM, *Lord and Peasant in Russia from the Ninth to the Nineteenth Century* (1961). A thorough and wide-ranging discussion.

F. BRAUDEL, *Capitalism and Material Life, 1400–1800* (1974). An investigation of the physical resources and human organization of preindustrial Europe.

P. DEANE, *The First Industrial Revolution* (1965). A well-balanced and systematic treatment.

F. FORD, *Robe and Sword: The Regrouping of the French Aristocracy After Louis XIV* (1953). An important treatment of the growing social tensions within the French nobility during the eighteenth century.

R. FORSTER, *The Nobility of Toulouse in the Eighteenth Century* (1960). A local study that displays the variety of noble economic activity.

R. FORSTER AND E. FORSTER, *European Society in the Eighteenth Century* (1969). An excellent collection of documents.

D. GEORGE, *London Life in the Eighteenth Century* (1925). A lively account.

D. V. GLASS AND D. E. C. EVERSLEY (Ed.), *Population in History: Essays in Historical Demography* (1965). Fundamental for an understanding of the eighteenth-century increase in population.

A. GOODWIN, *The European Nobility in the Eighteenth Century* (1953). Essays on the nobility in each state.

P. GOUBERT, *The Ancien Régime: French Society, 1600–1750,* tr. by Steve Cox (1974). A superb account of the peasant social order.

H. J. HABAKKUK AND M. POSTAN (Eds.), *The Cambridge Economic History of Europe* (1965). Separate chapters by different authors on major topics.

DOUGLAS HAY et al., *Albion's Fatal Tree: Crime and Society in Eighteenth-Century England* (1976). Separate essays on a previously little explored subject.

O. H. HUFTON, *The Poor of Eighteenth-Century France, 1750–1789* (1975). A brilliant study of poverty and the family economy.

E. L. JONES, *Agriculture and Economic Growth in England, 1650–1815* (1968). A good introduction to an important subject.

JOHN LOUGH, *An Introduction to Eighteenth-Century France* (1960). A systematic survey with good quotations (in French) from contemporaries.

S. POLLARD AND C. HOLMES, *Documents of European Economic History: The Process of Industrialization, 1750–1870* (1968). A very useful collection.

G. RUDÉ, *The Crowd in History, 1730–1848* (1964). This and the following work were pioneering studies.

G. RUDÉ, *Paris and London in the Eighteenth Century* (1973).

G. RUDÉ, *Europe in the Eighteenth Century* (1972). A survey with emphasis on social history.

C. WILSON, *England's Apprenticeship, 1603–1763* (1965). A broad survey of English economic life on the eve of industrialism.

A Declaration by the Representatives of the UNITED STATES OF AMERICA, in General Congress assembled.

When in the course of human events it becomes necessary for one people to dissolve the political bands which have connected them with another, and to ~~assume~~ assume among the powers of the earth the separate and equal station to which the laws of nature & of nature's god entitle them, a decent respect to the opinions of mankind requires that they should declare the causes which impel them to the separation.

We hold these truths to be self-evident; that all men are created equal & independent; that from that equal creation they derive rights inherent & inalienable, among which are the preservation of life, & liberty, & the pursuit of happiness; that to secure these rights, governments are instituted among men, deriving their just powers from the consent of the governed; that whenever any form of government shall becomes destructive of these ends, it is the right of the people to alter or to abolish it, & to institute new government, laying it's foundation on such principles & organising it's powers in such form, as to them shall seem most likely to effect their safety & happiness. prudence indeed will dictate that governments long established should not be changed for light & transient causes: and accordingly all experience hath shewn that mankind are more disposed to suffer while evils are sufferable, than to right themselves by abolishing the forms to which they are accustomed. but when a long train of abuses & usurpations [begun at a distinguished period, &] pursuing invariably the same object, evinces a design to subject reduce them to arbitrary power under absolute Despotism, it is their right, it is their duty, to throw off such government & to provide new guards for their future security. such has been the patient sufferance of these colonies; & such is now the necessity which constrains them to expunge their former systems of government. the history of the present king of Great Britain is a history of unremitting injuries and usurpations, [among which appears no solitary fact to contradict the uniform tenor of the rest but all have] in direct object the establishment of an absolute tyranny over these states. to prove this, let facts be submitted to a candid world, [for the truth of which we pledge a faith yet unsullied by falsehood]

544

21
Empire, War, and Colonial Rebellion

THE MIDDLE of the eighteenth century witnessed a renewal of European warfare on a worldwide scale. The conflict involved two separate but interrelated rivalries. Austria and Prussia fought for dominance in central Europe while Great Britain and France dueled for commercial and colonial supremacy. The wars were long, extensive, and very costly in both men and money. They resulted in a new balance of power on the Continent and on the high seas. Great Britain gained a world empire, and Prussia achieved the recognized status of a great power. Moreover the expense of these wars led every major European government after the Peace of Paris of 1763 to reconstruct in an extensive fashion their policies of taxation and finance. Those revised fiscal programs produced internal conditions for the monarchies of Europe that had most significant results for the rest of the century. They included the American Revolution, enlightened absolutism on the Continent, and a continuing financial crisis for the French monarchy.

Eighteenth-Century Empires
Periods of European Overseas Empires

Since the Renaissance, European contacts with the rest of the world have gone through four distinct stages. The first period was that of discovery, exploration, and initial conquest and settlement of the New World. It had closed by the end of the seventeenth century. The second era,

The American Revolution, proclaimed to the world through the Declaration of Independence, marked the climax of the eighteenth-century colonial wars and the beginning of a new democratic age in the West. This is the first page of Thomas Jefferson's rough draft of the declaration, with changes made by Benjamin Franklin and John Adams. [The Granger Collection.]

which is largely the concern of this chapter, was one of colonial trade rivalry among Spain, France, and Great Britain. The Anglo-French side of the contest has often been compared to a second hundred years' war. During this second period, which may be said to have closed during the 1820s, both the British colonies of the North American seaboard and the Spanish colonies of Central and South America emancipated themselves from European control. The third stage of European contact with the non-European world occurred in the late nineteenth century, when new formal empires involving European administration of indigenous peoples were carved out in Africa and Asia. Those nineteenth-century empires also included new areas of European settlement, such as Australia, New Zealand, and South Africa. The bases of these empires were trade, national honor, and military strategy. The last period of European empire came in the present century with the decolonization of peoples previously under European colonial rule.

During the four and one-half centuries before decolonization, Europeans exerted political dominance over much of the rest of the world. They frequently treated other peoples as social, intellectual, and economic inferiors. They ravaged existing cultures because of greed, religious zeal, or political ambition. These actions are major facts of European history and significant factors in the contemporary relationship of Europe and its former colonies. What allowed Europeans to exert such influence and domination for so long over so much of the world was not any innate cultural superiority but rather a technological supremacy closely related to naval power and gunpowder. Ships and guns allowed Europeans to exercise their will almost wherever they chose.

Mercantile Empires

Navies and merchant shipping were the keystone of the mercantile empires of the eighteenth century. These empires were meant to bring profit to a nation rather than to provide areas for settlement. The Treaty of Utrecht (1713) established the boundaries of empire during the first half of the century. Except for Brazil, which was governed by Portugal, Spain controlled all the mainland of South America and in North America controlled Florida, Mexico, and California. The Spanish also governed the island of Cuba and half of Hispaniola. The British Empire consisted of the colonies along the North Atlantic seaboard, Nova Scotia, Newfoundland, Jamaica, and Barbados. Britain also possessed a few trading stations on the Indian subcontinent. The French domains covered the St. Lawrence River valley; the Ohio and Mississippi river valleys; the West Indian islands of St. Domingue, Guadeloupe, and Martinique; and stations in India. All three powers also possessed numerous smaller islands in the Caribbean.

So far as any formal theory lay behind the conduct of these empires, it was mercantilism, that practical creed of hardheaded businessmen. The colonies were to provide markets and natural resources for the industries of the home country. In turn, the latter was to furnish military security and political administration for the colonies. For decades both sides assumed that the colonies were the inferior partner in the relationship. The mercantilist statesmen and traders regarded the world as an arena of scarce resources and economic limitation. They assumed

PL.XXXII.

Fig.2.

Fig.3.

This is the group of plans of a typical frigate of the mid-eighteenth century included by the Swede Frederik Henrik af Chapman in his monumental album of ship plans, *Architectura Navalis Mercatoria* (Stockholm, 1768) as plate 32. Although frigates were primarily planned as small fighting ships—note the single row of gun ports on the main deck—they could also be adapted for storing the goods of trade. (It is virtually impossible to find a cutaway view of a purely merchant vessel before the nineteenth century.) [Courtesy of George Campbell.]

that one national economy could grow only at the expense of others. Colonies and the home country were to trade only with each other. To that end they attempted to forge trade-tight systems of national commerce through navigation laws, tariffs, bounties to encourage production, and prohibitions against trading with subjects of other monarchs. National monopoly was the ruling principle.

Mercantilist ideas had always been neater on paper than in practice. By the early eighteenth century these assumptions were held only in the vaguest manner. They stood too far removed from the economic realities of the colonies and perhaps from human nature. The colonial

and home markets simply failed to mesh. Spain could not produce sufficient goods for South America. Economic production in the British North American colonies challenged English manufacturing and led to British attempts to limit certain colonial industries, such as iron and hat making. Colonists of different countries wished to trade with each other. English colonists could buy sugar more cheaply from the French West Indies than from English suppliers. Traders and merchants from one nation always hoped to break the monopoly of another. For all these reasons the eighteenth century became the "golden age of smugglers." [1] The governments could not control the activities of all their subjects. Clashes among colonists could and did bring about conflict between governments.

Areas of Rivalry and Conflict

The Spanish Empire stood on the defensive throughout the century. It was a sprawling expanse of territory over which the Spanish government wished to maintain a commercial monopoly without possessing the capacity to do so. Spanish colonists looked to illegal imports from French and British traders to supply needed goods. Both France and Britain assumed a very aggressive stance toward the Spanish Empire because they viewed it as a vast potential market and a major source of gold. Their rivalry for intrusion into the mainland Spanish markets were matched by other conflicts in North America, India, and the West Indies.

Neither the French nor the British colonies of North America fit particularly well into the mercantile pattern of empire. Trade with these areas during the early part of the century was smaller than with the West Indies. These mainland colonies were settlements rather than arenas for economic exploitation. The French lands of Canada were quite sparsely populated. Relations with the Indians were troublesome. The economic interests and the development of the colonies were not wholly com-

---

1 Walter Dorn, *Competition for Empire, 1740–1763* (New York: Harper, 1940), p. 266.

patible with those of the home countries. Nevertheless flash points existed between France and Britain on the North American continent. Their colonists quarreled endlessly with each other. Both groups of settlers were jealous over rights to the lower St. Lawrence River valley, upper New England, and later the Ohio River valley. There were other rivalries over fishing rights, fur trade, and relationships with the Indians.

Unlike North America or the West Indies, India was neither the home of migrating Europeans nor an integral part of their imperial schemes. The Indian subcontinent was an area where both France and Britain traded through privileged, chartered companies that enjoyed a legal monopoly. The East India Company was the English institution; the French equivalent was the Compagnie des Indes. The trade of India and Asia figured only marginally in the economics of empire. Some bullion gained by trade or piracy in the West Indies was shipped to India, where it was used to purchase cotton cloth that was shipped to England and then used to purchase slaves in Africa for the West Indies. The commercial problem with the states of India was that Europeans produced little or nothing wanted in the region.

Nevertheless throughout the century trade and involvement on the subcontinent continued. Enterprising Europeans always hoped that in some fashion profitable commerce with India might be developed. Others regarded India as a springboard into the even larger potential market of China. The original European footholds in India were trading posts called *factories*. They existed through privileges granted by the various Indian governments. Two circumstances arose during the middle of the eighteenth century to change this situation. First, in several of the Indian states there occurred decay in the indigenous administration and government. Second, Joseph Dupleix (1697–1763) for the French and Robert Clive (1725–1774) for the British saw these developments as opportunities for expanding the control of their companies. To maintain their own security and to expand their privileges, the companies began to fill the power

An English Mercantilist Views Trade Between Nations

It is not difficult for us to see mercantilism as a selfish and limited idea of what commerce should be. But seventeenth- and eighteenth-century theorists found it quite defensible. Its major tenet was the desirability of increasing the exports of a nation. This British pamphlet of 1721 praises the kind of trade that allows exports to grow and creates employment at home. It criticizes the trade that creates imports or that imports goods like those already produced at home or that could be produced at home.

I. That Trade which exports Manufactures made of the sole Product or Growth of the Country, is undoubtedly good . . . as much as those Exports amount to, so much is the clear Gain of the Nation.

II. That Trade which helps off the Consumption of our Superfluities, is also visibly advantageous . . . so much as the exported Superfluities amount unto, so much also is the clear National Profit.

III. The importing of foreign Materials to be manufactured at home, especially when the Goods, after they are manufactured, are mostly sent abroad, is also, without dispute, very beneficial. . . .

VI. A Trade may be call'd good which exchanges Manufactures for Manufactures, and Commodities for Commodities. . . . [B]y this means numbers of People are employ'd on both sides, to their mutual Advantage.

VIII. The carrying of Goods from one foreign Country to another, is a profitable Article in Trade. . . . But a Trade is disadvantageous to a Nation,

1. Which brings in things of mere Luxury and Pleasure, which are entirely, or for the most part, consumed among us. . . .

2. Much worse is that Trade which brings in a Commodity that is not only consumed amongst us, but hinders the consumption of the like quantity of ours. . . .

3. That Trade is eminently bad, which supplies the same Goods as we manufacture ourselves, especially if we can make enough for our Consumption. . . .

4. The Importation upon easy Terms of such Manufactures as are already introduc'd in a Country, must be of bad consequence, and check their progress. . . .

The British Merchant: A Collection of Papers, Charles King, (Ed.), cited in D. B. Horn and Mary Ransome, *English Historical Documents, 1715–1783* (London: Eyre and Spottiswoode, 1957), pp. 492–493.

The Custom House in Dublin, Ireland, is one of the most elegant political buildings of Europe. Its fine architecture suggests the importance that eighteenth-century governments attached to trade and the regulation of trade. [Irish Tourist Board, New York.]

vacuum and in effect took over the government of some regions. Each group of Europeans hoped to checkmate the other.

STRUGGLE FOR THE WEST INDIES. The heart of the eighteenth-century colonial rivalry was the West Indies. These islands, close to the American continents, constituted the jewels of empire. Here the colonial powers pursued their greedy ambitions in close proximity to each other. The West Indies raised tobacco, cotton, indigo, coffee, and sugar, for which there existed strong markets in Europe. Sugar in particular had become a product of standard consumption rather than a luxury. It was used in coffee, tea, and cocoa, for making candy and preserving fruits, and in the brewing industry. There seemed no limit to its uses. Sugar was also important to the domestic economy of Europe. Sugar refining had become a major industry in France. Sugar and tobacco figured prominently in the reexport industry. For example, large quantities of tobacco were shipped from Scotland to the Continent.

Basic to the economy of the West Indies as well as to that of South America and the British colonies on the south Atlantic seaboard of North America was the institution of slavery. Hundreds of thousands of slaves were imported into the Americas during the eighteenth century. Planters could not attract sufficient quantities of free labor to these areas. They became wholly dependent upon slaves. Slavery and the slave trade touched most of the economy of the transatlantic world. Cities such as Newport, Rhode Island; Liverpool, England; and Nantes,

France, enjoyed prosperity that rested almost entirely on the slave trade. All of the shippers who handled cotton, tobacco, and sugar were dependent on slavery, though they might have no direct contact with the institution. There was a general triangle of trade that consisted of carrying goods to Africa to be traded for slaves, who were then taken to the West Indies, where they were traded for sugar and other tropical produce, which were then shipped to Europe. Not all ships necessarily covered all three legs of the triangle. Another major trade pattern existed between New England and the West Indies. New England rum or ship stores were traded for sugar.

Within the rich commerce and agriculture of the West Indies there existed three varieties of colonial rivalry. Producers of different nations were intensely jealous of each other. The quantity of sugar being raised had expanded so as to depress the price in Europe. Consequently one group of planters hoped not to conquer the lands of their competitors but rather to destroy the productive capacity of those islands. There was a second form of rivalry among shippers in the Caribbean. Every captain hoped to transport as much sugar as possible to Europe. Finally, the West Indies possessions of France and Britain provided excellent bases for penetration of the trade of the Spanish Empire. Many French and British

Eighteenth-Century Empires 549

An eighteenth-century sugar press in Cuba. At this period it was tended by slaves. Most of the sugar would eventually end up in Europe where there was a growing market for the product. [Bettmann Archive.]

On a French West Indian plantation slaves pick cotton on the right while other slaves on the left remove the seeds from the fiber. The particular variety of cotton shown in this engraving grew on shrubs rather than on the bushes grown in the American south. [The Granger Collection.]

ship captains in the West Indies were admitted smugglers, and some were little better than pirates.

The close interrelationship of the West Indies and European economies meant that significant numbers of British, French, and Spanish subjects had an interest in the area. This "West Indian Interest," as it was called in England, consisted of absentee plantation owners, shippers, insurers, merchants, bankers, owners of domestic industry dependent on West Indian products, and all of those involved in the slave trade. In Great Britain it was an articulate and well-organized pressure group. In 1739 the West India Interest and political enemies of Robert Walpole succeeded in driving Britain into war with Spain, the War of Jenkins' Ear.

The Treaty of Utrecht (1713) included two special privileges for Great Britain in regard to the Spanish Empire. The British received a thirty-year contract known as the *asiento* to furnish slaves to the Spanish. Britain was also given the right to send one ship each year to the trading fair at Portobello, a major Caribbean seaport on the Panamanian coast. These two privileges allowed British traders and smugglers potential inroads into the Spanish market. Little but friction arose from these rights. The annual ship to Portobello was often supplied with additional goods during the night as it lay in port. Much to the chagrin of the British, the Spanish government took its own alleged trading monopoly seriously and maintained coastal patrols, which boarded and searched English vessels to look for contraband.

In 1731 during one such boarding operation there was a fight, and an English captain named Robert Jenkins had his ear cut off by the Spaniards. Thereafter he carried about his severed ear preserved in a jar of brandy. This incident was of little importance until 1738, when Jenkins appeared before the British Parliament, reportedly brandishing his ear as an example of Spanish atrocities to British merchants in the West Indies. The British merchant and West Indies interests put great pressure on Parliament to do something about Spanish intervention in their trade. Robert Walpole attempted to reach a solution through negotiations. However, Parliament—and especially members who believed that the war would drive Walpole from office—refused all accommodation. In late 1739 Great Britain went to war with Spain.

At the outbreak of hostilities France under the administration of Cardinal Fleury stood ready to profit from the British–Spanish conflict. They expected to see British trade harmed and eventually to receive Spanish commercial favors for aid. None of the major European powers except Britain had any present grudge against France. The years of Fleury's cautious policy were about to pay off. Then quite literally overnight the situation on the Continent changed.

Mid-Century Wars
The War of the Austrian Succession (1740–1748)

In December 1740, after possessing the throne of Prussia for less than seven months, Frederick II ordered his troops to occupy the Austrian province of Silesia. The invasion shattered the provisions of the Pragmatic Sanction and upset the continental balance of power as established by the Treaty of Utrecht. The young king of Prussia had treated the House of Hapsburg simply as another German state rather than as the leader of the Holy Roman Empire. The province of Silesia itself rounded out Prussia's possessions, and Frederick was determined to keep his ill-gotten prize. In 1740 the other European states were not sure whether to consider the Prussian invasion the act of a great power or that of a mere aggressive upstart. The wars of the next quarter century affirmed the former judgment.

Maria Theresa was twenty-three years old and had succeeded to the Austrian crown only two months before Frederick's move. Her army was weak, her bureaucracy inefficient, and the loyalty of her subjects uncertain. She herself was inexperienced and was more usually guided by the values of piety than by hardheaded statecraft. Yet she succeeded in rallying to her side the Magyars of Hungary and the aristocratic leaders of her other domains. They were genuinely sympathetic to her plight and inspired by her courage. Maria Theresa's great achievement was not the reconquest of Silesia, which eluded her, but rather the preservation of the Hapsburg Empire as a major political power.

The seizure of Silesia could have marked the opening of a general hunting season on Hapsburg holdings and the beginning of revolts by Hapsburg subjects. Instead it proved the occasion for new political allegiances. Those new loyalties, particularly between the Magyars and the empress, were not gained merely through heroism but more specifically by grants of privileges to the nobilities of the realm. The empress recognized Hungary as the most important of her crowns and promised the Magyars considerable local autonomy. However, the Hapsburg state was preserved at great cost to the power of the central monarchy. It would never become a unified modern political entity.

The war over the Austrian succession and the British–Spanish commercial conflict could have remained separate disputes. They were neither logically nor necessarily politically related. What ultimately united them was the role of France. Cardinal Fleury understood that the long-range interests of France lay in the direction of commercial growth. However, just as British merchant interests had pushed Robert Walpole into war, a group of court aristocrats led by the Comte de Belle Isle compelled the elderly Fleury to abandon his planned attack on British trade and to support the Prussian aggression against Austria. This proved to be one of the most fateful decisions in French history.

Even though the Hapsburgs had been the historic enemy of France, a war against Austria was not in the French interest in 1741. In the first place, aid to Prussia had the effect of consolidating a new powerful state in Germany. That new power could, and indeed later did, endanger France. Second, the French move against Austria brought Great Britain into the continental war. The

Prince Frederick Discusses Statecraft and European Affairs

King Frederick William I of Prussia thought at times he had reason for concern about the qualities of his flute-playing, philosophizing son, Prince Frederick. He need not have worried. The young prince was already able to write this hardnosed essay in 1738, two years before he became King Frederick II. He states the view common at the time that a monarch normally seeks to increase the power of his state. He also suggests that the major states of Europe were not in a healthy balance. Two years later he would follow up these thoughts by invading Silesia.

"I T IS *an unshaken principle among kings to aggrandize themselves as much as their power will permit; and, though such aggrandizement must be subject to different modifications, and infinitely varied according to the situation of princes, the power of neighboring states, or fortunate opportunities, the principle is not the less unchangeable, and is never abandoned by monarchs. Their pretended fame is part of this system. In a word, it is necessary they should increase in greatness."*

. . . .

From what has been said, it will be easy to perceive that the political body of Europe is in a perilous situation. It is deprived of its due equilibrium, and is in a state in which it cannot long remain, without great risk. The political body resembles the human body, which can only subsist by a mixture of equal quantities of the acid and the alkali. Whenever one of these two substances predominates, the body is made sensible of it, and the health is considerably injured: should that substance continue to increase, it may finally cause the destruction of the machine. Thus, whenever the policy and prudence of the princes of Europe lose sight of the maintenance of a just balance, between the principal powers, it is felt by the constitution of the whole body-politic. Violence on the one side, weakness on the other; the desire of invading on the one, and on the other the inability to prevent invasion. The most puissant [powerful] gives law, and the feeble are under the necessity of adding their signature. All finally concur in augmenting disorder and confusion. Force acts like an impetuous torrent, passes its bounds, carries everything with it, and exposes this unfortunate body-politic to the most fatal revolutions.

Frederick the Great, "Considerations on the Present State of the Body-Politic of Europe" (1738), in *Posthumous Works of Frederic II, King of Prussia*, trans. by Thomas Holcroft (London: G. G. J. and J. Robinson 1789), Vol. 4, pp. 364–365, 381–382.

Maria Theresa of Austria (seated right) and her husband, Emperor Francis I (seated left), with their very large family. Her son and successor, Joseph II, is the tall adolescent near her. The artist was Martin Meytens (1695–1770), court painter in Vienna. [Kunsthistorisches Museum, Vienna.]

British as usual wanted to see the Low Countries remain in friendly hands. In the eighteenth century that policy required continued Hapsburg control of the Austrian Netherlands. In 1744 the British–French conflict expanded beyond the Continent, as France decided to support Spain against Britain. As a result, French military and economic resources became badly divided. France could not bring sufficient strength to the colonial struggle. Having chosen to continue a struggle from the past with Austria, France lost the struggle for the future against Great Britain.

By 1748 the war had become a military stalemate for all concerned. Austria had not been able to regain Silesia, but it had fended off further aggression from other German states. The French army, led by Marshal Maurice de Saxe (1696–1750), won a series of splendid victories over the British and Austrians in the Netherlands during 1747 and 1748. Britain, for its part, had pursued a very suc-

Empire, War, and Colonial Rebellion

OPPOSITE: During the eighteenth century the various European nations continued to fight one another both by land and by sea with increasing professionalism and slaughter.

On land [ABOVE] eighteenth-century armies fought each other from carefully formed ranks. In this scene the two commanders of opposing forces formally pay their respects to each other before the battle. Note the fixed bayonets on the muskets for use in close fighting. [National Army Museum, London.]

At sea [BELOW] pitched battles were often fought between entire fleets. This picture is of a sea battle between Russian and Turkish forces in 1770; it is a nineteenth-century engraving based on an eighteenth-century painting by Richard Paton. [Bettmann Archive.]

cessful colonial campaign. Forces in America captured the fortress of Louisburg at the mouth of the St. Lawrence River. The British more than held their own on the Indian subcontinent. Warfare on French commerce had been highly effective. These victories overseas compensated for the poor showing on the Continent. Consequently the war was brought to a close by the Treaty of Aix-la-Chapelle (1748). In effect it restored conditions that had existed prior to the war, with the exception that Prussia retained Silesia. Spain renewed the *asiento* agreement with Great Britain. All observers believed that the treaty constituted a truce rather than a permanent peace.

The Diplomatic Revolution of 1756

Before the rivalries again erupted into war, a dramatic shift of alliances took place. In 1756 Prussia and Great Britain signed the Convention of Westminster. It was a defensive alliance aimed at preventing the entry of foreign troops into the Germanies. Frederick II feared invasions by both Russia and France. The convention meant that Great Britain, the ally of Austria since the wars of Louis XIV, had now joined forces with Austria's major eighteenth-century enemy.

Maria Theresa was despondent over this development. However, her foreign minister, Count Wenzel Anton Kaunitz (1711–1794), was delighted. This brilliant diplomat and servant of the Hapsburg dynasty had long hoped for an alliance between Austria and France for the dismemberment of Prussia. The Convention of Westminster made this alliance, unthinkable a few years earlier, possible. France was agreeable because Frederick had not consulted it before coming to his understanding with Britain. Consequently later in 1756 France and Austria signed a defensive alliance. Kaunitz had succeeded in completely reversing the direction of French foreign policy from Richelieu through Fleury. France would now fight to restore Austrian supremacy in central Europe. But the French monarchy, though having changed its German ally, would remain diverted from its commercial interests on the high seas.

Frederick the Great of Prussia in his later years displayed in his face the burden of personal hardship that his ambitious wars had brought to him and to his nation. Yet he did succeed in making Prussia a major power. [Culver Pictures.]

The Seven Years' War (1756–1763)

The Treaty of Aix-la-Chapelle had brought peace in Europe, but the conflict between France and Great Britain continued unofficially on the colonial front. There were continuous clashes between American and French settlers in the Ohio River valley and in upper New England. These were the prelude to what is known as the French and Indian War in American history. These colonial skirmishes would certainly have led in time to a broader conflict. However, once again the factor that opened a general European war that extended into a colonial theater was the action of the king of Prussia.

In August 1756 Frederick II invaded the kingdom of

Both the British general James Wolfe and the French general Montcalm died at the Battle of Quebec in September 1759, in which the British forces won the crucial encounter and thus drove the French out of their North American empire. The picture of the death of Wolfe is an engraving from a famous painting by the American artist Benjamin West (1738–1820). [Culver Pictures.]

Saxony. He regarded this invasion as a continuation of the defensive strategy of which the Convention of Westminster had been a part. Frederick believed that there existed an international conspiracy on the part of Saxony, Austria, and France to undermine and destroy Prussian power. The attack on Saxony was in Frederick's mind a preemptive strike. The invasion itself created the very destructive alliance that Frederick feared. In the spring of 1757 France and Austria made a new alliance dedicated to the destruction of Prussia. They were eventually joined by Sweden, Russia, and the smaller German states.

Prussia was surrounded by enemies, and Frederick II confronted the gravest crisis of his career. It was after these struggles that he came to be called Frederick the Great. He won several initial battles, the most famous of which was Rossbach, on November 5, 1757. Thereafter, however, the Prussians experienced a long series of defeats that might have destroyed the state. Two factors in addition to Frederick's stubborn leadership saved Prussia. The first was major financial aid from Great Britain. The British contributed as much to the Prussian war effort as did the Prussian treasury itself. Second, in 1762 Empress Elizabeth of Russia died. Her successor was Tsar Peter III (he also died in the same year), whose admiration for Frederick knew almost no bounds. He immediately made peace with Prussia, thus relieving the country of one enemy and allowing it to hold its own against Austria and France. The treaty of Hubertusburg of 1763 closed the continental conflict with no significant changes in prewar borders. Silesia remained Prussia's province, and Prussia clearly stood in the ranks of the great powers.

The survival of Prussia was less impressive to the rest of Europe than the victories of Great Britain over France in every theater of conflict. The architect of this victory was William Pitt the Elder (1708–1778). He came from a family that had made its fortune from commerce. His grandfather, "Diamond" Pitt, had laid the foundations of the family's wealth by commercial ventures in India. The grandson was no less dedicated to the growth of British trade and economic interests. Pitt was a person of colossal ego and administrative genius. From the time of the War of Jenkins' Ear he had criticized the government as being too timid in its colonial policy. He had been strongly critical of all continental involvement, including the Convention of Westminster. During the 1750s he had gained the favor of the London merchant interest. Once war had commenced again, these groups clamored for his appointment to the cabinet. In 1757 he was named prime minister, and he drew into his own hands all the power he could grasp. He was confident, as he told friends, that he and only he could lead the nation to victory.

Once in office Pitt changed his attitude toward British involvement on the Continent. He came to regard the German conflict as a way to divert French resources and attention from the colonial struggle. He pumped huge financial subsidies to Frederick the Great and later boasted of having won America on the plains of Germany. North America was the center of Pitt's real concern. Put quite simply, he wanted all of North America east of the Mississippi for Great Britain, and that was exactly what he won. In 1759 on the Plains of Abraham at Quebec the British army under General James Wolfe decisively defeated the French under Marshal Louis Joseph Montcalm. The French Empire in Canada had come to an end.

However, Pitt's colonial vision extended beyond the St. Lawrence valley and the Great Lakes basin. The major islands of the French West Indies fell to the British fleets. Income from the sale of captured sugar helped finance the British war effort. British slave interests captured the bulk of the French slave trade. Between 1755

France Turns Over French Canada to Great Britain

The Treaty of Paris (1763) concluded the French and English portion of the Seven Years' War. In this particular clause the previously French portion of Canada was turned over to Great Britain.

His *Most Christian Majesty [the King of France] renounces all pretensions which he has heretofore formed or might have formed to Nova Scotia or Acadia in all its parts, and guarantees the whole of it, and with all its dependencies, to the King of Great Britain: Moreover, His Most Christian Majesty cedes and guarantees to his said Britannic Majesty, in full right, Canada, with all its dependencies, as well as the island of Cape Breton, and all the other islands and coasts in the gulf and river of St. Laurence, and in general, everything that depends on the said countries, land, islands, and coasts, with the sovereignty, property, possession, and all rights acquired by treaty, or otherwise, which the Most Christian King and the Crown of France have had till now over the said countries, lands, islands, places, coasts, and their inhabitants, so that the Most Christian King cedes and makes over the whole to the said King, and to the Crown of Great Britain, and that in the most ample manner and form, without restriction, and without any liberty to depart from the said cession and guarantee under any pretence, or to disturb Great Britain in the possessions above mentioned. His Britannic Majesty, on his side, agrees to grant the liberty of the Catholic Religion, to the inhabitants of Canada: he will, in consequence, give the most precise and effectual orders, that his new Roman Catholic subjects may profess the worship of their religion according to the rights of the Romish Church, as far as the laws of Great Britain permit.*

H. Butterfield (Ed.), *Select Documents of European History, 1715–1920* (London: Methuen, 1931), pp. 29–30.

William Pitt the Elder guided the armies and navies of Great Britain to a stunning victory in the Seven Years' War. His portrait is from the studio of the artist Richard Brompton. [The Granger Collection.]

George II (1727–1760) was the British monarch during the great wars of the mid-century. The painting is by Thomas Worlidge, and the medal is by E. Hannibal. [The Granger Collection.]

and 1760 the value of the French colonial trade fell from thirty million to four million livres. On the Indian subcontinent the British forces under the command of Robert Clive defeated the French in 1757 at the Battle of Plassey. This victory opened the way for the eventual conquest of Bengal and later all of India by the British East India Company. Never had Great Britain or any other European power experienced such a complete worldwide military victory.

The Peace of Paris of 1763 reflected somewhat less of

a victory than Britain had won in the battle field. Pitt was no longer in office. George III (1760–1820) had succeeded to the British throne in 1760. He and Pitt had quarreled over policy, and the minister had departed. His replacement was the earl of Bute, a favorite of the new monarch. The new minister was responsible for the peace settlement. Britain received all of Canada, the Ohio River valley, and the eastern half of the Mississippi River valley. Britain partially surrendered the conquest in India by giving France footholds at Pondichéry and Chandernagore. The sugar islands of Guadeloupe and Martinique were restored to the French. Britain could have gained more territory only with further war involving more taxation, against which the country was already complaining.

The Seven Years' War had been a great conflict. Tens of thousands of soldiers had been killed or wounded. Major battles had been fought around the globe. At great internal sacrifice Prussia had permanently wrested Silesia from Austria and had turned the Holy Roman Empire into an empty shell. Hapsburg power now depended on the Hungarian domains. France, though still possessing sources of colonial income, was no longer a great colonial power. The Spanish Empire remained largely intact, but the British were still determined to penetrate its markets. On the Indian subcontinent the British East India Company was in a position to continue to press against the decaying indigenous governments and to impose its own authority. The results of that situation would be felt until the middle of the twentieth century. In North America the British government faced the task of organizing its new territories. From this time until World War II, Great Britain assumed the status not simply of a European but also of a world power.

The quarter century of warfare also caused a long series of domestic crises among the European powers. The French defeat impressed many people in the nation with a new sense of the necessity for political and administrative reform. The financial burdens of the wars had astounded all contemporaries. Every power had to begin to find ways to increase revenues to pay the war debt and to finance preparation for the next combat. Nowhere did this search for revenue lead to more far-ranging consequences than in the British colonies in North America.

The American Revolution and Europe
Events in the British Colonies

The revolt of the British colonies in North America was an event in transAtlantic and European history. It erupted from problems of revenue collection common to all the major powers after the Seven Years' War. The War of the American Revolution was a continuation of the conflict between France and Great Britain. The French support for the Americans deepened the existing financial and administrative difficulties of the monarchy.

The political ideals of the Americans had roots in the thought of John Locke and other English political theorists. The colonists raised questions of the most profound nature about monarchy, political authority, and constitutionalism. These questions had ramifications for all European states. Part of the difficulties from the British side arose because of the characteristic European political friction between the monarch and the aristocracy. Finally, the Americans were seen by many Europeans as inaugurating a new era in the history of European peoples and indeed of the world.

After the Treaty of Paris of 1763 the British government faced three imperial problems. The first was the sheer cost of empire, which the British felt they could no longer carry alone. The national debt had risen considerably and taxation had done likewise. The American colonies had been the chief beneficiaries of the conflict. It made rational sense that they should henceforth bear part of the cost of their protection and administration. The second problem was the vast expanse of new territory in North America that the British had to organize. There was all the land from the mouth of the St. Lawrence River to the Mississippi River with its French settlers and, more important, its Indian possessors.

The "Boston Massacre" of March 5, 1770 was depicted in an engraving quickly made and put on sale by Paul Revere. [The Granger Collection.]

As the British ministers pursued solutions to these difficulties, a third and more serious issue arose. The British colonists in North America resisted the taxation and were suspicious about the imperial policies toward the western lands. Consequently the British had to search for new ways to exert their authority over the colonies. The Americans became increasingly resistant because their economy had outgrown the framework of mercantilism, because the removal of the French relieved them of dependence on the British army, and because they believed that their liberty was in danger.

The British drive for revenue commenced in 1764 with the passage of the Sugar Act under the ministry of George Grenville (1712–1770). The measure was designed to produce more revenue from imports into the colonies. Smugglers who violated the law were to be tried in admiralty courts without juries. The next year Parliament passed the Stamp Act, which put a tax on legal documents and certain other items such as newspapers. The British considered these taxes legal because they had been passed by Parliament. The taxes seemed just because the money was to be spent in the colonies. The Americans responded that they had the right to tax themselves and that they were not represented in Parliament. Moreover, because most of the colonial charters had been granted by the king, the Americans claimed that their legal connection to Britain was through the monarch rather than the Parliament. The expenditure in the colonies of the revenue levied by Parliament did not reassure the colonists. They feared that if colonial government was financed from outside, they would lose control over their government. In October 1765 the Stamp Act Congress met in America and drew up a protest to the crown. There was much disorder in the colonies, particularly in Massachussetts. The colonists agreed to refuse to import British goods. In 1766 Parliament repealed the Stamp Act, but through the Declaratory Act it said that Parliament had the power to legislate for the colonies.

The Stamp Act crisis set the pattern for the next ten years. Parliament under the leadership of a royal minister would approve a piece of revenue or administrative legislation. The Americans would then resist by reasoned argument, economic pressure, and violence. Then the legislation would be repealed, and the process would commence again. Each time tempers on both sides became more frayed and positions more irreconcilable. In 1767 the ministry of Charles Townshend (1725–1767) passed a series of revenue acts relating to colonial imports. The colonists again resisted. The ministry sent over its own customs agents to administer the laws. To protect these new officers, British troops were sent to Boston in 1768. Tensions obviously resulted, and in March 1770 the Boston Massacre, in which British troops killed five citizens, took place. That same year all of the Townshend duties except for the one on tea were repealed.

In May 1773 Parliament passed a new law relating to the sale of tea by the East India Company. The measure permitted direct importation into the American colonies. It actually lowered the price of tea while retaining the tax. In some cities the colonists refused to permit the unloading of the tea; in Boston a shipload of tea was thrown into the harbor. The British ministry of Lord North (1732–1790) was determined to assert the authority of Parliament over the resistent colonies. During

COMMON SENSE;

ADDRESSED TO THE

INHABITANTS

OF

AMERICA,

On the following interesting

SUBJECTS.

I. Of the Origin and Design of Government in general,
with concise Remarks on the English Constitution.

II. Of Monarchy and Hereditary Succession.

III. Thoughts on the present State of American Affairs.

IV. Of the present Ability of America, with some miscellaneous Reflections.

Man knows no Master save creaing HEAVEN,
Or those whom choice and common good ordain.
THOMSON.

PHILADELPHIA;

Printed, and Sold, by R. BELL, in Third-Street.

MDCCLXXVI.

Common Sense, written by Tom Paine, was the most important political pamphlet published during 1776 when the American colonies were deciding to make a final break with Great Britain. [The Granger Collection.]

1774 Parliament passed a series of laws known in American history as the Intolerable Acts. These measures closed the port of Boston, reorganized the government of Massachussetts, allowed troops to be quartered in private homes, and removed trials of royal customs officials to England. The same year Parliament approved the Quebec Act for the future administration of that province. It extended the boundaries of Quebec to include the Ohio River valley. The Americans regarded the Quebec Act as an attempt to prevent the extension of their mode of self-government westward beyond the mountains.

During these years committees of correspondence composed of citizens critical of Britain had been established throughout the colonies. They made the various sections of the eastern seaboard aware of common problems and aided united action. In September 1774 these committees organized the gathering of the First Continental Congress in Philadelphia. This body hoped to persuade Parliament to restore self-government in the colonies and to abandon its attempt at direct supervision of colonial affairs. However, conciliation was not forthcoming. By April 1775 the battles of Lexington and Concord had been fought. In June the colonists had been defeated at the Battle of Bunker Hill. The colonial assemblies soon began to meet under their own authority rather than under that of the king.

The Second Continental Congress met in May 1775. It still sought conciliation with Britain, but the pressure of events led that assembly to begin to conduct the government of the colonies. By August 1775 George III had declared the colonies in rebellion. During the winter Thomas Paine's pamphlet *Common Sense* galvanized public opinion in favor of separation from Great Britain. A colonial army and navy were organized. In April 1776

Lord Cornwallis surrenders to General George Washington at Yorktown, Virginia, October 19, 1781. This is a romanticized nineteenth-century reconstruction of a scene that no contemporary pencil portrayed. [Culver Pictures.]

George III of Great Britain was distrusted by politicians at home and American colonists abroad. The 1767 portrait is by Allan Ramsay (1713–1784) and the medal is by C. H. Küchler. [Painting: Culver Pictures; medal: The Granger Collection.]

the Continental Congress opened American ports to the trade of all nations. And on July 4, 1776, the Continental Congress adopted the Declaration of Independence. Thereafter the war of the American Revolution continued until 1781, when the forces of George Washington defeated those of Lord Charles Cornwallis at Yorktown. However, early in 1778 the war had widened into a European conflict when Benjamin Franklin persuaded the French government to support the rebellion. In 1779 the Spanish also came to the aid of the colonies. In 1783 the Peace of Paris concluded the conflict, and the thirteen American colonies had established their independence.

This series of events is generally familiar to American readers. The relationship of the American Revolution to European affairs and the European roots of the American revolutionary ideals are less familiar.

The political theory of the American Declaration of Independence derived from the writings of seventeenth-century English Whig theorists, such as John Locke, and eighteenth-century Scottish moral philosophers, such as Francis Hutcheson. Their political ideas had in large measure arisen out of the struggle of seventeenth-century English aristocrats and gentry against the absolutism of the Stuarts. The American colonists looked to the English Revolution of 1688 as having established many of their own fundamental political liberties as well as those of England. The colonists claimed that through the measures imposed from 1763 to 1776 George III and the British parliament had attacked those liberties and dissolved the bonds of moral and political allegiance that had formerly united the two peoples. Consequently the Americans employed a theory developed to justify an aristocratic rebellion to support a popular revolution.

These Whig political ideas were only a part of the English ideological heritage that affected the Americans. Throughout the eighteenth century the colonists had become familiar with a series of British political writers called the *Commonwealthmen.* They held republican political ideas and had their intellectual roots in the most

radical thought of the Puritan revolution. During the early eighteenth century these writers had relentlessly criticized the government patronage and parliamentary management of Robert Walpole and his successors. They argued that such government was corrupt and that it undermined liberty. They regarded much parliamentary taxation as simply a means of financing corruption. They also attacked standing armies, which they considered instruments of tyranny. In Great Britain this political tradition had only a marginal impact. The writers were largely ignored because most British subjects regarded themselves as the freest people in the world. However, four thousand miles away in the colonies, these radical books and pamphlets were read widely and were often accepted at face value. The events in Great Britain following the accession of King George III made many colonists believe that the worst fears of the Commonwealth writers were coming true.

Events in Great Britain

George III (1760–1820) believed that his two immediate royal predecessors had been improperly bullied and controlled by their ministers. Royal power had in effect amounted to little more than the policies carried out by a few powerful Whig families. The new king intended to rule through Parliament, but he was determined to have ministers of his own choice. Moreover George III believed that Parliament should function under royal rather than under aristocratic management. When William Pitt resigned after disagreement over war policy, the king appointed the earl of Bute as his first minister. In doing so, he ignored the great Whig families that had run the country since 1715. The king sought the aid of politicians whom the Whigs hated. Moreover he attempted to use the same kind of patronage techniques developed by Walpole to achieve royal control of the House of Commons.

Between 1761 and 1770 George tried one minister after another, but each in turn failed to gain sufficient support from the various factions in the House of Com-

John Wilkes Esq.r
Drawn from the Life and Etch'd in Aquafortis by Will.m Hogarth.
Publish'd according to Act of Parliament. May 1.6.1763.

This satirical portrait etching of John Wilkes was made by William Hogarth. It suggests the unattractive personal character of Wilkes and also tends to question the sincerity of his calls for liberty. [Charles Farrell Collection.]

which he had been arrested was illegal. However, the House of Commons ruled that issue Number 45 of *The North Briton* was a libel and expelled Wilkes from the Commons. He soon fled the country and was outlawed. Throughout these procedures there was very widespread support for Wilkes, and many demonstrations were held in his cause.

In 1768 Wilkes returned to England and again stood for election to Parliament. He won the election, but the House of Commons, under the influence of George III's friends, refused to seat him. He was elected three more times. After the fourth election the House of Commons simply ignored the election results and seated the government-supported candidate. As earlier in the decade, large popular demonstrations of shopkeepers, artisans, and small property owners supported Wilkes. He was also aided by some aristocratic politicians who wished to humiliate George III. Wilkes himself contended during all of his troubles that his cause was the cause of English liberty. "Wilkes and Liberty" became the slogan of all political radicals and many noble opponents of the monarch. Wilkes was finally seated in 1774, after having become the lord mayor of London.

The American colonists followed all of these developments of the 1760s very closely. The contemporary events in Britain confirmed their fears about a monarchical and parliamentary conspiracy against liberty. The king, as their Whig friends told them, was behaving like a tyrant. The Wilkes affair displayed the arbitrary power of the monarch, the corruption of the House of Commons, and the contempt of both for popular electors. That same monarch and Parliament were attempting to overturn the traditional relationship of Great Britain to its colonies by imposing parliamentary taxes. The same government had then landed troops in Boston, changed the government of Massachussetts, and undermined the traditional right of jury trial. All of these events fulfilled too exactly the portrait of political tyranny that had developed over the years in the minds of articulate colonists.

mons. Finally, in 1770 he turned to Lord North (1732–1792), who remained the king's first minister until 1782. The reaction of the Whig families and political spokesmen was to proclaim that George III was attempting to impose a tyranny. What they meant was that the king was attempting to curb the power of a particular group of the aristocracy. George III certainly was seeking to restore more royal influence to the government of Great Britain, but he was not attempting to make himself a tyrant.

THE CHALLENGE OF JOHN WILKES. Then in 1763 began the affair of John Wilkes (1725–1797). This London political radical and member of Parliament published a newspaper called *The North Briton*. In issue Number 45 of this paper Wilkes strongly criticized Lord Bute's handling of the peace negotiations with France. Wilkes was arrested under authority of a general warrant issued by the secretary of state. He pled the privileges of a member of Parliament and was released. The courts also later ruled that the vague kind of general warrant by

Major John Cartwright (1740–1824) was the first English political reformer to call for universal manhood suffrage in parliamentary elections. [The Granger Collection.]

ical structure. Colonial arguments could be used by British subjects at home who were no more directly represented in the House of Commons than were the Americans. The colonial questioning of the taxing authority of the House of Commons was not unrelated to the protest of John Wilkes. Both the Americans and Wilkes were challenging the power of the monarch and the authority of Parliament. Moreover both the colonial leaders and Wilkes appealed over the head of legally constituted political authorities to popular opinion and popular demonstrations. Both were protesting the power of a largely self-selected aristocratic political body. The British ministry was fully aware of these broader implications of the American troubles.

The American colonists also demonstrated to Europe how a politically restive people in the old regime could fight tyranny and protect political liberty. They established revolutionary but orderly political bodies that would function outside the existing political framework. These revolutionary political institutions were the congress and the convention. These began with the Stamp Act Congress of 1765 and culminated in the Constitutional Convention of 1787. The legitimacy of those congresses and conventions lay not in existing law but rather with the alleged consent of the governed. This approach represented a new way to found a government.

Toward the end of the War of the American Revolution, calls for parliamentary reform were heard in Britain itself. The method proposed for changing the system was the extralegal Association Movement.

By the close of the 1770s there was much resentment

Movement for Parliamentary Reform in Britain. The political influences between America and Britain operated both ways. The colonial demand for no taxation without representation and the criticism of the adequacy of the British system of representation struck at the core of the eighteenth-century British politin Britain about the mismanagement of the war, the high taxes, and Lord North's ministry. In northern England in 1778 Christopher Wyvil (1740–1822), a landowner and retired clergyman, organized the Yorkshire Association Movement. Property owners or freeholders of Yorkshire met in a mass meeting to demand rather moderate changes in the corrupt system of parliamentary elections. They organized corresponding societies elsewhere. They intended that the Association examine, and suggest reforms for, the entire government. The Association Movement was thus a popular attempt to establish an extralegal institution to reform the government. The movement collapsed during the early 1780s because its supporters, unlike Wilkes and the American rebels, were not willing to appeal for broad popular support. Nonetheless the agitation of the Association Movement provided many people with experience in political protest. Several of its younger figures lived to raise the issue of parliamentary reform after 1815.

Parliament was not insensitive to the demands of the Association Movement. In April 1780 the Commons passed a resolution that called for lessening the power of the crown. In 1782 Parliament adopted a measure for "economical" reform, which abolished some patronage at the disposal of the monarch. However, these actions did not prevent George III from appointing a minister of his own choice. In 1782 Lord North had to form a ministry with Charles James Fox (1749–1806), a long-time critic of George III. The monarch was most unhappy with the arrangement. In 1783 he approached William Pitt the Younger (1759–1806), son of the victorious war minister, to manage the House of Commons. During the election of 1784 Pitt received immense patronage support from the crown and constructed a House of Commons favorable to the king. Thereafter Pitt sought to formulate trade policies that would give his ministry broad popularity. He attempted in 1785 one measure of modest parliamentary reform. When it failed, the young prime minister, who had been only twenty-two at the time of his appointment, abandoned the cause of reform.

By the mid-1780s George III had achieved what he sought beginning in 1761. He had restored the influence of the monarchy in political affairs. It proved a temporary victory because his own mental illness, which would finally require a regency, weakened the royal power. The cost of his years of dominance had been very high. On both sides of the Atlantic the issue of popular sovereignty had been raised and widely discussed. The American colonies had been lost. Economically this loss did not prove disastrous. American trade after independence actually increased. However, the Americans—through the state constitutions, the Articles of Confederation, and the federal Constitution—had demonstrated to Europe the possibility of government without kings and without aristocracies. They had established the example of a nation in which written documents based on popular consent and popular sovereignty rather than upon divine law, natural law, tradition, or the will of kings stood as the highest political and legal authority. Writers throughout western Europe sensed that a new kind of political era was dawning. It was to be an age of constituent assemblies, constitutions, and declarations of rights.

Colonies founded to serve the economic requirements of Britain and Europe repaid the debt by serving as examples of new political ideals and institutions. The ideas had generally been developed in Europe, but America was the first place where most of them were initially put into practice. America for a time served as an experiment station for the advanced political ideas of Europe. Soon the ideas would find their way back to the lands of their origins.

SUGGESTED READINGS

B. BAILYN, *The Ideological Origins of the American Revolution* (1967). An important work illustrating the role of English radical thought in the perceptions of the American colonists.

C. BECKER, *The Declaration of Independence: A Study in the History of Political Ideas* (1922). An examination of the political and imperial theory of the Declaration.

H. BUTTERFIELD, *George III, Lord North, and the People, 1779–1780* (1949). Explores the domestic unrest in Britain during the American Revolution.

WALTER DORN, *Competition for Empire, 1740–1763* (1940). Still one of the best accounts of the mid-century struggle.

L. H. GIPSON, *The British Empire Before the American Revolution*, 13 vols. (1936–1967). A magisterial account of the mid-century wars from an imperial viewpoint.

R. LODGE, *Great Britain and Prussia in the Eighteenth Century* (1923). The standard account.

E. MORGAN AND H. MORGAN, *The Stamp Act Crisis* (1953). A lively account of the incident from the viewpoint of both the colonies and England.

R. PARES, *War and Trade in the West Indies* (1936). Relates the West Indies to Britain's larger commercial and naval concerns.

R. PARES, *King George III and the Politicians* (1953). An important analysis of the constitutional and political structures.

J. H. PARRY, *Trade and Dominion: The European Overseas Empires in the Eighteenth Century* (1971). A comprehensive account with attention to the European impact on the rest of the world.

C. D. RICE, *The Rise and Fall of Black Slavery* (1975). An excellent survey of the subject with careful attention to the numerous historiographical controversies.

C. G. ROBERTSON, *Chatham and the British Empire* (1948). A brief study.

G. RUDÉ, *Wilkes and Political Liberty* (1962). A close analysis of popular political behavior.

J. S. WATSON, *The Reign of George III, 1760–1815* (1960). Covers the British domestic political scene.

G. WILLS, *Inventing America: Jefferson's Declaration of Independence* (1978). An important new study that challenges much of the analysis in the Becker volume noted above.

566

22

The Age of Enlightenment: Eighteenth-Century Thought

DURING the eighteenth century the conviction began to spread throughout the literate sectors of European society that change and reform were both possible and desirable. This attitude is now commonplace, but it came into its own only after 1700. It represents one of the primary intellectual inheritances from that age. The movement of people and ideas that fostered such thinking is called the *Enlightenment*. Its leading voices combined confidence in the human mind inspired by the Scientific Revolution and faith in the power of rational criticism to challenge the intellectual authority of tradition and the Christian past. These writers stood convinced that human beings could comprehend the operation of physical nature and mold it to the ends of material and moral improvement. The rationality of the physical universe became a standard against which the customs and traditions of society could be measured and criticized. Such criticism penetrated every corner of contemporary society, politics, and religious opinion. As a result the spirit of innovation and improvement came to characterize modern European and Western society.

The *Philosophes*

The writers and critics who forged this new attitude and who championed change and reform were the *philosophes*. They were not usually philosophers in a formal

Sir Isaac Newton's tomb in Westminster Abbey, London (1731) was the work of William Kent and Michael Rysbrack. With Newton, classically draped and with his books and the globe itself accompanying him, it both symbolizes the Enlightenment's mathematical and philosophical concerns and honors the man who defined some of nature's most important basic laws. There was hardly a thinker of the Enlightenment to whom Newton was not an intellectual hero. [By courtesy of the Dean and Chapter of Westminster.]

sense but rather were people who sought to apply the rules of reason and common sense to practically all the major institutions and social practices of the day. The most famous of their number included Voltaire, Montesquieu, Diderot, Rousseau, Hume, Gibbon, Smith, Bentham, Lessing, and Kant. A few of them occupied professorships in universities, but most were free agents who might be found in London coffeehouses, Edinburgh drinking spots, the salons of fashionable Parisian ladies, the country houses of reform-minded nobles, or the courts of the most powerful monarchs on the Continent. They were not an organized group; they disagreed on many issues. Their relationship with each other and with lesser figures of the same turn of mind has been quite appropriately compared to that of a family, in which despite quarrels and tensions a basic unity still remains.[1]

The chief unity of the *philosophes* lay in their desire to reform thought, society, and government for the sake of human liberty. As Peter Gay has suggested, this goal included "freedom from arbitrary power, freedom of speech, freedom of trade, freedom to realize one's talents, freedom of aesthetic response, freedom, in a word, of moral man to make his way in the world."[2] No other single set of ideas has done so much to shape the modern world. The literary vehicles through which the *philosophes* delivered their message included books, pamphlets, plays, novels, philosophical treatises, encyclopedias, newspapers, and magazines. During the Reformation and the religious wars the printed word had been used to debate the proper mode of faith in God. The *philosophes* of the Enlightenment employed the printed word to proclaim a new faith in the capacity of humankind to improve itself without the aid of God.

Most of the *philosophes* were middle class in their social origins. The bulk of their readership were also drawn from the prosperous commercial and professional people

1 Peter Gay, *The Enlightenment: An Interpretation* (New York: Alfred A. Knopf, 1967), Vol. 1, p. 4.
2 Ibid., 1, p. 3.

Edward Jenner (1749–1823), an English physician, discovered that by inoculating human beings with the relatively mild disease of cowpox he could make them immune to the dread disease of smallpox. That discovery eventually led to the practically complete removal of the danger of smallpox. [Culver Pictures.]

of the eighteenth-century towns and cities. These people discussed the reformers' writings and ideas in local philosophical societies, Freemason lodges, and clubs. They had sufficient income and leisure time to buy and read the *philosophes'* works. However, the writers of the Enlightenment did not consciously champion the goals or causes of the middle class. Nevertheless they did provide an intellectual ferment and a major source of ideas that could be used to undermine existing social practices and political structures. They taught their contemporaries how to pose pointed, critical questions. Moreover the *philosophes* generally supported the economic growth, the expansion of trade, and the improvement of transport that were transforming the society and economy of the eighteenth century.

Formative Influences

The Newtonian world view, the stability and prosperity of Great Britain after 1688, and the degradation that the wars of Louis XIV brought to France were the chief factors that favored discussion of reform throughout Europe.

Isaac Newton (1642–1727) and John Locke (1632–1704) were the major intellectual forerunners of the Enlightenment. Newton's formulation of the laws of universal gravitation exemplified the power of the human mind. His example and his writing encouraged Europeans to approach the study of nature directly and to avoid metaphysics and supernaturalism. Newton had formulated general laws but had always insisted upon a foundation of specific empirical evidence for those laws. Empirical experience had provided the constant check upon his

rational speculation. This emphasis on concrete experience became a keystone for Enlightenment thought. Moreover Newton had discerned a pattern of rationality in natural physical phenomena. During the eighteenth century the ancient idea of following nature became transformed under the Newtonian influence into the idea of following reason. Because nature was rational, society should be organized in a rational manner.

As explained in Chapter 18, Newton's scientific achievement had inspired his fellow countryman John Locke to seek a human psychology based on experience. In *An Essay Concerning Human Understanding* (1690), Locke argued that each human being enters the world as a *tabula rasa,* or blank page. His or her personality is consequently the product of the sensations that impinge from the external world throughout the course of life. The significant conclusion that followed from this psychology was that human nature is changeable and can be molded by modification of the surrounding physical and social environment. Locke's was a reformer's psychology. It suggested that improvement in the human situation was possible. Locke also in effect rejected the Christian view of humankind as creatures permanently flawed by sin. Human beings need not wait for the grace of God or other divine aid to better their lives.

Newton's physics and Locke's psychology provided the theoretical basis for reform. The domestic stability of Great Britain after the Revolution of 1688 furnished a living example of a society in which enlightened reforms functioned for the benefit of all concerned. England permitted religious toleration to all creeds except Unitarianism and Roman Catholicism, whose believers were not actually persecuted. Relative freedom of the press and free speech prevailed. The monarchy was limited in its authority, and political sovereignty resided in Parliament. Courts protected citizens from arbitrary government action. The army was quite small. These liberal policies had produced not disorder and instability but economic prosperity and loyalty to the political system. The continental view of England was somewhat idealized; never-

Voltaire challenged the authorities of eighteenth-century Europe with his mockery and bitter satire. Many of the *philosophes* considered him the leading figure in their effort to liberate European thought from the burden of the past. The statue is in the Théâtre Français in Paris. [Culver Pictures.]

theless the country was sufficiently freer than any other nation to make the point the reformers sought.

If the example of Great Britain proved that change need not be disastrous to a nation and society, France exhibited many of the practices and customs of European politics and society that needed to be reformed. Louis XIV had built his power on the grounds of absolute monarchy, religious unity involving persecution, a large standing army, and heavy taxation. However, the nation had been defeated in war by its enemies. Its people were miserable, and celebrations had marked the death of the great king. His successors had been unable to reform the state. Critics of the monarchy could be arbitrarily arrested. There was no freedom of worship. Political and religious censorship was frequently exercised over the press and other literary productions. Offending authors could be imprisoned, although some achieved co-operative relations with the authorities. State regulations hampered economic growth. Many aristocrats regarded themselves as a military class and upheld militaristic values. Yet throughout the French social structure there existed people who wanted to see changes brought about. These people read and supported the *philosophes* of their nation and of other countries. Consequently France became the major center for the Enlightenment. For there more than in any other state the demand for reform daily confronted writers and political thinkers.

Stages of the Enlightenment

The movement that came to be known as the Enlightenment evolved over the course of the century and involved a number of writers living at different times in various countries. Its early spokesmen popularized the rationalism and scientific ideas of the seventeenth century. They worked to expose contemporary social and political abuses and argued that reform was necessary and possible. The advancement of their cause and ideas was anything but steady. They confronted the obstacles of vested interests, political oppression, and religious con-

demnation. Yet by mid-century enlightened ideas had been brought to the public in a variety of formats. The *philosophes'* family had come into being. They corresponded with each other, wrote for each other as well as for the general public, and defended each other against the political and religious authorities.

By the second half of the century they were sufficiently safe to quarrel among themselves on occasion. They had stopped talking in generalities, and their major spokesmen were addressing themselves to specific abuses. Their books and articles had become more specialized and more practical. Having convinced Europeans that change was a good idea, they began to suggest exactly what changes were most desirable. They had become honored figures.

Voltaire

One of the earliest and by far the most influential of the *philosophes* was François Marie Arouet, known to posterity as Voltaire (1694–1778). During the 1720s Voltaire had offended the French authorities by certain of his writings. He was arrested and put in prison for a brief time.

Later Voltaire went to England, where he visited in the best literary circles, observed the tolerant intellectual and religious climate, felt free in its atmosphere of moderate politics, and admired its science and economic prosperity. In 1733 he published *Letters on the English,* which appeared in French the next year. The book praised the virtues of the English and indirectly criticized the abuses of French society. In 1738 he published *Elements of the Philosophy of Newton,* which popularized the thought of the great scientist. Both works were well received and gave Voltaire a reputation as an important writer.

Thereafter Voltaire lived part of the time in France and part near Geneva, just across the French border, where royal authorities could not bother him. He wrote essays, history, plays, stories, and letters that made him the literary dictator of Europe. He brought the bitter venom of his satire and sarcasm against one evil after another in French and European life. His most famous satire was *Candide* (1759), in which he attacked war, religious persecution, and unthinking optimism about the human condition. Like most *philosophes*, Voltaire believed that improvement of human society was necessary and possible. But he was never certain that reform, if achieved, would be permanent. The optimism of the Enlightenment constituted a tempered hopefulness rather than a glib certainty. Pessimism provided an undercurrent to most of the works of the period.

Montesquieu

Among the other pioneers of the early Enlightenment Charles de Secondat, Baron de Montesquieu (1689–1755) was outstanding. He was a lawyer, a noble of the robe, and a member of a provincial *parlement*. He also belonged to the Bordeaux Academy of Science, before which he presented papers on scientific topics. Although living comfortably within the bosom of French society, he saw the need for reform. In 1721 he published *The Persian Letters* to satirize contemporary institutions. The book consisted of letters purportedly written by two Persians visiting Europe. They explained to friends at home how European behavior contrasted with Persian life and customs. Behind the humor lay the cutting edge of criticism and an exposition of the cruelty and irrationality of much contemporary European life. In his most enduring work, *The Spirit of the Laws* (1748), Montesquieu held up the example of the British constitution as the wisest model for regulating the power of government. (We shall examine *The Spirit of the Laws* more closely later in this chapter.)

The Encyclopedia

The mid-century witnessed the publication of one of the greatest monuments of the Enlightenment. Under the heroic leadership of Denis Diderot (1713–1784), and Jean le Rond d'Alembert (1717–1783), the first volume of the *Encyclopedia* appeared in 1751. The project reached completion in 1772 with seventeen volumes of

---

The Encyclopedia *Discourses on Reason and Faith*

As illustrated in this passage from the *Encyclopedia* article on "Reason and Faith," the writers of the Enlightenment in the mid-eighteenth century wished to see human reason limit the excesses and fanaticism associated with religion. They wished to see reason as well as faith determine the practical character of religion.

EVERYTHING *within the province of revelation must prevail over our opinions, our prejudices and our interests, and is entitled to demand complete assent from the mind. But such submission of our reason to faith does not thereby reverse the limits of human knowledge and does not shake the foundations of reason; it allows us the freedom to employ our faculties in the areas of application for which they were given to us.*

If we are not careful in distinguishing between the different jurisdictions of faith and reason by means of these limits, reason will have no place in matters of religion, and we shall have no right to mock the extravagant opinions and ceremonies that we notice in most religions of the world. Who does not see that this opens a wide field to the most excessive fanaticism and the most insane superstition? With such a principle there is nothing so absurd that will not be believed. Hence it happens that religion, which is to the credit of humanity and the most excellent prerogative of our nature over the animals, is often the area in which men seem to be the most irrational.

Stephen J. Gendzier (Ed. and Trans.), *The Encyclopedia: Selections* (New York: Harper Torchbook, 1967), pp. 212–213.

OPPOSITE, LEFT: The title page of the first volume of the *Encyclopedia*. The early volumes of the text received the approval of the royal censor, as noted on the last line, but when it became evident that the work challenged many widely held religious and political views, its opponents obtained withholding of approval for later volumes which were eventually published. [The Mansell Collection.]

OPPOSITE, RIGHT: Denis Diderot, the principal editor who saw it through to the end; d'Alembert withdrew when the opposition turned nasty. [The Granger Collection.]

OPPOSITE, TOP: An extraordinary feature of the set was the plates, which set out the entire spectrum of contemporary technology in thousands of detailed etchings. This typical figure shows the contents of a chemical laboratory. [Giraudon.]

Gotthold Lessing (1729–1781) was a German dramatist and literary critic whose works made strong pleas for religious toleration. His 1760 portrait is by J. H. Tischbein. [The Granger Collection.]

text and eleven of plates. The *Encyclopedia* was the product of the collective effort of more than one hundred authors, and its editors had at one time or another solicited articles from all the major French *philosophes*. The project reached fruition only after numerous attempts to censor it and halt its publication. The *Encyclopedia* set forth the most advanced critical ideas in religion, government, and philosophy. This criticism often had to be hidden in obscure articles or under the cover of irony. The articles represented a collective plea for freedom of expression. However, the large volumes also provided important information on manufacturing, canal building, ship construction, and improved agriculture.

Between fourteen and sixteen thousand copies of various editions of the *Encyclopedia* were sold before 1789. The project had been constructed to secularize learning and to undermine the intellectual assumptions remaining from the Middle Ages and the Reformation. The articles on politics, ethics, and society ignored concerns about divine law and concentrated on humanity and its immediate well-being. The encyclopedists looked to antiquity rather than to the Christian centuries for their intellectual and ethical models. The future welfare of humankind lay not in pleasing God or following divine commandments but rather in harnessing the power of the earth and its resources and in living at peace with one's fellow human beings. The good life lay here and now and was to be achieved through the application of reason to human relationships.

With the publication of the *Encyclopedia*, enlightened thought was diffused over the Continent. Enlightened ideas penetrated German and Russian intellectual and political circles. The *philosophes* of the latter part of the century turned from championing the general cause of reform and discussed specific areas of practical application. Gotthold Lessing (1729–1781) wrote plays to plead for religious toleration. Adam Smith (1723–1790) attacked the mercantile system. Cesare Beccaria (1738–1794) and Jeremy Bentham (1748–1832) called for penal and legal reforms. By this time the concepts of

reform and the rationalization of existing institutions had become deeply impressed on European thinking and society. The issue then became and would remain for over a century how best to implement those reforms.

The Enlightenment and Religion

Throughout the century, in the eyes of the *philosophes* the chief enemy of the improvement of humankind and the enjoyment of happiness was the existence and influence of ecclesiastical institutions. The hatred of the *philosophes* for the church and Christianity was summed up in Voltaire's cry of "Crush the Infamous Thing." Almost all varieties of Christianity, but especially Roman Catholicism, invited the criticism of the *philosophes*. Intellectually the churches perpetuated a religious rather than a scientific view of humankind and physical nature. The clergy taught that human beings were basically depraved and that they required divine grace to become worthy creatures. The doctrine of original sin in either its Catholic or its Protestant formulation suggested that meaningful improvement in human nature on earth was impossible. Religious concerns turned human interest away from this world to the world to come. The concept of predestination suggested that the condition of the human soul after death had little or no relationship to virtuous living during this life. Through disagreements over obscure doctrines the various churches favored the politics of intolerance and bigotry that caused human suffering, torture, and war.

To attack the Christian churches in this manner was to raise major questions about the life and society of the old regime. Politically and socially the churches were deeply enmeshed in the power structure. They owned large amounts of land and collected tithes from peasants before any other taxes were collected. Most of the clergy were legally exempt from taxation, and made only annual voluntary grants to the government. The upper clergy in most countries were relatives of aristocrats. Churchmen were actively involved in politics, serving in the British

House of Lords and on the Continent advising princes. In Protestant countries the local clergyman of a particular parish was usually appointed by the local major landowner. Across the Continent membership in the predominant denomination of the kingdom gave certain subjects political advantages. Nonmembership often excluded other subjects from political participation. Clergymen of all faiths preached the sinfulness of political disobedience, and they provided the intellectual justification for the social and political status quo. They were active where possible in exerting religious and literary censorship. The churches were thus privileged and powerful corporate bodies of the old regime. The *philosophes* chose to attack both their ideas and their power.

Deism

The *philosophes* believed that religion should be reasonable and should lead to moral behavior. The Newtonian world view had convinced many writers that nature was rational. Therefore the God who had created nature must be rational and the religion through which that God was worshiped should also be rational. Moreover Lockean psychology, which limited human knowledge to empirical experience, raised the question whether such a thing as divine revelation to humankind was after all possible. These considerations gave rise to a movement for enlightened rational religion known as *deism*. The tenor of this religion is displayed in the title of one of its earliest expositions: *Christianity Not Mysterious* (1696) by John Toland. He and later writers wished to consider religion as a natural and rational rather than a supernatural phenomenon.

There were two major points in the deists' creed. The first was the belief in the existence of God. They thought that this belief could be empirically deduced from the contemplation of nature. Joseph Addison's poem on the spacious firmament (1712), illustrates this idea:

> The spacious firmament on high,
> With all the blue ethereal sky,

And spangled heav'n, a shining frame,
Their great Original proclaim:
Th' unwearied Sun, from day to day,
Does his Creator's power display,
And publishes to every land
The work of an Almighty hand.

Because nature provided evidence of a rational God, that deity must also favor rational morality. Consequently the second point in the deists' creed was the belief in life after death, when rewards and punishments would be meted out according to the virtue of the life a person led on this earth.

Deism was empirical, tolerant, reasonable, and capable of encouraging virtuous living. It was the major positive religious component of the Enlightenment. Voltaire declared:

> The great name of Deist, which is not sufficiently revered, is the only name one ought to take. The only gospel one ought to read is the great book of Nature, written by the hand of God and sealed with his seal. The only religion that ought to be professed is the religion of worshiping God and being a good man.[3]

If such a faith became widely accepted, the fanaticism and rivalry of the various Christian sects might be overcome. Religious conflict and persecutions encouraged by that fulsome zeal would end. There would also be little or no necessity for a priestly class to foment fanaticism, denominational hatred, and bigotry.

The *philosophes* did not rest with the formulation of a rational religious alternative to Christianity. They also attacked the churches and the clergy with great vehemence. Voltaire repeatedly questioned the truthfulness of priests and the morality of the Bible. In his *Philosophical Dictionary* (1764) he humorously pointed out inconsist-

---

3 Quoted in J. H. Randall, *The Making of the Modern Mind*, rev. ed. (New York: Houghton Mifflin, 1940), p. 292.

David Hume (1711–1776), a Scotsman, was one of the foremost philosophers of the Enlightenment. His essay on miracles was one of the key examples of religious scepticism. The painting is by Allan Ramsay. [The Granger Collection.]

Edward Gibbon (1737–1794), the English historian, was the author of *The History of the Decline and Fall of the Roman Empire,* published between 1776 and 1788. He is shown here as painted by Henry Walton.

encies in biblical narratives and immoral acts of the biblical heroes. In an *Essay on Miracles* (1748) the Scottish *philosophe* David Hume (1711–1776) argued that miracles, in which the churches put great store, were logically and naturally impossible. The greatest miracle was to believe in miracles. Edward Gibbon (1737–1794), the English historian, in *The Decline and Fall of the Roman Empire* (1776) examined the early history of Christianity and explained the rise of that faith in terms of natural causes rather than the influence of miracles and piety. A few *philosophes* went further. Baron d'Holbach (1723–1789) and Julien Offroy de La Mettre (1709–1751) embraced positions very near to atheism and materialism. Theirs was distinctly a minority position, however. Most of the *philosophes* sought not the abolition of religion but its transformation into a humane force that would encourage good living.

Toleration

A primary social condition for such a life was the establishment of religious toleration. Again Voltaire took the lead in championing this cause. In 1762 the Roman Catholic political authorities in Toulouse ordered the execution of a Huguenot named Jean Calas. He stood accused of having murdered his son to prevent him from converting to Roman Catholicism. Calas had been viciously tortured, broken on the wheel, and finally strangled to death without ever having confessed his guilt. The confession would not have saved his life, but it would

OPPOSITE: The elaborate Baroque splendor of the Kaisersaal in the episcopal, or bishop's, palace at Würzburg, West Germany, built in the early eighteenth century, displays the vast wealth and influence of the church in the society and the political structure of the old regime. The complex frescos were painted by the celebrated Italian artist Giovanni Battista Tiepolo and assistants in 1751. A close-up of the scene between the two circular windows is included in the color album. [Photo-Gundermann.]

Cesare Beccaria was an Italian advocate of the rational reform of criminal law and punishments. [The Granger Collection.]

have given the Catholics good propaganda to use against Protestants.

Voltaire learned of the case only after Calas's death. He made the dead man's cause his own. In 1763 he published a *Treatise on Tolerance* and hounded the authorities for a new investigation. Finally, in 1765, the judicial decision against the unfortunate man was reversed. For Voltaire the case illustrated the fruits of religious fanaticism and the need for rational reform of judicial processes. Somewhat later in the century the German playwright and critic Gotthold Lessing (1729–1781) wrote *Nathan the Wise* (1779) as a plea not only for toleration of different Christian sects but also of religious faiths other than Christianity. All of these calls for toleration stated in effect that life on earth and human relationships should not be subordinated to religion. Secular values and considerations were more important than religious ones.

The Enlightenment and Society

Although the *philosophes* wrote much on religion, humanity was the center of their interest. As one writer in the *Encyclopedia* observed, "Man is the unique point to which we must refer everything, if we wish to interest and please amongst considerations the most arid and

Beccaria Objects to Capital Punishment as Unenlightened

In the eighteenth century the death penalty was commonly applied throughout Europe for small as well as great crimes. The young north Italian nobleman Cesare Beccaria thought the penalty was unproductive of law and order and also unenlightened. *On Crimes and Punishments* appeared when he was only 26, and Voltaire, Bentham, and Catherine the Great professed to admire the work. His 1764 comments are a good example of the Enlightenment application of the criteria of reason and utility to social problems.

Is the *death penalty really* useful *and* necessary *for the security and good order of society? Are torture and torments* just, *and do they attain the* end *for which laws are instituted? What is the best way to prevent crimes? Are the same punishments equally effective for all times? What influence have they on customary behavior? These problems deserve to be analyzed with that geometric precision which the mist of sophisms, seductive eloquence, and timorous doubt cannot withstand. . . . If, by defending the rights of man and of unconquerable truth, I should help to save from the spasm and agonies of death some wretched victim of tyranny or of no less fatal ignorance, the thanks and tears of one innocent mortal in his transports of joy would console me for the contempt of all mankind.*

If one were to cite against me the example of all the ages and of almost all the nations that have applied the death penalty to certain crimes, my reply would be that the example reduced itself to nothing in the face of truth, against which there is no prescription; that the history of men leaves us with the impression of a vast sea of errors; among which, at great intervals, some rare and hardly intelligible truths appear to float on the surface. Human sacrifices were once common to almost all nations, yet who will dare to defend them? That only a few societies, and for a short time only, have abstained from applying the death penalty, stands in my favor rather than against me, for that conforms with the usual lot of great truths, which are about as long-lasting as a lightning flash in comparison with the long dark night that envelops mankind. The happy time has not yet arrived in which truth shall be the portion of the greatest number, as error has heretofore been.

Cesare Beccaria, *On Crimes and Punishments*, trans. by Henry M. Paolucci (Indianapolis: Bobbs Merrill, Inc., 1963), pp. 10, 51.

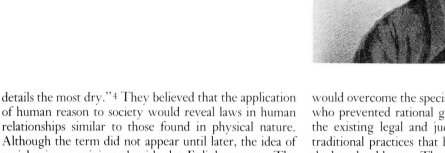

Jeremy Bentham applied the principle of "the greatest good for the greatest number" to his criticism of and attempts to reform English law. [The Granger Collection.]

details the most dry."[4] They believed that the application of human reason to society would reveal laws in human relationships similar to those found in physical nature. Although the term did not appear until later, the idea of social science originated with the Enlightenment. The purpose of discovering social laws was the removal of inhumanity that existed through ignorance of them. These concerns became especially evident in the work of the *philosophes* on law and prison procedures.

Beccaria

In 1764 Cesare Beccaria (1738–1794), an Italian *philosophe*, published *On Crimes and Punishments*, in which he applied critical analysis to the problem of making punishments both effective and just. He wanted the laws of monarchs and legislatures—that is, positive law—to conform with the rational laws of nature. He rigorously and eloquently attacked both torture and capital punishment. He thought that the criminal justice system should ensure speedy trial, sure punishment, and punishment intended to deter further crime. The purpose of law was not to impose the will of God or some other ideal of perfection; its purpose was to secure the greatest good or happiness for the greatest number of human beings. This utilitarian philosophy based on happiness in this life permeated most of the Enlightenment writing on practical reforms.

Bentham

Although utilitarianism did not originate with him, it is particularly associated with the English legal reformer Jeremy Bentham (1748–1832). He sought to create codes of scientific law that were founded on the principle of utility, that is, the greatest good for the greatest number. In the *Fragment on Government* (1776) and *The Principles of Morals and Legislation* (1789), Bentham explained that the application of the principle of utility

4 Quoted in F. L. Baumer, *Main Currents of Western Thought*, 4th ed. (New Haven: Yale University Press, 1978), p. 374.

would overcome the special interests or privileged groups who prevented rational government. Bentham regarded the existing legal and judicial systems as burdened by traditional practices that harmed the very people whom the law should serve. The application of reason and utility would remove the legal clutter that prevented justice from being realized.

The Physiocrats

Another area of social relationships where the *philosophes* saw existing legislation and administration preventing the operation of natural social laws was the field of economic policy. They believed trade, manufacture, and bountiful agriculture were hampered by the mercantilist legislation and labor regulations established by various governments and guilds. In France these economic reformers were called the *physiocrats*. Their leading spokesmen were François Quesnay (1694-1744) and Pierre Du Pont de Nemours (1739-1817). They believed that the primary role of government was to protect property and to permit freedom in the use of property. They particularly felt that all economic production was dependent on sound agriculture, and they favored the consolidation of small peasant holdings into larger, more efficient farms.

Adam Smith

The most important of Enlightenment discussions of economics was Adam Smith's (1723-1790) *Inquiry into the Nature and Causes of the Wealth of Nations* (1776). Smith, who was a professor at Edinburgh, urged that the mercantile system of England—including the navigation acts, the bounties, most tariffs, special trading monopolies, and the domestic regulation of labor and manufacture—be abolished. Smith believed that these modes of economic regulation by the state interfered with the natural system of economic liberty. They were intended to preserve the wealth of the nation, to capture wealth from other nations, and to preserve a minimum amount of work for the laborers of the country. However, Smith saw such regu-

Adam Smith was one of the most important members of
what may be called the Class of 1776—the astonishing
outburst of British historical writing that centered
on that year. In addition to Smith's *Inquiry into the
Nature and Causes of the Wealth of Nations*, Gibbon
published the first volume of *The Decline and Fall*,
Dr. Charles Burney (1726–1814) published the first
volume of *A General History of Music* (completed in
1789), and Sir John Hawkins (1719–1789) managed
to publish the entire five volumes of his *A General
History of the Science and Practice of Music*. Moreover, in 1774, Thomas Warton (1728–1790) published
the first volume of *The History of English Poetry*
(third volume, 1781; never completed), while in 1777
the Scottish historian William Robertson (1721–1793)
finished his career with the publication of his
History of America. [Culver Pictures.]

lations as preventing the wealth and production of the
country from growing. He wanted to see economic
growth and a consumer-oriented economy. The means to
those ends was the unleashing of individuals to pursue
their own selfish economic interest. Free pursuit of economic self-interest would ensure economic expansion as
each person attempted to enrich himself by meeting the
demands of the marketplace. Consumers would find their
wants met as manufacturers and merchants sought their
business.

Smith's book challenged the concept of scarce goods

and resources that lay behind mercantilism and the guilds.
Smith saw the realm of nature as a boundless expanse of
water, air, soil, and minerals. The physical resources of
the earth seemed to demand exploitation for the enrich-
ment and comfort of humankind. In effect, Smith was
saying that the nations and peoples of Europe need not be
poor. The idea of the infinite use of nature's goods for the
material benefit of humankind—a concept that has dominated Western life until recent years—stemmed directly
from the Enlightenment. When Smith wrote, the population of the world was smaller, its people were poorer,

Charles de Secondat, Baron de Montesquieu (1689–1755) was the author of *L'Esprit des Lois* (*The Spirit of the Laws*) (1748), which may have been the single most influential book of the Enlightenment, both in Europe and in America. The bust is the work of the sculptor LeComte. [Musée de Versailles. Cliché des Musées Nationaux.]

and the quantity of undeveloped resources per capita was much greater. For people of the eighteenth century it was in the uninhibited exploitation of natural resources that the true improvement of the human condition seemed to lie.

Smith is usually regarded as the founder of *laissez-faire* economics. However, the *Wealth of Nations* was a very complex book. Smith was no simple dogmatist. For example, he was not opposed to all government activity touching upon the economy. The state should provide schools, armies, navies, and roads. It should also undertake certain commercial ventures, such as the opening of dangerous new trade routes, that were economically desirable but the expense or risk of which discouraged private enterprise. His reasonable tone and recognition of the complexity of social and economic life displayed a very important point about the *philosophes*. Most of them were much less rigid and doctrinaire than any brief summary of their thought may tend to suggest. They recognized the passions of humanity as well as its reason. They adopted reason and nature as tools of criticism through which they might create a climate of opinion that would allow the fully developed human personality to flourish.

Political Thought of the *Philosophes*

Nowhere did the appreciation of the complexity of the problems of contemporary society become more evident than in the *philosophes'* political thought. Nor did any other area of their reformist enterprise so clearly illustrate the tension and conflict within the "family" of the Enlightenment. Most *philosophes* were discontent with certain political features of their countries, but they were especially discontent in France. There the corruptness of the royal court, the blundering of the bureaucracy, the less than glorious mid-century wars, and the power of the church compounded all problems. Consequently it was in France that the most important political thought of the Enlightenment occurred. However, the French *philo-*

sophes stood quite divided as to the proper solution. Their attitudes spanned the whole spectrum from aristocratic reform to democracy to constitutional monarchy.

The Spirit of the Laws

Montesquieu's *The Spirit of the Laws* (1748) may well have been the single most influential book of the century. It was a work that exhibited the internal tensions of the Enlightenment. Montesquieu pursued an empirical method, taking illustrative examples from the political experience of both ancient and modern nations. From these he concluded that there could be no single set of political laws that applied to all peoples at all times and in all places. Rather there existed a large number of political variables, and the good political life depended upon the relationship of those variables. Whether a monarchy or a republic was the best form of government was a matter of the size of the political unit and its population, the social and religious customs, the economic structure, the traditions, and the climate. Only a careful examination and evaluation of these elements could reveal what mode of government would prove most beneficial to a particular people. A century later such speculations would have been classified as sociology.

So far as France was concerned, Montesquieu had some rather definite ideas. He believed in monarchical government, but with a monarchy whose power was tempered and limited by various sets of intermediary institutions. The latter included the aristocracy, the towns, and the other corporate bodies that enjoyed particular liberties that the monarch must respect. These corporate bodies might be said to represent various segments of the general population and thus of public opinion. In France he regarded the aristocratic courts or *parlements* as the major example of an intermediary association. Their role was to limit the power of the monarchy and thus preserve the liberty of subjects. In championing these aristocratic bodies and the general role of the aristocracy, Montesquieu was a political reactionary. However, he adopted that stance in the hope of achieving

The writings of Jean Jacques Rousseau raised some of the most profound social and ethical questions of the Enlightenment. [Bettmann Archive.]

reform. For in his opinion it was the oppressive and inefficient absolutism of the monarchy that accounted for the degradation of French life.

One of Montesquieu's most influential ideas was that of division of power within any government. For his model of a government with power wisely separated among different branches, he took contemporary Great Britain. There he believed he had found a system in which executive power resided in the king, legislative power in the Parliament, and judicial power in the courts. He thought any two branches could check and balance the power of the other. His perception of the eighteenth-century British constitution was incorrect because he failed to see how patronage and electoral corruption allowed a handful of powerful aristocrats to dominate the government. Moreover, he was also unaware of the emerging cabinet system, which meant that the executive power was slowly becoming a creature of the Parliament. Nevertheless the analysis illustrated Montesquieu's strong sense of the need to limit the exercise of power through constitutionalism and the formation of law by legislatures rather than by monarchs. In this manner, although Montesquieu set out to defend the political privileges of the French aristocracy, his ideas had a profound and still lasting effect upon the liberal democracies of the next two centuries.

Rousseau

Jean Jacques Rousseau (1712–1778) held a view of the exercise and reform of political power quite different from Montesquieu's.

Rousseau was a strange isolated genius who never felt particularly comfortable with the other *philosophes*. Yet perhaps more than any other writer of the mid-eighteenth century he transcended the thought and values of his own time. Rousseau held a deep antipathy toward the world and the society in which he dwelled. It seemed impossible for human beings living according to contemporary commercial values to achieve moral, virtuous, or sincere lives. In 1750, in his *Discourse on the Moral Effects of the Arts and Sciences*, he contended that the process of civilization and enlightenment had corrupted human nature. Human beings in the state of nature had been more dignified. In 1755, in a *Discourse on the Origin of Inequality*, Rousseau blamed much of the evil in the world on maldistribution of property.

In both works Rousseau brilliantly and directly challenged the social fabric of the day. He drew into question the concepts of material and intellectual progress and the morality of a society in which commerce and industry were regarded as the most important of human activities. He felt that the real purpose of society was to nurture better people. In this respect Rousseau's vision of reform was much more radical than that of other contemporary writers. The other *philosophes* believed that human life would be improved if people could enjoy more of the fruits of the earth or could produce more goods. Rousseau raised the more fundamental question of what the good life is. This question has haunted European social thought ever since the eighteenth century. Much of the criticism of Europe's post-World War II society is rooted in this Rousseauean approach.

Rousseau carried these same concerns into his political thought. His most extensive discussion of politics appeared in *The Social Contract* (1762). Although the book attracted rather little immediate attention, it had by the end of the century become widely read in France. *The Social Contract*, as compared to Montesquieu's *Spirit of the Laws*, was a very abstract book. It did not propose specific reforms but outlined the kind of political structure that Rousseau believed would overcome the evils of contemporary politics and society.

Rousseau Argues that Inequality Is Not Natural

Jean Jacques Rousseau was one of the first writers to assert the social equality of human beings. He argued, as in this 1755 passage, that inequality had developed through the ages and was not "natural." He directly questioned the sanctity of property based on the assumed natural inquality of human beings.

I HAVE *endeavoured to trace the origin and progress of inequality, and the institution and abuse of political societies, as far as these are capable of being deduced from the nature of man merely by the light of reason, and independently of those sacred dogmas which give the sanction of divine right to sovereign authority. It follows from this survey that, as there is hardly any inequality in the state of nature, all the inequality which now prevails owes its strength and growth to the development of our faculties and the advance of the human mind, and becomes at last permanent and legitimate by the establishment of property and laws. Secondly, it follows that moral inequality, authorized by positive right alone, clashes with natural right, whenever it is not proportionate to physical inequality—a distinction which sufficiently determines what we think of that species of inequality which prevails in all civilized countries; since it is plainly contrary to the law of nature, however defined, that children should command old men, fools wise men, and that the privileged few should gorge themselves with superfluities while the starving multitude are in want of the bare necessities of life.*

Jean Jacques Rousseau, *The Social Contract and Discourses,* trans. by G. D. H. Cole, (New York: E. P. Dutton, 1950), pp. 271–272.

DU
CONTRACT SOCIAL;
OU,
PRINCIPES
DU
DROIT POLITIQUE.

PAR J. J. ROUSSEAU,
CITOYEN DE GENEVE.

—— *fœderis æquas*
Dicamus leges.
Æneid. XI

A AMSTERDAM,
Chez MARC MICHEL REY.
MDCCLXII.

Rousseau's *Social Contract* (1762) challenged the political thought of an aristocratic age by calling for radical political equality. Note that, like many other unorthodox works, it was published in relatively free Amsterdam. [The Granger Collection.]

Most eighteenth-century political thinkers, in the tradition of Thomas Hobbes and John Locke, regarded human beings as individuals and society as a collection of such independent individuals pursuing personal selfish goals. These writers wished to liberate these individuals from the undue bonds of government. Rousseau picked up the stick from the other end. His book opens with the declaration, "All men are born free, but everywhere they are in chains."[5] The rest of the volume constitutes *a*

5 Jean Jacques Rousseau, *The Social Contract and Discourses,* trans. by G. D. H. Cole (New York: E. P. Dutton, 1950), p. 3.

defense of the chains of society over its members. Rousseau suggested that society is more important than its individual members, because they are what they are only because of their relationship to the larger community. Independent human beings living alone can achieve very little. Through their relationship to the larger community, they become moral creatures capable of significant action. The question then becomes what kind of community allows people to behave morally. In his two previous discourses Rousseau had explained that contemporary European society was not such a community. It was rather merely an aggregate of competing individuals whose chief social goal was to preserve selfish independence in spite of all potential social bonds and obligations.

Rousseau sought to project the vision of a society in which each person could maintain his own personal freedom while at the same time behaving as a loyal member of the larger community. To that end Rousseau drew upon the traditions of Plato and Calvin to define freedom as obedience to law. In his case the law to be obeyed was that created by the general will. This concept normally meant the will of the majority of citizens as expressed through voting. Democratic participation in decision making would bind the individual citizen to the community. Rousseau believed that the general will must always be right and that to obey the general will was to be free. This argument led him to the notorious conclusion that under certain circumstances some people must be forced to be free. Rousseau's politics thus constituted a justification for radical direct democracy and for collective action against individual citizens.

Rousseau had in effect launched an assault on the eighteenth-century cult of the individual and the fruits of selfishness. He stood at odds with the commercial spirit that was transforming the society in which he lived. Rousseau would have disapproved the main thrust of Adam Smith's *Wealth of Nations,* which he may or may not have read, and would no doubt have preferred a study on the virtue of nations. Smith wanted people to be prosperous; Rousseau wanted them to be good even if that meant that they might remain economically poor. He saw human beings not as independent individuals but as creatures enmeshed in necessary social relationships. He believed that loyalty to the community should be encouraged. As one device to that end he suggested a civic religion based on the creed of Deism. Such a shared tolerant religious faith would provide unity for the society. Rousseau's chief intellectual inspiration arose from his study of Plato and the ancient Greek *polis.* Especially in Sparta he thought he had discovered human beings dwelling in a moral society inspired by a common purpose. He hoped that modern human beings might also create such a moral commonwealth in which virtuous living would become subordinate to commercial profit.

Rousseau's thought had only a marginal impact on his own time. The other *philosophes* questioned his critique of material improvement. Aristocrats and royal ministers could hardly be expected to welcome his proposal for radical democracy. Too many people were either making or hoping to make money to pay attention to his criticism of commercial values. However, he proved to be a figure to whom later generations returned. Many leaders in the French Revolution were familiar with his writing. Thereafter his ideas were important for most writers who felt called upon to criticize the general tenor and direction of Western culture. Rousseau hated much about the emerging modern society in Europe, but he contributed much to modernity by exemplifying for later generations the critic who dared to call into question the very foundations of social thought and action. Whatever our opinions of Rousseau, we have not yet escaped him.

Enlightened Absolutism

Most of the *philosophes* favored neither Montesquieu's reformed and revived aristocracy nor Rousseau's democracy as a solution to contemporary political problems. Like other thoughtful people of the day in other stations and occupations, they looked to the existing monarchies. The *philosophes* hoped in particular that the French monarchy might assert really effective power over the aristocracy and the church to bring about significant reform. Voltaire was a very strong monarchist. He and others—such as Diderot, who visited Catherine II of Russia, and physiocrats who were ministers to the French kings—did not wish to limit the power of monarchs but sought to redirect that power toward the rationalization of economic and political structures and the liberation of intellectual life. Most *philosophes* were not opposed to power if they could find a way of using it for their own purposes.

During the last third of the century it seemed to some

observers that several European rulers had actually embraced many of the reforms set forth by the *philosophes*. *Enlightened absolutism* is the term used to describe this phenomenon. The phrase indicates monarchical government dedicated to the rational strengthening of the central absolutist administration at the cost of other lesser centers of political power. However, the monarchs most closely associated with it—Frederick II of Prussia, Joseph II of Austria, and Catherine II of Russia—were neither genuinely enlightened nor truly absolute in the exercise of royal power. Their enlightenment was a veneer, and their absolutism was limited by the realities of political and economic life. Frederick II corresponded with the *philosophes,* for a time provided Voltaire with a place at his court, and even wrote history and political tracts. Catherine II, who was a master of what would later be called public relations, consciously sought to create the image of being enlightened. She read the works of the *philosophes,* became a friend of Diderot and Voltaire, and made frequent references to their ideas, all in the hope that her nation might seem more modern and Western. Joseph II undertook a series of religious, legal, and social reforms that contemporaries believed he had derived from suggestions of the *philosophes.*

Despite such appearances the policies of these monarchs were directed by the requirements of state security and political ambition rather than by the humanitarian and liberating zeal of the Enlightenment. They sought the rational economic and social integration of their realms so that they could wage more efficient future wars—a policy profoundly hateful to the *philosophes.* All of the states of Europe had emerged from the Seven Year's War understanding that they would require stronger armed forces for the next conflict and looking for new sources of taxation to finance those armies. The search for new revenues and further internal political support for their rule led these eastern monarchs to make "enlightened" reforms. They and their advisors used rationality to further what the *philosophes* considered irrational militarism.

Frederick the Great of Prussia

After the mid-century wars, during which Prussia had suffered badly and had almost been defeated, Frederick II (1740–1786) hoped to achieve recovery and consolidation. At grave cost he had succeeded in retaining Silesia, which he had seized from Austria in 1740. He worked to stimulate its potential as a manufacturing district. Like his Hohenzollern forebears he continued to import workers from outside Prussia. He directed new attention to Prussian agriculture. Under state supervision, swamps were drained, new crops introduced, and peasants encouraged and sometimes compelled to migrate. For the first time in Prussia potatoes and turnips came into general production. Frederick established a Land-Mortgage Credit Association to aid landowners in raising money for agricultural improvements.

Throughout this process, the impetus for development came from the state. The monarchy and its bureaucracy were the engine for change. Despite new policies and personal exhortations the general populace of Prussia did not prosper under Frederick's reign. The burden of taxation still fell disproportionally on peasants and townspeople.

In less material areas Frederick pursued enlightened policies with somewhat more success. He allowed Catholics and Jews to settle in his predominately Lutheran country, and he protected the Catholics residing in Silesia. He ordered a new codification of Prussian law, which was completed after his death. The policy of toleration allowed foreign workers to contribute to the economic growth of the state. The new legal code was to rationalize the existing system, to make it more efficient, to eliminate regional peculiarities, and to eliminate excessive aristocratic influence. The enlightened monarchs were very concerned about legal reforms, primarily as a means of extending and strengthening royal power.

Frederick liked to describe himself as "the first servant of the State." That image represented an important change in the European conception of monarchy. The idea of an impersonal state was beginning to replace the concept of a personal monarchy. Kings might come and go, but the impersonal apparatus of government—the bureaucracy, the armies, the rational laws, the courts, and the citizens' loyalty arising from fear and from appreciation of state services and protection—remained. The state as an entity separate from the personality of the ruler came into its own after the French Revolution, but it was born in the monarchies of the old regime.

Joseph II of Austria

No eighteenth-century ruler so embodied rational, impersonal force as the emperor Joseph II of Austria. He was the son of Maria Theresa and co-ruler with her from 1765 to 1780. During the next ten years he ruled alone. He has been aptly described as "an imperial puritan and a good deal of a prig."[6] During much of his life he slept on straw and ate little but beef. He prided himself on a narrow, passionless rationality, which he sought to impose by his own will on the various Hapsburg domains. The ultimate result of his well-intentioned efforts was a series of aristocratic and peasant rebellions extending from Hungary to the Austrian Netherlands.

As explained in Chapter 21, of all the rising states of the eighteenth century Austria was the most diverse in its people and problems. Robert Palmer has likened it to a "a vast holding company."[7] The Hapsburgs never succeeded in creating either a unified administrative structure or strong aristocratic loyalty. The price of the preservation of the monarchy during the War of the Austrian Succession (1740–1748) had been guarantees of considerable aristocratic independence. Joseph sought to overcome the pluralism of his holdings by increasing the power of the central monarchy. He also wished to expand

6 R. J. White, *Europe in the Eighteenth Century* (New York: St. Martin's, 1965), p. 214.

7 Robert R. Palmer, *The Age of Democratic Revolution* (Princeton: Princeton University Press, 1959), Vol. 1, p. 103.

Joseph II of Austria Promotes Toleration in His Realm

Toleration was frequently an important policy of enlightened absolutism. As shown in this 1787 passage, Joseph II of Austria believed toleration would remove religious fanaticism from his realms, lead to greater human knowledge, and at the same time make his subjects more loyal.

Till *now the Protestant religion has been opposed in my states; its adherents have been treated like foreigners; civil rights, possession of estates, titles, and appointments, all were refused them.*

I determined from the very commencement of my reign to adorn my diadem with the love of my people, to act in the administration of affairs according to just, impartial, and liberal principles; consequently, I granted toleration, and removed the yoke which had oppressed the protestants for centuries.

Fanaticism shall in future be known in my states only by the contempt I have for it; nobody shall any longer be exposed to hardships on account of his creed; no man shall be compelled in future to profess the religion of the state, if it be contrary to his persuasion, and if he have other ideas of the right way of insuring blessedness. . . .

Tolerance is an effect of that beneficent increase of knowledge which now enlightens Europe, and which is owing to philosophy and the efforts of great men; it is a convincing proof of the improvement of the human mind, which has boldly reopened a road through the dominions of superstition, which was trodden centuries ago by Zoroaster and Confucius, and which, fortunately for mankind, has now become the highway of monarchs.

"Letters of Joseph II," *The Pamphleteer*, Vol. 19 (1822), pp. 289–290.

---

the borders of his territory in the direction of Poland and the Ottoman Empire.

The first target of Joseph's reassertion of royal absolutism was the church. From the reign of Charles V in the sixteenth century to that of Maria Theresa, the Hapsburgs had been the single most important dynastic champion of Roman Catholicism. Maria Theresa had surrounded herself with pious and sometimes very superstitious advisers. Joseph changed these policies. He was a practicing and perhaps even a believing Catholic, but he rid himself of priestly advisers. He extended genuine toleration to all Christians and relieved Jews living in

Emperor Joseph II of Austria encouraged improved farming and industry in his domains. This propaganda painting portrayed him plowing a field and providing a good example to his subjects. [Austrian Information Service, New York.]

Austria of many special taxes and signs of degradation. He sought to undermine in every possible way the influence of the papacy in his lands. He drove monks and nuns from monasteries and reduced the number of religious holidays. While encouraging the construction of churches, he confiscated ecclesiastical lands. He considered church use of that property unproductive. Revenues traditionally going to the church were redirected to the state. Priests in effect became the employees of the state. The influence of the Roman Catholic Church as an independent institution came to a close. Joseph was willing for religious faith and practice to flourish, but religious institutions and the people they employed must stand subordinate to the power of the government. In many respects the ecclesiastical policies of Joseph II prefigured those of the French Revolution.

Like Frederick of Prussia, Joseph sought to improve the economic life of his domains. He abolished many internal tariffs and encouraged road building and the improvement of river transport. He went on personal inspection tours of farms and manufacturing districts.

Joseph also reconstructed the judicial system to make laws more uniform and rational and to lessen the influence of local landlords. National courts with power over landlord courts were established. All of these improvements were expected to bring new unity to the state and more taxes into the coffers at Vienna.

The most revolutionary of Joseph's departures was his attitude toward serfdom and the land. The emperor believed that if the peasantry were legally free and to some extent liberated from the special feudal payments to landlords, they would become more productive and industrious. However, to interfere with the landlord–serf relationship was to breach what had been one of the foundation stones of eastern European absolutism: the tradeoff of aristocratic support for the monarchy in exchange for a free hand with the serfs.

In 1781, 1783, and 1785 Jospeh issued a series of decrees giving legal freedom to serfs in Bohemia, Austria, Transylvania, and Hungary. They could marry and migrate without the permission of their landlords and could appeal decisions from manorial courts to the civil courts of the state. Between 1783 and 1789 Joseph went even further and drew up a tax list on which all occupiers of land were enumerated. Henceforth, all proprietors of the land were to be taxed regardless of social status. In 1789 by royal decree the emperor abolished *robot* or services

Empress Catherine the Great of Russia, born Sophia Augusta Frederica in the tiny German state of Anhalt-Zerbst, cultivated the friendship of the *philosophes* but pursued many policies of which they disapproved, including warfare and censorship. The artist represented here is Boroviloosky. [John R. Freeman.]

due landlords from serfs. The service was commuted to a tax, only part of which went to the landlord while the remainder reverted to the state. These measures brought turmoil to the Hapsburg domains. Peasants revolted against their landlords over the interpretation of their newly granted rights. Then the nobles of the various realms also rose up in rebellion over the emperor's decrees.

Having sowed the wind, Joseph died in 1790. His brother and successor Leopold II (1790–1792) reaped the noble whirlwind. Although quite sympathetic with Joseph's goals, Leopold repealed most of the reformist decrees to shore up the stability of his own rule. Serfdom persisted in the Austrian lands until 1848. Joseph II had possessed a narrow vision attached to an unbending will. For all his intellectual brilliance and hard work, he had failed to understand that except for a few royal bureaucrats his policies enjoyed no supporters. He had ruled without consulting any political constituency. The nobles, the church, the towns with their chartered liberties, and the absence of a strong bureaucracy or army stood as barriers to his absolutism. His was a mind of classical rationalism in conflict with political and social realities of baroque complexity.

Catherine the Great of Russia

Joseph II never grasped the practical necessity of cultivating political support for his policies. Catherine II (1762–1796) who had been born a German princess but who became empress of Russia understood only too well the fragility of the Romanov dynasty's base of power.

After the death of Peter the Great in 1725 the Russian succession had repeatedly been determined by court nobles and the army. The crown fell primarily into the hands of people with little talent. Peter's wife, Catherine I, ruled for two years (1725–1727) and was succeeded for three years by Peter's grandson Peter II. In 1730 the crown devolved on Anna, who was a niece of Peter the Great. During 1740 and 1741 a child named Ivan VI, who was less than a year old, was the nominal

The overriding territorial aim of Peter the Great in the first quarter and of Catherine the Great in the last half of the eighteenth century was the securing of northern and southern navigable-water outlets for the vast Russian Empire. Hence Peter's push to the Baltic Sea and Catherine's to the Black Sea. Catherine also managed to acquire large areas of Poland through the partitions of that country. (See pages 588–589.)

RUSSIAN EMPIRE, 1689

TERRITORIES ADDED, 1725–1762

TERRITORIES ADDED UNDER PETER THE GREAT, 1689–1725

TERRITORIES ADDED UNDER CATHERINE THE GREAT, 1762–1796

500 MI.

500 KM.

EXPANSION OF RUSSIA, 1689–1796

ruler. Finally, in 1741 Peter the Great's daughter Elizabeth came to the throne. She held the title of empress until 1762, but she did not rule. Her court was a shambles of political and romantic intrigue. Needless to say, much of the power possessed by the tsar at the opening of the century had vanished.

At her death in 1762 Elizabeth was succeeded by Peter III, one of her nephews. He was a weak ruler whom many contemporaries considered mad. He immediately exempted the nobles from compulsory military service and then made rapid peace with Frederick the Great, for whom he held unbounded admiration. That decision probably saved Prussia from military defeat. The one positive feature of this unbalanced creature's life was his marriage in 1745 to a young German princess born in Pomerania. This was the future Catherine the Great, who for almost twenty years lived in misery and frequent danger at the court of Elizabeth. During that time she befriended important nobles and read widely in the books of the *philosophes*. She was a shrewd person whose experience in a court crawling with rumors, intrigue, and conspiracy had taught her how to survive. She had neither love nor loyalty for her demented husband. After a few months of rule Peter III was deposed and murdered with the approval, if not the aid, of Catherine. On his death she was immediately proclaimed empress.

Catherine's familiarity with the Enlightenment and the general culture of Western Europe convinced her that Russia was very backward and that it must make major reforms if it were to remain a great power. She understood that any major reform must have a wide base of political and social support. In 1767 she summoned a Legislative Commission to revise the law and government of Russia. There were over five hundred delegates from all sectors of Russian life. Prior to the convening of the Commission she issued a set of *Instructions* partly written by herself. They contained numerous ideas drawn from the political writings of the *philosophes*. The Commission considered the *Instructions* as well as other ideas and complaints raised by its members. The revision of Rus-

sian law, however, did not occur for more than a half-century. In 1768 Catherine simply dismissed the Commission, which had reached few concrete decisions. Yet the meeting had not been useless, for considerable information had been gathered about the condition of the realm. The inconclusive debates and the absence of programs from the delegates themselves suggested that most Russians saw no alternative to an autocratic monarchy. Catherine proceeded to carry out limited reforms on her own authority. She gave strong support to the rights and local power of the nobility. In 1775 she reorganized local government to solve problems brought to light by the Legislative Commission. She put most local offices into the hands of nobles rather than creating a royal bureaucracy. In 1785 Catherine issued the Charter of the Nobility, which guaranteed many noble rights and privileges. In part the empress had no choice but to favor the nobles. They had the capacity to topple her from the throne. There were too few educated subjects in her realm to establish an independent bureaucracy. The treasury could not afford an army strictly loyal to the crown. So Catherine wisely made a virtue of necessity. She strengthened the stability of her crown by making convenient friends with her nobles.

Part and parcel of Catherine's program was a continuation of the economic development commenced under Peter the Great. She attempted to suppress internal barriers to trade. Exports of grain, flax, furs, and naval stores grew dramatically. She also favored the expansion of the small Russian middle class. Russian trade required such a vital urban class. And through all of these departures Catherine attempted to maintain ties of friendship and correspondence with the *philosophes*. She knew that if she treated them kindly, they would be sufficiently flattered and would give her a progressive reputation throughout Europe.

The limited administrative reforms and the policy of economic growth had a counterpart in the diplomatic sphere. The Russian drive for warm-water ports continued. This goal required warfare with the Turks. In 1769, as a result of a minor Russian incursion, the Ottoman Empire declared war on Russia. The Russians responded in a series of strikingly successful military moves. During 1769 and 1770 the Russian fleet sailed all the way from the Baltic Sea into the eastern Mediterranean. The Russian army won several major victories that by 1771 gave Russia control of Ottoman provinces on the Danube River and the Crimean coast of the Black Sea. The conflict dragged on until 1774, when it was closed by the Treaty of Kuchuk–Kainardji. The treaty gave Russia a direct outlet on the Black Sea, free navigation rights in its waters, and free access through the Bosporus. Moreover, the province of the Crimea became an independent state, which Catherine painlessly annexed in 1783.

The Partition of Poland

These military successes obviously brought the empress much domestic political support. However, they made the other states of eastern Europe uneasy. These anxieties were overcome by an extraordinary division of Polish territory known as the First Partition of Poland. The Russian victories along the Danube River were most unwelcome to Austria, which also harbored ambitions for territorial expansion in that direction. At the same time, the Ottoman Empire was pressing Prussia for aid against Russia. Frederick the Great made a proposal to Russia and Austria that would give each something it wanted, prevent conflict among the powers, and save appearances. After long, complicated, secret negotiations the three powers agreed that Russia would abandon the conquered Danubian provinces. In compensation Russia received a large portion of Polish territory with almost two million inhabitants. As a reward for remaining neutral Prussia annexed most of the territory between East Prussia and Prussia proper. This land allowed Frederick to unite two previously separate sections of his realm. Finally, Austria took Galicia, with its important salt mines, and other Polish territory with over two and one-half million inhabitants. In September 1773 the helpless Polish aristocracy, paying the price for the maintenance of their internal liberties, ratified this seizure of their territory. The Polish state had lost approximately one third of its territory.

There were two additional partitions of Poland by Russia, Prussia, and Austria. These occurred in 1793 and 1795 and removed Poland from the map of Europe. Each time the great powers contended that they were saving themselves and by implication the rest of Europe from Polish anarchy. The fact of the matter was that the

FIRST PARTITION 1772   SECOND PARTITION 1793   THIRD PARTITION 1795

TO PRUSSIA

TO AUSTRIA

TO RUSSIA

PARTITIONS OF POLAND,
1772–1793–1795

The callous eradication of Poland from the map displayed eighteenth-century power politics at its most extreme. Poland, without strong central governmental institutions, fell victim to those states in central and eastern Europe that *had* developed such institutions.

This French engraving is a satirical comment on the first partition of Poland (1772) by Russia, Austria, and Prussia. The distressed monarch attempting to retain his crown is Stanislaus of Poland. Catherine of Russia, Joseph of Austria, and Frederick of Prussia point out their respective shares of the loot.

political weakness of Poland made the country and its resources a rich field for plunderous aggression. The last two partitions took place during the French Revolution. The three eastern absolute monarchies objected to certain reforms undertaken by Polish nobles for fear that even minor Polish reform might endanger the stability of their own societies.

The End of the Eighteenth Century in Eastern Europe

During the last quarter of the eighteenth century all three regimes based on enlightened absolutism had become more repressive. Frederick lived much removed from his people during his old age. The aristocracy, looking out for its own self-interest, filled the major Prussian military and administrative posts. As Joseph II confronted growing frustration and political unrest over his plans for restructuring the society of his realms, he used more and more censorship and secret police. Catherine the Great never fully recovered from the fears raised by Pugachev's rebellion. Once the French Revolution broke out in 1789, the Russian empress censored books based on Enlightenment thought and sent offensive authors into Siberian exile.

By the close of the century all three states were characterized by autocracy, censorship, increasingly downtrodden serf populations, grasping nobilities, and fear of change permeating all the ruling classes. These attitudes had come into existence prior to 1789, but the events in France froze those points of view for almost half a century. Paradoxically nowhere did the humanity and liberalism of the Enlightenment ultimately have a more difficult time surviving and entering the mainstream of life and thought than in those states that had experienced "enlightened" rulers.

Although the enlightened absolute monarchs lacked the humanity of the *philosophes,* they had embraced the Enlightenment spirit of innovation. They wanted to change the political, social, and economic structures of their realms. From the close of the Seven Years' War (1763) until the opening of the French Revolution in 1789, the monarchies of both western and eastern Europe had been the major forces working for significant institutional change. In every case they had stirred up considerable aristocratic and some popular resistance and resentment. George III of Britain for years fought with Parliament and lost the colonies of North America in the process. Frederick II of Prussia carried out his program of reform only because he accepted new aristocratic influence over the bureaucracy and army. Catherine II of Russia had come to terms with her nobility. Joseph II had left his domains in turmoil by imposing changes without consulting the nobility.

These monarchs pushed for innovations because of their desires for increased revenue. The same problem existed in France. There the royal drive for adequate fiscal resources also led to aristocratic rebellion. However, in France neither the monarchy nor the aristocracy could control the social and political forces unleashed by their quarrel.

SUGGESTED READINGS

C. Becker, *The Heavenly City of the Eighteenth Century Philosophers* (1932). An influential, but very controversial discussion.

P. P. Bernard, *Joseph II* (1968). A brief biography.

T. Bestermann, *Voltaire* (1969). A recent biography by the editor of Voltaire's letters.

E. Cassirer, *The Philosophy of the Enlightenment* (1951). A brilliant but difficult work by one of the great philosophers of the twentieth century.

G. R. Cragg, *The Church and the Age of Reason* (1961). A general survey of eighteenth-century religious life.

P. Fussell, *The Rhetorical World of Augustan Humanism* (1969). Examines English writers during the Enlightenment.

J. Gagliardo, *Enlightened Despotism* (1967). A discussion of the subject in its European context.

P. Gay, *The Enlightenment: An Interpretation,* 2 vols. (1966, 1969). The most important and far-reaching recent treatment.

P. Gay, *The Enlightenment: A Comprehensive Anthology* (1973). A large, well-edited set of documents.

L. Gershoy, *From Despotism to Revolution, 1763–1793* (1944). A sound treatment of the political background.

N. Hampson, *A Cultural History of the Enlightenment* (1969). A useful introduction.

P. Hazard, *The European Mind: The Critical Years, 1680–1715* (1935), and *European Thought in the Eighteenth Century from Montesquieu to Lessing* (1946). The two volumes portray the century as the turning point for the emergence of the modern mind in Europe.

L. Krieger, *Kings and Philosophers, 1689–1789* (1970). A survey that relates the social and political thought of the Enlightenment writers to their immediate political setting.

K. Martin, *French Liberal Thought in the Eighteenth Century,* rev. ed. (1954). Surveys the political ideas of the French *philosophes.*

R. R. PALMER, *Catholics and Unbelievers in Eighteenth Century France* (1939). A discussion of the opponents of the *philosophes*.

G. RITTER, *Frederick the Great* (trans. 1968). A useful biography.

R. O. ROCKFORD (Ed.), *Carl Becker's Heavenly City Revisited* (1958). Important essays qualifying Becker's thesis.

G. S. THOMSON, *Catherine the Great and the Expansion of Russia* (1947). A short study that sets Catherine in the arena of general European politics.

A. M. WILSON, *Diderot* (1972). A splendid biography of the person behind the project for the *Encyclopedia* and other major Enlightenment publications.

592

23
The French Revolution

IN THE spring of 1789 the long-festering conflict between the French monarchy and aristocracy erupted into a new political crisis. This dispute, unlike earlier ones, quickly outgrew the issues of its origins and produced the wider disruption of the French Revolution. The quarrel that began as a struggle between the most exclusive elements of the political nation soon involved all sectors of French society and eventually every major state in Europe. Before the turmoil settled, small-town provincial lawyers and Parisian street orators exercised more influence over the fate of the Continent than did aristocrats, royal ministers, or monarchs. Armies commanded by persons of low birth and filled by conscripted village youths emerged victorious over forces composed of professional soldiers and directed by officers of noble birth. The very existence of the Roman Catholic faith in France was challenged. Politically and socially neither France nor Europe would ever be quite the same after these events.

The Crisis of the French Monarchy

The French Revolution constituted one of the central turning points in modern European history, but it originated from the basic tensions and problems that characterized practically all late eighteenth-century states. From the Seven Years' War (1756–1763) onward, the French monarchy was unable to handle its finances on a sound basis. It emerged from the conflict both defeated and in debt. The French support of the American revolt against

This nineteenth-century relief from the Arch of Triumph in Paris represents the spirit of the "Marseillaise" and the militant height in 1792 of the French Revolution. In contrast to earlier sculpture, its heroes are not aristocrats or mercenary soldiers but the people themselves, in bits of heroic antique armor, prepared to fight for liberty. The sculptor was François Rude (1784–1855). [Bettmann Archive.]

Great Britain further deepened the financial difficulties of the government. On the eve of the revolution the interest and payments on the royal debt amounted to just over one half of the entire budget. The annual deficit was in the vicinity of 126 million livres. Given the economic vitality of the nation, this debt was neither overly large nor disproportionate to those of other European powers. The problem lay with the inability of the royal government to tap the wealth of the French nation through taxes to service and repay the debt. Paradoxically France was a rich nation with an impoverished government.

The debt was symptomatic of the failure of the eighteenth-century French monarchy to come to terms with the resurgent social and political power of the aristocracy. For twenty-five years after the Seven Years' War there was a standoff between them. The monarchy attempted to pursue a program somewhat resembling that associated with enlightened absolutism in eastern Europe. However, both Louis XV (1715–1774) and Louis XVI (1774–1792) lacked the character and resolution for such a departure. The moral corruption of the former and the indecision of the latter meant that the monarchy could not rally the French public to its side. Generally speaking, the aristocratic *parlements* won the battle for public opinion. Whenever the king's ministers attacked the privileges or wealth of the nobility, the *parlements* represented themselves as the protectors of French liberty against the intrusion of absolute monarchical power.

In place of a consistent policy to deal with the growing debt, the monarchy gave way to hesitancy, retreat, and even duplicity. In 1763 the monarchy issued a new set of tax decrees that would have extended the collection of certain taxes that were supposed to have been discontinued at the close of the war. There were also new tax assessments. This search for revenue was not unlike the one that led the British government to attempt to tax the American colonies. Several of the provincial *parlements* and finally the Parlement of Paris—all controlled by nobles—declared the taxes illegal. During the ensuing dispute the aristocratic *parlements* set themselves up as the

Louis XVI of France (1774–1792) was unable to regain control of the political situation in France after the summer of 1789. The drawing is by Ducreux. [French Cultural Services, New York.]

spokesmen of the nation against the illegal assertion of monarchical power. Such was one of the political functions of the nobility that Montesquieu had outlined in *The Spirit of the Laws* (1748).

In 1770 Louis XV appointed René Maupeou (1714–1792) as chancellor. The new minister was determined to break the *parlements* and impose a greater part of the tax burden on the nobility. He abolished the *parlements* and exiled their members to different parts of the country. He then commenced an ambitious program of reform and efficiency. What ultimately doomed Maupeou's policy was less the resistance of the nobility than the death of Louis XV in 1774. His successor, Louis XVI, in an attempt to regain what he conceived to be popular support, restored all the *parlements* and confirmed their old powers. This action in conjunction with the later aid to the American colonies locked the monarchy into a continuing financial bind. Thereafter meaningful fiscal or political reform through existing institutions was probably doomed.

Louis XVI's first minister was the physiocrat Jacques Turgot (1727–1781), who attempted various economic reforms, including the removal of restrictions on the grain trade and the abolishment of the guilds. He transformed the *corvée* or road-working obligation of peasants into money payments. Turgot also intended to restructure the taxation system in order to tap the wealth of the nobility. These and other ideas represented a program of bold new departures for the monarchy. They proved too bold for the tremulous young king, who dismissed Turgot in 1776. By 1781 the debt, as a result of the aid to America, was larger and the sources of revenues unchanged. However, the new finance minister, Jacques Necker (1732–1804), a Swiss banker, produced a public report which suggested that the situation was not so bad as feared. He argued that if the expenditures for the American war were removed, the budget was in surplus. Soon after issuing this optimistic document, Necker left office. His financial sleight of hand made it more difficult for later ministers to claim the need for new taxes.

The Parlement *of Paris Makes Claims to Political Power*

The *Parlement* of Paris was a judicial court dominated by the French nobility. From the mid-eighteenth century until the French Revolution this court attempted to assert its power as a curb on the power of the monarchy. In this 1755 document, the Parlement argues that from time immemorial monarchs submitted their laws for the approval of the court and that stability and political harmony resulted. The Parlement has to appeal to very early times because under Louis XIV it had lost much power.

SIRE, *the monarchy has existed thirteen centuries. For thirteen centuries your* Parlement, *under whatever name it has been known by, always constituted the same tribunal and exercised the same functions in the State. Its administration, in regard to the management of the laws, has never ceased to be the same up to this moment. It has always preserved the glorious benefit of being the true Court of France because it was born with the empire of the French to be a branch of the essential pattern of government.*

. . . .

It is in accordance with this view, sire, that in order to enlighten and moderate the absolute power of sovereignty by the prudence of advisers, our monarchs in the past have always wisely granted their first magistrates [that is, the Parlement] *the right to check the possible extravagance of one man [that is, the monarch] against the fairness of princes [that is, the nobles of the* Parlement]. *Monarchs have perceived, they have recognized, that such ministers of their authority serve only to make monarchs rule justly and to win more and more people over to them.*

And what advantages have resulted, sire, from the birth of the monarchy to this day, from the happy mixture of sovereignty and prudence and from that wise moderation of one by the other? Constant and essential harmony as ancient as the French Empire and to which it is indebted for its progress and grandeur. Harmony is the principle and the pledge of the Empire's preservation. Harmony maintains authority without effort and assures sovereignty by justice.

Remonstrances du Parlement de Paris au XVIIIe Siècle, ed. by J. Flamermont. (Paris, 1898), Vol. 2, pp. 26, 86–87, cited in John Lough, *An Introduction to Eighteenth-Century France* (New York: David MacKay Company, 1964), pp. 174–175 (passage translated by Frank M. Turner).

Queen Marie Antoinette (1755–1793) was the daughter of Empress Maria Theresa of Austria and the wife of Louis XVI. Around her gathered many of the popularly believed unfavorable stories of the French court. The painting is by Elisabeth Vigée-Lebrun (1755–1842). [The Granger Collection.]

The monarchy hobbled along until 1786. By this time Charles Alexandre de Calonne (1734–1802) was the minister of finance. He was probably the most able administrator to serve Louis XVI. More carefully than previous ministers he charted the size of the debt and the deficit. He submitted a program for reform quite similar to that presented by Turgot a decade earlier. Calonne proposed to encourage internal trade, to lower some taxes such as the *gabelle* on salt, and to transform peasants' services to money payments.

More important, Calonne urged the introduction of a new land tax that would require payments from all landowners regardless of their social status. If this tax could be imposed, the monarchy would be able to abandon other indirect taxes. The government would also rarely have to seek approval for further new taxes from the aristocratically dominated *parlements*. Calonne also intended to establish new local assemblies to approve land taxes in which voting power would depend upon the amount of land owned rather than upon the social status of the owner. All of these proposals would have undermined both the political and the social power of the French aristocracy.

A new clash with the nobility was unavoidable, but the monarchy had very little room for maneuver. The creditors were at the door, and the treasury was nearly empty. Consequently, in 1787 Calonne met with an Assembly of Notables drawn from the upper ranks of the aristocracy and the church to seek support and approval for his plan. The assembly adamantly refused any such action. Rather

they demanded that the aristocracy be allowed a greater share in the government of the kingdom. They also called for the reappointment of Necker, whom they believed had left the country in sound fiscal condition. Finally, they demanded the convocation of the ancient Estates-General of France, which had not met since 1614.

Again Louis XVI backed off. He dismissed Calonne and replaced him with Étienne Charles Loménie de Brienne (1727–1794), who was archbishop of Toulouse and the chief opponent of Calonne at the Assembly of Notables. Once in office Brienne found to his astonishment that the situation was as bad as his predecessor had asserted. Brienne himself now sought to impose the land tax. However, the Parlement of Paris took the new position that it lacked authority to authorize the tax and said that only the Estates-General could do so. Shortly thereafter Brienne appealed to the Assembly of the

In the parks of the palace of Versailles was built an idealized farm village for Queen Marie Antoinette. There she and her friends could go to pretend for an afternoon that they were shepherds and milkmaids. Such extravagance was one of the reasons for resentment of the monarchy. This is a recent photograph of her restored hamlet. [The Granger Collection.]

The Crisis of the French Monarchy 595

Clergy to approve a large subsidy to allow funding of that part of the debt then coming due for payment. The clergy, like the Parlement dominated by aristocrats, not only refused the subsidy, but also reduced their existing contribution or *don gratuit* to the government. As these unfruitful negotiations were transpiring at the center of political life, local aristocratic *parlements* and estates in the provinces were demanding restoration of the privileges they had enjoyed during the early seventeenth century before Richelieu and Louis XIV had crushed their independent power. Consequently, in July 1788 the king, through Brienne, agreed to convoke the Estates-General the next year. Brienne resigned and was replaced by Necker. The institutions of the aristocracy and to a lesser degree of the church had brought the French monarchy to its knees. In the country of its origin, royal absolutism had been defeated.

The Revolutions of 1789
The Estates-General Becomes the National Assembly

The aristocratic triumph proved to be quite brief. It unloosed social and political forces that neither the nobles nor the monarchy could control. The new difficulties arose from clashes among the groups represented in the Estates-General. The body was composed of three divisions: the First Estate of the clergy, the Second Estate of the nobility, and the Third Estate, which represented everyone else in the kingdom. During the widespread public discussions preceding the meeting of the Estates-General, it became clear that the Third Estate, which included all the professional, commercial, and middle-class groups of the country, would not permit the monarchy and the aristocracy to decide the future course of the nation. Their spirit was best displayed in a pamphlet published during 1789 in which the Abbé Sieyès (1748–1836) declared, "What is the Third Estate? Everything. What has it been in the political order up to

1789

May 5	The Estates General opens at Versailles.
June 17	The Third Estate declares itself the National Assembly.
June 20	The National Assembly takes the Tennis Court Oath.
July 14	Fall of the Bastille in the city of Paris.
Late July	The Great Fear spreads in the countryside.
August 4	The nobles surrender their feudal rights in a meeting of the National Assembly.
August 27	Declaration of the Rights of Man and Citizen.
October 5–6	Parisian women march to Versailles and force Louis XVI and his family to return to Paris.

1790

July 12	Civil Constitution of the Clergy adopted.
July 14	A new constitution is accepted by the king.

1791

June 20–25	Louis XVI and his family attempt to flee France and are stopped at Varennes.
August 27	The Declaration of Pillnitz.
October 1	The Legislative Assembly meets.

1792

April 20	France declares war against Austria.
August 10	The Tuileries palace is stormed, and Louis XVI takes refuge with the Legislative Assembly.
September 2–7	The September Massacres.
September 20	France wins the battle of Valmy.
September 21	The Convention meets, and the monarchy is abolished.

1793

January 21	Louis XVI is executed.
February 1	France declares war against Great Britain.
March	Counterrevolution breaks out in the Vendée.
April	The Committee of Public Safety is formed.

The Estates-General opened at Versailles in 1789 with much pomp and splendor. In the old French print shown here, Louis XVI is on the throne. The First Estate, the clergy, is at the left; the Second Estate, the nobility, sits at the upper right; and the more numerous Third Estate, dressed in black suits and capes, sits at the lower right. [Culver Pictures.]

June 22	The Constitution of 1793 is adopted but not put into operation.
July	Robespierre enters the Committee of Public Safety.
August 23	*Levée en masse* proclaimed.
September 17	Maximum prices set on food and other commodities.
October 16	Queen Marie Antoinette is executed.
November 10	Worship of God is abolished, and the Cult of Reason is proclaimed.
	The revolutionary calendar beginning on September 22, 1792 is adopted.

1794

March 24	Execution of the Hébertist leaders of the *sans-culottes*.
April 6	Execution of Danton.
June 8	Robespierre leads the celebration of the Festival of the Supreme Being.
June 10	The Law of 22 Prairial is adopted.
July 27	The ninth of Thermidor and the fall of Robespierre.
July 28	Robespierre is executed.

1795

| August 22 | The Constitution of 1795 is adopted establishing the Directory. |

the present? Nothing. What does it ask? To become something."[1]

The split between the aristocracy and the Third Estate occurred before the Estates-General gathered. Debate over the proper organization of the body drew the lines of basic disagreement. Members of the aristocracy demanded an equal number of representatives for each estate. In September 1788 the Parlement of Paris ruled that voting in the Estates-General should be conducted by order rather than by head, that is, that each estate, or order, should have one vote, rather than that each member should have one vote. That procedure would ensure that the aristocratic First and Second Estates could always outvote the Third. Both moves on the part of the aristocracy unmasked its alleged concern for French liberty and exposed it as a group determined to maintain its privileges. After much public debate and private consultation, however, Louis XVI announced that the Third Estate would elect twice as many representatives as either the nobles or the clergy. This so-called doubling of the Third meant that the Third Estate could easily dominate the

1 Quoted in Leo Gershoy, *The French Revolution and Napoleon* (New York: Appleton, Century, Crofts, 1964), p. 102.

This well-known painting by Jacques Louis David (1748–1825) portrays the Tennis Court Oath, June 20. The emotion of the scene should be compared with the calm shown in the previous picture of the opening of the Estates-General. In the center foreground are members of *different* Estates joining hands in cooperation as equals. The presiding officer leading the oath is Jean Sylvain Bailly, soon to become mayor in a reorganized government of the city of Paris. The painting is in the Musée Carnavalet in Paris. [French Embassy Press and Information Division, New York.]

Estates-General if voting were allowed by head rather than by order. It was properly assumed that some liberal nobles and clergy would support the Third Estate. The method of voting was not settled until after the Estates-General gathered at Versailles in May 1789.

When the representatives came to the royal palace, they brought with them *cahiers*, or lists of grievances, registered by the local electors and to be presented to the king. Large numbers of these have survived to provide considerable information about the state of the country on the eve of the revolution. But those complaints could not be discussed until the questions of organization and voting had been decided. From the beginning, the Third Estate, whose members consisted largely of local officials, professional men, and lawyers, refused to sit as a separate order as the king desired. For several weeks there was a standoff. Then on June 1 the Third Estate invited the clergy and the nobles to join them in organizing a new legislative body. A few members of the lower clergy did so. On June 17 that body declared itself the National Assembly.

Three days later, locked out of their usual meeting place, the National Assembly moved to a nearby tennis court, where its members made an oath to continue to sit until they had given France a constitution. This was the famous "Tennis Court Oath." Louis XVI ordered the National Assembly to desist from their actions, but shortly afterward a majority of the clergy and a large group of nobles joined the Assembly. On June 27 the king capitulated and formally requested the First and Second Estates to meet with the National Assembly. Had

The fall of the Bastille on July 14, 1789 is recreated, possibly a bit romantically, in an early nineteenth-century French engraving. [The Granger Collection.]

nothing further occurred, the government of France would have been transformed. Government by privileged orders had come to an end. For the National Assembly, which renamed itself the National Constituent Assembly, was composed of persons from all three orders who possessed shared liberal goals for the administrative, constitutional, and economic reform of the country.

Fall of the Bastille

Two new factors soon intruded upon the scene. The first was Louis XVI himself, who attempted to regain the initiative by mustering royal troops in the vicinity of Versailles and Paris. It appeared that he might be contemplating the disruption of the National Constituent Assembly. Such was the advice of Queen Marie Antoinette, his brothers, and the most conservative nobles, with whom he had begun to consult. On July 11, without consultation with the Assembly leaders, Louis abruptly dismissed Necker. These actions marked the beginning of a steady, but consistently poorly executed, royal attempt to undermine the Assembly and halt the revolution. Most of the Constituent Assembly wished to create some form of constitutional monarchy, but from the start that effort was thwarted by Louis's refusal to cooperate. The king fatally decided to throw his lot in with the aristocracy against the nation.

The second new factor to impose itself on the events at Versailles was the populace of Paris. The mustering of royal troops created anxiety in the city, where throughout the winter and spring of 1789 there had been several riots. The Parisians who had elected their representatives to the Third Estate had continued to meet after the elections. By June they were organizing a citizen militia and collecting arms. They regarded the dismissal of Necker as the opening of a royal offensive against the National Constituent Assembly and the city. On July 14 somewhat over eight hundred people, most of whom were small shopkeepers, tradesmen, craftsmen, and wage earners, marched to the Bastille in search of weapons for the militia. This great fortress, with ten-foot-thick walls, had once held political prisoners. Through miscalculations and ineptitude on the part of the governor of the fortress, the troops in the Bastille fired into the crowd, killing ninety-eight people and wounding many others. Thereafter the crowd stormed the fortress and eventually gained entrance. They released the seven prisoners, none of whom were there for political reasons, and killed several troops and the governor. They found no weapons.

The attack on the Bastille marked the first of many crucial *journées*, or days, when the populace of Paris would redirect the course of the revolution. The fall of the fortress signaled that the political future of the nation would not be decided solely by the National Constituent Assembly. As the news of the Bastille spread, similar disturbances took place in the provincial cities. A few days later Louis XVI again bowed to the force of events and went to Paris, where he wore the revolutionary cockade and recognized the organized electors as the legitimate government of the city. The king also recognized the citizen militia, which under the command of Lafayette became the National Guard. The citizens of Paris were for the time being satisfied.

The Great Fear and the Surrender of Feudal Privileges

Simultaneous with the popular urban disturbances a movement known as the Great Fear swept across much of the French countryside. Rumors had spread that royal troops would be sent into the rural districts. The result was an intensification of peasant disturbances that had begun earlier during the spring. The Great Fear witnessed the burning of chateaux, the destruction of records and documents, and the refusal to pay feudal dues. The peasants were determined to take possession of food supplies and land that they considered to be rightfully theirs. They were reclaiming rights and property that they had lost through the aristocratic resurgence of the last quarter-century, as well as venting their general anger against the injustices of rural life.

The National Assembly Decrees Civic Equality in France

These famous decrees of August 4, 1789 in effect created civic equality in France. The special privileges previously possessed or controlled by the nobility were removed.

1. The National Assembly completely abolishes the feudal regime. It decrees that, among the rights and dues . . . all those originating in real or personal serfdom, personal servitude, and those which represent them, are abolished without indemnification; all others are declared redeemable, and that the price and mode of redemption shall be fixed by the National Assembly. . . .

2. The exclusive right to maintain pigeon-houses and dove-cotes is abolished. . . .

3. The exclusive right to hunt and to maintain unenclosed warrens is likewise abolished. . . .

4. All manorial courts are suppressed without indemnification. . . .

5. Tithes of every description and the dues which have been substituted for them . . . are abolished, on condition, however, that some other method be devised to provide for the expenses of divine worship, the support of the officiating clergy, the relief of the poor, repairs and rebuilding of churches and parsonages, and for all establishments, seminaries, schools, academies, asylums, communities, and other institutions, for the maintenance of which they are actually devoted. . . .

. . . .

7. The sale of judicial and municipal offices shall be suppressed forthwith. . . .

8. Pecuniary privileges, personal or real, in the payment of taxes are abolished forever. . . .

. . . .

11. All citizens, without distinction of birth, are eligible to any office or dignity, whether ecclesiastical, civil or military. . . .

Frank Maloy Anderson (Ed. and Trans.), *The Constitutions and Other Select Documents Illustrative of the History of France, 1789–1907*, 2nd ed., rev. and enlarged (Minneapolis: The H. W. Wilson Company, 1908), pp. 11–13.

On the night of August 4, 1789, aristocrats in the National Constituent Assembly attempted to halt the spreading disorder in the countryside. By prearrangement a number of liberal nobles and churchmen rose in the Assembly and renounced their feudal rights, dues, and tithes. In a scene of great emotion, hunting and fishing rights, judicial authority, and special exemptions were surrendered. In a sense these nobles gave up what they had already lost and what could not be regained without civil war in the rural areas. They would also in many cases receive compensation for their losses. Nonetheless, after the night of August 4 all Frenchmen were subject to the same and equal laws. That dramatic session of the Assembly paved the way for the legal and social reconstruction of the nation. Without those renunciations the constructive work of the National Constituent Assembly would have been much more difficult.

Both the attack on the Bastille and the Great Fear displayed varieties of rural and urban riots that had characterized much of eighteenth-century political and social life. Louis XVI first thought that the turmoil over the Bastille was simply another bread riot. The popular disturbances also were only partly related to the events at Versailles. A deep economic downturn had struck France during 1788 and had continued into 1789. The harvests for both years had been poor, and food prices in 1789 stood higher than at any time since 1703. Wages had not kept up with the rise in prices. Throughout the winter of 1788–1789, an unusually cold one, many people suffered from hunger. Several cities had experienced wage and food riots. These economic difficulties helped the revolution reach such vast proportions. The political, social, and economic grievances of numerous sections of the country became combined. The National Constituent Assembly could look to the popular forces as a source of strength against the king and the conservative aristocrats. As the various elements of the Assembly later fell into quarrels among themselves, their factions succumbed to the temptation of appealing to the politically sophisticated and well-organized shopkeeping and artisan classes for support. When this turn of events came to pass, the popular classes could demand a price for their cooperation.

The Declaration of the Rights of Man and Citizen

During late August 1789 the National Constituent Assembly decided that prior to the writing of a new constitution a statement of broad principles should be set forth. This task was accomplished on August 27 in the Declaration of the Rights of Man and Citizen. The declaration drew together much of the political language of the Enlightenment and was also influenced by the Declaration of Rights adopted by Virginia in America in June 1776. The French declaration proclaimed that all men were "born and remain free and equal in rights." The natural rights of men and citizens were "liberty, property, security, and resistence to oppression." Governments existed to protect those rights. All political sovereignty resided in the nation and its representatives. All citizens were to be equal before the law and were to be "equally admissible to all public dignities, offices and employments, according to their capacity, and with no other distinction than that of their virtues and talents." There were to be due process of law and presumption of innocence until proof of guilt. Freedom of religion was affirmed. Taxation was to be apportioned equally according to capacity to pay. Property constituted "an inviolable and sacred right."[2] Although these statements were rather abstract, practically all of them were directed against specific abuses of the old aristocratic and absolutist regime. If any two principles of the future governed the declaration, they were civic equality and protection of property. The Declaration of the Rights of Man and Citizen has often been considered the death certificate of the old regime.

Louis XVI stalled before ratifying both the declaration and the aristocratic renunciation of feudalism. The longer he hesitated, the larger existing suspicions grew that he might again try to resort to the use of troops. Moreover bread continued to be in short supply. On October 5 a large crowd of Parisian women marched to Versailles demanding more bread. They milled about the palace, and many stayed the night. Under this pressure the king agreed to sanction the decrees of the Assembly. The next day he and his family appeared on a balcony before the

2 Quoted in Georges Lefebvre, *The Coming of the French Revolution*, trans. by R. R. Palmer (Princeton, N.J.: Princeton University Press, 1967), pp. 221–223.

crowd. Finally, to satisfy the demands of the women, the monarch left Versailles for the last time and rode with his family to Paris, where they settled in the Tuileries Palace. The National Constituent Assembly soon followed. Thereafter both Paris and France remained relatively stable and peaceful until the summer of 1792.

An unknown contemporary German depicted the march of the women of Paris on the palace of Versailles in October 1789. On their return to the city they were accompanied by Louis XVI and his family. [The Granger Collection.]

The Reconstruction of France

Once established in Paris, the National Constituent Assembly set about reorganizing France. In government it pursued a policy of constitutional monarchy; in administration, rationalism; in economics, unregulated freedom; and in religion, anticlericalism. Throughout its proceedings the Assembly was determined to protect property and to limit the impact upon national life of the unpropertied elements of the nation and even of possessors of small amounts of property. While championing civic equality before the law, the Assembly spurned social equality and extensive democracy. In all these areas the Assembly charted a general course that to a greater or lesser degree nineteenth-century liberals across Europe would follow.

Political Reorganization

The Constitution of 1791, which was the product of the National Constituent Assembly's deliberations, established a constitutional monarchy. There was to be a unicameral Legislative Assembly in which all laws would originate and in which the major political authority of the

nation would reside. The monarch was allowed a suspensive veto that could delay but not halt legislation. Powers of war and peace were vested in the Assembly. The constitution provided for an elaborate system of indirect elections intended to thwart direct popular pressure on the government. The citizens of France were divided into active and passive categories. Only active citizens—that is, men paying annual taxes equal to three days of local labor wages—could vote. They chose electors who then in turn voted for the members of the legislature. At the levels of electors or members still further property qualifications were imposed. Only about fifty thousand citizens of a population of about twenty-five million could qualify as electors or members of the Legislative Assembly.

In reconstructing the local and judicial administration, the National Constituent Assembly applied the rational spirit of the Enlightenment. It abolished the ancient French provinces, such as Burgundy and Brittany, and established in their place eighty-three departments (*départements*) of generally equal size named after rivers, mountains, and other geographical features. The departments in turn were subdivided into districts, cantons, and communes. Most local elections were also indirect. The

ENGLAND

PAS-
DE-
CALAIS
NORD
SOMME
AISNE
ARDENNES
MEUSE
MOSELLE
MEURTHE
BAS
RHIN
SEINE
INFÉRIEURE
OISE
MARNE
HAUTE
MARNE
VOSGES
HAUT
RHIN
Paris
SEINE-
ET-
MARNE
AUBE
HAUTE
SAÔNE
MANCHE
CALVADOS
EURE
SEINE-
ET-
OISE
EURE-
ET-
LOIRE
ORNE
LOIRET
YONNE
CÔTE-
D'OR
DOUBS
JURA
LOIRE-
ET-
CHER
NIÈVRE
SAÔNE-
ET-
LOIRE
FINISTERRE
CÔTES-
DU-NORD
ILLE-ET-
VILAINE
MAYENNE
SARTHE
CHER
ALLIER
RHÔNE
AIN
MORBIHAN
INF-LOIRE
INFÉRIEURE
MAINE-
ET-
LOIRE
INDRE-
ET-
LOIRE
INDRE
CREUSE
PUY-
DE-
DÔME
LOIRE
ISÈRE
HAUTES
ALPES
FRENCH
DEPARTMENTS
AFTER
1789
VENDÉE
DEUX-
SÈVRES
VIENNE
HAUTE
VIENNE
CORRÈZE
CANTAL
HAUTE
LOIRE
ADRÈCHE
DRÔME
BASSES
ALPES
CHARENTE
INFÉRIEURE
CHARENTE
LOZÈRE
VAUCLUSE
VAR
DORDOGNE
LOT
AVEYRON
GARD
BOUCHES-
DU-RHÔNE
100 MI.
100 KM.
GIRONDE
LOT-ET-
GARONNE
TARN-ET-
GARONNE
TARN
HÉRAULT
LANDES
GERS
HAUTE
GARONNE
AUDE
GOLO
LIAMONE
BASSES
PYRÉNÉES
HAUTES
PYRÉNÉES
ARIÈGE
PYRÉNÉES
ORIENTALES

ENGLAND

FLANDERS
AND
HAINAUT
ARTOIS
PICARDY
METZ
AND
VERDUN
TOUL AND
LORRAINE
ALSACE
ISLE DE FRANCE
Paris
CHAMPAGNE
AND
BRIE
FRANCHE
COMTE
NORMANDIE
ORLÉANAIS
NIVERNAIS
BURGUNDY
BRETAGNE
MAINE
ANJOU
TOURAINE
BERRY
BOURBONNAIS
LYONNAIS
DAUPHINÉ
SAUMU-
ROIS
POITOU
MARCHE
LIMOUSIN
AUVERGNE
AUNIS
SAINTONGE AND
ANGOUMOIS
PROVENCE
GUIENNE
AND
GASCONY
LANGUEDOC
FRENCH
PROVINCES
BEFORE
1789
BEARN
FOIX
ROUSSILLON
CORSICA

FIRST
FRENCH
REPUBLIC,
1792-1799

PRUSSIA
BATAVIAN
REP.
Cologne
ENGLAND
Antwerp
Strasbourg
HELVETIAN REP. 1792-1799
AUSTRIA
Amiens
Lunéville
CISALPINE REP.
Paris
ETRURIAN
REP.
FRANCE
Marengo
ROMAN
REP.
Lyons
Avignon
Toulon
LIGURIAN
REP.
ITALY
PARTHENOPEAN
REP.
SPAIN

FRENCH
REPUBLIC,
1792
ANNEXATIONS
IN 1795
INDEPENDENT
REPUBLICS,
1799

200 MI.
200 KM.

The *assignats* were government bonds that were backed by confiscated church lands. They circulated as money. When the government printed too many of them, inflation resulted and their value fell. [Bettmann Archive.]

departmental reconstruction proved one of the most permanent achievements of the Assembly. The departments exist to the present day. All of the ancient judicial courts, including the seigneurial courts and the *parlements,* were also abolished. In their place were organized uniform courts with elected judges and prosecutors. Procedures were simplified, and the most degrading punishments were removed from the books.

Economic Policy

In economic matters the Assembly continued the policies attempted by Louis XVI's reformist ministers. The suppression of the guilds and the liberation of the grain trade were supported. The metric system was established to provide the nation with uniform weights and measures. These policies of economic freedom and uniformity disappointed both peasants and urban workers caught in the cycle of inflation. By decrees of 1790 the Assembly placed the burden of proof on the peasants to rid themselves of residual feudal dues for which compensation was to be paid. On June 14, 1791, the Assembly crushed the attempts of urban workers to protect their wages by enacting the Chapelier Law, which forbade worker associations. Peasants and workers were to be left to the freedom and mercy of the marketplace.

While these various reforms were put into effect, the original financial crisis that had occasioned the calling of the Estates-General persisted. The royal debt was not repudiated because it was owed to the bankers, the merchants, and the commercial traders of the Third Estate. The National Constituent Assembly had suppressed many of the old hated indirect taxes and had substituted new land taxes, but these proved insufficient. Moreover there were not enough officials to collect them. The continuing financial problem led the Assembly to take what may well have been for the future of French life and society its most decisive action. The Assembly decided to finance the debt by confiscating and then selling the land and property of the Roman Catholic Church in France. The results were further inflation, religious schism, and civil war. In effect, the National Constituent Assembly opened a new chapter in the relations of church and state in Europe.

Having chosen to plunder the land of the church, the Assembly in December 1790 authorized the issuance of *assignats,* or government bonds, the value of which was guaranteed by the revenue to be generated from the sale of church property. Initially a limit was set on the quantity of *assignats* to be issued. However, the bonds proved so acceptable to the public that they began to circulate as currency. The Assembly decided to issue an ever larger number of them to liquidate the national debt and to create a large body of new property owners with a direct stake in the revolution. However, within a few months the value of the *assignats* began to fall. Inflation increased and put new stress on the lives of the urban poor.

The Civil Constitution of the Clergy

The confiscation of church lands required an ecclesiastical reconstruction. In July 1790 the National Constituent Assembly issued the Civil Constitution of the Clergy, which transformed the Roman Catholic Church in France into a branch of the secular state. The number of bishoprics was reduced from 135 to 83, and the borders of the dioceses were brought into conformity with those of the new departments. Priests and bishops were to be elected and were henceforth regarded as salaried employees of the state. Neither the pope nor the clergy of France were consulted about these broad changes. The king approved the measure only with the greatest reluctance.

The Civil Constitution of the Clergy was the major blunder of the National Constituent Assembly. The measure created immense opposition within the French

Here, as seen by a contemporary Dutchman, Louis XVI and his family are being led back to Paris by armed escort after their attempt to flee France in June 1791 was foiled near Varennes. [The Granger Collection.]

church even from bishops who had long championed Gallican liberties over papal domination. In the face of this resistance, the assembly unwisely ruled that all clergy must take an oath to support the Civil Constitution. Only seven bishops and about half the regular clergy did so. In reprisal the Assembly designated the clergy who had not taken the oath as "refractory" and removed them from their clerical functions.

Further reaction was swift. Refractory priests attempted to celebrate mass. In February 1791 the pope condemned not only the Civil Constitution of the Clergy but also the Declaration of the Rights of Man and Citizen. That condemnation marked the opening of a Roman Catholic offensive against the revolution and liberalism that continued throughout the nineteenth century. Within France itself the pope's action created a crisis of conscience and political loyalty for all sincere Catholics. Religious devotion and revolutionary loyalty became incompatible for many people. French citizens were divided between those who supported the constitutional priests and those who resorted to refractory clergy. Louis XVI and his family favored the latter.

Counterrevolutionary Activity

The revolution had other enemies besides the pope and devout Catholics. As it became clear that the old political and social order was undergoing fundamental and probably permanent change, considerable numbers of aristocrats left France. Known as the *émigrés,* they settled in countries near the French border, where they sought to foment counterrevolution. Among the most important of their number was the king's younger brother, the Count of Artois (1757–1836). In the summer of 1791 he and the queen persuaded Louis XVI to attempt to flee the country. On the night of June 20, 1791, Louis and his immediate family, disguised as servants, left Paris. They traveled as far as Varennes on their way to Metz. At Varennes the king was recognized, and his flight was halted. On June 24 a company of soldiers escorted the royal family back to Paris. The leaders of the National Constituent Assembly, determined to save the constitutional monarchy, announced that the king had been abducted from the capital. However, such a convenient public fiction could not cloak the reality that the chief counterrevolutionary in France sat on the throne.

Two months later, on August 27, 1791, under pressure from a group of *émigrés,* Emperor Leopold II of Austria, who was the brother of Marie Antoinette, and Frederick William II the king of Prussia, issued the Declaration of Pillnitz. The two monarchs promised to intervene in

France to protect the royal family and to preserve the monarchy *if* the other major European powers agreed. The latter provision rendered the statement meaningless because at the time Great Britain would not have given its consent. However, the declaration was not so read in France, where the revolutionaries saw the nation surrounded by aristocratic and monarchical foes.

The National Constituent Assembly drew to a close in September 1791. Its task of restructuring the government and administration of France had been completed. One of its last acts was the passage of a measure disallowing any of its own members to sit in the Legislative Assembly then being elected. The new body met on October 1 and had to confront the immense problems that had emerged during the earlier part of the year. Within the Legislative Assembly there also soon developed a major political divisions about the future course of the nation and the revolution.

A Second Revolution

End of the Monarchy

The issues of the Civil Constitution of the Clergy and the trustworthiness of Louis XVI undermined the unity of the revolution. Much factionalism displayed itself throughout the short life of the Legislative Assembly (1791–1792). Ever since the original gathering of the Estates-General, deputies from the Third Estate had organized themselves into clubs composed of politically like-minded persons. The most famous and best organized of these were the Jacobins, whose name derived from the fact that Dominican friars were called Jacobins, and the group met in a Dominican monastery in Paris. The Jacobins had also established a network of local clubs throughout the provinces. They had constituted the most advanced political group in the National Constituent Assembly and had pressed for a republic rather than a constitutional monarchy. The events of the summer of 1791 led them to renew those demands.

In the Legislative Assembly a group of Jacobins known as the *Girondists* assumed leadership.[3] They were determined to oppose the forces of counterrevolution. They passed measures ordering the *émigrés* to return or suffer loss of property and requiring the refractory clergy to support the Civil Constitution or lose their state pensions. The king vetoed both acts. On April 20, 1792, the Girondists led the Assembly to declare war on Austria, by this time governed by Francis II (1768–1835) and allied to Prussia. The Girondists believed that the war would preserve the revolution from domestic enemies and bring the most advanced revolutionaries to power. Paradoxically Louis XVI and other monarchists also favored the war. They thought that the conflict would strengthen the executive. The king also entertained the hope that French forces might be defeated and the old regime restored. Both sides were playing dangerously foolish politics.

The war radicalized the revolution and led to what is usually called the second revolution, which overthrew the constitutional monarchy and established a republic. Initially the war effort went quite poorly. Both the country and the revolution seemed in danger. In July 1792 the Duke of Brunswick, commander of the Prussian forces, issued a manifesto promising the destruction of Paris if harm came to the French royal family. This statement stiffened support for the war and increased the already significant distrust of the king.

Late in July the government of the city of Paris passed from the elected council to a committee or commune of representatives from the sections of Paris. On August 10, 1792, a very large Paris crowd invaded the Tuileries Palace and forced Louis XVI and Marie Antoinette to take refuge in the Legislative Assembly itself. The crowd fought with the royal Swiss guards. When Louis was finally able to call off the troops, several hundred of them and a large number of Paris citizens lay dead. The monarchy itself was also a casualty of that melee. Thereafter

3 The Girondists are also frequently called the *Brissotins* after Jacques-Pierre Brissot (1754–1793), who was their chief spokesman in early 1792.

A Pamphleteer Describes What a Sans-Culotte Is

This pamphlet is a 1793 description of a *sans-culotte* written either by one or by a sympathizer. It describes the *sans-culotte* as a hardworking, useful, patriotic citizen who bravely sacrifices himself to the war effort. It contrasts those virtues to the lazy and unproductive luxury of the noble and the personally self-interested plottings of the politician.

A sans-culotte *you rogues? He is someone who always goes on foot, who has no millions as you would all like to have, no* chateaux, *no valets to serve him, and who lives simply with his wife and children, if he has any, on a fourth or fifth storey.*

He is useful, because he knows how to work in the field, to forge iron, to use a saw, to use a file, to roof a house, to make shoes, and to shed his last drop of blood for the safety of the Republic.

And because he works, you are sure not to meet his person in the Café de Chartres, or in the gaming houses where others conspire and game; nor at the National theatre . . . nor in the literary clubs. . . .

In the evening he goes to his section, not powdered or perfumed, or smartly booted in the hope of catching the eye of the citzenesses in the galleries, but ready to support good proposals with all his might, and to crush those which come from the abominable faction of politicians.

Finally, a sans-culotte always has his sabre sharp, to cut off the ears of all enemies of the Revolution; sometimes he even goes out with his pike; but at the first sound of the drum he is ready to leave for the Vendée, for the army of the Alps or for the army of the North. . . .

"Reply to an Impertinent Question: What Is a *sans-culotte?*" April 1793. Reprinted in Walter Markov and Albert Soboul (eds.), *Die Sansculotten von Paris,* and republished translated by Clive Emsley in Merryn Williams (ed.), *Revolutions: 1775–1830* (Baltimore: Penguin Books, in association with The Open University, 1971), pp. 100–101.

---

the royal family was imprisoned in comfortable quarters, but the king was allowed to perform none of his functions.

The Convention and the Role of the Sans-Culottes

Early in September the Paris crowd again made its will felt. During the first week of the month, in what are known as the September Massacres, the Paris Commune summarily executed or murdered about twelve hundred people who were in the city jails. Many of these people were aristocrats or priests, but the majority were simply common criminals. The crowd had assumed that the prisoners were all counterrevolutionaries. The Paris Commune then compelled the Legislative Assembly to call for the election by universal manhood suffrage of a new assembly to write a democratic constitution. That body, called the *Convention* after its American counterpart of 1787, met on September 21, 1792. The previous day the French Army had halted the Prussian advance at the battle of Valmy in eastern France. The victory of democratic forces at home had been confirmed by victory on the battlefield.

As its first act, the Convention declared France a republic, that is, a nation governed by an elected assembly without a king. The second revolution had been the work of Jacobins more radical than the Girondists and of the people of Paris known as the *sans-culottes.* The name of the latter means "without breeches" and derived from the long trousers that as working people they wore instead of aristocratic knee breeches. The sans-culottes were shopkeepers, artisans, wage earners, and in a few cases factory workers. The persistent food shortages and the revolutionary inflation had made their generally difficult lives even more burdensome. The politics of the old regime had ignored them, and the policies of the National Constituent Assembly had left them victims of unregulated economic liberty. However, the nation required their labor and their lives if the war was to succeed. From the summer of 1792 until the summer of 1794 their attitudes, desires, and ideals were the primary factors in the internal development of the revolution.

The sans-culottes generally knew what they wanted. The Paris tradesmen and craftsmen sought immediate relief from food shortages and rising prices through the vehicle of price controls. They believed that all people had a right to subsistence and profoundly resented most forms of social inequality. This attitude led them to intense hostility toward the aristocracy and toward the original leaders of the revolution who might have taken over the social privileges of the aristocracy. Their hatred of inequality did not go so far as a demand for the abolition of property. Rather they advocated a community of relatively small property owners. In politics they were strongly republican and even suspicious of representative government. In Paris, where their influence was most important, the sans-culottes' political experience had been gained in meetings of the Paris sections. Those gatherings exemplified direct community democracy and were not unlike a New England town meeting. The economic hardship of their lives made them impatient to see their demands met.

The goals of the sans-culottes were not wholly compatible with those of the Jacobins. The latter were republicans who sought representative government. Jacobin hatred of the aristocracy did not extend to a general suspicion of wealth. Basically the Jacobins favored an unregulated economy. However, from the time of the flight to Varennes onward, the more extreme Jacobins began to cooperate with leaders from the Paris sans-culottes and the Paris Commune for the overthrow of the monarchy. Once the Convention began its deliberations, these advanced Jacobins, known as the Mountain because of their seats high in the assembly hall, worked with the sans-culottes to carry the revolution forward and to win the war. This willingness to cooperate with the forces of the popular revolution separated the Mountain from the Girondists, who were also members of the Jacobin Club.

By the spring of 1793 several issues had brought the Mountain and its sans-culottes allies to domination of the Convention and the revolution. In December 1792 Louis XVI was put on trial as mere "Citizen Capet," the family name of extremely distant forebears of the royal family. The Girondists looked for some way to spare his life, but the Mountain defeated the effort. Louis was convicted by a very narrow majority, condemned to death, and beheaded on January 21, 1793. The next month the Convention declared war on Great Britain, Holland, and Spain. Soon thereafter the Prussians re-newed their offensive and drove the French out of Belgium. To make matters worse, General Dumouriez, the Girondist victor of Valmy, deserted to the enemy. Finally, in March 1793 a royalist revolt led by aristocratic officers and priests erupted in the Vendée in western France and roused much popular support. Consequently the revolution found itself at war with most of Europe and much of the French nation. The Girondists had led the country into the war but had proved themselves incapable of winning it and suppressing the enemies of revolution at home. The Mountain stood ready to take up the task. Every major European power was now hostile to the revolution.

The Revolution and Europe at War

Initially the attitude of the rest of Europe toward the revolutionary events in France had been ambivalent. Those people who favored political reform regarded the revolution as wisely and rationally reorganizing a corrupt and inefficient government. The major foreign governments thought that the revolution meant that France would cease to be an important factor in European affairs for several years. In 1790, however, the Irish-born writer and British statesman Edmund Burke (1729–1797) argued a different position in *Reflections on the Revolution in France*. Burke regarded the reconstruction of French administration as the application of a blind rationalism that ignored the historical realities of political development and the complexities of social relations. He also forecast further turmoil as persons without political experience attempted to govern France. As the revolutionaries proceeded to attack the church, the monarchy, and finally the rest of Europe, Burke's ideas came to have many admirers, and his *Reflections* became the handbook of European conservatives for decades.

By the time of the commencement of the war with Austria in April 1792, the other European monarchies recognized the danger of both the ideas and the aggression of revolutionary France. The ideals of the Rights of

Burke Condemns the Work of the French National Assembly

Burke was undoubtedly the most important and articulate foreign critic of the French Revolution. He believed that governments could not be quickly created or organized, as seemed to have occurred in France. He was also deeply opposed to democracy, which he thought would lead to unwise, extreme actions on the part of government. Burke left a legacy of brilliantly argued conservative thought that remained a comfort to many followers, a serious challenge to liberals in nineteenth-century Europe, and an important statement in political theory. This passage is from his 1790 *Reflections on the Revolution in France.*

To MAKE *a government requires no great prudence. Settle the seat of power; teach obedience: and the work is done. To give Freedom is still more easy. It is not necessary to guide; it only requires to let go the rein. But to form a free government; that is, to temper together these opposite elements of liberty and restraint in one consistent work, requires much thought, deep reflection, a sagacious, powerful, and combining mind. This I do not find in those who take the lead in the National Assembly. Perhaps they are not so miserably deficient as they appear. I rather believe it. It would put them below the common level of human understanding. But when the leaders choose to make themselves bidders at an auction of popularity, their talents, in the construction of the state, will be of no service. They will become flatterers instead of legislators; the instruments, not the guides, of the people. If any of them should happen to propose a scheme of liberty, soberly limited, and defined with proper qualifications, he will be immediately outbid by his competitors, who will produce something more splendidly popular. Suspicions will be raised of his fidelity to his cause. Moderation will be stigmatized as the virtue of cowards; and compromise as the prudence of traitors; until, in hopes of preserving the credit which may enable him to temper, and moderate, on some occasions, the popular leader is obliged to become active in propagating doctrines, and establishing powers, that will afterwards defeat any sober purpose at which he ultimately might have aimed.*

. . . The improvements of the National Assembly are superficial, their errors fundamental.

Edumund Burke, *Reflections on the Revolution in France,* in *The Works of the Right Honourable Edmund Burke* (London: Henry G. Bohn, 1864), Vol. 2, pp. 515–516.

Edmund Burke. The portrait is from the studio of Joshua Reynolds. [National Portrait Gallery, London.]

Man and Citizen were highly exportable and applicable to the rest of the Continent. One government after another turned to repressive domestic policies. In Great Britain William Pitt the Younger (1759–1806), who had unsuccessfully supported moderate reform of Parliament during the 1780s, turned against both reform and popular movements. The government suppressed the London Corresponding Society founded in 1792 as a working-class reform group. In Birmingham the government sponsored mob action to drive Joseph Priestley (1733–1804), the chemist and radical political thinker, out of the country. In early 1793 Pitt secured parliamentary approval for acts suspending habeas corpus and making it possible to commit treason in writing. With less success Pitt attempted to curb freedom of the press. All political groups who dared to oppose the action of the government were in danger of becoming associated with revolutionary sedition.

In eastern Europe the revolution brought to a close the life of enlightened absolutism. The aristocratic resistance to the reforms of Joseph II in the Hapsburg lands led his brother Leopold II to come to terms with the landowners. Leopold's successor, Francis II (1792–1835) became a major leader of the counterrevolution. In Prussia Frederick William II (1786–1797), the son of Frederick the Great, looked to the leaders of the Lutheran Church and the aristocracy to discourage any potential popular uprisings, such as those of the downtrodden Silesian weavers. In Russia Catherine the Great burned the works of her onetime friend Voltaire and exiled Alexander Radishchev (1749–1802) to Siberia for publishing *Journey from St. Petersburg to Moscow,* a work critical of Russian social conditions.

In 1792 and 1793 the three eastern powers once again combined against Poland. In that unhappy land aristocratic reformers had finally achieved the abolition of the *liberum veto* and had organized a new constitutional monarchy in 1791. Russia and Prussia, which already had designs on Polish territory, saw or pretended to see a threat of revolution in the new Polish constitution. In 1792 they annexed large sections of the country; in 1795 Austria joined the two other powers in a final partition that removed Poland from the map of Europe until after World War I. The governments of eastern Europe had used the widely shared fear of further revolutionary disorder to justify old-fashioned eighteenth-century aggression.

Consequently, in a paradoxical fashion the very success of the revolution in France brought to a rapid close reform movements in the rest of Europe. The French invasion of the Austrian Netherlands and the revolutionary reorganization of that territory roused the rest of Europe to the point of active hostility. In November 1792 the Convention declared that it would aid all peoples who wished to cast off the burdens of aristocratic and monarchical oppression. The Convention had also proclaimed the Scheldt River in the Netherlands open to the commerce of all nations and thus had broken a treaty that Great Britain had made with Austria and Holland. The British were on the point of declaring war on France over this issue when the Convention issued its own declaration of hostilities. By April 1793, when the Mountain began

to direct the French government, the nation stood at war with Austria, Prussia, Great Britain, Spain, Sardinia, and Holland. The governments of those nations were attempting to protect their social structures, political systems, and economic interests against the aggression of the revolution.

The Reign of Terror
The Republic Defended

In April 1793 the Convention established a Committee of General Security and a Committee of Public Safety to perform the executive duties of the government. The latter committee became more important and eventually enjoyed almost dictatorial power. The most prominent leaders of the Committee of Public Safety were Jacques Danton (1759–1794), who had provided heroic leadership in September 1792; Maximilien Robespierre (1758–1794), who became for a time the single most powerful member of the committee; and Lazare Carnot (1753–1823), who was in charge of the military. All of these men and the other figures on the committee were

Maximilien Robespierre was the dominant member of the Committee of Public Safety during the Reign of Terror. [Bettmann Archive.]

The major problem was to wage the war and to secure domestic support for the effort. In early June 1793 the Paris sans-culottes invaded the Convention and successfully demanded the expulsion of the Girondist members. That action further radicalized the Convention and gave the Mountain complete control. On June 22 the Convention approved a fully democratic constitution but suspended its operation until the conclusion of the war emergency. On August 23 Carnot began a mobilization for victory by issuing a *levée en masse*, which conscripted males into the army and directed economic production for military purposes. On September 17 a maximum on prices was established in accord with sans-culotte demands. During these same months the armies of the revolution also successfully crushed many of the counter-revolutionary disturbances in the provinces.

Never before had Europe seen a nation organized in this way nor one defended by a citizen army. Other events within France astounded Europeans even more. The Reign of Terror had begun. Those months of quasi-judicial executions and murders stretching from the autumn of 1793 to the midsummer of 1794 are probably the most famous or infamous period of the revolution. They can be understood only in the context of the war on the one hand and the revolutionary expectations of the Convention and the sans-culottes on the other.

The Republic of Virtue

The presence of armies closing in upon the nation created a situation in which it was relatively easy to dispense with legal due process. However, the people who sat in the Convention and composed the Committee of Public Safety also believed that they had made a new departure in world history. They had established a republic in which civic virtue rather than aristocratic and

strong republicans and had opposed the weak policies of the Girondists. They conceived of their task as saving the revolution from mortal enemies at home and abroad. They generally enjoyed a working political relationship with the sans-culottes of Paris, but this was an alliance of expediency on the part of the committee.

monarchical corruption might flourish. The republic of virtue manifested itself in the renaming of streets from the egalitarian vocabulary of the revolution, in republican dress copied from that of the sans-culottes or the Roman Republic, in the absence of powdered wigs, in the suppression of plays that were insufficiently republican, and in a general attack against crimes, such as prostitution, that were supposedly characteristic of aristocratic society.

The most dramatic departure of the republic of virtue and one that illustrates the imposition of political values that would justify the terror was an attempt by the Convention to dechristianize France. In November 1793 the Convention proclaimed a new calendar dating from the first day of the French Republic. There were twelve months of thirty days with names associated with the seasons and climate. Every tenth day rather than every seventh was a holiday. Many of the most important events of the next few years became known by their dates on the revolutionary calendar.[4] Also in November 1793 the convention abolished the worship of God and established a Cult of Reason. The legislature then sent trusted members known as *deputies on mission* into the provinces to enforce dechristianization by closing churches, persecuting clergy and believers, and occasionally forcing priests to marry. Needless to say, this religious policy roused much opposition and deeply separated the French provinces from the revolutionary government in Paris.

During the crucial months of late 1793 and early 1794 the person who emerged as the chief figure on the Committee of Public Safety was Robespierre. He was a complex person who has remained controversial to the present day. He was utterly selfless and from the earliest days of the revolution had favored a republic. The Jacobin Club provided his primary forum and base of power. A shrewd and sensitive politician, he had opposed the war in 1792 as a measure that might aid the monarchy. He largely depended upon the support of the sans-culottes of

Paris, but he continued to dress as he had prior to the revolution and opposed dechristianization as a political blunder. For him the republic of virtue meant wholehearted support of republican government and the renunciation of selfish gains from political life. He once told the Convention, "If the mainspring of popular government in peacetime is virtue, amid revolution it is at the same time virtue and *terror:* virtue, without which terror is fatal; terror, without which virtue is impotent. Terror is nothing but prompt, severe, inflexible justice; it is therefore an emanation of virtue."[5] He and those who supported his policies were among the first apostles of secular ideologies who in the name of humanity would bring so much suffering to European politics of the left and the right in the next two centuries.

Progress of the Terror

The Reign of Terror manifested itself through a series of revolutionary tribunals established by the Convention during the summer of 1793. They were to try the enemies of the republic, but the definition of *enemy* remained uncertain and shifted as the months passed. The enemies included those who might aid other European powers, those who endangered republican virtue, and finally good republicans who opposed the policies of the dominant faction of the government. In a very real sense the terror of the revolutionary tribunals systematized and channeled the popular resentment that had manifested itself in the September Massacres of 1792. The first victims were Marie Antoinette, other members of the royal family, and some aristocrats, who were executed in October 1793. They were followed by certain Girondist politicians who had been prominent in the Legislative Assembly.

By the early months of 1794 the Terror had moved to the provinces, where the deputies on mission presided over the summary execution of thousands of people who had allegedly supported internal opposition to the revolution. One of the most infamous incidents occurred in

4 From summer to spring the months on the revolutionary calendar were Messidor, Thermidor, Fructidor, Vendémiaire, Brumaire, Frimaire, Nivôse, Pluviôse, Ventôse, Germinal, Floréal, and Prairial.

5 Quoted in Richard T. Bienvenu, *The Ninth of Thermidor: The Fall of Robespierre* (New York: Oxford University Press, 1968), p. 38.

Marie Antoinette on the way to her execution, sketched from life by David, as her tumbril passed his window. [Bettmann Archive.]

Nantes, where several hundred people were simply tied to rafts and drowned in the river. By early 1794 the victims of the Terror came from every social class, including the sans-culottes.

In Paris during the late winter Robespierre began to orchestrate the Terror against republican political figures of the left and right. On March 24 he secured the execution of certain extreme sans-culottes leaders known as the *enragés*. They had wanted further measures regulating prices, securing social equality, and pressing dechristianization. Robespierre then turned against more conservative republicans, who included Danton. They were insufficiently militant on the war and had profited monetarily from the revolution. Danton was executed during the first week in April. In this fashion, Robespierre exterminated the leadership from both groups that might have threatened his position. Finally, on June 10, he secured passage of the Law of 22 Prairial, which permitted the revolutionary tribunal to convict suspects without even hearing evidence. The number of executions was growing steadily.

In June 1794, at the height of his power, Robespierre, considering the Cult of Reason too abstract for most citizens, abolished it and established the Cult of the Supreme Being. This deistic cult was in line with Rousseau's idea of a civic religion that would induce morality among citizens. However, Robespierre did not long preside over his new religion. On July 26 he made an ill-tempered speech in the Convention declaring there existed among other leaders of the government a conspiracy against himself and the revolution. Such accusations against unnamed persons had usually preceded his earlier attacks. On July 27—the Ninth of Thermidor—by prearrange-

Although many of the victims of the Reign of Terror were executed by other methods, the guillotine became the symbol of those frightening months in 1793 and 1794. Here prisoners are being prepared for decapitation, as the heads of those already executed are displayed to the crowd. [Bettmann Archive.]

The Festival of the Supreme Being took place in Paris in June 1794. It was one of the chief displays of the civic religion of the French Revolution. The painting is by P. A. de Machy. [Musée Carnavalet, Paris. Giraudon.]

ment, members of the Convention shouted him down when he rose to make another speech. That night Robespierre was arrested, and the next day he was executed. The revolutionary sans-culottes of Paris could not save him because he had deprived them of their chief leaders. The other Jacobins turned against him because after Danton's death they feared becoming the next victims. Robespierre had destroyed rivals for leadership without creating supporters for himself. In that regard he was the selfless creator of his own self-image.

The fall of Robespierre might simply have been one more shift in the turbulent politics of the revolution. Those who brought about his demise were motivated by instincts of self-preservation rather than by major policy differences. They had fully supported the Terror and the executions. Yet within a short time the Reign of Terror, which ultimately claimed over twenty-five thousand victims, did come to a close. The largest number of executions had involved peasants and sans-culottes who joined rebellions against the revolutionary government. By the late summer of 1794 those provincial uprisings had been crushed, and the war against foreign enemies was also going well. Those factors, combined with the feeling in Paris that the revolution had consumed enough of its children, brought the Terror to an end.

The Thermidorian Reaction
The End of the Terror and Establishment of the Directory

A tempering of the revolution called the *Thermidorian Reaction* began in July 1794. It consisted of the destruction of the machinery of terror and the institution of a new constitutional regime. Within days and weeks of Robespierre's execution the Convention allowed the Girondists who had been in prison or hiding to return to their seats. There was a general amnesty for political prisoners. The Committee of Public Safety was restructured under closer control of the Convention, and the notorious Law of 22 Prairial was repealed. Some, though by no means all, of the people responsible for the Terror were removed from public life. Leaders of the Paris Commune and certain deputies on mission were executed. The Paris Commune itself was outlawed. The Paris Jacobin Club was closed, and Jacobin clubs in the provinces were forbidden to correspond with each other.

One of the major events during the Thermidorian Reaction was the closing in November 1794 of the Jacobin Club in Paris. The structure was part of a former convent in the center of the city. [The Granger Collection.]

The executions of former terrorists marked the beginning of "the white terror." Throughout the country people who had been involved in the Reign of Terror were attacked and often murdered. Jacobins were executed with little more due process than they had extended to their victims a few months earlier. The Convention itself approved some of these trials. In other cases gangs of youths who had aristocratic connections or who had avoided serving in the army roamed the streets striking and beating known Jacobins. In Lyons, Toulon, and Marseilles these "bands of Jesus" dragged suspected terrorists from prisons and murdered them much as alleged royalists had been murdered during the September Massacres.

The republic of virtue gave way, if not to one of vice, at least to one of frivolous pleasures. The dress of the sans-culottes and the Roman Republic disappeared among the middle class and the aristocracy. New plays appeared in the theaters, and prostitutes again roamed the streets of Paris. Families of victims of the Reign of Terror gave parties in which they appeared with shaved necks like the victims of the guillotine and red ribbons tied about them. Although the Convention continued to favor the Cult of the Supreme Being, it allowed Catholic services to be held. Many refractory priests returned to the country. One of the unanticipated results of the Thermidorian Reaction was a genuine revival of Catholic worship.

The Thermidorian Reaction also involved a political reconstruction. The fully democratic constitution of 1793, which had never gone into effect, was abandoned. The Convention issued in its place the Constitution of the Year III, which reflected the Thermidorian determination to reject both constitutional monarchy and democracy. The new document provided for a legislature of two houses. Members of the upper body, or Council of Elders, were to be men over forty years of age who were either husbands or widowers. The lower Council of Five Hundred was to consist of married or single men at least thirty years old. The executive body was to be a five-person Directory chosen by the Elders from a list submitted by the Council of Five Hundred. Property qualifications limited the franchise except for soldiers, who even without property were permitted to vote.

Thermidor became a term associated with political reaction. However, if the French Revolution had originated in political conflicts characteristic of the eighteenth century, it had by 1795 become something very different. A society and a political structure based on rank and birth had given way to one based on civic equality and social status stemming from ownership or nonownership of property. People who had never been allowed direct, formal access to political power had to differing degrees been admitted to those activities. Their entrance had given rise to questions of property distribution and economic regulations that could not again be totally ignored. Representation had been established as a principle of practical politics. Henceforth the question before France and eventually before all of Europe would be which new groups would be admitted to representation. In the *levée en masse* the French had demonstrated to Europe the power of the secular ideal of nationhood.

All of these stunning changes in the political and social contours of Europe are not to be forgotten in a consideration of the post-Thermidorian course of the French Revolution. What triumphed in the Constitution of the Year III was the revolution of the holders of property. For this reason the French Revolution has usually been considered the victory of the bourgeoisie or middle class. However, the property that won the day was not industrial wealth but the wealth stemming from commerce and the professions. Moreover the largest new propertied class to emerge from the revolutionary turmoil was the peasantry, who as a result of the destruction of feudal privileges had achieved personal ownership of the land. Unlike peasants liberated from feudalism in other parts of Europe during the next century, French peasants had to pay no monetary compensation.

The most decisively reactionary element in the Thermidorian Reaction and the new constitution was the removal of the sans-culottes from political life. With the war effort succeeding, the Convention severed its ties with the sans-culottes. True to their belief in an unregulated economy, the Thermidorians repealed the ceiling on prices. As a result, the winter of 1794–1795 brought the worst food shortages of the period. There were numerous food riots, which the Convention put down with force to prove that the era of the sans-culottes *journées* had come to a close. On October 5, 1795–13 Vendémiaire—the sections of Paris rose up against the Convention. For the first time in the history of the revolution, artillery was turned against the people of Paris. A general named Napoleon Bonaparte (1769–1821) commanded the cannon, and with a "whiff of grapeshot" he dispersed the crowd.

By the Treaty of Basel in March 1795, the Convention concluded peace with Prussia and Spain. However, the legislators feared a resurgence of both radical democrats and royalists in the upcoming elections for the Council of Five Hundred. Consequently the Convention ruled that at least two thirds of the new legislature must have been members of the older body. The Thermidorians did not even trust the property owners as voters. The next year the newly established Directory again faced social unrest. In Paris Gracchus Babeuf (1760–1797) led the Conspiracy of Equals. He and his followers called for more radical democracy and for more equality of property. Babeuf was arrested, tried, and executed. This quite minor plot became famous many decades later when European socialists attempted to find their historical roots in the French Revolution.

The suppression of the sans-culottes, the narrow franchise of the constitution, the rule of the two thirds, and the Catholic royalist revival presented the Directory with problems that it never succeeded in overcoming. It lacked any broad base of meaningful political support. It particularly required active loyalty because France remained at war with Austria and Great Britain. Consequently the Directory came to depend upon the power of the army rather than upon constitutional processes for governing the country. All of the soldiers could vote. Moreover, within the army, created and sustained by the revolution, stood officers who were eager for power and ambitious for political conquest. The results of the instability of the Directory and the growing role of the army held profound consequences not only for France but for the entire Western world.

SUGGESTED READINGS

C. BRINTON, *The Jacobins: An Essay in the New History* (1930). An examination of the social background of these revolutionaries.

C. BRINTON, *A Decade of Revolution, 1789–1799* (1934). A general survey of Europe during the revolutionary years.

A. COBBAN, *Edmund Burke and the Revolt against the Eighteenth Century* (1929). Sets Burke's thought in a broader intellectual context.

A. COBBAN, *Aspects of the French Revolution* (1970). Essays on numerous subjects.

C. CONE, *The English Jacobins: Reformers in Late Eighteenth Century England* (1968). The fortunes of English radicals during the repression following the outbreak of war with France.

K. EPSTEIN, *The Genesis of German Conservatism* (1966). A major study of antiliberal forces in Germany before and during the revolution.

D. M. GREER, *The Incidence of the Terror During the French Revolution: A Statistical Interpretation* (1935). A study of what people in which regions became the victims of the Terror.

N. HAMPSON, *A Social History of the French Revolution* (1963). A clear account with much interesting detail.

G. LEFEBVRE, *The Coming of the French Revolution* (trans., 1947). An examination of the crisis of the French monarchy and the events of 1789.

G. LEFEBVRE, *The French Revolution*, 2 vols. (1962–1964). A major study by one of the most important modern writers on the subject.

R. R. PALMER, *Twelve Who Ruled: The Committee of Public Safety During the Terror* (1941). A clear narrative and analysis of the policies and problems of the committee.

R. R. PALMER, *The Age of Democratic Revolution: A Political History of Europe and America, 1760–1800*, 2 vols. (1959, 1964). An impressive survey of the political turmoil in the transAtlantic world.

G. RUDÉ, *The Crowd in the French Revolution* (1959). Examines who composed the revolutionary crowds and why.

ALBERT SOBOUL, *The French Revolution* (trans., 1975). An important work by a Marxist scholar.

J. H. STEWART, *A Documentary Survey of the French Revolution* (1951). Major sources in translation.

J. M. THOMPSON, *Robespierre*, 2 vols. (1935). The best biography.

C. TILLY, *The Vendée* (1964). A significant sociological investigation.

618

24
The Age of Napoleon and the Triumph of Romanticism

THE GOVERNMENT of the Directory represented a new class made up of politicians, merchants, bankers, war speculators, and profiteers sprung from the nonaristocratic order of the old regime, as well as a few undistinguished nobles. Together they formed a society of recently enriched and powerful people whose chief goal was to halt the revolutionary movement without rolling it back. They wanted to perpetuate their own rule. They sought to achieve peace and quiet in order to gain more wealth and to establish a society in which money would become the only requirement for eminence and power. They and their goals confronted a host of enemies.

The Rise of Napoleon Bonaparte

The chief danger to the Directory came from the royalists, who hoped to restore the Bourbon monarchy by legal means. Many of the *émigrés* had drifted back into France. Their plans for a restoration drew support from devout Catholics and from those citizens who had been disgusted by the excesses of the revolution. Monarchy seemed to hold the promise of stability. The spring elections of 1797 turned out most of the incumbents and replaced them with a majority of constitutional monarchists and their sympathizers. To prevent an end to the republic and a peaceful restoration of monarchy, the antimonarchist Directory staged a *coup d'état* on 18 Fructidor (September 4, 1797). They put their own supporters into the legislative seats won by their opponents. They then imposed censorship and exiled some of their enemies. These actions had been made possible by Napo-

leon Bonaparte who was the general in charge of the Italian military campaign. At the request of the Directors, he had sent one of his subordinates to Paris to guarantee the success of the *coup*. In 1797, as in 1795, the army and Bonaparte had saved the day for the government.

Napoleon Bonaparte was born in 1769 to a poor family of lesser nobles at Ajaccio, Corsica. Because France had annexed Corsica in the previous year, he went to French schools, pursued a military career, and in 1785 obtained a commission as a French artillery officer. He strongly favored the revolution and was a fiery Jacobin. In 1793 he played a leading role in recovering the port of Toulon from the British. In reward for his service the government appointed him a brigadier general. His radical associations threatened his career during the Therimidorian Reaction, but his defense of the new regime on 13 Vendémiaire restored him to favor and won him another promotion and a command in Italy.

By 1795 French arms and diplomacy had shattered the enemy coalition, but France's annexation of Belgium guaranteed continued fighting with Britain and Austria. The attack on Italy was aimed at depriving Austria of the provinces of Lombardy and Venetia. In a series of lightning victories Bonaparte crushed the Austrian and Sardinian armies. On his own initiative, and in many ways contrary to the wishes of the government in Paris, he concluded the treaty of Campo Formio in October 1797. The treaty took Austria out of the war and crowned Napoleon's campaign and independent policy with success. Before long all of Italy and Switzerland had fallen under French domination.

In November 1797 the triumphant Bonaparte returned to Paris to be hailed as a hero and to confront France's only remaining enemy, Britain. He judged it impossible to cross the channel and invade England at that time. Instead he chose to capture Egypt from the Ottoman Empire and thereby to drive the British fleet from the Mediterranean, cut off British communication with India, damage British trade, and threaten the British empire. The invasion of Egypt was a failure. Admiral

This portrait of Napoleon by the artist David illustrates the ruler as liberal reformer. Napoleon is shown working early into the morning on affairs of state. The *Code Napoléon* lies on the table at the right of the picture. [Bettmann Archive.]

Horatio Nelson (1758–1805) destroyed the French fleet at Abukir on August 1, 1798. The French army could then neither accomplish anything of importance in the Near East nor get home. To make matters worse, the situation in Europe was deteriorating. Russia, which also had ambitions in the Near East, was alarmed by the French invasion of Egypt. The Russians, the Austrians, and the Ottomans soon joined Britain to form the Second Coalition. In 1799 the Russian and Austrian armies defeated the French in Italy and Switzerland and threatened to invade France.

Economic troubles and the dangerous international situation eroded the already fragile support for the Directory. One of the Directors, the Abbé Sieyès, proposed a new constitution. The author of the pamphlet *What Is the Third Estate?* (1789) wanted to establish a vigorous executive body independent of the whims of electoral politics, a government based on the principle of "confidence from below, power from above." The change would require a *coup d'état* with military support. News of France's misfortunes had reached Napoleon in Egypt. Without orders and leaving his doomed army behind, he returned to France in October 1799. He received much popular acclaim, although some people thought he deserved a court-martial for desertion. He soon joined Sieyès. On 18 Brumaire (November 9, 1799) his troops drove out the legislators and permitted the success of the *coup*.

Sieyès appears to have thought Napoleon could be used and then dismissed, but if so he badly misjudged his man. The proposed constitution divided executive authority among three consuls. Bonaparte pushed it aside, as he did Sieyès, and in December 1799 put forth the Constitution of the Year VIII. Behind a screen of universal manhood suffrage that suggested democratic principles, a complicated system of checks and balances that appealed to republican theory, and a Council of State that evoked memories of Louis XIV, the constitution in fact established the rule of one man, the First Consul, Bonaparte. To find a reasonably close historical analogy one must go back to Caesar and Augustus and the earlier Greek

The Consuls Proclaim the End of the French Revolution

In this proclamation made by the three consuls on December 15, 1799 the end of the Revolution is ceremoniously announced and the Constitution of the Year VIII is commended to the French.

Frenchmen!

A Constitution is presented to you.

It terminates the uncertainties which the provisional government introduced into external relations, into the internal and military situation of the Republic.

It places in the institutions which it establishes first magistrates whose devotion has appeared necessary for its success.

The Constitution is founded on the true principles of representative government, on the sacred rights of property, equality, and liberty.

The powers which it institutes will be strong and stable, as they must be in order to guarantee the rights of citizens and the interests of the State.

Citizens, the Revolution is established upon the principles which began it: It is ended.

J. H. Stewart, *A Documentary Survey of the French Revolution* (New York: Macmillan, 1951), p. 780.

tyrants. The career of Bonaparte, however, pointed forward to the dictators of the twentieth century. He was the first modern political figure to employ the rhetoric of revolution and nationalism, to back it with military force, and to combine these elements into a mighty weapon of imperial expansion in the service of his own power and ambition.

The Consulate in France (1799–1804)

The establishment of the Consulate may be regarded as the end of the revolution in France. The leading elements of the Third Estate—that is, officials, landowners, doctors, lawyers, and financiers—had achieved most of their goals by 1799. Hereditary privilege had been abolished, and the career open to talent allowed them to achieve the wealth and status they sought. The peasants also were satisfied. They had acquired the land they had always wanted and had destroyed oppressive feudal privileges as well. The newly established dominant classes were profoundly conservative. They had little or no desire to share their recently won privileges with lower social orders. Bonaparte seemed just the person to give

Napoleon Describes Conditions Leading to the Consulate

November 1799 as described by Bonaparte.

On my *return to Paris I found division among all authorities, and agreement upon only one point, namely, that the Constitution was half destroyed and was unable to save liberty.*

All parties came to me, confided to me their designs, disclosed their secrets, and requested my support; I refused to be the man of a party.

The Council of Elders summoned me; I answered its appeal. A plan of general restoration had been devised by men whom the nation has been accustomed to regard as the defenders of liberty, equality, and property; this plan required an examination, calm, free, exempt from all influence and all fear. Accordingly, the Council of Elders resolved upon the removal of the Legislative Body to Saint-Cloud; it gave me the responsibility of disposing the force necessary for its independence. I believed it my duty to my fellow citizens, to the soldiers perishing in our armies, to the national glory acquired at the cost of their blood, to accept the command. . . .

I presented myself at the Council of Five Hundred, alone, unarmed, my head uncovered, just as the Elders had received and applauded me; I came to remind the majority of its wishes, and to assure it of its power.

The stilettos which menaced the deputies were instantly raised against their liberator; twenty assassins threw themselves upon me and aimed at my breast. The grenadiers of the Legislative Body whom I had left at the door of the hall ran forward, placed themselves between the assassins and myself. One of these brave grenadiers had his clothes pierced by a stiletto. They bore me out.

At the same moment cries of "Outlaw" were raised against the defender of the law. It was the fierce cry of assassins against the power destined to repress them.

They crowded around the president, uttering threats, arms in their hands; they commanded him to outlaw me; I was informed of this; I ordered him to be rescued from their fury, and six grenadiers of the Legislative Body secured him. Immediately afterwards some grenadiers of the Legislative Body charged into the hall and cleared it.

The factions, intimidated, dispersed and fled. . . .

Frenchmen, you will doubtless recognize in this conduct the zeal of a soldier of liberty, a citizen devoted to the Republic. Conservative, tutelary, and liberal ideas have been restored to their rights through the dispersal of the rebels who oppressed the Councils. . . .

J. H. Stewart, *A Documentary Survey of the French Revolution* (New York: Macmillan, 1951), pp. 763-765.

them security. When he submitted his constitution to the voters in a plebiscite, they approved it by 3,011,077 votes to 1,567.

Bonaparte quickly justified the public's confidence by setting about achieving peace with France's enemies. Russia had already quarreled with its allies and left the Second Coalition. A campaign in Italy brought another victory over Austria at Marengo in 1800. The Treaty of Lunéville early in 1801 took Austria out of the war and confirmed the earlier settlement of Campo Formio. Britain was now alone and, in 1802, concluded the Treaty of Amiens, which brought peace to Europe. Bonaparte was equally effective in restoring peace and order at home. He employed generosity, flattery, and bribery to win over some of his enemies. He issued a general amnesty and employed in his own service persons from all political factions. He required only that they be loyal to him. Some of the highest offices were occupied by persons who had been extreme radicals during the Reign of Terror, another by a person who had fled the Terror and favored constitutional monarchy, and still another by a former high official of the old regime.

On the other hand, Bonaparte was ruthless and efficient in suppressing opposition. He established a highly centralized administration in which all departments were managed by prefects directly responsible to the central government in Paris. He employed secret police. He stamped out the royalist rebellion in the west and made the rule of Paris effective in Brittany and the Vendée for the first time in many years. Nor was he above using or even inventing opportunities to destroy his enemies. When a bomb aimed at him exploded in 1804, he used the event as an excuse to attack the Jacobins, even though the bombing was the work of royalists. In 1804 his forces invaded the sovereignty of Baden to seize the Bourbon Duke of Enghien. The duke was accused of participation in a royalist plot and put to death, even though Bonaparte knew him to be innocent. The action was a flagrant violation of international law and of due process. Charles Maurice de Talleyrand-Périgord (1754-1838), Bona-

Charles Maurice de Talleyrand-Périgord, known to history as Talleyrand, was one of the most talented—or adaptable—political survivors of the Revolution. Before 1789 he had been a Roman Catholic bishop. Later he became a major diplomat, first for the revolutionary government, and then for Napoleon. Finally, in 1815, he represented the restored Bourbon government at the Congress of Vienna. The portrait is by Pierre-Paul Prud'hon. [The Granger Collection.]

parte's foreign minister, later termed the act "worse than a crime—a blunder," for it helped to provoke foreign opposition. On the other hand, it was popular with the former Jacobins, for it precluded the possibility of a Bourbon restoration. The person who killed a Bourbon was hardly likely to restore the royal family. The execution seems to have put an end to royalist plots.

A major obstacle to internal peace was the continued hostility of French Catholics. Refractory clergy continued to advocate counterrevolution. The religious revival that dated from the Thermidorian Reaction continued to increase discontent with the secular state created by the revolution. Bonaparte viewed religion as a political matter. He approved its role in preserving an orderly society but was suspicious of any such power independent of the state.

In 1801 Napoleon concluded a concordat with Pope Pius VII to the shock and dismay of his anticlerical supporters. The settlement gave Napoleon what he most wanted. Both refractory clergy and those who had accepted the revolution were forced to resign. Their replacements were given their spiritual investiture by the pope, but the state named the bishops and paid their salaries and the salary of one priest in each parish. In return the church gave up its claims on its confiscated property. The concordat declared that "Catholicism is the religion of the great majority of French citizens." This was merely a statement of fact and fell far short of what the pope had wanted, religious dominance for the

Roman Catholic Church. Clergy had to swear an oath of loyalty to the state, and the Organic Articles of 1802 established the supremacy of State over Church. Similar laws were applied to the Protestant and Jewish religious communities as well, reducing still further the privileged position of the Catholic Church.

Peace and efficient administration brought prosperity and security to the French and gratitude and popularity to Bonaparte. In 1802 a plebiscite appointed him consul for life, and he soon produced still another new constitution that granted him what amounted to full power. The years of the Consulate were employed in reforming and establishing the basic laws and institutions of France. The settlement imposed by Napoleon was an ambiguous combination of liberal principles derived from the Enlightenment and the early years of the revolution and conservative principles and practices going back to the old regime or adapted to the conservative spirit that had triumphed at Thermidor.

The abolition of all privileges based on birth, the establishment of equality before the law, the disappearance of all authority except that of the national state and all legal distinctions based on class or locality, the end of all purchased offices and the substitution of salaried officials chosen for merit represented the application of rationality and the achievement of goals sought by the people who had made the revolution. Most of these were embodied in the general codification of laws carried out under Bonaparte's direction. This was especially true of the Civil Code, usually called the Napoleonic Code. However, these laws stopped far short of full equality advocated by liberal rationalists. Fathers were granted extensive control over their children and men over their wives. Labor unions were still forbidden, and the rights of workers were inferior to those of their employers.

In the political arena and in administration Napoleonic institutions ran contrary to the tendencies of the revolution. They aimed at a kind of enlightened absolutism that was similar to but more effective than what had existed in the old regime. Representative government, local auton-

Napoleon Makes Peace with the Papacy

The following is part of the Concordat of 1802 between Napoleon's France and the papacy of Pius VII. It was announced in France on April 8, 1802 and was the cornerstone of Napoleon's religious settlement following the upheavals of the French Revolution.

THE *government of the French Republic recognizes that the Roman, catholic and apostolic religion is the religion of the great majority of French citizens.*

His Holiness likewise recognizes that this same religion has derived and in this moment again expects the greatest benefit and grandeur from the establishment of the catholic worship in France and from the personal profession of it which the consuls of the Republic make.

In consequence, after this mutual recognition, as well for the benefit of religion as for the maintenance of internal tranquility, they have agreed as follows:

1. The catholic, apostolic and Roman religion shall be freely exercised in France: its worship shall be public, and in conformity with the police regulations which the government shall deem necessary for the public tranquility.

. . . .

4. The First Consul of the Republic shall make appointments, within the three months which shall follow the publication of the bull of His Holiness, to the archbishoprics and bishoprics of the new circumscription. His Holiness shall confer the canonical institution, following the forms established in relation to France before the change of government.

. . . .

6. Before entering upon their functions, the bishops shall take directly, at the hands of the First Consul, the oath of fidelity which was in use before the change of government, expressed in the following terms:

"I swear and promise to God, upon the holy scriptures, to remain in obedience and fidelity to the government established by the constitution of the French Republic. I also promise not to have any intercourse, nor to assist by any counsel, nor to support any league, either within or without, which is inimical to the public tranquility; and if, within my diocese or elsewhere, I learn that anything to the prejudice of the state is being contrived, I will make it known to the government."

F. M. Anderson, *The Constitutions and Other Select Documents Illustrative of the History of France 1789–1907*, 2nd ed. (Minneapolis: H. W. Wilson Company, 1908), pp. 296–297.

---

omy, and personal freedom were rejected in favor of the centralization of all power and the subordination of personal rights and political freedom to the needs of the state as interpreted by the first consul. All of this was acceptable to the dominant bourgeoisie and the peasantry. They accepted censorship, the arbitrary and sometimes brutal suppression of dissent, and even the restoration of a new quasi nobility in the Legion of Honor so long as order, prosperity, and security of property were preserved.

In 1804 Bonaparte seized on the bomb attack on his life to make himself emperor. He argued that the establishment of a dynasty would make the new regime secure and make further attempts on his life useless. Another new constitution was promulgated in which Napoleon Bonaparte was called Emperor of the French, as well as First Consul of the Republic. This constitution was also overwhelmingly ratified in a plebiscite.

To conclude the drama, Napoleon invited the pope to Notre Dame to take part in the coronation. But at the last minute Napoleon snatched the crown away and placed it on his own head. Henceforth, he was called Napoleon I. This act was the natural goal of his career. His aims had always been profoundly selfish: power and glory for himself and his family. There was, moreover, a romantic streak in Napoleon. He thought of himself as a rival of Alexander the Great and Caesar, a conqueror as well as a ruler. Had Napoleon wished it, Europe might well have had peace; but his ambition would not permit it.

Napoleon's Empire (1804–1814)

In the decade between his coronation as emperor and his final defeat at Waterloo (1815), Napoleon conquered most of Europe in a series of campaigns that astonished the world. France's victories changed the map of Europe, put an end to the old regime and its feudal trappings in the west, and forced the eastern European states to reorganize themselves to resist Napoleon's armies. Everywhere Napoleon's advance unleashed the powerful force of nationalism. The French nation in arms, the invention of the revolution, was Napoleon's weapon. He could put as many as 700,000 men under arms at one time, risk as many as 100,000 troops in a single battle, endure heavy losses, and come back to fight again. He could conscript citizen soldiers in unprecedented numbers thanks to their loyalty to the nation and to their remarkable leader. No single enemy could match such resources, and even coalitions were unsuccessful until Napoleon at last overreached himself and made mistakes that led to his own defeat.

Napoleon deserves his reputation as one of the great commanders of all time. His genius did not lie in strategic or tactical invention, for the French military commanders of the eighteenth century had already pointed the course in that direction. Rather his brilliance lay in execution and leadership. His strategy depended on mobility and timing. He liked to divide his forces into units of moderate size, disperse them across the country, and use their superior speed and his skill in planning to unite them at the critical point at the right time. Self-sufficiency was an important Napoleonic principle that enabled him to disperse and reunite his armies swiftly as well as to outmaneuver his opponents.

The whole army, moreover, traveled light. By living off the country in which it fought, it was free of the need to establish and follow a chain of supply depots. This was a great advantage in fertile areas like western and central Europe but later proved a problem in the vast expanse of Russia during the winter and against guerrilla fighters in Spain. All of this speed of maneuver had a single goal: to bring the hostile armies together in a major battle swiftly. Napoleon departed from the usual eighteenth-century tactics, which emphasized maneuver and strategic position, fighting a battle only as a last resort. His aim was not to control territory nor to gain strong points but to destroy the enemy army. After that the rest would follow. So long as conditions permitted such warfare, Napoleon was unbeatable.

The Peace of Amiens (1802) was doomed to be merely a truce. Any hope that it might last was shattered

by Napoleon's unlimited ambitions. He sent an army to restore the rebellious island of Haiti to French rule. This move aroused British fears that he was planning the renewal of a French Empire in America, because Spain had restored Louisiana to France in 1800. More serious were his interventions in the Dutch Republic, Italy, and Switzerland and his role in the reorganization of Germany. The Treaty of Campo Formio had required a redistribution of territories along the Rhine River, and the petty princes of the region engaged in a shameful scramble to enlarge their holdings. Among the results were the reduction of Austrian influence in Germany and the emergence of a smaller number of larger German states in the west, all dependent on Napoleon.

The British found all of these developments alarming enough to justify an ultimatum. When Napoleon ignored it, Britain declared war in May 1803. William Pitt the Younger returned to office as prime minister in 1804 and began to construct the Third Coalition. By August 1805 he had persuaded Russia and Austria once again to move against French aggression. A great naval victory soon raised the fortunes of the allies. On October 21, 1805, the British admiral Lord Horatio Nelson (1758–1805) destroyed the combined French and Spanish fleets at the Battle of Trafalgar just off the Spanish coast. Nelson died in the battle, but the British lost no ships. The victory of Trafalgar put an end to all French hope of an invasion of Britain and guaranteed British control of the sea for the rest of the war.

On land the story was very different. Even before Trafalgar Napoleon had marched to the Danube River to

LEFT: William Pitt the Younger (1759–1806) led Great Britain in its struggle against the French Revolution and during the early years of Napoleon. [Culver Pictures.]

BELOW: British Admiral Horatio Nelson (1758–1805) was the brilliant naval strategist in the wars against Napoleonic France—wars in which he lost an eye, an arm, and finally his life. His last battle, in which he was killed, was a stunning victory over the combined French and Spanish fleets off Trafalgar on the coast of Spain, October 21, 1805, and ended any possible sea threat to England. The painting is by Lemuel Francis Abbott and is in the National Portrait Gallery, London. [The Granger Collection.]

attack his continental enemies. In mid-October he forced a large Austrian army to surrender at Ulm and soon occupied Vienna. On December 2, 1805, in perhaps his greatest victory, Napoleon defeated the combined Austrian and Russian forces at Austerlitz. The Treaty of Pressburg that followed took Russia out of the war and won major concessions from Austria. The Austrians withdrew from Italy and left Napoleon in control of everything north of Rome. He was recognized as king of Italy.

Extensive changes also came about in Germany. In July 1806 Napoleon organized the Confederation of the Rhine, which included most of the western German princes. The withdrawal of these princes from the Holy Roman Empire led Francis II of Austria to dissolve that ancient political body and henceforth to call himself only emperor of Austria.

Prussia, which had carefully remained neutral up to this point, was now provoked into war against France. The famous Prussian army was quickly crushed at the battles of Jena and Auerstädt in 1806. Two weeks later Napoleon was in Berlin. On June 13, 1807, Napoleon defeated the Russians at Friedland and was able to occupy Königsburg, the capital of East Prussia. The French emperor was master of all Germany.

Unable to fight another battle and unwilling to retreat into Russia, Tsar Alexander I (1801–1825) was ready to make peace. The two rulers met on a raft in the middle of the Niemen River while the two armies and the nervous king of Prussia watched. On July 7, 1807, they signed the Treaty of Tilsit, which confirmed France's gains. Moreover the Prussian state was reduced to half its size and was saved from extinction only by the support of Alexander. Prussia openly and Russia secretly became allies of Napoleon in his war against Britain.

Napoleon organized Europe much like the domain of a great Corsican family. The great French Empire was ruled directly by the head of the clan, Napoleon. On its borders were a number of satellite states carved out as the portions of the several family members. His stepson ruled

This painting of Napoleon and his officers at the
battle of Eylau in 1807 clearly shows the vast number
of troops that he customarily used in combat—although
in this picture the troops are included only as a
backdrop for a romantic rendering of the emperor and
his aides on the field of battle. The artist was
Antoine Jean Gros (1771–1835). [The Granger Collection.]

In 1807 Tsar Alexander I of Russia (center left) and
Napoleon (center right) met on a raft in the Niemen
River near Tilsit (on the Lithuanian border). At
that conference they signed a treaty in which they
divided Europe into spheres of French and Russian
influence. The scene is imagined here by the artist
Ludwig Wolf. [Bildarchiv Preussischer Kulturbesitz.]

Italy for him, while three of his brothers and his
brother-in-law were made kings of other conquered
states. Napoleon denied a kingdom to his brother Lucien
because he disapproved of his wife. The relatives were
expected to take orders without question. When they
failed to do so, they were rebuked and even punished.
The establishment of the Napoleonic family as the collective sovereign of Europe was offensive to the growing

national feeling in many states and helped to create it in others. The rule of puppet kings was unpopular and provoked opposition that needed only encouragement and assistance to flare up into serious resistance.

After the Peace of Tilsit such assistance could come only from Britain, and Napoleon knew he must defeat the British before he could feel safe. Unable to compete with the British navy, he turned to economic warfare. His plan was to cut off all British trade with the European continent. In this manner he hoped to cripple the commercial and financial power on which Britain depended, to cause domestic unrest and revolution, and so to drive the British from the war. For a time it appeared that this Continental System might work. British exports dropped, and riots broke out in England. But in the end the system failed and may even have contributed significantly to Napoleon's defeat.

The British economy survived because of its access to the growing markets of North and South America and of the eastern Mediterranean. At the same time, the Continental System did great harm to the European economies. The system was meant not only to hurt Britain but also to help France economically. Napoleon resisted advice to turn his empire into a free-trade area. Such a policy would have been both popular and helpful. Instead, his tariff policies favored France, increased the resentment of foreign merchants, and made them less willing to enforce the system and more ready to engage in smuggling. It was in part to prevent smuggling that Napoleon invaded Spain in 1808, and the resulting peninsular campaign in Spain and Portugal helped to bring on his ruin.

European Response to the Empire

Napoleon's conquests stimulated the two most powerful forces in nineteenth-century Europe: liberalism and nationalism. The export of his version of the French Revolution directly and indirectly spread the ideas and values of the Enlightenment and the principles of 1789. Wherever Napoleon ruled, the Napoleonic Code was imposed and class distinction abolished. Feudal dues disappeared and the peasants were freed from serfdom and manorial dues. In the towns the guilds and the local oligarchies that had dominated for centuries were dissolved or deprived of their power. New freedom thus came to serfs, artisans, workers, and entrepreneurs outside the privileged circles. Church monopoly of religion was replaced by general toleration. The established churches were deprived of their traditional independence, and made subordinate to the state.

These reforms were not undone by the fall of Napoleon and, along with the demand for representative, constitutional government, remained the basis for later liberal reforms. However, at the same time it became increasingly clear that Napoleon's policies were intended first and foremost for his own glory and that of France. The Continental System demonstrated that France rather than Europe generally was to be enriched by Napoleon's rule. Consequently, before long the conquered states and peoples became restive.

German Nationalism and Prussian Reform

The German response to Napoleon's success was particularly interesting and important. There had never been a unified German state. The great German writers of the Enlightenment, such as Kant, Schiller, and Lessing, were neither political nor nationalistic.

At the beginning of the nineteenth century the Romantic Movement had begun to take hold. One of its basic features in Germany was the emergence of nationalism. This movement went through two distinct stages. Initially, nationalistic writers emphasized the unique and admirable qualities of German culture, which, they argued, arose from the peculiar history of the German people. Such cultural nationalism prevailed until Napoleon's humiliation of Prussia at Jena in 1806. At that point many German intellectuals began to urge resistance to Napoleon on the basis of German nationality. The French conquest endangered the independence and achievements of the German people. Many nationalists

Baron Heinrich von Stein (1757–1831), on the left, and Prince Karl von Hardenberg (1750–1822) guided the reform of Prussia after the defeat by Napoleon at Jena in 1806. [The Granger Collection.]

were also critical of the German princes, who ruled selfishly and inefficiently and who seemed ever ready to lick the boots of Napoleon. No less important in forging a German national sentiment was the example of France, which had attained greatness by enlisting the active support of the entire people in the patriotic cause. Henceforth many Germans sought to solve their internal political problems by establishing a unified German state, reformed to harness the energies of the entire people.

After Tilsit only Prussia could arouse such patriotic feelings. Elsewhere German rulers were either under Napoleon's thumb or actively collaborating with him. Defeated, humiliated, and shrunken in size, Prussia continued to resist, however feebly. To Prussia fled German nationalists from other states, calling for reforms and unification that were, in fact, feared and hated by Frederick William III and the *Junker* nobility. Reforms came about in spite of such opposition because the defeat at Jena had made clear the necessity of new departures for the Prussian state.

The Prussian administrative and social reforms were the work of Baron von Stein (1757–1831) and Count von Hardenberg (1750–1822). The architects of military reform were General Gerhard von Scharnhorst (1755–

1813) and Count von Gneisenau (1760–1831). None of their reforms was intended to reduce the autocratic power of the Prussian monarch or to put an end to the dominance of the *Junkers,* who formed the bulwark of the state and of the army officer corps. Rather they aimed at fighting the revolution and French power with their own version of the French weapons. As Hardenburg declared:

> Our objective, our guiding principle, must be a revolution in the better sense, a revolution leading directly to the great goal, the elevation of humanity through the wisdom of those in authority. . . . Democratic rules of conduct in a monarchical administration, such is the formula . . . which will conform most comfortably with the spirit of the age.[1]

Although the reforms came from the top, they brought important changes in Prussian society.

Stein's reforms put an end to the existing system of Prussian landownership. The *Junker* monopoly of landholding was broken. Serfdom was generally abolished.

[1] Quoted in Geoffrey Brunn, *Europe and the French Imperium* (New York: Harper and Row, 1938), p. 174.

Arthur Wellesley, the duke of Wellington, first led troops against Napoleon in Spain and later defeated him at the battle of Waterloo, June 18, 1815. Unlike his great naval contemporary, Nelson, he lived to become an elder statesman of Britain. The portrait is by the celebrated Spanish painter Francisco Goya (1746–1828), another example of whose work is reproduced in the color album. [The Granger Collection.]

However, the power of the *Junkers* did not permit the total end of the system, as in the western principalities of Germany. Peasants remaining on the land were forced to continue manorial labor although they were free to leave the land if they chose. They could obtain the ownership of the land they worked only at the price of forfeiting a third of it to the lord. The result was that *Junker* holdings grew larger. Some peasants went to the cities to find work; others became agricultural laborers; and some did actually become small freeholding farmers. Serfdom had come to an end, but new social problems that would fester for another half century had been created as a landless labor force emerged.

The military reforms sought to increase the supply of soldiers and to improve their quality. Jena had shown that an army of free patriots commanded by officers chosen on merit rather than by birth could defeat an army of serfs and mercenaries commanded by incompetent nobles. To remedy the situation, the Prussian reformers abolished inhumane punishments, sought to inspire patriotic feelings in the soldiers, opened the officer corps to commoners, gave promotions on the basis of merit, and organized war colleges that developed new theories of strategy and tactics. These reforms soon put Prussia in a condition to regain its former power. However, because Napoleon had put a strict limit on the size of the Prussian army, universal conscription could not be introduced until 1813. Before that date the Prussians got around the limit of 42,000 men in arms by training one group each year, putting them into the reserves, and then training a new group the same size. In this manner Prussia could boast an army of 270,000 by 1814.

The Wars of Liberation

In Spain more than elsewhere in Europe national resistance to France had deep social roots. Spain had achieved political unity as early as the sixteenth century. The Spanish peasants were devoted to the ruling dynasty and especially to the Roman Catholic Church. France and Spain had been allies since 1796. In 1807, however, a

French army came into the Iberian Peninsula to force Portugal to abandon its traditional alliance with Britain. The army stayed in Spain to protect lines of supply and communication. When a revolt broke out in Madrid in 1808, Napoleon used it as a pretext to depose the Spanish Bourbon dynasty and place his brother Joseph on the Spanish throne. Public outrage was increased by attacks on the privileges of the church. Many members of the upper classes were prepared to collaborate with Napoleon, but the peasants, urged on by the lower clergy and the monks, rose in a general rebellion.

Napoleon faced a new kind of warfare not vulnerable to his usual tactics. Guerrilla bands cut lines of communication, killed stragglers, destroyed isolated units, and then disappeared into the mountains. The British landed an army under Sir Arthur Wellesley (1769–1852), later the duke of Wellington, to support the Spanish insurgents. Thus began the long peninsular campaign that would drain French strength from elsewhere in Europe and play a critical role in Napoleon's eventual defeat.

The French troubles in Spain encouraged the Austrians to renew the war in 1809. Since their defeat at Austerlitz they had sought a war of revenge. The Austrians counted on Napoleon's distraction in Spain, French war weariness, and aid from other German princes. However, Napoleon was fully in command in France;

When their marriage failed to produce a male heir, Napoleon divorced his first wife, Joséphine de Beauharnais (1763–1814) [LEFT]. Many considered the action one aspect of Napoleon's betrayal of the Revolution, especially because he then married Marie Louise (1791–1847) [RIGHT], daughter of the Hapsburg Emperor, who bore him a son. It was clear that Napoleon hoped to establish a new imperial dynasty in France. Joséphine's portrait is by F. P. Gérard and Marie Louise's is by J. B. Isabey. [The Granger Collection.]

and the German princes did not move. The French army marched swiftly into Austria and won the battle of Wagram. The resulting Peace of Schönbrunn deprived Austria of much territory and three and a half million subjects. Another spoil of victory was the Austrian Archduchess Marie Louise, daughter of the emperor. Napoleon's wife, Josephine de Beauharnais, was forty-six and had borne him no children. His dynastic ambitions, as well as the desire for a marriage matching his new position as master of Europe, led him to divorce his wife and to marry the eighteen-year-old Austrian heiress. Napoleon had also considered the sister of Tsar Alexander but had been politely rebuffed.

The failure of Napoleon's marriage negotiations with Russia emphasized the shakiness of the Franco-Russian alliance concluded at Tilsit. The alliance was unpopular with Russian nobles because of the liberal politics of France and because of the prohibition of the Continental System on timber sales to Britain. Only French aid in gaining Constantinople could justify the alliance in their eyes, but Napoleon gave them no help against the Ottoman Empire. The organization of the Grand Duchy of Warsaw as a Napoleonic satellite on the Russian doorstep and its enlargement in 1809 after the battle of Wagram angered Alexander I. Napoleon's annexation of Holland in violation of the Treaty of Tilsit, his recognition of the French Marshal Bernadotte as King Charles XIV of Sweden, and his marriage to an Austrian princess further

disturbed the tsar. At the end of 1810 Russia withdrew from the Continental System and began to prepare for war.

Napoleon was determined to put an end to the Russian military threat. He amassed an army of over 600,000 men, including a core of Frenchmen and over 400,000 other soldiers drawn from the rest of his empire. He intended the usual short campaign crowned by a decisive battle, but the Russians disappointed him by retreating before his advance. His vast superiority in numbers—the Russians had only about 160,000 troops—made it foolish for them to risk a battle. Instead they followed a "scorched-earth" policy, destroying all food and supplies as they retreated. The so-called Grand Army of Napoleon could not live off the country, and the expanse of Russia made supply lines too long to maintain. Terrible rains, fierce heat, shortages of food and water, and the courage of the Russian rear guard defending their country against the invader eroded the morale of Napoleon's army. Napoleon's advisers urged him to abandon the venture, but he feared that an unsuccessful campaign would undermine his position in the empire and in France. He pinned his faith on the Russians' unwillingness to abandon Moscow without a fight.

In September 1812 Russian public opinion forced the army to give Napoleon the battle he wanted in spite of the canny Russian General Kutuzov's wish to avoid the fight and to let the Russian winter defeat the invader. At

THE
CONTINENTAL
SYSTEM
1806 – 1810

AREAS IN WHICH
BRITISH EXPORTS
WERE PROHIBITED

THE
FRENCH EMPIRE

THE
GRAND EMPIRE

ALLIED WITH
NAPOLEON

300 MI.
300 KM.

NORWAY
Christiana
SWEDEN
Stockholm
Gothenburg
GOTHLAN

KINGDOM OF
DENMARK
AND
NORWAY

DENMARK
Copenhagen
BALTIC

SWEDISH
POMERANIA

SCOTLAND
Edinburgh

NORTH
SEA

HELIGO-
LAND
(U.K.)
Lübeck
MECK

Hamburg

PRUSSIA

THOR
GRA
Posen
BERLIN
SAXONY
Bres
LEIPZIG
BAUTZEN
DRESDEN

York

UNITED
KINGDOM

WALES

London
Dover
Boulogne

HOLLAND
OLDEN-
BURG
Brussels
WATERLOO
Cologne

WEST-
PHALIA
BERG
HESSE
Mainz
CONFEDERATION
OF THE
RHINE

JENA

Prague
BOHEMIA
AUSTERLITZ

Brest

Amiens
Reims
Paris
Versailles
Fontainebleau
Orléans

VALMY
Strasbourg

BADEN
ULM
Munich
RATISBON
HOHENLINDEN
BAVARIA
INNSBRUCK

WAGRAM
ASPERN
Vienna

EMPIR

QUIBERON

Nantes

FRANCE

SWITZ.
ST. GOTTHARD

SAVOY

LOMBARDY
Milan
LODI
VENETIA
SACILE

Trieste

BATTLE
SITES

VENDÉE

Rochefort

Bordeaux

BAY OF
BISCAY

Lyons

Turin
MARENGO
Genoa

Avignon
Marseilles
Nice
Leghorn
Toulon

LUCCA

K. OF
ITALY

Urbino

ILLYRIAN PROVIN
A D R I A
BO

ELBA
CORSICA

Rome

Bari
Naples
K. OF
NAPLES

CAPE
FINISTERRE
Corunna

Oporto

PORTUGAL

VIMEIRO
CINTRA
Lisbon

VITORIA
Burgos

ALMEIDA
SALAMANCA
CIUDAD
RODRIGO

SARAGOSSA
GERONA
Barcelona
TARRAGONA

ELVAS
BADAJOZ

TALAVERA
Madrid
SPAIN
OCAÑA
CIUDAD
REAL
VALENCIA
VALENCIA

Cordova
BAYLEN

Seville
MURCIA
ANDALUCIA

Cadiz

TRAFALGAR

GIBALTAR
(U.K.)

BALEARIC IS.

K. OF
SARDINIA
Cagliari

K. OF
SICILY

M E D I T E R R A N E A

Algiers

Tunis

632   *The Age of Napoleon and the Triumph of Romanticism*

NAPOLEONIC EUROPE IN LATE 1812

By mid-1812 the areas shown in black were incorporated into France, and most of the rest of Europe was directly controlled by or allied with Napoleon. But Russia had withdrawn from the failing Continental System, and the decline of Napoleon was about to begin.

CHRONOLOGY

1806 NOV. 21 — NAPOLEON ESTABLISHES THE CONTINENTAL SYSTEM PROHIBITING ALL TRADE WITH ENGLAND.

1807 JULY 7 — THE PEACE CONFERENCE AT TILSIT RESULTS IN RUSSIA JOINING THE CONTINENTAL SYSTEM AND BECOMING AN ALLY OF NAPOLEON.

1809 AND 1810 — NAPOLEON AT THE PEAK OF HIS POWER.

1810 DEC. 31 — RUSSIA WITHDRAWS FROM THE CONTINENTAL SYSTEM AND RESUMES RELATIONS WITH BRITAIN. NAPOLEON PLANS TO CRUSH RUSSIA MILITARILY.

1812 JUNE–DECEMBER — NAPOLEON INVADES RUSSIA. THE RUSSIANS ADOPT A SCORCHED-EARTH POLICY AND BURN MOSCOW. THE THWARTED NAPOLEON DESERTS HIS DWINDLING ARMY AND RUSHES BACK TO PARIS.

Borodino, not far west of Moscow, the bloodiest battle of the Napoleonic era cost the French 30,000 casualties and the Russians almost twice as many. Yet the Russian army was not destroyed, and Napoleon had won nothing substantial. The retreating Russians set fire to Moscow and left Napoleon far from home with a badly diminished army and lacking adequate supplies as winter came to a vast country whose people hated the invader. Napoleon addressed several peace offers to Alexander, but the tsar ignored them. By October what was left of the Grand Army was forced to retreat. By December Napoleon realized that the Russian fiasco would encourage plots against him at home and returned to Paris, leaving the remnants of his army to struggle westward. Perhaps only as many as 100,000 lived to tell the tale of their terrible ordeal.

Even as the news of the disaster reached the west, the total defeat of Napoleon was far from certain. He was able to put down his opponents in Paris and to raise another army of 350,000 men. Neither the Prussians nor the Austrians were eager to risk another bout with Napoleon, and even the Russians hesitated. The Austrian foreign minister, Prince Klemens von Metternich (1773–1859), would have been glad to make a negotiated peace that would leave Napoleon on the throne of a shrunken and chastened France rather than see Europe dominated by Russia. Napoleon might have won a reasonable settlement by negotiation had he been willing to make concessions that would have split his jealous opponents, but he would not consider that solution. As he explained to Metternich, "Your sovereigns born on the throne can let themselves be beaten twenty times and return to their capitals. I cannot do this because I am an

The leading figures of the Congress of Vienna are here portrayed in a single group. Talleyrand has his arm on the table at right, and Metternich, in white breeches, stands toward the left. The actual work of the Congress took place in small meetings, with only a few of these statesmen present. The artist was Isabey. [Austrian Information Service, New York.]

upstart soldier. My domination will not survive the day when I cease to be strong, and therefore feared."[2]

In 1813 patriotic pressure and national ambition brought together the last and most powerful coalition against Napoleon. The Russians drove westward and were joined by Prussia and then Austria. All were assisted by vast amounts of British money. From the west Wellington marched his peninsular army into France. Napoleon's new army was inexperienced and poorly equipped. His generals had lost confidence and were tired. The emperor himself was worn out and sick. Still he was able to wage a skillful campaign in central Europe and to defeat the allies at Dresden. In October, however, he met the combined armies of the enemy at Leipzig in what the Germans called the Battle of the Nations and was decisively defeated. At the end of March 1814 the allied army marched into Paris, and a few days later Napoleon abdicated and went into exile on the island of Elba off the coast of northern Italy.

2 Quoted in Felix Markham, *Napoleon and the Awakening of Europe* (New York: Macmillan, 1965), pp. 115–116.

The Congress of Vienna and the European Settlement

The victorious coalition had been held together by fear of Napoleon and hostility to his ambitions. As soon as he was removed, the allies began to pursue their own separate ambitions. The key person in achieving agreement was Robert Stewart Viscount Castlereagh (1769–1822), the British foreign secretary. Even before the victorious armies had entered Paris, he brought about the signing of the Treaty of Chaumont on March 9, 1814. It provided for the restoration of the Bourbon dynasty to the French throne and the contraction of France to its frontiers of 1792. Even more important was the agreement by Britain, Austria, Russia, and Prussia to form a Quadruple Alliance for twenty years to guarantee the peace terms and to act together to preserve whatever settlement they later agreed upon. Remaining problems, and they were many, and final details were left for a conference to be held at Vienna.

The Congress of Vienna assembled in September 1814, and its work was not concluded until November 1815. Although it was attended by a glittering array of heads of state, the important work of the conference was carried out by the four great powers. The only full session of the congress met to ratify the arrangements made by the big four. The easiest problem facing the great powers was France. All the victors were agreed that no single state should be allowed to dominate Europe, and all were determined to see that France should be pre-

Napoleon Looks Back from Exile on St. Helena

The following remarks are from the ex-emperor's final period of exile on St. Helena, 1815–1821.

FRANCE, *by her geographical situation, the fertility of her soil, the energy and intelligence of her inhabitants, is the arbitress of European states. She is among the nations of Europe what the lion is amongst the other animals. . . .*

Those who are called to hold the reins of such a kingdom should comprehend the full value and bearing of the favourable position which France enjoys, and never suffer a nation which was destined to be a sun, to degenerate into a satellite.

The whole of my policy was uniformly directed by this opinion, both during the consulate and the empire. . . .

Had I reigned twenty years longer, I would have shown the difference between a constitutional emperor and a king of France. The kings of France have never done anything save in the interests of their dynasty, and with a view [to] increasing their feudal power by the depression of the high nobility, the extinction of the great fiefs and their reunion with the crown. . . . I would have changed the face of France and of Europe. Archimedes promised to move the world, if they only furnished him with a fulcrum for his lever; I would have made a fulcrum for myself, wherever I could have [put into action] my energy, my perseverance, and my budgets. With budgets well employed, a world may be regenerated.

Napoleon, ed. by Maurice Hutt (Englewood Cliffs, N.J.: Prentice-Hall, 1972), pp. 55–56.

vented from doing so again. The restoration of the French Bourbon monarchy, which was again popular, and a nonvindictive boundary settlement kept France calm and satisfied. In addition the powers constructed a series of states to serve as barriers to any new French expansion. They established the kingdom of the Netherlands, including Belgium, in the north and added Genoa to Piedmont in the south. Prussia, whose power was increased by accessions in eastern Europe, was given important new territories in the west along the Rhine River to deter French aggression in that area. Austria was given full control of northern Italy to prevent a repetition of Napoleon's conquests there. As for the rest of Germany, most of Napoleon's arrangements were left un-

touched. The venerable Holy Roman Empire, which had been dissolved in 1806, was not revived. In all these areas the congress established the rule of legitimate monarchs and rejected any hint of the republican and democratic politics that had flowed from the French Revolution.

On these matters agreement was not difficult, but the settlement of eastern Europe sharply divided the victors. Alexander I of Russia wanted all Poland under his rule. Prussia was willing if she herself received all of Saxony. But Austria was unwilling to surrender its share of Poland or to see the growth of Prussian power and the penetration of Russia deeper into central Europe. The Polish–Saxon question brought the congress to a standstill and almost brought on a new war among the victors, but defeated France provided a way out. The wily Talleyrand, now representing France at Vienna, suggested that the weight of France added to that of Britain and Austria might bring Alexander to his senses. When news of a secret treaty among the three leaked out, the tsar agreed to become ruler of a smaller Poland, and Frederick William III of Prussia agreed to accept only part of Saxony. Thereafter France was included as a fifth great power in all deliberations.

Unity among the victors was further restored by Napoleon's return from Elba on March 1, 1815. The French army was still loyal to the former emperor, and many Frenchmen thought that their fortunes might be safer under his rule than under that of the restored Bourbons. The coalition seemed to be dissolving in Vienna. Napoleon seized the opportunity, escaped to France, and was soon restored to power. He promised a liberal constitution and a peaceful foreign policy. The allies were not convinced. They declared Napoleon an outlaw, a new device under international law, and sent their armies to crush him. Wellington, with the crucial help of the Prussians under Field Marshal von Blücher, defeated Napoleon at Waterloo in Belgium on June 18, 1815. Napoleon again abdicated and was sent into exile to St. Helena, a tiny Atlantic island off the coast of Africa, where he spent the rest of his life.

EUROPE
IN 1815

Bergen

NORWAY
AND
SWEDEN
1814

Christiania

Stockholm

FINLAND
RUSS., 18

NORTH

SCOTLAND

Edinburgh

DENMARK

SEA

BALTIC SEA

Belfast

SCHLESWIG

PRUSSIA

Danzig

IRELAND

Dublin

Liver-
pool

Manchester

BOUNDARY OF THE
GERMAN
CONFEDERATION

HOLSTEIN

EAST
PRUSSIA

HANOVER

(FORMER
DUTCH
REP.)

Warsaw

UNITED
KINGDOM

London

(FORMER
AUSTR.
NETHS.)

K. OF THE
NETHERLANDS

Berlin

Breslau

K. OF
POLAND
(RUSS.)

Cologne

ATLANTIC

Brussels

Cracow

Brest

Rouen

Prague

BOHEMIA

MORAVIA

Paris

Reims

LORRAINE

Rennes

Orléans

Strassburg

BAVARIA

AUSTRIAN

Nantes

FRANCE

ALSACE

Munich

AUSTRIA

Vienna

HUNGARY

Budapest

OCEAN

Berne

SWITZ.

EMPIRE

Lyons

SAVOY

TYROL

VENETIA

Trieste

Agram

CROATIA

Bordeaux

LOM-
BARDY

Montpelier

PIEDMONT

PAR.

MOD.

Bologna

BOSNIA

Belgrade

NICE

Marseilles

LUCCA

Sarajevo

SERBIA

Oviedo

ANDORRA

TUSCANY

STATES
OF THE
CHURCH

MONTE-
NEGRO

Burgos

ELBA

ITALY

PORTUGAL

Madrid

Barcelona

KINGDOM OF
SARDINIA

CORSICA
(FR.)

Rome

Lisbon

SPAIN

Naples

Valencia

BALEARIC IS.
(SP.)

SARDINIA

Cosenza

Cordova

KINGDOM OF THE
TWO SICILIES

Seville

MEDITE

SICILY

Tangier

GIBRALTAR (U.K.)

Ceuta
(SP.)

THE BARBARY STATES

Algiers

Tunis

Och

Ja

Fez

MOROCCO

ALGERIA
TURK TO 1830

TUNISIA
(TURK.)

MALTA
(U.K.)

T R MILLER

The Age of Napoleon and the Triumph of Romanticism

The Congress of Vienna achieved the post-Napoleonic territorial adjustments shown on the map. The most notable arrangements dealt with areas along France's borders (Netherlands, Prussia, Switzerland, and Piedmont) and in Poland and northern Italy.

The Hundred Days, as the period of Napoleon's return is called, frightened the great powers and hardened the peace settlement for France. In addition to some minor territorial adjustments, the victors imposed a war indemnity and an army of occupation on France. The Quadruple Alliance was renewed. Alexander also proposed a Holy Alliance, whereby the monarchs promised to act in accordance with Christian principles. Austria and Prussia signed; but Castlereagh thought it absurd, and England abstained. The tsar, who was then embracing mysticism, thought his proposal a valuable tool for international relations. The Holy Alliance soon became a symbol of extreme political reaction.

The chief aims of the Congress of Vienna were to prevent a recurrence of the Napoleonic nightmare and to arrange an acceptable settlement for Europe that might produce lasting peace. In achieving these goals it was remarkably successful. France accepted the new situation without undue resentment. The victorious powers settled difficult problems in a reasonable way. They established a legalistic balance of power and methods for adjusting to change. The work of the congress has been criticized for failing to recognize and provide for the great forces that would stir the nineteenth century—nationalism and democracy—but such criticism is inappropriate. The settlement, like all such agreements, was aimed at solving past ills, and in that it succeeded. If the powers failed to anticipate future problems or to yield to forces of which they disapproved, they would have been more than human to have done so. Perhaps it was unusual enough to produce a settlement that remained essentially intact for almost half a century and that allowed Europe to suffer no general war for one hundred years.

The Romantic Movement

The years of the French Revolution and the conquests of Napoleon saw the emergence of a new and very important intellectual movement throughout Europe. Romanticism in its various manifestations was a reaction against much of the thought of the Enlightenment. Romantic writers opposed what they considered the excessive scientific narrowness of the eighteenth-century *philosophes*. The latter stood accused of subjecting everything to geometrical and mathematical models and thereby demeaning the world of the feelings and of imagination. Romantic thinkers refused to conceive of human nature as primarily rational. They wanted to interpret both physical nature and human society in organic rather than in mechanical terms and categories. Where the Enlightenment spokesmen had often criticized religion and faith, the Romantics saw religion as basic to human nature and faith as a means to knowledge. Expressing this reaction to the rationalism of the previous century the German Romantic composer Franz Schubert (1797–1828) called the Enlightenment "that ugly skeleton without flesh or blood."

Some historians, most notably Arthur O. Lovejoy, have warned against speaking of a single European-wide Romantic Movement. They have pointed out that a variety of such movements, occurring almost simultaneously in Germany, England, and France, arose independently and had their own particular courses of development. Such considerations have not, however, prevented the designation of a specific historical period, dated roughly from 1780 to 1830, as the Age of Romanticism or the Romantic Movement. Despite national differences a shared reaction to the Enlightenment marked all of these writers and artists. They generally saw the imagination or some such intuitive intellectual faculty supplementing the reason as a means of perceiving and understanding the world. They urged a revival of Christianity such as had permeated Europe during the Middle Ages. And unlike the *philosophes*, the Romantics liked the art, the literature, and the architecture of medieval times. They were also deeply interested in folklore, folk songs, and fairy tales. The Romantics were also fascinated by dreams, hallucinations, sleepwalking, and other phenomena that suggested the existence of a world beyond that of empirical observation, sensory data, and discursive reasoning.

Several historical streams fed the Romantic movement. These included the individualism of the Renaissance and the Reformation and the Pietism of the seventeenth century and the eighteenth-century English Methodist movement, which encouraged a heartfelt, practical religion in place of dogmatism, rationalism, and deism. The sentimental novels of the eighteenth century, such as Samuel Richardson's *Clarissa,* also paved the way for thinkers who would emphasize feeling and emotion. The so-called *Sturm und Drang* ("storm and stress") period of German literature and German idealist philosophy were important for the Romantics. However, two writers who were also closely related to the Enlightenment provided the immediate intellectual foundations for Romanticism. They were Rousseau and Immanuel Kant, both of whom raised questions about the sufficiency of the rationalism so dear to the *philosophes*.

It has already been pointed out in Chapter 22 that Jean Jacques Rousseau, though sharing in some of the reformist spirit of the Enlightenment, opposed many of its other facets. What Romantic writers especially drew from Rousseau was his conviction that society had corrupted human nature. In the two *Discourses* and others of his works Rousseau had portrayed humankind as created happy and good by nature and originally living in a state of equilibrium, able to do what it desired and desiring only what it was able to do. For humankind to become happy again, it must remain true to its natural being, while still attempting to realize the new moral possibilities of life in society.

In the *Social Contract* (1762) Rousseau had provided his prescription for the reorganization of political life that would achieve that goal.

Immanuel Kant was the most important German philosopher of the late eighteenth century. His thought was the capstone of the philosophy of the Enlightenment and paved the way for Romanticism. [Bettmann Archive.]

Rousseau set forth his view on the individual's development toward the good and happy life in a novel entitled *Émile* (1762). Initially this treatise on education was far more influential than the *Social Contract*. In *Émile* Rousseau stressed the difference between children and adults. He distinguished the stages of human maturation and urged that in rearing children one must give them maximum individual freedom. Each child should be allowed to grow freely, like a plant, and to learn by trial and error what reality is and how best to deal with it. The parent or teacher would help most by providing the basic necessities of life and warding off what was manifestly harmful. Otherwise the adult should stay completely out of the way, like a gardener who waters and weeds his garden but otherwise lets nature take its course.

This was a revolutionary concept of education in an age accustomed to narrow, bookish, and highly regimented vocational education and learning. Rousseau thought that the child's sentiments as well as its reason should be permitted to flourish. To Romantic writers this concept of human development vindicated the rights of nature over those of artificial society and would eventually lead to a natural society. In its fully developed form this view of life led the Romantics to place a high value on the uniqueness of each individual person and to explore in great detail the experiences of childhood. Like Rousseau, the Romantics saw humankind, nature, and society as organically related to each other.

Immanuel Kant (1724–1804) wrote the two greatest philosophical works of the late eighteenth century: *The Critique of Pure Reason* (1781) and *The Critique of Practical Reason* (1788). He sought to accept the rationalism of the Enlightenment and still to preserve a belief in human freedom, immortality, and the existence of God. Against Locke and other philosophers who saw knowledge rooted in sensory experience alone, Kant successfully argued for the subjective character of human knowledge. For Kant the human mind did not simply reflect the world around it like a passive mirror: rather it actively imposed on the world of sensory experience "forms of sensibility" and "categories of understanding." These categories were generated by the mind itself. In other words, the human mind perceives the world as it does because of its own internal mental categories. What this meant was that human perceptions were radically subjective and as much the product of the mind's own activity as of sense experience.

Kant found the sphere of reality that was accessible to pure reason to be quite limited. However, he believed that beyond the phenomenal world over which "pure reason" was master there existed what he called the "noumenal" world. The latter was a sphere of moral and aesthetic reality known by "practical reason" and conscience. Kant thought that all men possessed an innate sense of moral duty or an awareness of what he called a "categorical imperative." This term referred to an inner command to act in every situation as one would have all other people always act in the same situation. The existence of this imperative of conscience was regarded by Kant as incontrovertible proof of humankind's natural freedom. On the basis of humankind's moral sense Kant went on to postulate the existence of God, eternal life, and future rewards and punishments. He believed that these transcendental truths could not be proved by discursive reasoning. Still he was convinced that they were realities to which every reasonable person could attest.

To many Romantic writers Kantian philosophy was a decisive refutation of the narrow rationality of the Enlightenment. Whether they called it "practical reason," "fancy," "imagination," "intuition," or simply "feeling," the Romantics believed in the presence of a special power in the human mind that could penetrate beyond the limits of human understanding as set forth by Hobbes, Locke, and Hume. Most of them also believed that poets and artists generally possessed these powers in particular abundance. Other Romantic writers appealed to the limits of human reason to set forth new religious ideas or political thought often at odds with that of Enlightenment writers.

An illustration made in 1825 for the Biblical book of Job by the English Romantic poet and engraver William Blake. [The Granger Collection.]

Romantic Literature

The term *romantic* appeared in English and French literature as early as the seventeenth century. Neoclassical writers used the word at that time to describe literature that they considered to be unreal, sentimental, or excessively fanciful. In the eighteenth century the English writer Thomas Warton associated *romantic* with medieval romances. In Germany, a major center of the Romantic literary movement, Johann Gottfried Herder used the terms *romantic* and *Gothic* interchangeably. In both England and Germany the term came to be applied to all literature that failed to observe classical forms and rules and gave free play to the imagination. English Romantic poets and essayists looked on the period of literature from John Dryden to Alexander Pope, roughly 1670–1750, as a classical "dark age." For both English and German Romantics the French Neoclassicists of the seventeenth century, such as Pierre Corneille and Jean Racine, were slavish imitators of the classics and represented all that literature should not be.

As an alternative to such dependence on the ancients August Wilhelm von Schlegel (1767–1845) praised the "romantic" literature of Dante, Petrarch, Boccaccio, Shakespeare, the Arthurian legends, Cervantes, and Calderón. According to Schlegel, Romantic literature was to classical literature what the organic and living were to the merely mechanical. He set forth his views in *Lectures on Dramatic Art and Literature* (1809–1811).

The Romantic Movement had peaked in Germany and England before it became a major force in France under the leadership of Madame de Staël (1766–1817) and Victor Hugo (1802–1885). So influential was the classical tradition in France that not until 1816 did a French writer openly declare himself a Romantic. That was Henri Beyle, who wrote under the pseudonym Stendahl (1783–1842). He praised Shakespeare and Lord Byron and criticized his own countryman, the seventeenth-century classical dramatist Racine.

The English Romantics believed that poetry was en-hanced by freely following the creative impulses of the mind. In this belief they directly opposed Lockean psychology, which regarded the mind as a passive receptor and poetry a mechanical exercise of "wit" following prescribed rules. For William Blake and Samuel Taylor Coleridge the artist's imagination was God at work in the mind. As Blake expressed his views, the imagination was "a repetition in the finite mind of the eternal act of creation in the infinite I AM." Percy Bysshe Shelley believed that "A poet participates in the eternal, the infinite, and the One." So conceived, poetry could not be considered idle play. It was the highest of human acts, man's self-fullfillment in a transcendental world.

William Blake (1757–1827) considered the poet a seer and poetry translated vision. He thought it a great tragedy that so many people understood the world only rationally and could perceive no innocence or beauty in it. In the 1790s he experienced a period of deep personal depression, which seems to have been related to his own inability to perceive the world as he believed it to be. The better one got to know the world, the more the life of the imagination and its spiritual values seemed to recede. Blake saw this problem as evidence of the materialism and injustice of English society. He was deeply impressed by

William Wordsworth was among the earliest and most influential of the English Romantic poets. He was particularly noted for his nature poetry. [Culver Pictures.]

the strong sense of contradiction between a true childlike vision of the world and conceptions of it based on actual experience. Through his own poetry he sought to bring childlike innocence and experience together and to transform experience by imagination. The conflict of which he was so much aware can be seen in *Songs of Innocence* (1789) and *Songs of Experience* (1794). In "The Tyger," published in the latter, he asked:

> Tyger, Tyger, burning bright
> In the forests of the night,
>
> . . . .
> When the stars threw down their spears
> And watered heaven with their tears,
> Did He smile His work to see?
> Did He who made the lamb make thee?

Samuel Taylor Coleridge (1772–1834) was the master of Gothic poems of the supernatural. His three poems, "Christabel," "The Ancient Mariner," and "Kubla Khan," are of this character. "The Ancient Mariner" relates the story of a sailor cursed for killing an albatross. The poem treats the subject as a crime against nature and God and raises the issues of guilt, punishment, and the redemptive possibilities of humility and penance. At the end of the poem the mariner discovers the unity and beauty of all things and, having repented, is delivered from his awful curse, which has been symbolized by the dead albatross hung around his neck:

> O happy living things! no tongue
> Their beauty might declare:
> A spring of love gushed from my heart,
> And I blessed them unaware . . .
> The self-same moment I could pray;
> And from my neck so free
> The Albatross fell off, and sank
> Like lead into the sea.

Coleridge also made major contributions to romantic literary criticism in his lectures on Shakespeare and in *Biographia Literaria* (1817), which presents his theories of poetry.

William Wordsworth (1770–1850) was Coleridge's closest friend. Together they published *Lyrical Ballads* in 1798 as a manifesto of poetry that rejected the rules of eighteenth-century criticism. Among Wordsworth's most important later poems is his "Ode on Intimations of Immortality" (1803), written in part to console Coleridge, who was in the midst of a deep personal crisis. Its subject is the loss of poetic vision, something Wordsworth also keenly felt at this time in himself. Nature, which he had worshiped, no longer spoke freely to him, and he feared that it might never speak to him again:

> There was a time when meadow, grove, and stream,
> The earth, and every common sight,
>   To me did seem
>   Appareled in celestial light,
> The glory and the freshness of a dream.
> It is not now as it hath been of yore—
>   Turn whereso'er I may,
>   By night or day,
> The things which I have seen I now can see no more.

What he had lost was the vision that he believed all human beings lose in the necessary process of maturation: their childlike vision and closeness to spiritual reality. For both Wordsworth and Coleridge childhood was the bright period of creative imagination. Wordsworth held a theory of the soul's preexistence in a celestial state prior to its creation. The child, being closer in time to its eternal origin and undistracted by much worldly experience, recollects the supernatural world much more easily. Aging and urban living corrupt and deaden the imagination and make one's inner feelings and the beauty of nature less important. Yet Wordsworth took consolation in the occasional moments of later life when he still found in nature "intimations of immortality," a brief glimpse of humankind's eternal origin and destiny:

George Gordon, Lord Byron not only wrote important Romantic poetry but also became a romantic hero in his own right by his death in the Greek revolution in 1824. The portrait by Richard Westall is itself a bit of Romanticism. [The Granger Collection.]

O joy! that in our embers
Is something that doth live,
That Nature yet remembers
What was so fugitive!

In his book-length poem *The Prelude* (1850) Wordsworth presented a long autobiographical account of the growth of the poet's mind.

Percy Bysshe Shelley (1792–1822), a very philosophical poet, lived in a Platonic world of ideas more real to him than anything in the sensible world. One of his greatest poetic works, *Prometheus Unbound* (1820), was written in Rome when he was twenty-seven years old. It was stimulated by Aeschylus's *Prometheus Bound*, the story of a defiant Titan who stole fire from the gods and paid for his crime by being eternally bound to a rock and attacked by savage birds. For Shelley, Prometheus was a symbol of all that was good in life, the principle of life itself. He was the friend of humanity, who like Christ suffered because he tried to improve humankind. He was the soul's unconquerable desire to create harmony in the world through reasonableness and love. In the poem Prometheus struggles against Jupiter, who represents tyranny and the power of evil in the world. He receives assistance in his struggle from Asia, a symbol of unspoiled nature, and from Mother Earth. In the end Jupiter is overthrown by his own son, Demogorgon, who rewards Prometheus's patience and endurance by setting him free. Demogorgon summarizes the poem's romantic message:

To suffer woes which Hope thinks infinite;
To forgive wrongs darker than death or night;
    To defy Power, which seems omnipotent;
To live, and bear; to hope til Hope creates
From its own wreck the thing it contemplates;
    Neither to change, nor falter, nor repent;
This, like thy glory, Titan, is to be
Good, great and joyous, beautiful and free;
This alone Life, Joy, Empire, and Victory.

A true rebel among the Romantic poets was Lord Byron (1788–1824). At home even the other Romantic writers distrusted and generally disliked him. He had little sympathy for their views of the imagination. However, outside England Byron was regarded as the embodiment of the new person of the French Revolution. He rejected the old traditions (he was divorced and famous for his amours) and championed the cause of personal liberty. Byron was outrageously skeptical and mocking, even of his own beliefs. In *Childe Harold's Pilgrimage* (1812) he created the the figure of a brooding, melancholy romantic hero. In *Don Juan* (1819) he wrote with ribald humor, acknowledged nature's cruelty as well as its beauty, and even expressed admiration for urban life. Byron tended to be content with the world as he directly knew it. He found his own experience of nature and love, objectively described and reported without embellishment, sufficient for poetic inspiration. He had the rare ability to encompass in his work the whole of his age and to write on subjects other Romantics considered unworthy of poetry.

The major figures of the early Romantic movement in Germany are August Wilhelm Schlegel and his brother Friedrich (1772–1829); Friedrich von Hardenberg, known under the pseudonym Novalis (1772–1801); Ludwig Tieck (1773–1853), famous for the story *Puss-in-Boots*; and Heinrich Wackenroder (1773–1798). In 1798 this group, under the leadership of the Schlegels, founded the principal organ of German Romanticism, the journal *Athenäum*. Their principles were derived from Shakespeare, Calderón, Johann Wolfgang von Goethe (1749–1832), Johann Christoph Friedrich von Schiller (1759–1805), and Friedrich Gottlieb Klopstock (1724–1803). *Athenäum* featured the most definitive Romantic views on art, literature, philosophy, and life, with contributions that were original, provocative, and seminal.

Much romantic poetry was also written on the continent, but almost all major German Romantics wrote at least one novel. Romantic novels tended to be highly sentimental and often borrowed material from medieval

The poetry of the German Johann Wolfgang von Goethe illustrated humankind striving with physical nature and attempting to discover the possibility of moral life on earth. The picture is a detail of a 1786 painting by Tischbein. [Bettmann Archive.]

romances. Novalis's *Heinrich von Ofterdingen* (1802), for example, was the story of a brooding poetical knight in search of a blue flower, symbolic of truth. The characters of Romantic novels were treated as symbols of the larger truth of life. Purely realistic description was avoided. The first German Romantic novel, Ludwig Tieck's *William Lovell* (1793–1795), contrasted the young Lovell, whose life is built on love and imagination, with those who live by cold reason alone and who thus become an easy prey to unbelief, misanthrophy, and egoism. As the novel rambles to its conclusion, Lovell is ruined by a mixture of philosophy, materialism, and skepticism, which are administered to him by two women he naively loves.

Friedrich Schlegel wrote a very progressive early Romantic novel, *Lucinde* (1799), which attacked contemporary prejudices against women as capable of being little more than lovers and domestics. Schlegel's novel reveals the ability of the Romantics to become involved in the social issues of their day. He depicted Lucinde as the perfect friend and companion, as well as the unsurpassed lover, of the hero. Like other early Romantic novels, the work shocked contemporary morals by frankly discussing sexual activity and by describing Lucinde as equal in all ways to the male hero.

Another important early Romantic novelist, E. T. A. Hoffmann (1776–1822), in *the Devil's Elixer* (1815–1816), traced in psychological detail the moral downfall of a monk aroused by sexuality. In these and other similiar works the Romantics attempted to repudiate many of the more widespread social values of their day. Their writings often reflect the world of dissolving certainties brought about by the continent-wide turmoil of the French Revolution and Napoleonic wars. What began as a movement in rebellion against literary norms became a movement in rebellion against social prejudices.

During the first three decades of the nineteenth century the Romantic Movement, begun in Berlin and Jena, established itself in major universities throughout Germany. Among other important nineteenth-century Romantics were Clemens Brentano (1778–1842) and

Achim von Arnim (1781–1831), famous for their collection of folk songs; the Grimm brothers, Jakob (1785–1863) and Wilhelm (1786–1859), famous for their collection of fairy tales; the tragic dramatist Heinrich von Kleist (1777–1811); and Heinrich Heine (1797–1856), the German master of satire and sarcasm.

Religion in the Romantic Period

During the Middle Ages the foundation of religion had been the church. The Reformation leaders had appealed to the authority of the Bible. Then, later Enlightenment writers had attempted to derive religion from the rational nature revealed by Newtonian physics. Romantic religious thinkers, on the other hand, appealed to the inner emotions of humankind for the foundation of religion. Their forerunners were the mystics of Western Christianity. One of the first great examples of a variety of Romantic religion—Methodism—occurred in England.

Methodism originated in the middle of the eighteenth century as a revolt against deism and rationalism in the Church of England. The Methodist revival formed an important part of the background of English Romanticism. The leader of the Methodist movement was John Wesley (1703–1791). His education and religious development had been carefully supervised by a remarkable mother, Susannah Wesley, who bore eighteen children in addition to John.

While at Oxford, Wesley organized a religious group known as the "Holy Club". He soon left England to give himself to missionary work in Georgia in America, where he arrived in 1735. While crossing the Atlantic, he had been deeply impressed by a group of German Moravians on the ship. These German pietists exhibited unshakable faith and confidence during a violent storm at sea while Wesley despaired of his life. Wesley concluded that they knew far better then he the meaning of justification by faith. When he returned to England in 1738 after an unhappy missionary career, Wesley began to worship with Moravians in London. There in 1739 he underwent a conversion experience that he described in the words,

John Wesley was the founder of the Methodist
movement in Great Britain. His preaching, teaching,
and revivals constituted—and expressed—one of the
major impulses toward Romantic religion.
[The Granger Collection.]

François René de Chateaubriand was the
author of *The Genius of Christianity,* one of the key
documents of the Roman Catholic revival of the
Romantic period. The portrait is by the Marquise de
Custine. [The Granger Collection.]

"My heart felt strangely warmed." From that point on he
felt assured of his own salvation.

Wesley discovered that he could not preach his version
of Christian conversion and practical piety in Anglican
Church pulpits. Therefore, late in 1739 he began to
preach in the open fields about the cities and towns of
western England. Literally thousands of humble people
responded to his message of repentance and good works.
Soon he and his brother Charles, who became famous for
his hymns, began to organize Methodist societies. By the
late eighteenth century the Methodists had become a
separate church. They ordained their own clergy and
sent missionaries to America, where the Methodists
eventually achieved their greatest success and most widespread influence.

The essence of Methodist teaching lay in its stress on
inward, heartfelt religion and the possibility of Christian
perfection in this life. John Wesley described Christianity
as "an inward principle . . . the image of God impressed
on a created spirit, a fountain of peace and love springing
up into everlasting life." True Christians were those who
were "saved in this world from all sin, from all unright-
eousness . . . and now in such a sense perfect as not to
commit sin and . . . freed from evil thoughts and evil
tempers."[3] Many people, weary of the dry rationalism
that derived from deism, found Wesley's ideal relevant to
their own lives. The Methodist preachers emphasized the
role of enthusiastic emotional experience as part of Christian conversion. After Wesley, religious revivals became
highly emotional in style and content.

Similar religion based on feeling appeared on the Continent. After the Thermidorian reaction a strong Roman
Catholic revival took place in France. Its followers were
people who had disapproved both the religious policy of
the revolution and the anticlericalism of the Enlightenment. The most important book to express these sentiments was *The Genius of Christianity* (1802) by Vicomte
François René de Chateaubriand (1768–1848). In this
work, which became known as the "Bible of Romanticism," Chateaubriand argued that the essence of religion
was "passion." The foundation of faith in the church was
the emotion that its teachings and sacraments inspired in
the heart of the Christian.

Against the Newtonian view of the world and of a
rational God, the Romantics found God immanent in
nature. No one stated the Romantic religious ideal more
eloquently or with greater impact on the modern world
than Friedrich Schleiermacher (1768–1834). In 1799 he
published *Speeches on Religion to Its Cultured Despisers.* It
was a response to Lutheran orthodoxy, on the one hand,
and to Enlightenment rationalism on the other. The
advocates of both were the "cultured despisers" of real or
heartfelt religion. According to Schleiermacher, religion
was neither dogma nor a system of ethics. It was an
intuition or feeling of absolute dependence on an infinite
reality. Religious institutions, doctrines, and moral activity expressed that primal religious feeling only in a secondary or indirect way.

Although Schleiermacher considered Christianity the
"religion of religion," he also believed that every world
religion was unique in its expression of the primal intuition of the infinite in the finite. He thus turned against
the universal natural religion of the Enlightenment,
which he termed "a name applied to loose, unconnected

3 Quoted in Albert C. Outler (Ed.), *John Wesley: A Representative
Collection of His Writings* (New York): Oxford University Press,
1964), p. 220.

Friedrich Schleiermacher of Germany was
the most important Protestant theologian of the
Romantic period. [The Granger Collection.]

impulses," and defended the meaningfulness of the numerous world religions. Every such religion was seen to
be a unique version of the emotional experience of dependence on an infinite being. In so arguing, Schleiermacher interpreted the religions of the world in the same
way that other Romantic writers interpreted the variety
of unique peoples and cultures.

Romantic Views of Nationalism and History

One of the most distinctive features of Romanticism,
especially in Germany, was its glorification of both the
individual person and individual cultures. Behind these
views lay the philosophy of German idealism, which
understood the world as the creation of subjective egos.
J. G. Fichte (1762–1814), an important German philosopher and nationalist, identified the individual ego with
the Absolute that underlay all existing things. According
to him and other similar philosophers, the world is truly
the creation of humankind. The world is as it is because
especially strong persons conceive of it in a particular way
and impose their wills on the world and other people.
Napoleon served as the contemporary example of such a
great person. This philosophy has ever since served to
justify the glorification of great people and their actions in
overriding all opposition to their wills and desires.

In addition to this philosophy the influence of new
historical studies lay behind the German glorification of
individual cultures. German Romantic writers went in
search of their own past in reaction to the copying of
French manners in eighteenth-century Germany, the
impact of the French Revolution, and the imperialism of
Napoleon. An early leader in this effort was Johann
Gottfried Herder (1744–1803). Herder had early resented the French cultural preponderance in Germany.

This feeling became widespread among German intellectuals after the arrival of Napoleon's armies. In 1778
Herder published an influential essay entitled "On the
Knowing and Feelings of the Human Soul." In it he
vigorously rejected the mechanical explanation of nature
so popular with Enlightenment writers. He saw human
beings and societies as developing organically over time.
Human beings were different at different times and
places.

Herder revived German folk culture by urging the
collection and preservation of distinctive German songs
and sayings. His most important followers in this regard
were the Grimm brothers. Believing that each language

Johann Gottfried von Herder was one of
the founders of nationalism in Europe. He thought
that each nationality had a particular contribution
to offer to the cultural life of the human race.
[Bettmann Archive.]

The Romantic Movement 645

Georg W. F. Hegel introduced the most influential philosophy of history written in the nineteenth century. [Bettmann Archive.]

and culture was the unique expression of a people, Herder opposed both the concept and the use of a "common" language, such as French, and "universal" institutions, such as those imposed on Europe by Napoleon. These, he believed, were forms of tyranny over the individuality of a people. Herder's writings led to a broad revival of interest in history and philosophy. While initially directed toward the identification of German origins, such work soon expanded to embrace other world cultures as well. Eventually the ability of the Romantic imagination to be at home in any age or culture spurred the study of non-Western religion, comparative literature, and philology.

Perhaps the most important person to write about history during the Romantic period was the German Georg Wilhelm Friedrich Hegel (1770–1831). He is one of the most difficult philosophers in the history of Western civilization. He is also one of the most important.

Hegel believed that ideas develop in an evolutionary fashion that involves conflict. At any given time a predominant set of ideas, which he termed the *thesis,* holds sway. They are challenged by other conflicting ideas, which he termed the *antithesis.* As these patterns of thought clash, there emerges a *synthesis,* which eventually becomes the new thesis. Then the process commences all over. Periods of world history receive their character from the patterns of thought predominating during them. A number of important philosophical conclusions followed from this analysis. One of the most significant was the belief that all periods of history have been of practically equal value because each was by definition necessary for the achievement of the civilization that came latter. Also all cultures are valuable because each contributes to the necessary clash of values and ideas that allows humankind to develop. Hegel discussed these concepts in *The Phenomenology of Mind* (1806), *Lectures on the Philosophy of History* (1822–1831), and numerous other works, many of which were published only after his death. During his lifetime his ideas became widely known through his university lectures at Berlin.

These various Romantic ideas made a major contribution to the emergence of nationalism, which proved to be one of the strongest motivating forces of the nineteenth and twentieth centuries. The writers of the Enlightenment had generally championed a cosmopolitan outlook on the world. But the emphasis of the Romantic thinkers was on the individuality and worth of each separate people and culture. The factors that helped to define a people or a nation were common language, common history, a homeland that possessed historical associations, and common customs. This cultural nationalism gradually became transformed into a political creed. It came to be widely believed that every people or nation should constitute a separate political entity and that only when it so existed could the nation be secure in its own character.

The example of France under the revolutionary government and then Napoleon had demonstrated the power of nationhood. Other peoples came to desire similar strength and confidence. Napoleon's toppling of ancient political structures, such as the Holy Roman Empire, demonstrated the need for new political organization in Europe. By 1815 these were the aspirations of only a few Europeans, but as time passed, such yearnings came to be shared by scores of peoples from Ireland to the Ukraine. The Congress of Vienna could ignore such feelings, but for the rest of the nineteenth century, statesmen had to confront the growing reality of their power.

SUGGESTED READINGS

MEYER H. ABRAMS, *The Mirror and the Lamp: Romantic Theory and the Critical Tradition* (New York, 1958). A standard text on Romantic literary theory that looks at English Romanticism in the context of German Romantic idealism.

C. M. BOWRA, *The Romantic Imagination* (Cambridge, 1949). Penetrating individual sketches of the major English romantics.

C. BRINTON, *The Lives of Talleyrand* (New York, 1932). A biography of the diplomat.

G. BRUUN, *Europe and the French Imperium, 1799–1814* (New York, 1938). A good survey.

D. G. CHANDLER, *The Campaigns of Napoleon* (New York, 1966). A good military study.

O. CONNELLY, *Napoleon's Satellite Kingdoms* (New York, 1965). The rule of Napoleon and his family in Europe.

H. C. DEUTSCH, *The Genesis of Napoleon's Imperialism, 1801–1805.* (Cambridge, 1938). Basic for foreign policy.

Dictionary of the History of Ideas, Vol. 4 (New York, 1973), pp. 198–208. Contributions by Rene Wellek, "Romanticism in Literature"; Franklin L. Baumer, "Romanticism (ca. 1780–ca. 1830)"; and Jacques Droz, "Political Romanticism in Germany." Excellent and succinct.

P. GEYL, *Napoleon: For and Against* (New Haven, Conn.: 1949). A fine survey of the historical debate.

E. HECKSCHER, *The Continental System: An Economic Interpretation* (Oxford, 1922). Napoleon's commercial policy.

J. C. HEROLD, *The Age of Napoleon* (New York, 1968). A lively, readable account.

R. HOLTMAN, *The Napoleonic Revolution* (Baton Rouge, La.: 1950). Good on domestic policy.

G. LEFEBVRE, *Napoleon,* 2 vols., trans. by H. Stockhold, (New York, 1969). The fullest and finest biography.

ARTHUR O. LOVEJOY, *"The Meaning of Romanticism for the Historian of Ideas," in Franklin L. Baumer, (Ed.), Intellectual Movements in Modern European History* (New York, 1965). A very influential summary of the basic characteristics of Romanticism.

F. MARKHAM, *Napoleon and the Awakening of Europe* (London, 1954). Emphasizes the growth of nationalism.

F. MARKHAM, *Napoleon* (New York, 1963). A good biography strong on military questions.

H. NICOLSON, *The Congress of Vienna* (London, 1946). A good, readable account.

SIEGBERT PRAWER (Ed.), *The Romantic Period in Germany* (London, 1970). Contributions covering all facets of the movement.

J. L. TALMON, *Romanticism and Revolt: Europe, 1815–1848* (London, 1967). An effort to sketch the Romantic movements and relate them to one another and to the larger political history of the period.

E. TARLE, *Napoleon's Invasion of Russia* (New York, 1942).

J. M. THOMPSON, *Napoleon Bonaparte: His Rise and Fall* (Oxford, 1952). A sound biography.

L. A. WILLOUGHBY, *The Romantic Movement in Germany* (London, 1930). An older but still very useful treatment.

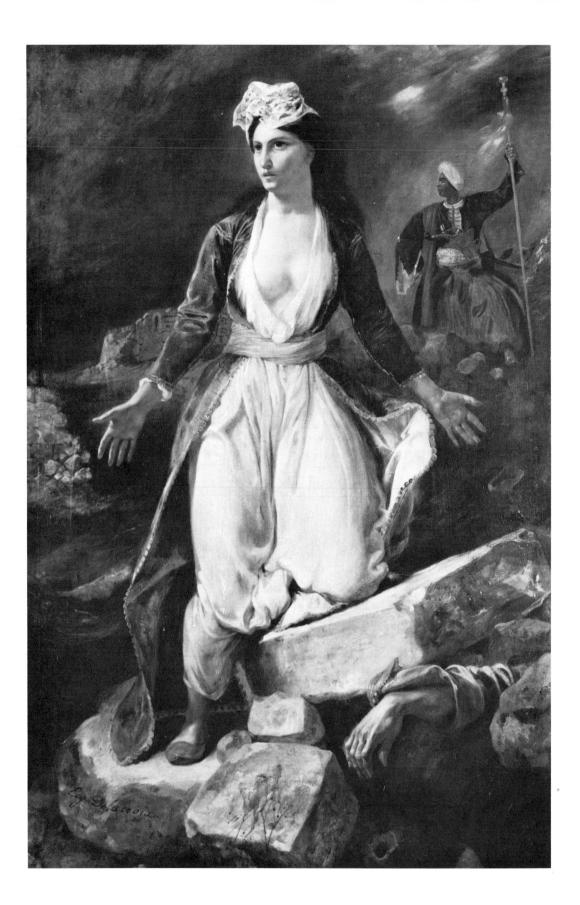

648

25
Restoration, Reaction, and Reform
(1815–1832)

THE DEFEAT of Napoleon and the diplomatic settlement of the Congress of Vienna restored a conservative political and social order in Europe. Legitimate monarchies, landed aristocracies, and established churches constituted the major pillars of conservatism. The institutions themselves were ancient, but the self-conscious alliance of throne, land, and altar was new. Throughout the eighteenth century these groups had been in frequent conflict. Only the upheaval of the French Revolution and the Napoleonic era transformed them into natural, if sometimes reluctant, allies. They retained their former arrogance but neither their former privileges nor their old confidence. They knew they could be toppled by the political groups who hated them. They understood that revolution in one country could spill over into another. The conservatives regarded themselves as surrounded by enemies and as standing permanently on the defensive against the forces of liberalism, nationalism, and popular sovereignty. These potential sources of unrest had to be confronted both at home and abroad.

Conservative Governments on the Domestic Scene

The course of nineteenth-century history is frequently associated with the emergence of the liberal, national state and industrial society. But the staying power of the restored conservative institutions, especially in Great Britain and eastern Europe, is an equally and perhaps even more striking feature of the century. Actually not

Greece Expiring on the Ruins of Missolonghi, by Eugène Delacroix (1799–1863) illustrates the manner in which small nationalities were idealized in sentimental liberal art in Western Europe. Greece is pictured as a beautiful, defenseless woman appealing for help against the dangers surrounding her. [Musée des Beaux-Arts, Bordeaux. A. Danvers.]

until World War I did their power and pervasive influence come to an end. One need not admire these institutions or the policies and personalities associated with them. Yet one must admit that their persistence constituted one of the most important features of nineteenth-century political and social life. To ignore or to disparage their relatively successful attempts at self-preservation is to underestimate the grave obstacles that confronted liberals and nationalists.

The more refined political and religious ideas of the conservative classes were associated with Romantic thinkers, such as Burke and Hegel. Conservatives shared other, less formal attitudes forged by the revolutionary experience. The fate of Louis XVI convinced most monarchs that they could trust only aristocratic governments or governments of aristocrats in alliance with the very wealthiest middle-class and professional people. The European aristocracies believed that their property and influence would rarely be safe under any form of genuinely representative government. All conservatives spurned the idea of a written constitution unless they were permitted to promulgate the document themselves. Even then some could not be reconciled to the concept.

The churches were equally apprehensive of popular movements except their own revivals. The ecclesiastical leaders throughout the Continent regarded themselves as entrusted with the educational task of supporting the social and political *status quo*. They also feared and hated most of the ideas associated with the Enlightenment because those rational concepts and reformist writings enshrined the critical spirit and undermined revealed religion. Conservative Europeans came to consider as *liberal* any idea or institution that they opposed. However, as will be seen, that word had rather different meanings in different countries.

Russia and Alexander I

The pursuit of Napoleon's army across Europe after the burning of Moscow created a new image of vast Russian power. The image remained until the Crimean

Tsar Alexander I of Russia began his reign with the reputation of a somewhat liberal reformer, but by the time of his death in 1825 he had become one of the most reactionary rulers in Europe. His portrait is by Gérard. [Bettmann Archive.]

War (1854–1856). In Vienna Tsar Alexander I had played a more important personal role than any other participating monarch. Both in those negotiations and in his governance of Russia, Alexander was and has remained an enigmatic figure. He was torn between an intellectual attraction to the doctrines of the Enlightenment and reform and a very pragmatic adherence to traditional autocracy. His own development as a person and as a ruler reflected the turn of eastern European states from enlightened absolutism to rigid conservatism and defense of the *status quo.*

Alexander I came to the Russian throne in 1801 after the murder of his father, Tsar Paul. The son had condoned the palace revolution. Paul had been an unstable person who ruled in an arbitrary and unpredictable manner. Paul had attempted to reverse the policies of his mother, Catherine the Great, whom he loathed. He attacked the privileges of the nobility. The result was a *coup d'état* led by court nobles and the army. Alexander I intended to return to the reformist policies of his grandmother. He confirmed the privileges of the nobles and abolished the security police. He was well educated in the ideas of the Enlightenment. In 1801 he appointed a government reform committee composed of liberal friends. Little came from the plans submitted by this group, and by 1803 Alexander declared that no group had a right to challenge the legality of the decrees of the tsar.

Once Alexander had led Russia into war against Napoleon, even the mild reformist tendencies began to wane. In 1807 the security police were, in effect, reestablished. Yet the military reverses of the campaign and his personal admiration for Napoleon's administrative genius convinced the tsar that a reconstruction of the Russian government was necessary. In 1808 he turned to Michael Speransky (1772–1839) to guide his thinking on matters of administrative reform. This enlightened minister, who held a series of government appointments, drew up a plan for constitutional government that included an elected legislative body. He even dared talk about an eventual,

Restoration, Reaction, and Reform (1815–1832)

Prince Klemens von Metternich (1773–1859), Foreign Minister, then Chancellor, of Austria, was the chief architect of reactionary politics in Europe between 1815 and 1848. [Culver Pictures.]

gradual abolition of serfdom. The tsar could not support such bold departures. Speransky had to be satisfied with a restructuring of the ministries and the bureaucracy. In 1812 he introduced new progressive taxes on landed income. Each of these policies alienated the nobility. In March 1812 Alexander dismissed his once-trusted minister. Again reform came to a close almost without having begun.

Thereafter Alexander, though occasionally using liberal rhetoric, became an increasingly hardened conservative. In the renewed struggle against Napoleon he needed the support of his nobility and the army. Also during this post-Speransky period he became deeply drawn to those mystical religious feelings that lay behind his project for the Holy Alliance. The tsar came to regard the Enlightenment, the French Revolution, and Napoleon as one vast attack on Christianity. His new chief adviser was Alexis Arakcheiev (1769–1834), a general and the opponent of Speransky. This reactionary military figure became the most powerful person in the country except for Alexander himself. Together they pursued a consistently conservative policy. Censorship and religiously dominated education became the order of the day. They also established "military farms." These institutions transformed whole districts of the country into military establishments where the army farmed and supported itself when not fighting. There was little or no toleration of political opposition or criticism of the regime. By the early 1820s the tsar, whose early years had been seen as holding the possible promise of reform, had become a leading symbol of conservative reaction.

Austria and the Germanies

The early nineteenth-century statesman who more than any other epitomized conservatism was the Austrian Prince Metternich whom we have already met at the Congress of Vienna. This devoted servant of the Hapsburg emperor had been, along with Castlereagh, the chief architect of the Vienna settlement. It was he who seemed to hold chief control over the forces of the European reaction. The conservative foreign and domestic policy that he forged for Austria stemmed from the pragmatic needs of that peculiar state rather than from ideology. To no other country were the programs of liberalism and nationalism potentially more dangerous. The Austrian government could make no serious compromises with the new political forces in Europe. Recognition of the rights and aspirations of the various national groups would mean probable dissolution of the empire. The Hapsburg domains were peopled with Poles, Hungarians, and several Slavic nationalities. Through puppet governments Austria also dominated the Italian peninsula. Hapsburg dynastic integrity required Austrian domination of the German Confederation to prevent the formation of a German national state that might absorb the heart of the empire. If Austria permitted representative government, Metternich and others feared that the national groups would fight their battles internally at the probable cost of Austrian international influence.

During the immediate postwar years Metternich's primary concern lay with Germany. The German Confederation had been created by the Congress of Vienna to replace the defunct Holy Roman Empire. It consisted of thirty-nine states under Austrian leadership. Each state remained more or less autonomous, but Austria was determined to prevent any movement toward constitutionalism in as many of them as possible.

The major victory for this holding policy came in Prussia. In 1815 Frederick William III (1797–1840), during the exhilaration after the War of Liberation, had promised his people some mode of constitutional government. However, he immediately stalled on keeping his pledge. In 1817 he formally reneged and created a new Council of State, which did bring about more efficient administration but which was not a constitutional mode of government. In 1819 the king moved further away from thoughts of reform. After a major disagreement over the organization of the army, his chief reform-minded ministers resigned. The monarch replaced them with hardened conservatives. On their advice in 1823

Frederick William III established eight provincial estates or diets, which were dominated by the *Junkers* and which exercised only an advisory function. The old alliance between the Prussian monarchy, the army, and the land-holders stood reestablished. This conservative alliance opposed German nationalist aspirations that seemed to threaten the social and political order.

Only two German states, Bavaria and Württemberg, enjoyed constitutional government. But the nationalist and liberal aspirations raised by the experience of defeating the French armies remained alive in the hearts and minds of many young Germans. The most important of these groups was university students. They had grown up during the days of the reforms of Stein and Hardenburg

and the initial circulation of the writings of Fichte and other German nationalists. Many of them had fought Napoleon. When they went to the universities, they continued to dream their dream of a united Germany. They formed various student clubs known as *Burschenschaften*. Like student groups today, these clubs served numerous social functions, but one of them was severing old provincial loyalties and replacing them with loyalty to the concept of a united German state.

In 1817 in Jena one such student club organized a large celebration of the fourth anniversary of the battle of Leipzig and of the tercentenary of Luther's Ninety-five Theses. There were bonfires, songs, and processions as more than five hundred people gathered for the festivities. The event made German rulers uneasy, for it was known that some republicans were involved with the student clubs. Two years later, in March 1819, a young man named Karl Sand, who was a *Burschenschaft* member assassinated the conservative dramatist August von Kotzebue. Sand, who was tried, condemned, and publicly executed, became a martyr. Although the assassin had acted alone, Metternich decided to use the incident to suppress the student clubs and other potential institutions of liberalism.

In August 1819 Metternich persuaded representatives of the major German states to issue the Carlsbad Decrees, which dissolved the *Burschenschaften*. The decrees also provided for university inspectors and press censors. The next year the German governments promulgated the Final Act, which limited the subjects that might be discussed in the constitutional chambers of Bavaria and Württemberg. The measure also asserted the right of the

In 1817 on the fourth anniversary of the defeat of Napoleon by Prussians, Austrians, and Russians at Leipzig, German students held a nationalist festival near the Wartburg Castle. Such meetings were considered very dangerous by conservative statesmen who opposed nationalism in Germany. [Bildarchiv Preussischer Kulturbesitz.]

Metternich Comments on Students and Professors

Metternich was the chief minister of the Austrian emperor and the leader of reactionary political policy after the Congress of Vienna. In 1819 he was attempting to suppress political activity in the universities. As he explained in this letter, he did not fear students but the later adults who during their student days had been taught liberal political ideas.

THAT *the students' folly declines or turns to some other side than that of politics does not surprise me. This is in the nature of things. The student, taken in himself, is a child, and the Burschenshaft is an unpractical puppet-show. Then, I have never . . . spoken of the students, but all my aim has been directed at the professors. Now, the professors, singly or united, are most unsuited to be conspirators. People only conspire profitably against things, not against theories. . . . Where they are political, they must be supported by deed, and the deed is the overthrow of existing institutions. . . .*

This is what learned men and professors cannot manage, and the class of lawyers is better suited to carry it on. I know hardly one learned man who knows the value of property; while, on the contrary, the lawyer class is always rummaging about in the property of others. Besides, the professors are, nearly without exception, given up to theory; while no people are more practical than the lawyers.

Consequently, I have never feared that the revolution would be engendered by the universities; but that at them a whole generation of revolutionaries must be formed, unless the evil is restrained, seems to me certain. I hope that the most mischievous symptoms of the evil at the universities may be met, and that perhaps from its own peculiar sources, for the measures of the Government will contribute to this less than the weariness of the students, the weakness of the professors, and the different direction which the studies may take. . . .

The greatest and consequently the most urgent evil now is the press.

Memoirs of Prince Metternich, trans. by Mrs. Napier (New York: Scribner, 1880–1881), Vol. 3, pp. 286–288.

aristocracy to protect monarchs from demands of constitutionalists. Thereafter, for many years the secret police of the various German states harassed potential dissidents. In the eyes of the princes these included practically anyone who sought even moderate social or political change.

Great Britain

The years 1819 and 1820 marked a high tide for conservative influence and repression in western as well as eastern Europe. After 1815 Great Britain experienced two years of poor harvests. There was also considerable industrial unemployment, to which discharged sailors and soldiers added their numbers.

The Tory ministry of Lord Liverpool (1770–1828) was unprepared to deal with these problems of postwar dislocation. Instead, it sought to protect the interests of the landed and other wealthy classes. In 1815 the Parliament passed a Corn Law to maintain high prices for domestically produced grain through import duties on foreign grain. The next year Parliament reduced the income tax and replaced it with excise taxes on consumer goods. These laws represented a continuation of previous legislation through which the British ruling class had abandoned its traditional role of paternalistic protector of the poor. In 1799 Parliament had passed the Combination Acts forbidding workers' organizations or unions. During the war, wage protection had been removed. The tax-paying classes grumbled about supporting the poor law; many people called for its abolition.

In light of these policies and the postwar economic downturn, it is hardly surprising that the lower social orders began to doubt the wisdom of their rulers and to call for a reform of the political system. Mass meetings calling for the reform of Parliament were held. Reform clubs were organized. Radical newspapers, such as William Cobbett's *Political Registrar,* demanded political change. In the hungry, restive agricultural and industrial workers the government could see only images of continental sans-culotte crowds ready to hang aristocrats from the nearest lamppost. Radical leaders, such as Cobbett (1763–1835), Major John Cartwright (1740–1824), and Henry "Orator" Hunt (1773–1835), were considered demagogues who were seducing the people away from allegiance to their natural leaders. The answer of the government to the discontent was repression. In Decem-

As regent and then monarch, George IV of Great
Britain (1820–1830) allowed scandal to come close
to the British crown and lower its prestige among
the general public. The medal by George Mills is
from the year of the king's accession. [The Granger
Collection.]

BELOW: The riots that occurred in London in 1815
at the time of the passage of the Corn Laws to
protect the interests of British landlords marked
the beginning of five years of political discontent,
with popular uprisings and demonstrations.
This contemporary picture shows an unruly crowd
at the entrance to the House of Commons in 1815.
[The Granger Collection.]

Restoration, Reaction, and Reform (1815–1832)

Scott Comments Unhappily on the New Industrial Labor Force

Sir Walter Scott (1771–1832) was a famous Scottish novelist. He was deeply disturbed by the conflict between workers and employers. In this passage from 1820 he blames that conflict largely on the steam engine. That new energy supply took manufacturing out of the countryside and into the cities where Scott believed employer-worker relations were much more impersonal.

THE *unhappy dislocation which has taken place betwixt the Employer and those in his employment has been attended with very fatal consequences. Much of this is owing to the steam engine. When the machinery was driven by water, the manufacturer had to seek out some sequestered spot where he could obtain a suitable fall of water, and then his workmen formed the inhabitants of a village around him, and he necessarily bestowed some attention, less or more, on their morals and on their necessities, had knowledge of their persons and characters, and exercised a salutary influence as over men depending on and intimately connected with him and his prospects. This is now quite changed; the manufacturers are transferred to great towns, where a man may assemble five hundred workmen one week and dismiss them the next, without having any further connection with them than to receive a week's work for a week's wages, nor any further solicitude about their future fate than if they were so many old shuttles. A superintendance of the workers considered as moral and rational beings is thus a matter totally unconnected with the employer's usual thoughts and cares. They have now seen the danger of suffering a great population to be thus entirely separated from the influence of their employers, and given over to the management of their own societies, in which the cleverest and most impudent fellows always get the management of the others, and become bell-wethers in every sort of mischief.*

Walter Scott, *Familiar Letters* (Boston: Houghton, Mifflin, 1894), Vol. 2, p. 78.

vests, brought calm for a time to the political landscape. However, by 1819 the people were restive again. Throughout the industrial north a large number of well-organized mass meetings were held to demand the reform of Parliament. Major radical leaders gave speeches to thousands of people. The radical reform campaign culminated on August 16, 1819, with a meeting in Manchester at St. Peter's Fields. Royal troops and the local militia were on hand to ensure order. Just as the speeches were about to begin, a local magistrate ordered the militia to move into the audience. The result was panic and death. At least eleven people in the crowd were killed; scores were injured. The event became known as the "Peterloo" Massacre through a contemptuous comparison with the victory at Waterloo.

Peterloo had been the act of the local Manchester officials. However, the Liverpool ministry felt that those officials must be supported. The Cabinet also decided to act once and for all to end these troubles. Most of the radical leaders were arrested and thus taken out of circulation. In December 1819, a few months after the German Carlsbad Decrees, Parliament passed a series of laws called the Six Acts. These forbade large meetings, raised the fines for seditious libel, speeded up the trials of political agitators, increased newspaper taxes, prohibited the training of armed groups, and allowed local officials to search homes in certain disturbed counties. In effect the Six Acts attempted to remove the instruments of agitation from the hands of radical leaders and to provide the authorities with new powers.

Two months after passage of the Six Acts, the Cato Street Conspiracy was unearthed. Under the guidance of a possibly demented figure named Thistlewood, a group of extreme radicals plotted to blow up the entire British Cabinet. The plot was foiled. The leaders were arrested and tried, and four of them were executed. The conspiracy was little more than a half-baked plot, but it provided new support for the repression of the government. More important, the conspiracy helped further to discredit the movement for parliamentary reform.

ber 1816 a very unruly mass meeting took place at Spa Fields near London. This disturbance provided an excuse to pass the Coercion Acts of March 1817. These measures temporarily suspended habeas corpus and extended existing laws against seditious gatherings.

This initial repression, accompanied by improved har-

This contemporary print depicting the "Peterloo"
Massacre of 1819 in Manchester, England, was intended
to evoke sympathy for political radicalism. Note that
in addition to being dedicated to Henry "Orator"
Hunt, it is also dedicated to women who supported
political reform. A large number of women and
children had been present at the political rally
the authorities turned into a massacre. [The Mansell
Collection.]

TO HENRY HUNT, ESQ.ᴿ

As Chairman of the Meeting assembled on St. Peter's Field, Manchester on the 16ᵗʰ of AUGUST, 1819,
and to the **Female Reformers** of MANCHESTER and the adjacent TOWNS who were exposed to and suffered from
THE WANTON and FURIOUS ATTACK MADE ON THEM BY THAT BRUTAL ARMED FORCE THE MANCHESTER and CHESHIRE YEOMANRY CAVALRY.

Louis XVIII of France. After his elevation to the throne of his executed brother, Louis XVI, he attempted to rule with moderation. [Bettmann Archive.]

Bourbon Restoration in France

The abdication of Napoleon in 1814 opened the way for a restoration of Bourbon rule in the homeland of the great revolution. The new king was the former Duke of Provence and brother of Louis XVI. The son of the executed monarch had died in prison. Royalists regarded the dead boy as Louis XVII, so his uncle became Louis XVIII (1814–1824). This fat, awkward man had become a political realist during his more than twenty years of exile. He understood that he could not govern if he attempted to turn back the clock. France had undergone too many irreversible changes. Consequently Louis XVIII agreed to become a constitutional monarch, but under a constitution of his own making.

The constitution of the French restoration was the Charter. It provided for a hereditary monarchy and a bicameral legislature. The upper house was appointed by the monarch. The lower chamber was elected according to a very narrow franchise that upheld a high property qualification. The Charter guaranteed most of the rights enumerated by the Declaration of the Rights of Man and Citizen. There was to be religious toleration, but Roman Catholicism was designated as the official religion of the nation. Most important for thousands of Frenchmen at various stations of life who had profited from the revolution, the Charter promised not to disturb the property changes brought about by the confiscation and sale of aristocratic and church land. In this manner Louis XVIII attempted to reconcile to his restored regime those classes who had benefited from the revolution.

This moderate spirit was not widely shared within the ranks of royalist supporters. Their families had suffered much at the hands of the revolution. They now demanded their revenge. The king's brother, the Count of Artois (1757–1836), served as a rallying point for those people who were more royalist than the monarch. In the months after Napoleon's final defeat at Waterloo, royalists in the south and west carried out a White Terror against former revolutionaries and supporters of the de-

posed emperor. The king could do little or nothing to halt this bloodbath of royalist revenge. Similar extreme royalist sentiment existed in the Chamber of Deputies. The ultraroyalist majority elected in 1816 proved so dangerously reactionary that the king soon dissolved the chamber. The majority returned by the second election were more moderate. Under the ministry of the Duke of Richelieu the country paid off the war indemnity to the allies, and the occupation troops were removed in 1818. Yet royalist discontent remained. Louis XVIII attempted to pursue a policy of mild accommodation with liberals through his minister Decazes, who took office in 1818, but the king's younger brother, the Count of Artois, pushed for reactionary departures.

This give and take might have continued for some time. However, in February 1820 the Duke of Berri, son of Artois and heir to the throne after his father, was murdered by a lone assassin. The ultraroyalists persuaded Louis XVIII that the murder was the result of Decazes's cooperation with liberal politicians. The Duke of Richelieu was recalled. The electoral laws were revised to give wealthy electors two votes. Press censorship was imposed. Persons suspected of dangerous political activity could be easily arrested. By 1821 the direction of secondary education in France was put under the control of the Roman Catholic bishops. All of these actions revealed the basic contradiction of the French restoration. There had been no intention of creating a genuinely parliamentary system. The king rather than the Chamber of Deputies chose the ministers. The government constantly tinkered with the electoral apparatus to disqualify opponents from voting. By the early 1820s the veneer of constitutionalism had worn away. Liberals were being driven out of legal political life and into near-illegal activity.

The Conservative International Order
The Congress System

At the Congress of Vienna the major powers—Russia, Austria, Prussia, and Great Britain—had agreed to consult

CENTERS OF REVOLUTION, 1820–1830

Conservative governments and cooperation among repressive great powers in post-Napoleonic Europe were challenged by uprisings and revolutions, beginning in 1820–1821 in Spain, Naples, and Greece and appearing in Russia, France, and Belgium later in the decade.

with each other from time to time on matters affecting Europe as a whole. The vehicle for this consultation was a series of postwar congresses. Later, as differences arose among the powers, consultation became more informal. This mode of working out issues of foreign policy was known as the Concert of Europe. It meant that no major move could be taken in international affairs by one nation without the assent of the others. The major goals of the Concert of Europe were to maintain the balance of power against new French aggression and against the military might of Russia. The Concert of Europe continued to function on large and small issues until the third quarter of the century.

The years that witnessed the domestic conservative consolidation of power also saw a generally successful functioning of the congress system. The first congress was held in 1818 at Aix-la-Chapelle. There the four major powers decided to remove their troops from France and to readmit that nation to good standing among European nations. Despite unanimity on these decisions, problems did arise during the conference. Tsar Alexander I, displaying his full reactionary colors, suggested that the Quadruple Alliance agree to uphold the borders and existing governments of all European countries. Britain, represented by Castlereagh, flatly rejected the proposal. He contended that the Quadruple Alliance was intended only to prevent future French aggression.

THE SPANISH REVOLUTION OF 1820. These disagreements appeared somewhat academic in 1818. But two years later a series of revolutions commenced in southern Europe. The Spanish rebelled against Ferdinand VII (1814–1833). When placed on his throne at the time of Napoleon's downfall, this Bourbon monarch had promised to govern according to a written constitution. Once securely in power Ferdinand simply ignored that pledge. He dissolved the parliament (the Cortes) and ruled alone. In 1820 a group of army officers about to be sent to suppress revolution in Spain's Latin American colonies rebelled. In March Ferdinand once again announced that he would abide by the provisions of the

constitution. For the time being the revolution had succeeded. Almost at the same time, in July 1820, the revolutionary spirit erupted in Naples where the King of the Two Sicilies very quickly accepted a constitution. There were other, lesser revolts in Italy, but none of them succeeded.

These events frightened the ever-nervous Metternich. Italian disturbances were especially troubling to him. Austria hoped to dominate the peninsula to provide a buffer against the spread of revolution on its southern flank. The other powers were divided on the best course of action. Britain opposed joint intervention in either Italy or Spain. Metternich turned to Prussia and Russia for support. The three eastern powers, along with unofficial delegations from Britain and France, met at the Congress of Troppau in late October 1820. The members of the Holy Alliance, led by Alexander of Russia, issued the Protocol of Troppau. This declaration asserted that stable governments might intervene to restore order in countries experiencing revolution. Yet even Russia hesitated to authorize Austrian intervention in Italian affairs. That decision was finally reached in January 1821 at the Congress of Laibach. Shortly thereafter Austrian troops marched into Naples and restored the King of the Two Sicilies to unconstitutional government.

The final postwar congress took place in October 1822 at Verona. Its primary purpose was to resolve the situation in Spain. Once again Britain balked at joint action. Shortly before the meeting Castlereagh had committed suicide. George Canning (1770–1827), the new foreign minister, was much less sympathetic to Metternich's goals. At Verona Britain, in effect, withdrew from continental affairs. Austria, Prussia, and Russia agreed to support French intervention in Spain. In April 1823 the French army crossed the Pyrenees and within a few months suppressed the Spanish revolution. Liberals and revolutionaries were tortured, executed, and driven from the country. The intervention in Spain in 1823 was one of the most bloody examples of reactionary politics during the entire century.

There was a second diplomatic result of the Congress of Verona and the Spanish intervention. George Canning was much more interested in the fate of British commerce and trade than Castlereagh had been. Consequently Canning sought to prevent the politics of European reaction from being extended to the Spanish colonies then revolting in Latin America. He intended to use those South American revolutions as the occasion for British penetration of the old Spanish trading monopoly in that area. To that end the British foreign minister supported the American Monroe Doctrine in 1823, prohibiting further colonization and intervention by European powers in the Americas. Britain soon recognized the Spanish colonies as independent states. Through the rest of the century British commercial interests dominated Latin America. In this fashion Canning may be said to have brought to a successful conclusion the War of Jenkins' Ear (1739).

The Greek Revolution of 1821

While the powers were plotting the new restorations in Italy and Spain, a third Mediterranean revolt had erupted in Greece. The Greek revolution became one of the most famous of the century because it attracted the support and participation of many illustrious literary figures. Liberals throughout Europe who were seeing their own hopes crushed at home imagined that ancient Greek democracy was being reborn. "The world's great age begins anew," wrote Shelley. Lord Byron went to fight and in 1824 died in the cause of Greek liberty. Philhellenic societies were founded in practically every major country.

The Greeks were rebelling against the Ottoman Empire. The weakness of that empire troubled Europe for the entire century and raised what was known as "the eastern question." The residue of the problem remains alive today in the tensions between Greece and Turkey and in the instability in the Middle East. Most of the major powers were interested in what happened to the Ottoman holdings for reasons less idealistic than the poets'. Russia and Austria coveted land in the Balkans. France and Britain were concerned with the empire's commerce and with control of key naval positions in the eastern Mediterranean. There was also the issue of protection of Christian access to the shrines in the Holy Land.

These conflicting interests, as well as mutual distrust, prevented any direct intervention in Greek affairs for several years. In 1827 a joint British, French, and Russian fleet supported the Greek revolt. The fleet was enforcing the Treaty of London of 1827, in which those powers demanded Turkish recognition of Greek independence. They had decided that their domestic security would not be endangered by an independent Greek state and that their several foreign policy concerns in the area would prosper from such a new nation. In 1828 Russia sent troops against the Ottoman holdings in what is today Romania. By the treaty of Adrianople of 1829 Russia gained effective control of that territory. The treaty further stipulated that the Turks would allow Britain, France, and Russia to decide the future of Greece.

In 1830 by a second Treaty of London Greece was declared an independent kingdom. Two years later Otto I (1832–1862), the son of the king of Bavaria, was chosen as the first king of the new Greek royal dynasty. The Greek revolt was the only successful national revolution of the first quarter of the century. Elsewhere the conservative powers had defeated the attempts at revolution.

Liberalism in the Early Nineteenth Century

The nineteenth century is frequently considered the great age of *isms*. Throughout the Western world secular ideologies began to take hold of the popular and learned imagination in opposition to the political and social *status quo*. These included liberalism, nationalism, socialism, republicanism, and communism. Other *isms* included conservatism, industrialism, and imperialism. One noted historian has called all such words "trouble-breeding and usually thought-obscuring terms."[1] They are just that if one uses them as an excuse to avoid thinking or if one fails to see the variety of opinions concealed beneath each word.

It was just such intellectual laziness that characterized European conservatives as they faced their political opposition after the Napoleonic wars. They tended to call "liberal" almost anything or anyone who drew into question their own political, social, or religious values. Moreover, the word *liberal* for twentieth-century Americans carries with it meanings and connotations that have little or nothing to do with its significance for nineteenth-century Europeans. European conservatives of the last century saw liberals as more radical than they actually were; present-day Americans consider them to be more conservative than they were.

Liberal Goals and Their Circumstances

POLITICS. The political ideas of liberals derived from the writers of the Enlightenment, the example of English liberties, and the so-called principles of 1789 as embodied in the French Declaration of the Rights of Man and Citizen. Liberal political figures sought to establish a framework of legal equality, religious toleration, and

1 Arthur O. Lovejoy, *The Great Chain of Being: A Study in the History of an Idea* (New York: Harper Torchbook, 1936), p. 6.

freedom of the press. Their general goal was a political structure that would limit the arbitrary power of the goverment against the persons and property of individual citizens. They generally believed that the legitimacy of government emanated from the freely given consent of the governed. The popular basis of such government was to be expressed through elected representative or parliamentary bodies. Most important, free government required that state or crown ministers must be responsible to the representatives rather than to the monarch.

These goals may seem very limited, and they were. However, such responsible government existed in none of the major European countries in 1815. Even in Great Britain the Cabinet ministers were at least as responsible to the monarch as to the House of Commons. The kinds of people who espoused these changes in government tended to be those who were excluded from the existing political processes but whose wealth and education made them feel that such exclusion was unjustified. Liberals tended to be academics, members of the learned professions, and people involved in the rapidly expanding commercial and manufacturing segments of the economy. They believed in and were products of the career open to talent. The existing monarchical and aristocratic regimes often failed to recognize sufficiently their new status and to provide for their economic and professional interests.

However, liberals were *not* advocates of democracy. Second only to their hostility to privileged aristocracies was their general contempt for the lower, unpropertied classes. Liberals transformed the eighteenth-century concept of aristocratic liberty into a new concept of privilege based on wealth and property instead of on birth. As the French liberal theorist Benjamin Constant (1767–1830) wrote in 1814:

Those whom poverty keeps in eternal dependence are no more enlightened on public affairs than children, nor are they more interested than foreigners in national prosperity, of which they do not understand the basis and of which they enjoy the advantages only indirectly. Property alone, by giving sufficient leisure, renders a man capable of exercising his political rights.[2]

By the middle of the century this widely shared attitude meant that throughout Europe liberals had separated themselves from both the rural and the urban working class.

ECONOMICS. The economic goals of liberals also furthered that important future split in European politics and society. Here again the pattern was set by the Enlightenment and by the economic thought deriving from Adam Smith. The manufacturers of Great Britain, the landed and manufacturing middle class of France, and the commercial interests of Germany and Italy sought the removal of the economic restraints associated with mercantilism. They wanted to be able to manufacture and sell goods freely. To that end they favored the general removal of internal barriers to trade and of international tariffs. Economic liberals opposed the old paternalistic legislation that established wages and labor practices by government regulation or by guild privileges. Labor was simply one more commodity to be bought and sold freely. Liberals sought an economic structure in which people were at liberty to use whatever talents and property they possessed to enrich themselves. By this means, they contended, there would be more goods and more services for everyone at lower prices. Such a system of economic liberty was to provide the basis for material progress.

NATIONALISM. Another major ingredient of liberalism as it developed in Germany, Italy, and the Austrian Empire was nationalism. The idea of nationhood was not necessarily or logically linked to liberalism. There were conservative nationalists. However, liberalism and nationalism were often complementary. Behind the concept of a people joined naturally together by the bonds of common language, customs, culture, and history lurked the idea of popular sovereignty. The idea of the career open to talent could be applied to suppressed national

2 Quoted in Frederick B. Artz, *Reaction and Revolution, 1814–1832* (New York: Harper, 1934), p. 94.

This poster is evidence of the industrial discontent that spread in some parts of Britain during the Napoleonic wars. That discontent became even sharper during the years of unemployment that followed Waterloo. [The Granger Collection.]

Protection
FOR THE
INDUSTRIOUS
Weavers.

INFORMATION having been received that a great number of industrious Weavers have been deterred by threats and acts of violence from the pursuit of their lawful occupations, and that in many instances their Shuttles have been taken, and their Materials damaged by persons acting under the existing Combinations :

Notice is hereby Given,

That every Protection will be afforded to persons so injured, upon giving Information to the Constables of Stockport : And a Reward of

FIFTY GUINEAS

Will be paid, on conviction, to the person who will come forward with such evidence as may be the means of convicting any one or more of the offences mentioned in the Act of Parliament, of which an Extract is subjoined : And a Reward of

TWENTY GUINEAS

Will be paid, on conviction, to the person who will come forward and inform of any person being guilty of assaulting or molesting industrious and honest Weavers, so as to prevent them from taking out or bringing in their Work peaceably.

Stockport, June 17th, 1808.　　PETER BROWN, } CONSTABLES.
　　　　　　　　　　　　　　　T. CARTWRIGHT, }

By the 22nd, Geo. 3, C. 40, S. 3.

It is enacted, " That if any person enter, by force, into any House or Shop, with intent to Cut and Destroy any Linen or Cotton, or Linen and Cotton mixed with any other Materials, in the Loom, or any Warp or Shute, Tools, Tackle, and Utensils, or shall Cut or Destroy the same, or shall Break and Destroy any Tools, Tackle, or Utensils, for Weaving, Preparing, or Making any such Manufactures, every such Offender shall be guilty of FELONY, without Benefit of Clergy".

groups who were not permitted to realize their cultural or political potential. The efficient government and administration required by commerce and industry would mean the replacement of the petty dynasties of the small German and Italian states with larger political units. Moreover nationalist groups in one country could gain the sympathy of liberals in other nations by espousing the cause of representative government and political liberty.

Because the social and political circumstances of various countries differed, the specific programs of liberals also differed. Great Britain already possessed institutions, such as Parliament, that could be reformed to provide more nearly representative government. The monarchy was already limited, and most individual liberties had been secured. Links between land, commerce, and industry existed. French liberals possessed a code of modern law in the Napoleonic Code. They could appeal to the widely accepted "principles of 1789." As in England, representatives of the different economic interests had worked together. Their problem was to protect the civil liberties by law and to define the respective powers of the monarch and the elected representative body.

The situation in Germany was quite different and very complex. Distinct social divisions existed between the aristocratic landowning classes, who filled the bureaucracies and officer corps, and the small middle-class commercial and industrial interests. There was little or no precedent for the latter groups' participating in the government or the army. There was no strong tradition of civil or individual liberty. From the time of Martin Luther through Kant and Hegel, freedom in Germany had meant conformity to a higher moral law rather than participation in politics. Consequently the mainstream of German liberalism differed from its British and French counterparts. There was much greater opposition from both the monarchs and the aristocracies. German liberals had little direct access to political influence. Most of them favored a united Germany that was to be created through the instrument of the Prussian monarchy. This policy meant that they tended to stress the power of the state and the monarchy rather more than did other liberals. Once unification had been achieved, a freer social and political order might be established. The great difficulty for German liberals was the refusal of the Prussian monarchy to cooperate. Thus in Germany liberals were generally frustrated and had to remain satisfied with the lowering of internal trade barriers.

Between 1819 and 1822 the institutions of the restored conservative order had held back the forces of liberalism. In the Germanies, Austria, and Italy the liberal challenge was smothered for at least another twenty-five years. However, during the twenties the conservative governments of Russia, France, and Great Britain faced new stirrings of political discontent. In Russia the result was suppression; in France, revolution; and in Britain, accommodation.

Russia: The Decembrist Revolt of 1825 and the Autocracy of Nicholas I

During the mid-twenties Russia took the lead in suppressing both liberal and nationalistic tendencies within its domains. In the process of driving Napoleon's army across Europe and then of occupying defeated France, many officers in the Russian army were introduced to the ideas of the French Revolution and the Enlightenment. They realized how economically backward and politically stifled their own nation remained. The domestic repression in Russia hardened as Alexander I became more conservative. Under these conditions secret societies were formed within the army officer corps. One such reformist coterie was the Southern Society. Led by an officer named Pestel, these men sought a representative government and the abolition of serfdom. Pestel himself favored democracy and a moderately independent Poland. The Northern Society was a second, more moderate group. It favored constitutional monarchy and the abolition of serfdom but with protection for the interests of the aristocracy. Both societies were very small; there was much friction between them. They agreed only that there must be a change in the government of Russia. Sometime

Tsar Nicholas I of Russia was the most conservative major ruler of the early nineteenth century. He resisted practically all attempts to reform Russia and offered the use of Russian troops to other European nations endangered by revolutionary disturbances. [Culver Pictures.]

during 1825 they seem to have decided to carry out a *coup d'état* in 1826.

Other events intervened. In late November 1825 Tsar Alexander I suddenly and unexpectedly died. His death created two crises. The first was a dynastic one. Alexander had no direct heir. His brother Constantine stood next in line to the throne. However, Constantine had been ruling Poland and did not want the Russian crown. Through a series of instructions made public after his death, Alexander had named his younger brother Nicholas (1825–1855) as the new tsar. However, Constantine had neither publicly repudiated the throne nor acknowledged Nicholas. Under these circumstances the Russian Senate declared Constantine to be the tsar, but he still would not refuse the throne. Moreover Constantine was so angered by the general ineptitude of the officials that he declined to come to St. Petersburg to proclaim Nicholas. The family muddle continued for about three weeks. Then during the early days of December, the army command reported to Nicholas the existence of a conspiracy among certain officers. Able to wait no longer for the working out of legal niceties, Nicholas had himself declared tsar.

The second crisis now proceeded to unfold. There was a plot devised by a number of junior officers intent upon rallying the troops under their command to the cause of reform. On December 26, 1825, the army was to take the oath of allegiance to Nicholas. Nearly all of the regiments did so. But the Moscow regiment, whose chief officers surprisingly were not secret society members, marched into the Senate Square in St. Petersburg and refused to swear allegiance. Rather they called for Constantine and a constitution. Attempts to settle the situation peacefully failed. Late in the afternoon Nicholas ordered the cavalry and artillery to attack the insurgents. Over sixty people were killed. Early in 1826 Nicholas himself presided over the commission that investigated the Decembrist Revolt and the secret army societies. Five of the plotters were executed and over one hundred other officers were exiled to Siberia.

Although the Decembrist Revolt completely failed, it was the first rebellion in modern Russian history whose instigators had specific political goals. They wanted constitutional government and the abolition of serfdom. As the century passed, the Decembrists in their political martyrdom came to symbolize the yearnings of all Russian liberals, whose numbers were always quite small. The more immediate result of the revolt was the crushing of liberalism as even a moderate political influence in Russia. Nicholas I was determined that never again would his power come under question. He eventually epitomized the most extreme form of nineteenth-century autocracy.

Nicholas was neither an ignorant nor a bigoted reactionary. He was quite simply afraid of change. He knew that Russia required reforms for economic growth and social improvement. In 1842 he told his State Council, "There is no doubt that serfdom, in its present form, is a flagrant evil which everyone realizes, yet to attempt to remedy it now would be, of course, an evil more disastrous."[3] To remove serfdom would necessarily in his

3 Quoted in Michael T. Florinsky, *Russia: A History and an Interpretation* (New York: Macmillan, 1953), Vol. 2, p. 755.

view have undermined the nobles' support for the tsar. Consequently Nicholas turned his back on this and practically all other reforms. Literary and political censorship and a widespread system of secret police flourished throughout his reign. There was little attempt to forge even an efficient and honest administration. The only significant reform of his rule was a codification of Russian law published in 1833.

In place of reform Nicholas and his closest advisers embraced a program called Official Nationalism. Its slogan, published repeatedly in government documents, newspapers, journals, and schoolbooks, was "Orthodoxy, Autocracy, and Nationalism." The Russian Orthodox faith was to provide the basis for morality, education, and intellectual life. The church, which since the days of Peter the Great had been an arm of the secular government, controlled the schools and universities. Young Russians were taught to accept their place in life and to spurn rising in the social structure. The program of autocracy championed the unrestrained power of the Tsar as the only authority that could hold the vast expanse of Russia and its peoples together in an orderly fashion. Political writers stressed that only under the autocracy of Peter the Great, Catherine the Great, and Alexander I had Russia prospered and exerted a major influence on world affairs. Through the glorification of Russian nationality, the country was urged to see its religion, language, and customs as a source of perennial wisdom that separated the nation from the moral corruption and political turmoil of the West. The person who presided over the program of Official Nationalism was Count S. S. Uvarov, minister of education from 1833 to 1849. The result of his efforts and those of the Tsar was the profound alienation of serious Russian intellectual life from the tsarist government.

Nicholas I also manifested extreme conservatism in foreign affairs. After the Congress of Vienna, Poland had been given a constitutional government but within the limits of the Russian domination that dated back to the eighteenth-century partitions of Poland. Grand Duke

Uvarov Praises the Policy of Official Nationality

Uvarov was the Russian minister of education under Nicholas I. In that capacity he was largely responsible for the policy of Official Nationality with its program of orthodoxy, autocracy, and nationality. In 1843 he explains that this ideology is to prevent Russia from experiencing the political turmoil that had occurred in western Europe.

IN THE *midst of rapid collapse in Europe of religious and civil institutions, at the time of a general spread of destructive ideas, at the sight of grievous phenomena surrounding us on all sides, it was necessary to establish our fatherland on firm foundations upon which is based the well-being, strength, and life of a people; it was necessary to find the principles which form the distinctive character of Russia, and which belong only to Russia; it was necessary to gather into one whole the sacred remnants of Russian nationality and to fasten to them the anchor of our salvation. Fortunately, Russia had retained a warm faith in the sacred principles without which she cannot prosper, gain in strength, live. Sincerely and deeply attached to the church of his fathers, the Russian has of old considered it the guarantee of social and family happiness. Without a love for the faith of its ancestors a people, as well as an individual must perish. A Russian devoted to his fatherland, will agree as little to the loss of a single dogma of our* Orthodoxy *as to the theft of a single pearl from the tsar's crown. Autocracy constitutes the main condition of the political existence of Russia. The Russian giant stands on it as on the cornerstone of his greatness. An innumerable majority of the subjects of Your Majesty feel this truth; they feel it in full measure although they are placed on different rungs of civil life and although they vary in education and in their relations to the government. The saving conviction that Russia lives and is protected by the spirit of a strong, humane, and enlightened autocracy must permeate popular education and must develop with it. Together with these two national principles there is a third, no less important, no less powerful:* nationality.

Cited in Nicholas Riasanovsky, *Nicholas I and Official Nationality in Russia, 1825–1855* (Berkeley: University of California Press, 1959), pp. 74–75.

Constantine, the brother of Alexander I and Nicholas I, was in charge of the Polish government by authority delegated by the tsars. Although both tsars frequently infringed upon the constitutional arrangement and quar-

Some of his subjects considered King Charles X of France to be the handsomest person in the nation. His reactionary policies prepared the way for the Revolution of 1830. [The Granger Collection.]

reled with the Polish Diet, the constitution itself remained. Nevertheless Polish nationalists continued to agitate for change.

In late November 1830, after the news of the French and Belgian revolutions of that summer had penetrated Poland, a small military insurrection broke out in Warsaw. Disturbances soon spread throughout the rest of the country. On December 18 the Polish Diet declared the revolution to be a nationalist movement. In early January 1831 the Diet voted to depose Nicholas as ruler of Poland. The tsar reacted by sending troops into the country. After several months the revolt was thoroughly suppressed. In February 1832 Nicholas issued the Organic Statute, which declared Poland to be an integral part of the Russian empire. The statute guaranteed certain Polish liberties, but they were systematically ignored. The Polish uprising had confirmed all the tsar's worst fears. Henceforth Russia and Nicholas became the gendarme of Europe, ever ready to provide troops to suppress liberal and nationalist movements.

Revolution in France (1830)

The Polish revolt was the most distant of several disturbances that flowed from the overthrow of the Bourbon dynasty in France during July 1830. In 1824 Louis XVIII had died. He was succeeded by his brother, the Count of Artois, who became Charles X (1824–1830). The new king, who had been the chief leader of the ultraroyalists at the time of the restoration, considered himself a monarch by divine right. He was crowned with elaborate ceremony and ritual at the Cathedral of Reims. At long last in power, he intended to roll back as much of the revolution as possible and to repay the loyalty of the French royalists.

His first action was to have the Chamber of Deputies in 1824 and 1825 provide for the indemnification of aristocrats who had lost their lands in the revolution. The existing land settlement was confirmed. However, by lowering the interest rates on government bonds, the Chamber created a fund from which the survivors of the

émigrés who had forfeited land would be paid, on the average, 1377 francs annually. This move was naturally resented by the middle-class bondholders, who lost income. Another measure restored the rule of primogeniture, whereby only the eldest son of an aristocrat inherited the family domains. Charles X supported the Roman Catholic Church by a law punishing sacrilege with sentences of imprisonment or death. Liberals disapproved of all of these measures.

The results of the elections of 1827 compelled Charles X to appease the liberals, who in conjunction with more moderate royalists could muster a majority in the Chamber of Deputies. He appointed a less conservative ministry. Laws directed against the press and those allowing the government to dominate education were eased. Yet the liberals, who wanted a genuinely constitutional regime, remained unsatisfied. In 1829 the king decided his policy of accommodation had failed. He dismissed his ministers and in their place appointed an ultraroyalist ministry headed by the Prince de Polignac (1780–1847). The opposition was now forced to the desperate action of opening negotiations with the liberal Orleanist branch of the royal family.

In 1830 Charles X called for new elections, in which the liberals scored a stunning victory. He might have relented and tried to accommodate the new Chamber of Deputies. Instead the king and his ministers decided to attempt a royalist seizure of power. In June and July 1830 Polignac had sent a naval expedition against Algeria. On July 9 reports of its victory reached Paris. The foundation of a French Empire in North Africa had been laid. On July 25, 1830, under the euphoria of this foreign diversion, Charles X issued the Four Ordinances, which amounted to a royal *coup d'état*. The ordinances restricted freedom of the press, dissolved the recently elected

LES POIRES,

Faites à la cour d'assises de Paris par le directeur de la CARICATURE.

Vendues pour payer les 6,000 fr. d'amende du journal le *Charivari.*

(CHEZ AUBERT, GALERIE VERO-DODAT.)

Si, pour reconnaître le monarque dans une caricature, vous n'attendez pas qu'il soit désigné autrement que par la ressemblance, vous tomberez dans l'absurde. Voyez ces croquis informes, auxquels j'aurais peut-être dû borner ma défense :

Ce croquis ressemble à Louis-Philippe, vous condamnerez donc ?   Alors il faudra condamner celui-ci, qui ressemble au premier.

Puis condamner cet autre, qui ressemble au second   Et enfin, si vous êtes conséquens, vous ne sauriez absoudre cette poire, qui ressemble aux croquis précédens.

Ainsi, pour une poire, pour une brioche, et pour toutes les têtes grotesques dans lesquelles le hasard ou la malice aura placé cette triste ressemblance, vous pourrez infliger à l'auteur cinq ans de prison et cinq mille francs d'amende !!
Avouez, Messieurs, que c'est là une singulière liberté de la presse !!

Political cartoonists found a superb subject in Louis Philippe. In this series of caricatures he is shown being transformed by progressive stages into a pear. The surrounding text and this group of drawings are primarily a satire on the so-called freedom of the press under which publishers were still in danger of heavy fines and the individual cartoonists liable to imprisonment for up to five years for lack of respect to the king. [The Granger Collection.]

Chamber of Deputies, restricted the franchise to the wealthiest people in the country, and called for new elections under the new royalist franchise.

The Four Ordinances provoked swift and decisive popular political reactions. Liberal newspapers called upon the nation to reject the monarch's actions. The laboring populace of Paris, burdened since 1827 by an economic downturn, took to the streets and erected barricades. The king called out troops, and over eighteen hundred people died during the ensuing battles in the city. On August 2 Charles X abdicated and left France for exile in England. The liberals in the Chamber of Deputies named a new ministry composed of constitutional monarchists. They proclaimed Louis Philippe (1830–1848), the Duke of Orleans, as the new monarch. The July Days had brought to a final close the rule of the Bourbon dynasty in France.

In the Revolution of 1830 the liberals of the Chamber of Deputies filled a power vacuum created by the popular Paris uprising and the failure of effective royal action. Had Charles X provided himself with sufficient troops in Paris, the outcome could have been quite different. Moreover had the liberals, who favored constitutional monarchy, not acted quickly, the workers and shopkeepers of Paris might have formed a republic. By seizing the moment, the middle class, the bureaucrats, and the moderate aristocratic liberals overthrew the restoration monarchy and still avoided a republic. These liberals feared a new popular revolution such as had swept France in 1792 on the overthrow of the old monarchy. They had no desire for another sans-culotte republic. However, the basic tension that existed between hard-pressed laborers and prosperous middle-class persons who had in a temporary alliance achieved the revolution continued to mark the new monarchy.

Politically the July Monarchy, as it was called, was more liberal than the restoration government. Louis Philippe was called the king of the French rather than of France. The tricolor flag of the revolution replaced the white flag of the Bourbons. The Charter was regarded as a right of the people rather than a concession of the monarch. Catholicism became the religion of the majority

Louis Philippe became King of the French by the Revolution of 1830 and was deposed by the Revolution of 1848. [The Granger Collection.]

of the people rather than the official religion. Censorship was abolished. The franchise became somewhat wider but remained on the whole restricted. The king had to cooperate with the Chamber of Deputies; he could not dispense with laws on his own authority.

Socially, however, the Revolution of 1830 proved quite conservative. The hereditary peerage was abolished in 1831, but the everyday economic, political, and social influence of the landed oligarchy continued. Money was the path to power and influence in the government. There was much corruption. Most important, the liberal monarchy displayed little or no sympathy for the lower and working classes. The Paris workers in 1830 had called for the protection of jobs, better wages, and the preservation of the traditional crafts rather than for the usual goals of political liberalism. The government of Louis Philippe ignored their demands and their plight. The laboring classes of Paris and the provincial cities seemed just one more possible source of disorder. In late 1831 a workers' revolt in the city of Lyons was suppressed by troops. In July 1832 an uprising occurred in Paris during the funeral of a popular Napoleonic general. Again troops were called out, and over eight hundred people were killed or wounded. In 1834 a very large strike of silkworkers in Lyons was crushed. Such discontent might be smothered for a time, but without attention to the social and economic conditions creating that tension new turmoil would eventually erupt.

Belgium Becomes Independent (1830)

The July Days in Paris sent sparks into other political tinder on the continent. The revolutionary fires first lighted in neighboring Belgium. The former Austrian Netherlands had in 1815 been merged with the kingdom of Holland. The upper classes of Belgium had never reconciled themselves to rule by a country with a different language, religion, and economic life. On August 25, 1830, disturbances broke out in Brussels following the performance of an opera that portrayed a rebellion of Naples against Spanish rule. To put an end to the rioting,

the municipal authorities and persons from the propertied classes formed a provisional national government. When compromise between the Belgians and the Dutch failed, William of Holland sent troops and ships against Belgium. By November 10, 1830, the Dutch had been defeated. A National Congress then wrote a liberal Belgian constitution, which was promulgated in 1831.

The major powers saw the revolution in Belgium as upsetting the boundaries established by the Congress of Vienna. Russia could not intervene because of the Polish revolt. Prussia and the other German states were suppressing small risings in their own domains. The Austrians were busy putting down disturbances in Italy. France under Louis Philippe favored an independent Belgium and hoped to dominate it. Britain felt that it could tolerate a liberal Belgium so long as it was free of foreign domination. In December 1830 Lord Palmerston (1784–1865), the British foreign minister, gathered representatives of the powers in London. Through skillful negotiations he persuaded them to recognize Belgium as an independent and neutral state. In July 1831 Leopold of Saxe-Coburg (1831–1865) became king of the Belgians. By the Convention of 1839 the great powers guaranteed the neutrality of Belgium. For almost a century Belgian neutrality remained one of the articles of faith in European international relations. In 1914 it was German violation of the neutrality convention that technically brought Great Britain into World War I.

The Great Reform Bill in Britain (1832)

The revolutionary year of 1830 saw in Great Britain the election of the House of Commons that passed the first major bill to reform Parliament. The death of George IV (1820–1830) and the accession of William IV (1830–1837) required the calling of an election. It was once believed that the July revolution in France had influenced the British elections in the summer of 1830. This theory has been shown to be incorrect through a close analysis of the time and character of individual county and borough elections. The passage of the great reform bill, which became law in 1832, was the result of a series of events very different from those that occurred on the continent. In Britain the forces of conservatism and reform made accommodations with each other.

Several factors made this situation possible and meant that Great Britain would become "the chief laboratory of liberal thought during the century."[4] First, there was a larger commercial and industrial class in Britain than in other countries. No matter what group might control the government, British prosperity required attention to those economic interests. Second, there existed in Britain the long tradition of liberal Whig aristocrats, who regarded themselves as the protectors of constitutional liberty. They saw their role as that of making moderate political changes that would render revolutionary changes unnecessary. Their influence had been harmed by early sympathy for the French Revolution. However, after 1815 they reentered the political arena and waited to be recalled to power. Finally, there also existed in British law, tradition, and public opinion a strong respect for the civil liberties.

In 1820, the year after the passage of the notorious Six Acts, Lord Liverpool shrewdly moved to change his cabinet. New faces began to appear. They included George Canning, Robert Peel (1788–1850), and William Huskisson (1770–1830). These men, sometimes called "liberal Tories," favored conservative politics but also knew that the nation and government must accommodate themselves to the new economic and political forces of the day. Canning introduced the more liberal foreign policy that led to the recognition of the Latin American republics. Peel set about reforming the criminal law and reducing the number of capital offenses. Huskisson was an economic liberal who commenced a slow process of lowering tariffs for the benefit of the commercial classes. In 1824 the Combination Acts were repealed, and labor organization became possible.

4 George L. Mosse, *The Culture of Western Europe: The Nineteenth and Twentieth Centuries* (New York: Rand McNally, 1965), p. 97.

Daniel O'Connell was the most dynamic and effective Irish nationalist leader in the first half of the nineteenth century. His portrait is by George Hayter and was made in 1834 when O'Connell was 59. [The Granger Collection.]

Economic considerations had generally led to these moderate reforms. English determination to maintain its union with Ireland brought about another key reform. England's relationship to Ireland was not unlike that of Russia's to Poland or Austria's to its several national groups. In 1800, fearful that Irish nationalists might again rebel as they had in 1798 and perhaps turn Ireland into a base for a French invasion, William Pitt the Younger had Parliament enact the Act of Union between England and Ireland. Ireland now sent more than eighty members to the House of Commons. However, because of the religious scruples of King George III, Pitt was unable to secure passage of a law to permit Roman Catholics to sit in the House of Commons. Consequently only Protestant Irishmen, who usually had close ties to England, could be elected to represent overwhelmingly Catholic Ireland.

During the 1820s, under the leadership of Daniel O'Connell (1775–1847), Irish nationalists organized the Catholic Association to agitate for Catholic emancipation. In 1828 O'Connell secured his own election to Parliament, where he could not legally take his seat. The British ministry of the Duke of Wellington realized that henceforth an entirely Catholic delegation might be elected from Ireland. If they were not seated, civil war

Charles, Earl Grey was the prime minister under whose leadership the British Parliament passed the Great Reform Bill. [The Granger Collection.]

might erupt across the Irish Sea. Consequently, in 1829 Wellington and Robert Peel steered the Catholic Emancipation Act through Parliament. Roman Catholics could now become Members of Parliament. This measure, together with the repeal in 1827 of restrictions against Protestant nonconformists, meant that the Anglican monopoly on British political life was over.

Catholic emancipation was a liberal measure that was passed for the conservative purpose of preserving order in Ireland. It included a provision raising the franchise in

Thomas Babbington Macaulay Defends the Great Reform Bill

Macaulay (1800–1859) was a member of the House of Commons that twice passed the Parliamentary Reform Bill in 1831 only to have it rejected by the House of Lords before a third measure was successfully enacted in 1832. His speeches in support of the bill derived from his views on the need for Parliament to give balanced representation to major elements in the population. Specifically, he supported the Reform Bill because it allowed the middle class to obtain political influence without creating a democratic government. He saw the reform of Parliament as a way to prevent political revolution in England. His argument had wide appeal.

[THE *principle of the ministers*] *is plain, rational, and consistent. It is this,—to admit the middle class to a large and direct share in the Representation, without any violent shock to the institutions of our country. . . . I hold it to be clearly expedient, that in a country like this, the right of suffrage should depend on a pecuniary qualification. Every argument . . . which would induce me to oppose Universal Suffrage, induces me to support the measure which is now before us. I oppose Universal Suffrage, because I think that it would produce a destructive revolution. I support this measure, because I am sure that it is our best security against a revolution. . . . I . . . do entertain great apprehension for the fate of my country. I do in my conscience believe, that unless this measure, or some similar measure, be speedily adopted, great and terrible calamities will befall us. Entertaining this opinion, I think myself bound to state it, not as a threat, but as a reason. I support this measure as a measure of Reform: but I support it still more as a measure of conservation. That we may exclude those whom it is necessary to exclude, we must admit those whom it may be safe to admit. . . . All history is full of revolutions, produced by causes similar to those which are now operating in England. A portion of the community which had been of no account, expands and becomes strong. It demands a place in the system, suited, not to its former weakness, but to its present power. If this is granted, all is well. If this is refused, then comes the struggle between the young energy of one class, and the ancient privileges of another. . . . Such . . . is the struggle which the middle classes in England are maintaining against an aristocracy of mere locality. . . .*

Hansard's Parliamentary Debates, 3rd series, Vol. 2, pp. 1191–1197.

When King William IV (1830–1837) agreed to create enough new peers to pass the Reform Bill, the House of Lords at last accepted the measure. His portrait is by an unknown artist, and his medal is by William Wyon. [The Granger Collection.]

Ireland so that only the wealthier Irish could vote. Nonetheless this measure alienated many of Wellington's Anglican Tory supporters in the House of Commons. In the election of 1830 a large number of supporters of parliamentary reform were returned to Parliament. Even some Tories believed that parliamentary reform was necessary because they had concluded that Catholic emancipation could have been passed only by a corrupt House of Commons. The Wellington ministry soon fell. The Tories were badly divided. Consequently King William IV turned to the Whigs under the leadership of Earl Grey (1764–1845) to form a government.

The Whig ministry soon presented the House of Commons with a major reform bill that had two broad goals. The first was to abolish "rotten" boroughs, which had small numbers of voters, and to replace them with representatives for the previously unrepresented manufacturing districts and cities. Second, the number of voters was about doubled through a series of new franchises. In 1831 the House of Commons passed the bill, but the measure was defeated in the House of Lords. Grey called for a new election, in which another majority in favor of the bill was returned. The House of Commons passed the reform bill a second time, and again the House of Lords rejected it. Mass meetings were held throughout the country. Riots broke out in several cities. Finally, William IV agreed to create enough new peers to give a third reform bill a majority in the House of Lords. Under this pressure the House of Lords yielded, and in 1832 the measure became law.

The Great Reform Bill expanded the size of the British electorate, but it was not a democratic measure. The number of voters was increased by over 200,000 persons or by almost 50 per cent. However, the basis of voting remained a property qualification. Some working-class voters actually were disenfranchised because of the abolition of certain old franchise rights. New urban boroughs were created to allow the growing cities to have a voice in the House of Commons. Yet the passage of the reform act did not, as it was once thought, constitute the triumph of

While less clamorous than the vigorous earlier demands for the Reform Bill, the celebrations after its passage in 1832 were none the less lively. These contemporary posters announce the different manners in which two English towns decided to mark the event. At Woodbridge the sobersided inhabitants elected to give a dinner to the poor. At Chippenham, however, they decided to give a vast "Old English Dinner" for two thousand of themselves, the menu for which they proudly announce, the dinner to be followed by a fine program of various sports and, finally, fireworks. [Courtesy Charles Farrell.]

the middle-class interest in Britain. For every new urban electoral district, a new rural district was also drawn. It was expected that the aristocracy would dominate the rural elections.

The success of the reform bill was its reconciliation of previously unrepresented property owners and economic interests to the existing political institutions of the country. The act created a political situation in which further reforms of the church, the municipal government, and commercial policy could be achieved in an orderly fashion. Revolution in Britain was unnecessary because the people who sought change had been admitted to the political forum that could legislate those changes. In this manner the historic institutions of Great Britain were maintained while the persons and groups who influenced them became more diverse.

SUGGESTED READINGS

F. B. Artz, *Reaction and Revolution, 1814–1832* (1934). A useful introduction.

A. Briggs, *The Making of Modern England* (1959). The best survey of English history during the first half of the nineteenth century.

M. Brock, *The Great Reform Act* (1974). The standard work.

G. A. Craig, *The Politics of the Prussian Army, 1640–1945* (1955). A splendid study of the conservative political influence of the army on Prussian development.

D. Dakin, *The Struggle for Greek Independence* (1973). An excellent explanation of the intricacies of the Greek independence question.

G. de Bertier de Sauvigny, *The Bourbon Restoration* (trans., 1966), and *Metternich and His Times* (1962). Sympathetic, but not uncritical studies of the forces of political conservatism.

G. de Ruggiero, *The History of European Liberalism* (1927). The major treatment of the subject.

J. Droz, *Europe between Revolutions, 1815–1848* (1967). An examination of Europe as created by the Vienna settlement.

Carlton J. Hayes, *Essays on Nationalism* (1926). Pioneering, but still useful studies.

E. J. Hobsbawm, *The Age of Revolution, 1789–1848* (1962). A very comprehensive survey emphasizing the social ramifications of the liberal democratic and industrial revolutions.

H. Kohn, *The Idea of Nationalism: A study in Its Origin and Background* (1944). An examination of the roots of nationalism in Western culture.

L. Krieger, *The German Idea of Freedom* (1957). A far-ranging examination of the problems and ideology of German liberalism.

J. Merriman (Ed.), *1830 in France* (1976). A collection of important essays on the Revolutions of 1830.

M. Raeff, *The Decembrist Movement* (1966). An examination of the unsuccessful uprising, with documents.

N. V. Riasanovsky, *Nicholas I and Official Nationality in Russia, 1825–1855* (1959). A lucid discussion of the conservative ideology that made Russia the major opponent of liberalism.

D. Thomson, *Europe Since Napoleon* (1962). A survey of political developments during the past century and a half.

Mack Walker, *Metternich's Europe* (1968). A useful collection of documents.

P. S. Wandycz, *The Lands of Partitioned Poland, 1795–1918* (1974). The best study of Poland during the nineteenth century.

674

26
Economic Advance and Social Unrest
(1830–1850)

By 1830 Europe was headed toward an industrial society. Only Great Britain had already attained that status, but the pounding of new machinery and the grinding of railway engines soon began to echo across the entire continent. Further urbanization, the disintegration of traditional social bonds and work habits, and eventually class conflict became part and parcel of the economic development. However, what characterized the second quarter of the century was not the triumph of industrialism but the final gasps of those groups who opposed it. Intellectually the period saw the formulation of the major creeds supporting and criticizing the new society. These were years of uncertainty for almost everyone. Even the most confident businessman knew that the trade cycle might bankrupt him in a matter of weeks. For industrial workers and the artisans unemployment became a haunting and recurring problem. For the peasants the question was sufficiency of food. It was a period of self-conscious transition that culminated in 1848 with a continentwide outbreak of revolution. People knew that one mode of life was passing, but they were uncertain what would replace it.

Toward an Industrial Society
Population and Migration

The Industrial Revolution had begun in eighteenth-century Great Britain with the advances in textile production described in Chapter 20. Natural resources, adequate capital, native technological skills, a growing food supply, a social structure that allowed considerable mobility, and strong foreign and domestic demand for goods had given Britain an edge in achieving a vast new capacity for production in manufacturing. Its factories and recently invented machines allowed British producers to furnish customers with more products and better products at lower prices than any competitors. The wars of the French Revolution and of Napoleon brought about the collapse of the French Atlantic trade. The same conflicts had destroyed capital, led to inflated currencies, and killed off much of the labor supply in continental countries. The restored conservative governments were fearful of the social and political unrest that might accompany major economic change. Consequently Britain's initial lead became further extended, so that in 1850 the nation still remained a generation ahead of its future continental competitors.

Despite the economic lag the continental nations were beginning to make material progress. By the 1830s in Belgium, France, and Germany the number of steam engines in use was growing steadily. Exploitation of the coalfields of the Ruhr and the Saar basins had commenced. Coke was replacing charcoal in iron and steel production. Industrial areas were generally less concentrated than in Britain. Large manufacturing districts, such as the British Midlands, did not yet exist across the English Channel. There were major pockets of production, such as the cities of Lyons, Rouen, Liège, and Lille, but most continental manufacturing still took place in the countryside. New machines were integrated into the existing domestic system. The extreme slowness of continental imitation of the British example meant that at mid-century peasants and urban artisans remained more important politically than industrial factory workers.

While the process of industrialization spread, the population of Europe continued to grow upon the base of the eighteenth-century population explosion. The number of people in France rose from 32.5 million in 1831 to 35.8 million in 1851. The population of Germany rose from

After 1830 railroads began to destroy the peace and quiet of the countryside. Here, in an 1837 illustration by John G. Bourne for his *Drawings of the London and Birmingham Railway,* rocks are being blasted to make way for new tracks. Once the railroads penetrated the countryside, people at last could move easily to the city and to other parts of the country, a factor that helped to undermine the stability of rural society and to modify the character of the cities themselves.

The Clifton Bridge, a great iron suspension bridge over the Avon River gorge near Bristol, England, was one of the many spectacular engineering accomplishments of the early nineteenth century. It was designed in 1831 by Isambard Kingdom Brunel (1806–1859), possibly the greatest engineer of his era. Construction began in 1836, and the bridge was completed in 1864. It is still in use. The bridge epitomizes the modern breakthrough in building such structures, as well as railways, subways, massive ships, and others—all dependent on new technologies. [British Tourist Authority, New York.]

26.5 million to 33.5 million during approximately the same period. That of Britain grew from 16.3 million to 20.8 million. More and more of the people of Europe lived in cities. By mid-century one half of the population of England and Wales had become town dwellers; the proportion for France and Germany was about one quarter. The sheer numbers of human beings put considerable pressure on the physical resources of the cities. Migration from the countryside meant that existing housing, water, sewers, food supply, and lighting were completely inadequate. Slums with indescribable filth grew, and disease, especially cholera, ravaged the population. Crime increased and became a way of life for those who could make a living in no other manner. Human misery and

degradation in numerous early nineteenth-century cities seemed to have no bounds.

The situation in the countryside was little or no better. During the first half of the century, land ownership and its productive use still remained the overwhelming facts of life for the majority of Europeans. The enclosures of the late eighteenth century, the land redistribution of the French Revolution, and the emancipation of serfs in Prussia and later in central Europe (Austria, 1848; Russia, 1861) commercialized landholding. Liberal reformers had hoped that the legal revolution in ownership would transform peasants into progressive, industrious farmers. Most of them had instead become very conservative landholders who possessed too little soil to innovate or in many cases even to support themselves. The specter of poor harvests still haunted Europe. The worst such experience of the century was the Irish famine of 1845–1847. Tens of thousands of Irish peasants with no land or small plots simply starved when disease blighted the potato crop. Hundreds of thousands emigrated. By mid-century the revolution in landholding had led not to greater agricultural production but to vast uprootings of peoples from the countryside into cities and from Europe into the rest of the world.

Railways

Industrial advance itself had also contributed to this migration. The decades of the thirties and forties were the great age of railway building. The Stockton and Darlington Line opened in England in 1825. By 1830 another major line had been built between Manchester and Liverpool with several hundred daily passengers. Belgium had undertaken railway construction by 1835. The first French line opened in 1832, but serious construction came only in the forties. Germany entered the railway age in 1835. At mid-century Britain had 9,797 kilometers of railway; France, 2,915; and Germany, 5,856. The railroads plus canals and improved regular roads meant that people could leave the place of their birth more easily than ever before. The improvement in transportation also allowed cheaper and more rapid passage of raw materials and finished products.

Railways epitomized the character of the industrial economy during the second quarter of the century. They represented investment in capital rather than in consumer goods. There was consequently somewhat of a shortage of consumer goods at cheap prices. This favoring of capital over consumer production was one reason that the working class often found itself able to purchase so little for its wages. The railways in and of themselves also brought about still more industrialization. They created a sharply increased demand for iron and steel and then for a more skilled labor force. The new iron and steel capacity soon permitted the construction of ironclad ships and iron rather than wooden machinery. These great capital industries led to the formation of vast industrial fortunes that would be invested in still newer enterprises. Industrialism had begun to grow upon itself.

Railroads literally cut into the cities of Europe. Here in Camden Town in London retaining walls are being built in a deep cut on either side of the newly laid tracks. The picture was made in 1838 by John G. Bourne.

The "Penny Black" with a portrait of Queen Victoria was the world's first adhesive postage stamp. Issued on May 6, 1840, it signified one small part of a world of more rapid communication. The engraver was Frederick Heath. [The Granger Collection.]

The Middle Classes

It was the age of the career open to talent. The middle class of businessmen, traders, shippers, factory owners, doctors, lawyers, shopkeepers, and schoolteachers benefited most from the economic and material progress. Their incomes, unlike those of laborers, allowed them to buy consumer goods. Their skills and education permitted them to rise socially. They often had sufficient savings to make either large or small investments in the railroads and other heavy industries. Many of them were able to rise well above the social status of their birth.

The middle *classes*—for the group was very diverse—believed that merit and competition should replace good birth and patronage as avenues to social position and political influence. In place of the former aristocratic value of leisure, they raised the values of thrift and hard work. They tended to measure success and respectability in terms of money. This attitude made them very unsympathetic toward the plight of the poor. They believed that the poor experienced poverty from either lack of ability or laziness. The middle classes were the people whom the English novelist Charles Dickens (1812–1870) pilloried in *Hard Times* and other novels and whose amoral existence the French novelist Honoré de Balzac (1799–1850) dissected in his fiction. But the confidence of the middle classes was a reflection of the new economic order that their members had created. They were also arrogant because they had learned from the aristocracy that pride and self-confidence were the marks of socially superior people.

Charles Dickens was the most popular novelist of mid-Victorian England. His works included many memorable, moving, and comic characters, but he was also deeply committed to exploring the evils of industrial and commercial society in which money and production had replaced love and imagination. The photograph was made during an American tour in the 1860s. [The Granger Collection.]

Frances Trollope, mother of the popular novelist Anthony Trollope, was herself an English novelist who wrote books portraying the harsh conditions in factories. The painting from the 1830s is by Augusta Hervieu. [The Granger Collection.]

Yet for all their economic success and apparent self-certainty, in several countries the middle classes at mid-century still generally lacked effective political power. They were best off in Britain, where aristocratic leaders did listen to them and where they were being absorbed into the political process, as the careers of Robert Peel, Richard Cobden, John Bright, and William Gladstone demonstrated.

In France, by contrast, a very small group of extremely wealthy persons affected politics. During the July Monarchy only about 250,000 persons had the right to vote. In the states of Germany, the Hapsburg Empire, and Russia the small middle classes were relatively powerless. Throughout Europe these people were coming increasingly to resent the lack of political influence equal to their wealth and ability. Their enemies were the aristocracy and inefficient royal administrations. Through philosophical and scientific societies, chambers of commerce, and where possible newspapers, they were by the late forties voicing their complaints and ambitions.

The early nineteenth-century middle class, however, was critical of the social conditions arising from industrialism as well as eager to enjoy economic profits. During the second quarter of the century numerous physicians who had to enter working-class districts to treat disease wrote books describing the suffering of the poor. Novelists—such as Dickens, Elizabeth Gaskell (1810–1865), Frances Trollope (1780–1863), and Benjamin Disraeli (1804–1881), who was also a notable statesman—featured the plight of the British working class in works such as *Mary Barton* and *Sybil.* Social commentators, such as Thomas Carlyle (1795–1881) in *Past and Present,* denounced the sacrifice of social welfare to the naked profit motive. Henry Mayhew (1812–1887), a reporter for the London *Morning Chronicle,* wrote a long series of articles in 1849–1850 about the life of the laboring poor in the city. He revealed a world of which middle-class readers had neither knowledge nor experience. Edwin Chadwick (1800–1890), a pioneer of sanitary reform, presented government reports on the degradation of urban and industrial life in Britain. Various parliamentary commissions also published papers describing the harsh realities of the conditions of the working class. All of these materials provided Karl Marx (1818–1883) with some of the most important sources for his denunciation of capitalism.

The Labor Force

The composition and experience of the early nineteenth-century labor force was quite varied. No single description could include all of the factory workers, urban artisans, domestic system craftsmen, household servants, countryside peddlers, farm workers, or railroad navvies. The work force was composed of some persons who were reasonably well off, enjoying steady employment and decent wages. It also numbered the "laboring poor," who held jobs but whose wages allowed them little more than subsistence. The condition of any particular working-class family depended upon the skills of its members, the nature of the local labor market, and the trade cycle. But all of these working people faced possible unemployment with little or no provision for their security. They confronted over the course of their lives the dissolution of many of the traditional social ties of custom and community. Most of the economic relationships in their lives became that of the marketplace, or as Thomas Carlyle said of the "cash nexus."

Within the variety of workers there are two broad categories about whom some general statements can be made: factory workers and artisans. The former were on the side of the future; the latter tried to hold onto the past. During the second quarter of the century the skilled artisans were more likely than the factory workers to be vocally discontent about their situation.

FACTORY WORKERS. Throughout the period there was a relative shortage of factory labor. Most of the new industries paid their workers higher wages than they would have received elsewhere. Moreover, contrary to opinions once held, the factory did not destroy the working-class family. For some time spinners and weavers working in factories were able to employ their own

Machinery in early mechanized cotton mills was often tended by women and children, as shown in this 1835 picture. If this picture is reasonably accurate, this mill, with its windows and the wide aisles between the machines, would have been considered a fairly good place to work. However, note that there are few safety devices on the machines to prevent injury to workers. [Bettmann Archive.]

The drabness of the exterior of the factory and the filth of the smoke from its stacks symbolized to many social critics the dark side of the industrial revolution. Nevertheless, factories, like this one in Manchester, England, also symbolized the vast new productive potential of European society. [E. Bains, *History of the Cotton Manufacture in Great Britain.* Courtesy Frank Cass & Co., London.]

children as helpers. In this manner to a certain extent the old family economy was transported into the mills. Only later on, when a laboring family became prosperous enough to send its own children to school, did it employ children outside its own family to tend the machines, thus splitting up a less prosperous family. There were also some factory owners who really cared about the lives and welfare of their employees.

Nonetheless there were many factories that were dangerous and unhealthy. Women and children were frequently employed for long hours at low wages. Factory laws were passed in Great Britain, France, and Prussia, but for many years they had only a marginal impact.

The harshest aspect of factory life, with the exception of the long hours, was the discipline of the machinery itself. Workers could no longer, as in the domestic system, set their own hours or speed of production. All work became determined by the machine. The closing of fac-

Friedrich Engels Describes the Plight of English Workers

As the most industrially advanced country, England offered a vast object lesson for study by social critics like Karl Marx and Friedrich Engels. Engels (1820–1895) had visited England where his father owned a factory. At age twenty-five he already believed the major difficulty confronting industrial workers was the almost total lack of security in their lives. They seemed to be the victims of chance and of the economic interest of the middle class.

INSECURITY *is even more demoralising than poverty. English wage-earners live from hand to mouth, and this is the distinguishing mark of their proletarian status. The lower ranks of the German peasantry are largely filled with men who are also poor, and often suffer want, but they are less subject to that sort of distress which is due solely to chance. They do at least enjoy some measure of security. But the proletarian is in quite a different position. He possesses nothing but his two hands and he consumes to-day what he earned yesterday. His future is at the mercy of chance. He has not the slightest guarantee that his skill will in the future enable him to earn even the bare necessities of life. Every commercial crisis, every whim of his master, can throw him out of work. He is placed in the most revolting and inhuman position imaginable. A slave is at least assured of his daily bread by the self-interest of his master. . . . Slaves and serfs are both guaranteed a basic minimum existence. The proletarian on the other hand is thrown wholly upon his own resources, and yet at the same time is placed in such a position that he cannot be sure that he can always use those resources to gain a livelihood for himself and his family. Everything that the factory worker can do to try and improve his position vanishes like a drop in the bucket in face of the flood of chance occurrences to which he is exposed and over which he has not the slightest control. He is the passive sufferer from every possible combination of mishaps, and can regard himself as fortunate if he keeps his head above water even for a short time. . . . He may fight for survival in this whirlpool; he may try to maintain his dignity as a human being. This he can do only by fighting the middle classes, who exploit him so ruthlessly and then condemn him to a fate which drives him to live in a way unworthy of a human being.*

Friedrich Engels, *The Condition of the Working Class in England*, trans. by W. O. Henderson and W. H. Chaloner (Stanford, Calif.: Stanford University Press, 1970), p. 131.

tory gates to late workers, the fines for such lateness, the dismissals for drunkenness, and the public scolding of faulty laborers constituted attempts to create human discipline and regularity that would match the demands of the cables, wheels, and pistons. To this psychological hardship in the plant must be added the haunting specter of unemployment.

URBAN ARTISANS. The plight of the urban artisans or craftsmen was different. They were attempting to maintain a traditional mode of life rather than adjusting to a new one. At mid-century there were still many more artisans working in small shops with fewer than ten employees than there were factory laborers. Often the introduction of new power machinery, such as the power loom, occurred so slowly that the artisan believed that he could still maintain his livelihood. By the time the true situation dawned on him, it was often too late for him to change skills.

The migration of rural domestic craftsmen into the cities created excessive hardship for urban artisans, such as weavers, metal workers, and construction laborers. The urban artisan already felt endangered by machines, and the new city dwellers increased the competition. Where possible, the guilds became more exclusive. Apprentices had difficulty becoming journeymen, and the latter found the ranks of the masters increasingly closed. The old framework of government control of wages and quality had been undermined by the economics of the middle class. With their skills threatened by machinery and with the old economic and social protections gone, these hard-pressed artisans, whose social forebears had been the revolutionary sans-culottes, became the most politically radical element in European society.

Early in the century the workers in traditional industries had attempted to protect their position by destroying the machines. These attacks on property failed, and swift repression often followed. By the twenties artisans and a few less-skilled workers were turning to unions. These efforts were only marginally successful during the first half of the century. In Germany liberal reformers

For a time it appeared that Chartism would become a violent political movement. However, riots, such as this one at Newport in 1839, eventually gave way to more peaceful demonstrations and mass petitions to Parliament to enact the Six Points of the Charter. [The Granger Collection.]

had attempted to break up the guilds. They succeeded in several states but not in Prussia. There the guilds remained effective until the middle of the forties and were legal until the sixties. In France the revolutionary legislation against workers' organizations remained on the books.

Workers' organizations again became legal in Great Britain after 1824. They made considerable headway until the early thirties. They then collapsed because they lacked sufficient funds to support long strikes. Equally important, the Whig government that passed the liberal Reform Act was most unsympathetic to organized labor. In 1833 that ministry mercilessly suppressed a revolt of farm workers called the Captain Swing uprising. In 1834 it transported to Australia four poor laborers, known as the Tolpuddle Martyrs, for attempting some vague kind of labor organization.

CHARTISM IN GREAT BRITAIN. By the late thirties, the British working class turned to direct political activity. They linked the solution of their economic plight to a program of political reform known as *Chartism*. In 1836 William Lovett (1800–1877) and other London radical artisans formed the London Working Men's Association. In 1838 the group issued the Charter, demanding six specific reforms. The Six Points of the Charter included universal manhood suffrage, annual election of the House of Commons, the secret ballot, equal electoral districts, abolition of property qualifications for Members of Parliament, and payment of members. For over ten years the Chartists, who were never tightly organized, agitated for their reforms. On three occasions the Charter was presented to Parliament, which refused to pass it. Mass petitions were presented to the House of Commons with millions of signatures. Strikes were called. A Chartist newspaper called *The Northern Star* was published. Feargus O'Connor (1794–1855), the most important Chartist spokesmen, made speeches up and down the island. Despite this vast activity Chartism as a national movement failed. Its ranks were split between those who favored violence and those who wanted to use peaceful tactics. However, locally the Chartists scored several successes and controlled the city councils in Leeds and Sheffield.

The economic foundation of Chartism had been the depression of the late thirties and early forties. As prosperity returned, many working people abandoned the movement. Chartism came to a close in March 1848. A mass march on Parliament planned for that month fizzled. The reviving economy took care of the rest of the problem. Nevertheless the Chartist movement constituted the first large-scale working-class political movement. It had specific goals and largely working-class leadership. Henceforth the British ruling classes knew that they could never again ignore the working class as a political factor. And eventually several of the Six Points were enacted into law. Continental working-class observers saw in Chartism the kind of mass movement that workers must eventually adopt if they were to improve their situation.

Intellectual Responses to Industrial Society

Classical Economics

Economists whose thought largely derived from Adam Smith's *Wealth of Nations* (1776) dominated private and public discussions of industrial and commercial policy. Their ideas are generally associated with the phrase *laissez-faire*. Although they thought that the government should perform many important functions, the classical economists favored economic growth through competitive free enterprise. Most economic decisions should be made through the mechanism of the marketplace. They distrusted government action, believing it to be mischievous and corrupt. The government should maintain a sound currency, enforce contracts, protect property, impose low tariffs and taxes, and leave the remainder of economic life to private initiative. The economists naturally assumed that the state would maintain sufficient armed forces and naval power to protect the economic structure and foreign trade of the nation.

The economists conceived of society as consisting of atomistic individuals from whose competitive efforts the demands of the consumers in the marketplace were met. Their theories supported the self-confidence of the middle class. The capitalist was the keystone of the whole economic system. The manufacturer or merchant, by making his capital produce, created jobs, goods, and income for other people. In contrast, the aristocrat or large landowner had a lazy, unproductive existence, as he lived off the rents from his land. The landlords had to do nothing to make their capital produce income. The logical conclusion of this theory was a seizure and redistribution of land. The economists, however, did not carry

their ideas that far because the seizure of land would lead to ideas about seizing middle-class capital.

What the classical economists said about the working class was more complicated and very pessimistic. Thomas Malthus (1766–1834) and David Ricardo (1772–1823), probably the most influential of all these writers, suggested in effect that the condition of the working class could not be improved. In 1798 Malthus published the first edition of his *Essay on Population*. His ideas have haunted the world ever since. He contended that population must outstrip the food supply. Although the human population grows geometrically, the food supply can expand only arithmetically. There was little hope of averting the disaster, in Malthus's eyes, except through late marriage, chastity, and contraception, the last of which he considered a vice. It took three quarters of a century before contraception became a socially acceptable method of containing the population explosion.

Malthus contended that the immediate plight of the working class could only become worse. If wages were raised, the workers would simply produce more children, who would in turn consume both the extra wages and more food. Later in his life Malthus suggested in a more optimistic vein that if the working class could be persuaded to adopt a higher standard of living, their increased wages might be spent on consumer goods rather than upon more children.

In the *Principles of Political Economy* (1817) David Ricardo transformed the concepts of Malthus into the Iron Law of Wages. If wages were raised, more children would be produced. They in turn would enter the labor market, thus expanding the number of workers and lowering wages. As wages fell, working people would produce fewer children. Wages would then rise, and the process would start all over. Consequently, in the long run wages would always tend toward a minimum level. These arguments simply confirmed employers in their natural hesitancy to raise wages. These concepts also provided strong theoretical support to opposition to labor unions. The ideas of the economists were spread to the

Harriet Martineau (1802–1876) was one of the most important popularizers of the ideas of the British classical economists. She illustrated their principles through moral tales [The Granger Collection.]

public during the thirties through journals, newspapers, and even short stories, such as Harriet Martineau's series of *Illustrations of Political Economy.*

The working class of France and Great Britain, needless to say, resented these attitudes, but the governments embraced them. Louis Philippe and his minister Francois Guizot (1787–1874) told Frenchmen to go forth and enrich themselves. If a person simply displayed sufficient energy, he need not be poor. A goodly number of the French middle class did just that. The July Monarchy saw the construction of major social overhead capital, such as roads, canals, and railways. Little was done about the poverty in the cities and the countryside.

In Germany the middle classes made less headway. However, the Prussian reformers after the Napoleonic wars had seen the desirability of abolishing internal tariffs that impeded economic growth. In 1834 all the major German states, with the exception of Austria, formed the *Zollverein* or free trading union.

Britain was the home of the major classical economists, and their policies were widely accepted. In 1834 the reformed House of Commons passed a new Poor Law. This measure established a Poor Law Commission, which set out to make poverty the most undesirable of all social situations. Government poor relief was to be dispersed only in workhouses. Life in the workhouse was consciously designed to be more unpleasant than life outside. Husbands and wives were separated. The food was bad, and the work assigned in the house was distasteful. The social stigma of the workhouse was even worse. The law and its administration presupposed that people would not work because they were lazy. The laboring class not unjustly regarded the workhouses as new "bastilles."

The second British monument to applied classical economics was the repeal of the Corn Laws in 1846. The Anti-Corn Law League, organized by manufacturers, had sought this goal for over six years. The league wanted the tariffs protecting the domestic price of grain to be abolished. That change would lead to lower food prices, which would then allow lower wages at no real

cost to the workers. In turn the prices on British manufactured goods could be lowered to allow a stronger competitive position in the world market. The actual reason for Robert Peel's repeal of the Corn Laws in 1846 was the Irish famine. He had to open British ports to foreign grain to feed the starving Irish. He realized that the Corn Laws could not be reimposed. Peel accompanied the abolition measure with a program for government aid to modernize British agriculture and to make it more efficient. The repeal of the Corn Laws was the culmination of the lowering of British tariffs that had begun during the 1820s. The repeal marked the opening of an era of free trade that continued until late in the century.

UTILITARIANISM. Closely related to the classical economists were the British utilitarians. Their major figures included Jeremy Bentham (1748–1832), James Mill (1773–1836), John Stuart Mill (1806–1873), and Sir Edwin Chadwick (1800–1890). They were a set of radical political reformers who urged that the principle of utility—the greatest good for the greatest number—should constitute the guiding principle of public policy. They lacked all reverence for tradition. They felt that political, economic, and social problems should be addressed rationally and without reference to the sinister interests of special or privileged groups. They have frequently been considered spokesmen for the middle class, but it would be more correct to see them as forerunners of an efficient bureaucracy. The utilitarians and their disciples were often civil servants, and they frequently worked on governmental commissions. They were the actual authors of much reform legislation, such as the Factory Act of 1833, the Poor Law of 1834, and the Sanitation Act of 1848.

The utilitarians have achieved a bad reputation for lacking an understanding of humanity and emotion. Some of this reputation is deserved. However, their most distinguished spokesman, John Stuart Mill, was anything but doctrinaire. As a young man he revolted against the rigid Benthamite education imposed on him by his father, James Mill. In his *Principles of Political Economy* (1848)

John Stuart Mill advocated the education of the working class as a means of raising their standard of living. He believed workers capable of as high moral existence as any other social group. He urged the formation of labor cooperatives. In 1859 Mill published *On Liberty* to plead for freedom of thought and expression and for the protection of the individual against the intrusion of the state. In 1869 he took up the cause of women's rights in a pioneering essay on *The Subjection of Women.* If utilitarianism had been narrow in its origins, by the close of Mill's life in 1873 the creed had proved itself capable of considerable moderation.

Socialism

Today the socialist movement, in the form of either communist or social democratic political parties, constitutes one of the major political influences in Europe. Less than 150 years ago the spokesmen for socialism lacked any meaningful political following. Their doctrines were blurred and often seemed silly to their contemporaries. The confusion in early socialist thought reflected its pioneering nature. The social and economic conditions being analyzed were new, and the exact problems to be solved still had to be defined. The early socialists generally applauded the new productive capacity of industrialism, but they denied that the free market could produce and distribute goods in the fashion claimed by the classical economists. The socialists saw primarily mismanagement, low wages, maldistribution of goods, and suffering emanating from the unregulated industrial system. Moreover the socialists thought that human society should be organized as a community rather than merely as a conglomerate of atomistic, selfish individuals.

UTOPIAN SOCIALISM. Among the earliest people to define the social question were a group of writers called the *utopian socialists.* They were considered utopian because their ideas were often visionary, and they frequently advocated the creation of ideal communities. They were called socialists because they questioned the structures and values of the existing capitalistic frame-work. In some cases they actually deserved neither description.

Claude Henri, Count of Saint-Simon (1760–1825), was the earliest of the socialist pioneers. As a young liberal French aristocrat he had fought in the American Revolution. Later he welcomed the French Revolution, during which he made and lost a fortune. By the time of Napoleon's ascendancy he had turned to a career of writing and social criticism. Saint-Simon believed that history oscillated between organic and critical periods. During organic periods, such as the Middle Ages, order, harmony, and shared values prevailed. During critical periods, such as the Reformation, the structures, values, and customs of a society underwent severe criticism and disintegration. He saw the late eighteenth and early nineteenth centuries as a critical age. He hoped to set forth a body of ideas and to organize a group of disciples that could project a social blueprint for the inevitable new organic period.

Above all else Saint-Simon believed that modern society would require rational management. Private wealth, property, and enterprise should be subject to administration other than that of its owners. His ideal government would have consisted of a large board of directors organizing and coordinating the activity of individuals and groups to achieve social harmony. In a sense he was the ideological father of technocracy. Not the redistribution of wealth but its management by experts would alleviate the poverty and social dislocation of the age. His faith in experts was similar to the Enlightenment *philosophes'* advocacy of political absolutism. Like his eighteenth-century forebears Saint-Simon had little sympathy with democracy. The order and harmony of the new organic age was to come from the genius of great thinkers such as himself. When Saint-Simon died in 1825, he had persuaded only a handful of people that his ideas were correct. Interestingly enough several of those disciples later became leaders in the French railway industry during the 1850s.

The major British contributor to the early socialist

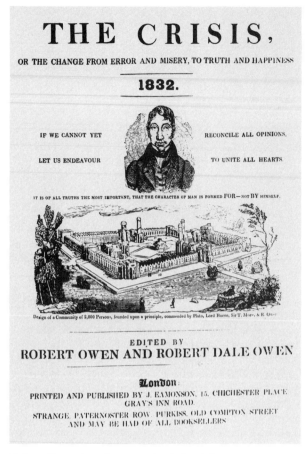

THE CRISIS,

OR THE CHANGE FROM ERROR AND MISERY, TO TRUTH AND HAPPINESS

1832.

IF WE CANNOT YET   RECONCILE ALL OPINIONS,

LET US ENDEAVOUR   TO UNITE ALL HEARTS.

IT IS OF ALL TRUTHS THE MOST IMPORTANT, THAT THE CHARACTER OF MAN IS FORMED FOR—NOT BY HIMSELF.

Design of a Community of 2,000 Persons, founded upon a principle, commended by Plato, Lord Bacon, Sir T. More, & R. Owen

EDITED BY
ROBERT OWEN AND ROBERT DALE OWEN

London:
PRINTED AND PUBLISHED BY J. EAMONSON, 15, CHICHESTER PLACE,
GRAY'S INN ROAD,
STRANGE, PATERNOSTER ROW, PURKISS, OLD COMPTON STREET
AND MAY BE HAD OF ALL BOOKSELLERS

Robert Owen hoped to organize industrial society into a series of small communities such as that pictured on the cover of his publication. He thought such communities would lead people to live by cooperation rather than by competition. [Bettmann Archive.]

tradition was Robert Owen (1771–1858), a self-made cotton manufacturer. In his early twenties Owen became a partner in New Lanark, one of the largest cotton factories in Britain. Owen was a firm believer in the environmentalist psychology of the Enlightenment. If human beings were placed in the correct surroundings, they and their character could be improved. Moreover Owen saw no incompatibility between creating a humane industrial environment and making a good profit. At New Lanark he put his ideas into practice. Workers were provided with good quarters. Recreational possibilities abounded, and the children were educated. There were several churches, although Owen himself was a notorious freethinker on matters of religion and sex. In the factory itself various rewards were given for good work. His plant made a fine profit. Visitors flocked from all over Europe to see what Owen had accomplished through enlightened management.

Robert Owen Attacks the Economic Ideal of Competition

Robert Owen owned a cotton mill in Scotland—a model of good working conditions for employees. In 1820, he argued, as throughout his life, that the principle of cooperation must replace self-interested competition in economic relationships. He saw competition as one of the chief causes of human suffering.

IT HAS *been, and still is, a received opinion among theorists in political economy, that man can provide better for himself, and more advantageously for the public, when left to his own individual exertions, opposed to and in competition with his fellows, than when aided by any social arrangement which shall unite his interests individually and generally with society. . . .*

Yet when they shall know themselves, and discover the wonderful effects which combination and union can produce, they will acknowledge that the present arrangement of society is the most anti-social, impolitic, and irrational, that can be devised; that under its influence all the superior and valuable qualities of human nature are repressed from infancy, and that the most unnatural means are used to bring out the most injurious propensities; in short, that the utmost pains are taken to make that which by nature is the most delightful compound for producing excellence and happiness, absurd, imbecile, and wretched. . . .

From this principle of individual interest have arisen all the divisions of mankind, the endless errors and mischiefs of class, sect, party, and of national antipathies, creating the angry and malevolent passions, and all the crimes and misery with which the human race have been hitherto afflicted.

In short, if there be one closet doctrine more contrary to truth than another, it is the notion that individual interest, as that term is now understood, is a more advantageous principle on which to found the social system, for the benefit of all, or of any, than the principle of union and mutual cooperation.

Robert Owen, *Report to the County of Lanark*, in V. A. C. Gatrell (Ed.), Robert Owen, *A New View of Society and Report to the County of Lanark* (Baltimore: Penguin Books, 1970), pp. 231–232.

In numerous articles and pamphlets as well as in letters to influential people, Owen pleaded for a reorganization of industry based on his own successful model. He envisioned a series of communities shaped like parallelograms in which factory and farm workers might live together and produce their goods in cooperation. During the

1820s Owen sold New Lanark and then went to the United States, where he established a community at New Harmony, Indiana. When it failed, he refused to give up his reformist causes. He returned to Britain, where he became the moving force behind the organization of the Grand National Union. This was an attempt to draw all British trade unions into a single body. It collapsed with other labor organizations during the early thirties. Owen possessed an exaggerated sense of his own importance and was a difficult person. His version of socialism amounted to little more than old-fashioned paternalism transported to the industrial setting. However, he contributed to the socialist tradition a strong belief in the practicality of cooperative production and proof that industrial production and humane working conditions were compatible.

Charles Fourier (1772–1837) was the French intellectual counterpart of Owen. He was a commercial salesman who never succeeded in attracting the same kind of public attention as Owen. He wrote his books and articles and returned home each day at noon, hoping to meet a patron who would undertake his program. No one ever arrived to meet him. Fourier believed that the industrial order ignored the passionate side of human nature. Social discipline ignored all the pleasures that human beings naturally seek. Fourier advocated the construction of communities, called *phalanxes,* in which liberated living would replace the boredom and dullness of industrial existence. Agrarian rather than industrial activity would predominate in these communities. Sexual activity would be relatively free, and marriage was to be reserved only for later life. Fourier also urged that no person be re-

Charles Fourier [BELOW], the French utopian socialist, believed that so far as possible work should be less boring and more pleasurable. His schemes for the ideal society were aimed at achieving this end.
A model for one of Fourier's phalansteries, in which the inhabitants would both live and work, is illustrated in this contemporary German print. [ABOVE]. [Both: The Granger Collection.]

quired to perform the same kind of work for the entire day. People would be both happier and more productive if they moved from one task to another. Through his emphasis on the problem of boredom Fourier isolated one of the key difficulties of modern economic life. Both he and Owen had raised the whole issue of the quality of life within the processes of industrial production.

Saint-Simon, Owen, and Fourier expected some existing government to carry out their ideas. They failed to confront the political difficulties of their envisioned social transformations. Other figures paid more attention to the politics of the situation. In 1839 Louis Blanc (1811–1882) published *The Organization of Labor.* Like other socialist writers this Frenchman demanded an end to competition, but he did not seek a wholly new society. He called for political reform that would give the vote to the working class. Once so empowered, workers could use the vote to turn the political processes to their own economic advantage. A state controlled by a working class electorate would finance workshops to employ the poor. In time such workshops might replace private enterprise. Industry could be organized to ensure jobs. Blanc recognized the power of the state to improve life and the conditions of labor. It could become the great employer of labor.

ANARCHISTS. Other writers and activists of the forties, however, rejected both industry and the dominance of government. These were the anarchists. They are usually included in the socialist tradition although they do not exactly fit. Some favored programs of violence; others were peaceful. Auguste Blanqui (1805–1881) was a major spokesman for terror and was one of Europe's earliest professional revolutionaries. He spent most of his adult life in jail. Blanqui urged the development of a professional revolutionary vanguard to attack capitalist society. He sought the abolition of both capitalism and the state. His ideas for the new society were quite vague, but in his call for professional revolutionaries he foreshadowed Lenin.

Pierre Joseph Proudhon (1809–1865) represented the other strain of anarchism. In his most famous work, *What Is Property?* (1840), Proudhon attacked the banking system, which so rarely extended credit to small property owners or the poor. He wanted credit expanded to allow such people to engage in economic enterprise. Society should be organized on the basis of mutualism, which amounted to a system of small businesses. There would be peaceful cooperation and exchange of goods among these groups. With such a social system the state as it then existed would be unnecessary. His ideas later influenced the French labor movement, which generally avoided political activity.

Pierre Joseph Proudhon, here portrayed with his children by the French realist painter Gustave Courbet (1819–1877), was the most important French contributor to anarchist thought. [The Granger Collection.]

These various strains of early socialist thought provided the background and the context for the emergence of Marxist socialism. But they did more than that. They influenced the ideas and activities of European socialists and trade unions well into the third quarter of the century. Too often the history of socialism is regarded as a linear development leading naturally or necessarily to the triumph of Marxism. Nothing could be further from the truth. Marxism did eventually triumph over much though not all of Europe but only through competition with other socialist formulas. At mid-century the ideas of Karl Marx were simply one more contribution to a heady mixture of concepts and programs criticizing the emerging industrial society. Marxist ideology differed from its competitors in the brilliance of its author, its claim to rigorous scientific accuracy, and its message of the inevitable collapse of the capitalistic order.

Marxism

Karl Marx was born in 1818 in the Rhineland. His Jewish middle-class parents sent him to the University of Berlin, where he became deeply involved with Hegelian philosophy and radical politics. During 1842 and 1843 he edited the radical *Rhineland Gazette* (*Rheinische Zeitung*). Soon the German authorities drove him from his native land. He lived as an exile in Paris, then in Brussels, and finally after 1847 in London.

In 1844 Marx met Friedrich Engels (1820–1895), another young middle-class German, whose father owned a textile factory in Manchester, England. The next year Engels published *The Condition of the Working Class in England,* which presented a devastating picture of industrial life. The two men became fast friends. Late in 1847 they were asked to write a pamphlet for a newly organized and ultimately short-lived secret Communist League. *The Communist Manifesto,* published in German, appeared early in 1848. This work of less than fifty pages would become the most influential political document of modern European history, but that development lay in the future. At the time it was simply one more political

The socialist philosophy of Karl Marx eventually triumphed over most alternative versions of socialism in Europe—even though varying interpretations, criticisms, and revisions of his monumental work continue to today. [Bettmann Archive.]

tract. Moreover neither Marx nor his thought had any effect on the revolutionary events of 1848.

The major ideas of the *Manifesto* and of Marx's later work, including *Capital* (1867), were derived from German Hegelianism, French socialism, and British classical economics. Marx applied to social and economic development Hegel's concept that thought develops from the clash of thesis and antithesis into a new intellectual synthesis. For Marx the conflict between dominant and lesser social groups generated conditions that led to the emergence of a new dominant social group. These new social relationships in turn generated new discontent, conflict, and development.

The French socialists provided Marx with a portrayal of the evils of capitalist society and had raised the issue of property redistribution. Both Hegel and Saint-Simon had led Marx to see society and economic conditions as developing through historical stages. The classical economists

The title page of the *Manifesto of the Communist Party* (February 1848), by Marx and Engels, called for the proletariat of all lands to unite. Although written in German, the *Manifesto* was printed in London where there was no political censorship. [Culver Pictures.]

had produced the analytical tools for empirical, scientific examination of industrial capitalist society. Marx later explained to a friend:

> What I did that was new was to prove: (1) that the *existence of classes* is bound up with *particular historical phases in the development of production*; (2) that the class struggle necessarily leads to the *dictatorship of the proletariat*; (3) that this dictatorship itself only constitutes the transition to the *abolition of all classes and to a classless society*.[1]

In *The Communist Manifesto* Marx and Engels contended that human history must be understood rationally and as a whole. It is the record of humankind coming to grips with physical nature to produce the goods necessary for survival. That basic productive process determines the structures, values, and ideas of a society. The organization of the means of production have historically always involved conflict between the classes who owned and controlled the means of production and those classes who work for them. That necessary conflict has provided the engine for historical development; it is not an accidental by-product of mismanagement or bad intentions. Consequently piecemeal reforms cannot eliminate the social and economic evils that are inherent in the very structures of production. What is required is a radical social transformation. Such a revolution will occur as the inevitable outcome of the development of capitalism.

In Marx's and Engels's eyes, during the nineteenth century the class conflict that had characterized previous Western history had become simplified into a struggle between the bourgeoisie and the proletariat, or between the middle class and the workers. The character of capitalism ensured the sharpening of the struggle. Capitalist production and competition would steadily increase the

1 Albert Fried and Ronald Sanders (Eds.), *Socialist Thought: A Documentary History* (Garden City, N.Y.: Anchor Doubleday, 1964), p. 295.

size of the unpropertied proletariat. Large-scale mechanical production crushed both traditional and smaller industrial producers into the ranks of the proletariat. As the business structures grew larger and larger, smaller middle-class units would be squeezed out by the competitive pressures. Competition among the few remaining giant concerns would lead to more intense suffering on the part of the proletariat. As the workers suffered increasingly from the competition among the ever-enlarging firms, they would eventually begin to foment revolution and finally overthrow the few remaining owners of the means of production. For a time the workers would organize the means of production through a dictatorship of the proletariat, which would eventually give way to a propertyless and classless communist society.

This proletarian revolution was inevitable, according to Marx and Engels. The structure of capitalism required competition and consolidation of enterprise. Although the class conflict involved in the contemporary process resembled that of the past, it differed in one major respect. The struggle between the capitalistic bourgeoisie and the industrial proletariat would culminate in a wholly new society that would be free of class conflict. The victorious proletariat by its very nature could not be a new oppressor class: "The proletarian movement is the self-conscious, independent movement of the immense majority, in the interest of the immense majority." [2] The result of the proletarian victory would be "an association, in which the free development of each is the condition for the free development of all." [3] The victory of the proletariat over the bourgeoisie represented the culmination of human history. For the first time in human history one group of people would not be oppressing another.

Marx's analysis was conditioned by his own economic environment. The 1840s had been a period of much unemployment and deprivation. However, capitalism did

not collapse as he predicted, nor did the middle class during the rest of the century become proletarianized. Rather, more and more people came to benefit from the industrial system. Nonetheless, within a generation Marxism had captured the imagination of many socialists and large segments of the working class. The doctrines were based on the empirical evidence of hard economic fact. This scientific aspect of Marxism helped the ideology as science became more influential during the second half of the century. Marx had made the ultimate victory of socialism seem certain. His writings had also portrayed for the first time the actual magnitude of the revolutionary transformation. Those works also suggested that the path to socialism lay with revolution rather than with reform. The days of the utopians were over.

Conservative Paternalism Reasserted

The socialists were not alone in their criticism of the liberal, capitalistic order. Many conservative Europeans also hated the atomistic view of society set forth by the classical economists and the liberal politicians. These conservatives saw that philosophy as undermining the influence of the aristocracy and the landowning classes. The middle-class concept of the poor was also at odds with the traditional Christian view of charity. These conservatives had much paternalistic sympathy for the working class. The writers who upheld this position were generally less brilliant than the liberals and the socialists. Their view of society had developed during the Romantic movement and harkened back to an idealized view of the Middle Ages. In many ways it was an obsolete view of social problems. However, their opinions permitted a temporary political alliance to be forged for a time between workers caught in the pressures of the labor market and spokesmen for political reaction.

England again provides important examples of this attitude. The movement to enact the first meaningful and enforceable factory legislation was led by Richard Oastler (1789–1861), Michael Sadler (1780–1835), and Lord Shaftesbury (1801–1885). These figures were conserva-

2 Robert C. Tucker (Ed.), *The Marx–Engels Reader* (New York: W. W. Norton, 1972), p. 344.

3 Ibid., p. 353.

Lord Shaftesbury (1801–1885) was one of the liberal
Victorian philanthropists and reformers. He sought
improvement in factory and mining conditions, a
shorter working day, and better sanitation. The
photograph was made about 1876. [The Granger Collection.]

tive politically and upheld the position of the church and
the aristocracy. After attaining the Factory Act of 1833,
Oastler led the Anti-Poor Law movement, which protested the stark utilitarian measures for the relief of the
unemployed. In 1843 Lord Shaftesbury fought for the
passage of the Mines Act, which removed women and
children from appalling labor conditions beneath the
earth. In 1847 Shaftesbury and Oastler were again active
in the campaign for the Ten Hours Act, which limited
the length of the workday.

Continental conservatives often adopted similar attitudes. In 1846 Joseph Maria von Radowitz (1797–1853)
published *Contemporary Talks on State and Church,* in
which he attacked competition. Conservatives used paternalistic social arguments against the demands of liberals for free trade and industrial development. The conservatives could pose as the protectors of the poor and the
industrial classes. They favored the preservation of guilds,
the regulation of industry, and the paternalistic relief of
poverty. The price of such protection, however, was
nonparticipation in politics by the industrial and rural
working classes. For sometime the working classes were
willing to accept that political cost because political liberals repeatedly ignored the social question.

March 23	Piedmont is defeated, and Charles Albert abdicates the crown of Piedmont in favor of Victor Emmanuel II.
March 27	The Frankfurt Parliament completes a constitution for Germany.
March 28	The Frankfurt Parliament elects Frederick William IV of Prussia to be emperor of Germany.
April 21	Frederick William IV of Prussia rejects the crown offered by the Frankfurt Parliament.
June 18	The remaining members of the Frankfurt Parliament are dispersed by troops.
July 3	Collapse of the Roman Republic after invasion by French troops.
August 9–13	The Hungarian forces are defeated by Austria aided by the troops of Russia.

1850

November 29	The Punctuation of Olmütz.

1851

December 2	*Coup d'état* of Louis Napoleon.

1848: Year of Revolutions

In 1848 a series of liberal and nationalistic revolutions spread across the Continent. No single factor caused this general revolutionary ground swell; rather, a number of similar conditions existed in several countries. Severe food shortages had prevailed since 1846. The harvests of grain and potatoes had been very poor. The famine in Ireland was simply the worst example of a more widespread situation. The commercial and industrial economy was also in a period of downturn. Unemployment was very widespread. All systems of poor relief were overburdened. These difficulties, added to the wretched living conditions in the cities, heightened the sense of frustration and discontent of the urban artisan and laboring classes.

However, the dynamic force for change in 1848 originated not with the working classes but with the political liberals, who were generally drawn from the middle classes. Throughout the Continent liberals were pushing for their program of more representative government, civil liberty, and an unregulated economic life. They had received much encouragement from the repeal of the English Corn Laws and the example of peaceful agitation by the Anti-Corn Law League. The liberals on the Continent wanted to pursue similar peaceful tactics. However, to put additional pressure on their governments, they began to appeal for the support of the urban working classes. The goals of the latter were improved working and economic conditions rather than a liberal framework of government. Moreover the tactics of the working classes were frequently violent rather than peaceful. The temporary alliance of liberals and workers in several states overthrew the old order; then the allies commenced to fight between themselves.

Finally, outside France nationalism was an important common factor in the uprisings. Germans, Hungarians, Italians, and smaller national groups in eastern Europe sought to create national states that would reorganize or replace existing political entities. The Austrian Empire was the state most profoundly endangered by nationalism. The nationalists were also frequently liberal and sometimes benefited from lower- and working-class economic discontent in the major cities.

The immediate results of the 1848 revolutions were quite stunning. The French monarchy fell, and many of the others were badly shaken. Never in a single year had

Conditions leading to revolutions in the 1820s and 1830s remained and by 1848 were fuelled by new nationalist and liberal political demands, as well as by severe economic conditions among the poor. Following Paris's lead, violence erupted in the centers shown here.

CENTERS OF REVOLUTION, 1848–1849

Europe known so many major uprisings. Yet the revolutions proved a false spring for progressive Europeans. Without exception they failed to establish new liberal or national states. The conservative order proved stronger and more resilient than anyone had expected. Moreover the liberal middle-class political malcontents in each country discovered that they could no longer push for political reform without at the same time raising the social question. The liberals refused to follow political revolution with social reform and thus isolated themselves from the working classes. Once separated from potential mass support, the liberal revolutions became an easy prey to the armies of the reactionary classes.

France: The Second Republic and Louis Napoleon

As twice before, the revolutionary tinder first blazed in Paris. The liberal political opponents of the corrupt regime of Louis Philippe and his minister Guizot had organized a series of political banquets. These occasions were used to criticize the government and to demand further middle-class admission to the political process. The poor harvests of 1846 and 1847 and the resulting high food prices and unemployment brought working-class support to the liberal campaign. On February 21, 1848, the government forbade further banquets. A very large one had been scheduled for the next day. On February 22 disgruntled Parisian workers paraded through the streets demanding reform and Guizot's ouster. The next morning the crowds grew, and by afternoon Guizot had resigned. Barricades had been erected, and numerous clashes had occurred between the citizenry and the mu-

nicipal guard. On February 24, 1848, Louis Philippe abdicated and fled to England.

The liberal opposition, led by the poet Alphonse de Lamartine (1790–1869), organized a provisional government. They intended to call an election for an assembly that would write a republican constitution. The various working-class groups in Paris had other ideas; they wanted a social as well as a political revolution. Led by Louis Blanc, they demanded representation in the Cabinet. Blanc and two other radical leaders were made ministers. Under their pressure the provisional government organized national workshops to provide work and relief for thousands of unemployed workers.

On Sunday, April 23, an election based on universal manhood suffrage chose the new National Assembly. The result was a legislature dominated by moderates and conservatives. In the French provinces there had been much resentment against the Paris radicals. The church and the local notables still exercised considerable influence. Small landowning peasants feared possible confiscation of their holdings by Parisian socialists. The new conservative National Assembly had little sympathy for the national workshops, which they incorrectly perceived to be socialistic. Throughout May government troops and the Parisian crowd of unemployed workers and artisans clashed. Late that month the assembly closed the workshops to new entrants and planned the removal of many enrolled workers. By the latter part of June barricades again appeared in Paris. On June 24, under orders from the government, General Cavaignac, with troops drawn largely from the conservative countryside, moved to destroy the barricades and to quell potential disturbances.

Paris Workers Complain About the Actions of their Government

In the late spring of 1848 the government of the recently formed French Republic abolished the national workshops that it had created a few weeks earlier to provide aid for the unemployed. The first selection below illustrates the anger caused by the abolition of the workshops and the sense of betrayal felt by the workers. The second document describes the experience of a cabinet-maker who had for a time enrolled in one of the workshops.

TO THE FINANCE MINISTER OF THE REPUBLIC

ARE *you really the man who was the first finance minister of the Republic, of the Republic won at the cost of blood thanks to the workers' courage, of this Republic whose first vow was to provide bread every day for all its children by proclaiming the universal right to work. Work, who will give it to us if not the state at a time when industry has everywhere closed its workshops, shops and factories? Yesterday martyrs for the Republic out on the barricades, today its defenders in the ranks of the national guard, the workers might consider it owed them something. . . .*

Why do the national workshops so rouse your reprobation . . . ? You are not asking for their reform, but for their total abolition. But what is to be done with this mass of 110,000 workers who are waiting each day for their modest pay, for the means of existence for themselves and their families? Are they to be left a prey to the evil influences of hunger and of the excesses that follow in the wake of despair?

A LETTER TO A NEWSPAPER EDITOR

I LIVE *in the fauborg; by trade I am a cabinet-maker and I am enrolled in the national workshops, waiting for trade to pick up again.*

I went into the workshops when I could no longer find bread elsewhere. Since then people have said we were given charity there. But when I went in I did not think that I was becoming a beggar. I believed that my brothers who were rich were giving me a little of what they had to spare simply because I was their brother.

I admit that I have not worked very hard in the national workshops, but then I have done what I could. I am too old now to change my trade easily—that is one explanation. But there is another: the fact is that, in the national workshops, there is absolutely nothing to do.

Roger Price (Ed. and Trans.), *1848 in France* (Ithaca, N.Y.: Cornell University Press, 1975), pp. 103–104.

During the next two days over four hundred people were killed. Thereafter troops hunted down another three thousand persons in street-to-street fighting. The drive for social revolution had come to an end.

The so-called June Days confirmed the political predominance of conservative property holders in French life. They wanted a republic, but a republic safe for small property. This search for social order received further confirmation late in 1848. The victor in the presidential election was Prince Louis Napoleon Bonaparte (1808–1873), a nephew of the great emperor. For most of his life he had been an adventurer living outside France. Twice he had unsuccessfully attempted to lead a *coup* against the July Monarchy. The disorder of 1848 provided him a new opportunity to enter the French political scene. After the corruption of Louis Philippe and the turmoil of the early months of the Second Republic, the voters turned to the name of Bonaparte as a source of stability and greatness.

The election of the "Little Napoleon" doomed the Second Republic. Louis Napoleon was dedicated to his own fame rather than to republican institutions. He was the first of the modern dictators who by playing upon unstable politics and social insecurity have so changed European life. He constantly quarreled with the National Assembly and claimed that he rather than they represented the will of the nation. In 1851 the assembly refused to amend the constitution to allow the president to succeed himself. Consequently, on December 2, 1851, the anniversary of the great Napoleon's victory at Austerlitz, Louis Napoleon seized personal power. Troops dispersed the assembly, and the president called for new elections. Over two hundred people died resisting the *coup*, and over twenty-six thousand persons were arrested. Yet in the plebiscite of December 21, 1851, over $7\frac{1}{2}$ million voters supported Louis Napoleon, who, as a result, became Emperor Napoleon III. Only about 600,000 opposed him. For the second time in just over fifty years France had turned from republicanism to caesarism.

In 1848 the populace of Paris erected barricades
at strategic points throughout the city to halt
the movement of troops used against revolutionaries.
This picture of one in the Montmartre section
purports to be by an eyewitness and appeared in a
London newspaper. [The Granger Collection.]

De Tocqueville Analyzes the June Revolution in Paris

Alexis de Tocqueville (1805–1859) was a French liberal politician, historian, political scientist and also a keen social observer. By the time of the 1848 uprising in Paris he had lived two years in the United States in the 1830s; *Democracy in America* is still an important analysis of our early institutions. In this passage from his memoirs he describes the manner in which the conflict of the June Days of 1848 in Paris differed from earlier political upheavals in France. He understood that what had occurred was a mode of class warfare and that it might characterize European political life for many decades to come.

I COME *at last to the insurrection of June. . . .*

What distinguished it also, among all the events of this kind which have succeeded one another in France for sixty years, is that it did not aim at changing the form of government, but at altering the order of society. . . . It was not, strictly speaking, a political struggle, in the sense which until then we have given to the word, but a combat of class against class, a sort of Servile War. It represented the facts of the Revolution of February in the same manner as the theories of Socialism represented its ideas; or rather it issued naturally from these ideas, as a son does from his mother. We beheld in it nothing more than a blind and rude, but powerful, effort on the part of the workmen to escape from the necessities of their condition, which had been depicted to them as one of unlawful oppression, and to open up by main force a road towards that imaginary comfort with which they had been deluded. It was this mixture of greed and false theory which first gave birth to the insurrection and then made it so formidable. These poor people had been told that the wealth of the rich was in some way the produce of a theft practised upon themselves. They had been assured that the inequality of fortunes was as opposed to morality and the welfare of society as it was to nature. Prompted by their needs and their passions, many had believed this obscure and erroneous notion of right, which, mingled with brute force, imparted to the latter an energy, a tenacity and a power which it would never have possessed unaided.

It must be observed that this formidable insurrection was not the enterprise of a certain number of conspirators, but the revolt of one whole section of the population against another.

Alexis de Tocqueville, *Recollections*, trans. by A. T. de Mattos (New York: Macmillan, 1896), pp. 187–188.

The Hapsburg Empire: Nationalism Resisted

The events of February 1848 in Paris immediately reverberated throughout the Hapsburg domains. The empire was susceptible to revolutionary challenge on every score. Its government eschewed liberal institutions. Its geographical borders ignored the principle of nationalism. Its society perpetuated serfdom. During the forties even Metternich had urged reform, but none was forthcoming. In 1848 the regime confronted major rebellions in Vienna, Prague, Hungary, and Italy. It was also intimately involved in the disturbances that broke out in Germany.

The Hapsburg troubles commenced on March 3, 1848, when Louis Kossuth (1802–1894), a Hungarian Magyar nationalist, attacked Austrian domination of Hungary. He called for Hungarian independence and a responsible ministry under the Hapsburg crown. Ten days later, inspired by Kossuth's demands, students led a series of major disturbances in Vienna. The army failed to restore order. Metternich resigned and fled the country. The feeble-minded Emperor Ferdinand (1835–1848) promised a moderately liberal constitution. Unsatisfied, the radical students then formed democratic clubs to press the revolution further. On May 17 the emperor and the imperial court fled to Innsbruck. The government of Vienna at this point lay in the hands of a committee of over two hundred persons primarily concerned with alleviating the economic plight of Viennese workers.

What the Hapsburg government most feared was not the urban rebellions but rather a potential uprising of the serfs. Already there had been isolated instances of peasants invading manor houses and burning records. Almost immediately after the Vienna uprising the imperial government had emancipated the serfs in large areas of Austria. The Hungarian Diet also abolished serfdom in March 1848. These actions smothered the most serious potential threat to order in the empire. The emancipated serfs now had little reason to support the revolutionary movement in the cities.

Louis Kossuth, a Hungarian nationalist, helped to lead the revolution of 1848 in Budapest. The portrait was made the following year. [The Granger Collection.]

The Vienna revolt had given encouragement to the Hungarians. The leaders of the Hungarian March revolution were primarily liberal Magyars supported by Magyar nobles who wanted their aristocratic liberties guaranteed against the central government in Vienna. The Hungarian Diet passed a series of March Laws that ensured equality of religion, jury trials, the election of a lower chamber, a relatively free press, and payment of taxes by the nobility. Emperor Ferdinand approved these measures because in the spring of 1848 he was in a position to do little else.

The Hungarian Magyars also hoped to establish a separate Hungarian state within the Hapsburg domains. They would retain considerable local autonomy while Ferdinand remained their emperor. As part of this scheme for a partially independent state, the Hungarians attempted to annex Transylvania, Croatia, and other territories on the eastern border of the Hapsburg Empire. That policy of annexation would bring Romanians, Croations, and Serbs under Magyar government. These national groups resisted the drive toward Magyarization. They believed that they had a better chance of maintaining their identity and self-interest under Hapsburg control. Consequently they turned against Hungary. In late March the Vienna government sent Baron Joseph Jellachich to aid the national groups who were rebelling against the rebellious Hungarians. By early September 1848 he was leading an invasion force against Hungary.

In the middle of March, 1848, with Vienna and Budapest in revolt, Czech nationalists had demanded that Bohemia, Moravia, and Silesia be permitted to constitute an autonomous Slavic state within the empire similar to that just constituted in Hungary. Conflict immediately developed, however, between the Czechs and the Germans living in these areas. The Czechs summoned a congress of the Slavs, which met in Prague during early June. On June 12, the day the congress closed, a radical insurrection broke out in the city. General Alfred Windischgratz, whose wife had been killed by a stray bullet, moved his troops to repress the uprising. The local middle class was happy to see the radicals suppressed. The Germans in the area approved the smothering of Czech nationalism. The policy of divide and conquer had succeeded.

While confronting the Hungarian and Czech bids for autonomy, the Hapsburg government also faced war in northern Italy. A revolution commenced in Milan on March 18. Five days later the Austrian commander General Joseph Wenzel Radetzky retreated from the city. King Charles Albert of Piedmont (1831–1849), who wanted to expand the influence of his kingdom in the area, aided the rebels in Lombardy. The Austrian force faired badly until July, when Radetzky, reenforced by new troops, defeated Piedmont and suppressed the revolution. For the time being Austria had held its position in northern Italy.

Vienna and Hungary remained to be recaptured. In midsummer the emperor returned to the capital. A newly elected assembly was attempting to write a constitution. However, within the city the radicals continued to press for further concessions. The imperial government decided to reassert its control. When a new insurrection occurred in October, it was crushed by the imperial army, which bombarded Vienna. On December 2 Emperor Ferdinand abdicated in favor of his young nephew Francis Joseph (1848–1916). The real power now lay with Prince Felix Schwarzenberg (1800–1852), who intended to use the army with full force. On January 5, 1849, Budapest was occupied. By March the triumphant Austrian forces had imposed military rule over Hungary, and the new emperor repudiated the recent constitution. The Magyar nobles attempted one last revolt. It was crushed by Austrian troops reenforced by 200,000 soldiers happily furnished by Tsar Nicholas I of Russia. The imperial Hapsburg government had survived its gravest internal challenge because of the divisions among its

Economic Advance and Social Unrest (1830–1850)

In this Dutch lithograph Pope Pius IX (1846–1878) is pictured as a vicious reactionary hiding behind the mask of the suffering Jesus. After 1848 the pope, who had once been thought liberal, followed a strongly reactionary policy in Italy and the Roman Catholic Church. [John R. Freeman.]

enemies and its own willingness to use military force with vengeance.

Italy: Republicanism Defeated

The brief Piedmont–Austrian war of 1848 marked only the first stage of the Italian revolution. Many Italians hoped that Piedmont would drive Austria from the peninsula and thus prepare the way for Italian unification. The defeat of Piedmont was a sharp disappointment. Liberal and nationalist hopes then shifted to the pope. Pius IX (1846–1878), who had become pope in 1846, had a liberal reputation. He had reformed the administration of the Papal States. Nationalists believed that some form of a united Italian state might emerge under the leadership of this pontiff.

In Rome, however, as in other cities, political radicalism was on the rise. On November 15, 1848, a democratic radical assassinated Count Pelligrino Rossi, the liberal minister of the Papal States. The next day popular demonstrations forced the pope to appoint a radical ministry. Shortly thereafter Pius IX fled to Naples for refuge. In February 1849 the radicals proclaimed the Roman Republic. Republican nationalists from all over Italy, including Giuseppe Mazzini (1805–1872) and Giuseppe Garibaldi (1807–1882), two of the most prominent nationalists, flocked to Rome. They hoped to use the new republic as a base of operations to unite the rest of the peninsula under a republican government.

In March 1849 radicals in Piedmont forced Charles Albert to renew the patriotic war against Austria. The almost immediate defeat at the battle of Novara gave the king an opportunity to abdicate in favor of his son, Victor Emmanuel II (1849–1878). The defeat of Piedmont meant that the Roman Republic must defend itself alone. The troops that attacked Rome and restored the pope came from France. The French wanted to prevent the rise of a strong, unified state on their southern border. Moreover protection of the pope was good domestic politics for the French Republic and its president, Louis Napoleon. In early June 1849 ten thousand French sol-

diers laid siege to the Eternal City. By the end of the month the Roman Republic had dissolved. Garibaldi attempted to lead an army north against Austria but was defeated. On July 3 Rome fell to the French forces, which continued to occupy it as protection for the pope until 1870. Pius IX returned, having renounced his previous liberalism. He became one of the archconservatives of the next quarter century. Leadership toward Italian unification would have to come from another direction.

Germany: Liberalism Frustrated

The revolutionary contagion had also spread rapidly through numerous states of Germany. Württemberg, Saxony, Hanover, and Bavaria all experienced insurrections calling for liberal government and greater German unity. The major revolution, however, occurred in Prussia. By March 15, 1848, large popular disturbances had erupted in Berlin. Frederick William IV (1840–1861), believing that the trouble stemmed from foreign conspirators, refused to turn his troops on the Berliners. He even announced certain limited reforms. Nevertheless, on March 18, several citizens were killed when troops cleared a square near the palace. The next day Frederick

King Frederick William IV of Prussia (1840–1861) disappointed the hopes of German nationalists by refusing to accept the crown of a united Germany offered by the Frankfurt Parliament. His portrait is by Franz Krüger. [Bildarchiv Preussischer Kulturbesitz.]

William IV was forced to salute the corpses of his slain subjects. He made further concessions and implied that henceforth Prussia would aid the movement toward German unification. The king also called for a Prussian constituent assembly to write a constitution. For all practical purposes the Prussian monarchy had capitulated.

Frederick William IV appointed a cabinet headed by David Hansemann (1790–1864), a widely respected moderate liberal. However, the Prussian constituent assembly proved to be radical and democratic. As time passed, the king and his conservative supporters decided that they would ignore the assembly. The liberal ministry resigned and was replaced by a conservative one. In April 1849 the assembly was dissolved, and the monarch proclaimed his own constitution. One of its key elements was a system of three-class voting. All adult males were allowed to vote. However, they voted according to three classes arranged by ability to pay taxes. Thus the largest taxpayers, who constituted only about 5 per cent of the population, elected one third of the Prussian Parliament. This system prevailed in Prussia until 1918. In the finally revised Prussian constitution of 1850, the ministry was responsible to the king alone. Moreover, the Prussian army and officer corps swore loyalty directly to the monarch.

While Prussia had moved from revolution to reaction, other events had unfolded in Germany as a whole. On May 18, 1848, representatives from all the German states had gathered in St. Paul's Church in Frankfurt to revise the organization of the German Confederation. The Frankfurt Parliament intended to write a moderately liberal constitution for a united Germany. The liberal character of the Frankfurt Parliament alienated both German conservatives and the German working class. The offense to the conservatives was simply the challenge to the existing political order. The Frankfurt Parliament lost the support of the industrial workers and artisans by refusing to restore the protection once afforded by the guilds. The liberals were too much attached to the concept of a free labor market to offer meaningful legislation to workers. This failure marked the beginning of a profound split between German liberals and the German working class. For the rest of the century German conservatives would be able to play upon that division.

As if to demonstrate its disaffection from workers, the Frankfurt Parliament in September, 1848, called in troops of the German Confederation to suppress a radical insurrection in the city. The liberals in the parliament wanted nothing to do with workers who erected barricades and threatened the safety of property.

The Frankfurt Parliament floundered on the issue of unification as well as upon the social question. Members differed over the inclusion of Austria in the projected united Germany. The large German (*grossdeutsch*) solution favored inclusion while the small German (*kleindeutsch*) solution advocated exclusion. The latter formula prevailed because Austria rejected the whole notion of German unification. It raised too many other nationality problems within the Hapsburg domains. Consequently the Frankfurt Parliament looked to Prussian leadership. On March 27, 1849, the parliament produced its constitution. Shortly thereafter its delegates offered the crown of a united Germany to Frederick William IV of Prussia. He rejected the offer, asserting that kings ruled by the grace of God rather than by the wisdom of man-made constitutions. Upon his refusal the Frankfurt Parliament began to dissolve. Not long afterwards troops drove off the remaining members.

German liberals never fully recovered from this defeat. The Frankfurt Parliament had alienated the artisans and the working class without gaining any compensating support from the conservatives. The liberals had proved themselves to be awkward, hesitant, unrealistic, and ultimately dependent on the armies of the monarchies. They

The Frankfurt Parliament met in a church in that city in September 1848. Its deputies wanted to create a liberal, united Germany. However, as their debates dragged out, the forces of reaction regained strength and the parliament failed. [Bettmann Archive.]

had failed to unite Germany or to confront effectively the realities of political power in the German states. What was achieved through the various revolutions was an extension of the franchise in some of the German states and the establishment of conservative constitutions. The gains were not negligible, but they were a far cry from the hopes of March 1848.

The events of 1848 and 1849 had one important footnote for Frederick William IV. He gave much more thought to possible German unification under Prussia. In 1850 he attempted to create a German federation, which would have been a union of princes headed by the king of Prussia and excluding Austria. The Austrian Empire firmly rejected the proposal, which would have diminished Hapsburg influence in Germany. In November 1850, in what is known as the Punctuation of Olmütz, the Prussian monarch renounced his scheme at the demand of Austria. Prussian historians later called this event the Humiliation of Olmütz.

The turmoil of 1848 through 1850 brought to a close the era of liberal revolution that had begun in 1789. Liberals and nationalists had discovered that rational argument and small insurrections would not achieve their goals. The political initiative passed for a time to the conservative political groups. Nationalists henceforth were less romantic and more hardheaded. Railways, commerce, guns, soldiers, and devious diplomacy rather than language and cultural heritage became the weapons of national unification. The working class also adopted new tactics and organization. The day of the riot and urban insurrection were coming to a close. In the future, workers would turn to trade unions and political parties to achieve their political and social goals. Perhaps most important, after 1848 the European middle class ceased to be revolutionary. It became increasingly concerned about the protection of its property against radical political and social movements. The middle class remained politically liberal only so long as liberalism seemed to promise economic stability and social security for its own style of life.

Schurz Explains the Failure of the Frankfurt Parliament

Carl Schurz (1829–1906) was a German liberal who had witnessed and daringly participated in the uprisings of 1848 while still a student. He later moved to the United States, became a citizen, entered politics in Wisconsin, and served as a diplomat, Union Army general, cabinet member, senator from Missouri, and journalist. In his memoirs he attempted to explain why the German Frankfurt Parliament had been unable to provide Germany with a viable constitution and national unity. The Parliament had possessed no bureaucracy or military forces of its own, and its members had missed the opportunity to move rapidly to achieve their goals. By prolonging debate, the Parliament gave its opponents time to organize and permitted divisions to develop in its own ranks and in those of its supporters.

FACE *to face with the princes and their parties stood the national parliament in Frankfurt, that child of the revolution which might then have almost been called the orphan of the revolution. It had at its immediate disposal no administrative machinery, no army, no treasury, only its moral authority; all the rest was in the hands of the different German state governments. The only power of the national parliament consisted in the will of the people; and this power was sufficient for the fulfillment of its mission so long as the will of the people proved itself strong enough, even through revolutionary action in case of necessity, to counteract the adverse interests of the princes. The Parliament would have been sure of success in creating a constitutional German Empire, if it had performed that task quickly and elected and put into office its Kaiser while the revolutionary prestige of the people was still unbroken. . . .*

But that Parliament was laboring under an overabundance of learning and virtue and under a want of . . . political experience and sagacity. . . . The world has probably never seen a political assembly that contained a larger number of noble, learned, conscientious and patriotic men. . . . But it did not possess the genius that promptly discerns opportunity and with quick resolution takes fortune by the forelock; it was not mindful of the fact that in time of great commotion the history of the world does not wait for the theoretical thinker. And thus it failed.

The Reminiscences of Carl Schurz (New York: The McClure Company, 1907), Vol. 1, pp. 162–163.

SUGGESTED READINGS

S. AVINERI, *The Social and Political Thought of Karl Marx* (1969). An advanced treatment.

I. BERLIN, *Karl Marx: His Life and Environment* (1948). An excellent introduction.

A. BRIGGS (Ed.), *Chartist Studies* (1959). An anthology of significant studies.

S. G. CHECKLAND, *The Rise of Industrial Society in England, 1815–1885* (1964). Strong on economic institutions.

G. D. H. COLE, *A History of Socialist Thought,* 5 vols. (1953–1960). An essential work that spans the entire nineteenth century.

G. DUVEAU, *The Making of a Revolution* (trans., 1968). A lively book that explores the attitudes of the various French social classes.

E. HALEVY, *The Growth of Philosophic Radicalism* (1928). The basic discussion of utilitarianism.

T. HAMEROW, *Restoration, Revolution, and Reaction: Economics and Politics in Germany, 1815–1871* (1958). Traces the forces that worked toward the failure of revolution in Germany.

J. F. C. HARRISON, *Quest for the New Moral World: Robert Owen and the Owenites in Britain and America* (1969).

R. HEILBRONER, *The Wordly Philosophers,* rev. ed. (1972). A useful, elementary introduction to nineteenth-century economic thought.

W. O. HENDERSON, *The Industrialization of Europe, 1780–1914* (1969). Emphasizes the Continent.

D. LANDES, *The Unbound Prometheus: Technological Change and Industrial Development in Western Europe from 1750 to the Present* (1969). The best one-volume treatment of technological development in a broad social and economic context.

W. L. LANGER, *Political and Social Upheaval, 1832–1852* (1969). A remarkably thorough survey strong in both social and intellectual history as well as political narrative.

F. MANUEL, *The Prophets of Paris* (1962). A stimulating treatment of French utopian socialism and social reform.

H. PERKIN, *The Origins of Modern English Society, 1780–1880* (1969). A provocative attempt to look at the society as a whole.

P. ROBERTSON, *Revolutions of 1848: A Social History* (1952). Covers the developments in each nation.

P. STEARNS, *Eighteen Forty Eight: The Tide of Revolution in Europe* (1974). A good discussion of the social background.

A. J. TAYLOR (Ed.), *The Standard of Living in Britain in the Industrial Revolution* (1975). A collection of major articles on the impact of industrialism.

E. P. THOMPSON, *The Making of the English Working Class* (1964). An important, influential, and controversial work.

704

27
The Age of Nation States

THE REVOLUTIONS of 1848 collapsed in defeat for both liberalism and nationalism. Throughout the early fifties authoritarian regimes entrenched themselves across the Continent. Yet only a quarter century later many of the major goals of early nineteenth-century liberals and nationalists stood accomplished. Italy and Germany were at long last united under constitutional monarchies. The Hapsburg emperor had accepted constitutional government; the Hungarian Magyars had attained recognition of their liberties. In Russia the serfs had been emancipated. France was again a republic. Liberalism and even democracy flourished in Great Britain.

Paradoxically, most of these developments occurred under the direction and leadership of conservative statesmen. Events within European international affairs compelled some of them to pursue new policies at home as well as abroad. They had to find novel methods of maintaining the loyalty of their subjects. In some cases conservative leaders preferred to carry out a popular policy on their own terms so that they rather than the liberals would receive credit. Finally, some political leaders moved as they did because they had no choice.

The Crimean War (1854–1856)

As has so often been true in modern European history, the impetus for change originated in war. The Crimean War (1854–1856) was rooted in the longstanding rivalry

The Victor Emmanuel Monument in Rome (completed 1911) honors the king under whose rule Italy was united. The massiveness of the grandiose structure may well have reminded some people that the large-scale nation-state had become the most important political institution of modern times. Note the contrasting ruined splendor of ancient Rome in the foreground—Emperor Trajan's forum and column. [Italian Government Travel Office, New York.]

between Russia and the Ottoman Empire. Russia wanted to extend its control over the provinces of Moldavia and Walachia (now in Romania). The tsar's duty to protect Orthodox Christians in the empire furnished the pretext for Russian aggression. The Ottoman Empire had recently granted Catholic France rather than Orthodox Russia oversight of shrines in the Holy Land. Russia occupied the provinces in the summer of 1853, and the other great powers soon became involved. Both France and Great Britain opposed Russian expansion in the eastern Mediterranean, where they had extensive naval and commercial interests. Napoleon III also thought that an activist foreign policy would shore up domestic support for his regime. On March 28, 1854, France and Britain declared war on Russia. Much to the chagrin of Tsar Nicholas I, Austria and Prussia remained neutral. The Austrians had their own ambitions in the Balkans, and Prussia after the Humiliation of Olmütz followed in the Austrian train.

The war was ineptly waged on both sides. The ill-equipped and poorly commanded armies became bogged down along the Crimean coast of the Black Sea. In September 1855, after a long siege, the Russian fortress of Sevastopol finally fell. In March 1856 the peace conference in Paris concluded a treaty highly unfavorable to Russia. It was required to surrender territory near the mouth of the Danube River, to recognize the neutrality of the Black Sea, and to renounce claims of protection over Christians in the Ottoman Empire. Even before the conference Austria had forced Russia to withdraw from Moldavia and Walachia. The image of an invincible Russia that had prevailed across Europe since the close of the Napoleonic wars was totally shattered.

Also shattered was the Concert of Europe as a means of dealing with international relations on the Continent. There was much less fear of revolution than in the early part of the century and consequently much less reverence for the Vienna settlement. As Gordon Craig has commented, "After 1856 there were more powers willing to fight to overthrow the existing order than there were to

Florence Nightingale (1820–1910) was a strong-willed English nurse who organized hospitals for English troops during the Crimean War and left an indelible influence on nursing as a profession. [The Granger Collection.]

take up arms to defend it."[1] Louis Napoleon had little respect for the Congress of Vienna and favored redrawing the map along lines of nationality. The Austrians hoped to compensate for the poor figure they had cut during the conflict by asserting more influence within the German Confederation. Prussia became increasingly discontented with a role in Germany subordinate to Austria's. Russia, who had been among the chief defenders of the Vienna settlement, now sought to overcome the disgrace of the 1856 Treaty of Paris. The mediocre display of British military prowess led that nation to hesitate about future continental involvement.

Consequently, for about twenty-five years after the Crimean War instability prevailed in European affairs. It allowed a largely unchecked adventurism in foreign policy. Without the restraining influence of the Concert of Europe, each nation believed that only the limits of its military power and diplomatic influence should act as constraints on its international ambitions. Moreover, foreign policy increasingly became an instrument of domestic policy. The two most significant achievements to result from this new international situation were the unifications of Italy and Germany. Those events in turn generated further pressures on neighboring countries.

Italian Unification

Nationalists had long wanted the small, absolutist principalities of the Italian peninsula united into a single state. However, during the first half of the century there had existed broad differences of opinion about the manner and goals of unification.

One approach to the issue had been that of romantic republicans. After the Congress of Vienna numerous secret republican societies were founded, the most famous of which was the *Carbonari*. They were singularly ineffective.

Following the failure of nationalist uprisings in 1831, the leadership of romantic republican nationalism passed to Giuseppe Mazzini (1805–1872). He became the most important nationalist leader in all Europe and brought to the cause of nationalism new emotional fervor. He once declared, "Nationality is the role assigned by God to a people in the work of humanity. It is its mission, its task on earth, to the end that God's thought may be realized in the world."[2] In 1831 he founded the Young Italy Society for the purposes of driving Austria from the peninsula and establishing an Italian republic. During the thirties and forties Mazzini and fellow republican Giuseppe Garibaldi (1807–1882) led insurrections. Both were deeply involved in the ill-fated Roman Republic of 1849. Throughout the next decade they continued to conduct what amounted to guerrilla warfare. Because both men spent much time in exile, they became well known across the Continent and in the United States.

Republican nationalism frightened the more moderate Italians, who wanted to rid themselves of Austrian domination but not at the cost of establishing a republic. For a time these people had looked to the pope as a possible vehicle for unification. That solution became impossible after the experience of Pius IX with the Roman Republic in 1849. Consequently, at mid-century "Italy" remained a geographical expression rather than a political entity. However, between 1854 and 1860 the area was transformed into a national state. The process was carried out not by Romantic republican nationalists but rather by Count Camillo Cavour (1810–1861), the moderately liberal and almost conservative prime minister of Piedmont. The method of unification was that of force of

1 *The New Cambridge Modern History*, Vol. 10 (Cambridge: Cambridge University Press, 1967), p. 273.

2 Quoted in William L. Langer, *Political and Social Upheaval, 1832–1852* (New York: Harper Torchbook, 1969), p. 115.

LEFT: Giuseppe Mazzini supported the cause of Italian unification with both pen and sword. His books and articles were widely read in nationalist circles. He also led guerilla bands of Italian nationalists against the petty princes of the Italian peninsula before unification. [The Granger Collection.]

LEFT BELOW: Garibaldi represented the popular forces of romantic Italian nationalism more than did anyone else. The landing of his Redshirts on Sicily and their subsequent invasion of southern Italy in 1860 forced Cavour to unite the entire peninsula sooner than he had intended. [Culver Pictures.]

BELOW: Cavour was the moderately liberal prime minister of the Kingdom of Piedmont. He was determined to make the idea of a united Italy respectable and acceptable to the rest of Europe. [Culver Pictures.]

arms tied to secret diplomacy. The spirit of Machiavelli must have smiled over the enterprise.

Cavour's Policy

Piedmont, in northwestern Italy, was the most independent state on the peninsula. The kingdom had been restored by the Congress of Vienna as a buffer between French and Austrian ambitions in the area. As we have seen, during 1848 and 1849 King Charles Albert, after having promulgated a conservative constitution, twice unsuccessfully fought Austria. Following the second defeat, he abdicated in favor of his son, Victor Emmanuel II. In 1852 the new monarch chose as his prime minister Count Camillo Cavour. This cunning statesman had begun political life as a strong conservative but had gradually moved toward a moderately liberal position. He made a personal fortune by investing in railroads, re-

forming agricultural methods on his own estates, and editing a newspaper. He was deeply embued with the ideas of the Enlightenment, classical economics, and utilitarianism. Cavour was a nationalist of a new breed who had no respect for Mazzini's ideals. A strong monarchist, Cavour rejected republicanism. It was economic and material progress rather than romantic ideals that required a large, unified state on the Italian peninsula.

Cavour believed that if Italians proved themselves to be efficient and economically progressive, the great powers might decide that Italy could govern itself. He joined the Piedmontese Cabinet in 1850 and became premier two years later. He worked for free trade, railway construction, credit expansion, and agricultural improvement. He felt that such material and economic bonds rather than fuzzy romantic yearnings must unite Italians. However, Cavour also recognized the need to capture the loyalties of the Italians who possessed other varieties of nationalistic feelings. To that end, he fostered the Nationalist Society, which established chapters in other Italian states to press for unification under the leadership of Piedmont. Finally, the prime minister believed that Italy could be unified only with the aid of France. The recent accession of Napoleon III in France seemed to open the way for such aid at some time in the future.

Cavour used the outbreak of the Crimean War to enter the larger European picture. In 1855 Piedmont joined the conflict on the side of France and Britain and sent ten thousand troops to the front. This small but significant participation in the war allowed Cavour to raise the Italian question at the Paris conference. He left Paris with no diplomatic reward, but he had impressed everyone with his intelligence and political capacity. Cavour also gained the sympathy of Napoleon III. During the rest of the decade Cavour achieved further international respectability for Piedmont by opposing various plots of Mazzini, who was still attempting to lead nationalist uprisings. By the close of the decade Cavour represented a moderate, conservatively liberal alternative to both republicanism and reactionary absolutism in Italy.

The Piedmontese prime minister continued to bide his time. Then in January 1858 an Italian named Orsini attempted to assassinate Napoleon III. The incident made the French emperor, who had once belonged to a nationalist group, newly aware of the Italian issue. He began to fancy himself as continuing his more famous uncle's liberation of the peninsula. He also saw Piedmont as a potential ally against Austria. In July 1858 Cavour and Napoleon III met at Plombiers. Riding alone in a carriage, with the emperor at the reins, the two men plotted

Cavour Explains Why Piedmont Should Enter the Crimean War

As Prime Minister of Piedmont, Cavour attempted to prove that Italians were capable of progressive government. In 1855 he urged entry into the Crimean War so that Europeans would also consider Piedmont a military power. Earlier politics in Italy had been characterized by petty absolute princes and romantic nationalist conspiracies, both of which Cavour scorned. He understood that in the nineteenth century a nation must possess good government, economic prosperity, and a strong army.

THE *experience of recent years and previous centuries has proved (at least in my opinion) how little Italy has benefited by conspiracies, revolutions and disorderly uprisings. Far from helping her, they have been a tremendous calamity for this beautiful part of Europe. And not only, gentlemen, because individual people so often suffered from them, not only because revolutions became the cause or pretext for repression, but above all because continual conspiracies, repeated revolutions and disorderly uprisings damaged the esteem and, up to a certain point, the sympathy that other European peoples cherished for Italy.*

Now, gentlemen, I believe that the principal condition for the improvement of Italy's fate, the condition that stands out above all others, is to lift up her reputation once more, so to act that all the peoples of the world, those governing and those governed, may do justice to her qualities. And for this two things are necessary: first, to prove to Europe that Italy has sufficient civic sense to govern herself freely and according to law, and that she is in a condition to adopt the very best forms of government; second, to prove that her military valor is as great as that of her ancestors.

You [the Parliament of Piedmont] have done Italy one service by your conduct over the last seven years. You have shown Europe in the most luminous way that Italians are capable of governing themselves with wisdom, prudence, and trustworthiness. But it still remains for you to do Italy an equal, if not a greater, service; it is our country's task to prove that Italy's sons can fight valiantly on battlefields where glory is to be won. And I am sure, gentlemen, that the laurels that our soldiers will win in Eastern Europe will help the future state of Italy more than all that has been done by those people who hoped to regenerate her by rhetorical speeches and writings.

Denis Mack Smith (Ed. and Trans.), *The Making of Italy, 1796–1870* (New York: Walker and Company, 1968), pp. 199–200.

THE UNIFICATION OF ITALY

Beginning with the association of Sardinia and Piedmont by the Congress of Vienna in 1815, unification was achieved through the expansion of Piedmont between 1859 and 1870. Both Cavour's statesmanship and the campaigns of ardent nationalists played large roles.

to provoke a war in Italy that would permit their two nations to intervene against Austria. A formal treaty in December 1858 confirmed the agreement. France was to receive Nice and Savoy for its aid.

During the winter and spring of 1859 tension grew between Austria and Piedmont as the latter country mobilized its army. On April 22 Austria presented Piedmont with an ultimatum ordering a halt to mobilization. That demand provided sufficient grounds to claim that Austria was provoking a war. France intervened to aid its ally. On June 4 the Austrians were defeated at Magenta and on June 24 at Solferino. In the meantime revolutions had broken out in Tuscany, Modena, Parma, and Romagna. With the Austrians in retreat and the new revo-

lutionary states calling for union with Piedmont, Napoleon III feared too extensive a Piedmontese victory. On July 11 he independently concluded a peace with Austria at Villafranca. Piedmont received Lombardy, but Venetia remained under Austrian control. Cavour felt betrayed by France, but nonetheless Austria had been driven from most of northern Italy. Later that summer Parma, Modena, Tuscany, and Romagna voted to unify with Piedmont.

At this point the forces of romantic republican nationalism entered the picture and compelled Cavour to pursue complete unification of northern and southern Italy. In May 1860 Garibaldi landed in Sicily with more than a thousand troops, who had been outfitted in the north. He captured Palermo and prepared to attack the mainland. By September the city and kingdom of Naples, probably the most corrupt example of Italian absolutism, lay under Garibaldi's control. The popular leader had for over two decades hoped to form a republican Italy, but Cavour moved to forestall that possibility. He rushed Piedmontese troops south to confront Garibaldi. On the way they conquered the Papal States. Garibaldi's nationalism won out over his republicanism, and he unhappily accepted the Piedmontese domination. In late 1860 the southern Italian states joined the northern union forged by Piedmont.

The New Italian State

In March 1861 Victor Emmanuel II was proclaimed king of Italy. Three months later Cavour died. The new state more than ever needed his skills because Italy had in effect been more nearly conquered than united by Piedmont. Republicans resented the treatment of Garibaldi. Clericals resented the conquest of the Papal States. In the south armed resistance continued until 1866 against the intrusion of Piedmontese administration. The economies of the two areas were incompatible. The south was rural, poor, and backward. In the north industrialism was under way. The social structures reflected those differences.

The political framework of the united Italy did little to help overcome the problems. The constitution, which was that promulgated for Piedmont in 1848, provided for a rather conservative constitutional monarchy. The Senate was appointed, and the Chamber of Deputies was elected on a very narrow franchise. Ministers were responsible to the monarch. These arrangements did not foster a vigorous parliamentary life. The major problems of the nation were often simply avoided by the political leaders. In place of efficient, progressive government such as Cavour had brought to Piedmont, a system of *transformiso* developed. This process meant the transformation of political opponents into government supporters through bribery and favors. Italian politics became a byword for corruption.

There also remained territories that many Italians believed should be added to their nation. The most important of these were Venetia and Rome. The former was gained in 1866 as one result of the Austro-Prussian War. Rome and the papacy continued to be guarded by French troops, first sent there in 1849, until the Franco-Prussian War of 1870 forced the withdrawal of the garrison. The Italian state then annexed Rome and transferred the capital there from Florence. By 1870 only the small territories of Trent and Trieste remained outside the state. In and of themselves these areas were not important, but they served to fuel the continued hostility of Italian patriots toward Austria. The desire to bring *Italia Irredenta* or "Unredeemed Italy" into the nation was one reason for the Italian support of the Allies against Austria and Germany in 1915. The papacy continued to remain at odds with the new secular state until the Lateran Accord of 1929.

German Unification

The construction of a united German nation was the single most important political development in Europe between 1848 and 1914. It transformed the balance of economic, military, and international power. Moreover, the character of the united German state was largely determined by the method of its creation. Germany was united by the conservative army, monarchy, and prime minister of Prussia among whose chief motives was the outflanking of Prussian liberals. The goal of a unified Germany sought for two generations by German liberals was actually achieved for the most illiberal of reasons.

During the 1850s German unification still seemed very far away. The major states continued to trade with each other through the *Zollverein,* and railways linked the

Bismarck was the most influential German and European statesman of the last half of the nineteenth century. [Culver Pictures.]

various economic regions. However, Frederick William IV of Prussia had given up his short-lived thoughts of unification under Prussian leadership. Austria continued to oppose any mode of closer union that might lessen its influence. Liberal nationalists had not recovered from the humiliating experiences of 1848 and 1849. What modified this situation rather quickly was a series of domestic political changes and problems within Prussia.

In 1858 Frederick William IV was adjudged insane, and his brother William assumed the regency. William I (1861–1888), who became king in his own right in 1861, was less of an idealist than his brother and rather more of a Prussian patriot. In the highest tradition of the Hohenzollern dynasty his first concern was for the strength of the Prussian army. In 1860 his war minister and chief of staff proposed to enlarge the army, to increase the number of officers, and to extend the period of conscription from two to three years. The Prussian Parliament, created by the Constitution of 1850, refused to approve the taxes necessary for the military expansion. The liberals, who dominated the body, did not wish to place so much additional power in the hands of the monarchy. A deadlock continued for two years between the monarch and the Parliament.

Bismarck

In September 1862 William I turned for help to the person who more than any other single individual shaped the next thirty years of European history: Otto von Bismarck (1815–1898). Born in 1815, Bismarck came from *Junker* stock. He attended the university, joined a *Burschenschaft*, and had for a time taken an interest in German unification. Then he retired to his father's estate. During the forties he had been elected to the local provincial diet. At the time of the revolutions of 1848 his stand was so reactionary as to disturb even the king and the leading state ministers. Yet he had made his mark. From 1851 to 1859 Bismarck was the Prussian minister to the Frankfurt Diet of the German Confederation. Later he served as Prussian ambassador to St. Petersburg.

Just before William I called him to become prime minister of Prussia, Bismarck had been transferred to the post of ambassador to Paris.

Although Bismarck entered public life as a reactionary, he had mellowed into a conservative. He opposed parliamentary government but not constitutionalism that provided a strong monarch. His origins were those of a *Junker*, but he understood that Prussia—and later, Germany—must have a strong industrial base. He was a strong Prussian patriot. His years in Frankfurt arguing with his Austrian counterpart had only hardened that patriotism. In politics he was a pragmatist who put more trust in power and action than in ideas. As he declared in his first speech as prime minister, "Germany is not looking to Prussia's liberalism but to her power. . . . The great questions of the day will not be decided by speeches and majority decisions—that was the mistake of 1848–1849—but by iron and blood."[3] Yet this same minister, after having led Prussia into three wars, spent the next nineteen years seeking to ensure peace.

After being appointed prime minister in 1862, Bismarck immediately moved against the liberal Parliament. He contended that in the absence of new levies the Prussian constitution permitted the government to carry out its functions on the basis of previously granted taxes. Therefore taxes could be collected and spent despite the parliamentary refusal to vote them. The army and most of the bureaucracy supported this outrageous interpretation of the constitution. However, in 1863 new elections

3 Quoted in Otto Pflanze, *Bismarck and the Development of Germany: The Period of Unification: 1815–1871* (Princeton: Princeton University Press, 1963), p. 177.

THE UNIFICATION OF GERMANY

Under Bismarck's leadership, and with the strong support of its royal house, Prussia used most of the available diplomatic and military means, on both the German and international stages, to force the unification of German states into a strong national entity.

sustained the liberal majority in the Parliament. Bismarck had to find some way to attract popular support away from the liberals and toward the monarchy and the army. To that end Bismarck set about uniting Germany through the conservative institutions of Prussia. The tactic amounted to diverting public attention from domestic matters to foreign affairs.

THE DANISH WAR (1864). Bismarck pursued a *kleindeutsch* or small German solution to the question of unification. Austria was to be excluded from German affairs. This maneuver required highly complex diplomacy. The Schleswig–Holstein problem provided the handle for Bismarck's policy. These two duchies had long been administered by Denmark without being incorpo-

rated into that kingdom. Their populations were a mixture of Germans and Danes. Holstein, where Germans predominated, belonged to the German Confederation. In 1863 the Danes moved to annex both duchies. The smaller states of the German Confederation proposed an all-German war to halt the annexation. Bismarck wanted Prussia to act alone or only in cooperation with Austria. Together the two large states defeated Denmark in a short war in 1864. They took over the joint administration of the provinces.

The Danish defeat gave Bismarck new personal prestige. The joint holding of the duchies allowed him to prod Austria into war with Prussia. In August 1865 the two powers negotiated the Convention of Gastein, which put Austria in charge of Holstein and Prussia in charge of Schleswig. Bismarck then moved to mend other diplomatic fences. He had gained Russian sympathy by supporting the 1863 suppression of the Polish revolt. Conversations with Napoleon III achieved promises of neutrality in case of an Austro-Prussian conflict. In April 1866 Bismarck concluded a treaty with Italy that provided for Italian annexation of Venetia in exchange for support of Prussia should war break out with Austria. Now the issue became provocation of hostilities.

THE AUSTRO-PRUSSIAN WAR (1866). There had been constant Austro-Prussian tension over the administration of Schleswig and Holstein. Bismarck ordered the Prussian forces to do whatever was necessary to be obnoxious to the Austrians. On June 1, 1866, Austria appealed to the German Confederation to intervene in the dispute. Bismarck claimed that the request violated the terms of the 1864 alliance and the Convention of Gastein. The Seven Weeks' War of the summer of 1866 led to the decisive defeat of Austria at Königgrätz. However, the Treaty of Prague, which ended the conflict on August 23, was quite lenient toward Austria. It lost no territory except Venetia, which was ceded to Napoleon III, who in turn ceded it to Italy. The exchange could not be direct because Austria had actually defeated Italy when the latter honored its commitment to Prussia. The defeat of Austria and the treaty permanently excluded the Hapsburgs from German affairs. Prussia had become the only major power among the German states.

THE NORTH GERMAN CONFEDERATION. The states of Hanover, Hesse, and Nassau, and the city of Frankfurt, which had supported Austria during the war, were incorporated into Prussia, and their ruling dynasties were deposed. Prussia and these newly incorporated territories plus Schleswig and Holstein constituted the North German Confederation. The constitution of this state provided for a federation under Prussian leadership. Each province retained its own local government, but the military forces were under federal control. The president of the federation was the king of Prussia, represented by his chancellor. There was a federal council or *Bundesrat* composed of nominated members. The lower house or *Reichstag* was chosen by universal manhood suffrage. Bismarck had little fear of this broad franchise because he sensed that the peasants would tend to vote conserva-

tively. Moreover the *Reichstag* had little real power because ministers were responsible only to the monarch. Even legislation did not originate in the *Reichstag*. The legislature did have the right to approve military budgets, but they were usually submitted to cover several years at a time. The constitution of the confederation, which after 1871 became the governing document of the German Empire, possessed some of the appearances but none of the substance of liberalism. Germany was in effect a military monarchy.

The spectacular success of Bismarck's policy overwhelmed the liberal opposition in the Prussian Parliament. The liberals split between those who prized liberalism and those who supported unification. In the end nationalism proved more attractive than liberalism. In 1866 the Prussian Parliament passed an indemnity measure that retroactively approved the earlier military budget. Bismarck had crushed the Prussian liberals by making the monarchy and the army the most popular institutions in the country. The drive toward unification had achieved Bismark's domestic political goal.

The Franco-Prussian War and the German Empire (1870–1871)

Bismarck now awaited an opportunity to complete unification by bringing the states of southern Germany into the confederation. Events in Spain provided the excuse. In 1868 a revolution led by conservatives deposed the corrupt Bourbon queen of Spain. In searching for a new monarch, the Spaniards chose Prince Leopold of Hohenzollern-Sigmaringen, a cousin of William I of Prussia. On June 19, 1870, Leopold accepted the Spanish crown with Prussian blessings. Bismarck knew that France would react strongly against the idea of a second bordering state ruled by a Hohenzollern. On July 2 the Spanish publicized Leopold's acceptance, and the French reacted as expected. France sent Count Vincent Benedetti (1817–1900) to consult with William I, who was vacationing at Bad Ems. They discussed the matter at several meetings. On July 12 William persuaded Leopold's father to renounce his son's candidacy for the Spanish throne.

There the matter might have rested had it not been for the impetuosity of the French and the guile of Bismarck. On July 13 the French government instructed Benedetti to ask William I for assurances that he would tolerate no future Spanish candidacy for Leopold. The king refused but said that he might take the question under further consideration. Later that day he sent Bismarck, who was in Berlin, a telegram reporting the substance of the meeting. The chancellor, who desperately wanted a war with France to complete unification, had been disappointed by the peaceful solution to the Spanish candidacy question. The telegram provided a new opportunity. Bismarck released an edited version of the dispatch. The revised Ems telegram made it appear that William I had insulted the French ambassador. The idea was to goad France into a declaration of war.

The French quickly fell for Bismarck's bait, and on July 19 they declared war. The armies of the south German states eagerly joined the northern cause against France whose defeat was not long in coming. On September 1 at the Battle of Sedan the Germans not only beat the French army but also captured the French emperor, Napoleon III. By late September Paris stood besieged; it finally capitulated on January 28, 1871. Ten days earlier, in the Hall of Mirrors at the Palace of Versailles, the German Empire had been declared. During the war the states of south Germany had joined the North German Confederation, and their princes had requested William I to accept the imperial title. The princes of the southern states retained their positions as heads of their respective states within the new federation. From the peace settlement with France, Germany received the additional territory of Alsace and Lorraine.

Both the fact and manner of German unification produced long-range effects in Europe. A powerful new state had been created in north central Europe. It was rich in natural resources and talented citizens. Militarily and

Bismarck Edits William I: The Two Versions of the Ems Telegram

On July 13, 1870 William I of Prussia sent Bismarck a telegram reporting his meeting with Benedetti, the French Ambassador, at Ems, a watering place in north-west Germany. Before releasing the dispatch to the press, Bismarck edited it so that the telegram appeared to report that the King of Prussia had treated the French ambassador in a brusque and insulting fashion. Bismarck thus hoped to goad France into a declaration of war. In the text of both telegrams "His Majesty" is William I, and "the Prince" is Charles Anthony, the father of Prince Leopold, the candidate for the Spanish throne. Throughout the negotiations Charles Anthony had spoken on behalf of his son.

THE ORIGINAL MESSAGE SENT BY WILLIAM I TO BISMARCK

M. BENEDETTI *intercepted me on the Promenade in order to demand of me most insistently that I should authorize him to telegraph immediately to Paris that I shall obligate myself for all future time never again to give my approval to the candidacy of the Hohenzollerns should it be renewed. I refused to agree to this, the last time somewhat severely, informing him that one dare not and cannot assume such obligations* à tout jamais [*forever*]. *Naturally, I informed him that I had received no news as yet, and since he had been informed earlier than I by way of Paris and Madrid, he could easily understand why my government was once again out of the matter.*

Since then His Majesty has received a dispatch from the Prince. As His Majesty has informed Count Benedetti that he was expecting news from the Prince, His Majesty himself, in view of the above-mentioned demand and in consonance with the advice of Count Eulenburg and myself, decided not to receive the French envoy again but to inform him through an adjutant that His Majesty had now received from the Prince confirmation of the news which Benedetti had already received from Paris, and that he had nothing further to say to the Ambassador. His Majesty leaves it to the judgement of Your Excellency whether or not to communicate at once the new demand by Benedetti and its rejection to our ambassadors and to the press.

BISMARCK'S EDITED VERSION RELEASED TO THE PRESS

AFTER *the reports of the renunciation by the Hereditary Prince of Hohenzollern had been officially transmitted by the Royal Government of Spain to the Imperial Govern-*

ment of France, the French Ambassador presented to His Majesty the King at Ems the demand to authorize him to telegraph to Paris that His Majesty the King would obligate himself for all future time never again to give his approval to the candidacy of the Hohenzollerns should it be renewed.

His Majesty the King thereupon refused to receive the French envoy again and informed him through an adjutant that His Majesty had nothing further to say to the Ambassador.

Louis L. Snyder (Ed. and Trans.), *Documents of German History* (New Brunswick, N.J. Rutgers University Press, 1958), pp. 215–216.

economically the German Empire would be stronger than Prussia had been alone. The unification of Germany was also a blow to European liberalism because the new state was a conservative creation. Conservative politics was now backed not by a weak Austria or an economically retrograde Russia but rather by the strongest state on the Continent. The two nations most immediately affected by German and also Italian unification were France and Austria. The emergence of the two new unified states revealed the weakness of both France and the Hapsburg Empire. Change had to come in each. France returned to republican government, and the Hapsburgs organized a dual monarchy.

France: From Liberal Empire to the Third Republic

The reign of Emperor Napoleon III (1851–1870) is traditionally divided into the years of the authoritarian empire and those of the liberal empire. The point of division is 1860. Initially, after the *coup* in December 1851, Napoleon III had kept a close rein on the legisla-

ture, had strictly controlled the press, and had made life difficult for political dissidents. His support came from property owners, the French Catholic Church, and businessmen. They approved the security he brought to property, his protection of the pope, and his aid to commerce and railroad construction. The French victory in the Crimean War had further confirmed the emperor's popularity.

From the late fifties onward Napoleon III began to modify his policy. In 1860 he concluded a free trade treaty with Britain and permitted the legislature to discuss matters of state more freely. By the late sixties he had relaxed the press laws. In 1870 he allowed the leaders of the moderates in the legislature to form a ministry. That same year Napoleon III agreed to a liberal constitution that made ministers responsible to the legislature. All of these liberal moves were closely related to problems in foreign policy. He had lost control of the diplomacy of Italian unification. Between 1861 and 1867 he had supported a military expedition against Mexico led by Archduke Maximilian of Austria. The venture ended in defeat and the execution of the archduke. In 1866 Napoleon III and France rather sat on the sideline while Bismarck and Prussia reorganized German affairs. The liberal concessions on domestic matters were attempts to compensate for an increasingly unsuccessful foreign policy.

Whether Napoleon III would have succeeded in sustaining liberal government or his own position became a moot point. The Second Empire, but not the war, came to an inglorious end with the Battle of Sedan in September 1870. The emperor was captured, imprisoned, and then allowed to go to England, where he died in 1873. Shortly after news of the Sedan disaster reached Paris, a republic was proclaimed and a Government of National Defense established. Paris itself was soon under Prussian siege. During the siege of Paris the French government was transferred to Bordeaux. Paris finally surrendered in January 1871, but the rest of France had been ready to sue for peace long before the capital.

[*Text continued on page 719*]

Emperor Napoleon III of France is here pictured with his wife and son. [Culver Pictures.]

At an exhibition in Paris in 1867 Napoleon III inspected cannons manufactured in Germany by the Krupp company. Three years later such weapons were used by Germany against France. [The Granger Collection.]

Walter Bagehot Analyzes the Power of Napoleon III

Walter Bagehot (1826–1877) was an astute English observer. This 1863 passage explains the manner in which Napoleon III had to please the various elements in French politics in order to remain in power.

THE *Emperor is the Crowned Democrat of Europe. The position is no doubt one of great elevation and of enormous power, but it is also one full of peril and full of exigencies. "The Masses," though an effective, and under many circumstances, an almost resistless servant make a capricious, exacting, and relentless master. Both at home and abroad Napoleon III has a contract with the agencies that have made him what he is and that sustain him where he is, the terms of which must be rigidly fulfilled. At home he rules over the middle classes, in defiance of the educated classes, and by the support of the lower classes and the army. In ultimate resort he may be said to reign by the right of numbers and by the instrumentality of bayonets. It is true that he has done much—perhaps as much as lay in his power—to widen the basis of his throne, and to make all classes interested in maintaining him. He has tentatively and modestly allowed the intellectual classes to raise their heads; he has conciliated the bourgeoisie by the material prosperity which he has so sagaciously and indefatigably fostered; and he has cancelled or moderated the hostility once felt towards him by the rich and great by convincing them that property was in habitual danger from the Rouges [Reds], and that his was the only hand that could avert that danger. So that beyond dispute the number of those who wish to overthrow him has largely diminished, and the number of those who desire to maintain him has largely increased, each year since 1852. Still it remains true that to retain his popularity and prestige with FRANCE, . . . he must be sedulous to please, or at all events careful not to offend, the populace, the peasantry, and the army.*

The Collected Works of Walter Bagehot, ed. Norman St. John-Stevas (Cambridge, Mass.: Harvard University Press, 1968), Vol. 4, p. 105.

The siege of Paris during the Franco-Prussian War led to extreme food shortages. Animals in the zoo were slaughtered, and domestic dogs and cats were butchered, to feed the hungry citizens. The sketches made early in 1871 were published in London newspapers after being sent from Paris by balloon post. [The Granger Collection.]

France: From Liberal Empire to the Third Republic 717

In October 1870 Gambetta, who was then chief of the new French government, and his secretary escaped by balloons from beseiged Paris. The city was surrounded by Prussian troops who attempted unsuccessfully to shoot down the balloons, the second of which was said to carry three wealthy Americans also fleeing the city. Gambetta eventually established a governmental headquarters in Tours and prepared to negotiate terms of surrender with Prussia. The drawing was made by an eye-witness, J. C. Palmuri, for the American periodical, *Leslie's Weekly*. [Culver Pictures.]

The Paris Commune

The division between the provinces and Paris became even more decided after the fighting stopped. The new National Assembly elected in February was dominated by monarchists. For the time being, executive power was turned over to Adolphe Thiers (1797–1877), who had been active in French politics since 1830. He negotiated a settlement with Prussia (the Treaty of Frankfurt) whereby France was charged with a large indemnity, remained occupied by Prussian troops until it had been paid, and surrendered the provinces of Alsace and Lorraine. The city of Paris, which had suffered much during the siege, resented what it regarded as a betrayal by the monarchist National Assembly sitting in Versailles. Thiers, familiar with a half-century of Parisian political turmoil, ordered the disarmament of the Paris National Guard on March 17. The attempt to seize the guard's cannon was bungled. Paris then regarded the National Assembly as its new enemy.

On March 26, 1871, a new government, called the Commune, was elected in Paris. Its goal was to administer the city separately from the rest of the country. Political radicals and socialists of all stripes participated in the Commune at one time or another. The National Assembly moved rapidly. By early April Paris was again a besieged city, but this time it was surrounded by a French army. On May 8 Paris was bombarded. On May 21, the day on which the formal treaty with Prussia was signed, the National Assembly forces broke through the city's defenses. During the next seven days the troops restored order to Paris and in the process killed about twenty thousand inhabitants. The communards claimed their own victims as well.

The short-lived Paris Commune very quickly became a legend throughout France and Europe. Marxists regarded it as a genuine proletarian government that had been suppressed by the troops of the French bourgeoisie. This interpretation is incorrect. The Commune, though of shifting composition, was dominated by petty bourgeois members. The socialism that was a part of the Commune had its roots in Blanqui and Proudhon rather than in Marx. The goal of the Commune was not a workers' republic but a nation composed of relatively independent, radically democratic enclaves. The suppression of the Commune consequently represented not only the protection of property but also the triumph of the centralized nation state over an alternative mode of political organization. Just as the armies of Piedmont and Prussia had united the small states of Italy and Germany, the army of the French National Assembly destroyed the particularistic political tendencies of Paris and by implication those of any other French community.

The Third Republic

The National Assembly put down the Commune directly, but it backed into a republican form of government indirectly and much against its will. The monarchists, who constituted its majority, were divided in loyalty between the House of Bourbon and the House of Orleans. This problem could have been surmounted because the Bourbon claimant had no children. He could have become king on the condition that the Orleanist heir would follow him to the throne. However, the Bourbon Duke of Chambord refused to become king if the revolutionary tricolor flag were retained. Even the conservative monarchists would not return to the white flag of the Bourbons, which symbolized extreme political reaction.

While the monarchists quarreled over the proper heir, and the heir over the proper flag, time passed and events marched on. By September 1873 the indemnity had been paid and the Prussian occupation troops withdrawn. Thiers was ousted from office because he had displayed clear republican sentiments. The monarchists wanted a more certain person to be executive. They elected as president Marshal MacMahon (1808–1893), who was conservative and who was expected to prepare for an eventual monarchist restoration. In 1875 the National Assembly, still monarchist in sentiment but unable to find a candidate for the throne, decided to regularize the

This English cartoon of 1889 portrays General Georges Boulanger as a mock-heroic Napoleon who might attempt to seize power in Paris. The expected Boulangerist coup never took place. [The Granger Collection.]

political system. It adopted a law that provided for a Chamber of Deputies elected by universal manhood suffrage, a Senate chosen indirectly, and a president elected by the two legislative houses. This relatively simple republican system had resulted from the bickering and frustration of the monarchists.

MacMahon remained as president. He would have liked to transform that office into a new emperorship. After numerous quarrels with the Chamber of Deputies, he resigned in 1879. His departure meant that people dedicated to a republic generally controlled the national government. But France remained an uncertain and unconfident republic. A considerable body of public opinion within the army, the church, and the wealthy families still favored government by a single strong figure. During the late eighties they looked to General Georges Boulanger (1837–1891) as such a leader. In 1886 and 1887 he had been a popular minister of war who initiated a number of military reforms. When a financial scandal touched several major political figures, Boulanger became all the more appealing for his honesty and integrity. He was elected to the Chamber of Deputies from numerous districts though afterwards he sat for only one. In 1889 there was much talk and expectation of his carrying out a *coup d'état*. Nothing came of these speculations. The good general had talked with too many different political

groups to be trusted by any. He also lacked real drive and political ambition. In the end he left France for life with his Belgian mistress and in 1891 committed suicide on her grave in Brussels.

The political structure of the Third Republic proved much stronger than many citizens suspected at the time. It was able to survive a series of major scandals. In the late eighties the son of the president was discovered to be selling positions in the Legion of Honor. Early in the next decade a number of ministers and deputies were implicated in the Panama affair. Ferdinand De Lesseps, who had constructed the Suez Canal, organized a company to build a canal in Panama. Various people in authority in France accepted bribes for their public support of the venture. These two *causes célèbres* made the republic look rather sleazy in the eyes of its conservative enemies. But the institutions of the republic allowed new ministers to replace those whose corruption was exposed.

THE DREYFUS AFFAIR. The greatest trauma of the republic occurred over the Dreyfus affair. On December 22, 1894, a French military court found Captain Alfred Dreyfus (1859–1935) guilty of passing secret information to the German army. The evidence supporting his guilt was at best flimsy and was later revealed to have been forged. Someone in the officer corps had been passing documents to the Germans, and it suited the army investigators to accuse Dreyfus, who was Jewish. However, after Dreyfus had been sent to Devil's Island, secrets continued to flow to the German army. In 1896 a new head of French counterintelligence reexamined the Dreyfus file and found evidence of forgery. A different officer was implicated, but a military court quickly acquitted him of all charges. The officer who had discovered the forgeries was transferred to a distant post. By then the matter had become one of widespread public interest. The army, the church, the anti-Semitic press, and political conservatives opposed Dreyfus. Liberals, radicals, and socialists demanded a new trial. They saw the conservative institutions of the nation as having denied Dreyfus the rights belonging to any citizen of the

The Palace of Justice in Brussels (completed in 1883), heavy and imposing, symbolizes the general assumption of police and judicial power by the modern central state. The architect was Joseph Poelaert. [Copyright A.C.L., Brussels.]

Captain Alfred Dreyfus was falsely accused of passing French military secrets to Germany. His several trials during the 1890s became the occasion for major clashes, with strong anti-Semitic overtones, between the political left and right in the Third French Republic. [Culver Pictures.]

republic. Moreover Dreyfus had been singled out in order to protect the guilty persons in the army. In August 1898 further evidence of forged material came to light. A new military trial took place, but Dreyfus was again convicted by officers who refused to admit the original mistake. The president of France immediately pardoned the captain, and in 1906 a civilian court set aside the results of both trials.

The Dreyfus case divided France as no issue had done since the Commune. But it also for the first time created broad popular political support for the republic. Liberals, radicals, republicans, and socialists developed an informal alliance that outlived the fight over Dreyfus himself. These groups realized that republican institutions must be preserved if the political left were to achieve any of its goals. Outside political circles ever larger numbers of French citizens understood that their rights and liberties were safer under a republic than under some alternative mode of conservative government.

The Hapsburg Empire: Formation of the Dual Monarchy

After 1848 the Hapsburg Empire remained a problem both to itself and to the rest of Europe. An ungenerous critic remarked that the empire was supported by a standing army of soldiers, a kneeling army of priests, and a crawling army of informers. In the age of national

NATIONALITIES WITHIN THE HAPSBURG EMPIRE

The patchwork appearance reflects the unusual problem
of the numerous ethnic groups that the Hapsburgs could
not, of course, meld into a modern national state. Only
the Magyars were recognized in 1867, leaving nationalist
Czechs, Slovaks, and the others chronically dissatisfied.

states, liberal institutions, and industrialism, the Hapsburg
domains remained primarily dynastic, absolutist, and
agrarian. The response to the revolts at the end of the
forties had been the reassertion of absolutism. Francis
Joseph, who became emperor in 1848 and ruled until
1916, was honest, hard-working, and unimaginative. He
reacted to events but rarely commanded them.

During the 1850s his ministers attempted to impose a
centralized administration on the empire. The system
amounted to military and bureaucratic government dominated by German-speaking Austrians. All internal tariffs

were abolished. Hungary was divided into military districts. Education was put under the control of the Roman
Catholic Church. Although creating much domestic resentment, this system of neoabsolutism actually floundered on a series of foreign policy setbacks. Austrian
refusal to support Russia during the Crimean War meant
that the new tsar would not help to preserve Hapsburg
rule in Hungary as Nicholas I had done in 1849. The
Austrian defeat in 1859 at the hands of France and
Piedmont and the subsequent loss of territory in Italy
pointed to the need for new structures of domestic
government. For seven years the emperor, civil servants,
aristocrats, and politicians attempted to construct a viable
system of government.

In 1860 Francis Joseph issued the October Diploma,
which created a federation among the states and provinces of the empire. There were to be local diets domi-

The Austrian Prime Minister Explains the Dual Monarchy

The multinational character of the Austrian Empire had long been a source of internal weakness and political discontent. After the defeat of Austria by Prussia in 1866, the Austrian government attempted to regain the loyalty of the Hungarians by making Hungary a separate kingdom within a dual monarchy known thereafter as Austria-Hungary.

THE *dangers which Austria has to face are of a two-fold nature. The first is presented by the tendency of her liberalminded German population to gravitate toward that larger portion of the German-speaking people. . . . the second is the diversity of language and race in the empire. Of Austria's large Slav population, the Poles have a natural craving for independence after having enjoyed and heroically fought for it for centuries; while the other nationalities are likely at a moment of dangerous crisis to develop pro-Russian tendencies.*

Now my object is to carry out a bloodless revolution— to show the various elements of this great empire that it is to the benefit of each of them to act in harmony with its neighbor. . . . But to this I have made one exception. Hungary is an ancient monarchy, more ancient as such than Austria proper. . . . I have endeavoured to give Hungary not a new position with regard to the Austrian empire, but to secure her in the one which she has occupied. The Emperor of Austria is King of Hungary; my idea was that he should revive in his person the Constitution of which he and his ancestors have been the heads. The leading principles of my plan are . . . the resuscitation of an old monarchy and an old Constitution; not the separation of one part of the empire from the other, but the drawing together of the two component parts by the recognition of their joint positions, the maintenance of their mutual obligations, their community in questions affecting the entire empire, and their proportional pecuniary responsibility for the liabilities of the whole State. It is no plan of separation that I have carried out: on the contrary, it is one of closer union, not by the creation of a new power, but by the recognition of an old one. . . .

Memoirs of Friedrich Ferdinand Count von Beust, Baron Henry de Worms (Ed.) (London: Remington 1887), Vol. 1, pp. xx–xxvi.

nated by the landed classes and a single imperial parliament. The Magyar nobility of Hungary rejected the plan. Consequently in 1861 the February Patent was promulgated. Technically it interpreted the Diploma, but in point of fact it constituted an entirely different form of government. It established a bicameral imperial parliament or *Reichsrat* with an appointed upper chamber and an indirectly elected lower chamber. Again the Magyars refused to cooperate in a system designed to permit German-speaking Austrian domination. The Hungarians sent no delegates to the legislature. Nevertheless, for six years, the February Patent governed the empire, and it prevailed in Austria proper until World War I. There was no ministerial responsibility to the *Reichsrat*. Few genuine guarantees existed for civil liberties. Armies could be levied and taxes raised without parliamentary consent. When the *Reichsrat* was not in session, the emperor could simply promulgate laws on his own authority.

Meanwhile negotiations continued between the emperor and the Magyars. These produced no concrete result until the defeat of Austria by Prussia in the summer of 1866 and the consequent exclusion of Austria from German affairs. The military disaster compelled Francis Joseph to come to terms with the Magyars. Through the *Ausgleich*, or Compromise, of 1867 the Hapsburg Empire was transformed into a dual monarchy. Francis Joseph was separately crowned king of Hungary in Budapest. Except for the common monarch, Austria and Hungary became almost wholly separate states. They shared ministers of foreign affairs, defense, and finance, but the other ministers were different for each state. There were also separate parliaments. Each year delegations of sixty parliamentary delegates from each state were to discuss matters of mutual interest. Every ten years Austria and Hungary were to renegotiate their trade relationship. By this cumbersome machinery, unique in all European history, the Hungarian Magyars were reconciled to Hapsburg rule. They had achieved the free hand they had long wanted in local Hungarian matters.

Many of the other national groups within the empire—including the Czechs, the Ruthenians, the Romanians, and the Serbo-Croatians—opposed the Compromise of 1867. The dual monarchy in effect permitted the

Tsar Alexander II of Russia emancipated the serfs in 1861 and began numerous other major reforms of the Russian government and army. He was assassinated by radicals who sought even more fundamental reforms of Russian life. [Culver Pictures.]

German-speaking Austrians and the Hungarian Magyars to dominate all other nationalities in their respective states. The most vocal critics were the Czechs of Bohemia. They favored a policy of trialism or triple monarchy. In 1871 Francis Joseph was willing to accept this concept. However, the Hungarian Magyars vetoed the proposal for fear they might have to make similar concessions to their own subject nationalities.

For over twenty years the Czechs were conciliated by an extension of generous Austrian patronage and admission to the Austrian bureaucracy. By the nineties Czech nationalism had again become more vocal. In 1897 a series of ordinances gave the Czechs and the Germans equality of language in various localities. The Germans in the Austrian *Reichsrat* set out on a course of parliamentary disruption to oppose these measures. The Czechs replied in kind. By the turn of the century this obstructionist activity had paralyzed parliamentary life. The emperor ruled by imperial decree with the support of the bureaucracy. In 1907 universal manhood suffrage was introduced into Austria, but it did not change the situation in the *Reichsrat*. In effect, by 1914 constitutionalism was a dead letter in Austria. It flourished in Hungary at the cost of Magyar political supremacy over all other national groups.

Russia: Emancipation and Revolutionary Stirrings
Reforms of Alexander II

The defeat in the Crimean War and the humiliation of the Treaty of Paris compelled the Russian government to reconsider its domestic situation. Nicholas I had died in 1855 during the conflict. Because of extensive travel in Russia and an early introduction to government procedures, Nicholas's son Alexander II (1855–1881) was quite familiar with the chief difficulties facing the nation. The debacle of the war had created a situation in which reform was both necessary and possible. Alexander II

took advantage of this turn of events to institute the most extensive restructuring of Russian society and administration since Peter the Great. Like Peter, Alexander imposed his reforms from the top.

In every area of economic and public life a profound cultural gap existed between Russia and the rest of Europe. Nowhere was this fact more true than in the matter of serfdom. Everywhere else on the Continent it had been abandoned. In Russia the institution had changed very little since the eighteenth century. Landowners had a very free hand with their serfs, and the serfs had little recourse against the lords. In March 1856, at the conclusion of the Crimean War, Alexander II announced his intention to abolish serfdom. For over five years government commissions wrestled over the way to implement the tsar's desire. Finally, in February 1861, against much opposition from the nobility and the landlords, Alexander II promulgated the long statute ending serfdom in Russia.

The technicalities of the emancipation statute meant that freedom was often more theoretical than practical. The procedures were so complicated and the results so limited that many serfs believed that real emancipation was still to come. Serfs immediately received the personal rights to marry, to purchase and sell property, to engage in court actions, and to pursue trades without securing their landlord's permission. What they did not receive

The harsh treatment of Russian serfs by their land-lords prior to emancipation was frequently criticized in the rest of Europe. This French cartoon of 1854 portrays Russian landlords using bundles of their serfs as stakes for a card game. [The Granger Collection.]

Even after emancipation, the life of Russian peasants was difficult. They attempted to secure a livelihood partly from farming and partly from small handcraft industries, such as those seen in this picture of a Russian village in the late nineteenth century. [Culver Pictures.]

immediately was free title to their land. They were to pay for frequently insufficient allotments of land over a period of forty-nine years. They were also charged interest during this period. The serfs made the payments to the government, which had already reimbursed the landlords for their losses. The serfs did not receive title to the land until the debt was paid. The redemption payments led to almost unending difficulty. Poor harvests caused the debts to fall into arrears. The situation was not remedied until 1906. With widespread unrest following the Japanese defeat of Russia in 1905, the government grudgingly completed the process of emancipation by canceling the remaining debts.

Abolition of serfdom required reorganization of local government and the judicial system. The authority of village communes replaced that of the landlord over the peasant. The village elders settled family quarrels, imposed fines, issued internal passports, and collected taxes. In many cases also, the land of the emancipated serfs was owned communally rather than individually. The nobility were permitted a larger role in local administration through a system of provincial and county *zemstvos*, or councils, organized in 1864. These councils were to oversee local matters such as bridge and road repair, education, and agricultural improvement. However, because the councils were not adequately funded, local government never became vigorous.

The flagrant inequities and abuses of the preemancipation judicial system could not continue. In 1864 Alexander II promulgated a new statute on the judiciary. For the first time principles of west European legal systems were introduced into Russia. These included equality before the law, impartial hearings, uniform procedures, judicial independence, and trial by jury. The new system was far from perfect. Judges were not genuinely independent, and the tsar could increase as well as reduce sentences. For certain offenses, such as those involving the press, jury trials were not held. Nonetheless the system was an improvement both in its efficiency and in its relative lack of the old corruption.

Reforms were also instituted in the army. Russia possessed the largest military establishment on the Continent, but it had floundered badly in the Crimea. The usual period of recruitment was twenty-five years. Villages had to provide quotas of serfs. Often recruiters had come to villages and simply seized serfs from their families. Once in the army, the recruits rarely saw their homes again. Life in the army was exceedingly harsh, even by the usually brutal standards of most mid-century armies. In the sixties the period of recruitment was lowered to fifteen years, and disciplinary procedures were slightly relaxed. In 1874 the enlistment period was lowered to six years of active duty, followed by nine years in the reserves. All males twenty years old were subject to military service.

Alexander's reformist departures came to a close shortly after the Polish Rebellion of 1863. As in 1830, Polish nationalists attempted to flout Russian dominance. Once again the Russian army suppressed the rebellion. Alexander II then moved to "russify" Poland. In 1864 he emancipated the Polish serfs as a move against the restive Polish nobility. Russian law, language, and administration were imposed on all areas of Polish life. Henceforth, until the close of World War I, Poland was treated merely as one other Russian province.

As revealed by the Polish suppression, Alexander II was a reformer only within the limits of his own autocracy. His changes in Russian life failed to create new loyalty or gratitude among his subjects. The serfs felt that emancipation had been inadequate. The nobles and the wealthier educated segments of Russian society resented the tsar's persistent refusal to allow them a meaningful role in government and policy making. Consequently, although Alexander II became known as the Tsar Liberator, he was never a popular ruler. He could be very indecisive and was rarely open to new ideas. These characteristics became more pronounced after 1866, when an attempt was made on his life. Thereafter Russia increasingly became a police state. This new repression fueled the activity of radical groups within Russia. Their actions in turn made the autocracy more reactionary.

Revolutionaries

The tsarist regime had long had its critics. One of the most prominent was Alexander Herzen (1812–1870),

who lived in exile. From London he published a newspaper called *The Bell* in which he set forth reformist positions. The initial reforms of Alexander II had raised great hopes among Russian students and intellectuals, but they soon became discontented with the limited character of the restructuring. Drawing upon the ideas of Herzen and

The new reactionary policies of Tsar Alexander III included use of police against political opponents. This English newspaper engraving of 1887 presents the Russian police in St. Petersburg discovering a printing press run by political radicals. [The Granger Collection.]

other radicals, these students formed a revolutionary movement known as Populism. They sought a social revolution based on the communal life of the Russian peasants. The chief radical society was called Land and Freedom. In the early 1870s hundreds of young Russians, including both men and women, took their revolutionary message into the countryside. They intended to live with the peasants, to gain their trust, and to teach them about the peasant role in the coming revolution. The bewildered and distrustful peasants turned most of the youths over to the police. In the winter of 1877–1878 almost two hundred students were tried. Most were acquitted or given very light sentences. Alexander II then changed the sentences and sent many of the defendants to Siberia.

Thereafter the revolutionaries decided that the tsarist regime must be attacked directly. They adopted a policy of terrorism. In January 1878 Vera Zasulich attempted to assassinate the military governor of St. Petersburg. At her trial the jury acquitted her. This verdict encouraged the terrorists. In 1879 Land and Freedom split into two groups. One held to the idea of educating the peasants, and it soon dissolved. The other, known as People's Will, was dedicated to the overthrow of the autocracy. Its members decided to assassinate the tsar himself. Several assassination attempts failed, but on March 1, 1881, a bomb hurled by a member of People's Will killed Tsar Alexander II. Four men and two women were sentenced to death for the deed. All of them had been willing to die for their cause. The emergence of such dedicated revolutionary opposition constituted as much a part of the reign of Alexander II as did his reforms, for the limited character of those reforms convinced many people from various walks of life that the autocracy could never truly redirect Russian society.

Alexander III, whose reign (1881–1894) further underscored that pessimistic conviction, possessed all the autocratic and repressive characteristics of his grandfather Nicholas I and none of the better qualities of his father. Some slight attention was directed toward the improvement of life in the Russian factories, but primarily Alexander III sought to roll back the reforms of the third quarter of the century. He favored centralized bureaucracy over the new limited modes of self-government. He

Russia: Emancipation and Revolutionary Stirrings

strengthened the secret police and increased press censorship. In effect, he confirmed all the evils that the revolutionaries saw inherent in autocratic government. His son, Nicholas II, who became tsar in 1894, would discover that autocracy could not survive the pressures of the twentieth century.

Alexander III (1881–1894) attempted to reimpose arbitrary rule after the reforms of Alexander II. The future Tsar Nicholas II (1894–1917) is standing directly behind his father. [The Granger Collection.]

Great Britain: Toward Democracy

While continental nations became unified and struggled toward internal political restructuring, Great Britain continued to symbolize the confident liberal state. Britain was not without its difficulties and domestic conflicts, but it seemed able to deal with these through existing political institutions. The general prosperity of the third quarter of the century took the edge off the class hostility of the forties. A large body of shared ideas emphasizing competition and individualism was accepted by the members of all classes. Even the leaders of trade unions during these years asked for little more than to receive a portion of the fruits of prosperity and to prove their own social respectability. Parliament itself continued to provide an institution that permitted the absorption of new groups and interests into the existing political processes. In short, the British did not have to create new liberal institutions and then learn how to live within them.

The major political figure of mid-century was Henry John Temple, Lord Palmerston (1784–1865). He became prime minister early in 1855 as the nation became weary of blunders in the conduct of the Crimean War. Except for a seventeen-month interlude in 1858 and 1859, he governed until late 1865. Palmerston was a liberal Whig, whose chief interest was foreign policy. He generally championed free trade and the right of European nationalities to determine their own political destinies. His bombastic patriotism made him very popular with voters; he rarely hesitated to parade British naval power before the world. Yet Palmerston was a person of the past. He had little sympathy with those political and working-class figures who wanted to extend the franchise beyond the limits of the Reform Act of 1832. By the time of his death in 1865 Palmerston had become the chief obstacle to further political and social reform.

The Second Reform Act (1867)

By the early sixties it had become clear to most observers that in one way or another the franchise would again

The young Queen Victoria is shown on a medal
by J. S. Wyon at the time of her accession.
[The Granger Collection.]

Prince Albert and Queen Victoria (1837–1901) of
Great Britain successfully accommodated the British
monarchy to new liberal democratic political
structures. Prince Albert died in 1861. The photograph, by Roger Fenton, is from 1854. [The Mansell
Collection.]

The new British Houses of Parliament in London were
completed in the middle of the nineteenth century.
The architectural style was that of the Gothic
revival. Until at least after World War II these
buildings symbolized political liberalism in the
West. [British Tourist Authority, New York.]

have to be expanded. The prosperity and the social respectability of the working class convinced many politicians that workers truly deserved the vote. Organizations
such as the Reform League, led by John Bright (1811–
1889), were agitating for parliamentary action. In 1866
Lord John Russell's Liberal ministry introduced a reform
bill that was defeated by a coalition of traditional Conservatives and antidemocratic liberals. Russell resigned,
and the Tory Lord Derby replaced him. What then
occurred surprised everyone.

The Conservative ministry, led in the House of Commons by Benjamin Disraeli (1804–1881), introduced its
own reform bill in 1867. As the debate proceeded, Disraeli accepted one amendment after another and expanded the electorate well beyond the limits earlier proposed by the Liberals. When the final measure was
passed, the number of voters had been increased from
approximately 1,430,000 to 2,470,000. Britain had taken

a major step toward democracy. Large numbers of working-class voters had been admitted to the electorate.
Disraeli hoped that by sponsoring the measure the Conservatives would receive the gratitude of the new voters.
Because reform was bound to come, it was best for the
Conservatives to enjoy the credit. Disraeli thought that
eventually the working class would support Conservative
candidates who proved themselves responsive to social
issues. In the long run, his intuition proved correct, for in
the past century the Conservative Party has dominated
British politics.

In the immediate election of 1868, however, Disraeli's
hopes were dashed. William Gladstone (1809–1898)
became the new prime minister. Gladstone had begun
political life in 1833 as a strong Tory, but over the next
thirty-five years he moved steadily toward liberalism. He
had supported Robert Peel, free trade, repeal of the Corn
Laws, and efficient administration. As chancellor of the
exchequer during the fifties and early sixties, he had
lowered taxes and government expenditure. He had also
championed Italian nationalism. For many years he continued to oppose a new reform bill. Yet by the early
sixties he had also modified his position on that issue. In
1866 he had been Russell's spokesman in the House of
Commons for the unsuccessful liberal reform bill.

Gladstone Praises the Education Act of 1870

The British Education Act of 1870 marked the creation of the first national system of schools. Prime Minister Gladstone and others admired the measure because it still permitted private religious schools, because it was relatively inexpensive, and because it depended largely on the initiative of local government. In other words, it permitted the liberty and the low taxes that liberals prized.

THE *great object of all was to make education universal and effective. This was to be done, and doing it we sought, and I think reason and common sense required us to seek, to turn to account for that purpose the vast machinery of education already existing in the country, which had been devised and mainly provided by the Christian philanthropy and the voluntary action of the people. That was the second condition under which the Act was framed. The third was, and I think it was not less wise than the two former, that we should endeavour to separate the action of the State in the matter of education, and the application of State funds, in which I include funds raised by rate [taxes], from all subjects on which, unhappily, religious differences prevail. Those, I may say, were three of the principles of the measure; and the fourth principle, not less important than the others, was this: that we should trust for the attainment of these great objects, as little as possible to the central Government, and as much as possible to the local authorities and the self-governing power of the people. And let me say in passing, that in my opinion if there be one portion of our institutions more precious in my view than another, it is that portion in which the people are locally organized for the purposes of acquiring the habits and instincts of political action, and applying their own free consciences and free understandings to dealing with the affairs of the community.*

A. T. Bassett (Ed.), *Gladstone's Speeches* (London: Methuen, 1916), pp. 412–413.

Gladstone's Great Ministry (1868–1874)

Gladstone's ministry of 1868–1874 witnessed the culmination of classical British liberalism. Those institutions that still remained the preserve of the aristocracy and the Anglican Church were opened to people from other classes and religious denominations. By an Order in Council of 1870 competitive examinations replaced patronage as a means of entering the civil service. In 1871 the purchase of officer ranks in the army was abolished. The same year saw the removal of religious texts from Oxford and Cambridge universities. The Ballot Act of 1872 introduced voting by secret ballot. The most momentous measure of Gladstone's first ministry was the Education Act of 1870. For the first time in British history the government assumed the responsibility for establishing and running elementary schools. Previously British education had been a task relegated to the religious denominations, which received small amounts of state support for the purpose.

All of these reforms were typically liberal. They sought to remove longstanding abuses without destroying existing institutions and to permit all able citizens to compete on the grounds of ability and merit. They attempted to protect the state from the potential dangers of democracy by providing for a literate citizenry. These reforms also constituted a mode of state building because they created new bonds of loyalty to the nation by abolishing many sources of present and future discontent. They made increasing numbers of people benefit positively from being British citizens.

Disraeli in Office (1874–1880)

The liberal policy of creating popular support for the nation through the extension of political liberty and reform of abuses had its conservative counterpart in concern about social reform. Disraeli succeeded Gladstone as prime minister in 1874. The two men had stood on different sides of most issues for over a quarter century. Whereas Gladstone looked to individualism, free trade, and competition to solve social problems, Disraeli had believed that the ruling classes of the country must confront those matters through paternalistic legislation. Disraeli believed in state action to protect weak groups of citizens. In his view such paternalistic legislation would alleviate class antagonism.

Disraeli personally talked a better line than he pro-

William Gladstone was on four separate occasions the Liberal Party Prime Minister of Great Britain in the period from the 1860s to the 1890s. He was one of the most effective orators of his day. He pursued policies of peace, low government spending, and reform of major British political institutions. The 1869 caricature, for the British periodical *Vanity Fair,* is by "Ape" (Carlo Pellegrini). [The Granger Collection.]

duced. He had very few specific programs or ideas. The significant social legislation of his ministry stemmed primarily from the efforts of his Home Secretary Richard Cross. The Public Health Act of 1875 consolidated previous sanitary legislation and reaffirmed the duty of the state to interfere with private property on matters of health and physical well-being. Through the Artisans Dwelling Act of 1875 the government became actively involved in providing housing for the working class. The same year, in an important symbolic gesture, the Conservative majority in Parliament passed a law that gave new protection to British trade unions and allowed them to raise picket lines. The Gladstone ministry, although recognizing the legality of unions, had refused such extensive protection.

The Irish Question

In 1880 a second Gladstone ministry took office as an agricultural depression and unpopular foreign policy undermined Disraeli's popularity. In 1884, with Conservative cooperation, a third reform act extending the vote to most male farm workers was passed. However, the major issue of the decade was Ireland. From the late sixties onward Irish nationalists had sought to achieve home rule for Ireland, by which they meant more Irish control of local government. During his first ministry Gladstone had addressed the Irish question through two major pieces of legislation. In 1869 he carried a measure to disestablish the Church of Ireland, which was the Irish

Benjamin Disraeli was the Conservative Party leader of the House of Commons in 1867 at the time of the passage of the Second Reform Act. As Prime Minister between 1874 and 1880 he led the government in early efforts to improve the condition of the working class. The 1869 caricature is by "Ape." [The Granger Collection.]

branch of the Anglican Church. Henceforth Irish Roman Catholics would not pay taxes to support the hated Protestant church, to which only a small fraction of the population belonged. Second, in 1870 the Liberal ministry sponsored a land act that provided compensation to evicted Irish tenants and loans for tenants who wished to purchase their land.

Throughout the seventies the Irish question continued to fester. Land remained the center of the agitation. Today, the matter of Irish economic development seems more complicated and who owned the land seems less important than the methods of management and cultivation. Nevertheless the organization of the Irish Land League in the late seventies brought a period of intense agitation and intimidation against the landlords, who were often English. The leader of the Irish movement for a just land settlement and for home rule was Charles Stewart Parnell (1846–1891). In 1881 the second Gladstone ministry passed another Irish land act, which provided further guarantees of tenant rights. This measure only partly satisfied Irish opinion because it was accompanied by a Coercion Act intended to restore law and order to Ireland.

By 1885 Parnell had organized the eighty-five Irish members of the House of Commons into a tightly disciplined party that often voted as a bloc. They pursued disruptive tactics to gain attention for the cause of home rule. They bargained with the two English parties. In the election of 1885 the Irish Party emerged with the balance

Charles Stewart Parnell, shown here in an 1880 *Vanity Fair* drawing by Theobald Chartran, was the leader of the Irish members of Parliament during the Home Rule crisis of the 1880s. [The Granger Collection.]

of power between the English Liberals and Conservatives. The Irish could decide which party would take office. In December 1885 Gladstone announced support of home rule for Ireland. Parnell gave his votes to the formation of a Liberal ministry. However, the issue split the Liberal Party. In 1886 a group of Liberals known as the Liberal Unionists joined with the Conservatives to defeat Gladstone's Home Rule Bill. Gladstone called for a new election, in which the Liberals were defeated. They remained a permanently divided party.

The new Conservative ministry of Lord Salisbury (1830–1903) attempted to reconcile the Irish to English government through public works and administrative reform. The policy, which was tied to further coercion, had only marginal success. In 1892 Gladstone returned to power. A second Home Rule Bill passed the House of Commons but was defeated in the House of Lords. There the Irish question stood until after the turn of the century. The Conservatives sponsored a land act in 1903 that carried out the final transfer of land to tenant ownership. Ireland became a country of small farms. In 1911 a Liberal ministry passed the third Home Rule Bill. Under the provisions of the House of Lords Act of 1911, which curbed the power of that body, the bill had to pass the Commons three times over the Lords veto to become law. The third passage occurred in the summer of 1914, and the operation of the bill was suspended for the duration of World War I.

The Irish question affected British politics in a manner not unlike that of the Austrian nationalities problem. Normal British domestic issues could not be adequately addressed because of the political divisions created by Ireland. The split of the Liberal Party proved especially harmful to the cause of further social and political reform. The people who could agree on matters of reform could not agree on Ireland, and the latter problem seemed more important. As the two traditional parties failed to deal with the social questions, by the turn of the century a newly organized Labor Party began to fill the vacuum.

The European Political Scene: 1850–1875

Between 1850 and 1875 the major contours of the political systems that would dominate Europe until World War I had been drawn. Those systems and political arrangements solved, so far as such matters can be solved, many of the political questions and problems that had troubled the Europeans during the first half of the nineteenth century. The concept of the nation state had on the whole triumphed. Support for governments no longer stemmed from loyalty to dynasties but from various degrees of citizen participation. Moreover the unity of nations was no longer based on dynastic links but on cultural, linguistic, and historical bonds. The parliamentary governments of western Europe and the autocracies of eastern Europe were quite different, but both political systems had been compelled to recognize the force of nationalism and the larger role of citizens in political affairs. Only Russia failed to make such concessions, but the emancipation of the serfs had constituted a concession to a mode of popular opinion. The major sources of future discontent would arise from the demands of labor to enter the political processes and the still unsatisfied aspirations of subject nationalities. Those two areas of unrest would trouble Europe for the next forty years and would eventually undermine the political structures created during the third quarter of the nineteenth century.

SUGGESTED READINGS

G. F. A. BEST, *Mid-Victorian Britain* (1972). A good book on the social structure.
R. C. BINKLEY, *Realism and Nationalism, 1852–1871* (1935). A useful, though somewhat dated survey.
R. BLAKE, *Disraeli* (1967). The best recent biography.
J. BLUM, *Lord and Peasant in Russia from the Ninth to the Nineteenth Century* (1961). A clear discussion of emancipation in the later chapters.

W. L. Burn, *The Age of Equipoise* (1964). A thoughtful and convincing discussion of Victorian social stability.

G. Kitson Clark, *The Making of Victorian England* (1962). The best introduction.

G. Craig, *Germany, 1866–1945* (1978). An excellent new survey.

R. A. Kann, *The Multinational Empire,* 2 vols. (1950). The basic treatment of the nationality problem of Austria–Hungary.

P. Magnus, *Gladstone: A Biography* (1955). A readable biography.

A. J. May, *The Hapsburg Monarchy, 1867–1914* (1951). Narrates in considerable detail and with much sympathy the fate of the dual monarchy.

W. N. Medlicott, *Bismarck and Modern Germany* (1965). An excellent brief biography.

W. E. Mosse, *Alexander II and the Modernization of Russia* (1958). A brief biography.

C. C. O'Brien, *Parnell and His Party* (1957). An excellent treatment of the Irish question.

O. Pflanze, *Bismarck and the Development of Germany* (1963). Carries the story through the achievement of unification.

N. Rich, *The Age of Nationalism and Reform,* rev. ed. (1976). A sound volume based on recent research.

D. Mack Smith, *Cavour and Garibaldi in 1860: A Study in Political Conflict* (1954). Explores the two key personalities in Italian unification.

D. Mack Smith, *The Making of Italy, 1796–1870* (1968). A narrative that incorporates the major documents.

A. J. P. Taylor, *The Hapsburg Monarchy, 1809–1918* (1941). An opiniated but highly readable work.

D. Thomsom, *Democracy in France since 1870,* rev. ed. (1969). A clear guide to a complex problem.

J. M. Thomson, *Louis Napoleon and the Second Empire* (1954). A straightforward account.

Venturi, *The Roots of Revolution* (trans., 1960). A major treatment of late nineteenth-century revolutionary movement.

H. Seton Watson, *The Russian Empire, 1801–1917* (1967). A far-ranging narrative.

A. J. Whyte, *The Evolution of Modern Italy* (1965). An interesting survey of the Italian problem in nineteenth-century diplomacy.

R. Williams, *The World of Napoleon III,* rev. ed. (1965). Examines the cultural setting.

C. B. Woodham-Smith, *The Reason Why* (1953). A lively account of the Crimean War and the charge of the Light Brigade.

T. Zeldin, *France: 1848–1945,* 2 vols. (1973, 1977). Emphasizes the social developments.

736

28

The Building of European Supremacy: Society and Politics to World War I

ETWEEN 1860 and 1914 European political, economic, and social life assumed many of the features characteristic of our world today. Nation states with large electorates, political parties, centralized bureaucracies, and universal military service emerged. Business adopted large-scale corporate structures, and the labor force organized itself into trade unions. Large numbers of white-collar workers appeared. Urban life came to predominate throughout western Europe. Socialism became a major ingredient in the political life of all nations. The foundations of the welfare state and of vast military establishments were laid. Taxation increased accordingly.

During this half century the extensive spread of industrialism created an unparalleled productive capacity in Europe. The age of the automobile, the airplane, the bicycle, the refrigerated ship, the telephone, the wireless, the typewriter, and the electric light bulb dawned. The world's economies, based on the gold standard, became increasingly interdependent. European goods flowed into markets all over the globe. In turn, foreign products, raw materials, and food stuffs were imported. Europe had also quietly become dependent on the resources and markets of the rest of the world. Changes in the weather conditions in Kansas, Argentina, or New Zealand might now effect the European economy. However, prior to World War I the dependence was concealed by Europe's industrial, military, and financial supremacy. At the time people rather assumed that such supremacy was a natural

situation, but the twentieth century would reveal it to have been quite temporary. Nevertheless, while that condition prevailed, Europeans were able to dominate most of the other peoples of the earth and to display the most extreme self-confidence.

Population Trends

There seem to have been more Europeans proportionally about 1900 than ever before or since. Europe then contained just under one quarter of the estimated world population. The demographic expansion to which so much attention has already been paid continued through the second half of the century. The number of Europeans rose from approximately 266 million in 1850 to 401 million in 1900 and 447 million in 1910. However, the rate of European growth began to slow while the population expansion elsewhere did not recede. Depending on the country in Europe, the birth rate either fell or remained stationary. The death rate did likewise. In the long run that ratio meant a more slowly growing population. This situation also meant that the grave demographic differential between the developed and the undeveloped world—which is so much a part of the present food and resource crisis—had been established.

During the second half of the nineteenth century the small family of two or three children became "normal." Knowledge about and means of contraception became more fully dispersed and its practice more widespread. The desire to maintain a high standard of living, the cost of rearing children, the smaller number of children in the work force, and the desire of women to limit the number of births contributed to the stabilization of population. It seems that more and more couples decided that they wanted to spend their incomes on consumer goods rather than on children. Moreover children brought fewer economic advantages to their parents than in the past. Further improvements in sanitation, housing, food processing, and medicine tended to lower the death rate at the

During the last half of the nineteenth century, thousands of Europeans lived in slums such as this one in Glasgow, Scotland, photographed about 1870. Such conditions stood as a living condemnation of the failure of Western industrial society to achieve a just distribution of its goods and services. As time passed, the socialist movement and government welfare programs would begin to address this problem —with results that many continued to feel were less than satisfactory. [The Mansell Collection.]

[*Text continued on page 740*]

After the street fighting of the revolutions of 1848, the old wall fortifications of Vienna were torn down. (See the illustration on page 501 which shows them.) In their place were built broad boulevards lined with fine buildings. The new streets were more beautiful—and were also better suited for rapid movement of troops against possible insurrection. This is an early photograph of a portion of the Ringstrasse, the street replacing the walls. [Austrian Information Service, New York.]

BELOW: The building of sewers for the disposal of urban waste was one of the great accomplishments of nineteenth-century sanitary engineering. This picture was made inside one of the sewers of Paris. [French Cultural Services, New York.]

A fashionable Paris boulevard in the late nineteenth century. Note the various kinds of horsedrawn carriages and the doubledecked horsedrawn bus. [French Cultural Services, New York.]

Pollution was one of the earliest results of indus-trialization and the resulting rapid population growth, and it became a major problem for nineteenth-century governments, as it has remained for those of today. This English cartoon of 1858 was published near the time of the passage by Parliament of an act to clean the River Thames. [The Granger Collection.]

THE "SILENT HIGHWAY"-MAN.
"YOUR *MONEY* OR YOUR *LIFE!*"

The first subway in the world was built in London between 1860 and 1863 and, although powered with steam-driven locomotives, was a success. However, subways did not become truly practicable until electricity was available as the source of power, and the great age of subway building began with the second London subway, opened in 1890. Within the next thirty years many of the great cities of Europe and America had subway systems in operation. This print shows construction work on the London Underground. The Houses of Parliament are in the background. [Mary Evans Picture Library.]

The great town halls, such as this one in Copenhagen, Denmark, built between 1905 and 1911, illustrate both civic pride and the important administrative and political role that cities acquired during the nineteenth century. [Danish Information Office, New York.]

same time. This vast, but stabilizing European population provided a large consumer market and an increasingly healthy work force.

Europe's peoples were on the move in the last half of the century as never before. Legal movement and migration became easier as the role of the landlords lessened. Railways, steamships, and better roads allowed greater physical mobility. The development of the European economy and those of North America, Latin America, and Australia meant better wages and cheap land, which enticed people to move. Within Europe the movement continued toward the cities.

GROWTH OF MAJOR EUROPEAN CITIES
(FIGURES IN THOUSANDS)

	1850	1880	1910
Berlin	419	1,122	2,071
Birmingham	233	437	840
Frankfurt	65	137	415
London	2,685	4,470	7,256
Madrid	281	398	600
Paris	1,053	2,269	2,888
Vienna	444	1,104	2,031

By about 1900 in all the major west European nations approximately 50 per cent of the people lived in urban areas. These city populations were largely uprooted from traditional social ties. They confronted poor housing, social anonymity, and potential unemployment. The migrants to cities in the last half of the century rarely possessed the artisan skills of urban immigrants fifty years earlier. Their problems and their social setting made them ripe for new kinds of political and economic organization. The failure of people to mix socially and the competition for too few jobs generated new varieties of urban discontent such as were experienced by the thousands of Russian Jews who migrated to western Europe. Much of the political anti-Semitism of the latter part of the century had its social roots in these problems of urban migration.

Europeans also migrated out of their continent in record numbers. Between 1846 and 1932 over fifty million Europeans left their homelands. The major areas to benefit from this movement were the United States, Canada, Australia, South Africa, Brazil, and Argentina. At mid-century most of the emigrants left from Great Britain (and especially Ireland), Germany, and Scandinavia. After 1885 the migration drew its numbers from southern and eastern Europe. This exodus helped to relieve the social and population pressures on the Continent. The outward movement of peoples in conjunction with Europe's economic and technological superiority contributed heavily to the Europeanization of the world. Not since the sixteenth century had European civilization produced such an impact on other cultures.

The Second Industrial Revolution

As David Landes has suggested, "The period from 1850 to 1873 was the Continental industry's coming-of-age."[1] The gap that had existed for half a century between British and continental economic development was closed. The basic heavy industries of Belgium, France, and Germany underwent major expansion. French development was relatively slow, but steady. The rate of growth became more rapid after the Franco-Prussian War. The expansion of German industry was stunning. Coal mining, iron and steel production, and the chemical industry made rapid progress. German steel production surpassed that of Britain in 1893 and had almost doubled the British effort by the outbreak of World War I. This emergence of an industrial Germany was the major fact of European economic and political life at the turn of the century.

The systematic spread of railways continued to make a key contribution to economic development during the third quarter of the century. Railways cheapened transport costs and made wider regional and continental marketing possible. Railway building by Europeans in other parts of the globe created new overseas markets. The money spent on railways created demand elsewhere in the economy. Rail transportation, besides fostering capital industry and investment, put new pressure on European

agriculture. Trains running into the great plains of the United States lowered the cost of grain imported into Europe. Continental producers now faced foreign competition for the market in food.

Factors other than continued railway construction also accounted for the prosperity that followed hard on the heels of the economic troubles of the 1840s. From the fifties to the early seventies numerous countries negotiated treaties lowering tariffs. Goods could flow more easily and cheaply from one nation to another. New laws permitting the formation of joint stock companies and easier business incorporation allowed the garnering of vast capital funds for investment. Such legal reforms favoring capital expansion were enacted in Britain in 1856, in France in 1863, and in Prussia in 1870. The gold standard, whereby any major currency could be exchanged for gold, brought new confidence to international trade. Throughout Europe the various national currencies became more uniform. Currency rationalization was a major achievement of German unification. Finally, large banks, such as the French Crédit Mobilier and the German Darmstäder Bank, channeled funds into capital investment rather than commerce. Finance capitalism had the power to determine to a large extent what enterprises would and would not be undertaken. Banks rather than individual entrepreneurs now seemed to guide the economy.

New Industries

Initially the economic expansion of the third quarter of the century constituted the spread of industries similar to those pioneered earlier in Great Britain. Thereafter, however, wholly new industries emerged. It is this latter development that is usually termed the *Second Industrial Revolution*. The first Industrial Revolution was associated with textiles, steam, and iron; the second with steel, chemicals, electricity, and oil. Steel began to replace iron in manufacture and construction. It was stronger, more flexible, and more adaptable. Its uses seemed infinite. In the 1850s Henry Bessemer (1830–1898) discovered a

1 David S. Landes, *The Unbound Prometheus: Technological Change and Industrial Development in Western Europe from 1750 to the Present* (Cambridge, England: Cambridge University Press, 1969), p. 193.

The Eiffel Tower built for a late-nineteenth-century exhibition in Paris seemed to symbolize the material confidence of the age. It dominated the skyline of Paris when it was built—as clearly shown in this 1900 photograph—and still does so today. [The Granger Collection.]

new process, named after him, for manufacturing steel cheaply in large quantities. In 1860 Great Britain, Belgium, France, and Germany had produced 125,000 tons of steel. By 1913 the figure had risen to 32,020,000 tons. Tied to the increased production were new processes for rolling and forming the molten metal for use in shipbuilding, machinery, and automobiles.

The chemical industry came of age during this period. The Solway process of alkali production replaced the older Leblanc process. More sulfuric acid could be produced and so could more laundry soap. New dyestuffs and plastics were also developed. The chemical industry, which has been so fundamental to the quality of life in the twentieth century, represented the earliest example of a combination of scientific and industrial development. Formal scientific research had played only the most minimal role in early industrial development. Trial-and-error amateurism was then the order of the day. By late in the second half of the century chemists and physicists were increasingly called upon to solve the problems of industry. This alliance of science, technology, and industry proved to be fundamental to economic development from the nineties onward. As in so many other fields of the Second Industrial Revolution, Germany led the way in fostering scientific research and education.

The most significant change for industry and eventually for everyday life was the application of electrical energy to production. Electricity was the most versatile and transportable source of power ever discovered. It could be employed to run either large or small machines and to make factory construction more efficient. Electricity was a mode of energy that could be taken to the machinery. The first major public power plant was constructed in Great Britain in 1881. Soon electric poles, lines, and generating stations dotted the European landscape. Electric lights were beginning to be used in homes. Streetcar and subway systems were electrified. The industries powered by electricity in turn produced more and more products that were run by electricity, so that the electrical industry grew rapidly on itself. Probably no

J. M. Keynes Describes Late-Nineteenth-Century Capitalism

In this passage, the great modern economist Keynes (1883–1946) describes the economy disrupted by World War I, with special attention to the inequality of wealth that had contributed to industrial development.

EUROPE *was so organized socially and economically as to secure the maximum accumulation of capital. While there was some continuous improvement in the daily conditions of life of the mass of the population, society was so framed as to throw a great part of the increased income into the control of the class least likely to consume it. The new rich of the nineteenth century were not brought up to large expenditures, and preferred the power which investment gave them to the pleasures of immediate consumption. In fact, it was precisely the* inequality *of the distribution of wealth which made possible those vast accumulations of fixed wealth and of capital improvements which distinguished that age from all others. Herein lay, in fact, the main justification of the capitalist system. If the rich had spent their new wealth on their own enjoyments, the world would long ago have found such a regime intolerable. But like bees they saved and accumulated, not less to the advantage of the whole community because they themselves held narrower ends in prospect.*

The immense accumulations of fixed capital, which to the great benefit of mankind, were built up during the half century before the [First World] war, could never have come about in a society where wealth was divided equitably. The railways of the world, which that age built as a monument to posterity, were, not less than the pyramids of Egypt, the work of labour which was not free to consume in immediate enjoyment the full equivalent of its efforts.

Thus this remarkable system depended for its growth on a double bluff or deception. On the one hand the labouring classes accepted from ignorance or powerlessness, or were compelled, persuaded, or cajoled by custom, convention, authority, and the well-established order of society into accepting, a situation in which they could call their own very little of the cake that they and nature and the capitalists were co-operating to produce. And on the other hand the capitalist classes were allowed to call the best part of the cake theirs and were theoretically free to consume it, on the tacit underlying conditions that they consumed very little of it in practice. . . .

J. M. Keynes, *The Economic Consequences of the Peace* (New York: Harcourt, Brace and Howe, 1919), pp. 18–20.

single late nineteenth-century development has so influenced the material life style of this century.

The turn of the century also saw the emergence of the first large European demand for petroleum. The internal combustion engine was invented in 1876. When the German engineer Gottlieb Daimler (1834–1900) put it on four wheels and obtained a French patent in 1885, the automobile was born. France initially took the lead in auto manufacture, but for many years the car remained a novelty item that only the wealthy could afford. It was the American Henry Ford (1863–1947) who later made the automobile accessible to large numbers of people. The automobile and the new industrial and chemical uses for oil greatly expanded the demand for petroleum. Before the nineties petroleum had been used primarily for lighting; soon it became the basis for transportation and much of the new chemical industry. Europe, then as now, was almost wholly dependent on imported oil. The major supplying companies were Standard Oil of the United States, British Shell Oil, and Royal Dutch.

The Second Industrial Revolution witnessed a shift in the European economic balance of power. In almost all areas of the new industrial expansion Great Britain, which had pioneered the first Industrial Revolution, fell behind the continent and especially Germany. Britain ceased to be a leader and became simply one more competitor. There was no lack of invention on the part of individual British citizens, but the early industrial lead meant that the nations's industries were often locked into existing productive processes and could not easily incorporate new techniques. The British did too little to encourage scientific and technical education. Its managers put too much faith in the inventive amateur, who had so brilliantly fostered the early Industrial Revolution. British investors put too little capital into new industry. Management was immensely complacent. There was too much dependence on old marketing techniques. Attempts to improve the situation came only after the lead had been lost. All of these factors meant that by 1900, while still a great industrial power, Britain was falling behind Ger-

Inflating Tubes

In the 1890s bicycles rapidly became a popular and low-cost means of transportation. They have remained so among the working class in Europe to the present day. Here women workers are inflating the rubber tubes. Since rubber does not grow in Europe, the rubber for the tires often came from colonial holdings. [Bettmann Archive.]

man competition. This situation had much to do with the international rivalry of the two powers.

Wider Economic Trends

Business Difficulties

The second half of the century was not a period of uninterrupted or smooth economic growth. The years from 1850 to 1873 saw a general boom in both industry and agriculture. The last quarter of the century witnessed economic advance but of a much slower nature. Bad weather and foreign competition put grave pressures on European agriculture. Grain producers suffered the most. In Britain thousands of acres of land went out of tillage. In eastern Europe the landlords demanded new protective tariffs. There were moves to specialize farming. Denmark, for example, at this time changed to dairy production. Other countries adopted more scientific and mechanized modes of agriculture. Fertilizers were more frequently used, and steam engines were taken into fields to aid plowing. These techniques made farming more costly, and the size of farms became larger. From the consumers' standpoint these developments meant lower food prices. Nevertheless the difficulties of the agricultural sector put a drag on the general economy.

During 1873 a number of major banks failed, and the rate of capital investment slowed. The major railway systems had been built. During the next two decades stagnation occurred in several industries. Prices and profits fell. Wages also became lower, but the simultaneous fall in prices meant that real wages generally held firm and in some countries even improved. There were pockets of unemployment. (In fact the word *unemployment* was coined during this period.) Despite the stagnation, the general standard of living in the industrialized nations improved, although many workers still lived and labored in abysmal conditions. What made this depression less cruel and disruptive than the turmoil of the forties was the greater availability of consumer goods and the assurance of a food supply. By the turn of the century the demand for consumer goods and the development of new employing industries made possible by the Second Industrial Revolution had lifted Europe from its economic doldrums.

What brought the economy out of the depression was a new expansion of demand from three primary sources. These were changes in marketing, the reorganization of economic enterprise, and imperialism. The lower food prices eventually allowed all classes to spend a marginally larger amount of their income on consumer goods. Urbanization in and of itself created a larger market. People living in cities simply saw more things that they wanted to buy than they would have if still dwelling in the countryside. The new industries of the late century were largely directed toward consumer goods. Retailing techniques changed. Department stores, retail chains, new packaging, mail-order catalogues, and advertising were developed. Marketing itself was creating new demand. The foundations of a consumer economy were being laid.

Drift away from Competition and Free Trade

The economic pressures of the last quarter of the century brought about a shift from economic competition to business consolidation. Big business firms and corporations were organized. They had no desire to compete

The first telephone exchange in Berlin exhibits the role of both communication and electricity in the second industrial revolution. In this picture men are attending the switchboard; soon, however, women took over these jobs. Telephone companies eventually opened a large area of employment for women. [Bettmann Archive.]

RIGHT: A scene in the Great Hall of the Berlin Stock Exchange at the turn of the century. Holdings of and income from stock had become a major feature of wealthy middle-class life in Western Europe. [Ullstein Bilderdienst.]

because they had far too much to lose. Cartels and trade associations, which were the European version of the American trusts, were organized. They attempted to divide markets and to fix prices so as not to drive each other out of business. The great examples of these were the German General Electric Company, the German Siemens Electric Company, the I. G. Farben chemical concern, and the British Glass Manufacturers' Association. Other industries, such as the Krupp armaments company, organized vertically in order to control the sources of raw materials and marketing as well as manufacturing. These new forms of business organization tended to stabilize industries, to make jobs more secure, and to increase consumer demand in that fashion. They did not, however, necessarily produce the lowest consumer prices.

The mid-century ideal of free trade also came under increasing attack as both farming and manufacturing interests sought to ensure a monopoly in their national markets. Protective tariffs were raised across the Continent. Austria and Russia turned to this device in 1874 and in 1877, respectively. In 1879 Bismarck imposed a tariff to protect German industry and the *Junker* landlords. Italy moved to protection in 1887, and the Third French Republic passed the Meline Tariff in 1892. Each of these measures was passed to bring new domestic political support to the various governments. Great Britain remained true to free trade. Yet even there, after the turn of the century Joseph Chamberlain (1836–1914) led a campaign for tariff reform. The drive for tariffs meant that business was seeking the kind of government aid that it had largely spurned half a century earlier.

Europeans also looked outside their continent for markets. The late century age of imperialism was closely related to internal economic problems. European bankers invested large amounts of money in the rest of the world, with the largest portion going to the development of the United States. But traders and investors also hoped to reap profits from Latin America, Asia, and Africa. The early British textile industry had depended to a great extent on foreign markets. Britain's emulators in the latter part of the century also believed they must penetrate those areas. They needed both raw materials and new outlets for finished goods.

It was once argued that Europeans carved out their colonies in order to create those needed markets. The process is now considered more complicated. In establishing sources for raw materials and in forging markets, Europeans undermined existing governments and traditional societies in the underdeveloped portions of the globe. The result was political instability in those areas. It was after such turmoil had been created that European governments moved in to protect the already existing commercial presence of their nationals. The foreign markets never proved to be as profitable as their promoters hoped. Right up to World War I, Europe itself was the single largest market for its own goods.

At the close of the nineteenth century Europe clearly predominated in the world economy. It had the most capital and its industries provided it with the military might to control other areas. However, within Europe two distinct economic zones had come into existence. One consisted of advanced industrial states, including Britain, Belgium, France, Germany, northern Italy, and the western part of Austria. These areas enjoyed a relatively high standard of living, good transport systems, and healthy, educated populations. The second area consisted of Ireland, the Iberian Peninsula, southern Italy, the Balkans, most of Austria–Hungary, and Russia. There agricultural production and education were backward. These areas exported grain and foodstuffs to the industrialized sector. This European economic division, which came into being in the late nineteenth century, was not overcome until after World War II and even then only partially.

Social Ramifications of the Second Industrial Revolution
The Middle Classes

The sixty years prior to World War I were definitively the age of the middle classes. The Great Exhibition of 1851 held in the Crystal Palace in London had displayed the products and the new material life they had forged. Thereafter the middle classes became the arbiter of taste and the defender of the *status quo*. After the revolutions of 1848 the middle classes ceased to be a revolutionary group. Most of their political goals had been attained, even if imperfectly. Once the question of social equality had been raised, large and small property owners across

The Crystal Palace, erected to house the Great Exhibition of 1851, was a fabulous structure of glass and iron designed by the horticulturist and architect Sir Joseph Paxton (1801–1865) and modeled after his greenhouses for the Duke of Devonshire. It originally stood in Hyde Park, London, but after the exhibition it was dismantled and re-erected at Sydenham, the location shown here. It was destroyed by fire in 1936. The Great Exhibition itself was an abundant display of the vast material accomplishments of the industrial revolution and liberal society. [The Granger Collection.]

the Continent moved to protect what they possessed. The drive toward protective tariffs, new business organization, militarism, and empire suggested that bourgeois Europeans had come to use the power of the state to look out for their own interests as the aristocracy had done before them.

DIVISIONS WITHIN THE MIDDLE CLASS. The middle classes, which had never been perfectly homogeneous, now became even more diverse. Their most prosperous members were the owners and managers of great businesses and banks. They lived in a splendor that rivaled and sometimes excelled that of the aristocracy. Some, such as W. H. Smith, the owner of railway newsstands in England, were made peers. The Krupp family of Germany were pillars of the state. Only a few hundred families acquired such wealth. Beneath them were the comfortable small businessmen and professional people, whose incomes permitted private homes, large quantities of furniture, pianos, pictures, books, journals, education for their children, and vacations. There were also the shopkeepers, the schoolteachers, the librarians, and others who had either a bit of property or a skill derived from education that provided respectable, nonmanual employment. Finally, there was a wholly new element in the white-collar workers. These included factory foremen, secretaries, retail clerks, and lower-level bureaucrats in business and government. The white-collar labor force was often working class in its origins and might even belong to unions, but its aspirations for life style were middle class. All of these middle-class groups yearned to consume the products made possible by the Second Industrial Revolution.

Considerable tension began to exist among the various strata of middle-class society during the latter part of the century. The small businessmen and shopkeepers, whose numbers rose steadily until shortly after 1900, often resented the power of the great capitalists. The little people of the middle class feared being edged out of the marketplace by large companies, with whom they could not hope to compete. The shopkeeping class always had to work very hard simply to maintain their life style and were often dependent upon banks for commercial credit. Department stores and mail-order catalogues endangered their livelihood. There is also good reason to believe that the learned professions were becoming overcrowded. To be a professional man no longer ensured a sound income. The new white-collar work force had just attained re-

The Gatling gun was a forerunner of the modern machine gun. It greatly increased the destructive power of a small military force. Its invention and incorporation into warfare illustrates the impact of technology on military power in the nineteenth century. In the picture, the American Professor Richard Jordon Gatling (1818–1903) demonstrates his invention. [Culver Pictures.]

The Krupp works at Essen, Germany, was one of the largest military manufacturing establishments in Europe. This late nineteenth-century photograph is taken in the gun shop. The massive production of such arms meant that in the early twentieth century Europeans would be able to turn on themselves more sheer physically destructive force than at any previous time in history. [Culver Pictures.]

spectability and a non-working-class status. They profoundly feared slipping back to their social origins.

Prior to World War I these social groups were reasonably secure but remained quite apprehensive. The business cycle might turn against them. The small supplementary incomes from stocks, bonds, or interest from savings might disappear. Somehow the socialists might confiscate their property. After World War I many of those fears were realized. The profound insecurity that the middle classes then experienced became one of the most significant factors of twentieth-century political life.

THE MIDDLE CLASS FAMILY AND WOMEN. During the late nineteenth century the life style of the middle classes set the tone of the day. Machine-made clothes allowed them to dress well and alike. Machine-made furniture and wallpaper allowed their homes to appear similar. The productive processes they directed allowed the world of everyday life to assume a regularity and a conformity never before quite so possible. At the center of their lives was the family. Although equality and independence were the keynotes of their politics, the opposite qualities predominated in their homes. The bourgeois father presided over his household as a patriarch. Throughout the Continent he controlled most of his wife's property. He could still generally determine whom his daughter married. His son depended on his allowance. He and his sons maintained a double standard of sexual morality, demanding chastity from their sisters and fidelity from their wives while perhaps frequenting brothels themselves. Women in the family setting were supposed to remain what the English poet Coventry Patmore termed "the angel of the house." Perhaps the middle-class male needed that firm structure of home life and domestic values because he knew that the business world in which he dwelled might collapse with the next trade cycle or bank panic.

Whatever the hypocrisy involved in this domestic situation, the nineteenth-century middle-class family, by providing a point of departure for social criticism, has proved a powerful force in forging the conscience of the modern world. There was little or no role in that family and home for an active, articulate, thinking woman. By allowing men to provide sufficient income for the entire family, the new industry and its related enterprises gave women only the most minimal economic role. Smaller families lessened child-rearing duties. The more idle the wife or daughter, the greater the evidence of the success of the husband and father. Yet both the ideology and the structures of liberal society generated a weakening of that situation.

Liberal society and its values neither automatically nor inevitably improved the lot of women. Those who pioneered female entry into the professions, activity on government commissions and school boards, or dispersal of birth control information faced grave social obstacles, personal humiliation, and often outright bigotry. However, the intellectual and political tools for their social critique were present in the society itself.

The rationalism and penchant for self-criticism that have characterized modern Western society manifested themselves in the movement to emancipate women. As early as 1792 in Britain Mary Wollstonecraft (1759–1797), in *The Vindication of the Rights of Woman,* had applied the revolutionary doctrines of the rights of man to the predicament of members of her own sex. John Stuart Mill (1806–1873), in conjunction with the thought of his wife, Harriet Taylor, had applied the logic of liberal freedom to the position of women in *The Subjection of Women* (1869). The arguments for utility and efficiency so dear to middle-class liberals could be used to expose the human and social waste implicit in the inferior role assigned to women. That waste was becoming increasingly demonstrated as women pursued jobs in the professions, schoolteaching, social work, and other employment formerly the preserves of men. New areas of female employment were also opened in clerical jobs. The growing consumer orientation of the economy gave women new indirect power while they were still in the home. Moreover the socialist critique of capitalist society also included

Mary Wollstonecraft (1759–1797) was one of the first writers to call for equal rights for women. Shortly before her early death she was married to William Godwin, the English political writer and novelist. Their child was the future Mary Shelley, author of *Frankenstein* and wife of the Romantic poet. The portrait by John Opie is in the National Portrait Gallery, London. [The Granger Collection.]

a harsh indictment of the social and economic position to which women had been relegated.

Much of the discussion of the social position of women remained merely theory and talk. Some women did gain meaningful employment, but their numbers were small. Women did not rise rapidly through the work force. However, to some extent theory was transformed into practice, or at least protest, so far as political life was concerned. The political tactics used by men to expand the electoral franchise and to influence the governing processes could be and were employed by women toward the same end. The claims to political participation set forth by the respectable, prosperous, and educated working class applied equally well to women.

The most important prewar example of such activity was the British women's suffrage movement led by Mrs. Emmeline Pankhurst (1858–1928). Her husband,

J. S. Mill Analyzes the Causes of the Subjection of Women

John Stuart Mill (1806–1873) was one of the key nineteenth-century spokesmen for women's rights. In this 1869 essay he was concerned that society benefit from the various talents and capacities that women could bring to the social, political, and intellectual problems of the day. He attempted to explain how custom, public opinion, and traditional education not only denied women their rightful place in society but also cunningly convinced them in numerous subtle ways that they could not achieve such a place.

M EN *do not want solely the obedience of women, they want their sentiments. . . . They have therefore put everything in practice to enslave their minds. . . . The masters of women wanted more than simple obedience, and they turned the whole force of education to effect their purpose. All women are brought up from the very earliest years in the belief that their ideal of character is the very opposite to that of men; not self-will, and government by self-control, but submission, and yielding to the control of others. All the moralities tell them that it is the duty of women, and all the current sentimentalities that it is their nature, to live for others; to make complete abnegation of themselves, and to have no life but in their affections. And by their affections are meant the only ones they are allowed to have—those to the men with whom they are connected, or to the children who constitute an additional and indefeasible tie between them and a man. When we put together three things—first, the natural attraction between opposite sexes; secondly, the wife's entire dependence on the husband, every privilege or pleasure she has being either his gift, or depending on his will; and lastly, that the principal object of human pursuit, consideration, and all objects of social ambition, can in general be sought or obtained by her only through him—it would be a miracle if the object of being attractive to men had not become the polar star of feminine education and formation of character. And, this great means of influence over the minds of women having been acquired, an instinct of selfishness made men avail themselves of it to the utmost as a means of holding women in subjection, by representing to them meekness, submissiveness, and resignation of all individual will into the hands of a man, as an essential part of sexual attractiveness.*

John Stuart Mill, *On Liberty, Representative Government, The Subjection of Women* (London: Oxford University Press, 1960), pp. 443–444.

A photograph of John Stuart Mill and his stepdaughter Helen Taylor. Mill was the foremost English rationalist philosopher of the nineteenth century. He was also one of the earliest outspoken advocates of women's rights. [Radio Times Hulton Picture Library.]

BELOW: In 1911 Mrs. Emmeline Pankhurst led major demonstrations of British suffragettes in favor of the vote for women. Several ended in violence. Here Mrs. Pankhurst is literally being carried off to jail. [Culver Pictures.]

who died near the close of the century, had been active in labor and Irish nationalist politics. In 1903 Mrs. Pankhurst and her daughters, Christabel and Sylvia, founded the Women's Social and Political Union. For several years they and their followers, known derisively as the *Suffragettes*, lobbied publicly and privately for the extension of the vote to women. By 1910, having failed to move the government, they turned to the violent tactics of arson, window breaking, and sabotage of postal boxes. They marched en masse on Parliament. The Liberal government of Henry Asquith imprisoned many of the women and force-fed those who went on hunger strikes in jail. The government refused to extend the franchise. Only in 1918 did some British women receive the vote as a result of their contribution to the war effort. Prior to the conflict women could vote only in Norway and Finland. It required the social and emotional upheaval of World War I to bring women in significant numbers to a place of prominence and acceptance in European political life.

The Working Classes

The late century industrial expansion wrought further changes in the life of the labor force. In all industrializing continental countries the numbers of the urban proletariat rose. Like the middle class, the working class became more differentiated in its composition. Proportionally there were many fewer artisans, craftsmen, and highly skilled workers. For the first time factory wage-earners came to predominate. The increasingly mechanized factories often required less highly technical skills from its operatives. There also occurred considerable growth in the very unskilled work associated with shipping, transportation, and building. Work assumed a more impersonal character. Factories were located in cities, and practically all links between factory or day-labor employment and home life dissolved. Large corporate enterprise meant less personal contact between employers and their workers.

On the whole, the standard of living improved throughout the second half of the century. However, that improvement was often more statistical than real. There still existed widespread poverty, poor housing, sweatshop working conditions, and the haunting fears of accident, disability, unemployment, and old age. Between 1900 and World War I, industrial labor discontent was distinctly on the rise as wages failed to keep up with rising prices. During the latter years of the nineteenth century a

This print by Gustave Doré from the third quarter of the nineteenth century portrays an institution in London where homeless persons might spend the night. The gentleman in the middle is reading the Bible to the derelicts who have come in off the street. Many such charitable institutions were closely connected to Christian churches.

few big businesses attempted to provide some security for their employees through company housing and pension plans. Although these efforts were in a few cases pioneering, they could not prove adequate for the mass of the labor force.

TRADE UNIONISM. Workers still had to look to themselves for improvement of their situation. However, after 1848 European workers ceased taking to the streets to voice their grievances in the form of riots. They also stopped trying to revive the paternal guilds and similar institutions of the past. After mid-century the labor force accepted the fact of modern industrial production and its general downgrading of skills and attempted to receive more benefits from that system. Workers turned to new institutions and ideologies. Chief among these were trade unions, democratic political parties, and socialism.

Trade unionism came of age as legal protections were extended throughout the second half of the century. Unions became legal in Great Britain in 1871 and were allowed to picket in 1875. In France Napoleon III had first used troops against strikes, but as his political power waned, he allowed weak labor associations in 1868. The Third French Republic fully legalized unions in 1884. After 1890 they could function in Germany with little disturbance. Initially most trade unions entered the political process in a rather marginal fashion. So long as representatives of the traditional governing classes looked after labor interests, members of the working class rarely sought office themselves.

The mid-century organizational efforts of the unions were directed toward skilled workers. The goal was immediate improvement of wages and working conditions. By the close of the century, industrial unions for unskilled workers were being organized. They were very large and included thousands of workers. They confronted extensive opposition from employers, and longer strikes were frequently required to bring about employer acceptance. In the prewar decade there were an exceedingly large number of strikes thoughout Europe as the unions attempted to raise wages to keep up with inflation.

However, despite the advances of unions and the growth of memberships in 1910 to approximately 3 million in Britain, 2 million in Germany, and 977,000 in France, they never included a majority of the industrial labor force. What the unions did represent was a new collective fashion in which workers could associate to confront the economic difficulties of their lives and to attain better security.

DEMOCRACY AND POLITICAL PARTIES. The democratic franchise provided workers with direct political influence, which meant that they could no longer be ignored. With the exception of Russia all the major European states adopted broad-based, if not perfectly democratic, electoral systems. Great Britain passed its second reform act in 1867 and its third in 1884. Bismarck brought universal manhood suffrage to the German Empire in 1871. The French Chamber of Deputies was democratically elected. Universal manhood suffrage was adopted in Switzerland in 1879, in Spain in 1890, in Belgium in 1893, in the Netherlands in 1896, and in Norway in 1898. Italy finally fell into line in 1912. Democracy brought new modes of popular pressure to bear on all governments. It meant that discontented groups could now voice their grievances and advocate their programs within the institutions of government rather than from the outside.

The advent of democracy witnessed the formation for the first time in Europe of organized mass political parties. These had existed throughout the nineteenth century in the United States. In the liberal European states of narrow electoral bases most voters had been people of property who knew what they had at stake in politics. Organization had been minimal. The new expansion of the electorate brought into the political processes many people whose level of political consciousness, awareness, and interest was quite low. This electorate had to be organized and taught the nature of power and influence in the liberal democratic state. The organized political party—with its workers, newspapers, offices, social life, and discipline—was the vehicle that mobilized the new voters. The largest single group in these mass electorates was the working class. The democratization of politics presented the socialists with opportunities and caused the traditional ruling classes to vie with the socialists for the support of the new voters.

Labor, Socialism, and Politics to World War I

Along with new opportunities, the trade unions and the democratic electorates created ideological and practical problems for European socialists. Early socialist doctrines had been conditioned by both the economic dislocation of early industrialization and the exclusion of the workers from politics. Socialists of various kinds had called for major social changes, often involving violent revolution. However, unions, democracy, and rising standards of living meant that the ends of socialism might be attained within the existing political framework and without violent revolution. Moreover, as the labor force began to receive direct benefits from the expanding economy, they were less likely to desire its destruction. It was while working out these ideological and tactical problems that European socialists entered the mainstream of European politics. The internal socialist conflicts of these years have continued to influence the movement in Europe and elsewhere to the present day.

Marx and the First International

Karl Marx himself made considerable accommodation to the new practical realities that developed during the third quarter of the century. He did not abandon the revolutionary doctrines of *The Communist Manifesto,* and in *Capital* (1867) he continued to predict the disintegration of capitalism. His private thoughts as revealed in his letters also remained quite revolutionary, but his practical, public political activity reflected a somewhat different approach.

In 1864 a group of British and French trade unionists founded the International Working Men's Association.

Known as the First International, its membership encompassed a vast array of radical political types, including socialists, anarchists, and Polish nationalists. The First International allowed Marx, who was by then quite active in the London radical community, to write its Inaugural Address. In it he urged radical social change and the economic emancipation of the working class, but he also supported and approved efforts by workers and trade unions to reform the conditions of labor within the existing political and economic processes. He urged revolution but tempered the means. Privately he often criticized such reformist activity, but those writings were not made public till near the end of the century, and after his death.

During the late sixties the First International gathered statistics, kept labor groups informed of mutual problems, provided a forum for debate of socialist doctrine, and extravagantly proclaimed its own size and influence. From these debates and activities Marxism emerged as the single most important strand of socialism. In 1872 Marx and his supporters drove the anarchists out of the International. Marx was determined to preserve the role of the state against the anarchist attack on authority and large political organizations. Through the meetings and discussions of the First International, German socialists became deeply impressed with Marx's thought. Because, as will be seen, they became the most important socialist party in Europe, they became the chief channel for the preservation and development of Marxist thought.

The First International proved to be a very fragile structure. The events surrounding the Paris Commune presented the final blow to its existence. Few socialists and no real Marxists were involved with the Commune. However, Marx in a major pamphlet glorified the Commune as a genuine proletarian uprising. British trade unionists, who in 1871 were finally receiving new legal protection, wanted no connection with the crimes of the Parisians. The French authorities used the uprising to suppress socialist activity. Throughout Europe the events in Paris cast a pall over socialism. The First International held its last European congress in 1873. Its offices were then transferred to the United States, where it was dissolved in 1876. Thereafter the fate of socialism and the labor movement depended largely on the economic and political conditions of the individual European countries.

Great Britain: Fabianism and Early Welfare Programs

Neither Marxism nor any other form of socialism made significant progress in Great Britain, the most advanced industrial society of the day. There trade unions grew steadily and members normally supported Liberal Party candidates. The "new unionism" of the late eighties and the nineties organized the dock workers, the gas workers, and similar unskilled groups. Employer resistance to unions heightened class antagonism. In 1892 Kier Hardie became the first independent working man to be elected to Parliament. The next year the small, socialist Independent Labor Party was founded, but it remained ineffective.

Until 1901 general political activity on the part of labor remained quite limited. The Taff Vale decision in that year by the House of Lords, however, removed the legal protection previously accorded union funds. The Trades Union Congress responded by launching the Labor Party. In the election of 1906 the fledgling party sent twenty-nine members to Parliament. Their goals as trade unionists did not yet encompass socialism. Along with this new political departure the British labor movement became more militant. There were scores of strikes before the war as workers fought for wages to meet the rising cost of living. The government took a larger role than ever before in mediating these strikes, which in 1911 and 1912 involved the railways, the docks, and the mines.

British socialism itself remained primarily the preserve of intellectuals. H. M. Hyndman (1842–1921), a wealthy graduate of Eton, and William Morris (1834–1896), the poet and designer, read Marx's works avidly, but their Social Democratic Federation, founded in 1881, never had more than a handful of members. The socialists who exerted the most influence were the Fabian Society, founded in 1884. Their leading members were Sydney (1859–1947) and Beatrice (1858–1943) Webb, H. G. Wells (1866–1946), Graham Wallas (1858–1932), and George Bernard Shaw (1856–1950). Many of the Fabians were civil servants who believed that the problems of industry, the expansion of ownership, and the state direction of production could be achieved gradually, peacefully, and democratically. They sought to educate the country to the rational wisdom of socialism. They were particularly interested in modes of collective ownership on the municipal level, the so-called gas and water socialism.

The British government and the major political parties responded slowly to these various pressures. In 1903 Joseph Chamberlain launched his unsuccessful tariff reform campaign to finance social reform through higher import duties. The campaign badly split the Conservative Party. After 1906 the Liberal Party, led by Henry Campbell-Bannerman (1836–1908) and after 1908 by Herbert Asquith (1852–1928), pursued a two-pronged policy. Fearful of losing seats in Parliament to the new Labor Party, they restored the former protection of unions. Then after 1909, with David Lloyd George (1863–1945) as the guiding light, the Liberal ministry undertook a broad program of social legislation. This included the establishment of labor exchanges, the regulation of the sweated labor trades, such as tailoring and lacemaking, and the National Insurance Act of 1911 to provide unemployment benefits and health care. The financing of these programs brought the House of Commons into conflict with the Conservative-dominated House of Lords. The result was the House of Lords Act of 1911, which allowed the Commons to override the legislative veto of the upper chamber. The new taxes and social programs meant that in Britain, the home of nineteenth-century liberalism, the state was taking on an expanded role in the life of its citizens. The early welfare legislation was only marginally satisfactory to labor, many of whose members still thought they could gain more from the direct action of strikes.

Sidney Webb Relates Socialism to Democracy

Members of the Fabian Society represented a major
force in British socialism. They believed that
through democracy the great social questions of the
day could be addressed. They hoped to replace
individualism by state action. In their view the goals
of socialism could be achieved without revolution.
Sidney Webb, whose views follow, and his wife
Beatrice were frequent voices for the Fabians.

THE *main stream which has borne European society
towards Socialism during the past 100 years is the irresistible progress of Democracy. . . .*

*In the present Socialist movement these two streams are
united: advocates of social reconstruction have learnt the
lesson of Democracy, and know that it is through the
slow and gradual turning of the popular mind to new
principles that social reorganization bit by bit comes. All
students of society who are abreast of their time, Socialists
as well as Individualists, realize that important organic
changes can only be (1) democratic, and thus acceptable to
a majority of the people, and prepared for in the minds of
all; (2) gradual, and thus causing no dislocation, however rapid may be the rate of progress; (3) not regarded
as immoral by the mass of the people, and thus not
subjectively demoralizing to them; and (4) in this country at any rate, constitutional and peaceful. Socialists may
therefore be quite one with Radicals in their political
methods. Radicals, on the other hand, are perforce realizing that mere political levelling is insufficient to save a
State from anarchy and despair. Both sections have been
driven to recognize that the root of the difficulty is economic; and there is every day a wider consensus that the
inevitable outcome of Democracy is the control by the
people themselves, not only of their own political organization, but, through that, also of the main instruments of
wealth production; the gradual substitution of organized
cooperation for the anarchy of the competitive struggle. . . . The economic side of the democratic ideal is, in
fact, Socialism itself.*

Sidney Webb, in *Fabian Essays in Socialism* (Gloucester, Mass.:
Peter Smith, 1967, originally published 1889), pp. 50–52.

RIGHT: Jean Jaurès was one of the most popular and influential socialist leaders in France. He was assassinated near the beginning of World War I. [The Granger Collection.]

France: "Opportunism" Rejected

French socialism gradually revived after the suppression of the Paris Commune. The institutions of the Third Republic provided a framework for legal activity. The major problem for French socialists was their own internal division rather than government opposition. There were no fewer than five separate parties, plus other independent socialists. They managed to elect approximately forty members to the Chamber of Deputies by the early nineties. Despite their lack of common policy, the socialist presence aided the passage of measures to relieve workers from carrying identity cards and to provide for factory inspection and limited working hours and health care. In 1910 the republic inaugurated a scheme for voluntary pensions. However, the most important developments of French labor and socialism were not legislative.

At the turn of the century the two major factions of French socialism were led by Jean Jaurès (1859–1914) and Jules Guesde (1845–1922). The former believed that socialists should cooperate with radical middle-class ministries to ensure the enactment of needed social legislation. Guesde opposed this policy, arguing that socialists could not with integrity support a bourgeois cabinet that they were theoretically dedicated to overthrow. The quarrel came to a head as a by-product of the Dreyfus affair. In 1899, as a means of uniting all supporters of Dreyfus, Prime Minister René Waldeck-Rousseau (1846–1904) appointed the socialist Allexander Millerand to the Cabinet. By 1904 the issue of "opportunism," as such cabinet participation by socialists was termed, came to be debated at the Amsterdam Congress of the Second International. This organization has been founded in 1889 in a new effort to unify the various national socialist parties and

Under a Dutch banner calling for the proletariat of all lands to unite, a congress of the Second Socialist International meets in Amsterdam in 1904 to debate ideology and practical tactics. [Internationaal Instituut voor Sociale Geschiedenis, Amsterdam.]

trade unions. The Amsterdam Congress condemned "opportunism" in France and ordered the French socialists to form a single party. Jaurès, believing socialist unity the most important issue in France, accepted the decision. French socialists began to work together, and by 1914 the United Socialist Party was the second largest group in the Chamber of Deputies. However, Socialist Party members would not again serve in a French cabinet until the Popular Front Government of 1936.

The French labor movement, with deep roots in the Proudhonian doctrines of anarchism, was uninterested in both politics and socialism. French workers tended to vote socialist, but the unions avoided active political participation. The Confédération Générale du Travail was founded in 1895 and regarded itself as a rival to the socialist parties. Its leaders sought to improve the workers' conditions through direct action. They embraced the doctrines of syndicalism, which were most persuasively expounded by Georges Sorel (1847–1922) in *Reflections on Violence* (1908). This book enshrined the idea of the general strike as a means of generating worker unity and power. The strike tactic was quite different from the socialist idea of aiding the situation of labor through the action of the state. Strike action on the part of unions flourished between 1905 and 1914, and the radical ministry on more than one occasion used troops against the strikers. Consequently, in France the forces of labor were suppressed by the liberal state, and the Socialist Party was locked into a doctrine of nonparticipation in the Cabinet, which effectively undermined its potential political influence.

Germany: Social Democrats and Revisionism

The hostile judgment rendered by the Second International against French socialist participation in bourgeois ministries reflected the policy previously adopted by the German Social Democratic Party, or SPD. The organizational success of this party more than any other single factor kept Marxist socialism alive into the latter part of the century. The party was founded in 1869. Its origins

The German Empire Legislates Against the Socialists

Through these 1878 laws Bismarck hoped to destroy the young Social Democratic Party. The measures were intended to make it difficult for the SPD to hold meetings, publish newspapers and pamphlets, and collect money to support its activities. The Anti-Socialist Laws remained in effect until 1891.

1. ASSOCIATIONS *which aim, by Social Democratic, Socialistic, or Communistic endeavours, at the destruction of the existing order in State or society, are to be forbidden.* . . .

.   .   .   .

9. *Meetings in which Social Democratic, Socialistic, or Communistic tendencies, directed to the destruction of the existing order in State or society, make their appearance, are to be dissolved.*

Meetings, of which facts justify the assumption that they are destined to further such tendencies, are to be forbidden.

Public festivities and processions are placed under the same restrictions.

.   .   .   .

11. *Printed matter, in which Social Democratic, Socialistic, or Communistic tendencies, directed to the destruction of the existing order in State and society in a manner dangerous to the peace, and, in particular, to the harmony between different classes of the population, make their appearance, is to be forbidden.*

In the case of periodical literature, the prohibition can be extended to any further issue, as soon as a single number has been forbidden under this law.

.   .   .   .

16. *The collection of contributions for the furthering of Social Democratic, Socialistic, or Communistic endeavours, directed toward the destruction of the existing order in State or society, as also the public instigation to the furnishing of such contributions, are [sic] to be forbidden by the police.*

.   .   .   .

28. *For districts or localities which are threatened, by the above-mentioned endeavours, with danger to the public safety, the following provisions can be made, for the space of a year at most, by the central police of the state in question, and subject to the permission of the Bundesrath [the upper chamber of the Parliament].*

(1) That meetings may only take place with the previous permission of the police; this prohibition does not extend to meetings for an election to the Reichstag or the Diet.

(2) That the distribution of printed matter may not

lay in the labor agitation of Ferdinand Lasalle (1825–1864), who wanted worker participation in German politics. His followers were joined by Wilhelm Liebknecht (1826–1900) and August Bebel (1840–1913), who were Marxists. Consequently the party was divided from its founding between those who wanted reformist political activity and those who advocated revolution.

The forging experience of the SPD was twelve years of persecution by Bismarck. The iron chancellor believed that socialism would undermine German politics and society. Less than a decade after its founding, he moved against the young SPD. In 1878 there was an attempt to assassinate William I. Although the socialists were not involved, Bismarck used the opportunity to steer an antisocialist law through the *Reichstag*. The organization, meetings, newspapers, and other public activities of the SPD were suppressed. To remain a socialist meant to remove oneself from the mainstream of respectable German life and possibly to lose one's job. The antisocialist legislation proved politically counterproductive. From the early eighties onward the SPD steadily polled more and more votes in elections to the *Reichstag*.

As simple repression failed to separate German workers from socialist loyalties, Bismarck undertook a program of social welfare legislation. In 1883 the German Empire adopted a health insurance measure. The next year saw the enactment of accident insurance legislation. Finally, in 1889 Bismarck sponsored a plan for old age and disability pensions. These programs, to which both workers and employers contributed, represented a paternalistic, conservative alternative to socialism. The state itself would organize a system of social security that did not require any change in the system of property holding or politics. Germany became the first major industrial nation to enjoy this kind of welfare program.

In 1890, after forcing Bismarck's resignation, Emperor William II (1888–1918) allowed the antisocialist legislation to expire in hope of thus building new support for the monarchy among the working class. Even under the repressive laws members of the SPD could sit in the *Reichstag*. Now, however, the question became what attitude the recently legalized party should assume toward the German Empire. The answer came in the Erfurt Program of 1891, formulated under the political guidance of Bebel and the ideological tutelage of Karl Kautsky (1854–1938). In good Marxist fashion the program declared the imminent doom of capitalism and the necessity of socialist ownership of the means of production. However, these goals were to be achieved by legal political participation rather than by revolutionary activity. Because by its very nature capitalism must fall, the immediate task of socialists was to work for the improvement of workers' lives rather than for the revolution, which was inevitable. In theory the SPD was vehemently hostile to the German Empire, but in practice the party functioned within its institutions. The SPD members of the *Reichstag* maintained clear consciences by refusing to enter the Cabinet, to which they were not invited anyway, and by refraining for many years from voting for the military budget.

The situation of the SPD, however, generated the most important internal socialist challenge to the orthodox Marxist analysis of capitalism and the socialist revolution. Eduard Bernstein (1850–1932) was the author of this socialist heresy. He had spent over a decade of his life in Great Britain and was quite familiar with the Fabians.

Eduard Bernstein, here shown late in life, was the father of democratic socialism in Europe. His revisionist theories sharply divided the German socialist camp at the turn of the century. [The Granger Collection.]

The German Social Democratic Party Presents a Program

After the Anti-Socialist Laws were repealed in 1891, the German Social Democratic Party could once more operate legally. Through the Erfurt Program of the same year the party again asserted a basically revolutionary program for the working class. In theory the Erfurt Program rejected the idea of compromising the goals of socialism with the existing social and economic structures of the German Empire. However, despite its rhetoric the SPD did not undertake revolutionary activity. Here is the important part of the Erfurt Program.

PRIVATE *property in the means of production, which was formerly the means of securing to the producer the possession of his own product, has to-day become the means of expropriating peasants, handicraftsmen and small producers, and of putting the non-workers, capitalists and great landlords in possession of the product of the workers. Only the conversion of capitalistic private property in the means of production . . . into common property, and the change of the production of goods into a socialistic production, worked for and through society, can bring it about that production on a large scale, and the ever-growing productiveness of human labour, shall develop, for the hitherto exploited classes, from a source of misery and oppression, into a source of the highest well-being and perfect universal harmony.*

This social change betokens the emancipation, not only of the proletariat, but of the whole human race, which is suffering under the present conditions. But it can only be the work of the working classes. . . .

The struggle of the working class against capitalistic exploitation is of necessity a political struggle. . . .

To give to this fight of the working class a conscious and unified form, and to show it its necessary goal—that is the task of the Social Democratic Party.

The interests of the working classes are the same in all countries with a capitalistic mode of production. . . . In recognition of this, the Social Democratic Party of Germany feels and declares itself to be one with the class-conscious workmen of all other countries.

The Social Democratic Party of Germany does not fight, accordingly, for new class-privileges and class-rights, but for the abolition of class-rule and of classes themselves, for equal rights and equal duties of all, without distinction of sex or descent.

Bertrand Russell, *German Social Democracy* (London: Longmans, Green, 1896), pp. 138–139.

Rosa Luxemburg (1870–1919) was a German radical who strongly supported the revolutionary concept of socialism. She was assassinated while in prison. [The Granger Collection.]

Bernstein questioned whether Marx and his later orthodox followers, such as Kautsky, had been correct in their pessimistic appraisal of capitalism and the necessity of revolution. In *Evolutionary Socialism* (1899) Bernstein pointed to the rising standard of living in Europe. Ownership of capitalist industry was becoming more widespread through stockholding. The middle class was not being forced into the ranks of the proletariat and was not identifying its problems with those of the workers. The inner contradictions of capitalism as expounded by Marx had simply not developed. Moreover the opening of the franchise to the working class meant that revolutionary change might be achieved through parliamentary methods. What was required to realize a humane socialist society was not revolution but more democracy and social reform.

Bernstein's doctrines, known as *revisionism*, were widely debated among German socialists and were finally condemned as theory. His critics argued that evolution toward social democracy might be possible in liberal, parliamentary Britain, but not in authoritarian, militaristic Germany, with its basically powerless *Reichstag*. The critics were probably correct about the German political scene. Nonetheless, while still calling for revolution, the SPD pursued a course of action similar to that advocated by Bernstein. Its trade union members prospering with the German economy did not want revolution. Its grassroots members wanted to consider themselves patriotic Germans as well as good socialists. Its leaders feared any actions that might renew the persecution that they had experienced under Bismarck. Consequently the party worked at elections, membership expansion, and short-term political and social reform. It prospered and became one of the most important institutions of imperial Germany. Even some middle-class Germans voted for it as a means of opposing the illiberal institutions of the empire. And in August 1914, after long debate among themselves, the SPD members of the *Reichstag* abandoned their former stance and unanimously voted for the war credits that would finance World War I.

Russia: Industrial Development and the Birth of Bolshevism

During the last decade of the nineteenth century Russia entered the industrial age and confronted many of the problems that the more advanced nations of the Continent had experienced fifty or seventy-five years earlier. Unlike those other countries Russia had to deal with major political discontent and economic development simultaneously. Russian socialism reflected that peculiar situation.

WITTE'S PROGRAM FOR INDUSTRIAL GROWTH. The emancipation of the serfs in 1861 had brought little agricultural progress. The peasants were burdened with redemption payments, local taxes, excessive national taxes, and falling grain prices. There were few attempts to educate the peasantry in the more advanced techniques of farming. Most of the land held by free peasants was owned communally through the *mir*, or village. This system of ownership was extremely inefficient and employed strip farming and the farming of small plots. Between 1860 and 1914 the population of European Russia rose from approximately 50 million to approximately 103 million people. Land hunger spread among the peasants. There was intense agrarian discontent.

Count Sergei Witte was the major planner of industrialism in late nineteenth-century Russia. [The Granger Collection.]

Peasants with too little land still had to work on larger noble estates or for more prosperous peasant farmers known as *kulaks*. Uprisings in the countryside were a frequent problem. The agricultural sector benefited little from the late-century industrialism.

Alexander III and Nicholas II were determined that Russia should become an industrial power. Only by this means could the country maintain its military position and its diplomatic role in Europe. The person who led Russia into the industrial age was Sergei Witte (1849–1915). After a career in railways and other private business, he was appointed finance minister in 1892. Witte epitomized the nineteenth-century modernizer who pursued a policy of planned economic development, protective tariffs, high taxes, the gold standard, and efficiency. He established a strong financial link with the French money market, which led to later diplomatic cooperation between Russia and France.

Witte favored heavy industries. Between 1890 and 1904 the Russian railway system grew from 30,596 kilometers to 59,616 kilometers. The 5000-mile Trans-Siberian Railroad was almost completed. Coal output more than tripled during the same period. There was a vast increase in pig-iron production, from 928,000 tons in 1890 to 4,641,000 tons in 1913. During the same period steel production rose from 378,000 tons to 4,918,000 tons. The textile industry continued to expand and still constituted the single largest industry. The factory system began to be used more extensively throughout the country.

Industrialism brought considerable social discontent to Russia, as it had elsewhere. Landowners felt that foreign capitalists were earning too much of the profits. The peasants saw their grain exports and tax payments finance development that did not measurably improve their lot. A small but significant industrial proletariat arose. At the turn of the century there were approximately three million factory workers in Russia. Their working and living conditions were very bad by any standard. They enjoyed little state protection, and trade unions were illegal. In 1897 Witte did enact a measure providing for an $11\frac{1}{2}$-hour workday. But needless to say, discontent and strikes continued.

The economic development was accompanied by new political departures. In 1901 the Social Revolutionary Party was founded. Its members and intellectual roots went back to the Populists of the seventies. The party was opposed to industrialism and looked to the communal life of rural Russia as a model for the future. In 1903 the Constitutional Democratic Party, or Cadets, was formed. They were liberal in outlook and were drawn from people who participated in the local *zemstvos*. They wanted a parliamentary regime with responsible ministries, civil liberties, and economic progress. The Cadets hoped to model themselves on the liberal parties of western Europe.

LENIN'S EARLY THOUGHT AND CAREER. The situation for Russian socialists differed radically from that in other major European countries. Russia had no representative institutions and only a small working class. The compromises and accommodations achieved elsewhere were meaningless in Russia, where socialism in both theory and practice had to be revolutionary. The Russian Social Democratic Party had been established in 1898, but the repressive policies of the tsarist regime meant that the party had to function in exile. It was Marxist and greatly admired the German Social Democratic Party.

The leading late nineteenth-century Russian Marxist

was Gregory Plekhanov (1857–1918), who wrote from his exile in Switzerland. At the turn of the century his chief disciple was Vladimir Illich Ulyanov (1870–1924), who later took the name of Lenin. The future leader of the Communist Revolution had been born in 1870 as the son of a high bureaucrat. His older brother while a student in St. Petersburg had become involved in radical politics. He was arrested for participating in a plot against Alexander III and was executed in 1887. In 1893 Lenin moved to St. Petersburg, where he studied to become a lawyer. Soon he too became drawn to the revolutionary groups among factory workers. He was arrested in 1895 and exiled to Siberia. In 1900, after his release, Lenin left Russia for the West. He spent most of the next eighteen years in Switzerland.

Once in Switzerland Lenin became deeply involved in the organizational and policy disputes of the exiled Russian Social Democrats. They all considered themselves Marxists, but they held differing positions on the proper nature of a Marxist revolution in primarily rural Russia and on the structure of their own party. Unlike the backward-looking Social Revolutionaries, the Social Democrats were modernizers who favored further industrial development. The majority believed that Russia must develop a large proletariat before the revolution could come. This same majority hoped to mold a mass political party like the German SPD.

Lenin dissented from both positions. In *What Is To Be Done?* (1902) he condemned any accommodations, such as those practiced by the German SPD. He also criticized trade unionism that settled for short-term gains rather than true revolutionary change for the working class. Lenin further rejected the concept of a mass party composed of workers. Revolutionary consciousness would not arise spontaneously from the working class. It must be carried to them by "people who make revolutionary activity their profession."[2] Only a small elite party would

possess the proper dedication to revolution and be able to resist penetration by police spies. The guiding principle of that party should be "the strictest secrecy, the strictest selection of members, and the training of professional revolutionaries."[3]

In 1903, at the London Congress of the Russian Social Democratic Party, Lenin forced a split in party ranks. The more moderate democratic revolutionary faction became known as the *Mensheviks,* or "minority," although they really constituted a majority of the congress. Lenin's faction assumed the name *Bolsheviks,* meaning "majority." In 1912 the Bolsheviks organized separately. In 1905 Lenin complemented his organizational theory with a program for revolution in Russia. *Two Tactics of Social Democracy in the Bourgeois-Democratic Revolution* urged that the socialist revolution unite the proletariat and the peasants. Lenin grasped better than any other revolutionary the profound discontent in the Russian countryside. He knew that an alliance of workers and peasants in rebellion probably could not be suppressed. Lenin's two principles of an elite party and a dual social revolution allowed the Bolsheviks in late 1917 to capture leadership of the Russian Revolution and to transform the political face of the modern world.

THE REVOLUTION OF 1905 AND ITS AFTERMATH. The quarrels among the Russian socialists and Lenin's doctrines had no immediate influence on events in their country itself. Industrialization proceeded and continued to stir resentment in many sectors. In 1903 Nicholas II dismissed Witte in hope of quelling the criticism. The next year Russia went to war with Japan, partly in expectation that public opinion would rally to the tsar. However, the result was Russian defeat and political crisis. The Japanese captured Port Arthur early in 1905. A few days later, on January 22, a priest named Father Gapon led several hundred workers to present a petition to the tsar for the improvement of industrial life. As the petitioners approached the Winter Palace in St. Petersburg, the tsar's troops opened fire. About one hundred

2 Quoted in Albert Fried and Ronald Sanders (Eds.), *Socialist Thought: A Documentary History* (Garden City, N.Y.: Anchor Doubleday, 1964), p. 459.

3 Ibid., p. 468.

people were shot down in cold blood, and many more were wounded. Never again would the Russian people see the tsar as their protector and "little father."

During the next ten months revolutionary disturbances spread throughout Russia. Sailors mutinied. Peasant revolts erupted, and property was attacked. The uncle of Nicholas II was assassinated. Liberal Constitutional Democrat leaders from the *zemstvos* demanded political reform. Student strikes occurred in the universities. Social Revolutionaries and Social Democrats were active among urban working groups. In early October 1905 strikes broke out in St. Petersburg, and for all practical purposes worker groups called *soviets* controlled the city. Nicholas II recalled Witte and issued the October Manifesto, which promised Russia constitutional government.

Early in 1906 Nicholas II announced the election of a Duma with two chambers. However, he reserved to himself the appointment of ministers, financial policy, military matters, and foreign affairs. The April elections returned a very radical group of representatives. The tsar dismissed Witte and replaced him with P. A. Stolypin (1862–1911), who had little sympathy for parliamentary government. Within four months Stolypin persuaded Nicholas to dissolve the Duma. A second assembly was elected in February 1907. Again cooperation proved impossible, and dissolution came in June of that year. The tsar then changed the franchise to ensure a conservative parliament. The third Duma elected on the new basis in late 1907 proved sufficiently pliable for the tsar and his minister. Thus within two years of the 1905 Revolution, Nicholas II had recaptured much of the ground he had conceded.

Stolypin set about repressing rebellion, removing some causes of the revolt, and rallying property owners behind the tsarist regime. Early in 1907 special field courts-martial tried rebellious peasants, with almost seven hundred executions resulting. Before turning to this repression, the minister had canceled the redemptive payments that peasants still owed to the government from the emancipation of the serfs in 1861. This step, undertaken in

Russian Workers Attempt to Present a Petition to the Tsar

Growing unrest in Russia led, among other things, to organization in 1903 of the Assembly of Russian Factory and Mill Workers of St. Petersburg under a priest, Father Gapon. On January 22, 1905 the Assembly was able to muster a large crowd of workers to converge on Tsar Nicholas II's Winter Palace in the hope of peacefully presenting a petition detailing urban grievances and outlining a program of widespread industrial, political, and economic reform. Rather than allow access to the tsar, security forces, commanded by the tsar's uncle, fired on the crowd. This is the petition's preamble.

WE, WORKING *men and inhabitants of St. Petersburg of various classes, our wives and our children and our helpless old parents, come to Thee, Sire, to seek for truth and defence. We have become beggars; we have been oppressed; we are burdened by toil beyond our powers; we are scoffed at; we are not recognized as human beings; we are treated as slaves who must suffer their bitter fate and who must keep silence. We suffered, but we are pushed farther into the den of beggary, lawlessness, and ignorance. We are choked by despotism and irresponsibility, and we are breathless. . . . The first request which we made was that our masters should discuss our needs with us; but this they refused, on the ground that no right to make this request is recognized by law. They also declared to be illegal our requests to diminish the working hours to eight hours daily, to agree with us about the prices for our work, to consider our misunderstandings with the inferior administration of the mills, to increase the wages for the labour of women and of general labourers, so that the minimum daily wage should be one ruble per day, to abolish overtime work, to give us medical attention without insulting us, to arrange the workshops so that it might be possible to work there, and not find in them death from awful draughts and from rain and snow. All these requests appeared to be, in the opinion of our masters and of the factory and mill administrations, illegal. Everyone of our requests was a crime, and the desire to improve our condition was regarded by them as impertinence, and as offensive to them.*

. . . In reality in us, as in all Russian people, there is not recognized any human right, not even the right of speaking, thinking, meeting, discussing our needs, taking measures for the improvement of our condition.

James Mavor, *An Economic History of Russia* (London: J. M. Dent & Sons, 1914), pp. 469–470.

On "Bloody Sunday," January 22, 1905, troops of Tsar Nicholas II fired on a peaceful procession of workers who sought to present a petition at the Winter Palace in St. Petersburg. After this day there was little chance that the Russian working class could be reconciled with the existing government. [*Soviet Life* from Sovfoto.]

Grigori Rasputin was the sinister Russian monk who claimed the power to heal the ill son of Tsar Nicholas II and acquired great influence at court. His presence alienated many politically important persons from support of Nicholas. Rasputin was finally assassinated by a group of Russian noblemen. [The Granger Collection.]

November 1906, was part of a more general policy to eradicate communal land ownership. The peasants were encouraged to assume individual proprietorship of their land holdings and to abandon the communal system associated with the *mirs*. Stolypin believed that farmers working for themselves would be more productive. Agriculture did improve through this policy and through instruction of the peasants in better farming methods. The very small peasant proprietors who sold their land increased the size of the industrial labor force.

Russian moderate liberals who sat in the Duma approved of the new land measures. They liked the idea of competition and individual property ownership. The Constitutional Democrats wanted a more genuinely parliamentary mode of government, but they compromised out of fear of new revolutionary disturbances. There still existed widespread hatred of Stolypin among the older conservative groups in the country. The industrial workers were antagonistic to the tsar. In 1911 Stolypin was shot by a Social Revolutionary, who may have been a police agent in the pay of conservatives. Nicholas II found no worthy successor. His government simply continued to muddle along. At court the monk Grigori Efimovich Rasputin (1871?–1916) came into ascendancy because of his alleged power to heal the tsar's hemophelic son. The undue influence of this strange and uncouth man, the continued social discontent, and the conservative resistance rendered the position and policy of the tsar uncertain after 1911. Once again, as in 1904, he and his ministers thought that some bold move on the diplomatic front might bring the regime the broad popular support that it so desperately needed.

The domestic political situation in Russia was only the most extreme version of a pattern that appeared in several of the major European states. Potential or actual political and social unrest existed in Great Britain, France, Germany, Austria, and Russia. It was not at all certain that moderate political concessions could quiet the unrest of the working classes. Conservative governments were looking for some means whereby they might overcome social divisions and avoid further social change and revolution. From the French Revolution onward, war had been the one vehicle that had overcome the social and political cleavages in nations. It would be incorrect to say that this desire for national unity led governments to adopt war policies in 1914, but those anxieties may have made them less eager to turn back from the wider conflict. In other words, the social problems experienced by the major governments of Europe were closely related to their diplomatic policy.

SUGGESTED READINGS

A. ASHWORTH, *A Short History of the International Economy Since 1850*, rev. ed. (1967). An introductory survey.

R. E. CAMERON, *France and the Industrial Development of Europe, 1800–1914*, rev. ed. (1968). The best treatment of the subject.

C. M. CIPOLLA, *The Economic History of World Population* (1962). A basic introduction.

P. Gay, *The Dilemma of Democratic Socialism: Eduard Bernstein's Challenge to Marx* (1952). A clear presentation of the problems raised by Bernstein's revisionism.

H. Goldby, *A Life of Jean Jaurés* (1962). A splendid biography that explains the problems of the French socialists.

O. J. Hale, *The Great Illusion, 1901–1914* (1971). An excellent treatment based on the most recent scholarship.

S. Harcave, *First Blood: The Russian Revolution of 1905* (1964). A useful introduction.

C. J. H. Hayes, *A Generation of Materialism, 1871–1900* (1941). A classic account of the close of the century.

W. Henderson, *The Rise of German Industrial Power* (1976). A straightforward account.

E. J. Hobsbawm, *The Age of Capital* (1975). Explores the consolidation of middle-class life after 1850.

L. Jenks, *The Migration of British Capital to 1875* (1927). The basic discussion of a key topic in European economic history.

J. Joll, *The Second International* (1954). A straightforward treatment of the divisions among socialists before World War I.

D. Landes, *The Unbound Prometheus: Technological Change and Industrial Development in Western Europe from 1750 to the Present* (1969). Includes excellent discussions of late-century development.

G. Lichtheim, *Marxism: An Historical and Critical Study* (1961). Perhaps the clearest one-volume discussion of the development of Marxist thought.

A. H. McBriar, *Fabian Socialism and English Politics, 1884–1918* (1962). The standard discussion.

H. Moller (Ed.), *Population Movements in Modern European History* (1964). A collection of helpful and important articles.

H. Pelling, *The Origins of the Labour Party, 1880–1900* (1965). Examines the sources of the party in the activities of British socialists and trade unionists.

C. E. Schorske, *German Social Democracy, 1907–1917* (1955). A brilliant study of the difficulties of the Social Democrats under the empire.

A. B. Ullam, *The Bolsheviks: The Intellectual and Political History of the Triumph of Communism in Russia* (1965). Early chapters discuss prewar developments and the formation of Lenin's doctrines.

T. H. Von Laue, *Sergei Witte and the Industrialization of Russia* (1963). A useful account of the last great minister of tsarist Russia.

ON

THE ORIGIN OF SPECIES.

BY MEANS OF NATURAL SELECTION,

OR THE

PRESERVATION OF FAVOURED RACES IN THE STRUGGLE FOR LIFE.

By CHARLES DARWIN, M.A.,

FELLOW OF THE ROYAL, GEOLOGICAL, LINNÆAN, ETC., SOCIETIES;
AUTHOR OF ' JOURNAL OF RESEARCHES DURING H. M. S. BEAGLE'S VOYAGE
ROUND THE WORLD.'

LONDON:
JOHN MURRAY, ALBEMARLE STREET.
1859.

29
The Birth of
Contemporary European Thought

Uring the same period that the modern nation state developed and the Second Industrial Revolution laid the foundations for the modern material life style, the contours of the European mind assumed what has become a familiar cast. Like previous intellectual changes, these arose from earlier patterns of thought. The Enlightenment provided late nineteenth-century Europeans with a heritage of rationalism, toleration, cosmopolitanism, and appreciation for science. Romanticism led them to value the feelings, imagination, national identity, and the autonomy of the artistic experience. By 1900 these strands of thought had become woven into a new fabric. Many of the traditional intellectual signposts were disappearing. The death of God had been proclaimed. Christianity had undergone the most severe attack in its history. The picture of the physical world that had dominated since Newton underwent major modification. The work of Darwin and Freud challenged the special place Western thinkers had assigned to humankind. The value long ascribed to rationality became questioned. The political and humanitarian ideals of liberalism and socialism for a time gave way to new aggressive nationalism. At the turn of the century European intellectuals were more daring than ever before, but they were also probably less certain and less optimistic.

Charles Darwin's *On the Origin of Species* revolutionized thought about the character and development of living organisms. As the subtitle indicates, struggle came to be seen as taking place throughout all the natural world; and validly or not this idea was soon picked up by some social scientists for use in their fields. Darwin had drafted an essay on the origin of species as early as 1842 but long hesitated to publish. He completed his final version only after learning that Alfred Russel Wallace had independently reached the same conclusions. This is the title page of his epoch-making work's first edition.

The New Reading Public

The social context of intellectual life changed in the last half of the nineteenth century. For the first time in Europe a mass reading public came into existence. In 1850 approximately half the population of western Europe and a much higher proportion of Russians were illiterate. Even those people who might technically be capable of reading and writing did so very poorly. The literacy of the Continent improved steadily, as from the sixties onward one government after another undertook state-financed education. Hungary provided elementary education in 1868; Britain, in 1870; Switzerland, in 1874; Italy, in 1877; and France, between 1878 and 1881. The already advanced education system of Prussia was extended in various ways throughout the German Empire after 1871. The attack on illiteracy proved most successful in Britain, France, Belgium, the Netherlands, Germany, and Scandinavia, where by 1900 approximately 85 per cent or more of the people could read. Italy, Spain, Russia, Austria–Hungary, and the Balkans lagged well behind, with illiteracy rates of between 30 and 60 percent.

The new primary education in the basic skills of reading and writing and elementary arithmetic both reflected and generated social change. Both liberals and conservatives regarded such minimal training as necessary for orderly political behavior on the part of the newly enfranchised voters. There was also hope that literacy might help the poor to help themselves and to create a better, more productive labor force. This side of the educational crusade embodied the rationalist faith that right knowledge will lead to right action. However, literacy and its extension soon became forces in their own right. The schoolteaching profession grew rapidly in numbers and prestige. Those people who learned to read the little they were taught could continue to read much more on their own. They soon discovered that the education that led to better jobs and political influence was still open only to those who could afford it. Having created systems of primary education, the major nations had to give further attention to secondary education by the time of World War I. In yet another generation the question would become one of democratic university instruction.

The expanding literate population created a vast market for new reading material. There was nothing less than an explosion of printed matter. Advances in printing and paper technology lowered production costs. The number of newspapers, books, quantities of editions, and libraries grew rapidly. Cheap mass-circulation newspapers, such as *Le Petit Journal* of Paris and the *Daily Mail* and *Daily Express* of London, enjoyed their first heyday. Newspapers with very specialized political or religious viewpoints were also published. The number of monthly and quarterly journals for families, women, and free-thinking intellectuals increased. Probably more people with more different kinds of ideas could get into print in the late nineteenth century than ever before in European history. And more people could read their ideas than ever before.

The quantity of readers and reading material did not ensure quality. The cheap newspapers prospered on sensational crimes, political scandal, and pages of advertising. Religious journals depended upon denominational bigotry. A brisk market existed for pornography. There was much cutthroat journalism as portrayed in George Gissing's (1857–1903) novel, *New Grub Street* (1892). Newspapers became major factors in the emerging mass politics. The news could be managed, but in central Europe more often by the government censor than by the publisher. Editorials appeared on the front page.

The mass audience and the new literary world created problems for the literary artist. Much of the contempt for democracy and for the "people" found in late nineteenth-century literature arose in reaction to the recently established conditions for publication. The new sense of distance between the artist and his public was in part a result of the changed character of the literate public. As publishers sought to make profits, they often feared offending the sensibilities of their potential readership.

Some writers accepted this situation and happily wrote harmless verbiage that supported current moral and political opinion. Others, such as Matthew Arnold (1822–1888), worked to raise the level of popular taste. Still others, such as the French novelist Émile Zola (1840–1902), self-consciously offended the values of their readers. These anxieties and tensions were closely related to writers' criticism of democracy, and the artist and his middle-class audience became the subjects of novels, such as James Joyce's (1882–1941) *Portrait of the Artist As a Young Man* (1914).

Because many of the new readers were only marginally literate and still quite ignorant on many scores, the books and journals catering to them seemed and often were thoroughly mediocre. Social and artistic critics were correct in pointing out this low level of public taste. Nevertheless the new education, the new readers, and the hundreds of new books and journals permitted a monumental popularization of knowledge that has become a hallmark of the contemporary world. The new literacy was the intellectual equivalent of the railroad and the steamship. People could leave their original intellectual surroundings.

Literacy is not an end in itself. It leads to other skills and the acquisition of other knowledge. People who can read may not necessarily change their world for the better, but they have a better chance to do so than those who remain illiterate.

Science at Mid-Century

In about 1850 Voltaire would still have felt at home in a general discussion of scientific concepts. The basic Newtonian picture of physical nature that he had popularized still prevailed. Scientists continued to believe that nature operated as a vast machine according to mechanical principles. During the first half of the century mechanistic explanation had been extended into several important areas. John Dalton (1766–1844) had formulated the modern theory of chemical composition. However, at

The geological theories of Sir Charles Lyell vastly expanded human understanding of the age of the earth and of the natural—and continuing—processes that have formed its geography. [Culver Pictures.]

BELOW, TOP: Charles Darwin, here portrayed at the age of forty, was the co-discoverer of the principle of evolution through natural selection. [Sidney W. Fox and Klaus Dose, *Molecular Evolution and the Origin of Life.* San Francisco: W. H. Freeman and Company. Copyright © 1972.]

BELOW, BOTTOM: Alfred Russel Wallace, here photographed in his later years, also came upon the principle of evolution by natural selection while working independently from Darwin. [The Granger Collection.]

mid-century and long thereafter atoms and molecules were considered to resemble billiard balls. During the 1840s several independent researchers had arrived at the concept of the conservation of energy, according to which energy is never lost in the universe but is simply transformed from one form to another. The principles of mechanism had been extended to geology through the work of Charles Lyell (1797–1875), whose *Principles of Geology* (1830) postulated that various changes in geological formation were the result of the mechanistic operation of natural causes over great spans of time.

At mid-century the physical world was thus regarded as rational, mechanical, and dependable. Its laws could be ascertained objectively through experiment and observation. Scientific theory purportedly described physical nature as it really existed. Moreover practically all scientists also believed like Newton and the Deists of the eighteenth century that their knowledge of nature demonstrated the existence of a God or a Supreme Being.

Darwin

In 1859 Charles Darwin (1809–1882) published *The Origin of Species,* which carried the mechanical interpretation of physical nature into the world of living things. The book proved to be one of the seminal works of Western thought and earned Darwin the honor of being regarded as the Newton of biology. Both Darwin and his book have been much misunderstood. He did not originate the concept of evolution, which had been discussed widely before he wrote. What he and Alfred Russel Wallace (1823–1913) did, working independently, was to formulate the principle of natural selection, which explained how species had changed or evolved over time. Earlier writers had believed that evolution might occur; Darwin and Wallace explained how it could occur.

Drawing upon Malthus, the two scientists contended that more seeds and living organisms came into existence than could survive in their environment. Those organisms possessing some marginal advantage in the struggle for existence lived long enough to propagate their kind. This

The Thinker, by the French sculptor Auguste Rodin (1840–1917), was completed in the late nineteenth century. The face and other physical features suggest one aspect of the impact of Darwinian thought, which taught that humankind developed from earlier forms of life, while the pose and serious expression affirm that despite lowly origins humankind is composed of thinking, rational creatures. [Bettmann Archive.]

principle of survival of the fittest Darwin called *natural selection*. The principle was naturalistic and mechanistic. Its operation required no guiding mind behind the development and change in organic nature. What neither Darwin nor anyone else in his day could explain was the origin of those chance variations that provided some living things with the marginal chance for survival. Only when the work of the Austrian monk Gregor Mendel (1822–1884) received public attention after 1900, several years following his death, did the mystery of heredity begin to be unraveled.

Darwin's and Wallace's theory represented the triumph of naturalistic explanation, which removed the idea of purpose from organic nature. Eyes were not made for seeing according to the rational wisdom and purpose of God but had developed mechanistically over the course of time. In this manner the theory of evolution through natural selection not only contradicted the biblical narrative of creation but also undermined the Deistic argument for the existence of God from the design of the universe. Moreover Darwin's work undermined the whole concept of fixity in nature or the universe at large. The world was a realm of flux and change. The fact that physical and organic nature might be constantly changing allowed people in the late nineteenth century to believe that society, values, customs, and beliefs should also change.

In 1871 Darwin carried his work a step further. In *The Descent of Man* he applied the principle of evolution by natural selection to human beings. Darwin was hardly the first person to treat human beings as animals, but his arguments brought greater plausibility to that point of view. He contended that humankind's moral nature and religious sentiments, as well as their physical frame, had developed naturalistically in response largely to the requirements of survival. Neither the origin nor the character of humankind on earth required the existence or role of God for their explanation. Not since Copernicus had removed the earth from the center of the universe had the pride of Western human beings received so sharp a blow.

The Prestige of Science

Darwin's ideas remained highly controversial. They were widely debated in popular and scientific journals. He changed some of them in the course of his writings. However, at issue was not only the correctness of the theory and the place of humankind in nature but also the role of science and scientists in society. The prestige of Darwin's achievement, progress in medicine, and the links of science to the technology of the Second Industrial Revolution made the general European public aware of science as never before. The British Fabian Socialist Beatrice Webb recalled from her youth:

Who will deny that the men of science were the leading British intellectuals of that period; that it was they who stood out as men of genius with international reputations; that it was they who were the self-confident militants of the period; that it was they who were routing the theologians, confounding the mystics, imposing their theories on philosophers, their inventions on capitalists, and their discoveries on medical men; whilst they were at the same time snubbing the artists, ignoring the poets, and even casting doubts on the capacity of the politicians?[1]

Contemporaries spoke of a religion of science that would explain all without resort to supernaturalism. Popularizers, such as Thomas Henry Huxley (1825–1895) and John Tyndall (1820–1893) in Britain and Ernst Haeckel (1834–1919) in Germany, wrote and lectured widely on scientific topics. They urged that science held the answer to the major questions of life and government. They worked for government support of scientific research and for inclusion of science in the schools and universities.

Scientific knowledge and theories became models for thought in other fields. The French philosopher Auguste

1 Beatrice Webb, *My Apprenticeship* (London: Longmans, Green, and Co., 1926), pp. 130–131.

Auguste Comte was the founder of Positivism. He urged that all knowledge be modeled on the empirical knowledge of science. Because he wanted the understanding of human society to assume a scientific character, he is often regarded as the founder of sociology. [French Cultural Services, New York.]

Comte (1798–1857), a late child of the Enlightenment and a onetime follower of Saint-Simon, developed a philosophy of human intellectual development that culminated in science. In *The Positive Philosophy* (1830–1842) Comte argued that human thought had gone through three stages of development. In the theological stage, physical nature was explained in terms of the action of divinities or spirits. In the second or metaphysical stage, abstract principles became regarded as the operative agencies of nature. In the final or positive stage, explanations of nature became matters of exact description of phenomena, without recourse to an unobservable operative principle. Physical science had, in Comte's view, entered the positive stage, and similar thinking should penetrate other areas of analysis. In particular Comte thought that positive laws of social behavior could be discovered in the same fashion as laws of physical nature. For this reason he is generally regarded as the father of sociology. Works like Comte's helped to convince learned Europeans that genuine knowledge in any area must resemble scientific knowledge. This belief had its roots in the Enlightenment and continues to permeate Western thought to the present day.

Theories of ethics became modeled upon science during the last half of the century. The concept of the struggle for survival was widely applied to human social relationships. The phrase "struggle for survival" predated Darwin and reflected the competitive outlook of classical economics. Darwin's use of the phrase gave it the prestige associated with advanced science.

The most famous advocate of evolutionary ethics was Herbert Spencer (1820–1903), the British philosopher. Spencer, a strong individualist, believed that human society progressed through competition. If the weak received too much protection, the rest of humankind was the loser. In Spencer's work, struggle against one's fellow human beings became a kind of ethical imperative. The concept could be applied to justify the avoidance of aiding the poor and the working class or to justify the domination of colonial peoples or to urge aggressively competitive rela-

tionships among nations. Evolutionary ethics often came very close to saying that might makes right.

Interestingly enough, one of the chief opponents of such thinking was Thomas Henry Huxley, the great defender of Darwin. In 1893 Huxley declared that the physical cosmic process of evolution was at odds with the process of human ethical development. The struggle in nature held no ethical implications except to demonstrate how human beings should not behave.

Scientific thought even affected the way in which authors wrote novels. The movement to literary realism, which is considered more fully later in this chapter, was a product of the influence of science. Certain writers wanted to portray the world as they observed it. In France, Gustave Flaubert's (1821–1880) *Madame Bovary* (1857); in England, George Eliot's (1819–1880) *Adam Bede* (1859); and in Russia, Ivan Turgenev's (1818–1883) *A Sportsman's Sketches* (1852) paid new attention to minute physical and natural details. Emile Zola (1840–1902) found artistic inspiration in Claude Bernard's (1813–1878) *An Introduction to the Study of Experimental Medicine* (1865). Zola, a French novelist, believed that he could write an experimental novel in which the characters and their actions would be observed and reported upon as the scientist might relate events within a laboratory experiment. Zola and others believed that absolute physical (and psychological) determinism ruled human events, just as in the physical world determinism prevailed.

Scientists and their admirers enjoyed a supreme confidence during the last half of the century. They genuinely believed that they had for all intents and purposes discovered all that might be discovered. The issues for science in the future would be the extension of acknowledged principles and the refinement of measurement. However, the turn of the century held a much more brilliant future for science. That confident, self-satisfied world of late nineteenth-century science and scientism vanished. A much more complicated picture of nature developed. Before examining those new departures, we must see how the cult of science affected religious thought and practice.

Christianity and the Church Under Siege

The nineteenth century was one of the most difficult periods in the history of the organized Christian churches. Many European intellectuals left the faith. The secular, liberal nation states attacked the political and social influence of the church. The expansion of population and the growth of cities challenged its organizational capacity to meet the modern age. Yet during all of this turmoil the Protestant and Catholic churches made considerable headway at the popular level.

The intellectual attack on Christianity arose on the grounds of its historical credibility, its scientific accuracy, and its pronounced morality. The *philosophes* of the Enlightenment had delighted in pointing out contradictions in the Bible. The historical scholarship of the nineteenth century brought new issues to the fore.

In 1835 David Friederich Strauss (1808–1874) published a *Life of Jesus* in which he questioned whether the Bible provided any genuine historical evidence about Jesus. Strauss contended that the story of Jesus was a myth that had arisen from the particular social and intellectual conditions of first-century Palestine. Jesus' character and life represented the aspirations of the people of that time and place rather than events that had occurred. Other skeptical lives of Jesus were written and published elsewhere.

During the second half of the century scholars such as Julius Wellhausen (1844–1918) in Germany, Ernst Renan (1823–1892) in France, and William Robertson Smith (1847–1894) in Great Britain contended that the books of the Bible had been written and revised as the problems of Jewish society and politics changed. They were not inspired books but had, like the Homeric epics, been written by normal human beings in a primitive society. This questioning of the historical validity of the

---

Matthew Arnold Contemplates the Loss of Intellectual Certainties

In this poem, written in 1867, Matthew Arnold (1822–1888) portrays a man and a woman looking across the waters of the English Channel on a moonlit night. The speaker in the poem notes that Sophocles, the ancient Greek dramatist, had drawn lessons about the misery of life from the ebb and flow of the Aegean Sea. The speaker then compares the movement of the sea to the withdrawal of the Christian faith from the lives of nineteenth-century men and women. Finally, he says that the world that seems so beautiful is really a place where there can be no certainty, love, light, or peace. This pessimism reflects the state of mind of many writers who were no longer sure of the truth of the Christian faith.

T*HE sea is calm to-night.*
The tide is full, the moon lies fair
Upon the Straits;—on the French coast the light
Gleams and is gone; the cliffs of England stand,
Glimmering and vast, out in the tranquil bay,
Come to the window, sweet is the night air!
Only, from the long line of spray
Where the sea meets the moon-blanch'd land,
Listen! you hear the grating roar
Of pebbles which the waves draw back, and fling,
At their return, up the high strand,
Begin, and cease, and then again begin,
With tremulous cadence slow, and bring
The eternal note of sadness in.

Sophocles long ago
Heard it on the Aegean, and it brought
Into his mind the turbid ebb and flow
Of human misery; we
Find also in the sound a thought,
Hearing it by this distant northern sea.

The Sea of Faith
Was once, too, at the full, and round earth's shore
Lay like the folds of a bright girdle furl'd.
But now I only hear
Its melancholy, long, withdrawing roar,
Retreating, to the breath
Of the night-wind, down the vast edges drear
And naked shingles of the world.

Ah, love, let us be true
To one another! for the world, which seems
To lie before us like a land of dreams,
So various, so beautiful, so new,

Bible caused more literate men and women to lose faith in Christianity than any other single cause.

The march of science also undermined Christianity. This blow was particularly cruel because eighteenth-century Deists had led Christians to believe that the scientific examination of nature provided a strong buttress for their faith. This belief had been enshrined in works such as William Paley's (1743–1805) *Natural Theology* (1802) and in books by numerous scientists. The geology of Charles Lyell (1797–1875) suggested that the earth was much older than the biblical records contended. By appealing to natural causes to explain floods, mountains, and valleys, Lyell removed the miraculous hand of God from the physical development of the earth. Darwin's theory cast doubt on the doctrine of the Creation. His ideas and those of other writers suggested that the moral nature of humankind could be explained without appeal to the role of God. Finally, anthropologists, psychologists, and sociologists suggested that religion itself and the religious sentiments were just one more set of natural phenomena.

Other intellectuals questioned the morality of Christianity. The old issue of immoral biblical stories was again raised. Much more important, the moral character of the Old Testament God came under fire. His cruelty and unpredictability did not fit well with the progressive, tolerant, rational values of liberals. They also wondered about the morality of the New Testament God, who would sacrifice to his own satisfaction the only perfect being ever to walk the earth. Many clergymen began to ask themselves if they could honestly preach doctrines they felt to be immoral.

During the last quarter of the century this moral attack on Christianity came from another direction. Writers like Friederich Nietzsche (1844–1900) in Germany portrayed Christianity as a religion of sheep that glorified weakness rather than the strength that life required. Christianity demanded a useless and debilitating sacrifice of the flesh and spirit rather than full-blooded heroic living and daring. Nietzsche once observed, "War and courage have accomplished more great things than love of neighbor." [2]

These widespread skeptical intellectual currents seem to have directly influenced only the upper levels of educated society. Yet they created a climate in which Christianity lost much of its intellectual respectability. Fewer educated people became clergymen. More and more people found that they could lead their lives with little or no reference to Christianity. The secularism of everyday life proved as harmful to the faith as the direct attacks. This situation especially prevailed in the cities, which were growing faster than the capacity of the churches to meet the challenge. There was not even enough room in urban churches for the potential worshipers to sit. Whole generations of urban poor grew up with little or no experience with the church as an institution or with Christianity as a religious faith.

Conflict of Church and State

The secular state of the nineteenth century clashed with both the Protestant and the Roman Catholic churches. Liberals generally disliked the dogma and political privileges of the established churches. National states were often suspicious of the supranational character

2 Walter Kaufman (Ed. and Trans.), *The Portable Nietzsche* (New York: Viking, 1967), p. 159.

of the Roman Catholic Church. However, the primary area for conflict between the state and the churches was the expanding systems of education. The churches feared that future generations would emerge from the schools without the rudiments of religious teaching. The advocates of secular education feared the production of future generations more loyal to religion or the church than to the nation. From 1870 through the turn of the century the issue of religious education was heatedly debated in every major country.

GREAT BRITAIN. In Great Britain the Education Act of 1870 provided for the construction of state supported-school-board schools. They were to be built in areas where the religious denominations failed to provide satisfactory education. There was rivalry not only between the Anglican Church and the state but also between the Anglican Church and the Nonconformist denominations. There was intense local hostility among all these groups. The churches of all denominations had to oppose improvements in education because these increased the costs of their own schools. In the Education Act of 1902 the government decided to provide state support for both religious and nonreligious schools but imposed the same standards on each.

FRANCE. The British conflict was relatively calm compared to that in France, where there existed a dual system of Catholic and public schools. Under the Falloux Law of 1850 the local priest provided religious education in the public schools. The very conservative French Catholic Church and the Third French Republic were mutually hostile to each other. Between 1878 and 1886 the government passed a series of educational laws sponsored by Jules Ferry (1832–1893). The Ferry Laws replaced religious instruction in the public schools with civic training. Members of religious orders were no longer permitted to teach in the public schools, the number of which was to be expanded. After the Dreyfus affair the French Catholic Church again paid a price for its reactionary politics. The religious orders were sup-

pressed. In 1905 the Napoleonic Concordat was terminated, and Church and State were totally separated.

GERMANY AND THE *KULTURKAMPF*. The most extreme example of Church–State conflict occurred in Germany during the 1870s. At the time of unification the German Catholic hierarchy had wanted freedom for the churches guaranteed in the constitution. Bismarck left the matter to the discretion of each federal state, but he soon felt the activity of the Roman Catholic Church and the Catholic Center Party to be a threat to the new state. Through administrative orders in 1870 and 1871 Bismarck removed both Catholic and Protestant clergy from overseeing local education and set education under state direction. The secularization of education was merely the beginning of a concerted attack on the independence of the Catholic Church in Germany.

The "May Laws" of 1873 required German priests to have attended German schools and universities and to pass state-administered examinations. The state could veto appointments of priests. The disciplinary power of the pope and the church over the clergy was abolished and transferred to the state. When the bishops and many of the clergy refused to obey these laws, Bismarck used the police against them. In 1876 he had either arrested or driven from the country all the Catholic bishops. In the end Bismarck's *Kulturkampf* ("cultural struggle") against the Catholic Church failed. Not for the first time Christian martyrs had aided resistance to persecution. By the close of the decade the chancellor had abandoned his attack. He had gained only state control of education and civil laws governing marriage at the price of lingering Catholic resentment against the German Empire. The *Kulturkampf* was probably the greatest blunder of Bismarck's career.

AREAS OF RELIGIOUS REVIVAL. The successful German Catholic resistance to the intrusions of the secular state illustrates the continuing vitality of Christianity during this period of intellectual and political hardship. In Great Britain both the Anglican Church and the Non-

conformist denominations experienced considerable growth in membership. Vast sums of money were raised for new churches and schools. In Ireland the seventies saw a widespread Catholic devotional revival. Priests in France after the defeat by Prussia organized special pilgrimages by trains for thousands of penitents who believed that France had lost because of their sins. The cult of the miracles of Lourdes originated during these years. There were efforts by churches of all denominations to give more attention to the urban poor.

In effect, the last half of the nineteenth century witnessed the final great effort to Christianize Europe. It was well organized, well led, and well financed. It failed not from want of effort but rather because the population had simply outstripped the resources of the churches. This persistent liveliness of the church accounts in part for the intense hostility of its enemies.

The Roman Catholic Church and the Modern World

Perhaps the most striking feature of this religious revival amidst turmoil and persecution was the resilience of the papacy. The brief hope for a liberal pontificate from Pope Pius IX (1846–1878) vanished on the night in 1848 when he fled the turmoil in Rome. In the sixties Pius IX, embittered by the mode of Italian unification, launched a counteroffensive against liberalism in thought and deed. In 1864 he issued the *Syllabus of Errors,* which condemned all the major tenets of political liberalism and modern thought. He set the Roman Catholic Church squarely against the worlds of contemporary science, philosophy, and politics. In 1869 the pope called into session the First Vatican Council of the church. The next year, through the political manipulations of the pontiff and against much opposition from numerous members, the council promulgated the dogma of the infallibility of the pope when speaking officially on matters of faith and morals. No earlier pope had gone so far. The First Vatican Council came to a close in 1870, when Italian troops invaded Rome at the outbreak of the Franco-Prussian War.

The First Vatican Council met in 1869–1870 and proclaimed the dogma of the pope's infallibility when speaking in his official position on matters of faith and morals. This event marked the high water mark of papal influence in the Roman Catholic Church. The council was the first general one of the church since that at Trent in the sixteenth century. As shown in this painting from the Vatican, its main sessions took place in one of the transepts of Saint Peter's in Rome, with Pope Pius IX presiding. [Archivio Fotografico, Musei Vaticani.]

Pius IX died in 1878 and was succeeded by Leo XIII (1878–1903). The new pope, who was sixty-eight years old at the time of his election, sought to make accommodation with the modern age and to address the great social questions. He looked to the philosophical tradition of Thomas Aquinas to reconcile the claims of faith and reason. His encyclicals of 1888 and 1890 permitted Catholics to participate in the politics of liberal states.

Leo XIII's most important pronouncement on public issues was the encyclical *Rerum Novarum* (1891). In that document Leo XIII defended private property, religious education, and religious control of marriage laws, and he condemned socialism and Marxism. However, he also declared that employers should treat their employees justly, pay them proper wages, and permit them to organize labor unions. He supported laws and regulations to protect the conditions of labor. The Pope urged that modern society be organized according to corporate groups, including people from various classes, which might cooperate according to Christian principles. The corporate society, derivative of medieval social organization, was to be an alternative to both competitive capitalism and socialism. On the basis of Leo XIII's pronouncements democratic Catholic parties and Catholic trade unions were founded throughout Europe.

The emphasis of Pius X, who reigned from 1903 to 1914 and who has been proclaimed a saint, was intellectually reactionary. He hoped to restore traditional devo-

Leo XIII Considers the Social Question in European Politics

In this 1891 encyclical Pope Leo XIII addressed the social question in European politics. It was the answer of the Catholic Church to secular calls for social reforms. The pope denied the socialist claim that class conflict was the natural state of affairs. He urged employers to seek just and peaceful relations with workers.

THE *great mistake that is made in the matter now under consideration is to possess oneself of the idea that class is naturally hostile to class; that rich and poor are intended by Nature to live at war with one another. So irrational and so false is this view that the exact contrary is the truth. . . . Each requires the other; capital cannot do without labour, nor labour without capital. Mutual agreement results in pleasantness and good order; perpetual conflict necessarily produces confusion and outrage. Now, in preventing such strife as this, and in making it impossible, the efficacy of Christianity is marvellous and manifold. . . . Religion teaches the labouring man and the workman to carry out honestly and well all equitable agreements freely made; never to injure capital, or to outrage the person of an employer; never to employ violence in representing his own cause, or to engage in riot or disorder; and to have nothing to do with men of evil principles, who work upon the people with artful promises and raise foolish hopes which usually end in disaster and in repentance when too late. Religion teaches the rich man and the employer that their work people are not their slaves; that they must respect in every man his dignity as a man and as a Christian; that labour is nothing to be ashamed of, if we listen to right reason and to Christian philosophy, but is an honourable employment, enabling a man to sustain his life in an upright and creditable way; and that it is shameful and inhuman to treat men like chattels to make money by, or to look upon them merely as so much muscle or physical power. Thus, again, Religion teaches that, as among the workman's concerns are Religion herself and things spiritual and mental, the employer is bound to see that he has time for the duties of piety; that he be not exposed to corrupting influences and dangerous occasions; and that he be not led away to neglect his home and family or to squander his wages. Then, again, the employer must never tax his work people beyond their strength, nor employ them in work unsuited to their sex or age. His great and principal obligation is to give every one that which is just.*

F. S. Nitti, *Catholic Socialism*, trans. by Mary Mackintosh (London: S. Sonnenschein & Co., 1895), p. 409.

tional life. Between 1903 and 1907 he condemned Catholic Modernism, a movement of modern biblical criticism within the church, and in 1910 he required an anti-Modernist oath from all priests. By these actions Pius X set the church squarely against the intellectual currents of the day, and the struggle between Catholicism and modern thought continued. However, Pius X did not retreat measurably from the social policy of Leo XIII, so the Catholic Church continued to permit its members active participation in social and political movements.

Pope Leo XIII led the Roman Catholic Church toward a limited recognition of the social and political problems brought on by industrial democracy. His encyclical *Rerum Novarum* was the major statement of the Church on the issues of social justice and class conflict. [Culver Pictures.]

In an early demonstration Roentgen took an X ray of the entire body of a male subject. Note the buckle of his belt, the keys he had attached to the belt, and tacks in the soles and heels of his shoes. [Deutsches Museum, Munich.]

Toward a Twentieth-Century Frame of Mind

World War I is often regarded as the point of departure into the contemporary world. Although this view is possibly true for political and social developments, it is an incorrect assessment for intellectual history. The last quarter of the nineteenth century and the first decade of the twentieth century constitute the crucible of contemporary Western and European thought. During this period the kind of fundamental reassessment that Darwin's work had previously made necessary in biology and in understanding the place of human beings in nature was writ large in other areas of thinking. Philosophers, scientists, psychologists, and novelists began to portray physical reality, human nature, and human society in ways quite different from in the past. Their new concepts challenged the major presuppositions of mid-nineteenth-century science, rationalism, liberalism, and bourgeois morality.

Science: The Revolution in Physics

The modifications in the scientific world view originated within the scientific community itself. By the late 1870s considerable discontent existed over the excessive realism of mid-century science. It became felt that too many scientists believed that their mechanistic models, atoms, and absolute time and space actually described the real universe. In 1883 Ernst Mach (1838–1916) published *The Science of Mechanics,* in which he urged that the concepts of science be considered descriptive not of the physical world but of the sensations experienced by the scientific observer. Science could describe only the sensations, not the physical world that underlay the sensations. In line with Mach, the French scientist and mathematician Henri Poincaré (1854–1912) urged that the concepts and theories of scientists be regarded as hypothetical constructs of the human mind rather than as descriptions of the true state of nature. In 1911 Hans Vaihinger (1852–1933) suggested that the concepts of

The British scientist Ernest Rutherford was one of the first persons to explore the internal structure of the atom. The portrait is a 1932 painting by Oswald Birley. [Culver Pictures.]

Marie Curie (1867–1934), who was born in Poland but worked most of her life in France, was one of the leading figures in the turn-of-the-century advance of physics and chemistry. She is credited with the discovery of radium. [The Granger Collection.]

science be considered "as if" descriptions of the physical world. By World War I few scientists believed any longer that they could portray the "truth" about physical reality. Rather they saw themselves as recording the observations of instruments and as setting forth useful hypothetical or symbolic models of nature.

New discoveries in the laboratory paralleled the philosophical challenge to nineteenth-century science. With those discoveries the comfortable world of supposedly "complete" nineteenth-century physics vanished forever. In December 1895, Wilhelm Roentgen (1845–1923) published a paper on his discovery of X rays, a form of energy that penetrated various opaque materials. The publication of his paper was followed within a matter of months by major steps in the exploration of radioactivity. In 1896 Henri Becquerel (1852–1908), through a series of experiments following upon Roentgen's work, found that uranium emitted a similar form of energy. The next year J. J. Thomson (1856–1940), working in the Cavendish Laboratory of Cambridge University, formulated the theory of the electron. The interior world of the atom had become a new area for human exploration. In 1902 Ernest Rutherford (1871–1937), who had been Thomson's assistant, explained the cause of radiation through

the disintegration of the atoms of radioactive materials. Shortly thereafter he speculated upon the immense store of energy present in the atom.

The discovery of radioactivity and discontent with the existing mechanical models led to revolutionary theories in physics. In 1900 Max Planck (1858–1947) pioneered the articulation of the quantum theory of energy, according to which energy is a series of discrete quantities or packets rather than a continuous stream. In 1905 Albert Einstein (1879–1955) published his first epoch-making papers on relativity. He contended that time and space exist not separately but rather as a combined continuum. Moreover the measurement of space and time depend upon the observer as well as upon the entities being measured. In 1927 Werner Heisenberg (b. 1901) set forth the uncertainty principle, according to which the behavior of subatomic particles is a matter of statistical probability rather than of exactly determinable cause and effect. So much that only fifty years earlier had seemed certain and unquestionable about the physical universe had now once again become problematical.

Nineteen-century popularizers of science had urged its importance as a path to rational living and decision making. By the early twentieth century such optimistic hopes

The work of the German scientist Albert Einstein, who is seen here in a 1934 photograph made during an American lecture, set the fundamental theory of physics in a new direction just after the turn of the century. [Bettmann Archive.]

had been dashed by the developments in the scientific world itself. The mathematical complexity of twentieth-century physics meant that despite valiant efforts science would rarely again be successfully popularized. However, at the same time, through applied technology and further research in physics and medicine, science affected daily living more than ever before in human history. Consequently nonscientists in legal, business, and public life have been called upon to make decisions involving technological matters about which they rarely can or do understand in depth or detail. By the middle of this century some writers—such as the English essayist, novelist, and physicist, C. P. Snow (b. 1905)—spoke of the emergence of "two cultures," one of the scientists and one of literary persons. The problem was establishing ways in which they could communicate meaningfully with each other to address the major problems of human life.

Literature: Realism and Naturalism

Between 1850 and 1914 the moral certainties of learned and middle-class Europeans underwent modifications no less radical than their concepts of the physical universe. The realist movement in literature portrayed the hypocrisy, the physical and psychic brutality, and the dullness that underlay bourgeois life and society. By bringing scientific objectivity and observation to their work, the realist or naturalist writers used the mid-century cult of science so vital to the middle class to confront those same people with the harsh realities of life about them. Realism was a rejection of the romantic idealization of nature, the poor, love, and polite society. Realist novelists portrayed the dark, degraded, and dirty side of life almost, so some people thought, for its own sake.

An earlier generation of writers, including Charles Dickens (1812–1870) and Honoré de Balzac (1799–1850), had portrayed the cruelty of industrial life and of a society based wholly on money. Other authors, such as George Eliot (1819–1880), had paid close attention to the details of the scenes and the characters portrayed.

George Eliot was the pen name of Mary Ann Evans (1819–1880). She was an important English novelist who portrayed the life of the English countryside with much realistic detail. She was also a significant English religious and ethical thinker. [The Granger Collection.]

Émile Zola of France was the master of the realistic novel. Although his depiction of the harsh details of working class and peasant life shocked many of his readers, his novels sold well. Near the close of his life, he became one of the strongest supporters of Captain Alfred Dreyfus and demanded that the President of France seek justice for the military officer. His splendid portrait is by the photographer Nadar. [Bettmann Archive.]

However, there had always been room in their works for the play of the imagination, fancy, and self-conscious artistry. They had felt a better moral world possible. The major figures of late-century realism—Émile Zola (1840–1902), Gustave Flaubert (1821–1880), Ivan Turgenev (1818–1883), Anton Chekhov (1860–1904), Maksim Gorki (1868–1936), Henrik Ibsen (1828–1906), Arnold Bennett (1867–1931), and George Moore (1852–1933)—examined the dreary and unseemly side of life without being certain whether a better life was possible. In good Darwinian fashion they regarded and portrayed human beings as animals, subject to the passions, materialistic determinism, and the pressures of environment like any other animals. However, most of them also saw society itself as perpetuating evil.

Flaubert's *Madame Bovary* (1856), with its story of colorless provincial life and a woman's hapless search for love inside and out of marriage, is often considered the first genuinely realistic novel. It portrayed life without heroism, purpose, or even simple civility.

Nevertheless the author who turned realism into a movement was Émile Zola. As noted earlier, he saw himself as creating human experiments in his novels. He once declared, "I have simply done on living bodies the work of analysis which surgeons perform on corpses." [3] Between 1871 and 1893 Zola published twenty volumes of novels exploring subjects normally untouched by writers. In *L'Assommoir* (1877) he discussed the problem of alchoholism, and in *Nana* (1880) he followed the life of a prostitute. Others of his works considered the defeat of the French army and the social strife arising from attempts at labor organization. Zola refused to turn his pen or his readers' thoughts from the most ugly aspects of life. Nothing in his purview received the light of hope or the aura of romance. Although polite critics faulted his taste and middle-class moralists his subject matter, Zola enjoyed a wide following in France and elsewhere.

3 Quoted in George J. Becker, *Documents of Modern Literary Realism* (Princeton, N.J.: Princeton University Press, 1963), p. 159.

Henrik Ibsen (1828–1906) used his considerable skill as a playwright to probe the hypocrisy of middle class morality and its attitude toward women. [The Granger Collection.]

Virginia Woolf (1882–1941), shown here at age twenty-one, was one of the major voices urging the pursuit of literary and artistic modernism in Great Britain. Her novels constitute one of the monuments of twentieth-century British literature. [The Granger Collection.]

Realism in sculpture, as well as rising awareness of the condition of working people, is represented by the huge Belgian monument to labor by Constantin Émile Meunier (1831–1905). This is a portion of the work dedicated to miners. [Copyright by A. C. L., Brussels.]

784 *The Birth of Contemporary European Thought*

Friedrich Nietzsche became the most influential German philosopher of the late nineteenth century. His books challenged existing morality and demanded a revaluation of values themselves. He has exerted a vast influence on twentieth-century literature and philosophy in both Europe and North America. [The Granger Collection.]

The Norwegian playwright Henrik Ibsen carried realism into the dramatic presentation of domestic life. He sought to achieve new modes of social awareness and to strip away the illusory mask of middle-class morality. His most famous play is *A Doll's House* (1879). Its chief character, Nora, is the spouse of a narrow-minded middle-class husband who cannot tolerate any independence of character or thought on her part. When for the first time she fully confronts this situation, the play ends as she leaves him, slamming the door behind her. In *Ghosts* (1881) a respectable middle-class woman must deal with a son suffering from syphilis inherited from her husband. In *The Master Builder* (1892) an aging architect kills himself while trying to impress a young woman who perhaps loves him. Ibsen's works were extremely controversial. He had dared to strike at sentimentality in life, the female angel of the house, and the cloak of respectability that hung so insecurely over the middle-class family.

One of Ibsen's greatest champions was the Irish writer George Bernard Shaw (1856–1950), who spent much of his life in England. During the late eighties he had vigorously defended Ibsen's work. He went on to make his own realistic onslaught against romanticism and false respectability. In *Mrs. Warren's Profession* (1893), a play long censored in England, he explored the matter of prostitution. In *Arms and the Man* (1894) and *Man and Superman* (1903) he heaped scorn on the romantic ideals of love and war, and in *Androcles and the Lion* (1913) he pilloried Christianity. Shaw added to the impact of his plays by writing long critical prefaces in which he drove home the point of his social criticism.

Realism struck the public ego in another fashion besides presenting unseemly social situations. The realists tended to see humankind as subject, and often helplessly so, to great physical or historical forces of determinism. Throughout *War and Peace* (1869) Leo Tolstoy (1828–1910) pictured his characters as being tossed upon the seas of historical change. The characters of Thomas Hardy's (1840–1928) novels are repeatedly challenged by curious turns of fate. Human beings in such settings could not control their lives and lacked the freedom to make conscious, meaningful moral choices. These characters possessed little or no nobility because the artists who created them had ceased to believe that human beings stood just a little lower than the angels or were creatures fully capable of rational behavior.

These writers and many others believed it the duty of the artist to portray reality and the commonplace. In dissecting what they considered the "real" world, they helped to change the moral perception of the good life. They refused to let existing public opinion dictate the subjects about which they wrote or the manner in which they treated them. By presenting their audiences with unmentionable subjects, they sought to remove the veneer of hypocrisy that had previously forbade such discussion. They hoped to destroy social and moral illusions and to compel the public to confront reality. That change in itself seemed good. However, few of the realist writers who raised the problems had solutions. They often left their readers unable to sustain old values and uncertain about the sources of new ones.

Philosophy: Revolt Against Reason

Within philosophical circles the adequacy of rational thinking to address the human situation was being questioned. No late nineteenth-century writer better exemplified this new attitude than the German philosopher Friedrich Nietzsche (1844–1900), who had been educated as a classicist rather than as an academic philosopher. His books remained unpopular until late in his life, when his brilliance had deteriorated into an almost totally silent insanity. He was a person wholly at odds with the predominant values of the age. At one time or another he attacked Christianity, democracy, nationalism, rationality, science, and progress. He sought less to change values than to probe the very sources of values in the human mind and character. He wanted not only to tear away the masks of respectable life but also to explore the ways in which human beings made such masks.

His first important work was *The Birth of Tragedy* (1872), in which he urged that the nonrational aspects of human nature were as important and noble as the rational characteristics. Here and elsewhere he insisted upon the positive function of instinct and ecstasy in human life. To limit human activity to strictly rational behavior was to impoverish human life and experience. In this work Nietzsche regarded Socrates as one of the major contributors to Western decadence because of the Greek philosopher's appeal for rationality in human affairs. In Nietzsche's view the strength for the heroic life and the highest artistic achievement arose from sources beyond rationality.

In later works, such as the prose poem *Thus Spake Zarathustra* (1883), Nietzsche criticized democracy and Christianity. Both would lead only to the mediocrity of sheepish masses. He announced the death of God and proclaimed the coming of the Overman (*Übermensch*), who would embody heroism and greatness. This latter term was frequently interpreted as some mode of superman or super race, but such was not Nietzsche's intention. He was highly critical of contemporary racism and anti-Semitism. What he sought was a return to the heroism that he associated with Greek life in the Homeric age. He thought that the values of Christianity and of bourgeois morality prevented humankind from achieving life on a heroic level. Those moralities forbade too much of human nature from fulfilling and expressing itself.

Two of Nietzsche's most profound works were *Beyond Good and Evil* (1886) and *The Genealogy of Morals* (1887). Both are difficult books. Much of the former was written in brief, ambiguous aphorisms. Nietzsche sought to discover not what is good and what is evil but rather the social and psychological sources of the judgment of good and evil. He declared, "There are no moral phenomena at all, but only a moral interpretation of phenomena."[4] He dared to raise the question of whether morality itself was valuable: "We need a critique of moral values; the value of these values themselves must first be called in question."[5] In Nietzsche's view the basis of values was not rationality or religion but practicality. Morality was a human convention that had no independent existence apart from humankind. For Nietzsche this discovery did not condemn morality but liberated human beings to create life-affirming instead of life-denying values. Christianity, utilitarianism, and middle-class respectability could in good conscience be abandoned, and human beings could, if they so willed, create a new moral order for themselves.

What Nietzsche said about morality was indicative of what other philosophers were saying about similar subjects. There was a growing tendency to see all conceptual categories as being useful creations rather than exact descriptions.

The American philosopher William James (1842–1910) was one of the most influential figures to question the adequacy of nineteenth-century rationalism and science. He and his philosophy of pragmatism were very influential in Europe. James suggested that the truth of an idea or a description depended primarily upon how well it worked. Knowledge was less an instrument for knowing than for acting.

The most important European philosopher to pursue such lines of thought was the Frenchman Henri Bergson (1859–1941). His most significant works were *Time and Free Will* (1889), *Creative Evolution* (1907), and *Two Sources of Morality and Religion* (1932). Bergson glorified instinct, will, and subjectivism. He regarded human beings as dwelling in a world of becoming, where the only certain thing was their sense of themselves. The world was permeated with a great vital force in which all things to a greater or lesser degree participated. The evolutionary nature of the universe meant that both the knower and the object of knowledge were constantly changing. What Bergson did was to set down much of the thought

---

4 Walter Kaufman (Ed. and Trans.), *The Basic Writings of Nietzsche* (New York: The Modern Library, 1968), p. 275.

5 Ibid., p. 456.

Henri Bergson Criticizes Science and Philosophy

Bergson (1859–1941) was a French philosopher who argued that the knowledge provided by science could not include all of the experiences of life. He thought science could properly examine and explain those natural phenomena that were regular or repetitious in nature; these included molecular action, organic growth, and planetary motion. However, he thought philosophy was required to explain nonrepetitious occurrences such as feelings, dreams, and other subjective experiences.

T*HE essential function of our intellect, as the evolution of life has fashioned it, is to be a light for our conduct, to make ready for our action on things, to foresee, for a given situation, the events, favorable or unfavorable, which may follow thereupon. Intellect therefore instinctively selects in a given situation whatever is like something already known; it seeks this out, in order that it may apply its principle that "like produces like." In just this does the prevision of the future by common sense consist. Science carries this faculty to the highest possible degree of exactitude and precision, but does not alter its essential character. Like ordinary knowledge, in dealing with things science is concerned only with the aspect of* repetition. *Though the whole be original, science will always manage to analyze it into elements or aspects which are approximately a reproduction of the past. Science can work only on what is supposed to repeat itself—that is to say, on what is withdrawn, by hypothesis, from the action of real time. Anything that is irreducible and irreversible in the successive moments of a history eludes science. To get a notion of this irreducibility and irreversibility, we must break with scientific habits which are adapted to the fundamental requirements of thought, we must do violence to the mind, go counter to the natural bent of the intellect. But that is just the function of philosophy.*

Henri Bergson, *Creative Evolution*, trans. by Arthur Mitchell (New York: The Modern Library, 1944), pp. 34–35. First published in 1907.

of earlier mystics in the language of evolutionary science.

In their appeal to the feelings and the emotions and in their questioning of the adequacy of rationalism, these writers drew upon the Romantic tradition. The kind of creative impulse earlier Romantics had considered the gift of artists, these latter writers saw as the burden of all human beings. The character of the human situation that these philosophers urged upon their contemporaries was that of an ever-changing flux in which little or nothing but change itself was permanent. Human beings from their own inner will and determination had to forge the truth and values that were to exist in the world. These philosophies in their impact upon twentieth-century developments threw into doubt not only the rigid domestic and religious morality of the nineteenth century but also the values of toleration, cosmopolitanism, and benevolence that had been championed during the Enlightenment.

The Birth of Psychoanalysis

A determination to probe beneath surface or public appearances united the major figures of late nineteenth-century science, literature, and philosophy. They sought to discern the various undercurrents, tensions, and complexities that lay beneath the smooth, calm surfaces of hard atoms, respectable families, rationality, and social relationships. Their theories and discoveries meant that articulate, educated Europeans could never again view the surface of life with smugness or complacency or even much confidence. No single intellectual development more clearly and stunningly exemplified this trend than the emergence of psychoanalysis through the work of Sigmund Freud.

Freud was born in 1856 into an Austrian Jewish family that shortly thereafter settled in Vienna. He originally planned to become a lawyer but soon moved to the study of physiology and then to medicine. In 1886 he opened his medical practice in Vienna, where he continued to live until driven out by the Nazis in 1938, a year before his death. All of Freud's research and writing was done from the base of his medical practice. His earliest medical interests had been psychic disorders, to which he sought to apply the critical method of science. In late 1885 he had studied for a few months in Paris with Jean-Martin Charcot, who used hypnosis to treat cases of hysteria. In

The Viennese physician Sigmund Freud (1856–1939) revolutionized the concept of human nature in the Western world. After his books, European thinkers have had to see rationality as only one aspect of human nature. [Bettmann Archive.]

Vienna he collaborated with another physician, Josef Breuer (1842–1925), and in 1895 they published *Studies in Hysteria*.

In the mid-nineties Freud changed the technique of his investigations. He abandoned hypnosis and allowed his patients to talk freely and spontaneously about themselves. Repeatedly he found that they associated their particular neurotic symptoms with experiences related to earlier experiences, going back to childhood. He also noticed that sexual matters were significant in his pa-

tients' problems. For a time he thought that perhaps some sexual incident during childhood accounted for the illness of his patients. However, by 1897 he had privately rejected this theory. In its place he formulated a theory of infantile sexuality, according to which sexual drives and energy exist in infants and do not simply emerge at puberty. In Freud's view human beings were creatures of sexuality from birth through adulthood. He thus questioned in the most radical manner the concept of childhood innocence. He also portrayed the little-discussed or -acknowledged matter of sex as one of the bases of mental order and disorder. In a classic example of the prejudices of everyday life holding back scientific inquiry, almost all of Freud's contemporaries heaped scorn and condemnation on his theory.

During the same decade Freud was also examining the psychic phenomena of dreams. Romantic writers had taken dreams very seriously, but most psychologists had not examined dreams scientifically. As a good rationalist Freud believed that there must exist a reasonable, scientific explanation for the irrational contents of dreams. That examination led him to a reconsideration of the general nature of the human mind. He came to the conclusion that during dreams unconscious wishes, desires, and drives that were excluded from everyday conscious life and experience enjoyed relatively free play in the mind. He argued, "The dream is the (disguised) fulfillment of a (suppressed, repressed) wish."[6] During the waking hours the mind repressed or censored those wishes, which were as important to our psychological makeup as conscious thought. In fact, those unconscious drives and desires contributed to conscious behavior. Freud developed these concepts and related them to his idea of infantile sexuality in *The Interpretation of Dreams*, published in 1900. It was his most important book.

In later books and essays Freud continued to urge the significance of the role played by the human unconscious.

6 *The Basic Writings of Sigmund Freud*, trans. by A. A. Brill (New York: The Modern Library, 1938), p. 235.

Freud Explains an Obstacle to Acceptance of Psychoanalysis

In addition to spawning numerous divergent views, the radical nature of Freud's theories caused them to be heard with misunderstanding, scorn, and opposition. Freud, in this 1915 passage, was at pains to give a rational explanation for the nonrational popular reaction to his work. He contended that civilization had been built largely through channeling sexual energies into nonsexual activity. For him, psychoanalysis revealed this important role of the sexual impulses. By so revealing them, psychoanalysis tended to make people uncomfortable. Consequently, public opinion played down the discoveries of psychoanalysis by claiming it was either dangerous or immoral.

W E BELIEVE *that civilization has been built up, under the pressure of the struggle for existence, by sacrifices in gratification of the primitive impulses, and that it is to a great extent for ever being recreated, as each individual, successively joining the community, repeats the sacrifice of his instinctive pleasures for the common good. The sexual are among the most important of the instinctive forces thus utilized: they are in this way sublimated, that is to say, their energy is turned aside from its sexual goal and diverted towards other ends, no longer sexual and socially more valuable. But the structure thus built up is insecure, for the sexual impulses are with difficulty controlled; in each individual who takes up his part in the work of civilization there is a danger that a rebellion of the sexual impulses may occur, against this diversion of their energy. Society can conceive of no more powerful menace to its culture than would arise from the liberation of the sexual impulses and a return of them to their original goal. Therefore society dislikes this sensitive place in its development being touched upon; that the power of the sexual instinct should be recognized, and the significance of the individual's sexual life revealed, is very far from its interests; with a view to discipline it has rather taken the course of diverting attention away from this whole field. For this reason, the revelations of psychoanalysis are not tolerated by it, and it would greatly prefer to brand them as aesthetically offensive, morally reprehensible, or dangerous. . . . It is characteristic of human nature to be inclined to regard anything which is disagreeable as untrue, and then without much difficulty to find arguments against it.*

Sigmund Freud, *A General Introduction to Psychoanalysis,* trans. by J. Riviere (Garden City, N.Y.: Garden City Publishing Company, 1943), pp. 23–24.

He portrayed a new internal organization of the mind. That inner realm was the arena for struggle and conflict among entities that he termed the *id,* the *ego,* and the *superego.* The first of these consisted of amoral, irrational, driving instincts for sexual gratification, aggression, and general physical and sensual pleasure. The superego constituted the external moral imperatives and expectations imposed upon the personality by its society and culture. The ego stood as the mediator between the impulses of the id and the asceticism of the superego. The ego allowed the personality to cope with the inner and outer demands of its existence. Consequently everyday behavior displayed the activity of the personality as its inner drives were partially repressed through the ego's coping with the external moral expectations as interpreted by the superego. It has been a grave misreading of Freud to see him as urging humankind to thrust off all repression. He believed that excessive repression could lead to mental disorder but that a certain degree of repression of sexuality and aggression was necessary for civilized living and the survival of humankind.

Freud's work led to nothing less than a revolution in the understanding of human nature. As his views gained adherents just before and after World War I, new dimensions of human life became widely recognized. Human beings were seen to be attaining rationality rather than merely exercising it. Civilization itself came to be regarded as a product of repressed or sublimated aggressions and sexual drive.

In Freud's appreciation of the role of instinct, will, dreams, and sexuality his thought pertained to the Romantic tradition of the nineteenth century. However, Freud must stand as a son of the Enlightenment. Like the *philosophes* he was a realist who wanted human beings to live free from fear and illusions by rationally understanding themselves and their world. He saw the personalities of human beings as being determined by finite physical and mental forces in a finite world. He was hostile to religion and spoke of it as an illusion. Freud, like the writers of the eighteenth century, wished to see civiliza-

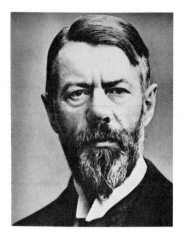

Georges Sorel was the French author of *Reflections on Violence*, which portrayed the general strike as the strongest weapon for social change. [Photo Harlingue–Viollet.]

Max Weber was one of the most influential writers contributing to sociology and economics in the late nineteenth and twentieth centuries. [The Granger Collection.]

tion and humane behavior prevail. However, more fully than those predecessors, he understood the immense sacrifice of instinctual drives required for civilized behavior. He understood how many previously unsuspected obstacles lay in the way of rationality. Freud believed that the sacrifice and struggle were worthwhile, but he was pessimistic about the future of civilization in the West.

Freud's work marked the beginning of the psychoanalytic movement. By 1910 he had gathered around him a small but highly able group of disciples. Several of his early followers soon moved toward theories of which the master disapproved. The most important of these dissenters was Carl Jung (1875–1961). He was a Swiss whom for many years Freud regarded as his most distinguished and promising student. Before World War I the two men had, however, come to a parting of the ways. Jung had begun to question the primacy of sexual drives in forming human personality and in contributing to mental disorder. He also put much less faith in the guiding light of reason. Jung believed that the human subconscious contained inherited memories from previous generations of human beings. These collective memories as well as the personal experience of a person constituted his soul. Jung regarded human beings in the twentieth century as alienated from these useful collective memories. One of his more famous books was entitled *Modern Man in Search of a Soul* (1933). Here and elsewhere Jung's thought tended toward mysticism and toward ascribing positive values to religion. Freud was highly critical of most of Jung's work. If Freud's thought derived primarily from the Enlightenment, Jung's was more dependent upon Romanticism.

By the 1920s psychoanalysis had become even more fragmented as a movement. Nonetheless, in its several varieties the movement touched not only psychology but also sociology, anthropology, religious studies, and literary theory. It has been the single most important set of ideas whereby men and women in the twentieth century have come to understand themselves and their civilization.

Retreat from Rationalism in Politics

Both nineteenth-century liberals and socialists agreed that society and politics could be guided according to rational principles. Rational analysis could discern the problems of society and prepare solutions. They generally felt that once given the vote individuals would behave in their rational political self-interest. Improvement of society and the human condition was possible through education. By the close of the century these views were under attack in both theory and practice. Political scientists and sociologists painted politics as frequently irrational. Racial theorists questioned whether rationality and education could affect human society at all.

In the realm of political theory the major figures contributing to this questioning of rational liberal assumptions were Gustave LeBon, Émile Durkheim, and Georges Sorel in France; Vilfredo Pareto in Italy; Max Weber in Germany; and Graham Wallas in England. LeBon (1841–1931) was a psychologist who explored the activity of crowds and mobs. He believed that in crowd situations rational behavior was abandoned. Sorel (1847–1922) argued in *Reflections on Violence* (1908) that people did not pursue rationally perceived goals but were led to action by collectively shared ideals. Durkheim (1858–1917) and Wallas (1858–1932) became deeply interested in the necessity for shared values and activities in a society. These elements rather than a logical analysis of the social situation bound human beings together. Instinct, habit, and affections instead of reason directed human social behavior. Weber (1864–1920) in his famous essay on *The Protestant Ethic and the Spirit of Capitalism* (1905) traced much of the rational character of capitalist enterprise to the ascetic religious doctrines of Puritanism. Besides playing down the function of reason in society, all of these theorists emphasized the role of collective groups in politics rather than that of the individual formerly championed by liberals.

The same tendencies to question or even to deny the constructive activity of reason in human affairs and to

Karl Pearson Justifies Social Darwinism and Racism

Writers such as Karl Pearson, in this passage from a 1901 book, took the Darwinian idea of the survival of the fittest and applied it to human relationships. They argued that the strong and healthy had a better right to survive and prosper than did the weak. They also regarded the white races as naturally superior and more worthy of survival than other races.

CONSCIOUSLY *or unconsciously, one type of life is fighting against a second type, and all life is struggle with its physical environment. The safety of a gregarious animal—and man is essentially such—depends upon the intensity with which the social instinct has been developed. The stability of a race depends entirely on the extent to which the social feelings have got a real hold on it. The race which allows the physically or mentally stronger Tom to make the existence of the somewhat inferior Jack impossible will never succeed when it comes into contest with a second race. Jack has no interests in common with Tom; the oppressed will hardly get worse terms from a new master. That is why no strong and permanent civilization can be built upon slave labor, why an inferior race doing mental labour for a superior race can give no stable community; that is why we shall never have a healthy social state in South Africa until the white man replaces the dark in the fields and in the minds, and the Kaffir is pushed back towards the equator. The nation organized for the struggle must be a* homogeneous *whole, not a mixture of superior and inferior races. For this reason every new land we colonize with white men is a source of strength; every land of coloured men we simply rule may be needful as a source of food and mineral wealth, but it is not an element of stability in our community, and must ever be regarded with grave anxiety by our statesmen.*

Karl Pearson, *National Life from the Standpoint of Science* (Cambridge England: Cambridge University Press, 1901), pp. 47–48.

sacrifice the individual to the group manifested themselves in theories of race. Racial thinking had long existed in Europe. Renaissance explorers had displayed considerable prejudice against nonwhite peoples. Since at least the eighteenth century biologists and anthropologists had classified human beings according to color of skin, language, and stage of civilization. Late eighteenth-century linguistic scholars had observed similarities between European languages and Sanskrit. They then postulated the existence of an ancient race called the *Aryans,* who had spoken the original language from which the rest derived. During the Romantic period writers had called the different cultures of Europe races. The debates over slavery in European colonies and the United States had given further opportunity for the development of racial theory. However, in the late nineteenth century the concept of race emerged as a single dominant explanation for history and the character of large groups of people.

Arthur Gobineau (1816–1882), a reactionary French diplomat, enunciated the first important theory of race as the major determinant of human history. In his four-volume *Essay on the Inequality of the Human Races* (1853–1854) Gobineau portrayed the troubles of Western civilization as the result of the long degeneration of the original white Aryan race. It had unwisely intermarried with the inferior yellow and black races, thus diluting the qualities of greatness and ability that originally existed in its blood. Gobineau was deeply pessimistic because he saw no way to reverse the degeneration that had taken place.

Gobineau's essay remained relatively obscure for many years. In the meantime a growing literature of anthropologists and explorers helped to spread racial thinking. In the wake of Darwin's theory, the concept of survival of the fittest was applied to races and nations. The recognition of the animal nature of humankind made the racial idea all the more persuasive. At the close of the century Houston Stewart Chamberlain (1855–1927), a German writer, drew together these strands of racial thought into the two volumes of his *Foundations of the Nineteenth Century* (1899). He championed the concept of biological determinism through race, but he was somewhat more optimistic than Gobineau. Chamberlain believed that through genetics the human race could be improved and that even a superior race could be developed. Chamberlain added another element. He pointed to the Jews as the major enemy of European racial regeneration. Chamberlain's book and the lesser works upon which it drew aided the spread of anti-Semitism in European political life.

Political and racial anti-Semitism, which have cast such dark shadows across the twentieth century, emerged in part from this atmosphere of racial thought and the retreat from rationality in politics. Religious anti-Semitism dated from at least the Middle Ages. Since the French Revolution west European Jews had gradually gained entry into the civil life of Britain, France, and Germany. Popular anti-Semitism continued to exist as the Jewish community was identified with money and banking interests. During the last third of the century as finance capitalism changed the economic structure of Europe, people pressured by the changes became hostile toward the Jewish community. This was especially true of the socially and economically insecure middle class. In Vienna Mayor Karl Leugar (1844–1910) used such anti-Semitism as a major attraction to his successful Christian Socialist Party. In Germany the ultraconservative Lutheran chaplain Adolf Stoecker (1835–1909) revived anti-Semitism. The Dreyfus affair in France allowed a new flowering of hatred toward the Jews.

To this already ugly atmosphere, racial thought contributed the belief that no matter to what extent a Jew assimilated himself or his family to the culture of his country, his Jewishness would remain and thus his alleged danger to the society. The problem of race was not in the character but in the blood of the Jew. An important Jewish response to this new, rabid outbreak of anti-Semitism was the launching by the Austro-Hungarian Theodor Herzl (1860–1904) in 1896 of the Zionist movement to found a separate Jewish state.

Racial thinking and revived anti-Semitism were part of a wider late-century movement toward more aggressive nationalism. Previously nationalism had been a movement among European literary figures and liberals. From the seventies onward it became a movement with mass support, well-financed organizations, and political parties. Nationalists often defined nationality in terms of race. The new nationalism opposed the internationalism of both liberalism and socialism. The ideal of nationality was used to overcome the pluralism of class, religion, and geography. The nation and its duties replaced religion in the lives of many secularized people. It became a secular religion in the hands of state schoolteachers who were replacing clergymen as instructors of the youth. Nationalism would prove to be the most powerful ideology of the early twentieth century.

SUGGESTED READINGS

R. ARON, *Main Currents in Sociological Thought,* 2 vols. (1965, 1967). A useful introduction to the founders of the science.

F. L. BAUMER, *Modern European Thought: Continuity and Change in Ideas, 1600–1950* (1977). The best work on the subject for this period.

F. L. BAUMER, *Religion and the Rise of Scepticism* (1960). Traces the development of religious doubt from the seventeenth to the twentieth centuries.

M. D. BIDDIS, *Father of Racist Ideology: The Social and Political Thought of Count Gobineau* (1970). Sets the subject in the more general context of nineteenth-century thought.

J. W. BURROW, *Evolution and Society: A Study in Victorian Social Theory* (1966). An important study of evolutionary sociology.

D. G. CHARLTON, *Positivist Thought in France During the Second Empire, 1852–1870* (1959), and *Secular Religions in France, 1815–1870* (1963). Two clear introductions to important subjects.

C. M. CIPOLLA, *Literacy and Development in the West* (1969). Traces the explosion of literacy in the past two centuries.

C. C. GILLISPIE, *Genesis and Geology* (1951). An excellent discussion of the impact of modern geological theory during the early nineteenth century.

C. C. GILLISPIE, *The Edge of Objectivity* (1960). One of the best one-volume treatments of modern scientific ideas.

J. C. GREENE, *The Death of Adam: Evolution and Its Impact on Western Thought* (1959). Emphasizes pre-Darwinian thought.

S. HUGHES, *Consciousness and Society: The Reorientation of*

European Social Thought, 1890–1930 (1958). A wide-ranging discussion of the revolt against positivism.

W. IRVINE, *Apes, Angels, and Victorians* (1955). A lively and sound account of Darwin and Huxley.

W. A. KAUFMANN, *Nietzsche: Philosopher, Psychologist, Antichrist,* rev. ed. (1968). An exposition of Nietzsche's thought and its sources.

J. T. MERZ, *A History of European Thought in the Nineteenth Century,* 4 vols. (1897–1914). Still a useful mine of information.

P. G. J. PULZER, *The Rise of Political Anti-Semitism in Germany and Austria* (1964). A sound discussion of anti-Semitism in the world of central European politics.

P. RIEF, *Freud: The Mind of the Moralist* (1959). Probably the best one-volume treatment.

L. SNYDER, *Race: A History of Modern Ethnic Theories* (1939). A good introductory treatment.

A. VIDLER, *The Church in an Age of Revolution* (1961). A sound account of the problems of Church and State in the nineteenth century.

R. WILLIAMS, *The Long Revolution* (1961). Explores the impact of literacy and popular publishing on English culture.

794

30
Imperialism, Alliances, and War

Expansion of European Power and the "New Imperialism"

URING the second half of the nineteenth century, and especially after 1870, European influence and control over the rest of the world grew to an unprecedented degree. North and South America, as well as Australia and New Zealand, became almost integral parts of the European world as the great streams of European immigrants populated them. Until the nineteenth century Asia, (with the significant exception of India) and most of Africa had gone their own ways, having little contact with Europe. But the latter part of that century brought the partition of Africa among a number of European nations and the establishment of European economic and political power from the eastern to the western borders of Asia. By the next century this growth of European dominance had brought every part of the globe into a single world economy and had made events in any corner of the world significant thousands of miles away.

The explosive developments in nineteenth-century science, technology, industry, agriculture, transportation, communication, and military weapons provided the chief sources of European power. They made it possible for a small number of Europeans (or Americans) to impose their will on other peoples many times their number by force or by the threat of force. Institutional as well as material advantages allowed Westerners to have their

This scene of trench warfare on the western front in World War I characterizes the twentieth century's first great international conflict. The trenches were defended by barbed wire and machine guns, the devices that gave the defense the advantage in this war. The masks worn by the French soldiers in this picture were the response to the German attempts to break a deadlock by using poison gas. [Collection Viollet.]

way. The growth of national states that commanded the loyalty, service, and resources of their inhabitants to a degree previously unknown was a Western phenomenon, and it permitted the European nations to deploy their resources in the most effective way. The Europeans also possessed another, less tangible weapon: a sense of the superiority of their civilization and way of life. This gave them a confidence that often took the form of an unpleasant arrogance but that fostered the expansionist mood.

The expansion of European influence was not anything new. Spain, Portugal, France, and Britain had controlled territories overseas for centuries, but by the mid-nineteenth century only Great Britain retained extensive holdings. The first half of the century was generally a period of hostility to colonial expansion. Even the British had been sobered by their loss of the American colonies. The French acquired Algeria and part of Indochina, and the British made some additional gains in territories adjacent to their holdings in Canada, India, Australia, and New Zealand. For the most part, however, the doctrine of free trade was dominant, and it opposed the idea of political interference in other lands.

Because Britain ruled the waves and had great commercial advantages as a result of being first in the Industrial Revolution, the British were usually content to let commerce go forward without annexations. Yet they were quite prepared to interfere forcefully if some "backward" country placed barriers in the way of their trade. Still at mid-century in Britain as elsewhere opinion stood predominantly against further political or military involvement overseas.

In the last third of the century, however, the European states swiftly spread their control over perhaps 10 million square miles and 150 million people, about a fifth of the world's land area and a tenth of its population. The movement has been called the *New Imperialism*.

The New Imperialism

Imperialism is a word that has come to be used so loosely as almost to be deprived of meaning. It may be useful to offer a definition that might be widely accepted: "The policy of extending a nation's authority by territorial acquisition or by the establishment of economic and political hegemony over other nations." [1] That definition seems to apply equally well to human actions as far back as ancient Egypt and Mesopotamia and to the performance of European nations in the late nineteenth century. But there were some new elements in the latter case. Previous imperialisms had either taken the form of seizing land and settling it with the conqueror's people or of establishing trading centers to exploit the resources of the dominated area. The New Imperialism did not completely abandon these devices, but it introduced new ones.

The usual pattern of the New Imperialism was for the European nation to invest capital in the "backward" country, to build productive enterprises and improved means of transportation, to employ great numbers of natives in the process, and thereby to transform the entire economy and culture of the dominated area. To guarantee their investments, the European states would make favorable arrangements with the local government either by enriching the rulers or by threatening them. If these arrangements proved inadequate, the dominant power established different degrees of political control, ranging from full annexation as a colony to protectorate status, whereby the local ruler was controlled by the dominant European state and maintained by its military power; to "spheres-of-influence" status, whereby the European state received special commercial and legal privileges without direct political involvement. Other novelties included the great speed with which European expansion went forward and the way in which participation in this expansion came to be regarded as necessary to retaining status as a great power.

MOTIVES FOR THE NEW IMPERIALISM. There has been considerable debate about the motives for the

1 *American Heritage Dictionary of the English Language* (New York: Houghton Mifflin Co., 1969), p. 660.

SUMMARY CHRONOLOGY FOR THE COMING OF WORLD WAR I

1871	The end of the Franco–Prussian war; creation of the German Empire; German annexation of Alsace–Lorraine.
1873	The Three Emperors' League.
1875	The Russo–Turkish War.
1878	The Congress of Berlin.
1879	The Dual Alliance between Germany and Austria.
1881	The Three Emperors' League is renewed.
1882	Italy joins Germany and Austria in the Triple Alliance.
1888	William II becomes German Emperor.
1890	Bismarck is dismissed.
1894	The Franco–Russian alliance.
1898	Germany begins to build a battleship navy.
1902	The British alliance with Japan.
1904	The *Entente Cordiale* between Britain and France.
1904–1905	The Russo–Japanese War.
1905	The first Moroccan Crisis.
1907	The British agreement with Russia.
1908–1909	The Bosnian Crisis.
1911	The second Moroccan Crisis. Italy attacks Turkey.
1912–1913	The First and Second Balkan Wars.
1914	Outbreak of World War I.

New Imperialism. The most widespread interpretation has been economic, most typically in the form given by the English radical economist J. A. Hobson and later adapted by Lenin. As Lenin put it, "Imperialism is the monopoly stage of capitalism," [2] the last stage of a dying capitalist system. According to this interpretation, competition inevitably led to the elimination of inefficient capitalists and, therefore, to monopoly. Powerful industrial and financial capitalists soon ran out of profitable areas of investment in their own countries and persuaded their governments to gain colonies in "backward" countries, where they could find higher profits from their investments, new markets for their products, and safe sources of the raw materials they needed.

The facts of the matter do not support this viewpoint. The European powers did export considerable amounts of capital in the form of investments abroad but not in such a manner as to fit the model of Hobson and Lenin.

2 V. I. Lenin, *Imperialism, the Highest Stage of Capitalism,* (New York: International Publishers Co., Inc., 1939), p. 88.

This British advertisement of 1887 unconsciously makes the point that, in the minds of some, empire and colonies were closely connected with economic gain. The advertising copy below the picture read, "Pears' Soap in the Soudan. Even if our invasion of the Soudan has done nothing else it has at any rate left the Arab with something to puzzle his fuzzy head over, for the legend Pears' Soap Is the Best, [is] inscribed in huge white characters on the rock which marks the farthest point of our advance . . ." [Thames and Hudson Ltd.]

THE FORMULA OF BRITISH CONQUEST

PEARS SOAP IS THE BEST

Britain, for example, made heavier investments abroad before 1875 than during the next two decades. Only a very small percentage of British and European investment overseas, moveover, went to the new colonial areas. Most went into Europe itself or into older, well-established areas like the United States, Canada, Australia, and New Zealand. Even when investments were made in the new areas, they were not necessarily put into colonies held by the investing country.

The facts are equally discouraging for those who emphasize the need for markets and raw materials. Colonies were not usually important markets for the great imperial nations, and all were forced to rely on areas that they did not control as sources of vital raw materials. It is not even clear that control of the new colonies was particularly profitable. As one of the leading students of the subject has said, "No one can determine whether the accounts of empire ultimately closed with a favorable cash balance." [3] That is true of the European imperial nations collectively, but it is certain that for some of them, like Italy and Germany, empire was a losing proposition. Some individuals and companies, of course, were able to make great profits from particular colonial ventures, but such people were able to influence national policy only occasionally. The motives for imperial policy must be sought elsewhere.

Advocates of imperialism put forth various justifications. Some argued that it was the responsibility of the advanced European nations to bring the benefits of their higher culture and superior civilization to the people of "backward" lands, but few people were influenced by such arrogant arguments, though many shared the intellectual assumptions. Religious groups argued for the responsibility of Western nations to bring the benefits of Christianity to the heathen with more extensive efforts and aid from their governments. Some politicians and diplomats argued for imperialism as a tool of social policy.

3 D. K. Fieldhouse, *The Colonial Empires* (New York: Delacorte Press, 1966), p. 393.

In Germany, for instance, a few conservatives suggested that imperial expansion might serve to deflect public interest away from domestic politics and social reform. But Germany acquired only a few colonies, and such considerations played little if any role.

In Britain such arguments were made, as was their opposite. The statesman Joseph Chamberlain (1836–1914) argued for the empire as a source of profit and economic security that would finance a great program of domestic reform and welfare. To the extent that they had any influence these arguments were not important as motives for imperialism because they were made well after the British had acquired most of their empire. Another common and apparently plausible justification was that colonies would provide a good place to settle surplus population. In fact, most European emigrants went to areas not controlled by their countries, chiefly to North and South America and Australia.

THE SCRAMBLE FOR AFRICA. Strategic and political considerations seem to have been more important in bringing on the New Imperialism. The scramble for Africa in the 1880s is one example. Britain was the only great power with extensive overseas holdings on the eve of the scramble. The completion of the Suez Canal in 1869 made Egypt an area of vital interest to the British

PARTITION OF AFRICA, 1880–1914

COLONIAL POWERS
- BRITISH
- FRENCH
- GERMAN
- PORTUGUESE
- ITALIAN
- BELGIAN
- SPANISH

Before 1880 European presence in Africa was largely the remains of early exploration by old imperialists and did not penetrate the heart of the continent. By 1914 the occupying powers included most large European states; only Liberia and Abyssinia remained independent.

because it sat astride the shortest route to India. Under Disraeli Britain purchased a major, but not a controlling, interest in the canal in 1875. When Egypt's stability was threatened by internal troubles in the 1880s, the British moved in and established a protectorate. Then to protect Egypt, they advanced into the Sudan.

France became involved in Africa in 1830 by sending a naval expedition to Algeria to attack the pirates based there. Before long French settlers arrived and established a colony but not because of economics or military security. By 1882 France was in full control of Algeria, and about the same time, to prevent Tunisia from falling into Italy's hand, France took over that area of North Africa also. Soon lesser states like Belgium, Portugal, Spain, and Italy were scrambling for African colonies. Their intervention had by the nineties compelled Britain to expand northward from the Cape of Good Hope into what is now Rhodesia. Britain may have had significant strategic reasons for protecting the Suez and Cape routes to India,

OPPOSITE, TOP: In this picture based on his own sketch, Henry M. Stanley (1841–1904), the explorer-adventurer sent in 1871 by the *New York Herald* to what was then called "darkest Africa" to find the supposedly lost missionary, David Livingston, arrives at an African village. The travels of these two men in Africa exemplify the diversity of motives that led westerners to explore the interior of the continent in the last half of the nineteenth century. [Radio Times Hulton Picture Library.]
OPPOSITE, BOTTOM: Christian missionaries were frequently part of the general pattern of European colonial penetration of Africa and Asia in the late nineteenth century. This print portrays a missionary in the West African German colony of Togoland, now part of the modern state of Ghana. [Culver Pictures.]

"Colonies for Germany, Too." This German cartoon of 1884 attacks Bismarck for neglecting imperial expansion overseas. He is shown attending to domestic social reform while the southern hemisphere is carved up by other nations. The caption to the cartoon read, "The Pacific Ocean is the Mediterranean of the future." [Thames and Hudson Ltd.]

but France and the smaller European nations did not have such reasons. Their motives were political, for they equated status as a great power (Britain stood as the chief model) with the possession of colonies. They therefore sought colonies as evidence of their own importance.

Bismarck appears to have pursued an imperial policy, however brief, from coldly political motives. In 1884 and 1885 Germany declared protectorates over Southwest Africa, Togoland, the Cameroons, and East Africa. None of these places was particularly valuable or of intrinsic strategic importance. Bismarck himself had no interest in overseas colonies and once compared them to fine furs worn by impoverished Polish noblemen who had no shirts underneath. His concern lay in Germany's exposed position in Europe. On one occasion he said, "My map of Africa lies in Europe. Here is Russia, and there is France, and here in the middle are we. That is my map of Africa."[4] He acquired colonies chiefly to improve Ger-

4 Quoted by J. Remak in *The Origins of World War I, 1871–1914*, (New York: Holt, Rhinehart and Winston, 1967), p. 5.

Bismarck Reminisces About His Foreign Policy

The following is Bismarck's own account of his foreign policy written during the years of his retirement, 1890–1898.

The *triple alliance which I originally sought to conclude after the peace of Frankfurt, and about which I had already sounded Vienna and St. Petersburg, from Meaux, in September 1870, was an alliance of the three emperors with the further idea of bringing into it monarchical Italy. It was designed for the struggle which, as I feared, was before us; between the two European tendencies which Napoleon called Republican and Cossack, and which I, according to our present ideas, should designate on the one side as the system of order on a monarchical basis, and on the other as the social republic to the level of which the antimonarchical development is wont to sink, either slowly or by leaps and bounds, until the conditions thus created become intolerable, and the disappointed populace are ready for a violent return to monarchical institutions in a Cæsarean form. I consider that the task of escaping from this* circulus vitiosus, *or, if possible, of sparing the present generation and their children an entrance into it, ought to be more closely incumbent on the strong existing monarchies, those monarchies which still have a vigorous life, than any rivalry over the fragments of nations which people the Balkan peninsula. If the monarchical governments have no understanding of the necessity for holding together in the interests of political and social order, but make themselves subservient to the chauvinistic impulses of their subjects, I fear that the international revolutionary and social struggles which will have to be fought out will be all the more dangerous, and take such a form that the victory on the part of monarchical order will be more difficult. Since 1871 I have sought for the most certain assurance against those struggles in the alliance of the three emperors, and also in the effort to impart to the monarchical principle in Italy a firm support in that alliance.*

Otto von Bismarck, *Reflections and Reminiscences*, ed. by Theodore S. Hamerow, (New York: Harper Torchbooks, 1968), pp. 236–237.

OPPOSITE: This is a satirical German cartoon of 1896 poking fun at German efficiency as applied to colonial adventures. In the upper picture is the deplorably idyllic jungle; in the bottom, the new and satisfactory tidiness brought about by German imperialism. [The Granger Collection.]

Expansion of European Power and the "New Imperialism" 8o1

many's diplomatic position in Europe. He tried to turn France from hostility against Germany by diverting the French toward colonial interests. At the same time German colonies in Africa could be used as a subtle weapon with which to persuade the British to be reasonable.

Germany's annexations started a wild scramble by the other European powers to establish claims on what was left of Africa. By 1890 almost all of the continent was parceled out. Great powers and small expanded into areas neither profitable nor strategic for reasons less calculating and rational than Bismarck's. "Empire in the modern period," D. K. Fieldhouse has observed, "was the product of European power: its reward was power or the sense of power."[5]

Such motives were not new. They had been well understood by the Athenian spokesman at Melos in 416 B.C., whose words are reported by Thucydides: "Of the gods we believe and of men we know clearly that by a necessity of their nature where they have the power they rule."[6]

IMPERIALISM IN THE PACIFIC. By the early years of the twentieth century the islands of the Pacific were also apportioned among the Western powers. Southeast Asia was divided among Britain in Burma, Malaya, and North Borneo, France in Indochina, and the Netherlands in the East Indies. China was able to maintain its territory and sovereignty in spite of European interference, in part because its central government continued to function, in part because of the antiforeign Boxer Rebellion of 1898–1900, but chiefly because of rivalry among the great powers. Still the powers established spheres of influence, opportunities for trade and investment immune from Chinese courts, and even military and naval bases. In addition to imperial nations of fairly long standing, China was of interest to two powers new on the international scene, Japan and the United States. Japan had been brought forcibly into contact with the Western world by

5 Fieldhouse, p. 393.
6 Thucydides, *The Peloponnesian War*, 5.105.2.

Kipling Advises the Americans: The Responsibility for Empire

THE WHITE MAN'S BURDEN
1899
(*The United States and the Philippine Islands*)

Take up the White Man's burden—
  Send forth the best ye breed—
Go bind your sons to exile
  To serve your captives' need;
To wait in heavy harness
  On fluttered folk and wild—
Your new-caught, sullen peoples,
  Half devil and half child.

Take up the White Man's Burden—
  In patience to abide,
To veil the threat of terror
  And check the show of pride;
By open speech and simple,
  An hundred times made plain,
To seek another's profit,
  And work another's gain.

Take up the White Man's burden—
  The savage wars of peace—
Fill full the mouth of Famine
  And bid the sickness cease;
And when your goal is nearest
  The end for others sought,
Watch Sloth and heathen Folly
  Bring all your hope to nought.

Take up the White Man's burden—
  No tawdry rule of kings,
But toil of serf and sweeper—
  The tale of common things.
The ports ye shall not enter,
  The roads ye shall not tread,
Go make them with your living,
  And mark them with your dead!

Take up the White Man's burden—
  And reap his old reward:
The blame of those ye better,
  The hate of those ye guard—
The cry of hosts ye humour
  (Ah, slowly!) toward the light:—
"Why brought ye us from bondage,
  "Our loved Egyptian night?"

Take up the White Man's burden—
Ye dare not stoop to less—
Nor call too loud on Freedom
To cloak your weariness;
By all ye cry or whisper,
By all ye leave or do,
The silent, sullen peoples
Shall weigh your Gods and you.

Take up the White Man's burden—
Have done with childish days—
The lightly proffered laurel,
The easy, ungrudged praise.
Comes now, to search your manhood
Through all the thankless years,
Cold-edged with dear-bought wisdom,
The judgment of your peers!

"The White Man's Burden (1899)," from *Rudyard Kipling's Verse: Definitive Edition,* (New York: Doubleday and Company, Inc., 1940) pp. 321–323.

The classical columns on the former British Viceroy's House in New Delhi, India, built in 1912, and now the residence of the President of India, illustrate the manner in which Western taste and design were imposed on much of the rest of the world during the age of imperialism. [Government of India Tourist Office, New York.]

the arrival in Tokyo Bay of an American naval force under Commodore Matthew Perry (1794–1858) in 1853. The constitutional and political reforms introduced in the Meiji era (1868–1912), as well as the rapid military and technological advance that accompanied it, swiftly made Japan a modern nation. Soon the Japanese adopted Western imperialism as well. In 1895 they defeated the Chinese in a one-sided war, took Formosa and the Liaotung Peninsula, and informally dominated the newly independent Korea.

The emergence of Japan frightened the other powers interested in China. The Russians were building a railroad across Siberia to Vladivostok and were afraid of any power that might threaten Manchuria. Together with France and Germany they applied diplomatic pressure

that forced Japan out of the Liaotung Peninsula and its harbor, Port Arthur, and all pressed feverishly for concessions in China. Fearing that China, its markets, and its investment opportunities would soon be closed to its citizens, the United States in 1899 proposed the "Open Door Policy," which opposed foreign annexations in China and allowed businessmen of all nations to trade there on equal terms. The support of Britain helped win acceptance of the policy by all the powers except Russia.

Expansion of European Power and the "New Imperialism" 803

RUSSIAN EMPIRE

EUROPE

OTTOMAN
EMPIRE

CYPRUS

EGYPT

PERSIA

AFGHA-
NISTAN

MONGOLIA

MANCHURIA

SAKHALIN

KURILE IS.
(JAP.)

JAPAN

Tokyo

KOREA

MANCHU
CHINA

Shanghai
Foochow   Ningpo
Amoy
Canton
Macao
(PORT.)   Hong Kong (BR.)

RYUKYU IS.
(JAP.)

TAIWAN

AFRICA

BAHREIN
(BR.)

NEJED

OMAN

HEJAZ

HADRAMAUT (BR.)

ADEN (BR.)

Bombay

Goa
(PORT.)

Mahé
(FR.)

NEPAL   SIKKIM   BHUTAN

Calcutta

INDIA

Pondicherry
(FR.)

CEYLON

MALDIVE IS.
(BR.)

BURMA

Rangoon

TONKIN
LAOS   ANNAM

SIAM

CAM-
BODIA

COCHIN-
CHINA

FEDERATED
MALAY STATES

SARAWAK

Singapore
(BR.)

PHILIPPINE IS.
(SPAIN)

DUTCH   EAST   INDIES

TIMOR

PORTUGUESE
TIMOR

ASIA, 1880 1914

BRITISH
COLONIES

PROTECTED STATES
IN INDIA

TREATY PORTS
IN CHINA

1000 MI.

1000 KM.

TRM

EUROPE

RUSSIAN   EMPIRE

OTTOMAN
EMPIRE

CYPRUS

AFGHANISTAN
(BR. INFLUENCE)

(RUSS.
INFLUENCE)

PERSIA

KUWAIT
(BR.)

BAHREIN
(BR.)

NEJED

HEJAZ

OMAN

YEMEN

HADRAMAUT (BR.)

ADEN (BR.)

AFRICA

Bombay

Goa
(PORT.)

Mahé
(FR.)

INDIA

Pondicherry
(FR.)

CEYLON
(BR.)

MALDIVE IS.
(BR.)

TIBET

NEPAL   SIKKIM   BHUTAN

BURMA

OUTER
MONGOLIA
1912

INNER MONGOLIA

MANCHURIA

SAKHALIN

KURILE IS.
(JAP.)

JAPAN

Vladi-
vostok

Tokyo

Port
Arthur

KOREA

REPUBLIC OF
CHINA

Hangchow

Macao
(PORT.)   Hong Kong (BR.)

RYUKYU IS.
(JAP.)

FORMOSA
(JAP.)

TONKIN

LAOS

SIAM

CAM-
BODIA

ANNAM

FRENCH
INDO-
CHINA

COCHIN-
CHINA
BRUNEI

FEDERATED
MALAY STATES

Singapore
(BR.)

BR.
N. BORNEO

PHILIPPINE IS.
(U.S.A.)

DUTCH   EAST   INDIES

PORT.
TIMOR

TIMOR

As in Africa, the decades before World War I saw imperialism spread widely and rapidly in Asia. Two new powers, Japan and the United States joined the British, French, and Dutch in extending control both to islands and to mainland and in exploiting an enfeebled China.

The United States had only recently emerged as a force in international affairs. After freeing itself from British rule and consolidating its independence during the Napoleonic Wars, the Americans had busied themselves with westward expansion on the North American continent until the end of the nineteenth century. The Monroe Doctrine of 1823, in effect, had made the entire Western Hemisphere an American protectorate. Cuba's attempt to gain independence from Spain was the spark for the new United States involvement in international affairs. Sympathy for the Cuban cause, American investments on the island, the desire for Cuban sugar, and concern over the island's strategic importance in the Carribean all helped win the Americans over to the idea of a war with Spain.

American victory in the Spanish–American War of 1898 brought an informal protectorate over Cuba and annexation of Puerto Rico and drove Spain completely out of the Western Hemisphere. The Americans also annexed the Philippine Islands and Guam, and Germany acquired the other Spanish islands in the Pacific. The Americans and the Germans also divided Samoa between them. What was left of the Pacific islands was soon taken by France and England. Hawaii had been under American influence for some time and had been asking for annexation, which was accomplished in 1898. This outburst of activity after the Spanish war made the United States an imperial and Pacific power. Soon after the turn of the century most of the world had come under the control of the advanced Western nations. The one remaining area of great vulnerability was the Ottoman Empire, but its fate was closely tied up with European developments and must be treated in that context.

Emergence of the German Empire and the Alliance Systems (1873–1890)

Prussia's victories over Austria and France and its creation of a large, powerful German Empire revolutionized European diplomacy. The sudden appearance of a vast new political unit that brought together the majority of the German people to form a nation of great and growing population, wealth, industrial capacity, and military power posed new problems. The balance of power created at the Congress of Vienna was altered radically. Britain retained its position and so did Russia, even though somewhat weakened by the Crimean War. Austria, however, had fallen quite a distance, and its position was destined to deteriorate further as the forces of nationalism threatened to disintegrate the Austro-Hungarian Empire. French power and prestige were badly damaged by the Franco-Prussian war and the German annexation of Alsace-Lorraine. The weakened French were both afraid of their powerful new neighbor and at the same time resentful of the defeat, the loss of territory and population, and the loss of their traditional position of dominance in Western Europe.

Until 1890 Bismarck continued to guide German policy. He insisted after 1871 that Germany was a satisfied power and wanted no further territorial gains, and he meant it. He only wanted to consolidate the new international situation by avoiding a new war that might undo his achievement. Aware of French resentment, he tried to assuage it by friendly relations and by supporting French colonial aspirations in order to turn French attention away from European discontents. At the same time he prepared for the worst. If France could not be conciliated, it must be isolated. The kernel of Bismarck's policy was to prevent an alliance between France and any other European power—especially Austria or Russia—that would threaten Germany with a war on two fronts.

WAR IN THE BALKANS. His first move was to establish the Three Emperors' League in 1873. It brought together the three great conservative empires of Germany, Austria, and Russia. The league soon collapsed as a result of the Russo-Turkish War, which broke out in 1875 because of an uprising in the Ottoman Balkan provinces of Bosnia and Herzegovina. The tottering Ottoman Empire was held together chiefly by the competing aims of those powers who awaited its demise. The weakness of the Ottoman Empire encouraged Serbia and Montenegro to come to the aid of their fellow Slavs. Soon the rebellion spread to Bulgaria. Then Russia entered the fray and turned it into a major international crisis. The Russians hoped to pursue their traditional policy of expansion at Ottoman expense and especially hoped to achieve their most cherished goal: control of Constantinople and the Dardanelles. The Russian intervention also reflected the influence of the Pan-Slav movement, which sought to bring together all the Slavic peoples, even those under Austrian or Ottoman rule, under the protection of Holy Mother Russia.

The Ottoman Empire was weak, and before long it was forced to ask for peace. The Treaty of San Stefano of March 1878 was a Russian triumph. The Slavic states in the Balkans were freed of Ottoman rule, and Russia itself obtained territorial gains and a heavy monetary indemnity. But the Russian victory was not lasting. The other great powers were alarmed by the terms of the settlement. Austria feared that the great Slavic victory and the

powerful increase in Russian influence in the Balkans would cause dangerous shock waves in its own Balkan provinces. The British were alarmed by the damage the Russian victory would do to the European balance of power and especially by the thought of possible Russian control of the Dardanelles and access to the Mediterranean and Black Seas. Disraeli was determined to resist, and British public opinion supported him. A music hall song that became popular gave the language a new word for superpatriotism: *jingoism.*

> We don't want to fight,
> But by jingo if we do,
> We've got the men,
> We've got the ships,
> We've got the money too!

THE CONGRESS OF BERLIN. Even before the Treaty of San Stefano, Disraeli sent a fleet to Constantinople. After the magnitude of Russia's appetite was

OPPOSITE: William I and Bismarck, victors over France, at Versailles as the new German Empire is proclaimed, January 18, 1871. Anton von Werner's painting shows the same hall in which would be signed the Versailles Treaty of 1919 after World War I. [John R. Freeman.]

At the Congress of Berlin in 1878 Bismarck acted as the "honest broker" to settle various foreign policy disputes of the major European powers. Disraeli of England is standing toward the left, facing forward with his hand on his hip. The painter is again Anton von Werner. [The Granger Collection.]

known, Britain and Austria forced Russia to agree to an international conference at which the provisions of the treaty would be reviewed by the other great powers. The resulting Congress of Berlin met in June and July of 1878 under the presidency of Bismarck. The choice of site and presiding officer was a clear recognition of Germany's new importance and of its chancellor's claim that his policy called for no further territorial gains and aimed at preserving the peace. Bismarck referred to himself as an "honest broker," and the title seems justified. He agreed to the congress simply because he wanted to avoid a war between Russia and Austria into which he feared Germany would be drawn with nothing to gain and much to lose. From the collapsing Ottoman Empire he wanted nothing. "The Eastern Question," he said, "is not worth the healthy bones of a single Pomeranian musketeer."[7]

The decisions of the congress were a blow to Russian

7 Quoted by Hajo Holborn, *A History of Modern Germany, 1840–1945,* (New York: Alfred A. Knopf, 1969), p. 239.

ambitions. Bulgaria was reduced in size by two thirds and was deprived of access to the Aegean Sea. Austria–Hungary was given Bosnia and Herzegovina to "occupy and administer." Britain received Cyprus, and France gained permission to expand into Tunisia. These privileges were compensation for the gains that Russia was permitted to keep. Germany asked for nothing but got little credit from Russia for its restraint. The Russians believed that they had saved Prussia in 1807 from complete dismemberment by Napoleon and had expected a show of German gratitude. They were bitterly disappointed, and the Three Emperors' League was dead.

All of the Balkan states were also annoyed by the Berlin settlement. Romania wanted Bessarabia; Bulgaria wanted a return to the borders of the Treaty of San Stefano; and Greece wanted a part of the Ottoman spoils. The major trouble spot, however, was in the south Slavic states of Serbia and Montenegro. They deeply resented the Austrian occupation of Bosnia and Herzegovina, as did many of the natives of those provinces. The south

Slavic question no less than the estrangement between Russia and Germany was a threat to the peace of Europe.

GERMAN ALLIANCES WITH RUSSIA AND AUSTRIA. For the moment Bismarck could ignore the Balkans, but he could not ignore the breach in his eastern alliance system. With Russia alienated, he turned to Austria and concluded a secret treaty in 1879. The resulting Dual Alliance was defensive in character and was aimed at Russia. If the signatory countries were attacked by someone else, each promised at least to maintain neutrality. The treaty was for five years and was renewed regularly until 1918. As the central point in German policy, it was criticized at the time, and some have judged it mistaken in retrospect. It appeared to tie German fortunes to those of the troubled Austro-Hungarian Empire and in that way to borrow trouble. At the same time, by isolating the Russians, it pushed them in the direction of seeking alliances in the West.

Bismarck was fully aware of these dangers but discounted them with good reason. At no time did he allow his Austrian alliance to drag Germany into Austria's Balkan quarrels. As he put it himself, in any alliance there is a horse and a rider, and in this one Bismarck meant Germany to be the rider. He made it clear to the Austrians that the alliance was purely defensive and that Germany would never be a party to an attack on Russia. "For us," he said, "Balkan questions can never be a motive for war." [8]

Bismarck believed that monarchical, reactionary Russia would not seek an alliance either with republican, revolutionary France or with increasingly democratic Britain. In fact, he expected news of Austro-German negotiations to frighten Russia into seeking closer relations with Germany, and he was right. Russian diplomats soon approached him, and by 1881 he had concluded a renewal of the Three Emperor's League on a firmer basis. The three powers promised to maintain friendly neutrality in case either of the others was attacked by a fourth power. Other clauses included the right of Austria to annex Bosnia–Herzegovina whenever it wished and closed the Dardanelles to all nations in case of war. The agreement allayed German fears of a Russian–French alliance and Russian fears of a combination of Austria and Britain against it, of Britain's fleet sailing into the Black Sea, and of a hostile combination of Germany and Austria. Most important of all, the agreement aimed at a resolution of the conflicts in the Balkans between Austria and Russia. Though it did not put an end to such conflicts, it was a significant step toward peace.

THE TRIPLE ALLIANCE. In 1882 Italy, ambitious for colonial expansion and annoyed by French preemption of Tunisia, asked to join the Dual Alliance. The provisions of its entry were defensive and directed against France. At this point Bismarck's policy was a complete success. He was allied with three of the great powers and friendly with the other, Great Britain, which held aloof from all alliances. France was isolated and no threat. Bismarck's diplomacy was a great achievement, but an even greater challenge was to maintain this complicated system of secret alliances in the face of the continuing rivalries among Germany's allies. In spite of another Balkan war that broke out in 1885 and again estranged Austria and Russia, he succeeded. Although the Three Emperors' League lapsed, the Triple Alliance (Germany, Austria, and Italy) was renewed for another five years. To restore German relations with Russia, he negotiated the Reinsurance Treaty of 1887, in which both powers promised to remain neutral if either was attacked. All seemed smooth, but a change in the German monarchy soon overturned everything.

In 1888 William II (1888–1918) came to the German throne. He was twenty-nine years old, ambitious and impetuous. He was imperious by temperament and believed in monarchy by divine right. He had suffered an injury at birth that left him with a withered arm, and he compensated for this disability by means of vigorous exercise, by a military bearing and outlook, and some-

8 Quoted by J. Remak in *The Origins of World War I 1871–1914*, (New York: Holt, Rinehart and Winston, 1967), p. 14.

times by an embarrassingly loud and bombastic rhetoric.

Like many Germans of his generation, William II was filled with a sense of Germany's destiny as the leading power of Europe. He wanted to achieve recognition at least of equality from Britain, the land of his mother and of his grandmother, Queen Victoria. To achieve a "place in the sun," he and his contemporaries wanted a navy and colonies like Britain's. These aims, of course, ran counter to Bismarck's limited continental policy. When William argued for a navy as a defense against a British landing in north Germany, Bismarck replied, "If the British should land on our soil, I should have them arrested."[9] This was only one example of the great distance between the young emperor, or Kaiser, and his chancellor. In 1890 William used a disagreement over domestic policy to dismiss Bismarck.

So long as Bismarck held power, Germany was secure and there was peace among the great European powers. Although he made mistakes and was not always successful, there was much to admire in his understanding and management of international relations in the hard world of reality. He had a clear and limited idea of his nation's goals. He resisted pressures for further expansion with few and insignificant exceptions. He understood and used the full range of diplomatic weapons: appeasement and deterrence, threats and promises, secrecy and openness. He understood the needs and hopes of other countries and, where possible, tried to help to accomplish them or use them to his own advantage. His system of alliances created a stalemate in the Balkans at the same time that it ensured German security.

During Bismarck's time Germany was a force for European peace and was increasingly understood to be so. This would not, of course, have been possible without its great military power, but it also required the leadership of a statesman who was willing and able to exercise restraint and who could make a realistic estimate of what his country needed and what was possible.

9 See Document on p. 810.

Forging of the Triple Entente (1890–1907)

FRANCO-PRUSSIAN ALLIANCE. Almost immediately after Bismarck's retirement his system of alliances collapsed. His successor was General Leo von Caprivi (1831–1899), who had once asked, "What kind of jackass will dare to be Bismarck's successor?" Caprivi refused the Russian request to renew the Reinsurance Treaty, in part because he felt incompetent to continue Bismarck's complicated policy and in part because he wished to draw Germany closer to Britain. The results were unfortunate, as Britain remained aloof and Russia was alienated. Even Bismarck had assumed that ideological differences were too great to permit a Franco-Russian alliance, but political isolation and the need for foreign capital unexpectedly drove the Russians toward France. The French, who were even more isolated, were glad to encourage their investors to pour capital into Russia if it would help produce an alliance and security against Germany. In 1894 the Franco-Russian alliance against Germany was signed.

BRITAIN AND GERMANY. Britain now became the key to the international situation. Colonial rivalries pitted the British against the Russians in Central Asia and against the French in Africa. Traditionally Britain had also opposed Russian control of Constantinople and the Dardanelles and French control of the Low Countries. There was no reason to think that Britain would soon become friendly with its traditional rivals or abandon its accustomed friendliness toward the Germans. Yet within a decade of William II's accession Germany had become the enemy in the minds of Englishmen. Before the turn of the century popular British thrillers about imaginary wars always portrayed the French as the invader; after the turn of the century the enemy was always German. This remarkable transformation has often been attributed to the economic rivalry, in which Germany made vast strides to challenge and even overtake British production in various materials and markets. There can be no doubt that Germany made such gains and that many Englishmen resented them, but the problem was not a serious cause of hostility and waned as the first decade of the century wore on. The real problem lay in the foreign and naval policies of the German emperor and his ministers.

William II's attitude toward Britain was respectful and admiring, especially with regard to its colonial empire and mighty fleet. At first Germany tried to win the British over to the Triple Alliance, but when Britain clung to its policy of "splendid isolation," German policy took a different tack. The idea was to demonstrate Germany's worthiness as an ally by withdrawing support and even making trouble for Britain. This odd manner of gaining

William II States His View of Germany's Future

Forced to abdicate in 1918, Emperor William II of Germany lived on quietly in the Netherlands until 1941. He was left with ample time to reflect on his life and on the background of World War I in which Germany was defeated. In his memoirs he contrasted his own and Bismarck's views on foreign policy during the short period between 1888 and 1890—that is, between William's accession to the throne and his dismissal of Bismarck.

I SPOKE *often with the Prince [Bismarck] about the colonial question and always found in him the intention to utilize the colonies as commercial objects, or objects for swapping purposes, other than to make them useful to the fatherland or utilize them as sources of raw materials. . . .*

I pointed out that steps must be taken for getting a fleet constructed in time, in order that German assets in foreign lands should not be without protection; that, since the Prince had unfurled the German flag in foreign parts, and the people stood behind it, there must also be a navy behind it. . . .

But the Prince turned a deaf ear to my statements and made use of his pet motto: "If the English should land on our soil I should have them arrested." His idea was that the colonies would be defended by us at home. . . .

The political interest of the Prince was, in fact, concentrated essentially upon continental Europe; England lay somewhat to one side among the cares that burdened him daily. . . .

Prince Bismarck did not realize that, through the acquisition of colonies for Germany, he would be obliged to look beyond Europe and be automatically forced to act, politically, on a large scale—with England especially. England, to be sure, was one of the five balls in his diplomatic-statesmanly game, but she was merely one of the five, and he did not grant her the special importance which was her due.

For this reason it was that the Foreign Office likewise was involved entirely in the continental interplay of politics, had not the requisite interest in colonies, navy, or England, and possessed no experience in world politics. The English psychology and mentality, as shown in the pursuit—constant, though concealed by all sorts of little cloaks—of world hegemony, was to the German Foreign Office a book sealed with seven seals.

William II, *The Kaiser's Memoirs*, trans. by Thomas R. Ybarra, (New York and London: Harper and Brothers, 1922), pp. 7–9.

King Edward VII of England and Emperor William II in Germany, August 1906. Edward was William's uncle, but the two men disliked each other. On learning of the outbreak of World War I, William wrote, "Edward VII dead is stronger after his death than I who am still alive!" [Bildarchiv Preussischer Kulturbesitz.]

an ally reflected the Kaiser's confused feelings toward Britain, which consisted of dislike and jealousy mixed with admiration. These feelings reflected those of many Germans, especially in the intellectual community, who like William were eager for Germany to pursue a "World Policy" rather than Bismarck's limited one that confined German interests to Europe. They too saw England as the barrier to German ambitions, and their influence in the schools, the universities, and the press guaranteed popular approval of actions and statements hostile to Britain.

The Germans began to exert pressure against Britain in Africa by barring British attempts to build a railroad from Capetown to Cairo. They also openly sympathized with the Boers of South Africa in their resistance to British expansion. In 1896 William insulted the British by sending a congratulatory telegram to Paul Kruger (1825–1904), president of the Transvaal, for repulsing a British raid "without having to appeal to friendly powers for assistance."

In 1898 William's dream of a German navy began to achieve reality with the passage of a naval law providing for nineteen battleships. In 1900 a second law doubled that figure. The architect of the new navy was Admiral

Alfred von Tirpitz (1849–1930), who openly proclaimed that Germany's naval policy was aimed at Britain. His "risk" theory argued that Germany could build a fleet strong enough not to defeat the British, but to do so much damage as to make the British navy inferior to other powers like France or the United States. The theory was, in fact, absurd because as Germany's fleet became menacing, the British would certainly build ships to maintain their advantage, and British resources were greater than Germany's. The naval policy, therefore, was doomed to failure. Over time its main achievements were to waste German resources and to begin a great naval race with Britain. It is not too much to say, moreover, that the threat posed by the German navy did more to antagonize British opinion than anything else. As the German navy grew and German policies seemed more threatening, the British became alarmed enough to abandon their traditional attitudes and policies.

Expansion of European Power and the "New Imperialism"

At first, however, Britain was not unduly concerned. The British were embarrassed by the general hostility of world opinion during the Boer War (1899–1902) and suddenly alarmed that their isolation no longer seemed so splendid. The Germans, with the exception of the Kruger telegram, had acted with restraint during the war. Between 1898 and 1901 Joseph Chamberlain, the colonial secretary, made several attempts to conclude an alliance with Germany. The Germans, confident that a British alliance with France or Russia was impossible, refused and expected the British to make greater concessions in the future.

THE *ENTENTE CORDIALE*. The first breach in Britain's isolation came in 1902, when an alliance was concluded with Japan to relieve the pressure of defending British interests in the Far East against Russia. Next Britain abandoned its traditional antagonism toward France and in 1904 concluded a series of agreements with the French, collectively called the *Entente Cordiale.* It was not a formal treaty and had no military provisions, but it settled all outstanding colonial differences between the two nations. The Entente Cordiale was a long step toward aligning the British with Germany's great potential enemy.

Britain's new relationship with France was surprising, but in 1904 hardly anyone believed that the British whale and the Russian bear would ever come together. The Russo-Japanese war of 1904–1905 made such a development seem even less likely because Britain was allied with Russia's enemy. But Britain had behaved with restraint, and the Russians were chastened by their unexpected and humiliating defeat. The defeat had also led to the Russian Revolution of 1905. Although the revolution was put down, it left Russia weak and reduced British apprehensions in that direction. At the same time the British were concerned that Russia might again drift into the German orbit.

THE FIRST MOROCCAN CRISIS. At this point Germany decided to test the new understanding between Britain and Germany and to press for colonial gains. In March 1905 Emperor William II landed at Tangier, challenged the French protectorate there, and by implication asserted Germany's right to participate in Morocco's destiny. Germany's chancellor, Prince Bernhard von Bülow (1849–1929), intended to show France how weak it was and how little it could expect from Britain and at the same time to gain significant colonial concessions.

The Germans might well have achieved their aims, but they pushed too far and demanded an international conference of concerned states to make their point more dramatically. The conference met in 1906 at Algeciras in Spain. Austria sided with its German ally, but Spain, Italy, and the United States voted with Britain and France. The Germans had overplayed their hand, receiving trivial concessions, and the French were confirmed in their position in Morocco. German bullying had, moreover, driven Britain and France closer together. In the face of the threat of a German attack on France, Sir Edward Grey, the British foreign secretary, without making a firm commitment, authorized conversations between the British and the French general staffs. Their agreements became technically and morally binding as the years passed. By 1914 French and British military and naval plans were so mutually dependent that they were effectively, if not formally, allies.

BRITISH AGREEMENT WITH RUSSIA. Britain's fear of Germany's growing naval power, its concern over German ambitions in the Near East as represented by the German-sponsored plan to build a railroad from Berlin to Baghdad, and its closer relations with France made it desirable for Britain to become more friendly with France's ally, Russia. With French support the British made overtures to the Russians and in 1907 concluded an agreement with them much like the Entente Cordiale with France. It settled Russo-British quarrels in central Asia and opened the door for wider cooperation. The Triple Entente was now ranged against the Triple Alliance. Because Italy was unreliable, Germany and Austria–Hungary stood surrounded by two great land powers and Great Britain.

H.M.S. *Dreadnought* was completed by the British navy in 1906. It initiated a whole new class of battleships and gave rise to a new arms race in the decade before World War I. [The Granger Collection.]

William II and his ministers had turned Bismarck's nightmare of the prospect of a two-front war with France and Russia into a reality and had made it more horrible by adding Britain to the hostile coalition. The equilibrium that Bismarck had worked so hard to achieve was destroyed. Britain could no longer support Austria in restraining Russian ambitions in the Balkans. Germany, increasingly terrified by a sense of encirclement, was less willing to restrain the Austrians for fear of alienating them. In the Dual Alliance of Germany and Austria it had become less clear who was horse and who rider. Bismarck's alliance system had been intended to maintain peace, but the new one increased the risk of war and made the Balkans a likely spot for it to break out. Bismarck's diplomacy left France isolated and impotent; the new arrangement found France associated with the two greatest powers in Europe apart from Germany. The Germans could rely only on Austria, and such was the condition of that troubled empire that it was less likely to provide aid than to need it.

The Road to War

Growing Tensions (1908–1914)

The situation in the Balkans in the first decade of this century was exceedingly complicated. The weak Ottoman Empire controlled the central strip running west from Constantinople to the Adriatic. North and south of it were the independent states of Romania, Serbia, and Greece, as well as Bulgaria, technically still part of the empire but legally autonomous and practically independent. The Austro-Hungarian Empire included Croatia and Slovenia and since 1878 had "occupied and administered" Bosnia and Herzegovina.

With the exception of the Greeks and the Romanians most of the inhabitants of the Balkans spoke variants of the same Slavic language and felt a cultural and historical kinship with one another. For centuries they had been ruled by Austrians, Hungarians, or Turks, and the growing nationalism that characterized late nineteenth-century Europe made many of them eager for liberty. The more radical among them longed for a union of the south Slavic or Yugoslav peoples in a single nation. They looked to independent Serbia as the center of the new nation and hoped to detach all the Slavic provinces from Austria and

"The Mailed Fist of the Kaiser Strikes Agadir." This cartoon refers to the landing of the German gunboat *Panther* at Agadir in Morocco in 1911. William II's purpose was to press the French to make colonial concessions to Germany in Africa and, perhaps, to break up the Entente between the French and the British. The result, instead, was the second Moroccan crisis, which drew the Entente closer together and helped bring on World War I.

OPPOSITE: Two maps show the Balkans before and after the two Balkan wars; note the Ottoman retreat. In the center we see the geographical relationship of the Central Powers and their Bulgarian and Turkish allies. Tables give relative strength of World War I combatants.

especially Bosnia, which bordered on Serbia. In this regard Serbia was to unite the Slavs at the expense of Austria, as Piedmont had united the Italians and Prussia the Germans.

In 1908 a group of modernizing reformers called the Young Turks brought about a revolution in the Ottoman Empire. Their actions threatened to revive the life of the empire and to interfere with the plans of the European jackals preparing to pounce on the Ottoman corpse. These events brought on the first of a series of Balkan crises that would eventually lead to war.

THE BOSNIAN CRISIS. In 1908 the Austrian and Russian governments decided to act quickly before Turkey became strong enough to resist. They struck a bargain in which it was agreed that they would call an international conference where each of them would support the other's demands. Russia would agree to the Austrian annexation of Bosnia and Herzegovina, and Austria would support Russia's request to open the Dardanelles to Russian warships.

Austria, however, declared the annexation before any conference was called. The British, ever concerned about their own position in the Mediterranean, refused to agree to the Russian demand. The Russians felt betrayed, humiliated, and furious. Their "little brothers," the Serbs, were frustrated and angry at the loss of Bosnia, and the Russians were too weak to do anything but accept the new situation. The Germans had not been warned in

advance of Austria's plans and were unhappy that the action threatened their relations with Russia. But Germany felt so dependent on the Dual Alliance that it assured Austria of its support. Austria had been given a free hand, and to an extent German policy was being made in Vienna. It was a dangerous precedent. At the same time, the failure of Britain and France to support Russia strained the Entente and made it harder for them to oppose Russian interests again in the future if they were to retain Russian friendship.

THE SECOND MOROCCAN CRISIS. The second Moroccan crisis in 1911 emphasized the French and British need for mutual support. When France sent in an army to put down a rebellion, Germany took the opportunity to assert its rights in Morocco as a means of extorting colonial concessions in the French Congo. To add force to their demands, they sent the gunboat *Panther* to the port of Agadir, allegedly to protect German citizens there. Once again, as in 1905, the Germans went too far. The *Panther*'s visit to Agadir provoked a strong reaction in Britain. For some time Anglo-German relations had been growing worse, chiefly because of the intensification of the naval race. In 1907 the Germans built the first new battleship of the dreadnought class, which Britain had developed in 1906. In 1908 Germany passed still another naval law, which accelerated the schedule of production to challenge British naval supremacy. These actions frightened and angered the British because of the clear threat to the security of the island kingdom and its empire. The German actions also forced Britain to increase taxes to pay for new armaments just when the Liberal government was launching its expensive program of social legislation. Negotiations failed to persuade William II and Tirpitz to slow down naval construction.

In this atmosphere the British heard of the *Panther*'s arrival in Morocco. They wrongly believed that the Germans meant to turn Agadir into a naval base on the Atlantic. The crisis passed when France yielded some insignificant bits of the Congo and Germany withdrew

	GREAT BRITAIN	FRANCE	ITALY	RUSSIA	BELGIUM	ROMANIA	GREECE
POPULATION (TOTAL)	OVERSEAS EMP. 390 MILLION / 45 000 000	OVERSEAS EMP. 58 MILLION / 40 000 000	OVERSEAS EMP. 2 MILLION / 35 000 000	164 000 000	7 500 000	7 500 000	5 000 000
SOLDIERS POTENTIALLY AVAILABLE	711 000	1 250 000	750 000	1 200 000	180 000	420 000	120 000
MILITARY EXPENDITURES 1913–1914 (MILLIONS OF $)	250 000 000	185 000 000	50 000 000	335 000 000	13 750 000	15 000 000	3 750 000
BATTLESHIPS IN SERVICE OR BEING BUILT	64	28	14	16			
CRUISERS	121	34	22	14			
SUBMARINES	64	73	12	29			
MERCHANT SHIPS MILLIONS OF TONS	20 000 000	2 000 000	1 750 000	750 000			

THE BALKANS 1912

1878 SERBIA
1878 ROMANIA
1878
1880 MONTENEGRO
1878 BULGARIA 1885
OTTOMAN EMPIRE
GREECE
100 MI.
TRM

CENTRAL EUROPE 1914

Berlin
GERMANY
AUSTRIA
HUNGARY
BULGARIA
OTTOMAN EMPIRE

CENTRAL POWERS
ALLIES

BERLIN – BAGHDAD RAILWAY

THE BALKANS 1913

ROMANIA
SERBIA
MONTE-NEGRO 1913
ALBANIA 1913
BULGARIA
1913
1913
GREECE
1913
OTTOMAN EMPIRE

	SERBIA	MONTE-NEGRO	UNITED STATES	GERMANY	AUSTRIA-HUNGARY	OTTOMAN EMPIRE	BULGARIA
POPULATION (TOTAL)	5 000 000	500 000	92 000 000	65 000 000	50 000 000	20 000 000	4 500 000
SOLDIERS POTENTIALLY AVAILABLE	195 000		150 000	2 200 000	810 000	360 000	340 000
MILITARY EXPENDITURES 1913–1914 (MILLIONS OF $)	5 250 000		150 000 000	300 000 000	110 000 000	40 000 000	5 500 000
BATTLESHIPS IN SERVICE OR BEING BUILT			37	40	16		
CRUISERS			35	57	12		
SUBMARINES			25	23	6		
MERCHANT SHIPS MILLIONS OF TONS			4 500 000	5 000 000	1 000 000		

from Morocco. The main result was to increase British fear and hostility and to draw them closer to France. Specific military plans were formulated for a British expeditionary force to defend France in case of German attack, and the British and French navies agreed to cooperate. Without any formal treaty the German naval construction and the Agadir crisis had turned the Entente Cordiale into an alliance that could not have been more binding. If France were attacked by Germany, Britain must defend the French, for its own security was inextricably tied up with that of France.

WAR IN THE BALKANS. The second Moroccan crisis also provoked another crisis in the Balkans. Italy had long sought to gain colonies and to take its place among the great powers. It had long wanted Libya, which though worth little at the time was at least available. Italy feared that the recognition of the French protectorate in Morocco would encourage France to move into Libya. Consequently, in 1911 Italy attacked the Ottoman Empire to anticipate the French, defeated the faltering Turks, and obtained Libya and the Dodecanese Islands. The Italian victory encouraged the Balkan states to try their luck. In 1912 Bulgaria, Greece, Montenegro, and Serbia joined an attack on the Ottoman Empire and won easily. After this First Balkan War the victors fell out among themselves. The Serbs and the Bulgarians quarreled about the division of Macedonia, and in 1913 a Second Balkan War erupted. This time Turkey and Romania joined the other states against Bulgaria and stripped away much of what the Bulgarians had gained since 1878.

After the First Balkan War the alarmed Austrians became determined to limit Serbian gains and especially to prevent the Serbs from gaining a port on the Adriatic. This policy meant keeping Serbia out of Albania, but the Russians backed the Serbs and tensions mounted. An international conference sponsored by Britain in early 1913 resolved the matter in Austria's favor and called for an independent kingdom of Albania. But Austria felt humiliated by the public airing of Serbian demands. Then

for some time the Serbs defied the powers and continued to occupy parts of Albania. Under Austrian pressure they withdrew, but in September 1913, after the Second Balkan War, the Serbs reoccupied sections of Albania. In mid-October Austria unilaterally issued an ultimatum to Serbia, and the latter country again withdrew its forces from Albania. During this crisis many people in Austria had wanted an all-out attack on Serbia to remove its threat once and for all from the empire. Those demands had been resisted by Emperor Francis Joseph and the heir to the throne, Archduke Francis Ferdinand. At the same time Pan-Slavic sentiment in Russia pressed Tsar Nicholas II to take a firm stand, but Russia once again let Austria have its way with Serbia. Throughout the crisis Britain, France, and Germany restrained their respective allies, although each worried about seeming too reluctant to help its friends.

The lessons learned from this crisis of 1913 profoundly influenced behavior in the final crisis, the crisis of 1914. The Russians had once again, as in 1908, been embarrassed by their passivity, and their allies were more reluctant to restrain them again. The Austrians were embarrassed by what had resulted from accepting an international conference and were determined not to repeat the experience. They had seen that better results might be obtained from a threat of direct force; they and their German allies did not miss the lesson.

Sarajevo and the Outbreak of War (June–August 1914)

THE ASSASSINATION. On June 28, 1914, a young Bosnian nationalist shot and killed the Austrian Archduke Francis Ferdinand, heir to the throne, and his wife as they drove in an open car through the Bosnian capital of Sarajevo. The assassin was a member of a conspiracy hatched by a political terrorist society called Union or Death, better known as the Black Hand. A major participant in the planning and preparation of the crime was the chief of intelligence of the Serbian army's general staff.

The Austrian Archduke Franz Ferdinand and his wife at Sarajevo, June 28, 1914. Later in the day the royal couple were assassinated by young Slavic revolutionaries trained and supplied in Serbia. The murders set off the crisis that led to World War I. [Popperfoto.]

Moments after the assassination of Archduke Ferdinand and his wife the Bosnian police captured one of the assassins in Sarajevo. [The Granger Collection.]

Even though his role was not actually known at the time, it was generally believed that Serbian officials were involved. The glee of the Serbian press lent support to that belief. The archduke was not a popular person in his own land, and his funeral evoked few signs of grief. He had been known to favor a form of federal government that would have given a higher status to the Slavs in the empire. This position alienated the conservatives and the Hungarians. It also alarmed radical Yugoslav nationalists,

who feared that reform might end their dream of an independent south Slav state.

THE CENTRAL POWERS' RESPONSE. News of the assassination produced outrage and condemnation everywhere. To those Austrians who had long favored an attack on Serbia as a solution to the empire's Slavic problem, the opportunity seemed irresistible. But it was never easy for the Dual Monarchy to make a decision. Conrad von Hötzendorf, chief of the Austrian general

Count Leopold Berchtold (on the left), the Austro-Hungarian Foreign Minister, and Theodor von Bethmann-Hollweg, German Chancellor, meet in 1912. Both men played crucial roles in the war crisis of 1914.
[Ullstein Bilderdienst.]

staff, urged an attack as he had often done before. Count Tisza, speaking for Hungary, resisted. Berchtold, the Austro-Hungarian foreign minister, felt the need for strong action, but he knew that German support would be required in the likely event that Russia should decide to intervene to protect Serbia. He also knew that nothing could be done without Tisza's approval and that only German support could persuade the Hungarians to accept the policy of war. The question of peace or war, therefore, had to be answered in Berlin.

William II and Chancellor Theobald von Bethmann-Hollweg (1856–1921) readily promised German support for an attack on Serbia. It has often been said that they gave the Austrians a "blank check," but their message was firmer than that. They urged the Austrians to move swiftly while the other powers were still angry at Serbia, and they made the Austrians feel that a failure to act would be taken as evidence of Austria–Hungary's weakness and uselessness as an ally. Therefore, the Austrians never wavered in their determination to make war on Serbia. They hoped, with the protection of Germany, to fight a limited war that would not bring on a general European conflict, but they were prepared to risk even the latter. The Germans also knew that they risked a general war, but they hoped to "localize" the fight between Austria and Serbia.

Some scholars believe that Germany had long been plotting war, and some even think that a specific plan for war in 1914 was set in motion as early as 1912. The vast body of evidence on the crisis of 1914 gives no support to such notions. The German leaders plainly reacted to a crisis that they had not foreseen and just as plainly made decisions in response to events. The fundamental decision to support Austria, which made it very difficult if not impossible to avoid war, was made by the emperor and the chancellor without significant consultation with either military or diplomatic advisers.

William II appears to have reacted violently to the assassination. He was moved by his friendship for the archduke and by outrage at an attack on royalty. It is

The Austrian Ambassador Gets a "Blank Check" from the Kaiser

It was at a meeting at Potsdam on July 5, 1914 that the Austrian ambassador received from the Kaiser assurance that Germany would support Austria in the Balkans, even at the risk of war.

AFTER *lunch, when I again called attention to the seriousness of the situation, the Kaiser authorised me to inform our gracious Majesty that we might in this case, as in all others, rely upon Germany's full support. He must, as he said before, first hear what the Imperial Chancellor has to say, but he did not doubt in the least that Herr von Bethmann Hollweg would agree with him. Especially as far as our action against Serbia was concerned. But it was his (Kaiser Wilhelm's) opinion that this action must not be delayed. Russia's attitude will no doubt be hostile, but to this he had been for years prepared, and should a war between Austria–Hungary and Russia be unavoidable, we might be convinced that Germany, our old faithful ally, would stand at our side. Russia at the present time was in no way prepared for war, and would think twice before it appealed to arms. But it will certainly set other powers on to the Triple Alliance and add fuel to the fire in the Balkans. He understands perfectly well that His Apostolic Majesty in his well-known love of peace would be reluctant to march into Serbia; but if we had really recognised the necessity of warlike action against Serbia, he (Kaiser Wilhelm) would regret if we did not make use of the present moment, which is all in our favour.*

Outbreak of the World War: German Documents Collected by Karl Kautsky, Max Montgelas and Walther Schücking (eds.) (New York: Carnegie Endowment for International Peace, 1924), p. 76.

doubtful that a different provocation would have moved him so much. Bethmann-Hollweg was less emotional but under severe pressure. To resist the decision would have meant flatly to oppose the emperor. The chancellor, moreover, was suspected of being "soft" in the powerful military circles favored by his master. A conciliatory position would have been difficult. Beyond these considerations Bethmann-Hollweg, like many other Germans, viewed the future with apprehension. Russia was recovering its strength and would reach a military peak in 1917. The Entente was growing more powerful, and Germany's only reliable ally was Austria. The chancellor recognized the danger of support for Austria, but he believed it to be even more dangerous to withhold that support. If Austria did not crush Serbia, the empire would soon collapse before the onslaught of Slavic nationalism defended by Russia. If Germany did not defend its ally, the Austrians might look elsewhere for help. His policy was one of "calculated risk."

The calculations proved to be incorrect. Bethmann-Hollweg hoped that the Austrians would strike swiftly and present the powers with a *fait accompli* while the outrage of the assassination was still fresh, and that German support would deter Russian involvement. Failing that, he was prepared for a continental war that would bring rapid victory over France and allow a full-scale attack on the Russians, who were always slow to bring their strength into action. All of this policy depended on British neutrality, and the German chancellor convinced himself that the British could be persuaded to stand aloof.

However, the Austrians were slow to act, as always, and did not even deliver their deliberately unacceptable ultimatum to Serbia until July 24, when the general hostility toward Serbia had begun to subside. Serbia further embarrassed the Austrians by returning so soft and conciliatory an answer that the mercurial German emperor thought it removed all reason for war. But it was too late for Austria to turn back, and on July 28 the Austrians declared war on Serbia even though they could not put an army into the field until mid-August.

THE ENTENTE'S RESPONSE. The Russians, previously so often forced to back off, angrily responded to the Austrian demands on Serbia. The most conservative elements of the Russian government opposed war, fearing that it would bring on revolution as it had in 1905. But nationalists, Pan-Slavs, and most of the politically conscious classes in general demanded action. The government responded by ordering partial mobilization, against Austria only. This policy was militarily impossible, but its intention was the diplomatic one of putting pressure on Austria to hold back its attack on Serbia. Mobilization of any kind, however, was a dangerous political weapon because it was generally understood to be equivalent to an act of war. It was especially alarming to General Helmuth von Moltke (1848–1916), head of the German general staff. The possibility that the Russians might start mobilization before the Germans could move would upset the delicate timing of Germany's only battle plan, the Schlieffen Plan, and put Germany in great danger. From this point on, Moltke pressed for German mobilization and war, and the pressure of military necessity mounted until it became irresistible.

The Western powers were not eager for war. France's president and prime minister were on their way back from a visit to Russia when the crisis flared up again on July 24. The Austrians had, in fact, timed their ultimatum precisely so that these two men would be at sea at the crucial moment. Had they been at their desks, they might have attempted to restrain the Russians, but the French ambassador to Russia gave the Russians the same assurances that Germany had given its ally. The British worked hard to avoid trouble by traditional means, a conference of the powers. Austria, still smarting from its humiliation after the London Conference of 1913, would not hear of it. The Germans privately supported the Austrians but publicly took on a conciliatory tone in the hope of keeping the British neutral. Soon, however, Bethmann-Hollweg came to realize what he should have known from the first: if Germany attacked France, Britain must fight. Until July 30 his public appeals to Austria for restraint were a sham. Thereafter he sincerely tried to persuade the Austrians to negotiate and to avoid a general war, but it was too late. While Bethmann-Hollweg was urging restraint on the Austrians, Moltke was pressing them to act. The Austrians wondered who was in charge in Berlin, but they could not turn back.

On July 30 Austria ordered mobilization against Russia. Bethmann-Hollweg resisted the enormous pressure to mobilize, not because he had any further hope of avoiding war but because he wanted Russia to mobilize against Germany first and appear to be the aggressor. Only in that way could he win the support of the German nation for war, especially the pacifistic Social Democrats. His luck was good for a change. The news of Russian general mobilization came only minutes before Germany would have mobilized in any case. The Schlieffen Plan went into effect. The Germans invaded Luxembourg on August 1 and Belgium on August 3. The latter invasion violated the treaty of 1839 in which the British had guaranteed Belgian neutrality. This factor undermined the considerable sentiment in Britain for neutrality and united the nation against Germany. Germany then invaded France, and on August 4 Britain declared war on Germany. The Great War had begun. As Lord Grey put it, the lights were going out all over Europe. They would come on again, but Europe would never be the same.

World War I (1914–1918)

Throughout Europe jubilation greeted the outbreak of war. No general war had been fought since Napoleon, and the horrors of modern warfare were not yet understood. The dominant memory was of Bismarck's swift and decisive campaigns, in which costs and casualties were light and the rewards great. After the repeated crises of recent years and the fears and resentments they had created, war came as a release of tension. The popular press had increased public awareness of and interest in foreign affairs and had fanned the flames of patriotism. The prospect of war moved even a rational man of science like Sigmund Freud to say, "My whole libido goes out to Austria–Hungary."[10]

Strategies and Stalemate: 1914–1917

The strategies of both sides rested on Karl von Clausewitz's (1780–1831) interpretation of the Napoleonic mode of war, which constituted the dominant military theory of the day. Both sides expected to take the offensive, force a battle on favorable ground, and win a quick victory. The Entente powers—or the Allies, as they came to be called—held superiority in numbers and financial

10 Quoted in Joachim Remak, *The Origins of World War I* (New York. Holt, Rinehart and Winston, 1967), p. 134.

Germany's grand strategy for quickly winning the war against France in 1914 is shown by the wheeling arrows on the map. The crushing blows at France were, in the original plan, to be followed by the release of troops for use against Russia on Germany's Eastern front. But the plan was not adequately implemented, and the war on the Western front became a long contest in place.

THE SCHLIEFFEN PLAN OF 1905

resources as well as command of the sea. Germany and Austria, the Central Powers, had the advantages of internal lines of communication and of having launched their attack first.

After 1905 Germany's only war plan was the one developed by Count Alfred von Schlieffen (1833–1913), chief of the German general staff from 1891 to 1906. It aimed at going around the French defenses by sweeping through Belgium to the channel, then wheeling to the south and east to envelop the French and to crush them against the German fortresses in Lorraine. The secret of success lay in making the German right wing immensely strong and deliberately weakening the left opposite the French frontier. The weakness of the left was meant to draw the French into the wrong place while the war was decided on the German right. As one keen military analyst has explained, "It would be like a revolving door—if a man pressed heavily on one side, the other side would spring round and strike him in the back. Here lay the real subtlety of the plan, not in the mere geographical detour." [11] In the east the Germans planned to stand on the defensive against Russia until France had been crushed, a task they thought would take only six weeks.

The apparent risk, besides the violation of Belgian neutrality and the consequent alienation of Britain, lay in weakening German defenses against a direct attack across the frontier. The strength of German fortresses and the superior firepower of German howitzers made that risk more apparent than real. The true danger was that the German striking force on the right through Belgium would not be powerful enough to make the swift progress vital to success. Schlieffen is said to have uttered the dying words: "It must come to a fight. Only make the right wing strong." The execution of his plan, however, was left to Helmuth von Moltke, the nephew of Bismarck's most effective general. The younger Moltke was a gloomy and nervous man who lacked the talent of his

11 B. H. Liddell Hart, *The Real War, 1914–1918* (Boston: Little, Brown and Co., 1964; first published in 1930), p. 47.

illustrious uncle and the theoretical daring of Schlieffen. He added divisions to the left wing and even weakened the Russian front for the same purpose. The consequence of this hesitant strategy was the failure of the Schlieffen Plan by a narrow margin.

THE WAR IN THE WEST. The French had also put their faith in the offensive, but with less reason than the Germans. They badly underestimated the numbers and effectiveness of the German reserves and set too much store by the importance of the courage and spirit of their troops. These proved insufficient against modern weapons, especially the machine gun. The French offensive on Germany's western frontier failed totally. In a sense this defeat was better than a partial success because it released troops for the use against the main German army. As a result the French and the British were able to stop the Germans at the Battle of the Marne in September 1914.

Thereafter the nature of the war in the west changed completely and became one of position instead of movement. Both sides dug in behind a wall of trenches protected by barbed wire that stretched from the North Sea to Switzerland. Strategically placed machine-gun nests made assaults difficult and dangerous. Both sides nonetheless attempted massive attacks prepared for by artillery barrages of unprecedented and horrible force and duration. Still the defense was always able to recover and bring up reserves fast enough to prevent a breakthrough. Sometimes assaults that cost hundreds of thousands of

WORLD WAR I IN EUROPE

T R MILLER

250 MI.
250 KM.

NORWAY
Christiania

SWEDEN
Stockholm
Göteborg

FINLAND
Petro...
ST. PETER...
Reval

ESTONIA

LATVIA

BALTIC SEA

NORTH SEA

Aberdeen

UNITED
KINGDOM
Edinburgh
Hull
Yarmouth
London
Dover

DENMARK
Copenhagen

HELIGOLAND

KIEL CANAL
Hamburg
Bremen
ELBE
Berlin
ODER

GERMAN EMPIRE
Essen
Cologne
Leipzig
Dresden
Koblenz
Frankfurt
RHINE
Mainz
Metz
LORRAINE
Nuremberg
Strassburg
ALSACE
Munich

Danzig
E. PRUSSIA
TANNENBERG

Memel
LITHUANIA
Kaunas
Vilna
Suwalki

FARTHEST
RUSSIAN ADVANCE
1914

BATTLE LINE
DEC., 1917

RUSS...

Warsaw
Brest-
Litovsk
Pinsk

BATTLE LINE
MAY, 1915

BRUSILOV'S
OFFENSIVE
AUG., 1916

Breslau
SILESIA

VISTULA

Cracow
GALICIA
Lemberg
Gorlice

Prague
BOHEMIA

MORAVIA

SLOVAKIA

Vienna

AUSTRIA-
HUNGARY

Budapest

Debrecen

TRAN-
SYLVANIA
Hermann-
stadt

NETH.
Amsterdam
Brussels
BELG.
Liége
Ypres
Arras
Sedan
LUX.
Compiègne
Versailles
Paris

Le
Havre

WESTERN
FRONT
SEE INSET

Verdun
Toul
Belfort

FRANCE
Clermont
Lyons

Berne
SWITZ.
Geneva

TYROL
AUG.
1917

Klagenfurt
Caporetto

Trieste
Fiume
CROATIA

Agram

BOSNIA
Sarajevo

Belgrade

Nish
MONTE-
NEGRO
SERBIA
Uskub
Strumitza
1917-18

ROMAN...
Bucharest
DANUBE

BULGARIA
Sofia

Milan
Turin
Genoa

Marseilles

ITALIAN
FRONT

PO
MAR.
1918.
Venice

ITALY
Rome

ADRIATIC SEA

ALBANIA

BALKAN
FRONT

1916

1915

GREECE

DARDA-
NELLES
GALLIPOLI
1915-16

Naples
Taranto

TRIPLE
ENTENTE

ALLIES OF THE
TRIPLE ENTENTE

CENTRAL
POWERS

ALLIES OF THE
CENTRAL POWERS

822 *Imperialism, Alliances, and War*

WORLD WAR I IN EUROPE
THE WESTERN FRONT
1914–1918

100 MI.

100 KM.

UNITED KINGDOM

Dover
Calais
Nieuport
Ghent
Antwerp
Brussels
BELGIUM
Lille
Mons
Liege
Namur
Vimy Ridge
Cambrai
St.Quentin
Laôn
Sedan
LUX.
Longwy
Compiègne
Reims
Metz
Verdun
Chateau Thierry
St. Mihiel
Versailles
Paris
FRANCE

② NIVELLE'S OFFENSIVE, SPRING, 1917

③ HINDENBURG LINE, (STABILIZED LINE) 1917–1918

① FARTHEST GERMAN ADVANCE, SEPT., 1914

⑥ ARMISTICE LINE NOV. 11, 1918

④ GERMAN GAINS, MARCH–JULY, 1918

⑤ MEUSE–ARGONNE MAJOR AMERICAN DRIVES CUT THE GERMAN SUPPLY LINE AT SEDAN AND END THE WAR, NOV. 11, 1918

RUSSIAN FRONT

Gomel
Kiev
Kharkov
Poltava
DNIEPER
DONETZ
Rostov
U K R A I N E
Odessa
SEA OF AZOV
BESSARABIA
DNIESTER
alatz
CRIMEA
Constantsa
B L A C K   S E A
Varna

FARTHEST GERMAN ADVANCE SUMMER, 1918

FARTHEST GERMAN ADVANCE DEC., 1917

Constantinople
OTTOMAN
Angora
EMPIRE

Despite the importance of military action in the Far East, in the Arab world, and at sea, the main theaters of activity in World War I were in the European areas shown here. The crucial Western front is seen in somewhat greater detail in the inset map.

lives produced advances that could be measured in hundreds of yards. The introduction of poison gas as a solution to the problem proved ineffective. Toward the end of the war the British introduced the tank, which proved to be the answer to the machine gun, but throughout the war defense was supreme. For three years after its establishment, the western front moved only a few miles in either direction.

THE WAR IN THE EAST. In the east the war began auspiciously for the Allies. The Russians advanced into Austrian territory and inflicted heavy casualties, but Russian incompetence and German energy soon reversed the situation. A young German officer, Erich Ludendorff (1865–1937), under the command of the elderly General Paul von Hindenburg (1847–1934), defeated the Russians at the Masurian Lakes and destroyed or captured an entire army at the Battle of Tannenberg. In 1915 the Central Powers pressed their advantage in the east and drove into the Baltic states and White Russia, inflicting over two million casualties in a single year. Russian confidence was badly shaken, but the Russian army stayed in the field.

As the battle lines hardened, both sides sought new allies. Turkey, because of its hostility to Russia, and Bulgaria, the enemy of Serbia, joined the Central Powers.

Italy seemed an especially valuable prize, and both sides bid for Italian support with promises of a division of the spoils of victory. Because what the Italians wanted most was held by Austria, it was easier for the Allies to make the more attractive promises. In a secret treaty of 1915 the Allies agreed to deliver to Italy most of *Italia Irredenta* (i.e., the Trentino, the South Tyrol, Trieste, and some of the Dalmatian Islands) after victory. By the spring of 1915 Italy was engaging Austrian armies. Although the Italian campaign drained the strength of the Central Powers to a degree, the alliance with Italy generally proved a disappointment to the Allies and never produced significant results.

Romania joined the Allies in 1916 but was quickly defeated and driven from the war.

World War I (1914–1918) 823

The military tank made its first appearance during World War I. It had the military advantages of giving its personnel armored protection, being able to cross many natural and manmade obstacles, and permitting a commander to advance fire power with some impunity closer to an enemy force than was possible by the traditional infantry charge. This photograph shows a light tank crossing an obstacle at a World War I British military experiment station. [Bettmann Archive.]

OPPOSITE: American soldiers in France. In 1918 the American army arrived in France in sufficient numbers to make a significant contribution. Here American forces take over a section in the Argonne forest, relieving tired Allied troops. [Radio Times Hulton Picture Library.]

In the Far East Japan honored its alliance with Britain and entered the war. The Japanese quickly overran the German colonies in China and the Pacific and used the opportunity to improve their own position against China.

Both sides also tried the tactic of subversion by appealing to nationalist sentiment in areas held by the enemy. The Germans supported nationalist movements among the Irish, the Flemings in Belgium, and the Poles and the Ukrainians under Russian rule. They even tried to persuade the Turks to lead a Moslem uprising against the British and the French in North Africa.

The Allies also used the device of subversion, with greater success. They sponsored movements of national autonomy for the Czechs, the Slovaks, the south Slavs, and the Poles that were under Austrian rule. They also favored a movement of Arab independence from Turkey. Led by Colonel T. E. Lawrence (1888–1935), this last scheme proved especially successful in the late years of the war.

In 1915 the Allies undertook to break the deadlock in the fighting by going around it. The idea came chiefly from Winston Churchill (1874–1965), first lord of the British Admiralty. He proposed an attack on the Dardanelles and the swift capture of Constantinople. This policy would knock Turkey from the war, bring help to the Balkan front, and ease communication with Russia. The plan was daring but promising and, in its original form, presented little risk. British naval superiority and the element of surprise would allow the forcing of the straits and the capture of Constantinople by purely naval action. Even if the scheme failed, the fleet could escape with little loss. Success depended on timing, speed, and daring leadership, but all of these were lacking. The execution of the attack was inept and overly cautious. Troops were landed, and as resistance continued, the

Allied commitment increased. Before the campaign was abandoned, the Allies lost almost 150,000 men and diverted three times that number from more useful occupation.

Both sides turned back to the west in 1916. General Erich von Falkenhayn (1861–1922), who had succeeded Moltke in September 1914, sought success by an attack on the French stronghold of Verdun. His plan was not to take the fortress or break through the line but rather to inflict enormously heavy casualties on the French, who must defend it against superior firepower coming from several directions. He, too, underestimated the superiority of the defense, and the French were able to hold Verdun with comparatively few men and to inflict almost as many casualties as they suffered. The commander of Verdun, Henri Pétain (1856–1951), became a national hero and "They shall not pass" a slogan of national defiance. The Allies tried to end the impasse by launching a major offensive along the River Somme in July. Aided by a Russian attack in the east that drew off some German strength and by an enormous artillery barrage, they hoped at last to break through. Once again the superiority of the defense was demonstrated. Enormous casualties on both sides brought no result. On all fronts losses were great and results meager. The war on land dragged on with no end in sight.

THE WAR AT SEA. As the war continued, control of the sea became more important. The British ignored the distinction between war supplies, which were contraband according to international law, and food or other peaceful cargo, which was not subject to seizure. They imposed a strict blockade meant to starve out the enemy, regardless of international law. The Germans responded with submarine warfare meant to destroy British shipping and starve the British. They declared the waters around the British Isles a war zone, where even neutral ships would not be safe. Both policies were unwelcome to neutrals, and especially to the United States, which conducted extensive trade in the Atlantic, but the sinking of neutral ships by German submarines was both more dramatic and more offensive. In 1915 the British liner *Lusitania* was torpedoed by a German submarine. Among the 1,200 drowned were 118 Americans. President Woodrow Wilson (1856–1924) warned Germany that a repetition would not be accepted, and the Germans desisted rather than further anger the United States. This development gave the Allies a considerable advantage. The German fleet that had cost so much money and caused so much trouble played no significant part in the war. The only battle it fought was at Jutland in the spring of 1916. The battle resulted in a standoff and confirmed British domination of the surface of the sea.

AMERICA ENTERS THE WAR. In December 1916 President Woodrow Wilson of the United States intervened in an attempt to bring about a negotiated peace, but neither side was willing to renounce war aims that its opponent found unacceptable. The war seemed likely to continue until one or both sides reached exhaustian. Two events early in 1917 changed the situation radically. On February 1 the Germans announced the resumption of unrestricted submarine warfare, which led the United States to break off diplomatic relations. On April 6 the United States declared war on the Central Powers. One of the barriers to an earlier American intervention had been the presence of autocratic tsarist Russia among the Allies. Wilson could conceive of the war only as an idealistic crusade "to make the world safe for democracy." That problem was resolved in March of 1917 by a revolution in Russia that overthrew the tsarist government.

World War I (1914–1918) 825

Field guns, under a red banner, in place in Petrograd (formerly St. Petersburg) during the Russian Revolution in March 1917. [The Granger Collection.]

Revolutions in Russia
(March and November 1917)

The March Revolution in Russia was neither planned nor led by any political faction. It was the result of the collapse of the monarchy's ability to govern. Although public opinion had strongly supported Russian entry into the war, the conflict put far too great demands on the resources of the country and the efficiency of the tsarist government. Nicholas II was weak, incompetent, and suspected of being under the domination of his German wife and the insidious monk Rasputin, who was assassinated by noblemen in 1916. Military and domestic failures produced massive casualties, widespread hunger, strikes by workers, and disorganization in the army. The peasant discontent that had plagued the countryside before 1914 did not subside during the conflict. In 1916 the tsar adjourned the Duma and proceeded to rule alone. All political factions were in one way or another discontented.

In early March 1917 strikes and worker demonstrations erupted in Petrograd, as St. Petersburg had been renamed. The ill-disciplined troops in the city refused to fire on the demonstrators, and the tsar abdicated on March 15. The government of Russia fell into the hands of members of the Duma who soon constructed a provisional government composed chiefly of Constitutional Democrats with Western sympathies. At the same time the various socialists, including both Social Revolutionaries and Social Democrats of the Menshevik wing, began to organize the workers into soviets. Initially they allowed the provisional government to function without actually supporting it. As relatively orthodox Marxists, they believed that a bourgeois stage of development must come to Russia before the revolution of the proletariat could be achieved.

In this climate the provisional government made the important decision to remain loyal to the existing Russian alliances and to continue the war against Germany. In this regard, the provisional government was accepting the tsarist foreign policy and was associating itself with the source of much domestic suffering and discontent. The fate of the provisional government was sealed by the collapse of the new offensive in the summer of 1917. Disillusionment with the war, shortages of food and other necessities at home, and the growing demand by peasants for land reform undermined the government, even after its leadership had been taken over by the moderate socialist Alexander Kerenski (1881–1970). Moreover, discipline in the army had badly disintegrated.

Ever since April the Bolshevik wing of the Social

During the May Day parade of 1917 in Petrograd soldiers march under a banner reading, "Down with the old!" [The Granger Collection.]

Alexander Kerensky headed the shortlived provisional government in Russia after the Revolution of March 1917 and before the Bolshevik victory later that year. The photograph was made during his summer of authority. [The Granger Collection.]

Democratic Party had been working against the provisional government. The Germans, in their most successful attempt at subversion, had rushed the brilliant Bolshevik leader V. I. Lenin (1870–1924) in a sealed train from his exile in Switzerland across Germany to Petrograd in the hope that he would cause trouble for the revolutionary government.

Lenin saw the opportunity to achieve the political alliance of workers and peasants that he had discussed theoretically before the war. In speech after speech he hammered away on the theme of peace, bread, and land. The Bolsheviks soon gained control of the soviets, or councils of workers and soldiers. They demanded that all political power should go to the soviets. The failure of the summer offensive encouraged them to attempt a *coup*, but the effort was premature and a failure. Lenin fled to Finland, and his chief collaborator, Leon Trotsky (1877–1940), was imprisoned.

The failure of a right-wing counter *coup* led by General Kornilov gave the Bolsheviks another chance. Trotsky came out of prison to lead the powerful Petrograd Soviet. Lenin returned in October, insisted to his doubting colleagues that the time was ripe to take power, and by the extraordinary force of his personality persuaded them to act. Trotsky organized the coup that took place on November 6 and concluded with an armed assault upon the provisional government. The Bolsheviks, almost as much to their own astonishment as to that of the rest of the world, had come to rule Russia.

The victors moved to fulfill their promises and to assure their own security. The provisional government had decreed an election for late November to select a Constituent Assembly. The Social Revolutionaries won a large majority over the Bolsheviks. When the assembly gathered in January, it met for only a day before the Red Army dispersed it. All other political parties also ceased to

Lenin here addresses a meeting in Moscow. Leon
Trotsky, his major collaborator, stands listening
on the right. [Popperfoto.]

*The Soviet Government Proclaims
the Bolshevik Victory*

On October 25 [November 7], 1917, through the
agency of the Military-Revolutionary Committee of
the Petrograd Soviet—headed by Trotsky—the Bolsheviks and their allies, the Left Socialist-Revolutionaries, forcibly overthrew Kerensky's government and assumed power in the name of the soviets.
A new cabinet, designated the "Council of People's
Commissars," was set up, with Lenin as chairman
and Trotsky as Commissar of Foreign Affairs. En-
dorsement of the coup was secured from the Second
All-Russian Congress of Soviets, which was con-
currently in session. This was the "October Revolution."

To the *Citizens of Russia!*
*The Provisional Government has been overthrown.
The power of state has passed into the hands of the organ
of the Petrograd Soviet of Workers' and Soldiers' Deputies, the Revolutionary Military Committee, which
stands at the head of the Petrograd proletariat and garrison.*
*The cause for which the people have fought—the
immediate proposal of a democratic peace, the abolition of
landed proprietorship, workers' control over production
and the creation of a Soviet government—is assured.*
*Long live the revolution of the soldiers, workers, and
peasants!*
Revolutionary Military Committee
of Petrograd
Soviet of Workers' and Soldiers' Deputies.

R. V. Daniels, ed., *A Documentary History of Communism* (New
York: Random House, 1960), Vol. 1, p. 117. The headnote in this
instance consists of R. V. Daniels's introductory comment to the
document.

function in any meaningful fashion. In November and
January the Bolshevik government promulgated decrees
that nationalized the land and turned it over to its peasant
proprietors. Factory workers were put in charge of their
plants. Banks were nationalized, and the debt of the
tsarist government repudiated. Property of the church
reverted to the state.

The Bolshevik government also took Russia out of the
war, which they believed benefited only capitalism. They
signed an armistice with Germany in December 1917.
On March 3, 1918, they accepted the Treaty of Brest-
Litovsk, by which Russia yielded Poland, the Baltic states,
and the Ukraine. Some territory in the Transcaucasus
region went to Turkey. In addition the Bolsheviks agreed
to pay a heavy war indemnity. These terms were a
terribly high price to pay for peace, but Lenin had no
choice. Russia was incapable of renewing the war effort,
and the Bolsheviks needed time to impose their rule on a
devastated and chaotic Russia. Moreover Lenin seemed to
believe that communist revolutions might soon sweep
across other nations in Europe as a result of the war and
the Russian example.

Until 1921 the new Bolshevik government confronted
major domestic resistance. A civil war erupted between
the "Red" Russians supporting the revolution and the
"White" Russians, who opposed the Bolshevik triumph.
In the summer of 1918 the tsar and his family were
murdered. Loyal army officers continued to press
against the revolution and eventually received aid
from the Allied armies. However, under the leadership
of Trotsky the Red Army eventually overcame the
domestic opposition. By 1921 Lenin and his supporters
were in firm control.

Lenin Establishes His Dictatorship

After the Bolshevik coup in October, elections for the Constituent Assembly were held in November. The results gave a majority to the Social Revolutionary Party and embarrassed the Bolsheviks. Using his control of the Red Army, Lenin closed the Constituent Assembly after only one day in January 1918 and established the rule of a revolutionary elite and his own dictatorship. Here is the crucial Bolshevik decree.

. . . *THE Constituent Assembly, elected on the basis of lists drawn up prior to the October Revolution, was an expression of the old relation of political forces which existed when power was held by the compromisers and the Cadets. When the people at that time voted for the candidates of the Socialist-Revolutionary Party, they were not in a position to choose between the Right Socialist-Revolutionaries, the supporters of the bourgeoisie, and the Left Socialist-Revolutionaries, the supporters of Socialism. Thus the Constituent Assembly, which was to have been the crown of the bourgeois parliamentary republic, could not but become an obstacle in the path of the October Revolution and the Soviet power.*

The October Revolution, by giving the power to the Soviets, and through the Soviets to the toiling and exploited classes, aroused the desperate resistance of the exploiters, and in the crushing of this resistance it fully revealed itself as the beginning of the socialist revolution . . . the majority in the Constituent Assembly which met on January 5 was secured by the party of the Right Socialist-Revolutionaries, the party of Kerensky, Avksentyev and Chernov. Naturally, this party refused to discuss the absolutely clear, precise and unambiguous proposal of the supreme organ of Soviet power, the Central Executive Committee of the Soviets, to recognize the program of the Soviet power, to recognize the "Declaration of Rights of the Toiling and Exploited People," to recognize the October Revolution and the Soviet power. . . .

The Right Socialist-Revolutionary and Menshevik parties are in fact waging outside the walls of the Constituent Assembly a most desperate struggle against the Soviet power. . . .

Accordingly, the Central Executive Committee resolves: The Constituent Assembly is hereby dissolved.

R. V. Daniels, ed., *A Documentary History of Communism* (New York: Random House, 1960), Vol. I, pp. 133–135.

The End of World War I

The internal collapse of Russia and the later Treaty of Brest-Litovsk brought Germany to the peak of its success. The Germans controlled eastern Europe and its resources, especially food, and they were free to concentrate their forces on the western front. This turn of events would probably have been decisive had it not been balanced by American intervention. Still American troops would not arrive in significant numbers for about a year, and both sides tried to win the war in 1917. An Allied attempt to break through failed disastrously, bringing heavy losses to the British and the French and causing a mutiny in the French army. The Austrians, supported by the Germans, defeated the Italians at Caporetto and threatened to overrun Italy, but they were checked with the aid of Allied troops. The deadlock continued, but time was running out for the Central Powers.

In 1918 the Germans—persuaded chiefly by Ludendorff, who was by then a general—decided to gamble everything on one last offensive. The German army pushed forward and even reached the Marne again but got no farther. They had no more reserves, and the entire nation was exhausted. The Allies, on the other hand, were bolstered by the arrival of American troops in ever-increasing numbers. They were able to launch a counteroffensive that proved to be irresistible. As the Austrian fronts in the Balkans and Italy collapsed, the German high command knew that the end was imminent.

Ludendorff was determined that peace should be made before the German army could be thoroughly defeated in the field and that the responsibility should fall on civilians. For some time he had been the effective ruler of Germany under the aegis of the emperor. He now insisted that William II authorize a new government to be established on democratic principles and to seek peace immediately. The new government, under Prince Max of Baden, asked for peace on the basis of the Fourteen

The birth of the Weimar Republic. On November 9, 1918, William II abdicated and the decision was made to establish a German republic. In this picture the Social Democratic leader Philipp Scheidemann (1865–1939) proclaims the republic to the people of Berlin from a window in the Chancellory. [Bildarchiv Preussischer Kulturbesitz.]

Points that President Wilson had declared as American war aims. These were idealistic principles, including self-determination for nationalities, open diplomacy, freedom of the seas, disarmament, and establishment of a league of nations to keep the peace. Wilson insisted that he would deal only with a democratic German government because he wanted to be sure that he was dealing with the German people and not merely their rulers.

Thus encouraged, the Germans, led by the Social Democrats, forced William II to abdicate on November 9, 1918, and established a republic. Two days later this republican, socialist-led government signed the armistice that ended the war by accepting German defeat. At the time of the armistice the German people were, in general, unaware that their army had been defeated in the field and was crumbling. No foreign soldier stood on German soil. It appeared to many Germans that they could expect a negotiated and mild settlement. The real peace was quite different and embittered the German people, many of whom came to believe that Germany had not been defeated but had been tricked by the enemy and betrayed—even stabbed in the back—by republicans and socialists at home.

The victors rejoiced, but they also had much to mourn. The casualties on all sides came to about ten million dead and twice as many wounded. The economic and financial resources of the European states were badly strained. The victorious Allies, formerly creditors to the world, became debtors to the new American colossus, itself barely touched by the calamities of war.

The old international order, moreover, was dead. Russia was ruled by a Bolshevik dictatorship that preached world revolution and the overthrow of capitalism everywhere. Germany was in chaos, and Austria–Hungary had disintegrated into a swarm of small national states competing for the remains of the ancient empire. The kinds of change stirred the colonial territories ruled by the European powers, and overseas empires would never again be so secure as they had seemed before the war. Europe was no longer the center of the world, free to

In 1919 President Woodrow Wilson left the United States on board the *George Washington* to take part in the peace negotiations being held at Versailles in France. [Culver Pictures.]

interfere when it wished or to ignore the outer regions if it chose. Its easy confidence in material and moral progress was shattered by the brutal reality of four years of horrible war. The memory of that war lived on to shake the nerve of the victorious Western powers as they confronted the new conditions of the postwar world.

The Settlement at Versailles

The representatives of the victorious states gathered at Versailles and other Parisian suburbs in the first half of 1919. Wilson speaking for the United States, David Lloyd George (1863–1945) for Britain, Georges Clemenceau (1841–1929) for France, and Vittorio Emanuele Orlando (1860–1952) for Italy made up the Big Four. Japan, now recognized for the first time as a great power, also had an important part in the discussions. The diplomats who met in Paris had a far more difficult task than the one facing those who had sat at Vienna a century earlier. Both groups attempted to restore order to the world after long and costly wars, but Metternich and his associates could confine their thoughts to Europe. France acknowledged defeat and was willing, even eager, to take part in and uphold the Vienna settlement. The diplomats at Vienna were not much affected by public opinion, and they could draw the new map of Europe along practical lines determined by the realities of power softened by compromise.

The Peacemakers

The negotiators at Paris in 1919 were not so fortunate. They represented constitutional, generally democratic governments, and public opinion had become a mighty force. Though there were secret sessions, the conference often worked in the full glare of publicity. Nationalism had become almost a secular religion, and Europe's many ethnic groups could not be relied on to remain quiet while they were distributed on the map at the whim of the great powers. World War I, moreover, had been transformed by propaganda and especially by the intervention of Woodrow Wilson into a moral crusade to achieve a peace that would be just as well as secure. The Fourteen Points set forth the right of nationalities to self-determination as an absolute value, in spite of the fact that there was no way to draw the map of Europe to match ethnic groups perfectly with their homelands. All these elements made compromise difficult.

Wilson's idealism, moreover, came into conflict with the more practical war aims of the victorious powers and with many of the secret treaties that had been made before and during the war. The British and French people had been told that Germany would be made to pay for the war, Russia had been promised control of Constantinople and the Dardanelles in return for recognition of the French claim to Alsace-Lorraine and British control of Egypt. Romania was promised Transylvania at the expense of Hungary. Some of the agreements contradicted others: Italy and Serbia had competing claims to the islands and shore of the Adriatic. During the war the British had encouraged Arab hopes of an independent Arab state carved out of the Ottoman Empire, but those plans conflicted with the Balfour Declaration (1917), in which the British seemed to accept Zionist ideology and to promise the Jews a national home in Palestine. Both of these plans stood in conflict with an Anglo-French agreement to divide the Near East between the two Western powers.

The continuing national goals of the victors presented further obstacles to an idealistic "peace without victors." France, keenly conscious of its numerical inferiority to Germany and of the low birth rate that would keep it inferior, was naturally eager to achieve a settlement that would permanently weaken Germany and preserve French superiority. Italy continued to seek the acquisition of *Italia Irredenta;* Britain continued to look to its imperial interests; Japan pursued its own advantage in Asia; and the United States insisted on freedom of the seas, which favored American commerce, while insisting on its right to maintain the Monroe Doctrine.

Finally, the peacemakers of 1919 faced a world still in turmoil. The greatest immediate threat appeared to be posed by the spread of Bolshevism. While Lenin and his colleagues were distracted by civil war, the Allies landed small armies at several places in Russia in the hope of overthrowing the Bolshevik regime. The revolution seemed likely to spread as Communist governments were established in Bavaria and Hungary, and Berlin experienced a dangerous Communist uprising led by the "Spartacus group." The Allies were sufficiently worried by these developments to allow and support suppression of these Communist movements by right-wing military forces, and they even allowed an army of German volunteers to operate against the Bolsheviks in the Baltic states. The fear of the spread of Communism played a part in the thinking of the diplomats at Versailles, but it was far from dominant. The Germans kept playing on such fears as a way of getting better terms, but the Allies, and especially the French, would not hear of it. Fear of Germany remained the chief concern for France, whereas attention to interests that were more traditional and more immediate governed the policies of the other Allies.

The Peace

The Versailles settlement consisted of five separate treaties between the victors and the defeated powers. Formal sessions began on January 18, 1919, and the last treaty was signed on August 10, 1920. Wilson arrived in Europe to unprecedented acclaim. Liberals and idealists expected a new kind of international order achieved in a new and better way, but they were soon disillusioned. "Open covenants openly arrived at" soon gave way to closed sessions in which Wilson, Clemenceau, and Lloyd George made arrangements that seemed cynical to outsiders. The notion of "a peace without victors" became a mockery when the Soviet Union (as Russia was now called) and Germany were excluded from the peace conference. The Germans were simply presented with a treaty and compelled to accept it in a manner that fully justified their complaint that the treaty had not been negotiated but dictated. The principle of national self-determination was violated many times, as was unavoidable, but the diplomats of the small nations were angered by their exclusion from decisions. The undeserved adulation accorded Wilson on his arrival gradually turned into equally undeserved scorn. He had not abandoned his ideals lightly but had merely given way to the irresistible force of reality.

THE LEAGUE OF NATIONS. Wilson was able to make unpalatable concessions without abandoning his ideals because he put great faith in a new instrument for peace and justice, the League of Nations. Its covenant was an essential part of the peace treaty. The League was not intended as an international government but as a body of sovereign states who agreed to pursue some common practices and to consult in the common interest, especially when war threatened. In that case the members promised to submit the matter to arbitration or to an international court or to the League Council. Refusal to abide by this agreement would justify League intervention in the form of economic and even military sanctions. But the League was unlikely to be effective because it had no armed forces at its disposal, and any action required the unanimous consent of its council, consisting of Britain, France, Italy, the United States, and Japan, as well as four other states who had temporary seats. The Covenant of the League bound its members to "respect and pre-

The Big Three at Versailles. Georges Clemenceau, French Prime Minister (left), American President Woodrow Wilson (center), and British Prime Minister David Lloyd George (right) tip their hats to the crowd after signing the Treaty of Versailles on June 28, 1919. [Culver Pictures.]

serve" the territorial integrity of all its members, and this was generally seen as a device to ensure the security of the victorious powers. The exclusion from the League Assembly of Germany and the Soviet Union further undermined the League's claim to evenhandedness.

COLONIES. Another provision of the covenant dealt with colonial areas. These were to be placed under the "tutelage" of one of the great powers under League supervision and encouraged to advance toward independence. Because there were no teeth in this provision, very little advance was made. Provisions for disarmament were doomed to be equally ineffective. Members of the League remained fully sovereign and continued to pursue their own national interests. Only Wilson seems to have put much faith in its future ability to produce peace and justice, and this belief allowed him to approve territorial settlements that violated his own principles.

GERMANY. In the west the main territorial issue was the fate of Germany. Although a united Germany was less than fifty years old, no one seems to have thought of undoing Bismarck's work and dividing it into its component parts. The French would have liked to detach the Rhineland and set it up as a separate buffer state, but Lloyd George and Wilson would not permit that. Still, they could not ignore France's need for protection against a resurgent Germany, France received Alsace-Lorraine and the right to work the coal mines of the Saar for fifteen years. Germany west of the Rhine and fifty kilometers east of it was to be a demilitarized zone, and Allied troops on the west bank could stay there for fifteen years. In addition to this physical barrier to a new German attack, the treaty provided that Britain and the United States would guarantee to aid France if it were attacked by Germany. Such an attack was made more unlikely by the permanent disarmament of Germany. Its army was limited to 100,000 men on long-term service; its fleet was all but eliminated; and it was forbidden to have war planes, submarines, tanks, heavy artillery, or poison gas. So long as these provisions were observed France would be safe.

THE EAST. The settlement in the east ratified the collapse of the great defeated empires that had ruled it for centuries. Germany's frontier was moved far to the west,

NORWAY
Oslo

NORTH SEA

SWEDEN
Stockholm

BALTIC SEA

FINLAND
Helsinki

KARELIA

WHITE SEA

Archangel

DVINA

L. ONEGA

L. LADOGA

UNITED KINGDOM

DENMARK

Reval

Leningrad
PETROGRAD
1914-1924

Perm

```
1914    1925
   ┌──────────┐
   │ GERMANY  │
   └──────────┘
```

ESTONIA

Riga
LATVIA

AREAS LOST BY RUSSIA

VOLGA

S O V I E T

KAMA

NETH.

Hamburg

Danzig

LITHUANIA
Kaunas

Moscow

URAL

BELG.

RHINE
RUHR
RHINELAND

Berlin

EAST PRUSSIA

Warsaw

Brest-Litovsk

Smolensk

WHITE RUSSIA

Samara

LUX.

Weimar

POLAND

Saratov

LORRAINE
FRANCE

Prague

U   N   I   O   N

ALSACE

Munich

CZECHOSLOVAKIA

GALICIA

Lvov

Kiev

DNIESTER

U K R A I N E

Tsaritsyn

VOLGA

SWITZ.

TYROL

Vienna
AUSTRIA

RUTHENIA

Rostov

DON

Astrakhan

Milan

Budapest
HUNGARY

TRANS-SYLVANIA

MOLDAVIA

BESSARABIA

DNIEPER

CASPIAN SEA

ITALY

Fiume
CROATIA

YUGOSLAVIA

BANAT

ROMANIA

Rome

BOSNIA
Belgrade

MONTE-NEGRO

SERBIA

WALLACHIA

Bucharest

DOBRUJA

CRIMEA

B L A C K   S E A

Batum

TRANSCAUCASIA

Baku

AUSTRIA-HUNGARY 1914

Tirana
ALBANIA

Sofia
BULGARIA

AZERBAIJAN

ADRIATIC SEA

ARMENIA

Tabriz

M E D I T E R R A N E A N   S E A

SICILY

GREECE

TURK. Istanbul

Angora
((ANKARA, 1930)

TURKEY
REPUBLIC, 1923

KURDISTAN

IRAN
PERSIA

TUNISIA
(FR.)

MALTA
(U.K.)

Smyrna
(IZMIR, 1930)

DODECANESE IS.
(IT.)

CRETE

CYPRUS
(U.K.)

Mosul

MESOPOTAMIA

TIGRIS
EUPHRATES

Baghdad

AREAS LOST BY THE OTTOMAN EMP.

SYRIA
(FR. MAND.)

IRAQ
(BR. MAND.)

PERSIAN GULF

500 MI.

500 KM.

LIBYA
(IT.)

PALESTINE
(BR. MAND.)

EGYPT
BR. INFLUENCE

Cairo

SUEZ CANAL

TRANS-JORDAN
(BR. MAND.)

SAUDI ARABIA
(1932)

RED SEA

WORLD WAR I PEACE SETTLEMENT IN EUROPE AND THE MIDDLE EAST

The map of central and Eastern Europe, as well as that of the Middle East, underwent drastic revision after World War I. The enormous geographical losses suffered by Germany, Austria-Hungary, the Ottoman Empire, Bulgaria, and Russia were the other side of the coin represented by gains for France, Italy, Greece, and Romania and the appearance, or reappearance, of at least eight new independent states from Finland in the north to Yugoslavia in the south. The mandate system for former Ottoman territories outside Turkey proper laid foundations for several new, mostly Arab, states in the Middle East.

excluding most of Silesia and much of East Prussia. What was left of East Prussia was cut off from the rest of Germany by a corridor carved out to give the revived state of Poland access to the sea. The Austro-Hungarian Empire disappeared entirely, giving way to many smaller successor states. Most of its German-speaking people were gathered in the small Republic of Austria, cut off from the Germans of Bohemia and forbidden to unite themselves with Germany. The Magyars occupied the Kingdom of Hungary. The Czechs of Bohemia and Moravia joined with the Slovaks and Ruthenians to the east to form Czechoslovakia, and this new state included several million unhappy Germans. The southern Slavs were united in the Kingdom of Serbs, Croats, and Slovenes, or Yugoslavia. Italy gained the Trentino and Trieste. Romania was enlarged by receiving Transylvania from Hungary and Bessarabia from Russia. Bulgaria was diminished by the loss of territory to Greece and Yugoslavia. Russia lost vast territories in the west. Finland, Estonia, Latvia, and Lithuania became independent states, and a good part of Poland was carved out of formerly Russian soil. The old Ottoman Empire disappeared. The new republic of Turkey was limited to little more than Constantinople and Asia Minor, while the former Ottoman territories of Palestine and Iraq came under British control and Syria and Lebanon under French control as mandates of the League. Germany's former colonies in Africa were divided among Britain, France, and South Africa, and her Pacific possessions went to Australia, New Zealand, and Japan.

REPARATIONS. Perhaps the most debated part of the peace settlement dealt with reparations for the damage done by Germany during the war. Before the armistice the Germans promised to pay compensation "for all damages done to the civilian population of the Allies and their property." The Americans judged that the amount would be between $15 billion and $25 billion and that Germany would be able to pay that amount. However, France and Britain, worried about repaying their war debts to the United States, were eager to have

Germany pay the full cost of the war, including pensions to survivors and dependents. There was general agreement that Germany could not afford to pay such a sum, whatever it might be, and no sum was fixed at the conference. In the meantime Germany was to pay $5 billion annually until 1921. At that time a final figure would be set, which Germany would have to pay in thirty years. The French did not regret the outcome. Either Germany would pay and be bled into impotence, or she would refuse to pay and justify French intervention.

To justify these huge reparations payments, the Allies inserted the notorious Clause 231 into the treaty:

> The Allied and Associated Governments affirm, and Germany accepts, the responsibility of Germany and her allies for causing all the loss and damage to which the Allied and Associated Governments and their nationals have been subjected as a consequence of the war imposed upon them by aggression of Germany and her allies.

The Germans, of course, did not believe that they were solely responsible for the war and bitterly resented the charge. They had suffered the loss of vast territories containing millions of Germans and great quantities of badly needed natural resources; they were presented with an astronomical and apparently unlimited reparations bill. To add insult to injury, they were required to admit to a war guilt that they did not feel. Finally, to heap insult upon insult, they were required to accept the entire treaty as it was written by the victors, without any opportunity for negotiation. Germany's Prime Minister Philipp Scheidemann (1865–1939) spoke of the treaty as the imprisonment of the German people and asked, "What hand would not wither that binds itself and us in these fetters?" But there was no choice. The Social Democrats and the Catholic Center Party formed a new government, and their representatives signed the treaty. These were the parties that formed the backbone of the Weimar government that ruled Germany until 1933, and they never overcame the stigma of accepting the Treaty of Versailles.

Evaluation of the Peace

Few peace settlements have undergone more severe attacks than the one negotiated in Paris in 1919. It is natural that the defeated powers should object to it, but the peace soon came under bitter criticism in the victorious countries as well. Many Frenchmen thought it failed to provide adequate security for France, because it tied that security to promises of aid from the unreliable Anglo-Saxon countries. In England and the United States a wave of bitter criticism arose in liberal quarters because the treaty seemed to violate the idealistic and liberal aims and principles that the Western leaders professed. It was not a peace without victors, did not put an end to imperialism, attempted to promote the national interests of the winning nations, and violated the principles of national self-determination by leaving significant pockets of minorities outside the borders of their national homelands.

The most influential critic was John Maynard Keynes (1883–1946), a brilliant British economist who took part in the peace conference. He resigned in disgust when he saw the direction it was taking and wrote a book called the *Economic Consequences of the Peace* (1919). It was a scathing attack, especially on reparations and the other economic aspects of the peace. It was also a skillful assault on the negotiators and particularly on Wilson, who was depicted as a fool and a hypocrite. Keynes argued that the Treaty of Versailles was both immoral and unworkable. It was a Carthaginian peace that would bring economic ruin and war to Europe unless it were repudiated. Keynes had a great effect on the British, who were already suspicious of France and glad of an excuse to withdraw from continental affairs. The decent and respectable position came to be one that aimed at revision of the treaty in favor of Germany. Even more important was the book's influence in the United States. It fed the traditional tendency toward isolationism and gave powerful weapons to Wilson's enemies. Wilson's own political mistakes helped prevent American ratification of the treaty. Consequently America was out of the League and not bound to defend France. Britain, therefore, was also free from its obligation to France. France was left to protect itself without adequate means to do so for long.

Many of the attacks on the Treaty of Versailles are unjustified. It was not a Carthaginian peace. Germany was neither dismembered nor ruined. Reparations could be and were scaled down, and until the great world depression of the 1930s, the Germans recovered a high level of prosperity. Complaints aginst the peace should also be measured against the peace that the victorious Germans imposed on Russia at Brest-Litovsk and the plans they made for a European settlement in case of victory. Both were far more severe than anything enacted at Versailles. The attempt at achieving self-determination for nationalities was less than perfect, but it was the best solution Europe had ever accomplished in that direction.

The peace, nevertheless, was unsatisfactory in important ways. The elimination of the Austro-Hungarian Empire, however inevitable that might seem, created a number of serious problems. Economically it was disastrous, for it separated raw materials from manufacturing areas and producers from their markets by new boundaries and tariff walls. In hard times this created friction and hostility that aggravated other quarrels also created by the peace treaties. Poland contained unhappy German minorities, and Czechoslovakia was a collection of nationalities who did not find it easy to live together as a nation. Disputes over territories in eastern Europe promoted further tension. The peace was inadequate on another level, as well. It rested on a victory that Germany did not admit. The Germans believed that they had been cheated rather than defeated. At the same time the high moral principles proclaimed by the Allies undercut the validity of the peace, for it plainly fell far short of those principles.

Finally, the great weakness of the peace was its failure to accept reality. Germany and Russia must inevitably play an important part in European affairs, yet they were excluded from the settlement and from the League of Nations. Given the many discontented parties, the peace was not self-enforcing; yet no satisfactory machinery for enforcing it was established. The league was never a serious force for this purpose. It was left to France, with no guarantee of support from Britain and no hope of help from the United States, to defend the new arrangements. Finland, the Baltic states, Poland, Romania, Czechoslovakia, and Yugoslavia were created as a barrier to the expansion westward of Russian Communism and as a threat in the rear to deter German revival. Most of these states, however, would have to rely on France in case of danger, and France was simply not strong enough for the task if Germany should rearm. The tragedy of Versailles was that it was neither conciliatory enough to remove the desire for change, even at the cost of war, nor harsh enough to make another war impossible. The only hope for a lasting peace required the enforcement of the disarmament of Germany while the more obnoxious clauses of the peace treaty were revised. Such a policy required continued attention to the problem, unity among the victors, and far-sighted leadership; but none of these was present in adequate supply during the next two decades.

SUGGESTED READINGS

L. ALBERTINI, *The Origins of the War of 1914*, 3 vols. (London, 1952, 1957). Discursive but invaluable.

M. BALFOUR, *The Kaiser and His Times* (New York, 1972). A fine biography of William II.

V. R. BERGHAHN, *Germany and the Approach of War in 1914* (New York, 1973). A work similar in spirit to Fischer's but stressing the importance of Germany's naval program.

V. DEDIJER, *The Road to Sarajevo* (London, 1967). A detailed study of the assassination of the Archduke Francis Ferdinand and its background.

S. B. FAY, *The Origins of the World War*, 2 vols. (New York, 1928). The best and most influential of the revisionist accounts.

D. K. FIELDHOUSE, *The Colonial Experience: A Compara-tive Study from the Eighteenth Century* (New York, 1966). An excellent recent study.

F. FISCHER, *Germany's Aims in the First World War* (New York, 1967). An influential interpretation that stirred a great controversy in Germany and around the world by emphasizing Germany's role in bringing on the war.

F. FISCHER, *War of Illusions* (New York, 1975). A long and diffuse book that tries to connect German responsibility for the war with internal social, economic, and political developments.

I. GEISS, *July 1914* (New York, 1967). A valuable collection of documents by a student of Fritz Fischer's. The emphasis is on German documents and responsibility.

O. J. HALE, *The Great Illusion 1900–1914* (New York, 1971). A fine survey of the period especially good on public opinion.

B. H. LIDDELL HART, *The Real War 1914–1918* (Boston, 1964). A fine short account by an outstanding military historian.

J. M. KEYNES, *The Economic Consequences of the Peace* (London, 1920). The famous and influential attack on the Versailles Treaty.

L. LAFORE, *The Long Fuse* (New York, 1965). A readable account of the origins of World War I that focuses on the problem of Austria–Hungary.

W. L. LANGER, *The Diplomacy of Imperialism* (New York, 1935). A continuation of the previous study for the years 1890–1902.

W. L. LANGER, *European Alliances and Allignments*, 2nd ed. (New York, 1966). A splendid diplomatic history of the years 1871–1890.

W. LAQUEUR AND G. L. MOSSE (Eds.), *1914; The Coming of the First World War* (New York, 1966). A collection of valuable essays.

E. MANTOUX, *The Carthaginian Peace* (Pittsburgh, 1952). A vigorous attack on Keynes's view.

J. STEINBERG, *Yesterday's Deterrent* (London, 1965). An excellent study of Germany's naval policy and its consequences.

A. J. P. TAYLOR, *The Struggle for Mastery in Europe, 1848–1918* (Oxford, 1954). Clever but controversial.

L. C. F. TURNER, *Origins of the First World War* (New York, 1970). Especially good on the significance of Russia and its military plans.

838

31
Political Experiments of the 1920s

Pursuit of experimentation in politics and of normality in economic life marked the decade following the conclusion of the Versailles Treaty. Many of the experiments failed, and the normality proved quite elusive. By the close of the decade the political path had been paved for the nightmares of brutally authoritarian governments and international aggression. Yet many of the people who had survived the Great War had hoped and worked for a better outcome. Totalitarianism and aggression were not the inexorable destiny of Europe. Their emergence was the result of failures in securing alternative modes of political life and international relations.

Political and Economic Factors After Versailles

New Governments

In 1919 experimental political regimes studded the map of Europe. From Ireland to Russia new governments were seeking to gain the active support of their citizens and to solve the grievous economic problems caused by the war. In the Soviet Union the Bolsheviks regarded themselves as forging nothing less than a new kind of civilization. They gave little significant consideration to anything but an authoritarian rule.

It was otherwise elsewhere on the Continent. Democratically elected parliamentary governments appeared where the autocratic, military empires of Germany and Austria–Hungary had previously held sway. Their goals

The signing of the Locarno Pacts in 1925 marked a high point in postwar international stability and cooperation for peace. The most prominent delegations are those of the Germans (left), the British (top), and the French (right). [United Press International Photo.]

were substantially more modest than those of the Bolsheviks. Yet to pursue parliamentary politics where it had never been meaningfully practiced proved no simple task. The Wilsonian vision of democratic, self-determined nations floundered on the harsh realities of economics, aggressive nationalism, and revived political conservatism. Too often the will for democratic, parliamentary government as well as experience in its exercise was absent from the nations on which it had been bestowed. Moreover, in many of the new democracies important sectors of the citizenry believed that parliamentary politics was by its very nature corrupt or unequal to great nationalistic enterprise.

Demands for Revision of Versailles

Several other Europe-wide problems haunted the early interwar period and directly affected the decisions and actions of individual nations. The Versailles settlement fostered both resentment and discontent in numerous countries. Germany had been humiliated. The arrangements for reparations led to seemingly endless haggling over payments. Various national groups in the successor states of eastern Europe felt that injustice had been done in their particular case of self-determination. There were demands for further border adjustments. On the other side, the victorious powers and especially France often believed that the provisions of the treaty were being inadequately enforced. Consequently, throughout the twenties calls both to revise or to enforce the Versailles Treaty contributed to domestic political turmoil across the Continent. All too many political figures were willing to fish in these troubled international waters for a large catch of domestic votes.

Post-War Economic Problems

Simultaneous with the move toward political experiment and demands for revision of the recently established international order was a widespread desire to return to the economic prosperity of the prewar years. However, after 1918 it was impossible to restore what American

President Warren Harding would shortly term "normalcy." During the conflict Europeans had turned against themselves and their civilization the vast physical power that they had created in the previous century. More than 750,000 British soldiers had perished. The combat deaths for France and Germany were 1,385,000 and 1,808,000, respectively. Russia had lost 1,700,000 troops. Scores of thousands more from other belligerent nations had also been killed. Still more millions had been wounded. These casualties meant not only the waste of human life and talent but also the loss of producers and consumers. There had also been widespread destruction of farmland, transport facilities, mines, and industry.

Another casualty of the conflict was the financial dominance and independence of Europe. At the opening of hostilities Europe had been the financial and credit center of the world. At the close of the fighting Europeans stood deeply in debt to each other and to the United States. The Bolsheviks had repudiated the debt of the tsarist government, much of which was owed to French creditors. Other nations could not pursue this revolutionary course. The Versailles settlement had imposed heavy financial obligations on Germany and its allies. The United States refused to ask reparations from Germany, but firmly demanded repayment of war debts from its own allies. On the one hand, the reparation and debt structure meant that no nation was fully in control of its own economic life. On the other hand, the absence of international economic cooperation meant that more than ever individual nations felt compelled to pursue or to attempt to pursue selfish, nationalistic economic aims. It was perhaps the worst of all possible international economic worlds.

The market and trade conditions that had prevailed before 1914 had also changed radically. Russia in large measure withdrew from the European economic order. The political reconstruction of eastern and central Europe into the multitude of small successor states broke up the trade region formerly encompassed by Germany and Austria–Hungary. Most of those new states had weak economies hardly capable of competing in modern economic life. The new boundaries separated raw materials from the factories using them. Railway systems on which finished and unfinished products traveled might now lie under the control of two or more nations. Political and economic nationalism went together. New customs barriers were raised.

International trade also followed new patterns. The United States became less dependent on European production and assumed the status of a major competitor. During the war the belligerents had been forced to sell many of their holdings on other continents to finance the conflict. As a consequence Europeans exercised less dominance over the world economy. Postwar economic growth within colonies or former colonies lowered the demand for European goods. The United States and Japan began to penetrate markets in Latin America and Asia previously dominated by European producers and traders.

New Roles for Government and Labor

The war effort in all countries occasioned new dimensions of state interference and direction in the economy. Large government bureaucracies had been organized to plan the course of production and distribution of goods. Prices had been controlled, raw materials stockpiled, consumer goods rationed, and economic priorities set by government technocrats. The mechanism of the freely operating market so dear to nineteenth-century liberals had been rejected as a vehicle for economic decision-making. The economic planning skills learned during the war could be transferred to peacetime operations. Moreover governments had learned about the immense productive and employment power of an economy placed under state control.

Labor had achieved new prominence within the wartime economic setting. The unions had actively supported the war effort of their nations. They had ensured labor peace for production. In turn, their members had received better wages, and their leaders had been admitted to high political councils. Although in peacetime wages might be lowered, they could not be reduced to prewar levels. European workers intended to receive their just share of the fruits of their labor. Collective bargaining and union recognition brought on by the war also could not be abandoned. This improvement in both the status and the effective influence of labor was one of the most significant social and political changes to flow from World War I. The social condition of the work force seemed to be improving while that of the middle class seemed to be stagnating or declining.

The war and peace settlement wrought one other major change that affected the course of political and economic life. The turn to liberal democracy and the extension of the franchise to women and previously disenfranchised males meant that for the first time in European history the governments handling economic matters were responsible to mass electorates. Economics and politics had become more intimately connected than ever before. The economic and social anxieties of the electorate could and eventually did overcome its political scruples. Whereas previously economic discontent had been articulated through riots and later through unions, it could now be voiced through the ballot box.

Joyless Victors

France and Great Britain, with the aid of the United States, had won the war. France became the strongest military power on the Continent. Britain had escaped with almost no physical damage. Both nations, however, had lost vast numbers of young men in the conflict. Their economies were weak, and their overseas wealth and power stood much diminished. Compared with contemporary events in Germany, Italy, and Russia, the interwar political development of the two major democracies seems rather tame. There was neither a revolution nor a shift to authoritarian government. Yet this surface calm was largely illusory. They were troubled democracies. To neither did victory in war bring the good life in peace.

France: The Search for Security

At the close of World War I, as after Waterloo, the revolution of 1848, and the defeat of 1871, the French voters elected a doggedly conservative Chamber of Deputies. The preponderance of military officers among its members led to the nickname of "the Horizon Blue Chamber." The overwelmingly conservative character of the chamber was registered in 1920 by its defeat of Georges Clemenceau's bid for the presidency. The crucial factor had been of all things the alleged leniency of the Versailles Treaty and the failure to establish a separate Rhineland state. The deputies wanted to achieve future security against Germany and Russian Communism. They intended to make as few concessions to domestic social reform as possible. The twenties were marked by fluctuations in ministries and a drift in domestic policy. The political turnstile remained ever active. Between the end of the war and January 1933, France was governed by no fewer than twenty-seven different cabinets.

NEW ALLIANCES. During the first five years after the Treaty of Versailles France accepted its role as the leading European power. The French plan was to enforce strictly the clauses of the treaty that were meant to keep Germany weak and, at the same time, to build a system of eastern alliances to replace the lost prewar alliance with Russia. In 1920 and 1921 three eastern states who had much to lose from revision of the treaty—Czechoslovakia, Romania, and Yugoslavia—formed the Little Entente. Before long France made military alliances with these states as well as with Poland. A dispute with Czechoslovakia over the control of Teschen prevented the Poles from joining the Little Entente, but the very existence of Poland depended on the maintenance of the Versailles settlement. This new system of eastern alliances was the best France could do, but it was far weaker than the old Russian alliance. The new states combined were no match for the former power of imperial Russia, and they were neither united nor reliable. Poland and Romania

POINCARÉ
Notre vaillant président

Cliché BERT
23

JN
PARIS

Raymond Poincaré (1860–1934) became a leading French politician in the first decade of this century. He was president from 1913 to 1920 during World War I, and three times Prime Minister (1912–1913, 1922–1924, 1926–1929), therefore the leader of France for much of the decade after the War. He was exceedingly nationalistic—as is suggested by the inscription on this photographic postcard made probably in 1914 and certainly after the War had begun. [The Granger Collection.]

QUEST FOR REPARATIONS. In 1923 the Germans failed to meet the schedule of reparation payments. Raymond Poincaré (1860–1934), France's powerful nationalist prime minister, took the opportunity to teach the Germans a lesson and force them to comply. He sent the French army to occupy the Ruhr, and when the Germans adopted a policy of passive resistance, he sent French civilians to run the mines and railroads. France got its way. The Germans paid, but France paid a great price for its victory. The English were alienated by French heavy-handedness and took no part in the occupation. They became more suspicious of France and more sympathetic to Germany. The cost of the Ruhr occupation, moreover, increased French as well as German inflation and damaged the French economy. As one scholar has explained: the French "threatened to choke Germany to death; the Germans threatened to die. Neither side dared carry its threat to extremity."[1] From the French viewpoint, consequently, victory in the war and achievement of considerable military power seemed to have brought the nation little of the prestige and effective influence it sought.

In 1924 the conservative ministry gave way to a coalition of leftist parties, the so-called *Cartel des Gauches*, led by Edouard Herriot (1872–1957). The chief policy changes of the new Cabinet were recognition of the Soviet Union and a more conciliatory policy toward Germany. Leadership on this score came from Aristide Briand (1862–1932), who was foreign minister for the remainder of the decade. He championed the League of Nations and attempted to persuade his nation that its military power did not give it unlimited influence on the foreign affairs of Europe. Under the leftist coalition a mild inflation also occurred. It had begun under the conservatives but picked up intensity in 1925. When the value of the franc fell sharply on the international money market in 1926, Poincaré returned to office as head of a national

were more concerned about Russia than about Germany, and the main target of the Little Entente was Hungary. If one of the eastern states were threatened by a resurgent Germany, there was considerable doubt that the others would be eager to come to its aid.

The formation of this new alliance system heightened the sense of danger and isolation felt by the two excluded powers, Germany and the Soviet Union. In 1922, while the European states were holding an economic conference at Genoa, the Russians and the Germans met at Rapallo nearby and signed a treaty of their own. It established diplomatic and economic relations that proved useful to both sides. Although the treaty contained no secret political or military clauses, such arrangements were suspected. And it is now known that the Germans helped train the Russian army and gave their own army valuable experience in the use of tanks and planes in the Soviet Union. The news of Rapallo confirmed the French in their growing belief that Germany was unwilling to live up to the terms of the Versailles Treaty and helped move them to strong action.

1 A. J. P. Taylor, *The Origins of the Second World War* (New York: Fawcett, 1961), p. 33.

Ramsay MacDonald was the first Labor Party Prime Minister of Great Britain. Although his first ministry lasted only a few months in 1924, he established Labor as the major alternative party to the Conservatives in Great Britain. He was again Prime Minister between 1929 and 1935. [Culver Pictures.]

government. The value of the franc recovered somewhat, and inflation cooled. For the rest of the twenties the conservatives remained in power. The country enjoyed a general prosperity that lasted until 1931, longer than in any other nation.

Great Britain

World War I profoundly changed British politics if not the political system. The electorate was expanded in 1918 to include all men aged twenty-one and women aged thirty. (In 1928 the age for women voters was also lowered to twenty-one.) The prewar structure of parties and leadership also shifted. A coalition Cabinet composed of Liberal, Conservative, and Labor ministers had directed the war effort. The wartime ministerial participation of the Labor Party did much to dispel its radical image. For the Liberal Party, however, the conflict brought unexpected division. Until 1916 Liberal Prime Minister Herbert Asquith had presided over the Cabinet. As disagreements over war management developed, he was ousted by fellow Liberal David Lloyd George. The party then became sharply split between followers of the two men. In 1918, against the wishes of both the Labor Party and the Asquith Liberals, Lloyd George decided to maintain the coalition through the tasks of the peace conference and the domestic reconstruction. The wartime coalition, now minus Labor members, won a stunning victory at the polls. However, Lloyd George could thereafter remain prime minister only so long as his dominant Conservative partners wished to keep him.

During the 1918 election campaign there had been much talk about creating "a land fit for heroes to live in." It did not happen. Except for the three years immediately after the war the British economy was depressed throughout the twenties. Genuine postwar recovery simply did not get under way. Unemployment never dipped below 10 per cent and often hovered near 11 per cent. There were never fewer than a million workers unemployed. Government insurance programs to cover unemployed workers, widows, and orphans were expanded.

But there was no similar meaningful expansion in the number of jobs available. From 1922 onward accepting the "dole" with little expectation of future employment became a wretched and degrading way of life for scores of thousands of poor British families.

THE FIRST LABOR GOVERNMENT. In October 1922 the Conservatives dropped Lloyd George and replaced him with Bonar Law (1858–1923), one of their own. A Liberal would never again be prime minister. Stanley Baldwin (1867–1947) soon replaced Law, who fell victim to throat cancer. Baldwin decided to attempt to cure Britain's economic plight by abandoning free trade and imposing protective tariffs. The voters rejected the proposed policy in 1923. At the election the Conservative Party lost its majority in the House of Commons, but only votes from both Liberal and Labor party members could provide an alternative majority. Labor had elected the second largest group of members to the Commons. Consequently, in December 1923, King George V (1910–1936) asked Ramsay MacDonald (1866–1937) to form the first Labor ministry in British history. The Liberal Party did not serve in the cabinet but provided the necessary votes in the House of Commons to give the Labor ministry a working majority.

The Labor Party was socialistic in its platform, but not revolutionary. The party had expanded beyond its early trade union base. MacDonald himself had opposed World War I and for a time had also broken with the party. His own version of socialism owed little, if anything, to Marx. His program consisted of plans for extensive social reform rather than for nationalization or public seizure of industry. A sensitive politician, if not a great leader, MacDonald understood that the most important task facing the ministry was proving to the nation that the Labor Party was both respectable and responsible. His nine months in office achieved just that goal if little else of major importance. The establishment of Labor as a viable governing party signaled the permanent demise of the Liberal Party. It has continued to exist, but the bulk of its voters have drifted into either the Conservative or the Labor ranks.

THE GENERAL STRIKE OF 1926. The Labor government fell in the autumn of 1924 over charges of inadequate prosecution of a communist writer. Stanley Baldwin returned to office, where he remained until 1929. The problem of the stagnant economy remained uppermost in the public mind. Business and political leaders continued to believe that all would be well if they could restore prewar conditions of trade. A major element in those conditions had been the gold standard as the basis for international trade. In 1925 the Conservative government returned to the gold standard in hopes of re-creating the former monetary stability. However, the government set the conversion rate for the pound against other currencies too high and thus in effect raised the price of British goods to foreign customers.

In order to make their products competitive on the world market, British management attempted to lower prices by cutting wages. The coal industry was the sector most directly effected by the wage cuts. It was inefficient and poorly managed and had been in trouble ever since the end of the war. Labor relations in the coal industry had been unruly for some time. In 1926, after cuts in wages and a breakdown in negotiations, the coal miners went out on strike. Soon thereafter, in May 1926, a general strike lasting nine days took place. There was much tension but little violence. In the end the miners and other unions capitulated. With such high levels of unemployment organized labor was in a relatively weak position. After the general strike the Baldwin government attempted to reconcile labor primarily through an expansion of housing and reforms in the poor laws. Despite the economic difficulties of these years the actual standard of living of most British workers, including those receiving government insurance payments, actually improved somewhat.

EMPIRE. World War I also modified Britain's imperial position. The aid given by the dominions, such as Canada and Australia, demonstrated a new independence on their part. Empire was a two-way proposition. The idea of self-determination as applied to Europe could not

---

Stanley Baldwin Reflects on the British General Strike

After halting much economic activity for more than a week in 1926, the British general strike came to a peaceful conclusion. Baldwin, who was the Conservative Prime Minister at the time, thought the outcome spoke well for British character and British freedom. In examining the impact of the strike, he was particularly concerned to present British institutions in a favorable light, as contrasted with the new social order then emerging in the Soviet Union. He hoped that communist doctrines would not come to influence the British labor movement.

IT MAY *have been a magnificent demonstration of the solidarity of labour, but it was at the same time a most pathetic evidence of the failure of all of us to live and work together for the good of all. . . . But if that strike showed solidarity, sympathy with the miners—whatever you like—it showed something else far greater. It proved the stability of the whole fabric of our own country, and to the amazement of the world not a shot was fired. We were saved by common sense and the good temper of our own people. We have been called a stupid people; but the moment the public grasped that what was at stake was not the solidarity of labour nor the fate of the miners, but the life of the State, then there was a response to the country's need deep and irresistible. And mark this: in my view there was that feeling in the country because the leaders of the strike and the men who were on strike felt it in their innermost hearts, too. They felt a conflict of loyalties. They knew that same conflict was raging in the breasts of thousands of men who had fought for their country ten years ago. Many of the strikers were uneasy in their minds and their consciences, because the British workman, as I know him, does not like breaking contracts, as so many of them did. I do not think many of them like stopping food supplies and shutting down the Press. I sometimes amuse myself with wondering what their language would have been like if these things had been done by the Government. And, after all, when all has been said about England, about the mistakes we make, and about our stupidity, and about how much better they do things in Russia, yet how many of those men or any of us, would prefer to have been born and brought up in any country in the world but this, or to send our children to be brought up there. In these post-war years, in spite of all the depression, in spite of all our troubles, never before has the wealth of this country, through the taxes and the rates, been so distributed to those less fortunate and for the provision of those thrown out of work. . . .*

I want to see our British Labour movement free from alien and foreign heresy. I want to see it pursued and developed on English lines, led by English men. The temptations that beset the growth of these vast organizations [the labor unions], in many respects as they are today outside the law, controlling multitudes of men and large sums of money—the temptation to set such a machine in motion and make people follow it is great indeed.

Stanley Baldwin, *Our Inheritance* (London: Hodder and Stoughton, 1928), pp. 222–224.

be prevented from filtering into imperial relationships. In India the Congress Party, led by Mohandas Gandhi (1869–1948), was beginning to attract widespread support. The British started to talk more about eventual self-government for the nation. Moreover, during the twenties the Indian government achieved the right to impose tariffs for the protection of its own industry rather than for the advantage of British manufacturers. The British textile producers no longer had totally free access to the vast Indian market.

IRELAND. A new chapter was written in the unhappy relations between Britain and Ireland during and after the war. In 1914 the Irish Home Rule Bill had passed Parliament, but its implementation was postponed for the duration of the conflict. As the war dragged on, Irish nationalists became determined to wait no longer. On Easter Monday 1916 a nationalist uprising occurred in Dublin. It was the only rebellion of a national group to occur against any government engaged in the war. The British suppressed it in less than a week but then made a grave tactical blunder. They executed the Irish nationalist leaders who had been responsible for the uprising. Overnight those rebels became national martyrs. Leadership of the nationalist cause quickly shifted from the Irish Party in Parliament to the extremist Sinn Fein ("Ourselves Alone") movement.

In the election of 1918 the Sinn Fein Party won all but four of the Irish parliamentary seats outside Ulster. They refused to go to the Parliament at Westminster. Instead they constituted themselves into a Dail Eireann, or Irish Parliament. On January 21, 1919, they declared Irish independence. The military wing of Sinn Fein became the Irish Republican Army (IRA). The first president was Eamon De Valera (1882–1975), who had been born in the United States. Very quickly what amounted to a guerrilla war broke out between the IRA and the British army supported by auxiliaries known as the Black and Tans. There was unusually intense bitterness and hatred on both sides.

In late 1921 secret negotiations commenced between the two governments. In the treaty concluded in December 1921 the Irish Free State took its place beside the earlier dominions in the British Commonwealth, Canada, Australia, New Zealand, and South Africa. The six counties of Ulster, or Northern Ireland, were permitted to remain part of what was now called the United Kingdom of Great Britain and Northern Ireland, with provisions for home rule. No sooner had the treaty been signed than a new Irish civil war broke out between Irish moderates and diehards. The moderates supported the treaty; the diehards wanted the oath to the British monarch abolished and a totally independent republic established. The second civil war continued until 1923. De Valera had supported the diehards, resigned the presidency, and organized resistance to the treaty. In 1932 he was again elected president. The next year the Dail Eireann abolished the oath of allegiance to the monarch.

During World War II Ireland remained neutral. In 1949 it declared itself the wholly independent republic of Eire.

Trials of the New Democracies

Both France and Great Britain had prewar experience in liberal democratic government. Their primary challenges lay in responding to economic pressures and allowing new groups, such as the Labor Party, to share political power. In Germany, Poland, Austria, Czechoslovakia, and the other successor states the issue for the twenties was to make new parliamentary governments function in a satisfactory and stable manner. Prior to the war both Germany and Austria–Hungary had possessed elected parliaments, but those bodies had not exercised genuine political power. The question after the war became whether those groups who had previously sat powerless in parliaments could assume both power and responsibility. Another question was how long conservative institutions, such as the armies and the conservative political groups, would tolerate or cooperate with the liberal experiments. At the same time all of these newly organized states confronted immense postwar economic difficulties.

Successor States in Eastern Europe

Only the barest outline can be given of the dreary political story of the successor states. It had been an article of faith among nineteenth-century liberals that only good could flow from the demise of Austria–Hungary. The new states in eastern Europe were to symbolize the principle of national self-determination and to provide a buffer against the westward spread of Bolshevism. However, they were in trouble from the beginning. They were poor, backward, and overwhelmingly rural nations dwelling in an industrialized world. Nationality problems continued to exist. The major social and political groups were generally unwilling to make compromises. With the exception of Czechoslovakia, all these states succumbed to some form of authoritarian government.

In Hungary during 1919 the Bolsheviks had erected a socialist government led by Béla Kun (1885–1937). The Allies quickly authorized an invasion by Romanian troops to remove the Communist danger. They then established Admiral Miklós Horty (1858–1957) as regent, a position he held until 1944. During the twenties the effective ruler of Hungary was Count Stephen Bethlen (1874–1947). He presided over a government that was parliamentary in form but aristocratic in character. In 1932 he was succeeded by General Julius Gömbös (1886–1936), who pursued policies of anti-Semitism and rigged elections. No matter how the popular vote turned out, the Gömbös party controlled the parliament. There was also deep resentment in Hungary over the territory it had lost to other nations at Versailles.

The situation in Austria was little better. The new Austria consisted of a capital city surrounded by some other territory. A quarter of the eight million Austrians lived in Vienna. Viable economic life was almost impossible, and union with Germany was forbidden by the Versailles Treaty. Throughout the twenties the leftist Social Democrats and the conservative Christian Socialists contended for power. Unwilling to use only normal political methods, both groups employed small armies to terrorize their opponents and to impress their followers. In 1933 the Christian Socialist Engelbert Dollfuss (1892–1934) became chancellor. He tried to steer a course between both the Communists and the German Nazis, who had begun to penetrate Austria. In 1934 he outlawed all political parties except those that composed his own Fatherland Front. He used government troops against the Social Democrats. During an unsuccessful Nazi *coup* in 1934, Dollfuss was shot. His successor, Kurt von Schuschnigg (b. 1897) presided over Austria until Hitler annexed it in 1938.

In southeastern Europe revision of the Versailles Treaty arrangements was somewhat less of an issue. Parliamentary government floundered nevertheless. In Yugoslavia (known as the Kingdom of the Serbs, Croats, and Slovenes until 1928), the clash of nationalities eventually led to the imposition of royal dictatorship in 1929 under King Alexander I (1921–1934). His dictatorship saw the outlawing of political parties and the jailing of popular politicians. Alexander I was assassinated in 1934, but the authoritarian government continued under the regency of his son. Other royal dictatorships were imposed in Romania by King Carol II (1930–1940) and in Bulgaria by King Boris III (1918–1943). They regarded their own illiberal regimes as countering even more extreme antiparliamentary movements and as quieting the discontent of nationalities within their borders. In Greece a parliamentary monarchy floundered amidst military coups and calls for a republic. In 1936 General John Metaxas (1871–1941) instituted a dictatorship that for the time being ended parliamentary life in Greece.

The nation whose postwar fortunes probably most disappointed liberal Europeans was Poland. For over a hundred years the country had been erased from the map. Restoration of an independent Poland had been one of Woodrow Wilson's Fourteen Points. When the country was finally reconstructed in 1919, nationalism proved

Thomas Masaryk (1850–1937) was the widely respected president of the democracy of Czechoslovakia after World War I. [The Granger Collection.]

an insufficient bond to overcome political disagreements stemming from class, diverse economic interests, and regionalism. The new parliament was plagued with a vast number of small political parties. The constitution assigned too little power to the executive. In 1926 General Josef Pilsudski (1857–1935) carried out a military *coup*. He ruled personally until the close of the decade, when the government passed into the hands of a group of military leaders.

Only one central European successor state escaped the fate of self-imposed authoritarian government. Czechoslovakia possessed a strong industrial base, a substantial middle class, and a tradition of liberal values. During the war Czechs and Slovaks had cooperated to aid the Allies. They had learned to work together and to trust each other. After the war the new government had carried out agrarian reform and had broken up large estates in favor of small peasant holdings. In the person of Thomas Masaryk (1850–1937) the nation possessed a gifted leader of immense integrity and fairness. The country had a real chance of constructing a viable modern nation state. However, it was plagued with discontent among its smaller national groups. The parliamentary regime might very well have been able to deal with this problem, but extreme German nationalists looked to Hitler for aid. For his part, the German dictator wished to expand into eastern Europe. In 1938 at Munich the great powers divided liberal Czechoslovakia to appease the aggressive instincts of Hitler.

The fate of the successor states proved most disappointing to those who had hoped for political liberty to result from the dissolution of the Hapsburg Empire and other border adjustments in eastern Europe. By the early thirties in most of those states the authoritarianism of the Hapsburgs had been replaced by that of other rulers. However, the most momentous democratic experiment between the wars was conducted in Germany. There, after a century of frustration and disappointment, a liberal state had been constructed. It was in Germany that

parliamentary democracy and its future in Western civilization faced its major trial.

The Weimar Republic

The German Weimar Republic was born from the defeat of the imperial army, the revolution of 1918 against the Hohenzollerns, and the hopes of German Liberals and Social Democrats. Its name derived from the city in which its constitution was written and promulgated in August 1919. While the constitution was being debated, the republic, headed by the Social Democrats, accepted the humiliating terms of the Versailles Treaty. Although its officials had signed only under the threat of an Allied invasion, the republic was nevertheless permanently associated with the national disgrace and the economic burdens of the treaty. Throughout the twenties the government of the republic was required to fulfill the economic and military provisions imposed by the Versailles settlement. It became all too easy for nationalists and military figures whose policies had brought on the tragedy and defeat of the war to blame the young republic and the socialists for the results of the conflict. In Germany more than in other countries the desire to revise the treaty was closely related to a desire to change the mode of domestic government.

The Weimar Constitution was a highly enlightened document. It guaranteed the civil liberties and provided for direct election, by universal suffrage, of the *Reichstag* and the president. However, it also contained certain crucial structural flaws that allowed the eventual overthrow of its institutions. Within the *Reichstag* a complicated system of proportional representation was adopted. It resulted in shifting party combinations that led to considerable instability. Ministers were technically responsible to the *Reichstag*, but the president appointed and removed the chancellor. Perhaps most important, Article 48 allowed the president in times of emergency to rule by decree. In this manner the constitution permitted the possibility of presidential dictatorship.

Beyond the burden of the Versailles Treaty and the potential constitutional pitfalls, the Weimar Republic suffered from a lack of sympathy and a lack of loyalty on the part of many Germans. A social revolution had not accompanied the changes in political structure. Many important political figures actually favored a constitutional monarchy. The schoolteachers, civil servants, and judicial officials of the republic were generally the same people who had previously served the Kaiser and the empire. Prior to the war they had distrusted or even hated the Social Democratic Party, which figured so prominently in the politics of the republic. The officer corps was deeply suspicious of the government and profoundly resentful of the military provisions of the peace settlement. They and other nationalistic Germans perpetuated the myth that the German army had surrendered on foreign soil only because it had been stabbed in the back by civilians at home. In other words, large numbers of Germans in significant social and political positions wanted both to revise the peace treaty and to modify the system of government. The early years of the republic only solidified those sentiments.

A number of major and minor humiliations as well as considerable economic instability impinged on the new government. In March 1920 the right-wing Kapp *Putsch* erupted in Berlin. Led by a conservative civil servant and supported by army officers, the attempted *coup* failed. But the collapse occurred only after government officials had fled the city. The same month a series of strikes took place in the Ruhr mining district. The government sent in troops. Such extremism from both the left and the right would haunt the republic for all its days. In May 1921 the Allies presented a reparations bill for 132 billion gold marks. The German republican government accepted this preposterous demand only after new Allied threats of occupation. Throughout the early twenties there were numerous assassinations or attempted assassinations of important republican leaders. Violence was the hallmark of the first five years of the republic.

This is a characteristic drawing, made in 1921, by the German artist George Grosz (1893–1959). His art expressed hatred of the bourgeoisie, militarism, and capitalism; here he views the exploitation of the poor and the working class by overfed, callous property owners. [The Granger Collection.]

Lilo Linke Recalls the Mad Days of the German Inflation

In 1923 the presses that were printing paper currency in Germany could hardly keep up with the rising prices. This memoir recounts the difficulties of those days and the resentments that arose as money became worth less than the paper on which it was printed.

THE *whole population had suddenly turned into maniacs. Everyone was buying, selling, speculating, bargaining, and dollar, dollar, dollar was the magic word which dominated every conversation, every newspaper, every poster in Germany. Nobody understood what was happening. There seemed to be no sense, no rules in the mad game, but one had to take part in it if one did not want to be trampled underfoot at once. Only a few people were able to carry through to the end and gain by the inflation. The majority lost everything and broke down, impoverished and bewildered.*

The middle class was hurt more than any other, the savings of a lifetime and their small fortunes melted into a few coppers. They had to sell their most precious belongings for ten milliard inflated marks to buy a bit of food or an absolutely necessary coat, and their pride and dignity were bleeding out of many wounds. Bitterness remained for ever in their hearts. Full of hatred, they accused the international financiers, the Jews and Socialists—their old enemies—of having exploited their distress. They never forgot and never forgave and were the first to lend a willing ear to Hitler's fervent preaching.

In the shop, notices announced that we should receive our salaries in weekly parts, after a while we queued up at the cashier's desk every evening, and before long we were paid twice daily and ran out during the lunch hour to buy a few things, because as soon as the new rate of exchange became known in the early afternoon our money had again lost half its value.

Lilo Linke, *Restless Days* (New York: Alfred A. Knopf, 1935) pp. 131–132.

In 1923 German inflation became so extreme that eventually money was not worth the paper on which it was printed. In these photographs from that time, [ABOVE] a German housewife finds it cheaper to use the inflated currency to light her stove than to spend it on kindling wood, while [BELOW] poor citizens sell tin cans to raise money. [TOP: United Press International Photo; BOTTOM: The Granger Collection.]

In January 1923 French troops occupied the Ruhr region of Germany because of alleged defaults in the delivery of reparations to France. [The Granger Collection.]

The sensitive French-Belgian-German border area between the two world wars. In spite of efforts to restrain tension in the twenty-year period, there were persistent difficulties related to the Ruhr, Rhineland, Saar, and Eupen-Malmédy regions that necessitated strong defenses.

GERMANY'S WESTERN FRONTIER

INVASION OF THE RUHR AND INFLATION. Inflation brought the major crisis of this period. The financing of the war and the continued postwar deficit spending generated an immense rise in prices. Consequently the value of German currency fell. By early 1921 the German mark traded against the American dollar at a ratio of 64 to 1, compared with a ratio of 4.2 to 1 in 1914. The German financial community contended that the value of the currency could not be stabilized until the reparations issue had been solved. In the meantime the printing presses kept pouring forth paper money, which was used to redeem government bonds as they fell due. In 1923 the Allies and France in particular declared Germany to be in technical default on its reparations payments. On January 11, to ensure receipt of the hard-won reparations, the French government ordered its troops to occupy the Ruhr mining and manufacturing district. The response of the Weimar Republic was to order passive resistance. This policy amounted to calling a general strike in the largest industrial region of the nation.

The invasion and the passive resistance produced cataclysmic inflation. The government paid subsidies to the Ruhr labor force, who had laid down their tools. Unemployment soon spread from the Ruhr to other parts of the country, creating a new drain on the treasury and also reducing tax revenues. The printing presses by this point had difficulty providing enough paper currency to keep up with the daily rise in prices. In November 1923 an American dollar was worth more than 800 million German marks. Money was literally not worth the paper it was printed on. Stores were unwilling to exchange goods for the worthless currency, and farmers withheld produce from the market. The moral and social values of thrift and prudence were thoroughly undermined. The security of middle-class savings, pensions, and insurance policies was wiped out. Simultaneously debts and mortgages could be paid off. Speculators in land, real estate, and industry made great fortunes. Union contracts generally allowed workers to keep up with rising prices. Inflation was not a disaster to everyone. However, to the middle class and the lower middle class the inflation was still one more traumatic experience coming hard on the heels of the military defeat and the peace treaty. Only when the social and economic upheaval of these months is grasped can the later German desire for order and security at almost any cost be comprehended.

HITLER'S EARLY CAREER. Late in 1923 Adolf Hitler (1889–1945) made his first major appearance on the German political scene. In 1889 he had been born the son of a minor Austrian customs official. By 1907 he had gone to Vienna, where his hopes of becoming an artist were soon dashed. He lived off money sent by his widowed mother and later off an Austrian orphan's allowance. He also painted postcards for further income and later found work as a day laborer. In Vienna he became acquainted with Mayor Karl Leugar's Christian Social Party which prospered on an ideology of anti-Semitism and from the social anxieties of the lower middle class. Hitler's own precarious situation and his observations taught him how desperately the lower middle class feared slipping into a proletarian condition. He also absorbed the rabid German nationalism and extreme anti-Semitism that flourished in Vienna. He came to hate socialism and Marxism, which he associated with Jews. During World War I Hitler fought with the German army, was wounded, was promoted to the rank of corporal, and was awarded the Iron Cross for bravery.

After the conflict Hitler settled in Munich. In the new surroundings he became associated with a small nationalistic, anti-Semitic political party that in 1920 adopted the name of National Socialist German Workers Party. The same year the group began to parade under a red banner with a black swastika. It issued a platform or program of

---

The National Socialist German Worker's Party Issues a Platform

These statements from the Nazi Party Twenty-five Points of 1920 illustrate the calls for nationalism, territorial expansion, anti-Semitic public policy, and aid for the poor and lower middle class that in time attracted broad support throughout Germany.

1. WE DEMAND *the union of all Germans to form a Great Germany on the basis of self-determination enjoyed by nations.*

2. *We demand equality of rights for the German people in its dealings with other nations, and abolition of the peace treaties of Versailles and Saint-Germain.*

3. *We demand land and territory (colonies) for the nourishment of our people and for settling our excess population.*

4. *None but members of the nation may be citizens of the state. None but those of German blood, whatever their creed, may be members of the nation. No Jew, therefore, may be a member of the nation.*

5. *Anyone who is not a citizen of the state may live in Germany only as a guest and must be regarded as being subject to foreign laws.*

.   .   .   .   .   .

7. *We demand that the state shall make it its first duty to promote the industry and livelihood of citizens of the state. If it is not possible to nourish the entire population of the state, foreign nationals (non-citizens of the state) must be excluded from the Reich.*

.   .   .   .   .   .

10. *It must be the first duty of each citizen of the state to work with his mind or with his body. The activities of the individual may not clash with the interests of the whole, but must proceed within the frame of the community and be for the general good.*

.   .   .   .   .   .

15. *We demand extensive development of provision for old age.*

16. *We demand creation and maintenance of a healthy middle class, immediate communalization of wholesale business premises, and their lease at a cheap rate to small traders, and that extreme considerations shall be shown to all small purveyors to the state, district authorities, and smaller localities.*

.   .   .   .   .   .

22. *We demand abolition of a paid army and formation of a national army.*

.   .   .   .

Raymond E. Murphy (Ed.), *National Socialism*, U.S. Department of State, Publication 1864 (Washington, 1943), pp. 222–224.

This picture of Adolf Hitler was made in May 1927. At the time he was not yet a major political figure, and the Nazi movement was relatively small. [United Press International Photo.]

Twenty-five Points. Among other things these called for the repudiation of the Versailles Treaty, the unification of Austria and Germany, the exclusion of Jews from German citizenship, agrarian reform, the prohibition of land speculation, the confiscation of war profits, the state administration of the giant cartels, and the replacement of department stores with small tradespeople. The "socialism" that Hitler and the Nazis had in mind was not state ownership of the means of production but the subordination of all economic enterprise to the welfare of the nation. It implied protection for very small economic enterprise. The social appeal of Nazism was to the lower middle class, which found itself squeezed between well-organized big business and socialist labor unions or political parties.

Soon after the promulgation of the Twenty-five Points, the Stormtroopers, or SA, were organized under the leadership of Captain Ernest Roehm. It was a paramilitary organization that initially provided members with food and uniforms and later in the decade with wages. In the mid-twenties the SA adopted its famous brown-shirted uniform. The Stormtroopers were the chief Nazi instrument for terror and intimidation before the party came into control of the government. They were a law unto themselves. The organization constituted a means of preserving military discipline and values outside the small army permitted by the Versailles settlement. The exist-

ence of such a private party army was a sign of the potential for violence in the Weimar Republic and the widespread contempt for the law and the institutions of the republic.

The economic turmoil following the Ruhr occupation provided the fledgling party, by now under Hitler's personal dominance, with an opportunity for direct action against the republic. On November 9, 1923, Hitler and a band of followers, accompanied by General Ludendorff, attempted an unsuccessful *Putsch* in Munich. When the local authorities crushed the rising, sixteen Naxis were killed. Hitler and Ludendorff were arrested and tried for treason. The general was acquitted. Hitler employed the trial to make himself into a national figure. In his defense he condemned the republic, the Versailles Treaty, the Jews, and the weakened condition of his adopted country. He was convicted and sentenced to five years in prison. He actually spent only a few months in jail, during which time he wrote *Mein Kampf* ("My Battle"). Another result of the brief imprisonment was a decision on Hitler's part that in the future he and his party must seek to seize political power by legal methods.

Gustav Stresemann addressed the League of Nations in 1926 upon the admission of Germany to that international body. This event was one of the major outcomes of the Locarno agreements. [Bildarchiv Preussischer Kulturbesitz. Herbert Hoffmann.]

THE STRESEMANN YEARS. Elsewhere the officials of the republic were attempting to repair the damage from the inflation. Gustav Stresemann (1878–1929) was primarily responsible for the reconstruction of the republic and for its achievement of self-confidence. He served as chancellor only from August to November 1923, but he provided the nation with a new basis for stability. Stresemann abandoned the policy of passive resistance in the Ruhr. The country simply could not afford it. Then with the aid of banker Hjalmar Schacht, he introduced a new German currency. The rate of exchange was one trillion of the old German marks for one new *Rentenmark*. Stresemann also moved against challenges from both the left and the right. He supported the crushing of Hitler's abortive *Putsch* and smaller communist disturbances. In late November 1923 he resigned as chancellor and assumed the position of foreign minister, a post that he held until his death in 1929. In that office he exercised considerable influence over the affairs of the republic.

In 1924 the Weimar Republic and the Allies agreed to a new systematization of the reparation payments. The Dawes Plan, submitted by the American banker Charles Dawes, lowered the annual payments and allowed them to fluctuate according to the fortunes of the German economy. The Ruhr was to be evacuated, and the last French troops left that region in 1925. The same year Friedrich Ebert (1871–1925), the Social Democratic president of the republic, died. Field Marshal Paul von Hindenburg (1847–1934), a military hero and a conservative monarchist, was elected as his successor. He governed in strict accordance with the constitution, but his election suggested that a new conservative tenor had come to German politics. It looked as if conservative Germans had become reconciled to the republic. This conservatism was in line with the prosperity of the latter part of the decade. Foreign capital flowed into Germany, and employment, which had been poor throughout most of the postwar years, improved smartly. Giant industrial combines spread. The prosperity helped to establish broader acceptance and appreciation of the republic.

In foreign affairs Stresemann pursued a conciliatory course. He was committed to a policy of fulfilling the provisions of the Versailles Treaty, even as he attempted to revise it by diplomacy. He was willing to accept the settlement in the west but was a determined, if sometimes secret, revisionist in the east. He aimed to recover German territories lost to Poland and Czechoslovakia and possibly to unite with Austria, chiefly by diplomatic means. The first step, however, was to achieve respectability and economic recovery. That goal required a policy of accommodation and "Fulfillment," for the moment at least.

With the exception of the modernistic wing (toward the upper part of the picture), these buildings were the headquarters of the post-World War I League of Nations in Geneva, Switzerland. Today they house agencies of the United Nations. [United Nations.]

LOCARNO. These developments gave rise to the Locarno Agreements of October 1925. The spirit of conciliation led politicians Austen Chamberlain for Britain and Aristide Briand for France to accept Stresemann's proposal for a fresh start. France and Germany both accepted the western frontier established at Versailles as legitimate. Britain and Italy agreed to intervene against the aggressor if either side violated the frontier or if Germany sent troops into the demilitarized Rhineland. Significantly no such agreement was made about Germany's eastern frontier, but the Germans made treaties of arbitration with Poland and Czechoslovakia, and France strengthened its ties with the Little Entente. France supported German membership in the League of Nations and agreed to withdraw its troops from the Rhineland in 1930, five years earlier than specified at Versailles.

Germany was pleased to have achieved respectability and a guarantee against another Ruhr occupation, as well as the possibility of revision in the east. Britain was pleased to be allowed to play a more evenhanded role. Italy was glad to be recognized as a great power. The French were happy, too, because the Germans voluntarily accepted the permanence of their western frontier, which was also guaranteed by Britain and Italy, while France maintained its allies in the east. As A. J. P. Taylor has put it, "Any French statesman of 1914 could have been bewildered with delight by such an achievement."[2]

The Locarno Agreements brought a new spirit of hope to Europe. Germany's entry into the League of Nations was greeted with enthusiasm. Chamberlain, Briand, and Stresemann jointly received the Nobel Peace Prize in 1926. The spirit of Locarno was carried even further

2 Taylor, p. 58.

when the leading European states, Japan, and the United States signed the Kellogg–Briand Pact in 1928, renouncing "war as an instrument of national policy." The joy and optimism were not justified. France had merely recognized its inability to coerce Germany without help. Britain had shown its unwillingness to uphold the settlement in the east. Austen Chamberlain declared that no British government ever would "risk the bones of a British grenadier" for the Polish corridor. Germany was by no means reconciled to the eastern settlement. It continued its clandestine military connections with the Soviet Union, which had commenced with the Treaty of Rapallo, and planned to continue to press for revision.

In both France and Germany, moreover, the conciliatory politicians represented only a part of the nation. In Germany, especially, most people continued to reject Versailles and regarded Locarno as only an extension of it. When the Dawes Plan ran out in 1929, it was replaced by the Young Plan, which lowered the reparation payments, put a term on how long they must be made, and removed Germany entirely from outside supervision and control. The intensity of the outcry in Germany against the continuation of any reparations showed how far the Germans were from accepting their situation. In spite of these problems, major war was by no means inevitable. Europe, aided by American loans, was returning to prosperity. German leaders like Stresemann would certainly have continued to press for change, but there is little reason to think that they would have resorted to force, much less to a general war. Continued prosperity and diplomatic success might have won the loyalty of the German people for the Weimar Republic and moderate revisionism, but the Great Depression of the thirties brought new forces to power.

The Fascist Experiment in Italy

While its wartime allies continued to pursue parliamentary politics and its former enemies set out on the troubled path of democracy, Italy moved toward a new form of authoritarian government. From the Italian Fascist movement of Benito Mussolini (1883–1945) was derived the general term of *fascist*, which has frequently been used to describe the various right-wing dictatorships that arose between the wars.

The exact meaning of *fascism* as a political term remains much disputed among both historians and political scientists. However, a certain consensus does exist. The governments regarded as fascist were antidemocratic, anti-Marxist, antiparliamentary, and frequently anti-Semitic. They hoped to hold back the spread of Bolshevism, which seemed at the time a very real threat. They sought a world safe for the middle class, small businesses, owners of moderate amounts of property, and small farmers. The fascist regimes rejected the political inheritance of the French Revolution and of nineteenth-century liberalism. Their adherents believed that normal parliamentary politics and parties sacrificed national honor and greatness to petty party disputes. They wanted to overcome the class conflict of Marxism and the party conflict of liberalism by consolidating the various groups and classes within the nation for great national purposes. As Mussolini declared in 1931, "The fascist conception of the state is all-embracing, and outside of the state no human or spiritual values can exist, let alone be desirable."[3] Fascism was also highly elitist. The fascist governments were usually single-party dictatorships characterized by terrorism and police surveillance.

The Rise of Mussolini

The Italian *Fasci di Combattimento* ("Band of Combat") was founded in 1919 in Milan. Its members came largely from Italian war veterans who felt that the sacrifices of the conflict had been in vain. They resented the failure of Italy to gain the city of Fiume, toward the northern end of the Adriatic Sea, at the Paris conference. They feared socialism and inflation.

3 Quoted in Denis Mack Smith, *Italy: A Modern History* (Ann Arbor: University of Michigan Press, 1959), p. 412.

Their leader, Benito Mussolini, had been born the son of a blacksmith. For a time he had been a schoolteacher, then a day laborer. He became active in Italian socialist politics and by 1912 had become editor of the socialist newspaper *Avanti*. In 1914 Mussolini broke with the socialists and supported Italian entry into the war on the side of the Allies. His interventionist position lost him the editorship of *Avanti*. He then established his own paper, *Il Popolo d'Italia*. Later he served in the army and was wounded. In 1919, although of some prewar political stature, Mussolini was simply one of many Italian politicians. His *Fasci* organization was for its part simply one of numerous small political groups in a country characterized by such entities. As a politician Mussolini was an opportunist par excellence. He proved capable of changing his ideas and principles to suit every new occasion. Action for him was always more important than thought or rational justification. His one real rule was that of political survival.

Postwar Italian politics was a muddle. During the conflict the Italian Parliament had for all intents and purposes ceased to function. It had been quite willing to allow ministers to rule by decree. However, the parliamentary system as it then existed had begun to prove quite unsatisfactory to large sectors of the citizenry. Many Italians besides those in Mussolini's band of followers felt that Italy had emerged from the war as less than a victorious nation and had not been treated as a great power at the peace conference. The main spokesman for this discontent was the extreme nationalist poet and novelist Gabriele D'Annunzio (1863–1938). In 1919 he successfully led a force of patriotic Italians in an assault on Fiume. Troops of the Italian parliamentary government eventually drove him out. D'Annunzio had provided the example of the political use of a nongovernmental military force. The action of the government in removing him from Fiume gave the parliamentary ministry a somewhat less than patriotic appearance.

Between 1919 and 1921 Italy also experienced considerable internal social turmoil. Numerous industrial strikes

Gabriele D'Annunzio was an Italian poet and fervent nationalist. In 1919 he led a private military raid against Fiume, which he believed had wrongfully been denied to Italy by the Versailles Treaty. The painting is by Romaine Brooks. [The Granger Collection.]

occurred, and workers occupied factories. Peasants seized uncultivated land from large estates. Parliamentary and constitutional government seemed incapable of dealing with this unrest. The Socialist Party had captured a plurality of seats in the Chamber of Deputies during the 1919 election. A new Catholic Popular Party had also done quite well. Both appealed to the working and agrarian classes. However, neither party would cooperate with the other, and parliamentary deadlock resulted. Under these conditions many Italians honestly and still others conveniently believed there existed the danger of a communist revolution.

Initially Mussolini was uncertain of the direction of the political winds. He first supported the factory occupations and land seizures. However, never one to be concerned with consistency, he soon reversed himself. He had discovered that large numbers of both upper-class and middle-class Italians who were pressured by inflation and who feared property loss had no sympathy for the workers or the peasants. They wanted order rather than some vague social justice that might harm their own interests. Consequently Mussolini and his Fascists took direct action in the face of the government inaction. They formed local squads of terrorists who disrupted Socialist meetings, mugged Socialist leaders, and terrorized Socialist supporters. They attacked strikers and farm workers and protected strikebreakers. Conservative land and factory owners were grateful. The officers and institutions of the law simply ignored the crimes of the Fascist squads. By early 1922 the Fascists had turned their intimidation against local officials in cities, such as Ferrara, Ravenna, and Milan. They controlled the local government in many parts of northern Italy.

In the election of 1921 Mussolini and thirty-four of his followers were sent to the Chamber of Deputies. Their importance grew as the local Fascists gained more direct power. The movement now had hundreds of thousands of supporters. In October 1922 the Fascists, dressed in their characteristic black shirts, began a march on Rome. King Victor Emmanuel III (1900–1946) refused to sign

a decree that would have authorized the use of the army against the marchers. Probably no other single decision so ensured a Fascist seizure of power. The cabinet resigned in protest. On October 29 the monarch telegraphed Mussolini in Milan and asked him to become prime minister. The next day Mussolini arrived in Rome by sleeping car and greeted his followers as head of the government when they entered the city.

Technically Mussolini had come into office by legal means. The monarch did possess the power to appoint the prime minister. However, Mussolini had no majority or even near majority in the Chamber of Deputies. Behind the legal façade of his assumption of power lay the months of terrorist disruption and intimidation and the threat of the Fascist march itself. The non-Fascist politicians, whose ineptitude had prepared the way for Mussolini, believed that his regime like others of previous months would be temporary. They failed to comprehend that he was not a traditional Italian politician.

The Fascists in Power

Mussolini had not really expected to be appointed prime minister. He moved cautiously to shore up his support and to consolidate his power. His success was the result of the impotence of his rivals, his own effective use of his office, his power over the masses, and his sheer ruthlessness. On November 23, 1922, the king and parliament granted Mussolini dictatorial authority for one year to bring order to the lower levels of the government. Wherever possible Mussolini appointed Fascists to office. Late in 1924, under Mussolini's guidance, the parliament changed the election law. Previously parties had been represented in the Chamber of Deputies in proportion to the popular vote cast for them. According to the new election law, the party that gained the largest popular vote (with a minimum of at least 25 per cent) received two thirds of the seats in the chamber. Coalition government, with all its compromises and hesitant policies, would no longer be necessary. In the election of 1924 the Fascists won a great victory and complete control of the

Mussolini was a powerful public orator. His gestures, which often appear comic in hindsight, were part of a carefully cultivated public image designed to make him appear at all times a leader. [Culver Pictures.]

Chamber of Deputies. They used that majority to end legitimate parliamentary life. A series of laws passed in 1925 and 1926 permitted Mussolini, in effect, to rule by decree. In 1926 all other political parties were dissolved. By the close of that year Italy had been transformed into a single-party, dictatorial state.

Their growing dominance over the government had not, however, diverted the Fascists from the course of violence and terror. They were put in charge of the police force, and the terrorist squads became institutionalized into government militia. In late 1924 their thugs murdered Giacomo Matteotti (1885–1924), a major non-Communist socialist leader. He had persistently criticized Mussolini and had exposed the criminality of the Fascist movement. In protest against the murder, a number of opposition deputies withdrew from the chamber. That tactic gave the prime minister an even freer hand. The deputies were refused readmission.

Support for the regime was sustained by the parallel organization of the party and the government. For every government institution there existed a corresponding party organization. In this manner the Fascist Party dominated the political structure at every level. As all other political parties were outlawed, citizens had to look to the Fascists in their community for political favors. They also knew the high price of opposition. By the late twenties the Grand Council of the party had become an organ of the state. It drew up and presented the list of persons who would stand for election to the Chamber of Deputies. Major policies to be approved by the chamber first passed the Grand Council. And Mussolini himself controlled the council.

The party used propaganda quite effectively. A cult of personality surrounded Mussolini. His skills in oratory and his general intelligence allowed him to hold his own with both large crowds and the leaders of the more respectable portions of the community. The latter tolerated and often admired him in the belief that he had saved them from Bolshevism. The persons who did have the courage to oppose Mussolini were usually driven into exile, and some were murdered.

The Italian Fascists Establish a New Set of Ten Commandments

These commandments of 1934 clearly illustrate the aggressive and authoritarian character of Italian Fascism. They also display the intense importance attached to Mussolini himself.

1. KNOW *that the Fascist, and in particular the soldier, must not believe in perpetual peace.*
2. *Days of imprisonment are always deserved.*
3. *The nation serves even as sentinel over a can of petrol.*
4. *A companion must be a brother, first, because he lives with you, and secondly because he thinks like you.*
5. *The rifle and cartridge belt, and the rest, are confided to you not to rust in leisure, but to be preserved in war.*
6. *Do not ever say "The Government will pay . . ." because it is you who pay; and the Government is that which you willed to have, and for which you put on a uniform.*
7. *Discipline is the soul of armies; without it there are no soldiers, only confusion and defeat.*
8. *Mussolini is always right.*
9. *For a volunteer there are no extenuating circumstances when he is disobedient.*
10. *One thing must be dear to you above all: the life of the Duce.*

Michael Oakeshott (Ed.), *The Social and Political Doctrines of Contemporary Europe* (Cambridge, England: Cambridge University Press, 1939), p. 180.

The Italian dictator made one important domestic departure that brought him significant political dividends. Through the Lateran Pact of February 1929, the Roman Catholic Church and the Italian state made peace with each other. Ever since the armies of Italian unification had seized papal lands in the 1860s, the church had been hostile to the state. The popes had remained virtual prisoners in the Vatican. The agreement of 1929 recognized the pope as the temporal ruler of Vatican City. The Italian government agreed to pay an indemnity to the papacy for confiscated land. The state also recognized Catholicism as the religion of the nation, exempted church property from taxes, and allowed church law to govern the institution of marriage. The Lateran Pact brought further respectability to Mussolini's authoritarian regime.

The Beginning of the Soviet Experiment

The political right had no monopoly on authoritarianism between the wars. The consolidation of the Bolshevik Revolution in Russia established the most extensive and durable of all twentieth-century authoritarian governments. However, the dictatorships of the left and the right did differ from each other. Unlike the Italian Fascists or the German National Socialists, the Bolsheviks had seized power illegally through revolution. For several years they confronted effective opposition, and their leaders long felt insecure about their hold on the country. The Communist Party was not a mass party nor a nationalistic one. Its early membership rarely exceeded more than 1 per cent of the Russian population. The Bolsheviks confronted a much less industrialized economy than existed in Italy or Germany. They believed in and practiced the collectivization of economic life attacked by the right-wing dictatorships. The Marxist–Leninist ideology was far more all-encompassing than the nationalism of the Fascists and the racism of the Nazis. Communism was an exportable commodity. The Communists regarded their government and their revolution not as local events in a national history but rather as an epoch-making event in the history of the world and the development of humanity.

The Third International

In a curious manner, however, certain policies of the early Russian Communist Revolution directly affected the rise of the Fascists and the Nazis in western Europe. The success of the revolution in Russia had the paradoxical effect of dividing socialist parties and socialist movements in the rest of Europe. In 1919 the Soviet Communists founded the Third International of the European socialist movement. It became better known as the Comintern. A year after its inception the Comintern imposed its Twenty-one Conditions upon any other socialist party that wished to become a member. The conditions included acknowledgement of leadership from Moscow, rejection of reformist or revisionist socialism, and repudiation of previous socialist leaders. The Comintern wished to make the Russian model of socialism as developed by Lenin the rule for all socialist parties outside the Soviet Union.

The decision whether to join or not to join the Comintern under these conditions split every major socialist party on the continent. As a result, separate communist parties and social democratic parties emerged. The former modeled themselves after the Soviet party and pursued policies dictated by Moscow. The social democratic parties attempted to pursue both social reform and liberal parliamentary politics. Throughout the twenties and early thirties the communists and the social democrats tended to fight each other more intensely than they fought either capitalism or conservative political parties. This division of the European political left meant that right-wing political movements rarely had to confront a united opposition on the political left.

War Communism

Within the Soviet Union the Red Armies under the organizational genius of Leon Trotsky had suppressed internal and foreign military opposition to the new government. Throughout the civil war Lenin had declared that the Bolshevik Party, as the vanguard of the revolution, was imposing the dictatorship of the proletariat. Political and economic administration became highly centralized. All major decisions flowed from the top in a nondemocratic manner. Under the economic policy of "War Communism" the revolutionary government confiscated and then operated the banks, the transport facilities, and heavy industry. The state also forcibly requisitioned grain produced by the peasants and shipped it from the countryside to feed the army and the workers in the cities. The fact of the civil war permitted suppression of possible resistance to this economic policy.

"War Communism" aided the victory of the Red Army over its opponents. The revolution had survived

The Third International Issues Conditions of Membership

After the Russian Revolution, the Russian Communist Party organized the Third Communist International. Any communist party outside the Soviet Union was required to accept these Twenty-one Conditions, adopted in 1919, in order to join the International. In effect, this program demanded that all such parties adopt a distinctly revolutionary program and cease operating as legal parties within their various countries. By this means, the Soviet Union sought to achieve leadership of the socialist movement throughout Europe. As non-Russian socialist parties debated whether to join the Third International, they quickly split into social democratic parties that remained independent of Moscow and communist parties that adopted the policy imposed by the Russian Communist Party.

1. THE *daily propaganda and agitation must bear a truly communist character and correspond to the program and all the decisions of the Third International. All the organs of the press that are in the hands of the party must be edited by reliable communists who have proved their loyalty to the cause of the proletarian revolution. . . .*

3. *The class struggle in almost all of the countries of Europe and America is entering the phase of civil war. Under such conditions the communists can have no confidence in bourgeois law. They must everywhere create a parallel illegal apparatus, which at the decisive moment could assist the party in performing its duty of revolution. . . .*

4. *The obligation to spread communist ideas includes the particular necessity of persistent, systematic propaganda in the army. . . .*

5. *It is necessary to carry on systematic and steady agitation in the rural districts. . . .*

7. *The parties desiring to belong to the Communist International must recognize the necessity of a complete and absolute rupture with reformism . . . , and they must carry on propaganda in favor of this rupture among the broadest circles of the party membership. . . .*

8. *. . . Every party desirous of belonging to the Third International must ruthlessly denounce the methods of "their own" imperialists in the colonies, supporting, not in words, but in deeds, every independence movement in the colonies. . . .*

14. *Every party that desires to belong to the Communist International must give every possible support to the*

Lenin addressing a May Day demonstration in Moscow in 1918. [Culver Pictures.]

Soviet Republics in their struggle against all counter-revolutionary forces. . . .

. . . .

16. All decisions of the congresses of the Communist International . . . are binding on all parties affiliated to the Communist International. . . .

17. In connection with all this, all parties desiring to join the Communist International must change their names. Every party that wishes to join the Communist International must bear the name: Communist party *of such-and-such country. This question as to name is not merely a formal one, but a political one of great importance. The Communist International has declared a decisive war against the entire bourgeois world and all the yellow, social democratic parties. Every rank-and-file worker must clearly understand the difference between the communist parties and the old official "social democratic" or "socialist" parties which have betrayed the cause of the working class.*

18. Members of the party who reject the conditions and thesis of the Communist International, on principle, must be expelled from the party.

International Communism in the Era of Lenin: A Documentary History, ed. by Helmut Gruber (Garden City, N.Y.: Doubleday, 1972), pp. 241–246.

and triumphed. However, the policy generated domestic opposition to the Bolsheviks, who in 1920 numbered only about 600,000 members. The alliance of workers and peasants forged by the slogan of "Peace, Bread, and Land" had begun to come apart at the seams. Many Russians were no longer willing to make the sacrifices demanded by the central party bureaucrats. In 1920 and 1921 major strikes occurred in numerous factories. Peasants were discontented and resisted the requisition of grain. In March 1921 the navy mutinied at Kronstadt. Its rebellion was crushed by the Red Army with grave loss of life. Each of these incidents suggested that the proletariat itself was opposing the dictatorship of the proletariat. Also, by late 1920 it had become clear that further revolution would not sweep across the rest of Europe. For the time being the Soviet Union would constitute a vast island of revolutionary socialism in the larger sea of worldwide capitalism.

The New Economic Policy

Under these difficult conditions Lenin made a crucial strategic retreat. In March 1921, following the Kronstadt mutiny, he outlined the New Economic Policy, normally referred to as *NEP*. Apart from what he termed "the commanding heights" of banking, heavy industry, transportation, and international commerce, there was to be considerable private economic enterprise. In particular, peasants were to be permitted to farm for a profit. They would pay taxes like other citizens, but they could sell their surplus grain on the open market. The NEP was in line with Lenin's earlier conviction that the Russian peasantry held the key to the success of revolution in the nation. After 1921 the countryside did become more stabilized, and a secure food supply seemed assured for the cities. Similar free enterprise flourished within light industry and domestic retail trade. By 1927 industrial production had reached its 1913 level. The revolution seemed to have transformed Russia into a land of small family farms and small privately owned shops and businesses.

An early tractor arrives on a Russian farm during the 1920s. [The Granger Collection.]

Stalin versus Trotsky

The New Economic Policy had caused sharp disputes within the Politburo, the highest governing committee of the Communist Party. The partial return to capitalism seemed to some members nothing less than a betrayal of sound Marxist principles. These frictions increased as Lenin's firm hand disappeared. In 1922 he suffered a stroke that broke his health. He returned to work but never again dominated party affairs. In 1924 Lenin died. As the power vacuum developed, an intense struggle for future leadership of the party commenced. Two factions emerged. One was led by Trotsky; the other by Josef Stalin (1879–1953), who had become General Secretary of the party in 1922. Shortly before his death Lenin had criticized both men. He was especially harsh toward Stalin. However, the General Secretary's base of power lay with the party membership and with the daily management of party affairs. Consequently he was able to withstand the posthumous strictures of Lenin.

The issue between the two factions was power within the party, but the struggle was fought out over the question of Russia's path toward industrialization and the future of the communist revolutionary movement. Trotsky, speaking for what became known as the left wing, urged rapid industrialization financed through the expropriation of farm production. Agriculture should be collectivised, and the peasants should be made to pay for industrialization. Trotsky further argued that the revolution in Russia could succeed only if new revolutions took place elsewhere in the world. Russia needed the skills and wealth of other nations to build its own economy. As Trotsky's influence within the party began to wane, he also demanded that party members be permitted to criticize the policies of the government and the party. However, Trotsky was very much a latecomer to the advocacy of open discussion. When in control of the Red Army, he had been known as an unflinching disciplinarian.

A right-wing faction opposed Trotsky. Its chief ideological voice was that of Nikolai Bukharin (1888–1938), the editor of *Pravda*. Stalin was the major political manipulator. In the mid-twenties this group pressed for the continuation of Lenin's NEP and a policy of relatively slow industrialization. Stalin emerged as the victor in these intraparty rivalries.

Stalin had been born in 1879 into a very poor family. Unlike the other early Bolshevik leaders, he had not spent a long period of exile in western Europe. He was much less of an intellectual and internationalist. He was also much more brutal. His handling of various recalcitrant national groups within Russia after the revolution had even shocked Lenin. Stalin's power lay in his command of bureaucratic and administrative methods. He was neither a brilliant writer nor an effective public speaker; however, he mastered the crucial, if dull, details of party structure, including admission and promotion. That mastery meant that he could draw upon the support of the lower levels of the party apparatus when he came into conflict with other leaders.

In the middle of the decade Stalin supported Bukharin's position on economic development. In 1924 he also enunciated in opposition to Trotsky the doctrine of "socialism in one country." He urged that socialism could be achieved in Russia alone. Russian success did not depend upon the fate of the revolution elsewhere. In this manner Stalin nationalized the previously international scope of the Marxist revolution. Stalin cunningly used the apparatus of the party and his control over the Central Committee of the Communist Party to edge out Trotsky and his supporters. By 1927 Trotsky had been removed from all his offices, expelled from the party, and exiled to Siberia. In 1929 he was sent out of Russia and eventually took up residence in Mexico, where he was murdered in 1940, presumably by one of Stalin's agents. With the removal of Trotsky from all positions of influence Stalin was firmly in control of the Soviet state. It remained to be seen where he would direct its course and what "socialism in one country" would mean in practice.

Results of the Decade of Experiment

At the close of the twenties it appeared that Europe had finally emerged from the difficulties of the World War I era. The initial resentments over the peace settlement seemed to have abated. The major powers were cooperating. Democracy was still functioning in Germany. The Labor Party was about to form its second ministry in Britain. France had settled into a less assertive international role. Mussolini's Fascism seemed to have little relevance to the rest of the continent. The successor states had not fulfilled the democratic hopes of the Versailles conference, but their troubles seemed their own. The Soviet Union, though still harboring a communist menace, stood largely withdrawn into its own internal development and power struggles.

The European economy seemed finally to be on an even keel. The frightening inflation was over, and unemployment had eased. American capital was flowing into the continent. The reparations payments had been systematized by the Young Plan. Yet both this economic and this political stability proved illusory and temporary. What brought them to an end was the deepest economic depression in the modern history of the West. As the governments and electorates responded to the economic collapse, the search for liberty gave way in more than one instance to a search for security. The political experiments of the twenties gave way to the political tragedies of the thirties.

SUGGESTED READINGS

K. D. BRACHER, *The German Dictatorship* (1970). A comprehensive treatment of both the origins and the functioning of the Nazi movement and government.

A. BULLOCK, *Hitler: A Study in Tyranny*, rev. ed. (1964). The best biography.

E. H. CARR, *A History of Soviet Russia*, 9 vols. (1950–19–). An extensive and important study.

G. D. H. COLE, *A History of the Labour Party from 1914* (1948). A straightforward account by a sympathetic supporter.

R. DAHRENDORF, *Society and Democracy in Germany* (1967). An important commentary by a leading sociologist.

I. DEUTSCHER, *The Prophet Armed* (1954), *The Prophet Unarmed* (1959), and *The Prophet Outcast* (1963). A major biography of Trotsky.

E. EYCK, *A History of the Weimar Republic*, 2 vols. (trans., 1963). The story as narrated by a liberal.

L. FISCHER, *The Life of Lenin* (1964). A sound biography by an American journalist.

P. GAY, *Weimar Culture: The Outsider as Insider* (1968). A sensitive analysis of the intellectual life of Weimar.

N. GREENE, *From Versailles to Vichy: The Third Republic, 1919–1940* (1970). A useful introduction to a difficult subject.

H. GRUBER, *International Communism in the Era of Lenin: A Documentary History* (1967). An excellent collection of otherwise difficult-to-find documents.

C. A. MACARTNEY AND A. W. PALMER, *Independent Eastern Europe: A History* (1962). The best one-volume survey.

A. MARWICK, *The Deluge: British Society and the First World War* (1965). Full of insights into both major and more subtle minor social changes.

E. NOLTE, *Three Faces of Fascism* (1963). An important, influential, and difficult work on France, Italy, and Germany.

R. PIPES, *The Formation of the Soviet Union*, 2nd ed. (1964). A study of internal policy with emphasis on Soviet minorities.

H. ROGGER AND E. WEBER (Eds.), *The European Right: A Historical Profile* (1965). An anthology of articles on right-wing political movements in various European countries.

H. Seton-Watson, *Eastern Europe Between the Wars, 1918–1941* (1946). Somewhat dated but still a useful work.

D. Mack Smith, *Italy: A Modern History,* rev. ed. (1969). Very good chapters on the Fascists and Mussolini.

R. J. Sontag, *A Broken World, 1919–1939* (1971). An exceptionally thoughtful and well-organized survey.

A. J. P. Taylor, *English History, 1914–1945* (1965). Lively and opinionated.

H. A. Turner, Jr. (Ed.), *Reappraisals of Fascism* (1975). A collection of very important recent articles on Fascist movements.

T. Wilson, *The Downfall of the Liberal Party, 1914–1935* (1966). A close examination of the surprising demise of a political party in Britain.

E. Wiskemann, *Fascism in Italy: Its Development and Influence* (1969). A comprehensive treatment.

For works on diplomatic developments, see Chapter 33.

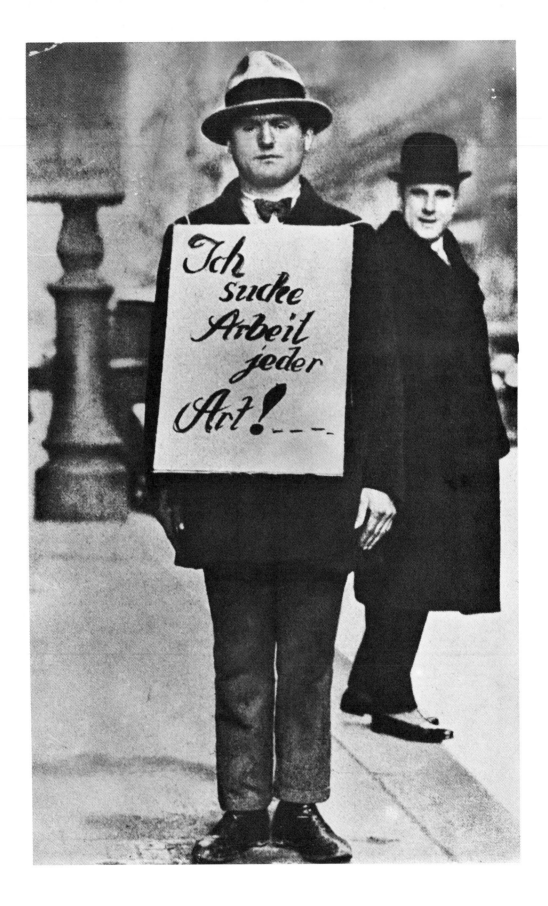

868

32
Europe and the Depression of the 1930s

IN EUROPE, unlike the United States, the 1920s had not been "roaring." Economically they had been a decade of much insecurity, of a search for elusive stability, of a short-lived upswing, and then of collapse in finance and production. The depression that commenced in 1929 was the most severe downturn ever experienced by the capitalist economies. The unemployment, low production levels, financial instability, and contracted trade arrived and would not depart. Marxists thought that the final downfall of capitalism was at hand. Capitalist businessmen and political leaders despaired over the failure of the market mechanism to save them. Voters looked for new ways out of the doldrums, and statesmen sought escapes from the political pressures that the depression had brought upon them. One result of the fight for economic security was the establishment of the Nazi dictatorship in Germany. Another was the piecemeal construction of what has since become known as the *mixed economy;* that is, governments became directly involved in economic decisions. In both cases most of the political and economic guidelines of nineteenth-century liberalism were abandoned for good. Two other casualties of these years were decency and civility in political life.

Toward the Great Depression

Three factors combined to bring about the intense severity and the extended length of the depression. There was a financial crisis that stemmed directly from the war and the peace settlement. To this was added a crisis in the production and distribution of goods in the world market. These two problems became intertwined in 1929, and so far as Europe was concerned they reached the breaking point in 1931. Finally, both of these difficulties became worse than might have been necessary because of the absence of strong economic leadership and responsibility on the part of any major west European country or the United States. Without cooperation or leadership in the Atlantic economic community, the economic collapse in finance and production simply lingered and deepened.

The Financial Tailspin

Most European nations emerged from World War I with inflated currencies. Immediately after the armistice the unleashed demand for consumer and industrial goods continued to drive up prices. The price and wage increases generally subsided after 1921, but the problem of maintaining the value of their currencies still haunted political leaders—and even more so after the German financial disaster of 1923. This frightening experience in part accounted for the refusal of most governments to run budget deficits when the depression struck. They feared inflation as a political danger in the same manner that European governments since World War II have feared unemployment.

The problems of reparation payments and international war-debt settlement further complicated the picture. France and the United States provided the stumbling blocks in these matters. France had paid reparations as a defeated nation after 1815 and 1871. As a victor it now intended to receive reparations and to finance its postwar recovery through them. The 1923 invasion of the Ruhr demonstrated French determination on this question.

The United States was no less determined that it receive repayments of the wartime loans extended to its allies. There were also various debts that the European Allies owed to each other. It soon became apparent that German reparations were to provide the means of repay-

An unemployed German in Berlin photographed about 1930 wearing a sign declaring "I seek work of any kind!" As his dress indicates, he was from either the upper working class or the lower middle class, and such people had rarely known unemployment during earlier periods of economic hardship in Europe. [Bildarchiv Preussischer Kulturbesitz. Herbert Hoffmann.]

This cartoon drawn in 1923 by Rollin Kirby pictures the attitude of the United States toward Europe. The Americans refused to join the League of Nations and demanded that their former European allies repay their war debts. [The Granger Collection.]

"I SYMPATHIZE DEEPLY WITH YOU, MADAME, BUT I CANNOT ASSOCIATE WITH YOU"

ment of the American and other Allied debts. Most of the money the Allies collected from each other also went to the United States.

In 1922 Great Britain announced that it would collect payment on its own debts only to the extent that the United States required payments from Britain. However, the American government would not relent. The reparations and the war debts made normal business, capital investment, and international trade very difficult and expensive for European nations. Various modes of government controls were exercised over credit, trade, and currency. Speculation in currency drew funds away from capital investment in productive enterprise. The monetary problems served to reinforce the general tendency toward high tariff policies. If a nation imported too many goods from abroad, it might have difficulty meeting those costs and the expenses of debt or reparations payments. The financial and money muddle thus discouraged trade and production and in turn harmed employment.

In 1924 the Dawes Plan brought more system to the administration and transfer of reparations. Those procedures in turn smoothed the debt repayments to the United States. Thereafter large amounts of private American capital flowed into Europe and especially into Germany. Much of this money, which provided the basis for Europe's brief prosperity after 1925, was in the form of short-term loans. In 1928 this lending began to contract as American money became diverted from European investments into the booming New York stock market. The crash of Wall Street in October 1929 saw the loss of large amounts of money. Within the United States there occurred a major contraction of credit and numerous bank failures. Henceforth little American capital was available for investment in Europe. Loans already made to Europe were not renewed, as American banks used their funds to cover domestic shortages.

As the credit to Europe began to run out, a major financial crisis struck the continent. In May 1931 the Kreditanstalt, a major bank in Vienna, collapsed. It was a primary lending institution for much of central and eastern Europe. The German banking system came under severe pressure and was saved only through government guarantees. However, it became clear that under this crisis situation Germany would be unable to make its next reparation payment as stipulated in the 1929 Young Plan. As the German difficulties reached such large proportions, American President Herbert Hoover announced in June 1931 a one-year moratorium on all payments of international debts. The Hoover moratorium was a prelude to the end of reparations. Hoover's action was a sharp blow to the French economy, for which reparations had continued to be important. The Lausanne Conference of the summer of 1932 in effect brought the era of reparations to a close. The next year the debts owed to the United States were settled either through small token payments or simply through default. Nevertheless the financial politics of the twenties had done its damage.

Problems in Agricultural Commodities

In addition to the dramatic financial turmoil and collapse there was also a less dramatic, but equally fundamental downturn in production and trade. The twenties witnessed a contraction in the market demand for European goods relative to the continent's productive capacity. Part of this problem originated within Europe and part outside. In both instances the difficulty arose from agriculture. Better methods of farming, improved strains of wheat, expanded tillage, and more extensive transport facilities all over the globe vastly increased the quantity of grain produced. World wheat prices fell to record lows.

The League of Nations Reports the Collapse of European Agriculture

A crisis in agriculture was as much a cause of the Depression as was the turmoil in the financial community. The League of Nations reported in 1931 how, in part, the desperate situation in agriculture developed.

IT IS *the lowness of prices that constitutes the agricultural crisis. It is becoming difficult to sell products, and in many cases prices have reached a level at which they are scarcely, if at all, sufficient to cover the cost of production.*

The reason for the crisis and for its continuance is to be found in the fact that agricultural prices are low in comparision with the expenditure which the farmer must meet. . . . Agricultural products cost a lot to produce and then fetch very little in the market. In spite of the great technical progress achieved, operating costs remain implacably higher than selling prices, farmers obtain no longer a fair return on their labour or on their capital. Frequently the returns of agricultural undertakings are not enough to cover the necessary outlay for the purchase of the material or products necessary for continued operation or for the payment of wages and taxes and so forth.

This disproportion between the income and expenditure of agricultural undertakings . . . appears to constitute the dominant and decisive element of the prevailing agricultural depression.

Until 1929, prices were low as compared with prices of industrial products, but were above pre-war prices. The predominating tendency to a fall which was observed was not altogether general nor was it abnormally rapid. The general character of the price movement completely changed in 1930. A fall, sometimes catastrophic, spread with extreme violence to almost all agricultural produce. It was so rapid that at the end of the year, whilst some products reached the pre-war level of prices, others fell as low as one-quarter or one-half below the 1913 level. . . . Farmers throughout the world have suffered from it.

League of Nations, Economic Committee, *The Agricultural Crisis,* (1931), Vol. 1, pp. 7–8, reprinted in S. B. Clough, T. Moodie, and C. G. Moodie, *Economic History of Europe: The Twentieth Century* (New York: Harper and Row, 1968), pp. 216–217.

This development was, of course, initially good for consumers. However, it meant lower incomes for European farmers and especially for those of central and eastern Europe. At the same time higher industrial wages raised the cost of the industrial goods used by the farmer or peasant. The farmers could not purchase those products.

Moreover farmers began to have difficulty paying off their mortgages and normal annual operation debts. They borrowed money to plant their fields, expecting to pay the debt when the crops were sold. The fall in commodity prices raised problems of repayment.

The difficulties of agricultural finance became especially pressing in eastern Europe. Immediately after the war numerous land reform programs had been undertaken in this region. The democratic franchise in the successor states had opened the way for considerable redistribution of tillable soil. In Romania and Czechoslovakia large amounts of land changed hands. This occurred to a lesser extent in Hungary and Poland. However, the new relatively small farmers proved to be inefficient and were unable to earn sufficient incomes. Protective tariffs often prevented the export of grain among European countries. The credit and cost squeeze on east European farmers and on their counterparts in Germany played a major role in their disillusionment with liberal politics. For example, in Germany farmers provided the Nazis with a major source of political support.

Outside of Europe similar problems affected other producers of agricultural commodities. The prices they received for their products plummeted. Government-held reserves accumulated to record levels. This glut of major world commodities involved the supplies of wheat, sugar, coffee, rubber, wool, and lard. The people who produced these goods in underdeveloped nations could no longer make enough money to buy finished goods from industrial Europe. As world credit collapsed, the economic position of these commodity producers became all the worse. Commodity production had simply outstripped world demand.

The result of the collapse in the agricultural sector of the world economy and the financial turmoil was stagnation and depression for European industry. Coal, iron, and textiles had depended largely on international markets. Unemployment spread from these industries to those producing finished consumer goods. The persistent unemployment of Great Britain and to a lesser extent of Germany during the twenties already meant "soft" domestic markets. The policies of reduced government spending with which the governments confronted the depression further weakened domestic demand. By the early thirties the depression was growing on itself.

Areas of Growth Within the Depressed Economies

Despite the depression some economic growth did take place between the wars. Depression did not mean economic regression. The economic growth was spotty, unsteady, and concentrated in special areas. Three of these industries deserve brief mention. They were radio, automobiles, and synthetic goods. The technological basis for each of them had been developed prior to World War I but their major impact on the economy occurred afterwards.

RADIO. Radio and radio technology came of age in the twenties and thirties. The wartime requirements for communication had speeded up development and production of the wireless. In 1922 broadcasting facilities had been established in Britain. The nationalized British Broadcasting System was organized in 1926. Other radio broadcasting facilities spread across the continent during the same years. The radio was a consumer gadget of the first order. The expanding electric systems made its use possible. The radio itself was sold and then required other businesses to supply service and parts. The radio industry in turn expanded the scope and transformed the nature of advertising. By the end of the twenties millions of radios were in European homes. It was a product bought not by the wealthy, who had various other modes of leisure, but by the relatively poor and middle-class groups of the population. It was the first product of sophisticated electrical technology to capture the mass market. Radio—like its successor, television—transformed European life and tended to produce a more nearly uniform culture. Radio also helped to make the propaganda programs of the authoritarian states possible.

"All Germany listens to the Führer with the people's radio receiver," declares a sales poster in 1936 for a cheap radio. Instruments such as this were pushed by the Nazis because they quickly came to realize that the efficient exploitation of such a medium of mass electronic communication was of fundamental importance to an authoritarian regime and that the presence of these receivers in nearly every home allowed the Nazi propaganda to penetrate virtually the entire German nation at will. [Bildarchiv Preussischer Kulturbesitz.]

Ganz Deutschland hört den Führer mit dem Volksempfänger

AUTOMOBILES. Automobiles were a second interwar growth industry. Only during those years did the motor car become a product of widespread consumption. In France Louis Renault and André Citroën built cars that the middle class wanted and could afford to buy. The automobile revolutionized European life rather less than it did American life. But the auto did bring new mobility and also possessed obvious military uses. Its production called forth new demand for steel, glass, rubber, petroleum, and highways. The automobile, like the radio, required a sales and service—as well as a production—industry.

SYNTHETICS. During these years the production of synthetic goods began to assume major economic significance. Rayon, invented before World War I, led the way in this area. Its production and consumption for hose and underwear grew rapidly. The product itself was soon much improved through the acetate process. Rayon began to replace cotton as the cheap textile for everyday use. The production of this synthetic fabric proved especially attractive to governments, such as those of Germany and Italy, that sought economic self-sufficiency. The prospect of war in the late thirties led various governments to encourage chemical industries to search for other synthetic substances that might replace natural products if foreign sources for the latter were shut off.

Depression and Government Policy

It is important to remember these areas of industrial expansion between the wars. The depression did not mean absolute economic decline. Nor did it mean that everyone was out of a job. The numbers of employed always well exceeded those without work. What the economic downturn did mean was the spread of actual or potential insecurity. People in practically all walks of life feared that their own economic security and life style might be the next to go. The depression also brought on a frustration of social and economic expectations. People with jobs frequently improved their standard of living or received promotion much more slowly than they might have under sound economic conditions. Although they were employed, they seemed in their own eyes to be going nowhere. Their anxieties created a major source of social discontent.

The governments of the late twenties and early thirties were not particularly well fitted in either structure or ideology to confront these problems. The demand from the electorates was to do something. What the government did in large measure depended on the severity of the depression in a particular country and the self-confidence of the nation's political system. The Keynesian solution of governments' spending the economy out of depression was not yet available. John Maynard Keynes's *General Theory of Employment, Interest, and Money* was not published until 1936. The orthodox economic policy of the day called for cuts in government spending so as to avoid inflation. It was then expected that eventually the market mechanism would bring the economy back to prosperity. However, the length and severity of the depression, plus the possibility of direct democratic political pressure, led governments across Europe to interfere with the economy as never before.

Government participation in economic life was not new. One need only recall the policies of mercantilism or government encouragement of railway building. But from the early thirties onward government involvement increased rapidly. Private economic enterprise became subject to new trade, labor, and currency regulations. The political goals of restoration of employment and provision for defense established new state-related economic priorities. Generally speaking, as in the past, the extent of state intervention increased as one moved from west to east across the continent. These new economic policies in most cases also involved further political experimentation.

Confronting the Depression in the Democracies

The depression brought to an end the business-as-usual attitude that had marked the political life of Great Britain and France during the late twenties. In Britain the emer-gency led to a new coalition government and the abandonment of economic policies considered almost untouchable for a century. The economic stagnation in France proved the occasion for a bold political and economic program sponsored by the parties of the left. The relative success of the British venture gave the nation new confidence in the democratic processes; the new departures in France created social and political hostilities that undermined faith in republican institutions.

Great Britain: The National Government

In 1929 a second minority Labor government headed by Ramsay MacDonald assumed office. As the number of British unemployed rose to more than 2.5 million workers in 1931, the ministry became divided over the remedy for the problem. MacDonald believed that the budget should be slashed, government salaries reduced, and the benefits to people on government insurance lowered. This was a bleak program for a Labor government. MacDonald's strong desire to make the Labor Party respectable led him away from more radical programs. Many of the Cabinet ministers rejected MacDonald's proposals. They would not consent to taking income away from the poor and the unemployed. The prime minister requested the resignations of his cabinet and arranged for a meeting with King George V.

Everyone assumed that the Labor ministry was about to leave office. However, to the surprise of his party and the nation, MacDonald did not resign. At the urging of the king and probably of his own ambition, MacDonald formed a coalition ministry called the National Government composed of Labor, Conservative, and Liberal ministers. The bulk of the Labor Party believed that their leader had sold out. In the election of 1931 the National Government received a very comfortable majority. After the election, however, MacDonald, who remained prime minister until 1935, was little more than the tool of the Conservatives. They held a majority in their own right in the House of Commons, but the appearance of a coalition was useful for imposing unpleasant programs.

Although Great Britain was beginning to emerge from the Great Depression by the late thirties, there remained much poverty and human degradation. This scene described in 1937 by the social critic George Orwell (1903–1950) captures a glimpse of the sadness and hopelessness that many British citizens experienced every day of their lives.

THE *train bore me away, through the monstrous scenery of slag-heaps, chimneys, piled scrap-iron, foul canals, paths of cindery mud criss-crossed by the prints of clogs. . . . As we moved slowly through the outskirts of the town we passed row after row of little grey slum houses running at right angles to the embankment. At the back of one of the houses a young woman was kneeling on the stones, poking a stick up the leaden waste-pipe which ran from the sink inside, and which I suppose was blocked. I had time to see everything about her—her sacking apron, her clumsy clogs, her arms reddened by the cold. . . . She had a round pale face, the usual exhausted face of the slum girl who is twenty-five and looks forty, thanks to miscarriages and drudgery; and it wore, for the second in which I saw it, the most desolate, hopeless expression I have ever seen. It struck me then that we are mistaken when we say that "It isn't the same for them as it would be for us," and that people bred in the slums can imagine nothing but the slums. For what I saw in her face was not the ignorant suffering of an animal. She knew well enough what was happening to her—understood as well as I did how dreadful a destiny it was to be kneeling there in the bitter cold, on the slimy stones of a slum backyard, poking a stick up a foul drain-pipe.*

George Orwell, *The Road to Wigan Pier* (New York: Berkeley Medallion Books, 1967, originally printed in 1937), p. 29.

The National Government took three decisive steps to attack the depression. To balance the budget, it raised taxes, cut insurance benefits to the unemployed and the elderly, and lowered government salaries. Its leaders argued that the fall in prices that had taken place meant that lowering those benefits and salaries did not appreciably cut real income. In September 1931 the National Government went off the gold standard. The value of the British pound on the international money market fell by about 30 per cent. Exports were somewhat stimulated by this move. In 1932 Parliament passed the Import Duties Bill, which placed a 10 per cent *ad valorum* tariff on all imports except those from the empire. In the context of previous British policy all of these steps were nothing less than extraordinary. Gold and free trade, the hallmarks of almost a century of British commercial policy, had been abandoned.

The policies of the National Government produced significant results. Great Britain avoided the banking crisis that hit other countries. By 1934 industrial production had expanded somewhat beyond the level for 1929. Britain was the first nation to achieve restoration of that level of production. Of course, the mediocre British industrial performance of the twenties made the British task easier. The government also encouraged lower interest rates. Those in turn led to the largest private housing boom in British history. Industries related to housing and the furnishing of homes prospered. Those people who were employed generally experienced an improvement in their standard of living. Nonetheless the hard core of unemployment remained. In 1937 the number of jobless had fallen to just below 1.5 million. That same year, when George Orwell described the laboring districts of the nation in *The Road to Wigan Pier*, his picture was dominated by the poverty and the workless days of the people whom he met.

Britain had entered the depression with a stagnant economy and left the era with a stagnant economy. Yet the political system itself was not fundamentally challenged. There were demonstrations of the unemployed, but social insurance, though hardly generous did support them. To the employed citizens of the country the National Government seemed to pursue a policy that avoided the extreme wings of both the Labor and the Conservative parties. When MacDonald retired in 1935, Stanley Baldwin again took office. He was succeeded in 1937 by Neville Chamberlain (1869–1940). The new prime minister is today known for the disaster of the Munich agreement. When he took office, he was known as one of the more progressive thinkers on social issues in the Conservative Party.

Oswald Mosley in May 1939 leads a demonstration
in London of his British Union of Fascists and
National Socialists. [United Press International
Photo.]

Britain did see one movement that flirted with the
extreme right-wing politics of the continent. In 1932 Sir
Oswald Mosley (b. 1896) founded the British Union of
Fascists. He had held a minor position in the second
Labor government and was disappointed in its feeble
attack on unemployment. Mosley urged a program of
direct action through a new corporate structure for the
economy. His group wore black shirts and attempted to
hold mass meetings. He gained only a few thousand
adherents. Mosley's popularity reached its height in 1934.
Thereafter his anti-Semitism began to alienate supporters, and by the close of the decade he had become little
more than a political oddity.

France: The Popular Front

The timing of the depression in France was the reverse
of that in Britain. It came later and lasted much longer.
Only in 1931 did the economic slide begin to affect the
French economy. Even then unemployment did not become the major problem it did elsewhere. Rarely were
more than a half million workers without jobs. However,
in one industry after another wages were lowered. Tariffs
were raised to protect French goods and especially
French agriculture. Ever since that time French farmers
have enjoyed unusual protection from the government.
These measures helped maintain the home market but
did little to overcome industrial stagnation. Relations
between labor and management were tense.

The first political fallout of the depression was the
election of another radical coalition government in 1932.
Fearful of contributing to inflation as it had after 1924,
the radical government pursued a generally deflationary

In February 1934 right-wing street riots broke out in Paris as a result of the political handling of the Stavisky Affair. Within a year these riots had given rise to new cooperation among French left-wing parties who feared the threat from the right. [The Granger Collection.]

policy. In the same year that the new ministry took office, reparation payments had stopped. As the economic crisis tightened, normal parliamentary and political life became a shambles.

Outside the Chamber of Deputies politics assumed a very ugly face. The old divisions between left and right hardened. Various right-wing groups with authoritarian tendencies became active. These leagues included the *Action Française,* founded prior to World War I in the wake of the Dreyfus Affair, and the *Croix de Feu,* composed of army veterans. The memberships of these and other similar groups numbered somewhat more than two million persons. Some wanted a monarchy; others favored what would have amounted to military rule. They were hostile to the idea of parliamentary government, socialism, and communism. They wanted what they regarded as the greater good and glory of the nation to be set above the petty machinations of political parties. In this regard they resembled the Fascists and the Nazis. Their activities and propaganda aided the dissolution of loyalty to republican government and injected bitterness and vindictiveness into French political life. The leagues also created one moment of extraordinary havoc that produced important long-range political consequences.

The incident grew out of the Stavisky affair, the last of those curious *causes célèbres* that punctuated the political fortunes of the Third Republic. Serge Stavisky was a small-time gangster who appears to have had good connections within the government. In 1933 he became involved in a fraudulent bond scheme. When finally tracked down by the police, he committed suicide in January 1934. The official handling of the matter suggested a political coverup. It was alleged that people in high places wished to halt the investigation. To the right wing in France the Stavisky incident symbolized all the seaminess, immorality, and corruption of republican politics. On February 6, 1934, a very large demonstration of the right-wing leagues took place in Paris. The exact purpose and circumstances of the rally remain uncertain, but the crowd did attempt to march on the Chamber of

Deputies. Violence occurred. Fourteen demonstrators were killed; scores of others were injured. It was the largest disturbance in Paris since the Commune of 1871.

In the wake of the night of February 6, the radical ministry of Edouard Daladier (1884–1970) resigned and was replaced by a national coalition government composed of all living former premiers. The Chamber of Deputies permitted the ministry to deal with economic matters by decree. However, the major result of the right-wing demonstrations was a political self-reassessment by the parties of the left. Radicals, socialists, and communists began to realize that a right-wing *coup* might be possible in France. Consequently, between 1934 and 1936 the French left began to make peace within its own ranks. This was no easy task. French Socialists, led by Léon Blum (1872–1950), had been the major target of the French Communists since the split over joining the Comintern in 1920. Only Stalin's fear of fascism as a danger to the Soviet Union made this new cooperation possible. In spite of deep suspicions on all sides, the Popular Front had been established by Bastille Day in 1935. Its purpose was to preserve the republic and to press for social reform.

The election of 1936 gave the Popular Front a majority in the Chamber of Deputies. The Socialists were the largest single party for the first time in French history. Consequently they organized the cabinet as they had long promised they would do when they constituted the majority party of a coalition. Léon Blum assumed the premiership on June 5, 1936. From the early twenties this Jewish intellectual and humanitarian had opposed the communist version of socialism. Cast as the successor to

Confronting the Depression in the Democracies

Jean Jaurès, who had been assassinated in 1914, Blum wanted socialism in the context of democratic, parliamentary government. He hoped to bring France a program akin to the New Deal that President Franklin Roosevelt had carried out in the United States.

During May 1936, before the Popular Front came to power, strikes had begun to spread throughout French industry. Immediately after assuming office on June 6, the Blum government faced further spontaneous work stoppages involving over a half million workers who had occupied factories in sit-down strikes. These were the most extensive labor disturbances in the history of the Third Republic. They aroused new fears in the conservative business community, which had already been frightened by the election of the Popular Front. Blum acted swiftly to bring together representatives of labor and management. On June 8 he announced the conclusion of the Matignon Accord, which reorganized labor-management relations in France. Wages were immediately raised from 7 to 15 per cent, depending on the job involved. Workers became free to join unions and to bargain collectively with employers. Annual paid two-week vacations for workers were adopted. The forty-hour week was established throughout French industry. Blum hoped to overcome labor hostility to French society, to establish a foundation for justice in labor–management relations, and to increase the domestic consumer demand of the nation.

Blum's labor policy was followed by other bold departures. He raised the salaries of civil servants and instituted a program of public works. Government loans were extended to small industry. Spending on armaments was increased, and some armament industries were nationalized. To aid agriculture, he set up a National Wheat Board to rationalize the production and sale of grain. Initially he had promised to resist devaluation of the franc. However, by the autumn of 1936 international monetary pressure forced him to devalue. He did so again in the spring of 1937. The devaluations brought little aid to French exports because they came too late. All of these

French Management and Labor Reach an Agreement

When the Popular Front government came to power in France in 1936, it immediately confronted widespread strikes. Premier Léon Blum called together the representatives of labor and management. The result of these negotiations was the Matignon Accord, which gave the unions more secure rights, raised wages, and brought the strikes to an end.

THE *delegates of the General Confederation of French Production (CGPF) and the General Confederation of Labour (CGT) have met under the chairmanship of the Premier (Léon Blum) and have concluded the following agreement, after arbitration by the Premier:*

1. The employer delegation agrees to the immediate conclusion of collective agreements.

2. These agreements must include, in particular, articles 3 and 5 below.

3. All citizens being required to abide by law, the employers recognize the freedom of opinion of workers and their right to freely join and belong to trade unions.

In their decisions on hiring, organization or assignment of work, disciplinary measures or dismissals, employers agree not to take into consideration the fact of membership or nonmembership in a union. . . .

The exercise of trade union rights must not give rise to acts contrary to law.

4. The wages actually paid to all workers as of 25 May 1936 will be raised, as of the resumption of work, by a decreasing percentage ranging from 15 per cent for the lowest rates down to 7 per cent for the highest rates. In no case must the total increase in any establishment exceed 12 per cent. . . .

The negotiations, which are to be launched at once, for the determination by collective agreement of minimum wages by regions and by occupations must take up, in particular, the necessary revision of abnormally low wages. . . .

. . . .

6. The employer delegation promises that there will be no sanctions for strike activities.

7. The CGT delegation will ask the workers on strike to return to work as soon as the managements of establishments have accepted this general agreement and as soon as negotiations for its application have begun between the managements and the personnel of the establishments.

V. R. Lorwin, *The French Labour Movement* (Cambridge, Mass.: Harvard University Press, 1954), pp. 313–315.

A display of unity by leaders of the French Popular
Front at a Bastille Day rally in Paris, July 14,
1937. Léon Blum of the Socialist Party is on the
left with Mme. Blum, and Maurice Thorez (1900–1964),
the Secretary of the French Communist Party, stands
beside him on the right. [Photo Trends.]

moves enraged the conservative banking and business
community. In March 1937 they brought sufficient influence to bear upon the ministry to cause Blum to halt
the program of reform. It was not taken up again. Blum's
Popular Front colleagues considered the pause in reform
an unnecessary compromise. In June 1937 Blum resigned. The Popular Front ministry itself held on until
April 1938, when it was replaced by a radical ministry
under Daladier.

The Popular Front had brought much hope to labor
and to socialists, but it did not lead France out of the
depression. Some of its programs actually harmed production. The business community, because of its apprehensions and hostility, became even less venturesome
after the Popular Front reforms. Not until 1939 did
French industrial production reach the level of 1929. In a
sense the Popular Front had come too late to give either
the economy or French political life new vitality. Internal
divisions and conservative opposition meant that the Popular Front had enjoyed less than a free hand. By the close
of the thirties citizens from all walks of life had begun to
wonder if the republic was worth preserving. The left
continued to remain divided. Businessmen found the
republic inefficient and in their opinion too much subject
to socialist pressures. The right wing hated the republic
in principle. When the time came in 1940 to defend the
republic, there were too many citizens who were less
than sure that it was worth defending.

Germany: The Nazi Seizure of Power
Depression and Political Deadlock

The outflow of foreign, and especially American, capital from Germany commencing in 1928 undermined the economic prosperity of the Weimar Republic. The resulting economic crisis brought parliamentary government to an end. In 1928 a coalition of center parties and the Social Democrats governed. All went reasonably well until the depression struck. Then the coalition partners differed sharply on economic policy. The Social Democrats wanted no reduction in social and unemployment insurance. The more conservative parties, remembering the inflation of 1923, insisted upon a balanced budget. The coalition dissolved in March 1930. To resolve the parliamentary deadlock in the *Reichstag*, President von Hindenburg appointed Heinrich Bruening (1885–1970) as chancellor. Lacking a majority in the *Reichstag*, the new chancellor governed through emergency presidential decrees as authorized by Article 48 of the constitution. The party divisions in the *Reichstag* prevented the overriding of the decrees. In this manner the Weimar Republic was transformed into a presidential dictatorship.

German unemployment rose from 2,258,000 in March 1930 to over 6,000,000 in March 1932. There had been persistent unemployment during the twenties, but nothing of such magnitude or duration. The economic downturn and the parliamentary deadlock worked to the advantage of the more extreme political parties. In the election of 1928 the Nazis had won only 12 seats in the *Reichstag*, and the Communists had won 54 seats. Two years later, after the election of 1930, the Nazis held 107 seats and the Communists 77.

The power of the Nazis in the streets was also on the rise. The unemployment fed thousands of men into the Stormtroopers, which had 100,000 members in 1930 and almost 1 million in 1933. The SA freely and viciously attacked Communists and Social Democrats. For the Nazis politics meant the capture of power through the instruments of terror and intimidation as well as by legal elections. Anything resembling decency and civility in political life vanished. The Nazis held rallies that resembled secular religious revivals. They paraded through the streets and the countryside. They gained powerful supporters and sympathizers in the business, military, and newspaper communities. Some intellectuals were also sympathetic. The Nazis were able to transform this discipline and enthusiasm born of economic despair and nationalistic frustration into impressive electoral results.

Hitler Comes to Power

For two years Bruening continued to govern through the confidence of Hindenburg. The economy did not improve, and the political situation deteriorated. In 1932 the eighty-three-year-old president stood for reelection. Hitler ran against him and forced a runoff. In the first election the Nazi leader garnered 30.1 per cent of the vote, and he later gained 36.8 per cent in the second. Although Hindenburg was returned to office, the results of the poll convinced him that Bruening no longer commanded sufficient confidence from conservative German voters. On May 30, 1932, he dismissed Bruening and appointed Franz von Papen (1879–1969) in his place. The new chancellor was one of a small group of extremely conservative advisers upon whom the aged Hindenburg had become increasingly dependent. Others included the president's son and several military figures. With the continued paralysis in the *Reichstag*, their influence over the president virtually amounted to control of the government. Consequently the crucial decisions of the next several months were made by only a handful of people.

Von Papen and the circle around the president wanted to find some way to draw the Nazis into cooperation with them without giving any effective power to Hitler. The government needed the mass popular support that only the Nazis seemed able to generate. The Hindenburg circle decided to convince Hitler that the Nazis could not come to power on their own. Von Papen removed the ban on Nazi meetings that Bruening had imposed and

Hitler and President von Hindenburg pictured riding together in an open carriage in 1933 shortly after the aged president had appointed Hitler chancellor. After von Hindenburg's death the next year, Hitler assumed the powers of the presidency as well as those of the chancellorship. [Culver Pictures.]

then called an election for July 1932. The Nazis won 230 seats and polled 37.2 per cent of the vote. As the price for his entry into the cabinet, Hitler demanded appointment as chancellor. Hindenburg refused. Another election was called in November, partly as a means of wearing down the Nazis' financial resources. It was successful in that regard. The number of Nazi seats fell to 196, and their percentage of the popular vote dipped to 33.1 per cent. The advisers around Hindenburg still refused to appoint Hitler to office.

In late December 1932 Von Papen resigned, and Kurt von Schleicher (1882–1934) became chancellor. There now existed much fear of civil war between groups on the left and right. Von Schleicher decided to attempt the construction of a broad-based coalition of conservative groups and trade unionists. The prospect of such a coalition, including groups from the political left, frightened the Hindenburg circle even more than the prospect of Hitler. They did not trust Von Schleicher's motives, which have never been very clear. Consequently they persuaded Hindenburg to appoint Hitler as chancellor. To control him and to see that he did little mischief, Von Papen was to be named vice-chancellor. On January 30, 1933, Adolph Hitler became the chancellor of Germany.

Hitler's Consolidation of Power

Hitler had come into office by legal means. All of the proper legal forms and procedures had been observed. This fact was very important, for it permitted the civil service, the courts, and the other agencies of the government to support him with good conscience. He had forged a rigidly disciplined party structure and had mastered the techniques of mass politics and propaganda. He understood how to touch the raw social and political nerves of the electorate. His major support came from the lower middle class, the farmers, and the young. Each of these groups had especially suffered from the insecurity of the twenties and the depression of the early thirties. Hitler promised them security against communists and socialists, effective government in place of the petty poli-

The Reichstag fire of February 27, 1933 created fear of a Communist revolution in Germany. In this political atmosphere the Nazis completed their seizure of power. [The Granger Collection.]

tics of the other parties, and an uncompromising nationalist vision of a strong, restored Germany.

Much credit was once given to German big business for the rise of Hitler. However, little evidence exists that business money financed the Nazis in a fashion that made any crucial difference to their success or failure. Hitler's supporters were frequently suspicious of business and giant capitalism. They wanted a simpler world and one in which small property would be safe from both socialism and large-scale capitalist consolidation. These people looked to Hitler and the Nazis rather than to the Social Democrats because the latter, though concerned with social issues, never appeared sufficiently nationalistic. The Nazis won out over other conservative nationalistic parties because, unlike the latter, they did address themselves to the problem of lower-middle-class social insecurity.

Once in office Hitler moved with almost lightning speed to consolidate his control. There were three facets to this process: the capture of full legal authority, the crushing of alternative political groups, and the purging of rivals within the Nazi Party itself.

On February 23, 1933, a mentally ill Dutch communist set fire to the *Reichstag* building in Berlin. The Nazis quickly turned the incident to their own advantage by claiming that the fire proved the existence of an immediate communist threat against the government. To the public it seemed plausible that the Communists might attempt some action against the state now that the Nazis

were in power. Under Article 48 Hitler suspended the civil liberties and proceeded to arrest Communists or alleged Communists. This decree was not revoked for as long as Hitler ruled Germany.

In early March another *Reichstag* election took place. The Nazis still received only 43.9 per cent of the vote. However, the arrest of the newly elected Communist deputies and the fear stemming from the fire meant that Hitler could control the *Reichstag* without a formal coalition. On March 23, 1933, the *Reichstag* passed an Enabling Act that permitted Hitler to rule by decree. Thereafter there were no legal limits on his exercise of power. The Weimar Constitution was never formally repealed or amended. It had simply been supplanted by the February Emergency Decree and the March Enabling Act.

Perhaps better than anyone else Hitler understood that he and his party had not inevitably come to power. All of his potential opponents had stood divided between 1929 and 1933. He intended to prevent them from regrouping. In a series of complex moves Hitler outlawed or undermined various German institutions that might have served as rallying points for opposition. In early May 1933 the offices, banks, and newspapers of the free trade unions were seized, and their leaders were arrested. This action was taken by the Nazi Party itself rather than by any government agency. In late June and early July all of the other German political parties were outlawed. By July 14, 1933, the National Socialists were the only legal party in Germany. During the same months the Nazis had moved against the governments of the individual federal states in Germany. By the close of 1933 all major institutions of potential opposition had been eliminated.

The final element in Hitler's consolidation of power involved the Nazi Party itself. By late 1933 the SA, or Stormtroopers, consisted of approximately one million active members and a larger number of reserves. The commander of this party army was Ernst Roehm, a possible rival to Hitler himself. The German army officer corps, upon whom Hitler depended to rebuild the national army, were jealous of the SA leadership. Conse-

The Nazi Party utilized massive rallies as one of
the major ways in which to show off its power. This
one took place in Nuremberg in 1938, and the
particular day shown in this photograph was devoted
to the Nazi youth movement. [Bildarchiv Preussischer
Kulturbesitz.]

quently, to protect his own position and to shore up support with the regular army, on June 30, 1934, Hitler personally ordered the murder of key SA officers, including Roehm. Others killed between June 30 and July 2 included the former chancellor General Kurt von Schleicher and his wife. The exact number of victims purged is unknown, but it has been estimated to have exceeded one hundred persons. The German army, which was the only institution in the nation that might have prevented the murders, did nothing. A month later, on August 2, 1934, President Von Hindenburg died. Thereafter the offices of chancellor and president were combined. Hitler was now the sole ruler of Germany and of the Nazi Party.

The Police State

Terror and intimidation had been a major factor in the Nazi march to office. As Hitler consolidated his power, he oversaw the organization of a police state. The chief vehicle of police surveillance was the SS, or security units, commanded by Heinrich Himmler (1900–1945). This group had originated in the mid-twenties as a bodyguard for Hitler and became a more elite paramilitary organization than the larger SA. In 1933 the SS was composed of approximately fifty-two thousand members. It was the instrument that carried out the blood purges of the party in 1934. By 1936 Himmler had become head of all police matters in Germany and stood second only to Hitler in power and influence.

The police character of the Nazi regime was all-pervasive, but the people who most consistently experienced the terror of the police state were German Jews. Anti-Semitism had been a key plank of the Nazi program. It was anti-Semitism based on biological racial theories stemming from late nineteenth-century thought rather than from religious discrimination. Prior to World War II the Nazi attack on the Jews went through three stages of increasing intensity. In 1933, shortly after assuming power, the Nazis excluded Jews from offices in the civil service. For a time they also attempted to enforce

The Nazis Pass Their Racial Legislation

Anti-Semitism had been a fundamental tenet of the Nazi Party and became a major policy of the Nazi government. This comprehensive legislation of September 15, 1935 carried anti-Semitism into all areas of public life and into some of the most personal areas of private life as well. It was characteristically titled the Law for the Protection of German Blood and Honor. Hardly any aspect of Nazi thought and action was as shocking to the non-German world as was their policy toward Jews.

IMBUED *with the knowledge that the purity of German blood is the necessary prerequisite for the existence of the German nation, and inspired by an inflexible will to maintain the existence of the German nation for all future times, the Reichstag has unanimously adopted the following law, which is now enacted:*

ARTICLE I: *(1) Any marriages between Jews and citizens of German or kindred blood are herewith forbidden. Marriages entered into despite this law are invalid, even if they are arranged abroad as a means of circumventing this law.*

(2) Annulment proceedings for marriages may be initiated only by the Public Prosecutor.

ARTICLE II: *Extramarital relations between Jews and citizens of German or kindred blood are herewith forbidden.*

ARTICLE III: *Jews are forbidden to employ as servants to their households female subjects of German or kindred blood who are under the age of forty-five years.*

ARTICLE IV: *(1) Jews are prohibited from displaying the Reich and national flag and from showing the national colors.*

(2) However, they may display the Jewish colors. The exercise of this right is under state protection.

ARTICLE V: *(1) Anyone who acts contrary to the prohibition noted in Article I renders himself liable to penal servitude.*

(2) The man who acts contrary to the prohibiton of Article II will be punished by sentence to either a jail or penitentiary.

(3) Anyone who acts contrary to the provisions of Articles III and IV will be punished with a jail sentence up to a year and with a fine, or with one of these penalties.

ARTICLE VI: *The Reich Minister of Interior, in conjunction with the Deputy to the Führer and the Reich Minister of Justice, will issue the required legal and administrative decrees for the implementation and amplification of this law.*

Two of Hitler's chief henchmen: [LEFT] Heinrich Himmler (1900–1945), who was head of the Nazi secret police; and [RIGHT] Joseph Goebbels (1897–1945), who headed the Nazi propaganda drive at home and abroad. [BOTH: The Granger Collection.]

ARTICLE *VII: This law shall go into effect on the day following its promulgation, with the exception of Article III, which shall go into effect on January 1, 1936.*

Louis L. Snyder (Ed. and Trans.), *Documents of German History* (New Brunswick, N.J.: Rutgers University Press, 1958), pp. 427–428.

During the night of November 9, 1938, all across Germany the windows of stores owned by Jewish businessmen were smashed in one of the major Nazi pre-war outbursts of anti-Semitism. This photograph was made in Berlin the following day. The Nazis then confiscated the insurance money and refused to allow the Jewish businesses to be compensated for their losses. [The Granger Collection.]

boycotts of Jewish shops and businesses. In 1935 a series of measures known as the Nuremberg Laws robbed German Jews of their citizenship. All persons with at least three Jewish grandparents were defined as Jews. The professions and the major occupations were closed to Jews. Marriage and sexual intercourse between Jews and non-Jews were prohibited. Legal exclusion and humiliation of Jews became the order of the day.

The persecution of the Jews increased again in 1938. Business careers were forbidden. In November 1938, under orders from the Nazi Party, thousands of Jewish stores and synagogues were burned or otherwise destroyed. The Jewish community itself was required to pay for the damage because the government confiscated the insurance money. In all manner of other ways, large and petty, the German Jews were harassed. This persecution allowed the Nazis to inculcate the rest of the population with the concept of a master race of pure German "Aryans" and also to display their own contempt for civil liberties. After the war broke out, Hitler decided in 1942 to destroy the Jews in Europe. It is thought that over six million Jews, mostly from east European nations, died as a result of that staggering decision, unprecedented in its scope and implementation.

Nazi Economic Policy

Besides consolidating power and persecuting allegedly inferior races, Hitler still had to confront the reality of the depression. German unemployment had been a major factor in his rise to power. The Nazis attacked this problem and achieved a degree of success that astonished and frightened the rest of Europe. By 1936, while the rest of the European economy continued to stagnate, the specter of unemployment and other difficulties associated with the depression for all intents and purposes no longer haunted Germany. So far as the economic crisis was concerned, Hitler had become the most effective political leader in Europe. This fact was a most important element in accounting for the internal strength and support of his tyrannical regime. The Nazi success against the depression provided the regime with considerable contemporary credibility. As might be expected, the cost in terms of liberty and human dignity had been very high.

Hitler reversed the deflationary policy of the cabinets that had preceded him. He instituted what amounted to a massive program of public works and spending. Many of these projects related directly or indirectly to rearmament. Canals were built, and land was reclaimed. Construction of a large system of highways with clear military uses was begun. Some unemployed workers were sent back to farms if they had originally come from there. Other laborers were frozen in their jobs and were not permitted to change employment. Renunciation of the military provisions of the Versailles Treaty in 1935 led to open rearmament and expansion of the army with little opposition, as will be explained in Chapter 33. These measures essentially restored full employment. In 1936 Hitler instructed Hermann Goering (1893–1946), who had headed the air force since 1933, to undertake a Four-Year Plan to prepare the army and the economy for war. The state determined that Germany must be economically self-sufficient. Armaments received top priority. This economic program satisfied both the yearning for social and economic security and the desire for national fulfillment.

Nazi economic policies maintained private property and private capitalism. However, all significant economic enterprise and decisions became subordinated to the goals of the state. Prices were controlled and investments restricted. Currency regulation interfered with trade. Production that related to the military buildup received top priority and even redirected some industries. For exam-

ple, in the late thirties, the German chemical producers diverted a large proportion of their resources toward the manufacture of various synthetics. With the crushing of the trade unions in 1933, strikes became illegal. There was no genuine collective bargaining. The government handled labor disputes through compulsory arbitration. Both workers and employers were required to participate in the Labor Front, the existence of which was intended to prove that class conflict had ended. It sponsored a "Strength Through Joy" program that provided vacations and other forms of recreation for the labor force. However, behind the direction of both business and labor stood the Nazi terror and police. The Nazi economic experiment proved that with the sacrifice of all political and civil liberty, of a free trade union movement, of private exercise of capital, and of consumer satisfaction, full employment for the purposes of war and aggression could be achieved.

The architect Albert Speer (born 1905) became a favored member of Hitler's inner circle. He and Hitler developed plans for an entire new design for the city of Berlin. On the [LEFT] is a photograph of the model designed by Speer for the new capital of Hitler's Reich. In the center is the Brandenburg Gate, the only major structure planned for preservation from Berlin's past. Beyond the gate is Unter den Linden running up the picture to a vast domed structure on the site of the former royal palace and lined left and right with the massive offices of the government.

On the [RIGHT] is one of the few structures actually to be completed, the German Chancellory, used by the Nazis until its destruction in World War II.

[CHANCELLORY: Ullstein Bilderdienst. MODEL: Courtesy Albert Speer. Photo Hermann Speer.]

Hermann Göring (1893–1946), Hitler's second in command, is here photographed flanked by other Nazi officers. [United Press International Photo.]

Fascist Economics in Italy

The Fascists had promised to bring order to the instability of Italian social and economic life. Discipline was a substitute for economic policy and creativity. During the twenties Mussolini undertook programs of public works, such as draining the Pontine Marshes for settlement. The shipping industry was subsidized, and protective tariffs were introduced. Mussolini desperately sought to make Italy self-sufficient. He embarked on the "battle of wheat" to prevent foreign grain from appearing in products on Italian tables. There was an extraordinary expansion of wheat farming in Italy. However, these policies did not keep the depression from affecting Italy. Production, exports, and wages fell. Even the increased wheat production backfired. So much poor marginal land that was expensive to cultivate came into production that the domestic price of wheat and thus of much food actually rose.

Both before and during the depression the Fascists sought to steer an economic course between socialism and a liberal *laissez-faire* system. Their policy was known as *Corporatism.* It constituted a planned economy linked to the private ownership of capital and to government arbitration of labor disputes. Major industries were first organized into syndicates representing labor and management. The two groups negotiated labor settlements within this framework and submitted differences to compulsory government arbitration. The Fascists contended that class conflict would be avoided if both labor and management looked to the greater goal of productivity for the nation. It is a matter of considerable dispute whether this arrangement favored workers or managers. What is certain is that from the mid-twenties Italian labor unions lost the right to strike and to pursue their own independent economic goals.

After 1930 these industrial syndicates were further organized into entities called *corporations.* These bodies included all industries relating to a major area of production, such as sugar beets or metallurgy, from raw materials through finished product and distribution. A total of twenty-two such corporations were established to encompass the whole economy. In 1938 Mussolini abolished the Italian Chamber of Deputies and replaced it with a Chamber of Corporations. This vast organization framework did not increase production; instead, it led to excessive bureaucracy and corruption. The corporate state allowed the government to direct much of the nation's economic life without a formal change in ownership. Consumers and owners simply no longer could determine what was to be produced. The Fascist government gained further direct economic power through the Institute for Industrial Reconstruction, which extended loans to businesses in financial difficulty. The loans, in effect, established partial state ownership.

How corporatism might have affected the Italian economy in the long run cannot really be calculated. In 1935 Italy invaded Ethiopia. Economic life was put on a formal wartime footing. The League of Nations imposed economic sanctions, urging member nations to refrain from purchasing Italian goods. Thereafter taxes rose. During 1935 the government imposed a forced loan on the citizenry by requiring property owners to purchase bonds. Wages continued to be depressed. As the international tensions increased during the late thirties, the Italian state assumed more and more direction over the economy. The order of Facism in Italy had not proved to be an order of prosperity. It had brought economic dislocation and a falling standard of living.

Stalin's Five-Year Plans and Purges

While the capitalist economies of western Europe floundered in the doldrums of the depression, the Soviet Union entered upon a period of tremendous industrial advance. Like similar eras of past Russian economic progress, the direction and impetus came from the top. Stalin far exceeded his tsarist predecessors in the intensity of state coercion and terror he brought to the task. Russia achieved its stunning economic growth during the thirties only at the cost of literally millions of human lives and the degradation of still other millions. Stalin's economic policy clearly proved that his earlier rivalry with Trotsky had been a matter of political power rather than one of substantial ideological difference.

The Decision for Rapid Industrialization

Through 1928 Lenin's New Economic Policy, as championed by Bukharin with Stalin's support, had charted the course of Soviet economic development. Private ownership and enterprise were permitted to flourish in the countryside as a means of ensuring an adequate food supply for workers in the cities. A few farmers, the *kulaks,* had become quite prosperous. They probably numbered less than 5 per cent of the rural population. During 1928 and 1929 these and other farmers withheld grain from the market because of dissatisfaction with prices. Food shortages occurred in the cities and provided a cause of potential unrest against the regime. The goals of NEP were no longer being fulfilled. Sometime during these troubled months Stalin came to a momentous decision. Russia must industrialize rapidly in order to match the economic and military power of the West. Agriculture must be collectivized to produce sufficient grain for food and export and to free peasant labor for factories. This program, which basically embraced Trotsky's earlier economic position, unleashed nothing less than a second Russian revolution. The costs and character of "Socialism in One Country" now became clear.

AGRICULTURAL POLICY. In 1929 Stalin ordered party agents into the countryside to confiscate any hoarded wheat. The *kulaks* were blamed for the grain shortages. As part of the general plan to erase the private ownership of land and to collectivize farming, a program was undertaken to eliminate the *kulaks* as a class. However, the definition of a *kulak* soon embraced anyone who opposed Stalin's policy. In the countryside there was extensive resistance from peasants and farmers at all levels of wealth. The stubborn peasants were determined to keep their land. They wreaked their own vengeance on the policy of collectivization by slaughtering more than 100 million horses and cattle between 1929 and 1933. The situation in the countryside amounted to nothing less than open warfare. The peasant resistance caused Stalin to call a brief halt to the process in March 1930. He justified the slowdown on the grounds of "dizziness from success."

Soon thereafter the drive to collectivize the farms was renewed with vehemence, but the costs remained very high. As many as ten million peasants were killed, and millions of others were sent forcibly to collective farms or labor camps. Initially, because of the turmoil on the land, agricultural production fell. There was famine in 1932 and 1933. Milk and meat remained in short supply because of the livestock slaughter. Yet Stalin persevered. The uprooted peasants were moved to thousand-acre collective farms. The machinery for these units was provided by the state through machine-tractor stations. In this fashion the state retained control over major farm machines. That monopoly was a powerful weapon.

The upheaval of collectivization did change Russian farming in a very dramatic way. In 1928 approximately 98 per cent of Russian farmland consisted of small peasant holdings. Ten years later, despite all of the opposition, over 90 per cent of the land had been collectivized. During the same period agricultural production had increased approximately 15 per cent, but the quantity of farm produce directly handled by the government had risen by 40 per cent. Those shifts in control meant that the government now had primary direction over the food supply. The farmers and peasants could no longer determine whether there would be stability or unrest in the cities. Stalin and the Communist Party had won the battle of the wheat fields, but they had not solved the problem of producing sufficient quantities of grain. That difficulty has continued to plague the Soviet Union to the present day.

THE FIVE-YEAR PLANS. The revolution in agriculture had been undertaken for the sake of industrialization. The increased grain supply was to feed the labor force and provide exports to finance the imports required for industrial development. The scope of the industrial achievement of the Soviet Union between 1928 and World War II stands as one of the most striking accomplishments of the twentieth century. Russia made a more rapid advance toward economic growth than any other nation in the Western world has ever achieved during any similar period of time. By even the conservative estimates of Western observers, Soviet industrial production rose approximately 400 per cent between 1928 and 1940. Emphasis was placed on the production of iron, steel, coal, electrical power, tractors, combines, railway cars, and other heavy machinery. Few consumer goods were produced. The labor for this development was supplied internally. Capital was raised from the export of grain even at the cost of internal shortage. The technology was generally borrowed from already-industrialized nations.

The organizational vehicle for industrialization was a series of Five-Year Plans first begun in 1928. The State Planning Commission, or Gosplan, oversaw the program. It set goals of production and organized the economy to meet them. The task of coordinating all facets of production was immensely difficult and complicated. Deliveries of materials from mines or factories had to be assured before the next unit could carry out its part of the plan. There was many a slip between the cup and the lip. The troubles in the countryside were harmful. A vast program of propaganda was undertaken to sell the Five-Year Plans to the Russian people and to elicit cooperation. However, the industrial labor force soon became subject to regimentation similar to that being imposed on the peasants. By the close of the thirties the accomplishment of the three Five-Year Plans was truly impressive and probably allowed the Soviet Union to survive the German invasion. Industries that had never existed in Russia now challenged and in some cases, such as tractor production, surpassed their counterparts in the rest of the world. Large, new industrial cities had been built and populated by hundreds of thousands of people.

Stalin Explains the Problem of Agriculture

By the late 1920s Stalin had changed his earlier views and had decided that the Soviet Union must industrialize rapidly. That shift meant that the agricultural sector must also be modernized in order to feed industrial workers and to pay for needed imports. Stalin saw the means to improved farming in the large scale collectivization of agriculture and the introduction of farm machinery. When implemented, this policy led to widespread peasant resistance in the countryside.

T HE *characteristic feature of the present state of our national economy is that we are faced by the fact of an* excessive *lag in the rate of development of grain farming behind the rate of development of industry, while at the same time the demand for marketable grain on the part of the growing towns and industrial areas is increasing by leaps and bounds. The task then is not to* lower *the rate of development of industry to the level of the development of grain farming . . . , but to bring the rate of development of grain farming into line with the rate of development of industry and to* raise *the rate of development of grain farming to a level that will guarantee rapid progress of the entire national economy, both industry and agriculture.*

Either we accomplish this task, and thereby solve the grain problem, or we do not accomplish it, and then a rupture between the socialist town and the small-peasant countryside will be inevitable.

. . . .

What ways and means are necessary to accelerate the rate of development of agriculture in general, and of grain farming in particular?

There are three such ways, or channels:

(a) *By increasing crop yields and enlarging the area sown by the individual poor and middle peasants.*
(b) *By further development of collective farms.*
(c) *By enlarging the old and establishing new state farms.*

. . . .

I should like to draw your attention to the collective farms, and especially to the states farms, as levers which facilitate the reconstruction of agriculture on a new technical basis, causing a revolution in the minds of the peasants and helping them to shake off conservatism, routine. The appearance of tractors, large agricultural machines and tractor columns in our grain regions cannot but have its effect on the surrounding peasant farms. Assistance rendered the surrounding peasants in the way of seed, machines and tractors will undoubtedly be appre-

By the late 1930s the cult of Stalin was an ever-present fact of Soviet life. Even at beach resorts his picture was always near. In this 1950 photograph swimmers in the Black Sea carry large pictures of him on small rafts. Notice the war ships in the background. [Sovfoto.]

ciated by the peasants and taken as a sign of the power and strength of the Soviet State, which is trying to lead them on to the high road of a substantial improvement of agriculture.

J. Stalin, *Collected Works* (Moscow: Foreign Language Publishing House, 1952–1956), Vol. 11 pp. 268–269, 272, 279. Originally written in 1928.

Many non-Russian contemporaries looked at the Soviet economic experiment quite uncritically. While the capitalist world lay in the throes of depression, the Soviet economy had grown at a pace never realized in the West. The American writer Lincoln Steffens reported after a trip to Russia, "I have seen the future and it works." Beatrice and Sydney Webb, the British Fabian socialists, spoke of "a new civilization" in the Soviet Union. These and other similar writers ignored the shortages in consumer goods and the poor housing. More important, they seem to have had little idea of the social cost of the Soviet achievement. Millions of human beings had been killed and millions more uprooted. The total picture of suffering and human loss during those years will probably never be known; however, the deprivation and sacrifice of Soviet citizens far exceeded anything described by Marx and Engels in relation to nineteenth-century industrialization in western Europe.

The internal difficulties caused by collectivization and industrialization led Stalin to make an important shift in foreign policy. In 1934 he began to fear that the nation might be left isolated against future aggression by Nazi Germany. The Soviet Union was not yet strong enough to withstand such an attack. Consequently that year he ordered the Comintern to permit communist parties in other countries to cooperate with non-communist political parties against Nazism and fascism. This marked a reversal of the Comintern policy established by Lenin as part of the Twenty-one Conditions in 1919. The new Stalinist policy originating from Moscow allowed the formation of the Popular Front government in France.

Stalin's Five-Year Plans and Purges 891

After more than a decade of vicious rivalry between communists and democratic socialists, for a few years the two groups would attempt to cooperate against the common right-wing foe.

The Purges

Stalin's decisions to industrialize rapidly, to move against the peasants, and to reverse the Comintern policy did arouse internal political opposition. They were all departures from the policies of Lenin. In 1929 Stalin forced Bukharin, the fervent supporter of NEP and his own former ally, off the Politburo. Little detailed information is known about further opposition, but it does seem to have existed among lower-level party followers of Bukharin and other previous opponents of rapid industrialization. Sometime in 1933 Stalin began to fear loss of control over the party apparatus and the emergence of possibly effective rivals. These fears were probably produced as much by his own paranoia as by real plots. Nevertheless they resulted in the Great Purges, one of the most mysterious and horrendous political events of this century. The purges were not understood at the time and have not been fully comprehended either inside or outside the Soviet Union to the present day.

On December 1, 1934, Sergei Kirov (1888–1934), the popular party chief of Leningrad and a member of the Politburo, was assassinated. In the wake of the shooting thousands of people were arrested, and still larger numbers were expelled from the party and sent to labor camps. At the time it was believed that Kirov had been murdered by opponents of the regime. Direct or indirect complicity in the crime became the normal accusation against the persons whom Stalin attacked. It now seems practically certain that Stalin himself authorized Kirov's assassination in fear of eventual rivalry with the Leningrad leader.

The purges after Kirov's death were just the beginning of a larger process. Between 1936 and 1938 a series of spectacular show trials were held in Moscow. Previous high Soviet leaders, including former members of the Politburo, publicly confessed all manner of political crimes. They were convicted and executed. It is still not certain why they made their palpably false confessions. Still other leaders and lower-level party members were tried in private and shot. Thousands of people received no trial at all. The purges touched persons in all areas of party life. There was apparently little rhyme or reason as to why some were executed, others sent to labor camps, and still others left unmolested. After the civilian party members had been purged, the prosecutors turned against the army. Important officers, including heroes of the civil war, were sent to their deaths. Within the party itself hundreds of thousands of members were expelled, and applicants for membership were removed from the rolls. The exact figures for executions, imprisonments, and expulsions are unknown but certainly ran into the millions.

The trials and purges astonished Western observers. Nothing quite like this phenomenon had been seen before. Political murders and executions were not new, but the absurd confessions were novel. The scale of the political turmoil was also unprecedented. Russians themselves did not believe or comprehend what was occurring. There existed no national emergency or crisis. There were only accusations of sympathy for Trotsky or of complicity in Kirov's murder or of other nameless crimes. If a rational explanation is to be sought, it probably must be found in Stalin's concern over his own power. In effect, the purges created a new party structure absolutely loyal to him. The "old Bolsheviks" of the October Revolution were among his earliest targets. They and others active in the first years of the revolution knew how far Stalin had moved from Lenin's policies. New, younger members appeared to replace all of the party members executed or expelled. The newcomers had little knowledge of old Russia or of the ideals of the original Bolsheviks. They had not been loyal to Lenin, to Trotsky, or to any other Soviet leader except Stalin himself.

Scope of the Dictatorships

By the middle of the thirties dictators of the right and the left had established themselves across much of Europe. Political tyranny was hardly new to Europe, but several factors combined to give these rulers unique characteristics. They drew their immediate support from well-organized political parties. Except for the Bolsheviks, these were mass parties. The roots of the popularity of the dictators lay in nationalism, the social frustration of the depression, and political ideologies that promised to transform the social and political orders. So long as the new rulers seemed successful, they were not lacking in support. They had in the eyes of many citizens brought an end to the pettiness of everyday politics.

After coming to power, these dictators possessed a practical monopoly over mass communications. Through the armies, police forces, and party discipline they also held a monopoly on terror and coercive power. They could propagandize large populations and compel large groups of people to obey them and their followers. Finally, as a result of the Second Industrial Revolution, they commanded a vast amount of technology and a capacity for immense destruction. Earlier rulers in Europe may have shared the ruthless ambitions of Hitler, Mussolini, and Stalin, but they had not found at their disposal the ready implements of physical force to impose their wills. Mass political support, monopoly on police and military power, and technological capacity meant that the dictators of the thirties held more extensive sway over their nations than any other group of rulers who had ever governed on the continent. Soon the issue would become whether they would be able to maintain peace among themselves and with their democratic neighbors.

SUGGESTED READINGS

W. S. ALLEN, *The Nazi Seizure of Power: The Experience of a Single German Town, 1930–1935* (1965). A classic treatment of Nazism in a microcosmic setting.

J. COLTON, *Léon Blum: Humanist in Politics* (1966). One of the best biographies of any twentieth-century political figure.

R. CONQUEST, *The Great Terror: Stalin's Purges of the Thirties* (1968). The best treatment of the subject to this date.

G. CRAIG, *Germany, 1866–1945* (1978). An important new survey.

I. DEUTSCHER, *Stalin: A Political Biography*, 2nd ed. (1967). The best biography in English.

M. DOBB, *Soviet Economic Development Since 1917*, 6th ed. (1966). A basic introduction.

H. HOLBORN, *A History of Modern Germany: 1840–1945* (1969). A very comprehensive treatment.

C. KINDLEBERGER, *The World in Depression, 1929–1939* (1973). An account by a leading economist whose analysis is comprehensible to the layman.

D. LANDES, *The Unbound Prometheus: Technological Change and Industrial Development in Western Europe from 1750 to the Present* (1969). Includes an excellent analysis of both the Great Depression and the few areas of economic growth.

W. LAQUEUR AND G. L. MOSSE (Eds.), *The Great Depression* (1970). A useful collection of articles.

V. R. LORWIN, *The French Labor Movement* (1954). A good introduction.

D. SCHOENBAUM, *Hitler's Social Revolution: Class and Status in Nazi Germany* (1966). A fascinating analysis of Hitler's appeal to various social classes.

Reference should also be made to the works cited in Chapter 31.

894

33
World War II and the Cold War

Again the Road to War (1933–1939)

WORLD WAR I and the Versailles Treaty in and of themselves had only a marginal relationship to the world depression of the thirties. But in Germany, where the reparations settlement had contributed to the vast inflation of 1923, economic and social discontent focused on the Versailles settlement as the cause of all ills. Throughout the late twenties Adolf Hitler and the Nazi Party had never ceased denouncing Versailles as the source of all Germany's trouble, and the economic woes of the early thirties seemed to bear them out. Nationalism and attention to the social question, along with party discipline, had been the sources of Nazi success. They would continue to influence Hitler's foreign policy after he became chancellor in early 1933. Moreover the Nazi destruction of the Weimar Constitution and of political opposition meant that to an extraordinary degree German foreign policy lay in Hitler's own hands. Consequently it is important to know what his goals were and what plans he had for achieving them.

Hitler's Goals

For almost twenty years after the outbreak of World War II there was general agreement that the war was the outcome of Hitler's expansionist ambitions, which might have been unlimited but which certainly included vast conquests in eastern Europe and dominance of the European continent. A more recent view is that Hitler was not very much different from any other German statesman,

wanting only a revision of Germany's eastern boundaries, elimination of the restrictions of the Versailles Treaty, "and then to make Germany the greatest power in Europe by her natural weight."[1] The same view asserts that Hitler did not have a consistent plan in foreign policy but was an opportunist who went the way that events and opportunity took him, emphasizing his own statement: "I go the way that Providence dictates with the assurance of a sleepwalker."[2]

The truth appears to be a combination of these apparently contradictory views. From the first expression of his goals in *Mein Kampf* to his last days in the bunker where he died, Hitler's racial theories and goals held the central place in his thought. He meant to go far beyond Germany's 1914 boundaries, which were the limit of the vision of his predecessors. He meant to bring the entire German people (*Volk*), understood as a racial group, together into a single nation. The new Germany would include all the Germanic parts of the old Hapsburg Empire, including Austria. This virile and growing nation would need more space to live (*Lebensraum*), which would be taken from the Slavs, a lesser race, fit only for servitude. The new Germany would be purified by the removal of the Jews, another inferior race in Nazi theory. The plan always required the conquest of Poland and the Ukraine as the primary areas for the settlement of Germans and for the provision of badly needed food. Neither *Mein Kampf* nor later statements of policy were blueprints for action. Hitler was a brilliant improviser who sought after and made good use of opportunities as they arose, but he never lost sight of his goal, which would almost certainly require a major war.

THE DESTRUCTION OF VERSAILLES. When Hitler came to power, Germany was far too weak to

During the 1930s Mussolini of Italy and Hitler of Germany believed they could impose a new political order on Europe. In the end, however, they brought war to the world and destruction and defeat to their nations. [The Granger Collection.]

1 A. J. P. Taylor, *The Origins of the Second World War,* (New York: Atheneum, 1968), p. 70.
2 Quoted by Alan Bullock in "Hitler and the Origins of the Second World War," in E. M. Robertson, ed., *The Origins of the Second World War,* (London: Macmillan and Co., 1971), p. 192.

permit the direct approach. The first problem was to shake off the fetters of Versailles and to make Germany a formidable military power. In October of 1933 Germany withdrew from an international disarmament conference and also from the League of Nations. Hitler argued that because the other powers had not disarmed as they had promised, it was wrong to keep Germany helpless. These acts alarmed the French but were merely symbolic. In January of 1934 Germany made a nonaggression pact with Poland that was of greater concern, for it put into question France's chief means of containing the Germans. At last, in March 1935, Hitler formally renounced the disarmament provisions of the Versailles Treaty with the formation of a German Air Force, and soon he reinstated conscription, which aimed at an army of half a million men.

His path was made easier by growing evidence that the League of Nations was ineffective as a device for keeping the peace and that collective security was a myth. In September 1931 Japan occupied Manchuria, provoking an appeal to the League of Nations by China. The league responded by sending out a commission under the Earl of Lytton. The Lytton Report condemned the Japanese for resorting to force, but the powers were unwilling to impose sanctions. Japan withdrew from the league and kept control of Manchuria.

When Hitler announced his decision to rearm Germany, the league formally condemned that action, but it took no action to prevent Germany's rearming. The Allies' response was hostile, but they felt unable to object because they had not carried out their own promises to disarm. Instead, the Allies met with Mussolini in June to form the so-called Stresa Front, making an agreement even to use force to maintain the *status quo* in Europe. But Britain soon made a separate naval agreement with Hitler, allowing him to rebuild the German fleet to an acceptable size, and Italy's expansionist ambitions in Africa soon brought it into conflict with the Western powers. Hitler had taken a major step toward his goal without provoking serious opposition.

Hitler Describes His Goals in Foreign Policy

From his early career, Hitler had certain long-term general views and goals. They were set forth in his *Mein Kampf*, which appeared in 1925, and included consolidation of the German *Volk*, provision of more land for the Germans, contempt for such "races" as Slavs and Jews, and so on. Here are some views on land.

THE *National Socialist movement must strive to eliminate the disproportion between our population and our area—viewing this latter as a source of food as well as a basis for power politics—between our historical past and the hopelessness of our present impotence. . . .*

The demand for restoration of the frontiers of 1914 is a political absurdity of such proportions and consequences as to make it seem a crime. Quite aside from the fact that the Reich's frontiers in 1914 were anything but logical. For in reality they were neither complete in the sense of embracing the people of German nationality, nor sensible with regard to geo-military expediency. . . .

As opposed to this, we National Socialists must hold unflinchingly to our aim in foreign policy, namely, *to secure for the German people the land and soil to which they are entitled on this earth. . . .*

. . . The soil on which some day German generations of peasants can beget powerful sons will sanction the investment of the sons of today, and will some day acquit the responsible statesmen of blood-guilt and sacrifice of the people, even if they are persecuted by their contemporaries. . . .

Much as all of us today recognize the necessity of a reckoning with France, it would remain ineffectual in the long run if it represented the whole of our aim in foreign policy. It can and will achieve meaning only if it offers the rear cover for an enlargement of our people's living space in Europe. . . .

If we speak of soil in Europe today, we can primarily have in mind only Russia *and her vassal border states. . . .*

. . . See to it that the strength of our nation is founded, not on colonies, but on the soil of our European homeland. Never regard the Reich as secure unless for centuries to come it can give every scion of our people his own parcel of soil. Never forget that the most sacred right on this earth is a man's right to have earth to till with his own hands, and the most sacred sacrifice the blood that a man sheds for this earth.

Adolf Hitler, *Mein Kampf*, trans. by Ralph Manheim (Boston: Houghton, Mifflin, 1943), pp. 646, 649, 652, 653, 656.

In 1936, Haile Selassie (1891–1976), the Emperor of Ethiopia, addressed the League of Nations and asked for aid against Italian aggression in his nation. [The Granger Collection.]

Italy Attacks Ethiopia

The Italian attack on Ethiopia made the impotence of the League of Nations and the timidity of the Allies even clearer. Using a border incident as an excuse, Mussolini attacked Ethiopia in October 1935 to avenge the humiliating defeat at Adowa in 1896, to begin the restoration of Roman imperial glory, and, perhaps, to turn the thoughts of Italians away from the corruption of the Fascist regime and their economic misery. France and Britain were eager to appease Mussolini in order to offset the growing power of Germany. They were prepared to allow him the substance of conquest if he would only maintain Ethiopia's formal independence, but for Mussolini the form was more important than the substance. His attack outraged opinion in the West, and the French and British governments were forced at least to appear to resist. The League condemned Italian aggression and, for the first time, voted economic sanctions. It imposed an arms embargo that limited loans and credits to and imports from Italy. But Britain and France were afraid of alienating Mussolini, so they refused to place an embargo on oil, the one economic sanction that could have prevented Italian victory. Even more important, the British fleet did not prevent the movement of Italian troops and munitions through the Suez Canal. The results of this wavering policy were disastrous. The League and collective security were totally discredited, and Mussolini was alienated as well. He now turned to Germany, and by November 1, 1936, he could speak publicly of a Rome–Berlin "Axis."

Remilitarization of the Rhineland

No less important a result of the Ethiopian affair was its effect on Hitler's evaluation of the strength and determination of the Western powers. On March 7, 1936, he took his greatest risk yet, sending a small armed force into the demilitarized Rhineland. This was a breach not only of the Versailles Treaty but of the Locarno Agreements of 1925 as well, agreements that Germany had made voluntarily. It also removed one of the most impor-

Pablo Picasso's Guernica is the artist's vision of the terror-bombing in the Spanish Civil War of the Basque town of Guernica in northern Spain on April 26, 1937 by German airplanes aiding Franco— one of the first calculated aerial bombardments of civilians. It was painted by Picasso in May and June 1937. [Oil on canvas; 11′ 5½″ × 25′ 5¾″. On extended loan to The Museum of Modern Art, New York, from the artist's estate.] (Another Picasso painting will be found in the color album.)

OPPOSITE: The dotted area on the map shows the large portion of Spain quickly overrun by Franco's insurgent armies during the first year of the war. In the following two years, progress came more slowly for the fascists as the war became a kind of international rehearsal for the coming World War II. Madrid's fall to Franco in the spring of 1939 had been preceded by that of Barcelona a few weeks earlier.

tant elements of French security. France and Britain had every right to resist, and the French especially had a claim to retain the only element of security left after the failure of the Allies to guarantee her defense, yet neither did anything but make a feeble protest with the League. British opinion would not permit any support for France. The French themselves were paralyzed by internal division and by military ideas that concentrated on defense and feared taking the offensive. Both countries were further weakened by a growing pacifism.

In retrospect it appears that the Allies lost a great opportunity to stop Hitler before he became a serious menace. The failure of his gamble, taken against the advice of his generals, might have led to his overthrow; at the least it would have made German expansion to the east dangerous if not impossible. Nor is there much reason to doubt that the French army could easily have routed the tiny German force in the Rhineland. As the German General Alfred Jodl said some years later, "The French covering army would have blown us to bits."[3]

A Germany that was rapidly rearming and had a defensible western frontier presented a completely new problem to the Western powers. Their response was the policy of "appeasement." It was based on the assumption that Germany had real grievances, that Hitler's goals were limited and ultimately acceptable, and that the correct policy was to bring about revision by negotiation and concession before a crisis could arise and lead to war. Behind this approach was the general horror at the thought of another war. Memories of the losses in the last war were still fresh, and the advent of aerial bombard-

ment made the thought of a new war terrifying. A firmer policy, moreover, would have required rapid rearmament, but British leaders especially were reluctant to pursue this path because of the expense and because of the widespread belief that the arms race had been a major cause of the last war. As Germany armed, the French huddled behind their newly constructed defensive wall, the Maginot Line, and the British hoped things would go well.

The Spanish Civil War

The new European alignment that found the Western democracies on one side and the fascist states on the other was made clearer by the Spanish Civil War, which broke out in July 1936. In 1931 the Spaniards had driven out their king and established a democratic republic. The

3 Quoted by W. L. Shirer in *The Collapse of the Third Republic,* (New York: Simon and Schuster, 1969), p. 281.

Winston Churchill Warns on the Effects of the Munich Agreement

Churchill delivered his speech on the Munich agreement before the House of Commons on October 5, 1938. The following are excerpts from it.

T*HE Chancellor of the Exchequer [Sir John Simon] said it was the first time Herr Hitler had been made to retract—I think that was the word—in any degree. We really must not waste time after all this long Debate upon the difference between the positions reached at Berchtesgaden, at Godesberg and at Munich. They can be very simply epitomized, if the House will permit me to vary the metaphor. One pound was demanded at the pistol's point. When it was given, £2 were demanded at the pistol's point. Finally, the dictator consented to take £1 17s. 6d. and the rest in promises of good will for the future. . . .*

. . . .

I do not grudge our loyal, brave people, who were ready to do their duty no matter what the cost, who never flinched under the strain of last week—I do not grudge them the natural, spontaneous outburst of joy and relief when they learned that the hard ordeal would no longer be required of them at the moment; but they should know the truth. They should know that there has been gross neglect and deficiency in our defenses; they should know that we have sustained a defeat without a war, the consequences of which will travel far with us along our road; they should know that we have passed an awful milestone in our history, when the whole equilibrium of Europe has been deranged, and that the terrible words have for the time being been pronounced against the Western democracies: "Thou art weighed in the balance and found wanting." And do not suppose that this is the end. This is only the beginning of the reckoning. This is only the first sip, the first foretaste of a bitter cup which will be proffered to us year by year unless, by a supreme recovery of moral health and martial vigor, we arise again and take our stand for freedom as in the olden time.

Winston S. Churchill, *Blood, Sweat, and Tears* (New York: G. P. Putnam's Sons, 1941), pp. 56, 66.

avoid war. At Hitler's mountain retreat, Berchtesgaden, on September 15 Chamberlain accepted the separation of the Sudetenland from Czechoslovakia. And he and the French premier, Daladier, forced the Czechs to agree by threatening to desert them if they did not. A week later Chamberlain flew yet again to Germany only to find that Hitler had raised his demands: he wanted cession of the Sudetenland in three days and immediate occupation by the German army.

Munich

Chamberlain returned to England thinking that he had failed, and France and Britain prepared for war. Almost at the last moment Mussolini proposed a conference of Germany, Italy, France, and Britain. It met on September 29 at Munich. Hitler received almost everything he had demanded. The Sudetenland, the key to Czech security, became part of Germany, thus depriving the Czechs of any chance of self-defense. In return the powers agreed to spare the rest of Czechoslovakia. Hitler promised: "I have no more territorial demands to make in Europe." Chamberlain returned to England and told a cheering crowd that he had brought "peace with honour. I believe it is peace for our time."

Even in the short run the appeasement of Hitler at Munich was a failure. Soon Poland and Hungary tore bits of territory from Czechoslovakia, and the Slovaks demanded autonomy. Finally, on March 15, 1939, Hitler broke his promise and occupied Prague, putting an end to Czechoslovakia and to illusions that his only goal was to restore Germans to the Reich. Defenders of the appeasers have argued that their policy was justified because it bought valuable time in which the West could prepare for war. But that argument was not made by the appeasers themselves, who thought that they were achieving peace, nor does the evidence appear to support it.

If the French and the British had been willing to attack Germany from the west while the Czechs fought in their own defense, there is reason to think that their efforts might have been successful. High officers in the German army were opposed to Hitler's risky policies and might have overthrown him. Even failing such developments, a war begun in October 1938 would have forced Hitler to fight without the friendly neutrality and material assistance of the Soviet Union and without the resources of eastern Europe that became available to him as a result of

The Munich Conference, October 1938. The figures in front are, from left to right, Chamberlain of Great Britain, Daladier of France, Hitler of Germany, and Mussolini of Italy. [Imperial War Museum, London.]

appeasement. If, moreover, the West ever had a chance of alliance with the Soviet Union against Hitler, the exclusion of the Russians from Munich and the appeasement policy helped destroy it. Munich remains an example of short-sighted policy that helped bring on a war in disadvantageous circumstances because of the very fear of war and the failure to prepare for it.

Hitler's occupation of Prague discredited appeasement in the eyes of the British people. In the summer of 1939 a Gallup Poll showed that three quarters of the British public believed it worth a war to stop Hitler. Though Chamberlain himself had not lost all faith in his policy, he felt the need to respond to public opinion, and he responded to excess. It was apparent that Poland was the next target of German expansion. In the spring of 1939 the Germans put pressure on Poland to restore Danzig and to allow a railroad and a highway through the Polish Corridor to connect East Prussia with the rest of Germany. When the Poles would not yield, the usual propaganda campaign began, and the pressure mounted. On

March 31 Chamberlain announced a Franco-British guarantee of Polish independence. Hitler appears to have expected to fight a war with Poland but not with the Western allies, for he did not take their guarantee seriously. He had come to hold their leaders in contempt. He knew that both countries were unprepared for war and that large segments of their populations were opposed to fighting a war to save Poland.

Belief in the Polish guarantee was further undermined by the inability of the Allies to get effective help to the Poles. An attack on Germany's western front was out of the question for the French, still dominated by the defensive mentality of the Maginot Line. The only way to defend Poland was to bring Russia into the alliance

PARTITIONS OF CZECHOSLOVAKIA AND POLAND, 1938–1939

The immediate background of World War II is found in the complex international drama unfolding on Germany's eastern frontier in 1938 and 1939. Germany's expansion inevitably meant the victimization of Austria, Czechoslovakia, and Poland. With the failure of the Western powers' appeasement policy and the signing of a German-Soviet pact, the stage for the war was set.

against Hitler, but a Russian alliance posed many problems. Each side was profoundly suspicious of the other. The French and the British were hostile to Russia's communist ideology, and since Stalin's purge of the officer corps of the Red Army, they stood unconvinced of the military value of an alliance with Russia. Besides, the Russians could not help Poland without the right of transit through Romania and the right of entry into Poland. Both nations, suspicious of Russian intentions, and with good reason, refused to grant these rights. As a result Western negotiations with Russia moved forward slowly and cautiously.

Nazi-Soviet Pact

The Russians had at least equally good reason to hesitate. They resented being left out of the Munich agreement. They were annoyed by the low priority the West seemed to give to negotiations with Russia compared with the urgency with which they dealt with Hitler. They feared, quite rightly, that the Western powers meant them to bear the burden of the war against Germany. As a result they opened negotiations with Hitler, and on August 23, 1939, the world was shocked to learn of a Nazi–Soviet nonaggression pact. Its secret provisions, which were easily guessed and soon carried out, divided Poland between the two powers and allowed Russia to take over the Baltic states and to take Bessarabia from Romania. The most bitter ideological enemies had become allies. Communist parties in the West changed their line overnight from the ardent advocacy of resistance to Hitler to a policy of peace and quiet. Ideology gave way to political and military reality. The West offered the

On the eve of World War II, in August 1939, the Soviet Union and Nazi Germany shocked the rest of the world by signing a non-aggression pact. For years National Socialists and Communists had been the most bitter enemies and regularly hurled insults at each other, but now they came together in a marriage of convenience. This British cartoon by David Low (1891–1963) emphasizes the ironic character of the new relationship. [Cartoon by David Low. By arrangement with the Trustees and the London *Evening Standard*.]

RENDEZVOUS

Russians danger without much prospect of gain. Hitler offered Stalin gain without immediate danger. There could be little doubt as to the decision.

The Nazi–Soviet pact sealed the fate of Poland, and the Franco-British commitment guaranteed a general war. On September 1, 1939, the Germans invaded Poland. Two days later Britain and France declared war on Germany. World War II had begun.

World War II (1939–1945)

World War II has a better claim to its name than its predecessor, for it was truly global. Fighting took place in Europe and Asia, the Atlantic and the Pacific oceans, the Northern and Southern Hemispheres. The demand for the fullest exploitation of material and human resources for increased production, the use of blockades, and the intensive bombing of civilian targets made the war of 1939 even more "total," that is, comprehensive and intense, than that of 1914.

The German Conquest of Europe

The German attack on Poland produced swift success. The new style of "lightning warfare," or *Blitzkrieg*, employed fast-moving, massed armored columns supported by airpower. The Poles were inferior in tanks and planes, and their defense soon collapsed. The speed of the German victory astonished everyone, not least the Russians, who hastened to collect their share of the booty before Hitler could deprive them of it. On September 17 they invaded Poland from the east, dividing the country with the Germans. They then forced the encircled Baltic countries to sign treaties with them. By 1940 Estonia, Latvia, and Lithuania were absorbed as constituent republics into the USSR. In November 1940 the Russians invaded Finland, but the Finns put up a surprisingly effective resistance. Although they were finally worn down and compelled to yield territory and bases to Russia, they retained their independence. Russian difficulties in Finland may well have encouraged Hitler to invade the

Soviets just twenty-two months after the 1939 treaty.

Meanwhile the western front was quiet. The French huddled behind the Maginot Line while Hitler and Stalin swallowed Poland and the Baltic states. Britain hastily rearmed and organized the traditional naval blockade. Cynics in the West called it the phony war, or *"Sitzkrieg,"* but Hitler shattered the stillness in the spring of 1940. In April, without warning and with swift success, the Germans invaded Denmark and Norway. Hitler's northern front was secure, and he now had both air and naval bases closer to Britain. A month later a combined land and air attack struck Belgium, the Netherlands, and Luxembourg. German airpower and armored divisions were irresistible. The Dutch surrendered in a few days, and the Belgians, though aided by the French and the British, surrendered less than two weeks later. The British and French armies were forced to flee to the English Channel to seek escape from the beaches of Dunkerque. By the heroic effort of hundreds of Britons manning small boats, over 200,000 British and 100,000 French soldiers were saved, but casualties were high and much valuable equipment was abandoned.

The Maginot Line ran from Switzerland to the Belgian frontier. The French had always expected the Belgians to

OPPOSITE: Dunkirk. Late in May 1940 the German army, having broken through the French defenses, reached the coast of the English Channel. The Germans might have destroyed the Allied armies, but their indecision allowed over 200,000 British troops and about two-thirds as many French to escape by sea to England. The British Navy, aided by countless civilian boats, rescued these men from the beach at Dunkirk, France. [Imperial War Museum, London.]

continue the fortifications along their German border. After Hitler remilitarized the Rhineland without opposition, the Belgians lost faith in their French alliance and returned to neutrality, leaving the Maginot Line exposed on the left flank. Hitler's swift advance through Belgium therefore circumvented France's main line of defense. The French army, poorly and hesitantly led by superannuated generals who lacked a proper understanding of the use of tanks and planes, quickly collapsed. Mussolini, eager to claim the spoils of victory when it was clearly safe to do so, sent an army across the French border on June 10, less than a week before the new French government, under the ancient hero of Verdun, Henri Philippe Pétain, asked for an armistice. In two months Hitler had accomplished what Germany had failed to achieve in four years of bitter fighting in the previous war.

The terms of the armistice, signed June 22, allowed the Germans to occupy more than half of France, including the Atlantic and English Channel coasts. In order to prevent many Frenchmen from fleeing to North Africa to continue the fight, and even more to prevent the French from turning their fleet over to Britain, Hitler left southern France unoccupied. Pétain set up a dictatorial regime at the resort city of Vichy and followed a policy of collaboration with the Germans in order to preserve as much autonomy as possible. Most Frenchmen were too stunned to resist. Many thought that Hitler's victory was certain and saw no alternative to collaboration. A few, most notably General Charles de Gaulle (1890–1969), fled to Britain, where they organized the French National Committee of Liberation, or "Free French." Vichy controlled most of French North Africa and the navy, but the Free French began operating in central Africa and from London beamed messages of hope and defiance to their countrymen in France. As the passage of time dispelled expectations of a quick German victory, a French underground movement arose that organized many forms of resistance.

The Battle of Britain

The fall of France left Britain isolated, and Hitler expected the British to come to terms. He was prepared to allow Britain to retain its empire in return for a free hand for Germany on the continent. The British had never been willing to accept such an arrangement and had fought the long and difficult war against Napoleon to prevent it. If there was any chance that the British would consider such terms, that chance disappeared when Winston Churchill (1874–1965) replaced Chamberlain as prime minister in May of 1940.

In May 1940 Winston Churchill replaced Neville Chamberlain as Prime Minister of Great Britain. The spirit of appeasement was dead, and David Low's cartoon celebrates the new spirit of determination and resistance Churchill inspired. The recognizable faces in the first three or four rows are those of the then leading British politicians of all parties; in the front row to the right of Churchill, who was a Conservative, are Clement Atlee and Ernest Bevin, the leaders of Labor. Chamberlain is behind Churchill. [Cartoon by David Low. By arrangement with the Trustees and the London *Evening Standard*.]

Churchill had been an early and forceful critic of Hitler, the Nazis, and the policy of appeasement. A descendant and biographer of the Duke of Marlborough (1650–1722), who had fought to prevent the domination of Europe by Louis XIV in the seventeenth century, Churchill's sense of history, his feeling for British greatness, and his hatred of tyranny and love of freedom rejected any thought of compromise. His skill as a speaker and a writer allowed him to infuse the British people with his own courage and determination and to undertake what seemed almost a hopeless fight. Hitler and his allies, including the Soviet Union, controlled all of Europe. Japan was having its way in Asia. The United States was neutral, dominated by isolationist sentiment, and determined to avoid involvement outside the Western Hemisphere.

One of Churchill's greatest achievements was establishing a close relationship with the American President Franklin D. Roosevelt who found ways to help the British in spite of strong political opposition. In 1940 and 1941,

ALL BEHIND YOU, WINSTON

before the United States was at war, America sent military supplies, traded badly needed warships for leases on British naval bases, and even convoyed ships across the Atlantic to help the British survive.

As weeks passed and Britain remained defiant, Hitler was forced to contemplate an invasion, and that required control of the air. The first strikes by the German air force, directed against the airfields and fighter planes in southeastern England, began in August. There is reason to think that if these attacks had continued, Germany might soon have gained control of the air and with it the chance of a successful invasion. In early September, however, seeking revenge for some British bombing raids on German cities, the *Luftwaffe* made London its major target. For two months London was bombed every night. Much of the city was destroyed and about fifteen thousand people were killed, but the theories of victory through airpower alone proved vain. Casualties were many times fewer than expected and morale was not shattered. In fact, the bombings brought the British people together and made them more resolute. At the same time, the Royal Air Force inflicted heavy losses on the *Luftwaffe.* Aided by the newly developed radar and an excellent system of communications, the Spitfire and Hurricane fighter planes destroyed more than twice as many enemy planes than were lost by the RAF. Hitler had lost the Battle of Britain in the air and was forced to abandon his plans for invasion.

The German Attack on Russia

From the first, the defeat of Russia and the conquest of the Ukraine to provide *Lebensraum* for the German people had been a major goal for Hitler. Even before the assault on Britain, he had informed his staff of his intention to attack Russia as soon as conditions were favorable. In December of 1940, even while the bombing of England continued, he ordered his generals to prepare for an invasion of Russia by May 15, 1941. He appears to have thought that a *Blitzkrieg* victory in the east would destroy all hope and bring the British to their senses.

Operation Barbarossa, the code name for the invasion of Russia, aimed at knocking Russia out of the war before winter could set in. Success depended in part on an early start, but here Hitler's Italian alliance proved costly. Mussolini was jealous of Hitler's success and annoyed by the treatment he had received. Unable to make progress against the French army even while Hitler was crushing the part of it on his own frontier, Mussolini was not allowed any gain at the expense of France or even of French Africa. Instead he launched an attack against the British in Egypt and drove them back some sixty miles. Encouraged by this success, he invaded Greece from his base in Albania. His purpose was revealed by his remark to his son-in-law, Count Ciano: "Hitler always faces me with a *fait accompli.* This time I am going to pay him back in his own coin. He will find out in the newspapers that I have occupied Greece."[5] But in north Africa the British drove the Italians back into Libya, and the Greeks themselves pushed into Albania. In March 1941 the British sent help to the Greeks, and Hitler was forced to divert his attention to the Balkans and to Africa. General Erwin Rommel (1891–1944), later to earn the title "The Desert Fox," went to Africa and soon got the British out of Libya and back into Egypt. In the Balkans the German army swiftly occupied Yugoslavia and crushed Greek resistance, but the price was a delay of six weeks. The diversion caused by Mussolini's vanity proved to be costly the following winter.

Operation Barbarossa was launched against Russia on June 22, 1941, and it came very close to success. In spite of their deep suspicion of Germany and the allegation that the Nazi–Soviet Pact was meant to give Russia time to prepare, the Russians were taken quite by surprise. Stalin appears to have panicked. He had not fortified his frontier nor had he issued orders for his troops to withdraw when attacked. In the first two days some two thousand planes were destroyed on the ground. By No-

5 Quoted in Gordon Wright, *The Ordeal of Total War,* (New York: Harper and Row, 1968), pp. 35–36.

AXIS STATES
AND
ANNEXED AREA

AXIS
ALLIES

AXIS-
OCCUPIED

AXIS EUROPE, 1941

vember Hitler had gone further into Russia than Napoleon: the German army stood at the gates of Leningrad,
on the outskirts of Moscow, and on the Don River. Of
the 4.5 million troops with which the Russians had begun
the fighting, they had lost 2.5 million; of their 15,000
tanks only 700 were left. Moscow was in panic, and a
German victory seemed imminent.

But the Germans could not deliver the final blow. In
August there was a delay in their advance to decide on a
course of action. One plan was to drive directly for
Moscow and take it before winter. There is some reason

to think that such a plan might have worked and brought
victory, for unlike the situation in Napoleon's time, Moscow was the hub of the Russian system of transportation.
Hitler, however, imposed his own view on his generals,
and diverted a significant part of his forces to the south.
By the time he was ready to return to the offensive near
Moscow, it was too late. Winter struck the German
army, which was neither dressed nor equipped to face it.
Given precious time, Stalin was able to restore order and
build defenses for the city. Even more important, there
was time for troops to come from Siberia, where they had

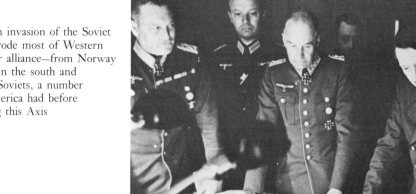

OPPOSITE: On the eve of the German invasion of the Soviet Union the Germany–Italy Axis bestrode most of Western Europe by annexation, occupation, or alliance—from Norway and Finland in the north to Greece in the south and from Poland to France. Britain, the Soviets, a number of insurgent groups, and, finally, America had before them the long struggle of conquering this Axis "fortress Europe."

Moscow or the Ukraine? Hitler and his generals study a map of the Russian front in August 1941. From left to right are Keitel, Brauchitsch, Warlimont, and Hitler. [Bibliothek für Zeitgeschichte, Stuttgart.]

been placed to check a possible Japanese attack. In November and December the Russians were able to counterattack. The *Blitzkrieg* had turned into a war of attrition, and the Germans began to have visions of Napoleon's retreat.

Hitler's Europe

Hitler often spoke of the "new order" that he meant to impose after he had established his Third Reich throughout Europe. The first two German empires (*Reichs*) were those of Charlemagne in the ninth century and William II in the nineteenth, and Hitler predicted that his own would last for a thousand years. If his organization of Germany before the war is a proper index, he had no single plan of government but relied frequently on intuition and pragmatism. His organization of conquered Europe had the same characteristics of spontaneity and patchwork. Some conquered territory was annexed to Germany; some was administered directly by German officials; some lands were nominally autonomous but were ruled by puppet governments.

The demands and distractions of war and the fact that Hitler's defeat prevented him from carrying out his plans fully make it hard to be sure what his intentions were, but the measures he took before his death provide indications. They give evidence of a regime probably unmatched in history for carefully planned terror and inhumanity. To accomplish his plan of giving *Lebensraum* to the Germans at the expense of people he deemed inferior, Hitler established colonies of Germans in parts of Poland, driving the local people from their land and employing them as cheap labor. He had similar plans on an even higher scale for Russia. The Russians would be driven eastward to central Asia and Siberia; they would be kept in check by frontier colonies of German war veterans, and the more desirable lands of European Russia would be settled by Germans.

Hitler's long-range plans included Germanization as well as colonization. In lands inhabited by people racially akin to the Germans, like the Scandinavian countries, the

Netherlands, and Switzerland, the natives would be absorbed into the German nation. Such peoples would be reeducated and purged of dissenting elements, but there would be little or no colonization. He even had plans, only slightly realized, of adopting selected people from the lesser races into the master race. One of these plans involved bringing half a million Ukrainian girls into Germany as servants and finding German husbands for them; about fifteen thousand actually did reach Germany.

In the economic sphere Hitler regarded the conquered lands merely as a source of plunder. He removed everything useful, including entire industries. In Russia and Poland the Germans simply confiscated the land. In the west the conquered countries were forced to support the occupying army at a rate several times the real cost. The Germans used the profits to buy up everything useful and desirable, stripping the conquered peoples of most necessities. The Nazis were frank about their policies. One of Hitler's high officials said, "Whether nations live in prosperity or starve to death interests me only insofar as we need them as slaves for our culture."[6]

The most horrible aspect of the Nazi rule in Europe arose not from military or economic necessity but from the inhumanity and brutality inherent in Hitler's racial doctrines. He considered the Slavs *Untermenschen*, subhuman creatures like beasts who need not be thought of or treated like people. In parts of Poland the upper and professional classes were entirely removed, either jailed, deported, or killed. Schools and churches were closed; marriage was controlled by the Nazis to keep down the Polish birth rate; and harsh living conditions were imposed. In Russia things were even worse. Hitler spoke of his Russian campaign as a war of extermination. Heinrich Himmler (1900–1945), head of Hitler's elite SS guard, planned the elimination of thirty million Slavs to make room for the Germans, and he formed extermination

---

6 Quoted by Gordon Wright, *The Ordeal of Total War, 1939–1945*, (New York: Harper and Row, 1968), p. 117.

World War II (1939–1945) 909

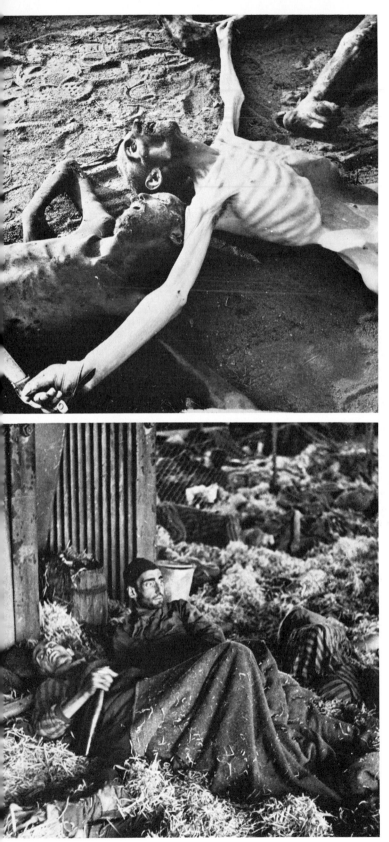

squads for the purpose. The number of Russian prisoners of war and deported civilian workers who died under Nazi rule may have reached six million.

Hitler had special plans for the Jews. He meant to make all Europe *Judenrein* ("free of Jews"). For a time he thought of sending them to the island of Madagascar, but later he arrived at the "final solution of the Jewish problem"—extermination. The Nazis built extermination camps in Germany and Poland and used the latest technology to achieve the most efficient means of killing millions of men, women, and children for no other reason than their birth into the designated group. Before the war was over, perhaps six million Jews had died in what has come to be called the Holocaust. Only about a million remained alive, those mostly in a pitiable condition.

World War II was unmatched in modern times in cruelty. When Stalin's armies conquered Poland and entered Germany, they raped, pillaged, and deported millions to the east. The British and American bombing of Germany killed thousands of civilians, and the dropping of atomic bombs on Japan inflicted terrible harm on civilian populations. The bombings, however, were thought of as acts of war that would help defeat the enemy. Stalin's atrocities were not widely known in the West at the time and are not even today. Little wonder,

German concentration camps—the dead and the dying as found by Western armies in 1945. The Nazis set up their first concentration camps in Germany to hold the German opponents of their regime, but later, after the war had begun and had moved east into non-German territory, the new camps established in Poland were deliberately planned as part of Hitler's "final solution," the extermination of the Jews, although Jews were not his only victims. Even in those camps not avowedly dedicated to extermination the conditions were brutal in the extreme, and the armies that liberated them in 1945 found in all of them scenes such as those in these photographs. [United Press International Photo.]

Hitler States His Plans for Russia

As was revealed in detail only after World War II, Hitler had definite, if vainglorious, views on Russians and positive plans for Germany's exploitation of Russia in the event of Germany's victory.

THE *German colonists ought to live on handsome, spacious farms. The German services will be lodged in marvelous buildings, the governors in palaces. Beneath the shelter of the administrative services, we shall gradually organize all that is indispensable to the maintenance of a certain standard of living. Around the city, to a depth of thirty to forty kilometers, we shall have a belt of handsome villages connected by the best roads. What exists beyond that will be another world, in which we mean to let the Russians live as they like. It is merely necessary that we should rule them. In the event of a revolution, we shall only have to drop a few bombs on their cities, and the affair will be liquidated. Once a year we shall lead a troop of Kirghizes through the capital of the Reich, in order to strike their imaginations with the size of our monuments.*

What India was for England, the territories of Russia will be for us.

When one contemplates this primitive world, one is convinced that nothing will drag it out of its indolence unless one compels the people to work. The Slavs are a mass of born slaves, who feel the need of a master. . . . It's better not to teach them to read. They won't love us for tormenting them with schools. Even to give them a locomotive to drive would be a mistake. . . .

The Germans—this is essential—will have to constitute amongst themselves a closed society, like a fortress. The least of our stable-lads must be superior to any native.

For German youth, this will be a magnificent field of experiment. We'll attract to the Ukraine Danes, Dutch, Norwegians, Swedes. The army will find areas for maneuvers there, and our aviation will have the space it needs.

Hitler's Secret Conversations, 1941–1944, trans. by Norman Cameron and R. H. Stevens (New York: Farrar, Straus and Young, 1953) pp. 20, 28–29.

then, that the victorious Western Allies were shocked by what they saw when they came upon the Nazi extermination camps and their pitiful survivors, and little wonder that they were convinced that the effort of resistance to the Nazis and all the pain it cost were well worth it.

Japan and America's Entry into the War

The sympathies of the American government were very much on the British side, and the various forms of assistance that Roosevelt gave Britain would have justified a German declaration of war. Hitler, however, held back, and it is not clear that the United States government would have overcome isolationist sentiment and entered the war in the Atlantic if war had not been thrust on America in the Pacific. Since the Japanese conquest of Manchuria in 1931, American policy toward Japan had been suspicious and unfriendly. The outbreak of the war in Europe emboldened the Japanese to move forward more quickly in their drive to dominate Asia. They allied themselves with Germany and Italy, made a treaty of neutrality with the Soviet Union, and penetrated into Indochina at the expense of defeated France. At the same time they continued their war in China and made plans to gain control of Malaya and the East Indies at the expense of beleaguered Britain and the conquered Netherlands. The only barrier to Japanese expansion was the United States.

The Americans had temporized, unwilling to cut off vital supplies of oil and other materials for fear of provoking a Japanese attack on Southeast Asia and Indonesia. The Japanese seizure of Indochina in July 1941 changed that policy. The United States froze Japanese assets and cut off oil supplies; the British and Dutch did the same. Japanese plans for expansion could not continue without the conquest of the Indonesian oil fields and Malayan rubber and tin. In October a war faction led by General Tojo took power in Japan and decided to risk a war rather than yield. On Sunday morning, December 7, 1941, even while Japanese representatives were discussing negotiation in Washington, Japan launched an air attack on Pearl Harbor, Hawaii, the chief American naval base in the Pacific. The technique was similar to the one Japan had used against the Russian fleet at Port Arthur in 1904, and it caught the Americans equally by surprise. A large part of the American fleet and many airplanes were

Pearl Harbor, December 7, 1941. The successful Japanese attack on the American base at Pearl Harbor in Hawaii, together with simultaneous attacks on other Pacific bases, brought the United States into war against the Axis powers. This picture shows the effects of the Japanese bombing upon the battleships *Arizona, Tennessee,* and *West Virginia.* [Official United States Navy Photograph.]

Marshal Tito of Yugoslavia (born 1892, and whose original name was Josip Broz), on the right, led his country's partisan resistance against the Nazis during World War II. [The Granger Collection.]

destroyed, and the American capacity to wage war in the Pacific was destroyed for the time being. The next day the United States and Britain declared war on Japan, and three days later Germany and Italy declared war on the United States.

The Tide Turns

The potential power of the United States was enormous, but right after Pearl Harbor America was ill prepared for war. Though conscription had been introduced in 1940, the army was tiny, inexperienced, and ill supplied. American industry was not on a war footing. The Japanese swiftly captured Guam, Wake Island, and the Philippine Islands. At the same time they attacked Hong Kong, Malaya, Burma, and Indonesia. By the spring of 1942 they controlled these places and the Southwest Pacific as far as New Guinea. They were poised for an attack on Australia, and it seemed that nothing could stop them.

In the same year the Germans advanced deeper into Russia and almost reached the Caspian Sea in their drive for Russia's oil fields. In Africa, too, Axis fortunes were high. Rommel drove the British back into Egypt toward the Suez Canal and finally was stopped at El Alamein, only seventy miles from Alexandria. Relations between the democracies and their Soviet ally were still far from close; German submarine warfare was threatening British supplies; the Allies were being thrown back on every front; and the future looked bleak.

The first good news for the Allied cause in the Pacific came in the spring of 1942. A naval battle in the Coral Sea sent many Japanese ships to the bottom and gave security to Australia. A month later the United States defeated the Japanese in a fierce air and naval battle off Midway Island, blunting the chance of another assault on Hawaii and doing enough damage to halt the Japanese advance. Soon American Marines landed on Guadalcanal in the Solomon Islands and began in a small way to reverse the momentum of the war. The war in the Pacific was far from over, but Japan was checked sufficiently to

allow the Allies to concentrate their efforts first in Europe.

The nations opposed to the Axis powers numbered more than twenty and were located all over the world, but the main combatants were Great Britain, the Soviet Union, and the United States. The two Western democracies cooperated in everything to an unprecedented degree, but suspicion between them and their Soviet ally continued. Although the Russians accepted all the aid they could get, they did not trust their allies, complained of inadequate help, and demanded that the democracies open a "second front" on the mainland of Europe. In 1942 American preparation and production were inadequate for an invasion of Europe, and control of the Atlantic by German submarines was such as to prevent safe crossing by the required number of troops. Not until 1944 were conditions right for the invasion, but in the meantime other developments forecast the doom of the Axis.

ALLIED LANDINGS IN AFRICA, SICILY, AND ITALY. In November 1942 an Allied force landed in French North Africa. Even before that landing the British General Bernard Montgomery (1887–1976), after stopping Rommel at El Alamein, had begun a drive to the west, and the American General Dwight D. Eisenhower (1890–1969) pushed eastward through Morocco and Algeria. The two armies caught the German army between them in Tunisia and crushed it. The Suez Canal and the Mediterranean were now under Allied control, and southern Europe was exposed. In July and August 1943 the Allies took Sicily. Mussolini was driven from power, and the new government tried to make peace, but

1942, NOV. 10 GERMAN AND ITALIAN TROOPS OCCUPY VICHY FRANCE AND CORSICA. ③

1942, NOV. TO AUG. 1943 ALLIED AIR AND NAVAL POWER HARRASS THE ENEMY SUPPLY LINE FROM ITALY VIA SICILY. ④

1943, JULY–AUG. SICILY IS CLEARED OF AXIS FORCES. MUSSOLINI IS OUSTED AS ITALY'S RULER. ⑥

1943, AFTER SEPT 9 THE MEDITERRANEAN IS NOW OPEN TO ALLIED SHIPPING, AND AIR BASES ARE AVAILABLE FOR ATTACK ON SOUTHERN EUROPE.

AXIS-OCCUPIED EUROPE, 1943.

1943, FEB.–MAY 300,000 AXIS TROOPS ARE TRAPPED IN TUNISIA BETWEEN THE AMERICANS AND THE BRITISH. THEY SURRENDER ON MAY 13. ⑤

1942, NOV. 8 AMERICANS AND BRITISH LAND IN FR. MOROCCO AND ALGERIA AGAINST SPORADIC RESISTANCE. ②

1943, SEPT. 8 ITALY SURRENDERS ON MALTA. ALLIED LANDINGS AT SALERNO AND ON THE ITALIAN BOOT, SEPT. 9 ⑦

1942, OCT. 23 THE BRITISH BEGIN THEIR DRIVE TO PUSH ROMMEL OUT OF EGYPT, THEN ACROSS 1,000 MILES OF DESERT TO TUNISIA. ①

FREE FRENCH FROM EQUATORIAL AFRICA.

500 MI.
500 KM.

NORTH AFRICAN CAMPAIGNS, 1942–1945

Control of North Africa was important to the Allies in order to have access to Europe from the south. The map diagrams this theater of the war from Morocco to Egypt and the Suez Canal.

Stalingrad after the battle: Russians returning to the ruined city in February 1943. In this crucial battle the Russians suffered terrible losses but stopped the German advance and cut off and destroyed an entire German army. This battle is generally regarded as the turning point of the war in the East. [Sovfoto.]

the Germans moved into Italy. The Allies landed in Italy and Marshal Badoglio, the leader of the new Italian government went over to their side, declaring war on Germany. Churchill had spoken of Italy as the "soft underbelly" of the Axis, but German resistance was tough and determined. Still the need to defend Italy put a strain on the Germans' manpower and resources and left them vulnerable on other fronts.

BATTLE OF STALINGRAD. The Russian campaign became especially demanding. In the summer of 1942 the Germans resumed the offensive on all fronts but were unable to get very far except in the south. The goal was the oil fields near the Caspian Sea, and they got as far as Stalingrad on the Volga, a key point for the protection of the flank of the German army in the south. Hitler was determined to take the city and Stalin to hold it. The battle raged for months with unexampled ferocity. The Russians lost more men than the Americans lost in combat during the entire war, but their heroic defense prevailed. Because Hitler again overruled his generals and would not allow a retreat, an entire German army was lost. Stalingrad marked the turning point of the Russian campaign. Thereafter Lend Lease help from America and, even more, increased production from their own industry, which had been built in or moved to the safety of central and eastern Russia, allowed the Russians to gain and keep the offensive. As German manpower and material resources dwindled, the Russians advanced westward inexorably.

STRATEGIC BOMBING. In 1943 the Allies began to gain ground in production and logistics as well. The industrial might of the United States began to come into full force, and at the same time new technology and tactics made great strides in eliminating the submarine menace. In the same year the American and British air forces began a series of massive bombardments of Germany by night and day. The Americans were more committed to the theory of "precision bombing" of military and industrial targets vital to the enemy war effort, so they flew the day missions. The British regarded precision bombing as impossible and therefore useless. They preferred indiscriminate "area bombing" aimed at destroying the morale of the German people, and this kind of mission could be done at night. It does not appear that either kind of bombing had much effect on the war until 1944. Then the Americans introduced long-range fighters that could protect the bombers and allow accurate missions by day. By 1945 the Allies had cleared the skies of German planes and could bomb at will. Concen-

Dresden in ruins. In February 1945, with the end of the war in sight, the Allies launched a series of air raids on Dresden in Germany, which was without defense. The raids destroyed the heart of the city and are thought to have caused twice as many casualties as those caused by the first atomic bomb dropped on Hiroshima, Japan, in August of the same year. [Bildarchiv Preussischer Kulturbesitz.]

trated attacks on industrial targets, especially communications centers and oil refineries, did very real damage and helped shorten the war. Terror bombing continued, too, but seems not to have had any useful result. The bombardment of Dresden in February 1945 was especially savage and destructive. It was much debated within the British government and has raised moral questions since, for it seems to have had no military value.

As this scene from Cologne, Germany, illustrates, World War II witnessed unprecedented destruction. Scores of bridges across major European rivers were destroyed, including all of the bridges across the Rhine, among them this one. [Bettmann Archive.]

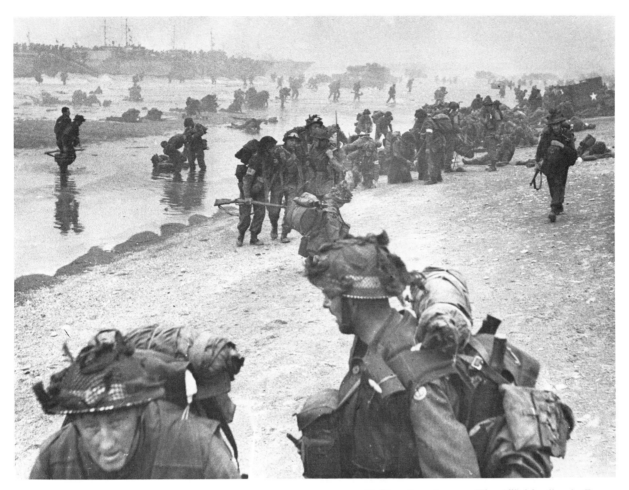

D-Day, June 6, 1944. The Allied landing in France on the coast of Normandy. [Imperial War Museum, London.]

The Defeat of Nazi Germany

On June 6, 1944 ("D-Day"), American, British, and Canadian troops landed in force on the coast of Normandy. The "second front" was opened. General Dwight D. Eisenhower, the commander of the Allied armies, faced a difficult problem. The European coast was heavily fortified, and excellent communications systems allowed the Germans to move reserves swiftly to whatever point might be attacked. Amphibious assaults, moreover, are especially vulnerable to changes of wind and weather. Success depended on meticulous planning, advance preparation by heavy bombing, and successful feints to mask the point of attack. The German defense was strong, but the Allies were able to establish a beachhead and then to break out of it. In mid-August the Allies landed in southern France to put more pressure on the enemy. By the beginning of September France had been liberated.

All went smoothly until December, when the Germans launched a counterattack on the Belgian front through the Forest of Ardennes. Because the Germans were able to push forward into the Allied line, this was called the Battle of the Bulge, and it brought heavy losses and considerable alarm to the Allies. That effort, however, was the last gasp for the Germans. The Allies recovered the momentum and pushed eastward. They crossed the Rhine in March of 1945, and German resistance crumbled. This time there could be no doubt that the Germans had lost the war on the battlefield.

In the east the Russians swept forward no less swiftly. By March 1945 they were within reach of Berlin. Because the Allies insisted on unconditional surrender, the Germans fought on until May. Hitler and his intimates committed suicide in an underground hideaway in Berlin. The Russians occupied Berlin by agreement with their Western allies. The Third Reich had lasted a dozen years instead of the milennium predicted by Hitler.

[*Text continued on page 921*]

500 MI.

500 KM.

N O R T H S E A

N. IRELAND

EIRE

UNITED KINGDOM

Liverpool   Hull

Coventry

London

Trondheim

NORWAY

Oslo

Stavanger

SWEDEN

Stockholm

DENMARK

Copenhagen

B A L T I C   S E A

FINLAND

L. ONEGA

L. LADOGA

Viborg   Leningrad

Helsinki

Reval   Novgorod

ESTONIA

Riga   Rzhev

LATVIA

LITHUANIA   Smolensk

Memel   Vitebsk

Kaunas   KATYN FOREST

BYELO-   Brya

Vilna   RUSSIA

GERMAN SURRENDER IN REIMS, MAY 7, 1945 BERLIN, MAY 8, 1945

NETH.

Rotterdam

BELG.

Dunkirk

NORMANDY INV. JUNE 6, 1944

BATTLE OF THE BULGE DEC. 1944

Hamburg   Danzig   EAST PRUSSIA

Bremen

GREATER   Berlin   GERMANY

Essen   Torgau   POSEN

Cologne   Dresden   Warsaw

Remagen   Breslau

RHINE CROSSING, MAR. 7, 1945

Nürnberg   BOHEMIA   Cracow

Strassburg   MORAVIA   Lemberg

Reims   Munich   SLOVAKIA

Paris

St. Nazaire

Orléans   SWITZ.   TYROL   AUSTRIA   Vienna

Tours

FRANCE   Vichy   HUNGARY

Budapest

Gomel

Kiev

Odessa

RUSSIAN FRONT JUNE 23, 1944

BESSARABIA   Kir

DNIESTER

Jassi

Lyons

Bordeaux

AXIS TROOPS OC- CUPY VICHY FRANCE, NOV. 10 AND 11, 1942

PROVENCE

Marseilles   Toulon

SPAIN

Barcelona

Valencia

BALEARIC IS.

M E D I T E R

Algiers

ALGERIA (VICHY)

Bizerte

AXIS TROOPS EVACUATED, MAY 1943

Tunis

TUNISIA (VICHY)

CORSICA (VICHY)

ALLIES LAND IN PROVENCE, AUG. 15, 1944

Milan

Bologna

Florence

ITALY

Rome

Anzio   Cassino

Naples   Salerno

SARDINIA (IT.)

ALLIES INVADE SICILY & ITALY, JULY–SEPT. 1943

SICILY   ITALIAN SURRENDER, SEPT. 8, 1943

MALTA (U.K.)

A D R I A

CROATIA

YUGOSLAVIA   SERBIA

MONTE- NEGRO

Tirana

ALBANIA

S E A

CALABRIA

R A N E A N   *S E A*

ROMANIA

Bucharest

Belgrade   Varna

BULGARIA

Sofia

Skoplje   (TURK.)

Istanbu

Salonika

GREECE   *AEGEAN*

SEA   Izmir

Athens

RHODE

Candia

CRETE

DEFEAT OF THE AXIS
IN EUROPE,
1942–1945

THE
AXIS

ALLIED
WITH
THE AXIS

OCCUPIED
BY
THE AXIS

Jaroslavl

VOLGA

'OVIET
• Moscow

Kuibyshev
(WARTIME
CAPITAL)

DEC., 1941
FARTHEST
AXIS ADVANCE
NOV. 1942

ula

• Voronezh

el

ursk

• Stalingrad

UNION

VOLGA

• Kharkov

• Astrakhan

NE

DON

• Rostov
• Elista

CASPIAN
SEA

• Kerch
• Maikop

• Grozny

CRIMEA

TRANSCAUCASIA

• Yalta

BLACK
SEA

• Batum
• Tiflis

• Sinop
• Kars

IRAN

• Ankara

TURKEY

• Mosul

TIGRIS

• Adana

EUPHRATES

talya
• Aleppo

SYRIA

IRAQ

CYPRUS
(U.K.)

LEBANON

T R MILLER

This is the sequel to the map on page 908. Here we see some major steps in the progress toward Allied victory against Axis Europe. From the south through Italy, from the west through France, and from the east through Russia the Allies gradually conquered the continent to bring the war in Europe to a close.

The Red Flag flies over the Reichstag in Berlin. This picture shows a ceremony duplicating the scene of the Russian capture of Berlin on May 8, 1945, held on the twentieth anniversary of that event. The division of Germany for the purpose of military occupation hardened into a political division of Germany into two nations. [United Press International Photo.]

World War II (1939–1945) 919

AFGHANISTAN

S O V I E T   U N I O N

Irkutsk

L. BALKASH

L. BAIKAL

Chita

TRANS-SIBERIAN R.R.

OUTER MONGOLIA

SINKIANG

SOVIET UNION ENTERS WAR, 8/9/1945

SAKHALIN

KARAFUTO

KURILE IS.

ETORFU

Karachi

TIBET C H I N A

Peiping

Kirin

Mukden

Vladivostok

MANCHOUKUO

Bombay

NEPAL

Yenan

HOKKAIDO

INDIA

Sadiya

(U.K.)

LEDO ROAD

Chungking

BURMA ROAD

Hankow

KOREA (OCC. 8/16/45)

8/6/45

JAPAN

HONSHU

1930

JAPANESE EMPIRE

1946

Calcutta

Lashio

1941-1943

Hiroshima

ATOMIC BOMBINGS

Tokyo

JAPANESE SURRENDER, 9/2/1945

JAPANESE EMPIRE DEC. 6 1941

Madras

Kunming

BURMA (U.K.)

Nagasaki 8/9/45

Rangoon

Hanoi

Canton

FORMOSA

RYUKYU IS.

Hong Kong

OKINAWA 4/1/45

BONIN IS.

CEYLON

SIAM

Bangkok

HAINAN

FRENCH INDOCHINA

P A C I F I C   O C E A N

IWO JIMA 3/16/45

Saigon

PHILIPPINES

LUZON 6/30/45

Manila, 2/24/45

CORREGIDOR

MINDORO 12/15/44

SPRATLY I.

MALAYA

MARIANAS IS.

Singapore (U.K.)

SARAWAK

SUMATRA

BORNEO

LEYTE 10/20/44

MINDANAO

SAIPAN 6/15/44

GUAM 7/21/44

ENIWETOK 2/17/44

I N D I A N

CELEBES

PALAU 9/15/44

YAP

O C E A N

N E T H E R L A N D S   E A S T   I N D I E S

JAVA

TRUK

Darwin

NEW GUINEA

PAPUA

Hollandia 4/22/44

ADMIRALTY 2/29/44 IS.

BISMARCK ARCH.

SOLOMON IS.

Lae

Port Moresby

C O R A L

GUADAL-CANAL 8/7/42

WORLD WAR II IN THE PACIFIC

AUSTRALIA

S E A

NEW CALEDON.

Brisbane

Sydney

ALLIED SUPPL

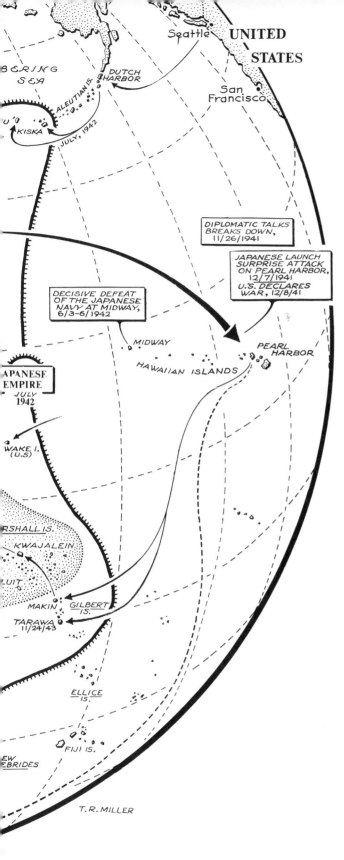

As in Europe, the Pacific war was a problem in Allied recapture of areas that had been quickly taken earlier by the enemy. The enormous area represented by the map shows the initial expansion of Japanese holdings to cover half the Pacific and its islands, as well as huge sections of eastern Asia, and the long struggle to push the Japanese back to their homeland and defeat them by the summer of 1945.

Fall of the Japanese Empire

The war in Europe ended on May 8, 1945, and by then victory over Japan was in sight. The original Japanese attack on the United States had been a calculated risk against the odds. The longer the war lasted, the greater the advantage to the American superiority in industrial production and manpower. Beginning in 1943 the American forces, still relatively small in number, began a campaign of "island hopping." They did not try to recapture every Pacific island held by the Japanese but selected major bases and places strategically located along the enemy supply line. Starting from the Solomons, they moved northeast toward the Japanese homeland. By June of 1944 they had reached the Mariana Islands, which they could use as bases for bombing the Japanese in the Philippines, in China, and in Japan itself. In October of the same year the Americans recaptured the Philippines and drove the Japanese fleet back into its home waters. In 1945 Iwo Jima and Okinawa fell, in spite of determined Japanese resistance that included "kamikaze" attacks, suicide missions in which specially trained pilots deliberately flew their explosive-filled planes into American warships. From these new bases, closer to Japan, the American bombers launched a terrible wave of bombings that destroyed Japanese industry and disabled the navy, but still the Japanese government, dominated by a military clique, refused to surrender.

Confronted with Japan's determination, the Americans made plans for a frontal assault on the Japanese homeland, which, they calculated, might cost a million American casualties and even greater losses for the Japanese. At this point science and technology presented the Americans with another choice. Since early in the war a secret program had been in progress. Its staff, made up in significant part by exiles from Hitler's Europe, was working to use atomic energy for military purposes. On August 6, 1945, an American plane dropped an atomic bomb on the city of Hiroshima. The city of 200,000 was destroyed and over 70,000 people were killed. Two days

The mushroom-shaped cloud of the atomic bomb has come to symbolize the possibility of total human destruction that has haunted the statesmen and peoples of the world since 1945. This photograph shows one of the post-war test explosions held on remote atolls in the Pacific. [Official United States Navy Photograph.]

later the Soviet Union declared war on Japan and invaded Manchuria. The next day a second atomic bomb fell, this time on Nagasaki. Even then the Japanese did not yield. The Japanese cabinet was prepared to resist further, to face an invasion rather than give up. It was only the unprecedented and unconstitutional intervention of Emperor Hirohito that convinced the government to surrender on August 14. Even then they made the condition that Japan could keep its emperor. Although the Allies had continued to insist on unconditional surrender, President Harry S. Truman who had come to office on April 12, 1945, on the death of Franklin D. Roosevelt, accepted the condition, and peace was formally signed aboard the *USS Missouri* in Tokyo Bay on September 2, 1945.

Revulsion and horror at the only use of atomic bombs, as well as hindsight arising from the Cold War have surrounded the decision to use the bomb against Japanese cities with debate. Some have suggested that the bombings were unnecessary to win the war and that their main purpose was to frighten the Russians into a more cooperative attitude after the war. Others have emphasized the bureaucratic, almost automatic nature of the decision, once it had been decided to develop the bomb. To the decision makers and their contemporaries, however, matters were simpler. The bomb was a way to end the war swiftly without the need of invasion or an extended period of bombardment, and it would save American lives. The decision to use it was conscious, not automatic, and required no ulterior motive.

The Cost of War

World War II was the most terrible war in history. Military deaths are estimated at some fifteen million, and at least as many civilians were killed. If deaths linked indirectly to the war are included, the figure of victims might reach as high as forty million. Most of Europe and significant parts of Asia were devastated. Yet the end of so terrible a war brought little opportunity for relaxation. The dawn of the Atomic Age and the dramatic end it brought to the war made men conscious that another major war might bring an end to humanity. Everything depended on the conclusion of a stable peace, but even as the fighting came to an end, conflicts among the victors made the prospects of a lasting peace doubtful.

Preparations for Peace and the Onset of the Cold War

The split between the Soviet Union and its wartime allies should cause no surprise. As the self-proclaimed center of world Communism, the Soviet Union was openly dedicated to the overthrow of the capitalist nations, though this message was muted when the occasion demanded. On the other side, the Western allies were no less open about their hostility to Communism and its chief purveyor, the Soviet Union. Though they had been friendly to the early stages of the Russian Revolution, they had sent troops in hopes of overthrowing the Bolshevik regime. The United States did not grant formal recognition to the USSR until 1933. The Western powers' exclusion of the Soviets from the Munich conference and Stalin's pact with Hitler did nothing to improve relations.

Though cooperation against a common enemy and strenuous propaganda efforts in the West helped improve western feeling toward the Soviet ally, Stalin remained suspicious and critical of the Western war effort, and Churchill never ceased planning to contain the Soviet

President Roosevelt and Prime Minister Churchill meeting on a warship at Placentia Bay, Newfoundland, in August 1941. There they signed the Atlantic Charter, a vague and general statement of liberal aims for the post-war world. [Imperial War Museum, London.]

advance into Europe. For some time Roosevelt seems to have been hopeful that the Allies could continue to work together after the war, but even he was losing faith as the war and his life drew to a close. Differences in historical development and ideology, as well as traditional conflicts over political power and influence, soon dashed whatever hopes there were of a mutually satisfactory peace settlement and continued cooperation to uphold it.

The Atlantic Charter

In August 1941, even before the Americans were at war, Roosevelt and Churchill had met on a ship off Newfoundland and agreed to the Atlantic Charter, a broad set of principles in the spirit of Wilson's Fourteen Points, which provided a theoretical basis for the peace they sought. When Russia and the United States joined Britain in the war, the three powers entered a purely military alliance in May 1942, leaving all political questions aside. The first political conference was the meeting of foreign ministers in Moscow in October 1943. The ministers reaffirmed earlier agreements to fight on until the enemy surrendered without condition and to continue cooperating after the war in a United Nations organization.

Teheran

The first meeting of the three leaders of state took place at Teheran, the capital of Iran, in 1943. Western promises to open a second front in France the next summer and Stalin's agreement to join in the war against Japan when Germany was defeated created an atmosphere of goodwill in which to discuss a postwar settlement. Stalin wanted to retain what he had gained in his pact with Hitler and to dismember Germany. Roosevelt and Churchill were conciliatory, but they made no firm commitments. The most important decision was the one that chose Europe's west coast as the point of attack instead of southern Europe, by the way of the Mediterranean. That meant, in retrospect, that Soviet forces would occupy eastern Europe and control its destiny. At Teheran in 1943 the Western allies did not foresee this clearly, for the Russians were still fighting deep within their own frontiers, and military considerations were paramount everywhere.

By 1944 the situation was different. In August Soviet armies were in sight of Warsaw, which had risen in expectation of liberation. But the Russians halted, allowing the Polish rebels to be annihilated while they turned south into the Balkans. They gained control of Romania and Hungary, advances of which centuries of expansionist tsars had only dreamed. Alarmed by these developments, Churchill went to Moscow and met with Stalin in October. They agreed to share power in the Balkans on the basis of Soviet predominance in Romania and Bulgaria, Western predominance in Greece, and equality of influence in Yugoslavia and Hungary. These agreements were not enforceable without American approval, and the Americans were known to be hostile to such un-Wilsonian devices as "spheres of influence."

Yalta

The next meeting of the "Big Three" was at Yalta in the Crimea in February 1945. The Western armies had not yet crossed the Rhine, and the Soviet army was within a hundred miles of Berlin. The war with Japan continued, and no atomic explosion had yet taken place. Roosevelt, faced with an invasion of Japan and heavy losses, was eager to bring the Russians into the Pacific war as soon as possible. As a true Wilsonian he also suspected Churchill's determination to maintain the British Empire and Britain's colonial advantages. The Americans thought that Churchill's plan to set up British spheres of influence in Europe would encourage the Russians to do the same and lead to friction and war. To encourage Russian participation in the war against Japan, Roosevelt and Churchill made extensive concessions to Russia in Sakhalin and the Kurile Islands, in Korea, and in Manchuria. Again in the tradition of Wilson, Roosevelt laid great stress on a United Nations organization: "Through the United Nations, he hoped to achieve a self-enforcing peace settlement that would not require American troops, as well as an open world without spheres of influence in which American enterprise could work freely." [7] Soviet agreement on these points seemed well worth concessions elsewhere.

Agreement on European questions was more difficult. On Germany the three powers easily agreed on its disarmament and denazification and on its division into four zones of occupation by France and the Big Three. Churchill, however, began to balk at Stalin's plan to dismember Germany and objected to his demand for reparations in the amount of $20 billion as well as forced labor from all the zones and Russia to get half of everything. These matters were left undecided to fester and cause dissension in the future.

The settlement of Eastern Europe was no less a problem. Everyone agreed that the Soviet Union deserved neighboring governments that were friendly, but the West insisted that they also be independent, autonomous, and democratic. The Western leaders, and especially Churchill, were not eager to see Eastern Europe fall under Russian domination; they were also, especially Roosevelt, truly committed to democracy and self-determination. But Stalin knew that independent, freely elected governments in Poland and Romania would not be safely friendly to Russia. He had already established a subservient government in Poland at Lublin in competition with the Polish government-in-exile in London. Under pressure from the Western leaders, however, he agreed to reorganize the government and include some Poles friendly to the West. He also signed a Declaration on Liberated Europe promising self-determination and free democratic elections. Stalin may have been eager to avoid conflict before the war with Germany was over—he never was free of the fear that the Allies might still make an arrangement with Germany and betray him—and he probably thought it worth endorsing some meaningless principles as the price of continued harmony. In any case, he wasted little time in violating these agreements.

7 Robert O. Paxton, *Europe in the Twentieth Century*, (New York: Harcourt Brace, Jovanovich, Inc., 1975), p. 487.

The map pictures the shifts in territory following the defeat of the Axis. No treaty of peace has formally ended the war with Germany. (See also the map on page 930.)

At the Yalta Conference in February 1945 President Roosevelt and Stalin await the arrival of Churchill. Speaking to the President is Edward Stettinius, the American Secretary of State. [The Granger Collection.]

POST–WORLD WAR II
BOUNDARIES

TERRITORIAL CHANGES
RESULTING FROM
WORLD WAR II

BERLIN AND VIENNA WERE
UNDER 4-POWER CONTROL

THE SAAR AND THE
FREE TERRITORY OF TRIESTE
WERE UNDER SPECIAL CONTROL

THE SAAR WAS RETURNED
TO GERMANY IN 1957

TERRITORIAL CHANGES
AFTER WORLD WAR II

President Harry Truman stands between Stalin and Churchill at the Potsdam Conference in July 1945. [The Granger Collection.]

Potsdam

The Big Three met for the last time in the Berlin suburb of Potsdam in July 1945. Much had changed since the last conference. Germany was defeated, and news of the successful explosion of an atomic weapon reached the American president during the meetings. The cast of characters was also different; Truman replaced Roosevelt, and Clement Attlee (1883–1967), leader of the Labour Party that had defeated Churchill's Conservatives in a general election, spoke for Britain. Previous agreements were reaffirmed but progress on undecided questions was slow.

Russia's western frontier was moved far into what had been Poland and included part of German East Prussia. In compensation Poland was allowed "temporary administration" over the rest of East Prussia and Germany east of the Oder–Neisse river line, a condition that became permanent. In effect Poland was moved about a hundred miles west, at the expense of Germany, to accommodate the Soviet Union. The Allies agreed that Germany would be divided into occupation zones until the final peace treaty was signed. As no such treaty has ever been made, Germany remains divided to this day.

A Council of Foreign Ministers was established to draft peace treaties for Germany's allies. Growing disagreements made the job difficult, and it was not until February 1946 that Italy, Romania, Hungary, Bulgaria, and Finland signed treaties. The Russians were dissatisfied with the treaty made with Japan in 1951 and signed their own agreements with the Japanese in 1956. These disagreements were foreshadowed at Potsdam.

Causes of the Cold War

Some scholars attribute the hardening of the atmosphere to the advent of Truman in place of the more sympathetic Roosevelt and to the American possession of an effective atomic bomb. The fact is that Truman was trying to carry Roosevelt's policies forward, and there is evidence that Roosevelt himself had become distressed by Soviet actions in Eastern Europe. Nor did Truman use the successful test of the atomic bomb to try to keep Russia out of the Pacific. On the contrary, he worked hard to ensure Russian intervention against Japan. In part the new coldness among the Allies arose from the mutual feeling that each had violated previous agreements. The Russians were plainly asserting permanent control of Poland and Romania under puppet Communist governments. The United States, on the other hand, was taking a harder line on the extent of German reparations to the Soviet Union.

In retrospect, however, it appears unlikely that friendlier styles on either side could have avoided a split that rested on basic differences of ideology and interest. The Soviet Union's attempt to extend its control westward into central Europe and the Balkans and southward into the Middle East was a continuation of the policy of tsarist Russia. It had been Britain's traditional role to try to restrain Russian expansion into these areas, and it was not surprising that the United States should inherit that task as Britain's power waned. The alternative was to permit a major change in the balance of power in the world in favor of a huge nation, traditionally hostile, dedicated in its official ideology to overthrow nations like the United States, governed by an absolute dictator who had already demonstrated many times his capacity for the most amazing deceptions and the most horrible cruelties. Few nations would be likely to take such risks.

Nevertheless the Americans made no attempt to roll back Soviet power where it existed, though American military forces were the greatest in their history, their industrial power was unmatched in the world, and atomic weapons were an American monopoly. In less than a year from the war's end American forces in Europe were reduced from 3.5 million to half a million men. The speed of the withdrawal was the result of pressure to "get the boys home" but was fully in accord with American plans and peacetime goals. These were the traditional ones of support for self-determination, autonomy and democracy in the political area, free trade, freedom of the seas, no barriers to investment, and the Open Door in the economic sphere. These goals agreed with American principles, and they also served American interests well. As the strongest, richest nation in the world, the one with the greatest industrial plant and the strongest currency, the United States would benefit handsomely if such an international order were established.

American hostility to colonial empires created tension with France and Britain, but these were minor. The main conflict came with the Soviet Union. From the Soviet perspective the extension of its frontiers and the domination of formerly independent states in Eastern Europe were necessary for the security of the USSR and a proper compensation for the fearful losses the Russians had suffered in the war. American resistance to the new state of things could be seen as a threat to Soviet security and legitimate aims. American objections about Poland and other states could be seen as attempts to undermine regimes friendly to Russia and to encircle the Soviet Union with hostile neighbors. Such behavior might be seen to justify attempts to overthrow regimes friendly to the United States in Western Europe and elsewhere.

The growth in France and Italy of large Communist parties plainly taking orders from Moscow led the Americans to believe that Stalin was engaged in a great worldwide plot to destroy capitalism and democracy by subversion. In the absence of reliable evidence about Stalin's intentions certainty is not possible, but most people in the West thought the suspicions plausible. Rivalry between the Soviet Union and the United States dominated international relations for the next three decades, and in the flawed world of reality it is hard to see how things could have been otherwise. The important question was whether the conflict would take a diplomatic or a military form.

Cold War

Evidence of the new mood of hostility among the former allies was not long in coming. In February 1946 both Stalin and Molotov gave public speeches in which they spoke of the Western democracies as enemies. A month later Churchill gave a speech in Fulton, Missouri, in which he viewed Russian actions in eastern Europe with alarm. He spoke of an Iron Curtain that had descended upon Europe, dividing a free and democratic West from an East under totalitarian rule. He warned against Communist subversion and urged Western unity and strength as a response to the new menace. In this atmosphere difficulties grew.

The attempt to deal with the problem of atomic energy was an early victim of the Cold War. The Americans put forward a plan to place the manufacture and control of atomic weapons under international control, but the Russians balked at the proposed requirements for on-site inspection and for limits on the veto power in the United Nations. The plan fell through. The United States continued to develop its own atomic weapons in secrecy, and the Russians did the same. By 1949, with the help of information obtained by Soviet spies in Britain and the United States, the Soviet Union exploded its own atomic bomb, and the race to nuclear explosions was on.

Any hopes that the new United Nations organization, with its headquarters in New York as a symbol of firm American adherence to international responsibility, would resolve the world's conflicts were soon disappointed. Like the League of Nations, it is dependent on voluntary contributions of money and troops. The UN Charter, moreover, forbids interference in the internal affairs of nations, and many of the problems of the 1940s were internal in nature. Finally, the Security Council, which is responsible for maintaining world peace, gives a veto to each of the permanent members. Because the Soviet Union was generally in the minority, it used the veto repeatedly, making it clear that the United Nations was not adequate to resolve existing problems.

Western resistance to what the West increasingly perceived as Soviet intransigence and Communist plans for subversion and expansion took clearer form in 1947. Since 1944 civil war had been raging in Greece between the royalist government restored by Britain and insurgents supported by Communist countries, chiefly Yugoslavia. In 1947 Britain informed the United States that it was financially no longer able to support the Greeks. On March 12 President Truman asked Congress for legislation to support Greece and also Turkey, which was under Soviet pressure to yield control of the Dardanelles. Congress voted funds only to aid Greece and Turkey, but the Truman Doctrine, as enunciated in the speech of March 12 had a broader significance. The president advocated a policy of supporting "free people who are resisting attempted subjugation by armed minorities or by outside pressures," by implication anywhere in the world.

American aid to Greece and Turkey took the form of military equipment and advisers, but the threat in Western Europe was the growth of Communist parties fed by postwar poverty and hunger. To deal with this menace, the Americans devised the European Recovery Program, named the Marshall Plan after George C. Marshall, the secretary of state who introduced it. This was a plan for broad economic aid to European states on condition only that they work together for their mutual benefit. The invitation included the Soviet Union and its satellites. Finland and Czechoslovakia were willing to participate, and Poland and Hungary showed interest. The Soviets, fearing that American economic aid would attract many satellites out of their orbits, forbade them to take part. The Marshall Plan was a great success in restoring prosperity to Western Europe and setting the stage for its unprecedented economic growth since that time. It also

Churchill Invents the Iron Curtain; Cold War Declared

Winston Churchill chose an American audience (at Westminster College in Fulton, Missouri) for his March 5, 1946 speech that contributed "iron curtain" to the language and, more important, defined the existence of what came to be known as the "cold war" between the communist and the democratic camps.

A SHADOW *has fallen upon the scenes so lately lighted by the Allied victory. Nobody knows what Soviet Russia and its Communist international organization intends to do in the immediate future, or what are the limits, if any, to their expansive and proselytizing tendencies. . . .*

From Stettin in the Baltic to Trieste in the Adriatic, an iron curtain has descended across the Continent. Behind that line lie all the capitals of the ancient states of central and eastern Europe. Warsaw, Berlin, Prague, Vienna, Budapest, Belgrade, Bucharest and Sofia, all these famous cities and the populations around them lie in the Soviet sphere and all are subject in one form or another, not only to Soviet influence but to a very high and increasing measure of control from Moscow. Athens alone, with its immortal glories, is free to decide its future at an election under British, American and French observation. The Russian dominated Polish government has been encouraged to make enormous and wrongful inroads upon Germany, and mass expulsions of millions of Germans on a scale grievous and undreamed of are now taking place. The Communist parties, which were very small in all these eastern states of Europe, have been raised to pre-eminence and power far beyond their numbers and are seeking everywhere to obtain totalitarian control. Police governments are prevailing in nearly every case, and so far, except in Czechoslovakia, there is no true democracy. . . .

. . . I do not believe that Soviet Russia desires war. What they desire is the fruits of war and the indefinite expansion of their power and doctrines. . . .

. . . If the western democracies stand together in strict adherence to the principles of the United Nations Charter, their influence for furthering these principles will be immense and no one is likely to molest them. If, however, they become divided or falter in their duty, and if these all-important years are allowed to slip away, then indeed catastrophe may overwhelm us all.

"Winston Churchill's Speech at Fulton," in *Vital Speeches of the Day*, Vol. 12 (March 15, 1946) (New York: City News Publishing Co.), pp. 331–332.

The headquarters of the United Nations in New York City. [United Nations.]

Josef Cardinal Mindszenty was one of the major anti-communist heroes of the Cold War. As Roman Catholic primate of Hungary he was tried in 1949 by the Communists for treason, convicted, and imprisoned. This picture shows him at his trial flanked by two guards. During the 1956 uprising he escaped and took refuge in the American Embassy in Budapest, where he remained until 1971 when he was permitted to fly to Rome. [United Press International Photo.]

led to the waning of communist strength in the West and to the establishment of solid democratic regimes.

From the Western viewpoint this policy of "containment" was a new and successful response to the Soviet and communist challenge. To Stalin it may have seemed a renewal of the old Western attempt to isolate and encircle the USSR. His answer was to put an end to all multiparty governments behind the Iron Curtain and to replace them with thoroughly communist regimes completely under his control. He also called a meeting of all communist parties around the world at Warsaw in the autumn of 1947. There they organized the Communist Information Bureau (Cominform), a revival of the old Comintern, dedicated to spreading revolutionary communism throughout the world. The era of the popular front was officially over. Communist leaders in the West who favored friendship, collaboration, and reform were replaced by hard-liners who attempted to sabotage the new structures.

In February 1948 a more dramatic and brutal display of Stalin's new policy took place in Prague. The communists expelled the democratic members of what had been a coalition government and murdered Jan Masaryk, the foreign minister and son of the founder of Czechoslo-

BRITISH

Berlin

RUSSIAN

P O L A N D

FARTHEST ADVANCE OF
THE ALLIES, MAY 6, 1945,
BEFORE WITHDRAWAL IS
ORDERED ON JULY 1, 1945.

AMERICAN

FRENCH

Vienna

200 MI.

200 KM.

BERLIN AND VIENNA
WERE JOINTLY
OCCUPIED

UNITED
STATES   UNITED
KINGDOM   FRANCE   SOVIET
UNION

OCCUPIED GERMANY AND AUSTRIA

At the war's end, defeated Germany, including Austria, was occupied by the victorious Allies in the several zones shown here. Austria, by prompt agreement, was re-erected into an independent, neutral state and no longer occupied. But the German zones have hardened into an "East" Germany (the former Soviet zone) and a "West" Germany (the former British, French, and American zones). The city of Berlin, within the Soviet zone, was similarly divided.

vakia, Thomas Masaryk. President Beneš was also forced to resign, and Czechoslovakia was brought fully under Soviet rule.

These Soviet actions, especially those in Czechoslovakia, increased American determination to go ahead with its own arrangements in Germany. The wartime Allies had never agreed on the details of a German settlement and kept putting off decisions. At first they all agreed on the dismemberment of Germany but not on the form it should take. By the time of Yalta, Churchill had come to fear Russian control of Eastern and Central Europe and began to oppose dismemberment. There were differences in economic policy too. The Russians proceeded swiftly to dismantle German industry in the eastern zone, but the Americans acted differently. They concluded that such a policy would require the United States to support Germany for the foreseeable future. It would also cause political chaos and open the way for Communism. They preferred, therefore, to try to make Germany self-sufficient, and this meant restoring rather than destroying its industrial capacity. To the Soviets the restoration of a powerful industrial Germany, even in the western zones only, was frightening and unacceptable. The same difference of approach hampered agreement on reparations because the Soviets claimed the right to industrial equipment in all the zones, and the Americans resisted their demands.

Disagreement over Germany produced the most heated of postwar debates. When the Western powers agreed to go forward with a separate constitution for

Germany in the west in February 1948, the Soviets walked out of the joint Allied Control Commission. In the summer of that year the Western powers issued a new currency in their zone. Berlin, though well within the Soviet zone, was governed by all four powers. The Soviets feared the new currency circulating in Berlin at better rates than their own and chose to seal the city off by closing all railroads and highways to West Germany. The Western allies responded with an airlift of supplies to the city that lasted almost a year. In May 1949 the Russians were forced to back down and open access to Berlin, but the incident was decisive. It greatly increased tensions and suspicions between the opponents, and it hastened the lasting separation of Germany into two states. West Germany formally became the German Federal Republic in September 1949, and the eastern region became the German Democratic Republic a month later. Ironically Germany had been dismembered in a way no one had planned or expected.

NATO AND THE WARSAW PACT. Meanwhile the nations of Western Europe had been coming closer together. The Marshall Plan encouraged international cooperation, and in March 1948 Belgium, the Netherlands, Luxembourg, France, and Britain signed the Treaty of Brussels, providing for cooperation in economic and military matters. In April 1949 these nations joined with Italy, Denmark, Norway, Portugal, and Iceland to sign a treaty with Canada and the United States that formed the North Atlantic Treaty Organization (NATO). NATO committed its members to mutual assistance in case any was attacked. For the first time in history the United States was committed to defend allies outside the Western Hemisphere. The NATO treaty formed the West into a bloc. A few years later West Germany, Greece, and Turkey joined the alliance.

Soviet relations with the states of Eastern Europe were governed by a series of bilateral treaties providing for close ties and mutual assistance in case of attack. In 1949 the Council of Mutual Assistance (COMECON) was formed to integrate the economies of these states. Unlike

The North Atlantic Treaty Organization, which includes both Canada and the United States, stretches as far east as Turkey. By contrast, the Warsaw Pact nations are contiguous communist states of eastern Europe, with the Soviet Union, of course, as the dominant member.

NATO NATIONS   WARSAW PACT NATIONS   OTHER COMMUNIST NATIONS

- NON-EUROPEAN MEMBERS OF NATO:
  · UNITED STATES
  · CANADA
- SPECIAL TREATY BETWEEN THE UNITED STATES AND SPAIN.
- OTHER COMMUNIST NATIONS:
  · YUGOSLAVIA—NOT A MEMBER OF THE WARSAW PACT.
  · ALBANIA—WITHDREW FROM THE WARSAW PACT IN 1968.

MAJOR EUROPEAN ALLIANCE SYSTEMS

the NATO states the Eastern alliance system was under direct Soviet domination through local communist parties controlled from Moscow and overawed by the presence of the Red Army. The Warsaw Pact of May 1955, which included Albania, Bulgaria, Czechoslovakia, East Germany, Hungary, Poland, Romania, and the Soviet Union, merely gave formal recognition to a system that already existed. Europe was divided into two unfriendly blocs. The Cold War had taken firm shape in Europe.

SUGGESTED READINGS

A. BULLOCK, *Hitler: A Study in Tyranny*, rev. ed. (New York, 1964). A brilliant biography.

W. S. CHURCHILL, *The Second World War*, 6 vols. (London, 1948–1954). The memoirs of the great British leader.

H. FEIS, *From Trust to Terror: The Onset of the Cold War, 1945–1950* (Princeton, 1970). The best general account.

H. W. GATZKE, *Stresemann and the Rearmament of Germany* (Baltimore, 1954). An important monograph.

H. W. GATZKE (Ed.), *European Diplomacy Between Two Wars* (Chicago, 1972). A collection of important essays.

M. GILBERT, *The Roots of Appeasement* (New York, 1966). A study of diplomacy and opinion in the 1920s.

M. GILBERT AND R. GOTT, *The Appeasers*, rev. ed. (Boston, 1963). A revealing study of British policy in the 1930s.

B. H. LIDDELL HART, *History of the Second World War*, 2 vols. (New York, 1971). A good military history.

K. HILDEBRAND, *The Foreign Policy of the Third Reich* (Berkeley, 1970).

G. KOLKO, *The Politics of War* (New York, 1968). An interesting example of the new revisionist school that finds the causes of the Cold War in economic considerations and emphasizes American responsibility.

L. LAFORE, *The End of Glory* (Philadelphia and New York, 1970). A well-written interpretive essay on the origins of World War II.

W. L. LANGER AND S. E. GLEASON, *The Challenge of Isolation* (New York, 1952). American foreign policy in the 1930s.

E. M. ROBERTSON, *Hitler's Pre-War Policy and Military Plans* (London, 1963).

E. M. ROBERTSON (Ed.), *The Origins of the Second World War* (New York, 1971). A valuable collection of essays.

R. J. SONTAG, *A Broken World 1919–1939* (New York, 1971). An excellent survey.

A. J. P. TAYLOR, *The Origins of the Second World War* (New York, 1966). A lively, controversial, even perverse study.

C. THORNE, *The Approach of War 1938–1939* (London, 1967). A careful analysis of diplomacy.

J. W. WHEELER-BENNET, *Munich: Prologue to Tragedy* (London, 1966). A fine study of the crisis.

A. WOLFERS, *Britain and France Between Two Wars* (New York, 1940). Still a valuable study of the policy of the Western powers.

G. WRIGHT, *The Ordeal of Total War 1939–1945* (New York, 1968). An excellent survey.

932

34
Europe in the Era of the Superpowers

ABOUT thirty-five years have passed since the conclusion of World War II and the onset of the Cold War. In this period of considerably more than a human generation, Europe has remained divided between communist and noncommunist states and between allies of the United States and those of the Soviet Union. Such division is hardly a new feature of European history. For centuries the continent was separated into Roman and barbarian areas, later into Christian and Islamic spheres, then into Protestant, Catholic, and Orthodox camps, and finally into liberal and conservative states. Each of these divisions left an imprint on the culture of Europe. This seems no less true of the Cold War separation, although the latter may prove less long-lived than the previous divisions.

The three decades of the Cold War have witnessed extraordinary changes in European political and economic life. These in turn have produced significant results for the rest of the world once dominated by Europeans. Leadership in the western part of the Continent shifted to the United States and in the eastern part to the Soviet Union. The successor states of the Austria–Hungarian Empire previously coveted by Hitler fell under Soviet domination. Britain, France, Belgium, the Netherlands, and Portugal have conducted what is no doubt a permanent retreat from world empire. They have thus concluded an era of European world dominance that had commenced during the Renaissance.

Many of those same nations began to cooperate eco-

This vast statue, Worker and Peasant, by the Soviet sculptor V. Mukhina, stands in Moscow outside the Soviet Economics Achievement Exhibition. The sheer size of the monument is meant to suggest the subduing of physical nature by the workers and peasants and the productive power of the Soviet system. It may also symbolize the dominance of the Soviet Union over much of Europe since 1945. [Tass from Sovfoto.]

nomically and politically with each other as at no time in previous European experience. Peaceful economic integration and possible political unity became facts of everyday life. These same years also saw much of the Continent experience the most extensive material prosperity in its history. Even though the relative power of Europe has clearly declined since 1939, the Cold War rivalry, decolonization, the movement toward unity, and the economic growth have led to a continuing European influence elsewhere in the world.

Europe and the Soviet–American Rivalry

From approximately 1848 to 1948 the nation-state characterized European political life and rivalry. Generally these countries sought to expand their political influence and economic power at each other's expense. During the same century Europe's economic and technological supremacy allowed certain of its states to rule or administer a vast area of the globe inhabited by non-European peoples. These nation-states have obviously continued to exist, but the economic and political collapse occasioned by World War II led them to become more interrelated and interdependent. The loss of economic and military superiority coincided with and in some cases aided the rise of nationalism throughout the colonial world. The United States and the Soviet Union—with their extensive economic resources, military forces, and nuclear capacities—have filled the power vacuum created by the European collapse.

The new situation of Europe lying between two superpowers marked a genuine turning point in the history of the Continent. Prior to 1939 Great Britain, France, and Germany had been, in the context of the times, "world" powers. During the thirties even Italy through its ventures in Ethiopia had aspired to that position. By the onset of the 1960s it had become evident that all of these nations had become simply "European" powers and were no longer wholly independent states even in that

The "spirit of Geneva" is displayed in this picture
of the four major leaders who met there in the summer
of 1955 for a summit conference. From left to right
they are Nikolai Bulganin of the Soviet Union,
Dwight Eisenhower of the United States, Edgar Faure
of France, and Anthony Eden of Great Britain. [United
Press International Photo.]

position. The impact of the Marshall Plan and the nuclear deterrent power of America meant that the United States would exert a relatively permanent influence on Europe. There was to be no return to the isolationism that had characterized American policy after World War I. Europe as a whole, and more particularly Germany, became an arena for continuing confrontation and tension between the United States and the Soviet Union. The kind of direct and indirect power that European nations had once exerted elsewhere in the world was now being exercised over them.

The first round of Cold War confrontations culminated in the formation of NATO (1949) and the intervention of United States and United Nations forces in Korea (1950). In 1953 Stalin died, and later that year an armistice was concluded in Korea. Both events produced hope that international tensions might lessen. In early 1955 Austria agreed to become a neutral state, and Soviet occupation forces left. Later that year the leaders of France, Great Britain, the Soviet Union, and the United States held a summit conference at Geneva. Nuclear weapons and the future of divided Germany were the chief items on the agenda. Although there was much public display of friendliness among the participants, there were few substantial agreements on major problems. Nonetheless the fact that statesmen were discussing problems and issues produced the so-called "spirit of Geneva." This atmosphere proved short-lived, and the rivalry of power and polemics soon resumed.

The year 1956 was one of considerable significance for both the Cold War and the recognition of the realities of European power in the postwar era. In July President Gamal Nasser (1918–1970) of Egypt nationalized the Suez Canal. Great Britain and France feared that this action would close the canal to their supplies of oil in the Persian Gulf. In October 1956 war broke out between Egypt and the eight-year-old state of Israel. The British and the French seized the opportunity of this conflict to intervene. Publicly they spoke of acting to separate the combatants, but their real motive was to recapture the canal. The Anglo-French military operation was a fiasco of the first order and resulted in a humiliating diplomatic defeat. The United States refused to support their action. The Soviet Union protested in the most severe terms. The Anglo-French forces had to be withdrawn, and control of the canal remained with Egypt. The Suez intervention proved that without the support of the United States the nations of Western Europe could no longer undertake meaningful military operations. They could no longer impose their will on the rest of the world. At the same time, it appeared that the United States and the Soviet Union had acted to restrain allies from undertaking actions that might result in a wider conflict. The fact that neither of the superpowers wanted war put limitations on the actions of both Egypt and the Anglo-French forces.

The autumn of 1956 also saw important developments in Eastern Europe. These demonstrated in a similar fashion the limitations on independent action among the Soviet bloc nations. When the prime minister of Poland died, the Polish Communist Party leaders refused to choose as his successor the person selected by Moscow. Considerable tension developed. The Soviet leaders even visited Warsaw to make their opinions known. In the end Wladislav Gomulka (b. 1905) emerged as the new Communist leader of Poland. He was the choice of the Poles, and he proved acceptable to the Soviets because he promised continued economic and military cooperation. Within those limits he moved to halt collectivization of Polish agriculture and to improve the relationship between the Communist government and the Polish Roman Catholic Church.

Hungary provided the second trouble spot for the Soviet Union. In late October, as the Polish problem was approaching a solution, demonstrations and street fighting erupted in Budapest. A new government headed by former premier Imre Nagy (1896–1958) was installed. He was a communist who sought a more independent position for Hungary. He called for the removal of Soviet troops and the ultimate neutralization of Hungary. These

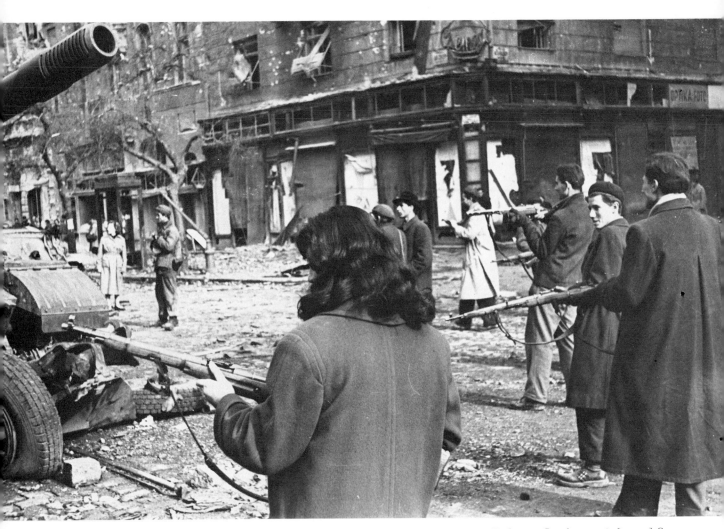

Budapest, October 1956. [ABOVE] Street battles raged for several days until Soviet tanks finally put down the Hungarian revolt. [LEFT] A woman carrying flowers and followed by a black flag leads a procession of mourners in an anti-Soviet demonstration in Marx Square. [BOTH: Raymond Darolle. Sygma.]

This passage is from President John F. Kennedy's speech at the time of the Berlin Wall crisis of 1961. He called for a democratic challenge to communism throughout the world. The commitment to Southeast Asia would later lead to the major war in Vietnam.

THE *immediate threat to free men is in West Berlin. But that isolated outpost is not an isolated problem. The threat is worldwide. Our effort must be equally wide and strong, and not be obsessed by any single manufactured crisis. We face a challenge in Berlin, but there is also a challenge in Southeast Asia, where the borders are less guarded, the enemy harder to find, and the dangers of Communism less apparent to those who have so little. We face a challenge in our own hemisphere, and indeed wherever else the freedom of human beings is at stake.*

Public Papers of the Presidents of the United States, John F. Kennedy. January 20 to December 31, 1961, ed. by Wayne C. Gover (Washington: U.S. Government Printing Office, 1962), pp. 533.

demands were wholly unacceptable to the Soviet Union. In early November Soviet troops invaded the country; deposed Nagy, who was later executed; and imposed Janos Kadar (b. 1912) as premier. The Suez intervention had provided an international diversion that helped to permit free action by the Soviet Union. The Polish and Hungarian disturbances had several results. They demonstrated the limitations of independence within the Soviet bloc, but they did not bring an end to independent action. They also demonstrated that the example of Austrian neutrality would not be imitated elsewhere in eastern Europe. Finally, the failure of the United States to take any action in the Hungarian uprising proved the hollowness of American political rhetoric about liberating the captive nations of eastern Europe.

The events of 1956 brought to a close the era of fully autonomous action by the European nation-states. In very different ways and to differing degrees the two superpowers had demonstrated the new political realities. After 1956 the Soviet Union began to talk about "peaceful coexistence" with the United States. In 1958 negotiations commenced between the two countries for limitations on the testing of nuclear weapons. However, that same year the Soviet Union announced that the status of West Berlin must be changed and the Allied occupation forces withdrawn. The demand was refused. In 1959 tensions relaxed sufficiently for several Western leaders to visit Moscow and for Soviet Premier Nikita Khrushchev (1894–1971) to tour the United States. A summit meeting was scheduled for May 1960, and American President Eisenhower was to go to Moscow.

The Paris Summit Conference of 1960 proved anything but a repetition of the friendly days of 1955. Just before the gathering, the Soviet Union shot down an American U-2 aircraft that was flying reconnaissance over Soviet territory. Khrushchev demanded an apology from President Eisenhower and aborted the summit conference as the participants arrived in the French capital. Eisenhower's trip to the Soviet Union never took place.

The Soviets had long been aware of the American flights but chose to protest at this time for two reasons. Khrushchev had hoped that the leaders of Britain, France, and the United States would be sufficiently divided over the future of Germany so that a united Allied front would be impossible. The divisions did not come about as he had hoped. Consequently the conference would have been of little use to him. Second, by 1960 the communist world itself had become split between the Soviets and the Chinese. The latter were portraying the Russians as lacking sufficient revolutionary zeal. Khrushchev's action was in part a response to those charges and proof of the hard-line attitude of the Soviet Union toward the capitalist world.

The abortive Paris conference opened the most difficult period of the Cold War. In 1961 the new U.S. president, John F. Kennedy, and Premier Khrushchev met in Vienna. The conference was inconclusive, but the American president left wondering if the two nations could avoid war. Throughout 1961 thousands of refugees from East Germany were crossing the border into West Berlin. This outflow was a political embarrassment to East Germany and a detriment to its economic life. In August 1961 the East Germans erected a concrete wall along the border between East and West Berlin. Henceforth it was possible to cross only at designated checkpoints and with proper papers. The United States protested and sent Vice President Lyndon Johnson to Berlin to reassure its citizens, but the wall remained—and does so to the present day. The refugee stream was halted, and the United States commitment to West Germany was brought into doubt.

A year later the most dangerous days of the Cold War occurred during the Cuban missile crisis. The Soviet Union attempted to place missiles in Cuba, which was a nation friendly to Soviet aims lying less than a hundred miles from the United States. The United States blockaded Cuba, halted the shipment of new missiles, and demanded the removal of existing installations. After a very tense week, with numerous threats and messages between Moscow and Washington, the crisis ended and the Soviets backed down.

The Cuban missile crisis was the last major Cold War confrontation that would have involved Europe directly. Thereafter the American–Soviet rivalry shifted to the war in Vietnam and the Arab–Israeli conflict in the Near East. A "hotline" communications system was installed between Moscow and Washington for more rapid and direct exchange of diplomatic messages in times of crisis.

In 1963 the two powers concluded a Nuclear Test Ban treaty. This agreement marked the beginning of a lessening in the tensions between the United States and the Soviet Union. The German problem somewhat subsided in the late sixties as West Germany under Premier Willy Brandt (b. 1913) moved to improve its relations with the Soviet Union and eastern Europe. In 1968 the Soviet Union invaded Czechoslovakia to prevent its emergence into further independence. Although deplored by the United States, this action led to no renewal of tensions. During the presidency of Richard Nixon (1969–1974) the United States embarked on a policy of detente or reduction of tension with the Soviet Union. This policy involved trade agreements and mutual reduction of strategic armaments. In 1975 President Gerald Ford attended a conference in Helsinki, Finland, that in effect recognized the Soviet sphere of influence in eastern Eu-

rope. The Helsinki Treaty also committed its signatory powers, including the Soviet Union, to recognize and protect the human rights of their citizens. The foreign policy of President Jimmy Carter has stressed the observance of these human rights clauses.

The late sixties and early seventies saw other changes in postwar relations between Europe and the United States. The NATO alliance became somewhat weaker as France moved to oppose United States influence over Europeans. The unpopularity of United States involvement in Vietnam strained its relations with NATO allies. Moreover the genuine possibility of Communist governments in Portugal and Italy after 1974 raised new questions about the strength and unity of NATO. During the late seventies the influence of the United States over Western Europe remained, but it was clear that the desires of Europeans as well as of Americans would have to be taken into greater account as policy was formulated for the future.

Decolonization and the Cold War
Retreat from Empire

At the onset of World War II many of the nations of Europe were still imperial powers. Great Britain, France, the Netherlands, Belgium, Italy, and Portugal governed millions of non-European peoples. One of the most striking and significant postwar developments has been the decolonization of these imperial holdings and the consequent emergence of the so-called Third World political bloc. The process of retreat from empire involved the colonial powers in three major stages of difficulties. The first was the turmoil created by nationalist movements and revolts in the colonies. The second was the injection of Cold War diplomacy and rivalries into the power vacuums formed by the European withdrawals. Finally, in recent years the control of important natural resources and particularly of oil by the new nations of the Third World has put considerable economic pressure on both Western Europe and the United States. This last condi-

MOROCCO 1956
ALGERIA 1962
TUNISIA, 1956
MALTA 1964
CYPRUS 1959
MAURITANIA 1960
SENEGAL, 1959
GAMBIA, 1965
GUINEA-BISS. 1974
MALI 1959
GUINEA 1958
SIERRA LEONE 1961
NIGER 1960
UPPER VOLTA 1960
LI-BERIA
IVORY COAST 1960
GHANA 1957
TOGO 1960
DAHOMEY 1960
NIGERIA 1960
LIBYA 1951
EGYPT
CHAD 1960
AFRICA
SUDAN 1956
CAMEROON 1960
EQ. GUINEA 1968
CENT. AFRICAN-REP. 1960
GABON 1960
CONGO 1960
ZAIRE 1960
YEMEN 1967
DJIBOUTI 1977
ETHIOPIA
SOUTH YEMEN 1967
SOMALIA 1960
UGANDA 1962
RWANDA 1962
BURUNDI 1962
KENYA 1963
TANZANIA, 1961
ANGOLA 1976
ZAMBIA 1964
MALAWI 1964
NAMIBIA
RHODESIA
MOZAMBIQUE 1974
MADAGASCAR 1960
MAURITIUS 1968
BOTSWANA 1966
SOUTH AFRICA
SWAZILAND 1968
LESOTHO 1965
BAHREIN 1971
UNITED ARAB EMIRATES 1971
QATAR 1971
KUWAIT 1961
OMAN 1977
PAKISTAN 1947
INDIA 1945
SRI LANKA 1948
MALDIVES 1965
BANG-LADESH 1973
BURMA 1948
LAOS 1954
KHMER 1954
VIETNAM 1954
SINGAPORE 1965
MALAYSIA 1963
PHILIPPINES 1946
INDONESIA 1950

EUROPE

ASIA

BEFORE 1950
1950 - 1959
1960 - 1969
AFTER 1970

T R MILLER

DECOLONIZATION SINCE WORLD WAR II

tion may well prove the most important factor in world politics for the remainder of this century.

The decolonization that has occurred since 1945 has been a direct result of both the war itself and the rise of indigenous nationalist movements within the European colonial world. The conflict drew the military forces of the colonial powers back to Europe. The Japanese conquests of Asia helped to turn out the European powers in that area. After the military and political dislocations of the war came the postwar economic collapse. The latter meant that the colonial powers could no longer afford to maintain their positions abroad.

Finally, the war aims of the Allies undermined colonialism. It was difficult to fight against tyranny in Europe while maintaining colonial dominance abroad. Moreover the postwar policy of the United States generally opposed continuation of European empires. Within the colonies there had also arisen nationalist movements of varying strengths. These were often led by gifted persons who had been educated in Europe. The values and political ideologies they had learned in Europe itself helped them to present effective critiques of the colonial situation. Such leadership, as well as the frequently blatant injustice

imposed upon colonial peoples, paved the way for effective nationalist movements.

There was a wide variety in decolonization. Some cases were relatively systematic; in others the European powers simply beat a hasty retreat. In 1947 Britain left India. The result of internal disputes, including religious differences, was the creation of two states, India and Pakistan. In 1948 Burma became independent. During the fifties the British attempted to prepare colonies for self-government. Ghana (formerly the Gold Coast) and Nigeria—which became self-governing in 1957 and 1960, respectively—were the major examples of planned decolonization. In other areas, such as Malta and Cyprus, the British withdrawal occurred under the pressure of militant nationalist movements.

The smaller colonial powers had much less choice. The Dutch were forced from Indonesia in 1950. In 1960 the Belgian Congo, now Zaire, became independent in the midst of great turmoil. For a considerable time, as will be seen, France attempted to maintain its position in Southeast Asia but met defeat in 1954. It was similarly driven from North Africa. President De Gaulle carried out a policy of referendums within remaining French colonial

Decolonization and the Cold War 939

possessions. By the late sixties only Portugal remained a traditional colonial power. In 1975 it finally abandoned its African colony of Angola.

The retreat from empire represents a major turning point in both European and world history. European and Western influences remain active in the former colonial world. Multinational corporations can and do exert considerable power over developing economies. The trade policies of the major Western industrial nations can do likewise. However, it now seems certain that in the future the command over natural resources possessed by these new nations will mean a considerable loss of independence by European and Western nations generally. At the end of the nineteenth century the technological power of Europe allowed certain nations to become colonial powers. At the close of the twentieth century the dependence of European industry and technology upon the resources of the underdeveloped world may very well mean that the former colonies will exert immense influence over the destiny of Europeans. The oil embargo of 1973 imposed on Europe by the oil-producing countries of the world demonstrated the potential for such powerful influence. The rest of this century will be largely devoted to the working out of this new economic balance. Although the political power of Europe will thus be lessened, the impact of its culture and of the technology originally developed in Europe will continue to expand as nations throughout the world continue to become westernized.

France, the United States, and Vietnam

So far as the general history of the West is concerned, the decolonization policies of France produced the major postwar upheavals. French decolonization became an integral part of the Cold War and led directly to the involvement of the United States in the Southeast Asian country of Vietnam. The problem of decolonization helped to transfer the Cold War rivalry that had developed in Europe to other continents. Nowhere did those rivalries become more intense than in Asia. Moreover, there was a close relationship between events in Asia and in Europe.

KOREA. To elucidate how the United States became so deeply involved in the French attempt to maintain its position in Vietnam, brief attention must first be given to the Korean War.

Between 1910 and 1945 Japan as an Asian colonial power in its own right occupied and exploited Korea. By the close of World War II the Japanese had been driven out of the Korean peninsula. At home, under the direction of the United States, the Japanese nation was politically reconstructed into a democracy. The influence of the army and of large business combines was reduced. Women were allowed to vote, and representative institutions were imposed. General Douglas MacArthur was the representative of the United States during this crucial period. Maintenance of a democratic Japan was to be a cornerstone of postwar United States policy.

The Japanese empire still had to be dealt with. Consequently the United States and the Soviet Union presided over the division of Korea into two parts with the thirty-eighth parallel as the line of separation. It was anticipated that the country would eventually be reunited. However, by 1948 two separate states had been organized: the Democratic People's Republic of Korea under Kim Il-sung in the north and the Republic of Korea under Syngman Rhee in the south. The former was supported by the Soviet Union and the latter by the United States.

Numerous border clashes occurred between the two states. In late June 1950 forces from North Korea crossed the thirty-eighth parallel. The United States intervened and was soon supported by the mandate of the United Nations. Great Britain, Turkey, and Australia sent token forces. The troops were commanded by General MacArthur. The Korean police action was technically a United Nations venture to halt aggression. (It had been made possible by a boycott of the Soviet ambassador to the United Nations at the time of the key vote.) From the standpoint of the United States the point of the Korean conflict was to contain the spread and to halt the

The North Korean invasion of South Korea in 1950 and the bitter three-year war to repulse the invasion and stabilize a firm boundary near the thirty-eighth parallel are outlined here. The war was a dramatic application of the American policy of "containment" of communism.

KOREA,
1950–1953

aggression of communism. The United States policy makers tended to conceive of the communist world as a single unit directed from Moscow. The movement of forces into South Korea was simply another example of communist pressure against a noncommunist state similar to that previously confronted in Europe.

General MacArthur's forces had initially repelled the North Koreans. He then pushed them almost to Manchuria. Late in 1950, however, the Chinese, responding to the pressure against their border, sent troops to support North Korea. The American forces had to retreat. The United States policymakers believed that the Chinese, who since 1949 had been under the communist government of Mao Tse-tung (1893–1976), were simply the puppets of Moscow. For over two years the war bogged down. Eventually a border near the thirty-eighth parallel was restored. The war lasted until June 26, 1953, when an armistice was signed. In Korea limited military action had halted and contained the military advance of a communist nation. The lessons of the Cold War learned in Europe had been successfully applied to Asia. The American government was confirmed in its faith in a policy of containment.

VIETNAM. During the years of the Korean conflict another war was being fought in Asia between France and the Viet Minh nationalist movement in Indochina. France, in its push for empire, had occupied this territory, including Laos, Cambodia, and Vietnam, between 1857 and 1883. It had administered the area and invested heavily in it, but the economy of Indochina remained overwhelmingly agrarian. During World War I tens of thousands of Indochinese troops supported France. The French also educated many people from the colony. However, neither the aid during the war nor the achievement of Western education allowed the Vietnamese to escape discrimination from their French colonial rulers. By the time of World War II, resistance to French government had developed in Vietnam.

By 1930 a movement against French colonial rule had been organized by Ho Chi Minh (1892–1969) into the

Indochinese Communist Party. Ho had traveled throughout the world and had held jobs in several places in Europe prior to World War I. He and other Indochinese had lobbied at the Versailles Conference in 1919 to have the principle of self-determination applied to their country. In 1920 he was part of the wing of the French Socialist Party that formed the French Communist Party. In 1923 he was sent to Moscow. By 1925 he had formed the Vietnam Revolutionary Youth. After organizing the

Indochinese Communist Party, he traveled in Asia and spent considerable time in the Soviet Union. Throughout the thirties, however, the French succeeded in suppressing most activities by the Communist Party in their colony.

World War II provided new opportunities for Ho Chi Minh and other nationalists. When Japan invaded, it found the pro-Vichy French colonial administration ready to collaborate. Consequently action against the Japanese thereafter meshed quite neatly with action against the French. It was during these wartime circumstances that Ho Chi Minh established his position as a major nationalist leader. He was a Communist to be sure, but he was first and foremost a nationalist. Most important, he had achieved his position in Vietnam during the war independent of the support of the Chinese Communist movement.

In September 1945 Ho Chi Minh declared the independence of Vietnam under the Viet Minh. There was considerable internal Vietnamese resistance to this claim of political control. The opposition arose from religious groups and noncommunist nationalists. After the war the French immediately took advantage of these divisions to establish a government favorable to their own interests. The United States, in line with its wartime anticolonialist position, urged the French to make some kind of accommodation with Ho Chi Minh. In 1946 France and the Viet Minh reached an armistice. It proved quite temporary, and in 1947 full-fledged war broke out. The next year the French established a friendly Vietnamese government under Bao Dai. It was to be independent within a loose union with France. This arrangement would have meant very limited independence and was clearly unacceptable to both the Viet Minh and most other nationalists.

Until 1949 the United States had displayed only the most minimal concern in the Indochina War. However, the defeat in China of Chiang Kai-shek (1887–1975) in 1949 and the victors' establishment of the communist People's Republic of China changed that situation dra-matically. This turn of events led the United States to regard the French colonial war against Ho Chi Minh as a integral part of the Cold War conflict. The French government, hoping for United States support, worked to maintain that point of view. Early in 1950 the United States recognized the Bao Dai government. At approximately the same time the Soviet Union and the People's Republic of China recognized the governement of Ho Chi Minh. Indochina was thus transformed from a colonial battleground into an area of Cold War confrontation.

In May 1950 the United States announced that it would supply financial aid to the French war effort. Between that time and 1954 more than $4 billion flowed from the United States to France. However, the war itself deteriorated for the French. In the spring of 1954 their army was overrun by the Viet Minh forces at the battle of Dien Bien Phu. Psychologically and militarily the French could not muster new energy for the war. Pierre Mendès-France (b. 1907) was elected premier in Paris on the promise of concluding the conflict. At this point the United States government was badly divided, but it decided against military intervention.

During the late spring and early summer of 1954 a conference was held at Geneva to settle the Indochina conflict. All in all it proved a most unsatisfactory gathering. To one degree or another, all of the major powers were involved in the proceedings, but they did not sign the agreements. Technically the agreements existed between the armed forces of France and those of the Viet Minh. The precedents for such arrangements were the surrender of the German army in 1945 and the Korean armistice of 1953. The Geneva conference provided for the division of Vietnam at the seventeenth parallel. This was to be a temporary border. By 1956 elections were to be held to reunify the country. North of the parallel, centered on the city of Hanoi, the Viet Minh were in charge; below it, the French were in charge, with Saigon the major city. The prospect of elections meant that theoretically both groups could function politically in the

The Southeast Asia scene of the long and complex struggle centered in Vietnam is shown by the map.

VIETNAM AND ITS NEIGHBORS

territory of the other. In effect, the conference attempted to transform a military conflict into a political one.

The United States was less than happy about the results of the Geneva discussions. Its first major response came in September 1954, with the formation of the Southeast Asia Treaty Organization (SEATO). It was a collective security agreement that in some respects paralleled the European NATO alliance. However, it did not involve the integration of forces achieved in NATO, nor did it include all the major states of the region. Its membership consisted of the United States, Great Britain, France, Australia, New Zealand, Thailand, Pakistan, and the Philippines.

By 1955 American policy makers had begun to think about the Indochina region, and more especially Vietnam, largely in terms of the Korean example. The United States government assumed that the government being established in North Vietnam was, like the government of North Korea, basically a communist puppet state. The same year French troops began to withdraw from the south. As they left, the various Vietnamese political groups began to fight for power. Into the turmoil of the power vacuum stepped the United States with military and economic aid. Among the Vietnamese politicians, it chose to support Ngo Dinh Diem. He was a strong noncommunist nationalist who had not collaborated with the French. The Americans hoped that he would become a leader around whom a noncommunist Vietnamese nationalist movement might rally. However, because the United States had publicly been deeply committed to the French, any government it supported would be and was viewed with suspicion by Vietnamese nationalists. In October 1955 Diem established a Republic of Vietnam in the territory for which the Geneva conference had made France responsible. By 1956 the United States was training troops and government officials, paying salaries, and providing military equipment.

In the meantime Diem announced that he and his newly established government were not bound by the Geneva agreements and that elections would not be held in 1956. The American government, which had not signed the Geneva documents, supported his position. Diem undertook an anticommunist campaign, attacking many citizens who had earlier resisted the French. This was the beginning of a program of political repression that characterized his regime and those that followed. There was a long series of ordinances that gave the government extraordinary power over its citizens. Diem alienated the peasants by restoring rents to landlords and generally strengthening large landowners. He abolished elected village councils and replaced them with his own officials, who had often come from the north. In fact, Diem's major base of political support lay with the more

Soldiers of the United States equipped with sophisticated weapons examine a Viet Cong guerilla booby trap in Vietnam. One of the great frustrations of the war for the Americans was the ability of relatively simple guerilla tactics of sabotage to slow or even halt altogether technologically advanced American operations. [Official United States Navy Photograph.]

than one million Vietnamese who had migrated to the south after 1954.

By 1960 Diem's policy had created considerable internal resistance in South Vietnam. In that year the National Liberation Front was founded, with the goals of overthrowing Diem, unifying the country, reforming the economy, and ousting the Americans. It was anticolonial, nationalist, and communist. Its military arm was called the Viet Cong. Sometime in the very late fifties the government of North Vietnam began to aid the insurgent forces of the south. The Viet Cong and their supporters carried out a program of widespread terrorism and political disruption. They imposed an informal government through much of the countryside. Many peasants voluntarily supported them; others supported them from fear of reprisals. In addition to the communist opposition, Diem confronted mounting criticism from noncommunist citizens. The Buddhists agitated against the Roman Catholic president. The army was less than satisfied with him. Diem's response to all of these pressures was further repression and dependence on an ever smaller group of advisers.

The Eisenhower and early Kennedy administrations in America continued to support Diem while demanding reforms. The American military presence grew from somewhat more than six hundred persons in early 1961 to over sixteen thousand troops in late 1963. The political situation in Vietnam became increasingly unstable. On November 1, 1963, Diem was overthrown and murdered in an army *coup*. The United States was deeply involved in this plot. Its officials hoped that if the Diem regime were eliminated, the path would be opened for the establishment of a new government in South Vietnam capable of generating popular support. Thereafter the political goal of the United States was to find a leader who could fill this need. It finally settled on Nguyen Van Thieu, who governed South Vietnam from 1966 to 1975.

President Kennedy was assassinated on November 22, 1963. His successor, Lyndon Johnson, continued and vastly expanded the commitment to South Vietnam. In

August 1964, after an attack on an American ship in the Gulf of Tonkin, the first bombing of North Vietnam was authorized. In February 1965 major bombing attacks began that continued with only brief pauses until the early weeks of 1973. The land war grew in extent, with over 500,000 Americans stationed in South Vietnam. In 1969 President Richard Nixon commenced a policy of gradual withdrawal of troops. The program was called *Vietnamization*. From the spring of 1968 onwards long-drawn-out peace negotiations were conducted in Paris. In January 1973 a cease-fire was finally arranged. The troops of the United States were pulled back, and prisoners of war held in North Vietnam were returned. Thereafter violations of the cease-fire occurred on both sides. In early 1975 an evacuation of South Vietnamese troops from the northern part of their country turned into a complete rout. On April 30, 1975 the city of Saigon fell to the troops of the Viet Cong and North Vietnam. The Second Indochina war had come to an end.

The Second Indochina War, which was in effect a continuation of the first war, which the French had lost, was an event of immense controversy and complexity. It was widely debated throughout the world at the time and will continue to be debated for many years. The United States saw the conflict as part of the Cold War and as a repetition of Korea. Aggression from the north had to be halted. There was also hope that the military power of the United States might buy time so that a strong nationalist, noncommunist regime could be established in South Vietnam. However, the United States misread the situation in Vietnam and especially its superficial resemblance to what had taken place in Korea. The United States ignored the basic colonial character of the Vietnamese political scene. It also overlooked the larger size of Vietnam, the different topography, the weakness of the South Vietnamese army, and the corruption of the government of South Vietnam.

The war grew out of a power vacuum left by decolonization. It produced a major impact on all the Western world. For a decade after the Cuban missile crisis the attention of the United States was largely diverted from Europe. American prestige suffered, and the American commitment to Western Europe came into question. Moreover the blundering of American policy in Southeast Asia made many Europeans wonder about the basic wisdom of the American government. Many young Europeans—and not a few Americans—born after World War II came to consider the United States not as a protector of liberty but as an ambitious, aggressive, and cruel power trying to keep colonialism alive after the end of the colonial era. The American involvement in Vietnam probably proved fundamental to the emergence of a new commitment to unity and economic integration in Europe. That involvement allowed Europeans still living in the shadow of American power and influence to reassert their own independence and to strike out in new directions.

Toward West-European Unification

Since 1945 the nations of Western Europe have taken unprecedented steps toward cooperation and potential unity. The idea of a single Europe is as old as Latin Christendom and as recent as the military exploits of Napoleon and Hitler. However, what has occurred since World War II fits into none of these patterns. The steps toward unification have related primarily to economic integration. These moves have arisen from American encouragement, in response to the Soviet domination of Eastern Europe, and from a sense of lack of effective political power by the states of Western Europe. The process of integration has not been steady, nor is it near completion, but it has provided a major factor in the domestic politics of the states involved.

The Marshall Plan of the United States created the Organization for European Economic Cooperation. It was a vehicle set up to require common planning and cooperation among the participating countries and to discourage a return to the prewar economic nationalism. The OEEC and later NATO gave the countries involved new experience working with each other and demonstrated the productivity, the efficiency, and the simple possibility of cooperative action. Although neither organization provided a means for political or economic integration, the experience was most important.

The movement toward unity could have occurred in at least three ways: politically, militarily, or economically. In 1949 ten European states organized the Council of Europe, which meets in Strasbourg, France. Its organization involved foreign ministers and a Consultative Assembly elected by the parliaments of the participants. The Council of Europe was and continues to be only an advisory body. It had been hoped by some persons that the council might become a parliament of Europe, but during the early fifties none of the major states was willing to surrender any of its sovereignty to the newly organized body. The initial failure of the council to bring about significant political cooperation meant that for the time being unity would not come about by political or parliamentary routes.

Between 1950 and 1954 there was some interest in a more thorough integration of the military forces of NATO. When the Korean War broke out, the United States began to urge the rearmament of Germany. The German forces would provide Western Europe with further protection against possible Soviet aggression while the United States was involved in Korea. France continued to fear a German army. In 1951 the French government suggested the creation of a European Defense Community that would constitute a supranational military organization. It would require a permanent British commitment of forces to the Continent to help France, in effect, counter any future German threat. The proposal continued to be considered for some time, but in 1954 the French Parliament itself vetoed the program. In 1955 Germany was permitted to rearm and to enter NATO. Supranational military organization had not been achieved.

Rather than in politics or the military the major moves toward European cooperation and potential unity came in the economic sphere. Unlike the other two possible paths of cooperation, economic activity involved little or no immediate loss of political sovereignty. Moreover the material benefits of combined economic activity would bring new popular support to all of the governments involved. Among European leaders and civil servants there existed a large body of opinion that only through the abandonment of economic nationalism could the newly organized democratic states avoid the economic turmoil that had proved such fertile ground for dictator-

The European Economic Community Is Established

The 1957 Treaty of Rome identified the major goals of the European Economic Community (Common Market) for the six (later nine) members.

ARTICLE 2: *It shall be the aim of the Community, by establishing a Common Market and progressively approximating the economic policies of Member States, to promote throughout the Community a harmonious development of economic activities, a continuous and balanced expansion, an increased stability, an accelerated raising of the standard of living and closer relations between its Member States.*

ARTICLE 3: *For the purposes set out in the preceding Article, the activities of the Community shall include, under the conditions and with the timing provided for in this Treaty:*

(a) the elimination, as between Member States, of customs duties and of quantitative restrictions in regard to the importation and exportation of goods, as well as of all other measures with equivalent effect;

(b) the establishment of a common customs tariff and a common commercial policy towards third countries;

(c) the abolition, as between Member States, of the obstacles to the free movement of persons, services and capital;

(d) the inauguration of a common agricultural policy;

(e) the inauguration of a common transport policy;

(f) the establishment of a system ensuring that competition shall not be distorted in the Common Market;

(g) the application of procedures which shall make it possible to co-ordinate the economic policies of Member States and to remedy disequilibria in their balances of payments;

(h) the approximation of their respective municipal law to the extent necessary for the functioning of the Common Market;

(i) the creation of a European Social Fund in order to improve the possibilities of employment for workers and to contribute to the raising of their standard of living;

(j) the establishment of a European Investment Bank intended to facilitate the economic expansion of the Community through the creation of new resources; and

(k) the association of overseas countries and territories with the Community with a view to increasing trade and to pursuing jointly their effort towards economic and social development.

Treaty Establishing the European Economic Community (Brussels: Secretariat of the Interim Committee for the Common Market and Euratom, 1957), pp. 17–18.

ship. Economic cooperation carried the possibility of greater efficiency, prosperity, and employment. The leading figures holding these opinions were Robert Schuman (1886–1963), the foreign minister of France; Konrad Adenauer (1876–1967), the chancellor of the Federal Republic of Germany; Alcide De Gasperi (1881–1954), the prime minister of Italy; and Paul-Henri Spaak (1899–1972), the prime minister of Belgium. Among major civil servants and bureaucrats, Jean Monnet (b. 1885) of France was the leading spokesman.

In 1950 Schuman proposed that the coal and steel production of Western Europe be undertaken on an integrated, cooperative basis. The next year France, West Germany, Italy, and the "Benelux" countries (Belgium, the Netherlands, and Luxembourg) organized the European Coal and Steel Community. Its activity was limited to a single part of the economy, but that was a sector that affected practically all other industrial production. An agency called the High Authority administered the plan. The authority was genuinely supranational, and its members could not be removed during their appointed terms. The Coal and Steel Community prospered. By 1955 coal production had grown by 23 per cent. Iron and steel production was up by almost 150 per cent. The community both benefited from and contributed to the immense growth of material production in Western Europe during this period. Its success reduced the suspicions of government and business groups about the concept of coordination and economic integration.

It took more than the prosperity of the European Coal and Steel Community to draw European leaders toward further unity. The unsuccessful Suez intervention and the resulting diplomatic isolation of France and Britain persuaded many Europeans that only through unified action could they exert any significant influence on the two superpowers or control their own destinies. Consequently, in 1957, through the Treaty of Rome, the six members of the Coal and Steel Community agreed to form a new organization. It was the European Economic Community. The *Common Market*, as the EEC soon

THE COMMON MARKET

The single most important development since World War II looking toward peaceful European cooperation and unity has been the Common Market, which by 1973 included the nine states shown here. Partly overlapping the Common Market is the European Free Trade Area. Greece is to become a Common Market member in 1981, and Spain and Portugal will probably be seeking membership thereafter.

Konrad Adenauer of West Germany and Charles De Gaulle of France were the two major West European statesmen of the late 1950s and early 1960s. They pursued policies of reconciliation between their two nations and a policy of a more nearly united Europe based on the Common Market. [United Press International Photo.]

came to be called, envisioned more than a free-trade union. Its members sought to achieve eventual elimination of tariffs, free flow of capital and labor, and similar wage and social benefits in all participating countries. Its chief institutions were a Council of Foreign Ministers and a High Commission composed of technocrats. The former came to be the dominant body.

The problems of the world-wide noncommunist economy are discussed by the participants in a summit conference in Bonn, West Germany, in July 1978. Here are (from left to right) Prime Minister Fukuda of Japan; President Carter of the United States; Prime Ministers Callaghan, Trudeau, and Andreotti of Great Britain, Canada, and Italy; President Giscard d'Estaing of France; and Chancellor Schmidt of West Germany. [United Press International Photo.]

The Common Market achieved a stunning degree of success during its early years. By 1968 all tariffs among the six members had been abolished well ahead of the planned schedule. Trade and labor migration among the members grew steadily. Moreover nonmember states began to copy the community and later to seek membership. In 1959 Britain, Denmark, Norway, Sweden, Switzerland, Austria, and Portugal formed the European Free Trade Area. However, by 1961 Great Britain had decided to seek Common Market membership. Twice, in 1963 and 1967, British membership was vetoed by President De Gaulle of France. The French president felt that Britain was too closely related to the United States and its policies to support the European Economic Community wholeheartedly.

The French veto of British membership demonstrated the major difficulty confronting the Common Market during the sixties. The Council of Ministers, representing the individual national interests of member states, came to have more influence than the High Commission. Political as well as economic factors increasingly entered into decision making. France particularly was unwilling to compromise on any matter that it regarded as pertaining to its sovereignty. On more than one occasion President De Gaulle demanded his own policies and refused French participation under any other conditions. This attitude caused major problems over agricultural policy.

Despite the French actions the Common Market survived and continued to prosper. In 1973 Great Britain, Ireland, and Denmark became members. Discussions continue on further steps toward integration, including a common currency. The future for the EEC may well be filled with difficulties, but there is little doubt that it will continue to be one of the major economic units of the world. The full ramifications of economic integration still remain to be seen, but the direction for the rest of this century will be almost certainly toward greater unity.

Internal Political Developments in Western Europe

After the war, with the exceptions of Portugal and Spain, which remained dictatorships until the mid-1970s, the nations of Western Europe continued to pursue the path of liberal democracy. But their leaders realized that the prewar democratic political structures alone had been insufficient to ensure peace, stability, material prosperity, and domestic liberty for their peoples. It had become clear that democracy required a social and economic base as well as a political structure. Economic prosperity and social security in the eyes of most Europeans became a duty of government as a way of staving off the kind of turmoil that had brought on tyranny and war. They also regarded such programs as a means of avoiding communism.

Except for the British Labor Party the vehicles of the new postwar politics were not, as might have been expected, the democratic socialist parties. On the whole those parties did not prosper after the onset of the Cold War. They stood opposed by both communists and groups more conservative than themselves. Rather the new departures were led by various Christian Democratic parties, usually leading coalition governments. These Christian Democratic political parties were a major new feature of postwar politics. They were largely Roman Catholic in leadership and membership. Catholic parties had previously existed in Europe. But from the late nineteenth century through the 1930s they had been very conservative and had tended to protect the social, political, and educational interests of the church. They had traditionally opposed communism but had few positive programs of their own. The postwar Christian Democratic parties of Germany, France, and Italy were progressive. They accepted democracy and advocated social reform. They welcomed non-Catholics to membership. Democracy, social reform, economic growth, and anti-communism were their hallmarks. Only in the late sixties were those goals seriously challenged or questioned.

The events of the war years in large measure determined the political leadership of the postwar decade. On the continent those groups and parties which had been active in the resistance against Nazis and fascism held an initial advantage. Until the Prague *coup* of 1948 those groups frequently included the Communist Party. Thereafter communists were quite systematically excluded from all Western European governments. This policy was quite naturally favored and encouraged by the United States. The immediate domestic problems after the war included not only those created by the physical damage of the conflict but often those that had existed in 1939. The war in most cases had not solved those prewar difficulties, but it had often opened new opportunities or possibilities for solution.

Great Britain: Power in Decline

In July 1945 the British electorate overwhelmingly voted for a Labor Party government. For the first time the Labor Party commanded in its own right a majority of the House of Commons. Clement Attlee (1883–1967) replaced Churchill as prime minister. The British had not so much rejected the great wartime leader as they had renounced the Conservative Party, which had in effect governed since 1931. In the public mind the Conservatives were associated with the economic problems of the thirties. For purposes of postwar reconstruction and redirection the Labor Party seemed to have a better program.

Attlee's ministry was socialist but clearly non-Marxist. It made a number of bold departures in both economic and social policy. The government nationalized major industries, including the Bank of England, the airlines, public transport, coal, electricity, and steel. The ministry also undertook a major housing program. Probably its most popular accomplishment was the establishment of a major program of welfare legislation. This involved further unemployment assistance, old-age pensions, school lunches, and, most important, free medical service to all citizens. All of these departures were expensive, and immediate postwar economic recovery was slow. By the

The British Labor Party Issues a Cautious Platform

The Labor Party was committed to a program of socialism in 1945. However, its platform of that year made clear that the party would move cautiously in carrying out its policy. Both the commitment to social change and the promise of caution proved attractive to the electorate, with the result that Labor came to power.

By the *test of war some industries have shown themselves capable of rising to new heights of efficiency and expansion. Others, including some of our older industries fundamental to our economic structure, have wholly or partly failed. . . .*

Each industry must have applied to it the test of national service. If it serves the nation, well and good; if it is inefficient and falls down on its job, the nation must see that things are put right.

These propositions seem indisputable, but for years before the war anti-Labour Governments set them aside, so that British industry over a large field fell into a state of depression, muddle and decay. Millions of working and middle-class people went through the horrors of unemployment and insecurity. It is not enough to sympathise with these victims: we must develop an acute feeling of national shame—and act.

The Labour Party is a Socialist Party, and proud of it. Its ultimate purpose at home is the establishment of the Socialist Commonwealth of Great Britain—free, democratic, efficient, progressive, public-spirited, its material resources organised in the service of the British people.

But Socialism cannot come overnight, as the product of a week-end revolution. The members of the Labour Party, like the British people, are practical-minded men and women.

There are basic industries ripe and over-ripe for public ownership and management in direct service of the nation. There are many smaller businesses rendering good service which can be left to go on with their useful work.

There are big industries not yet ripe for public ownership which must nevertheless be required by constructive supervision to further the nation's needs and not to prejudice national interests by restrictive anti-social monopoly or cartel agreements—caring for their own capital structures and profits at the cost of a lower standard of living for all.

Let Us Face the Future, cited in J. F. C. Harrison, *Society and Politics in England, 1780–1960* (New York: Harper and Row, 1965), pp. 450–451.

close of 1948 the drive toward further social reform had come to a halt. During the next several years the Labor Party itself became badly divided between one wing that advocated more socialism and government services and another that contended that the nation could for the time being afford few or no new programs.

The forward domestic policy of the Labor government was matched by a policy of gradual retreat on the world scene. In 1947 the enunciation of the Truman Doctrine in regard to Greece and Turkey marked the British admission that it could not afford to oversee the security of those areas. In the same year Britain recognized the independence of Pakistan and India. In the postwar era Britain would be repeatedly confronted by nationalist movements within the empire and would gradually and usually gracefully retreat from those outposts. In 1949 the government devalued the pound sterling from $4.03 to $2.80. The once-strong economy was clearly in trouble; the nation could earn insufficient foreign exchange from its exports to pay for its imports. The military, imperial, and economic power that had once made Britain the foremost of European nations had eroded and would continue to do so for the next three decades.

In 1951 the Conservative Party under Churchill returned to office and remained there until 1964. This was the longest period of continuous government by any party in modern British history. Internal Labor Party divisions contributed to this development, but so did the policies of the Conservatives. Under Churchill and then under his successors, Anthony Eden in 1955–1957, Harold Macmillan in 1957–1963, and Alec Douglas-Home in 1963–1964, the Conservatives attempted to draw a picture of major differences between themselves and the Labor Party. In reality, the differences were ones of degree rather than of kind. The Conservative government did denationalize steel, but it did not return to a free economy. The program of national welfare and health services continued, and the Conservatives actually undertook a building program larger than that of the Labor Party.

Wrecked ships were strewn throughout the Suez Canal after the Franco-British attack of 1956. [United Press International Photo.]

The problem of decline of power and prestige continued. From the mid-fifties onward one part of the empire after another became independent. The Suez intervention of 1956 brought an end to independent British military intervention. Increasingly British policy was made subservient to that of the United States. However, the economy constituted the most persistent difficulty. Throughout the decade the slogan "Export or die" was heard. Exports did grow rapidly, yet more slowly than imports. Productivity remained discouragingly low. British unions were old-fashioned and less forward-looking than those on the Continent. Management was quite timid. Perhaps most important, there was a low rate of capital investment in both privately and nationally owned industries. The trade unions were often more interested in carving up existing wealth than in creating new wealth to be distributed. The government too often favored economic programs that were not aimed at long-term growth.

In 1964 the Labor Party returned to office under Harold Wilson. It promised to right the economic situation, but the economy only worsened. The pound was devalued further. Wilson renewed the attempt to join the Common Market, which Macmillan had begun in 1963. Labor, like the Conservatives, confronted the veto of France. In 1970 the electorate again turned to the Conservative Party, then led by Edward Heath. His major accomplishment was to take Britain into the Common Market in 1973. However, domestically Heath floundered badly in his dealings with the trade unions. The country suffered a crippling coal strike in the winter of 1973-1974.

In 1974 Wilson returned to office, primarily on the grounds that the Labor Party might have better relations with the unions. The Labor government was able to reach some agreements on limitations for pay raises. Still inflation raged and in 1976 the value of the pound sterling dipped below $1.60. The same year Wilson voluntarily resigned and was replaced by James Callaghan. In 1975 Margaret Thatcher had replaced Heath as leader of the Conservative Party. The future political direction of the nation remains unclear, as does its economic situation. The discovery of oil in the North Sea off Scotland may well give new strength to the economy.

In addition to the gravest economic situation in the Western world, Britain has also had to confront in recent years a major internal disturbance in Northern Ireland. By the treaty of 1921 the Ulster counties remained a part of the United Kingdom while retaining a large measure of self-government. The Protestant majority used its power to discriminate systematically against the Roman Catholic minority in the province. In 1968 a Catholic civil rights movement was launched. Demonstrations and counterdemonstrations resulted. Units of the Provisional Wing of the Irish Republican Army became active in seeking to unite Ulster with the Irish Republic. In turn militant Protestant organizations became mobilized. The British government sent in units of the army to restore order. Soon the army units became the target of both groups of militant Irish. Thus far the troops remain, and well over thirteen hundred people have been killed in terrorist activity. A peaceful solution has not yet proved forthcoming.

West Germany: The Economic Miracle

No country in Europe since the war has so contrasted with Britain as the Federal Republic of Germany. The nation was organized in 1949 from the three Western Allied occupation sectors. Its amazing material progress from the ruins of the conflict has become known as the economic miracle of postwar Europe. Between 1948 and 1964 West German industrial production grew by 600 per cent. Unemployment became practically unknown. All of this time the country remained the center of Cold War disputes and was occupied by thousands of foreign troops. In the midst of Cold War tensions the Germans prospered.

The economic growth of the nation stemmed from a number of favorable factors. The Marshall Plan provided an initial impetus to recovery. The government of the republic throughout the fifties and sixties pursued a policy of giving private industry a relatively free hand while providing sufficient planning to avoid economic crisis. The goods produced by Germany proved attractive to the customers of other nations. *Volkswagen* became a household word throughout the world. Moreover domestic demand was vigorous, and skilled labor and energetic management were available. The war had destroyed vast amounts of equipment. The replacements could employ the most advanced technology. Finally, Germany had very few foreign commitments or responsibilities. A relatively small portion of its national income had to be spent on defense. This situation aided capital formation.

In a very real sense postwar West Germany indulged in economic expansion rather than in politics or active international policy. Unlike the Weimar Constitution, the constitution of the Federal Republic did not permit the proliferation of splinter parties. Nor did the president possess extraordinary power. The Federal Republic returned to the arena of nations very slowly. In 1949 it participated in the Marshall Plan and two years later in the European Coal and Steel Community. In 1955 the nation joined NATO, and in 1957 it was one of the charter members of the European Economic Community. The Federal Republic has been perhaps the major champion of European cooperation.

Throughout this period political initiative lay with the Christian Democrats led by Konrad Adenauer. His policies were relatively simple and consistent. West Germany must become genuinely democratic and economically stable and prosperous. His foreign policy was profoundly anticommunist. Under what was known as the Hallstein Doctrine, the Federal Republic refused to have diplomatic ties with any nation, except the Soviet Union, that extended diplomatic recognition to East Germany. Adenauer's position on East Germany contributed to the Cold War climate, and it may have led the United States to overestimate the threat of communist aggression in Europe. The Hallstein Doctrine separated the Federal Republic from all the nations of Eastern Europe.

Few sights better illustrate the astounding economic recovery of Europe after 1945 than the contrast between these two views of Berlin. The ghostly picture [ABOVE] shows the heavy destruction caused by the intense wartime bombing of the city. The contrasting photograph [BELOW] shows the rebuilt center of West Berlin that emerged in the following decade. Only the ruins of the Emperor William I Memorial Church were left as they stood to serve as a permanent monument and a reminder of war's destruction. [ABOVE: United Press International Photo; BELOW: German Information Center, New York.]

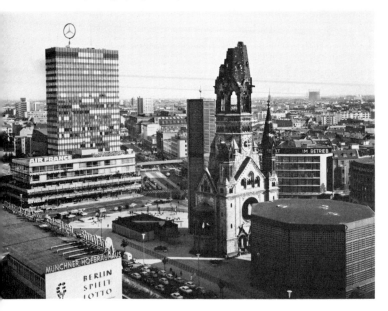

Adenauer remained in office until 1963, when he retired at the age of eighty-seven. The Christian Democrats remained in power, led first by Ludwig Erhard and later by Kurt Kiesinger. In 1966, however, they were compelled to form a coalition with the Social Democrats (SDP). After the war this party had revived but had been unable to capture a parliamentary majority. By the early sixties the SDP had expanded their base beyond the working class and had become more a party of social and economic reform than a party of socialism. This shift reflected the growing prosperity of the German working class. The major leader of the SDP in the sixties was Willy Brandt, the mayor of West Berlin. In 1966 he became vice-chancellor in the coalition government. In 1969 Brandt and the SDP carried the election in their own right.

In one of the most moving events of Willy Brandt's effort to improve German relations with the states of eastern Europe, the German chancellor knelt at the memorial to Warsaw Jews killed by the Germans during World War II. He was in Poland in December 1970 to sign a treaty that would lead to regular diplomatic relations between the two countries. [United Press International Photo.]

The most significant departure of the SDP occurred in the area of foreign policy. While continuing to urge further Western unity through the Common Market, Brandt moved carefully but swiftly to establish better relations with eastern Europe (*Ostpolitik*). In 1970 he met with the leadership of East Germany. Later that year he went to Moscow to sign a treaty of cooperation. By November 1970 Brandt had completed a reconciliation treaty with Poland that recognized the Oder-Neisse River line as the Polish western border. A treaty with Czechoslovakia soon followed. In 1973 both the Federal Republic of Germany and the German Democratic Republic were admitted to the United Nations. Brandt's policy of *Ostpolitik* to a large extent regularized the German situation, but that regularity will probably remain only so long as the two superpowers desire it. Brandt's moves were in part a subdevelopment of the policy of detente on the part of the United States and the Soviet Union. In 1974 Brandt resigned. His successor was Helmut Schmidt.

France: Search for Stability and Glory

France experienced the most troubled postwar domestic political scene of any major European nation. The Third Republic had been in very deep difficulty in 1939. It had come to satisfy neither the left nor the right of the political world. More important, the republic had been incapable of staving off military defeat. To these inherited problems was added after the war the fact of wide-scale collaboration with the Nazi conquerors. A few trials, executions, and prison sentences superficially handled the problem of the Vichy collaborators, but much bitterness remained.

After the defeat of 1940 a little-known general named Charles De Gaulle (1890–1970) had organized a free French government in London. In 1944 De Gaulle presided over the provisional government in liberated France. He was an immensely proud, patriotic person who seemed to regard himself as personally embodying the spirit of France. He had a low regard for traditional liberal democratic politics and hated the machinations of political parties, which he thought unnecessarily divided the nation. In 1946 De Gaulle suddenly resigned from the government, believing that the newly organized Fourth Republic, like the Third, gave far too little power to the executive. The Fourth French Republic thus lost the single strong leader it had possessed. After De Gaulle's departure the republic returned to the rapid turnover of ministries that had characterized the Third Republic during the twenties and thirties. Between 1948 and 1958 there were no less than nineteen ministries. The faces of the ministers changed, but the problems remained.

A major source of domestic discontent related to colonial problems in North Africa and Indochina. Between 1947 and 1954 France fought the long, bitter war to retain some measure of control over Indochina. That conflict has been examined more closely earlier in this chapter. By 1954, however, Premier Mendès-France's government admitted defeat and began to preside over a withdrawal from the region. It marked a major defeat for a Western nation by a former colony. The Mendès-France government also granted independence to Tunisia. Morocco was soon moving toward independence. The Suez fiasco of 1956 marked another conspicuous loss of power and prestige for France.

Indochina, Tunisia, and Morocco were regarded as colonial problems by the French. However, in their eyes Algeria, conquered in 1830 and now possessing over a million French citizens, was not a colony but an integral part of France. In 1954 a revolt broke out in Algeria, led by the Algerian Liberation Movement (the FLN). The revolt deeply divided France. The army and right-wing political groups were determined to hold Algeria. Nevertheless the war, which was intensely bitter and brutal, became increasingly unpopular. There were demands for a negotiated settlement. When the civilian government began to make moves in that direction in 1958, an army mutiny occurred in Algeria and unrest soon spread to Corsica. France seemed on the brink of civil war.

At this point the politicians in Paris turned to General De Gaulle, whom the army trusted would uphold their cause. The general accepted office only on the conditions that he be given a free hand to govern and to submit a new constitution to the nation. De Gaulle created the Fifth French Republic, in which the president possessed extraordinary power. He could appoint and dismiss the premier and dissolve the Chamber of Deputies. De Gaulle submitted the constitution to a popular referendum, in which it was overwhelmingly approved. Having secured his own power, De Gaulle moved to attack the Algerian problem. He made large concessions to the FLN, and by 1962 Algeria was independent. There was much domestic opposition to De Gaulle's policy. Hundreds of thousands of French citizens in Algeria returned to France, putting new pressures on its economy and resources. However, the president of the republic held the nation behind him. He had become a symbol of stability and nationalism. There always existed the fear in the late fifties and early sixties that De Gaulle might again resign and leave the nation subject to possible disruptive forces.

De Gaulle combined the methods of Louis Napoleon with the patriotism of Clemenceau. Throughout the 1960s he pursued a policy of making France the leading nation in a united Europe. Often De Gaulle pursued

President De Gaulle Insists on Maintaining French Autonomy

De Gaulle was determined to maintain the national independence of France both in Europe and in the Atlantic community. In this 1966 speech he criticizes those who would compromise that independence by having France subordinate itself to various international organizations, such as NATO and the United Nations. He particularly resented the influence of the United States in European affairs.

I<small>T IS</small> *true that, among our contemporaries, there are many minds—and often some of the best—who have envisaged that our country renounce its independence under the cover of one or another international grouping. Having thus handed over to foreign bodies the responsibility for our destiny, our leaders would—according to the expression sanctioned by that school of thought—have nothing more to do than "plead France's case."*

". . . Thus some—exalting in the dream of the international—wanted to see our country itself, as they placed themselves, under the obedience of Moscow. Thus others—invoking either the supranational myth, or the danger from the East, or the advantage that the Atlantic West could derive from unifying its economy, or even the imposing utility of world arbitration—maintained that France should allow her policy to be dissolved in a tailor-made Europe, her defense in NATO, her monetary concepts in the Washington Fund, her personality in the United Nations, et cetera.

Certainly, it is a good thing that such institutions exist, and it is only in our interest to belong to them; but if we had listened to their extreme apostles, these organs in which, as everyone knows, the political protection, military protection, economic power and multiform aid of the United States predominate—these organs would have been for us only a cover for our submission to American hegemony. Thus, France would disappear swept away by illusion.

Cited in Ronald C. Monticone, *Charles De Gaulle* (Boston: Twayne Publishers, 1975), pp. 67–68.

strictly nationalist goals that frustrated those who favored united action. His nationalism was probably necessary as a means of healing the internal wounds to French pride and prestige brought about by the colonial and Algerian defeats. He pursued systematically good relations with Germany but was never friendly with Great Britain. He deeply resented the influence of the United States in Western Europe.

De Gaulle wanted Europe to become a third force in the world between the superpowers. For that reason he pushed for the development of a French nuclear capacity and refused to become a party to the 1963 Nuclear Test Ban Treaty. He took French forces out of NATO in 1967 and caused its headquarters to be moved from Paris to Brussels. He was highly critical of the American involvement in Vietnam. That American adventure served to convince him even further that Europe under French leadership must prepare to fend for itself.

It is not certain that the rest of the world ever understood De Gaulle or he them. He imposed a kind of presidential dictatorship on France but permitted the civil liberties to be observed and parliamentary politics to function. Yet what was important was what the president and his ministers decided. For ten years he succeeded. Then in 1968 he confronted a domestic unrest in France that was even more widespread than that confronted by Léon Blum in the spring of 1936. The troubles commenced among student groups in Paris, and then they spread to other major sectors of French life. Hundreds of thousands of workers went on strike. Having assured himself of the support of the army, De Gaulle made a brief television speech to rally his followers. Soon they too came into the streets to demonstrate for De Gaulle and stability. The strikes ended. Police often moved against the student groups. The government itself quickly moved to improve the wages and benefits to workers. May 1968 had revealed the fragile strength of the Fifth Republic. It had also revealed that the economic progress of France since the war had created a large body of citizens with sufficient stake in the *status quo* to fear and prevent its disruption.

In 1969 President De Gaulle resigned after some relatively minor constitutional changes were rejected in a referendum. The next election returned Georges Pompidou (1911–1974) to the presidency. He was a strong supporter of De Gaulle and his policies. He and his own successor, Valéry Giscard D'Estaing (b. 1926), set about to improve the economic conditions that had fostered discontent among factory workers in 1968. They have also continued to favor a strong policy favoring European unity. In 1973, three years after De Gaulle's death in political retirement, France permitted Great Britain to join the Common Market.

The center-right government of Valéry Giscard d'Estaing was elected in 1974 on a platform of social reform. The new president also spoke of an "opening" to the political left. It would seem that he might be willing to accept the support of the French Socialist Party for his programs. Giscard d'Estaing is essentially a technocrat who would like to see the traditionally harsh ideological split in France healed. He and others of his persuasion see such splits as preventing the serious handling of major economic problems. Yet to date his interest in some mode of alliance with the left has remained a matter of rhetoric. Indeed, during the parliamentary elections of 1978 he made major election-eve speeches deploring the possibility of a political victory for the left.

Such a victory had for a time seemed possible, on the one hand, because of disillusionment with Giscard d'Estaing's timid policies and, on the other, because of new cooperation between the French Socialist Party and the French Communist Party. Beginning in the late sixties François Mitterand led an impressive drive to reorganize the Socialist Party. Its membership increased, as did its performance at the polls. In 1972 the Socialist Party and the Communist Party led by Georges Marchais formed a Common Front and agreed on a social and economic program that they would enact if they were elected. The Socialists accepted the alliance because it seemed the only way that a left-wing majority could be achieved. The motives of the Communists were less clear, but it would seem they thought such an alliance would give them considerable political leverage within left-wing politics. They hoped to become the tail that wagged the dog.

However, after 1972 the strength of the Socialist Party

continued to grow while that of the Communist Party did not. It became clear by 1977 that if the proposed coalition won the election, the Communists would be able to exert relatively little pressure within the cabinet. Consequently in the middle of 1977 the Communist Party resumed its traditional stance of harshly criticizing the Socialists. In September 1977 the Common Front in effect came to an end. During the elections of 1978 the two left-wing parties failed to cooperate. Communists refused to vote for Socialists, and Socialists refused to vote for Communists. The result of the election was a victory for the right and the center. Since the election there have been pressures from French Communist intellectuals to reform and democratize the internal structures of the French Communist Party. These critics believe the Communist destruction of the alliance with the Socialists destroyed a major opportunity for a left-wing victory. Perhaps the major result of the election will be a continuation for some time of distrust between the Socialists and the Communists. Moreover, the possibility of a left-wing victory seems to have hardened the center and right-wing parties' resolve to prevent such victory in the future.

Instability in the Mediterranean World

For a quarter century after World War II the major Mediterranean states were stable, though for very different reasons. Spain and Portugal remained governed by General Francisco Franco (1892–1975) and Antonio Salazar (1889–1970), respectively. They had established themselves during the turmoil between the wars and continued to preside over illiberal regimes. Italy had attained a course of reasonably steady progress under the leadership of the Christian Democrats. Greece had become stabilized during the fifties, primarily thanks to American military and economic aid. By the middle of the sixties each of these nations had begun to experience internal tensions that have since led to considerable turmoil throughout the region. Moreover, at the far southeastern end of the Mediterranean the Arab-Israeli conflict has proved a continuing source of instability.

Salazar ruled Portugal with an iron hand until 1968, when a stroke removed him from the political scene. His successor, Marcelo Caetono, continued to pursue authoritarian policies. The government remained determined to hold its possessions in Africa long after other European states had abandoned traditional colonial policies. Both at home and abroad major opposition to the government developed within the army officer corps. In 1974 General Antonio de Spinola led an army revolt against Caetono.

Since that time Portugal has indulged itself in the kind of political activity that had been forbidden for almost half a century. There have been large numbers of popular demonstrations, intense political party activity, and broad discussion of economic, social, and political problems. The Portuguese Communist Party proved to be exceedingly well organized. It was able to contribute to the overthrow of the Spinola government. However, in the elections of 1975 the Communists did not do well. The government came under the control of the Socialists, led by Mario Soares. Whether they will remain in power for a substantial period remains to be seen. For the immediate future the two major problems confronting Portugal are the establishment of central political authority and the reviving of the economy, which has suffered from the turmoil since 1974.

Spain has also entered upon a period of considerable uncertainty. So long as he lived, Franco tolerated little or no political life outside that of his own supporters. The Spanish police were active against any political opposition. Many political activists remained either in exile or in jail. However, opposition continued to grow. A large number of illegal political parties had been organized. Franco died in 1976. As he had provided, his successor was Juan Carlos, from the old Bourbon royal family of Spain, who became king. The new monarch, though trained by Franco, has made it clear that he wishes Spain to be liberalized both politically and culturally. In December 1976 the Spanish voters approved a more liberal constitution. The question has now become whether Juan Carlos can obtain the cooperation and trust of the recently legalized political parties. If the monarch is successful, Spain might move to the path of some form of liberal democracy. Otherwise a period of great unrest and violence may commence. It is still too early to say in which direction Spain will go.

At the other end of the Mediterranean, Greece has also experienced a decade of upheaval. In 1965 King Constantine II (b. 1940) came into conflict with the officer corps of the army. During the next several months leftist and liberal Greek politicians hoped to exert new influence on the monarch. In the spring of 1967 conservative army officers deposed Constantine. They claimed to be acting to save the country from a communist takeover. The army junta imposed strongly authoritarian control over the entire population. Political opponents were imprisoned. In the summer of 1974, however, confrontation between Greece and Turkey over the future of Cyprus led to the collapse of the Greek military government. Turkey had invaded Cyprus under the pretext of protecting the Turkish part of the population. The Greek junta were incapable of dealing with the crisis. A civilian government took over. It was headed by Constantine Karamanlis (b. 1907), a former premier. In 1975 a referendum of the Greek people decided against restoration of the monarchy. The problem of the future of Cyprus remains a source of friction between Greece and Turkey.

Instability has threatened Italy from different sources. The transformation from a fascist to a nonfascist government commenced during the war. In 1943 the Grand Fascist Council had ousted Mussolini. He was later summarily executed by Italian partisans. A government friendly to the Allies was installed in southern Italy, and it expanded its control as the Allied armies moved northward. At the close of the conflict the prefascist political parties quickly reemerged. In 1946 the nation voted to abolish the monarchy.

The Christian Democrats governed under the leadership of Alcide de Gasperi. Until 1947 the Italian Communist Party served in the coalition, but it was excluded after the elections of that year. Thereafter Italy remained a nation with a single major large political party, the Christian Democrats, who formed coalitions with other smaller parties. Government by bargained coalition became the order of the day. Under this system, which resembled the system of *transformiso* that had prevailed before Mussolini, the Italian economy experienced a period of growth not unlike that of West Germany. Italy became a genuinely modern nation. It manufactured autos, refrigerators, and office equipment. The nation was very active in the drive for European unity.

However, by the late sixties and early seventies discontent was stirring against the Christian Democrats. Their methods of government had led to corruption, inefficiency, and political paralysis. Inflation became intense as economic growth stagnated. As a result, the Italian Communist Party, the largest and best organized in Western Europe, began to make significant inroads into political life. It won a considerable number of municipal elections. During 1976 the communists won over 35 per cent of the popular vote for the Chamber of Deputies. They were refused admission to the cabinet but were granted several important posts within the Chamber of Deputies.

The architect of the Communist advance within Italian politics was Enrico Berlinguer. He set forth a policy known as the "historic compromise." The policy represented a major break not only with the previous stand of the Italian Communist Party but also with a Moscow-dominated Communist movement. By the "historic compromise" Berlinguer announced the willingness of the Italian Communist Party to enter a coalition government with the Christian Democrats and other noncommunist parties. In other words, the Italian Communists have for the time being renounced revolution as the path to political power. They have also agreed to participate in a government that they would not dominate or control. The Italian Communist Party has also promised that as a partner in a coalition or as the governing party, should it be elected, it will govern constitutionally and will respect individuals' civil liberties. It has also urged continued Italian participation in NATO. To date these promises have not been put to the test. The compromises, however, represent an important example of the strains emerging among Communist Parties in Europe, just as a Communist electoral victory in Italy would be a major change from the postwar noncommunist solidarity of Western Europe.

The Italian Communist success stemming from its announced willingness to cooperate with middle class and Christian political parties has led to a further radicalization of the political left in Italy. The "historic compromise" has made the Italian Communist Party seem quite conservative to the unknown numbers of people who wish to see radical, but so far unclearly defined, political and social change in the nation. These groups have resorted to terrorism to make their power felt and to illustrate how the Communists have now become a pillar of the existing establishment. The best known of the terror-

ist organizations is the Red Brigades. In the spring of 1978 while several members of the Red Brigades were on trial for earlier violence, other members kidnapped Aldo Moro, a former premier of Italy and a major leader of the Christian Democratic Party. The government refused to negotiate for his release. After several weeks of captivity Moro was assassinated, and his body was left in a car on a street in Rome. During the crisis both the Christian Democratic Party and the Italian Communist Party condemned terrorism.

The unrest in so much of Mediterranean Europe has been a cause of considerable concern for the United States and for many of its NATO allies. The conflict between Greece and Turkey over Cyprus constituted an intra-NATO dispute. The possibility of communist government in Italy has led to much rethinking about European defense arrangements. No matter what the political future of Spain may hold, there will be difficulties over agreements about the stationing of United States forces that would not have occurred under Franco. Taken as a whole, the Mediterranean turmoil is the most potent example of the disintegration of the framework of European alliances and political suppositions that have guided postwar Western European international relations. A period of considerable flux no doubt lies ahead.

A final source of instability in the Mediterranean world is the Arab-Israeli conflict. This dispute involves Europe because many of the citizens of Israel are immigrants from Europe and because Europe, like the United States, is highly dependent upon oil from Arab countries. Moreover, the Middle East also remains an arena for poten-

On May 9, 1978, the body of former Italian premier Aldo Moro was found in the rear of an automobile on a street in Rome. He had been kidnapped on March 16 by an Italian terrorist organization known as the Red Brigades and was murdered when the Italian government refused to negotiate for his release. [United Press International Photo.]

ISRAEL AND ITS NEIGHBORS

The map shows the geography of the difficult problem of Israel and its surrounding Arab neighbors. Syria, Jordan, and Egypt are the states with lands now occupied by Israel. The future of those lands and of earlier Palestinian refugees makes up the major set of problems still unresolved in the area.

cal parties, press, labor unions, and educational system. There were numerous conflicts with the Arabs already living in Palestine, for they considered the Jewish settlers as intruders. The British rather unsuccessfully attempted to mediate those clashes.

This situation might have prevailed longer in Palestine except for the outbreak of World War II and the attempt by Hitler to exterminate the Jewish population of central and eastern Europe. The Nazi persecution united Jews throughout the world behind the Zionist ideal of a Jewish state in Palestine. At the same time the knowledge of Nazi atrocities mobilized the conscience of the United States and the other Western powers. It seemed morally right that something be done for Jewish refugees from Nazi concentration camps. In 1947 the British turned over to the United Nations the whole problem of the relationship of Arabs and Jews in Palestine. That same year the United Nations passed a resolution calling for a division of the territory into a Jewish state and an Arab state.

The Arabs in Palestine and the surrounding area resisted the United Nations resolution. Not unnaturally, they resented the influx of new settlers. Large numbers of Palestinian Arabs were displaced and themselves became refugees. In May 1948 the Yishuv declared the independence of a new Jewish state called Israel. The United States through President Truman almost immediately recognized the new nation, whose first prime minister was David Ben Gurion. During 1948 and 1949 Israel fought its war of independence against the Arabs. In that war Israel expanded its borders beyond the limits originally set forth by the United Nations. By 1949 Israel had, through force of arms, secured its existence and peace, but it had not secured diplomatic recognition by its Arab neighbors—Egypt, Jordan, Syria, Saudi Arabia, to name the closest. The peace amounted to little more than an armed truce.

Then in 1952 a group of Egyptian army officers seized power in Egypt. Their leader was Gamal Abdel Nasser. He established himself as a dictator and, more important,

tial problems between the United States and the Soviet Union.

The modern state of Israel was the achievement of the world Zionist movement founded in 1897 by Theodore Herzl and later led by Chaim Weizmann. The British Balfour Declaration of 1917 had favored the establishment of a national home for the Jewish people in Palestine. Between the wars thousands of Jews, mainly from Europe, immigrated into the area, which was then governed by Great Britain under a mandate of the League of Nations. During the interwar period the Yishuv or Jewish community in Palestine developed its own politi-

President Carter was host to Prime Minister Begin of Israel and President Sadat of Egypt in September 1978 at a series of meetings that raised hopes for a peace treaty between the two eastern Mediterranean nations but left many unresolved difficulties between Israel and her neighbors. [United Press International Photo.]

as a spokesman for militant Arab nationalism. His policy was marked by a clear hatred of all the old imperial powers. In 1956 Nasser nationalized the Suez Canal. That same year, as noted previously, Great Britain and France responded to Nasser's action by attacking the canal. Israel joined with France and Britain. This alliance helped Israel fend off certain Arab guerilla attacks but associated Israel with the former imperial powers. After 1956 a United Nations peacekeeping force separated the armies of Israel and Egypt. The bases of the U.N. force were located in Egypt. Still there was no official Arab recognition of the existence of Israel.

An uneasy peace continued until 1967. Meanwhile, the Soviet Union increased its influence in Egypt, and the United States increased its influence in Israel. Both great powers supplied weapons to their friends in the area. In 1967 President Nasser made the calculation, which proved to be quite wrong, that the Arab nations could defeat Israel, which by then was nearly two decades old. He began to mass troops in the Sinai Peninsula, and he attempted to close the Gulf of Aqaba to Israeli shipping. He also demanded the withdrawal of the U.N. peacekeeping force. Diplomatic activity failed to stem the crisis and the Arab attempt to isolate Israel. On June 5, 1967 the armed forces of Israel, under the direction of Defense Minister Moshe Dayan, attacked Egyptian airfields rather than endure additional provocation by Egypt. Almost immediately Syria and Jordan entered the war on the side of Egypt. Yet by June 11 the Six Days' War was over, and Israel had won a stunning victory. The military forces of Egypt lay in shambles. Moreover, Israel occupied the entire Egyptian Sinai Peninsula, as well as the West Bank region along the Jordon River that had previously been part of the state of Jordan. This victory marked the height of Israeli power and prestige.

In 1970 President Nasser died. He was succeeded by Anwar el-Sadat. Sadat had first to shore up his support at home. The existing tensions between Israel and the defeated Egypt of course continued, and the Soviet Union still poured weapons into Egypt. However, Sadat deeply distrusted the Russians and in 1972 ordered them to leave the country. He and his advisors also felt that only another war with Israel could return to Egypt the lands lost in 1967. In October 1973, on the Jewish holy day of Yom Kippur, the military forces of Egypt launched an attack across the Suez Canal into Israeli-held territory. The invasion came as a complete surprise to the Israelis. Initially the Egyptian forces made considerable headway. Then the Israeli army thrust back the invasion. In November 1973 a truce was signed between the forces in the Sinai. Although Israel had been successful in repelling the Egyptians, the cost in troops and prestige was very high.

The Yom Kippur War added a major new element to the Middle East problem. In the fall of 1973 when the war broke out, the major Arab oil-producing states shut off the flow of oil to the United States and Europe. This dramatic move was an attempt to force the Western powers to use their influence to moderate the policy of Israel. The threat of the loss of oil was particularly frightening to Europeans, who possess almost no major sources of oil on which their industry depends. In the future this Arab oil can be expected to play an even more influential part in Middle East developments.

The most recent important development in the troubled area occurred in November 1977. President Sadat of Egypt, in a dramatic personal gesture, flew to Israel, addressed the Israeli parliament, and held discussions with Prime Minister Menahem Begin, although the two states were still technically at war. In effect, for the first time the head of a major Arab state recognized the existence of Israel. Previously all contacts had taken place either through the United Nations or other third parties. The Sadat initiative, roundly condemned in many Arab quarters, resulted in direct conversations, the most important of which occurred at Camp David in the United States under the direction of President Carter. Whether the Camp David accords of September 1978 will succeed in achieving peace remains to be seen. Tensions are still high. The Arab refugee problem is perhaps the major stumbling block, as the Palestine Liberation Organization demands the creation of a separate Palestinian state in the region. The Arab states to a greater or lesser degree have supported this position, but Israel believes such a state would inevitably become another major enemy rather than a "neighbor."

Eurocommunism in Western Europe

Within West European politics the past decade has witnessed the emergence of what may be a new version of Communism. Termed Eurocommunism, this development has characterized the policy and rhetoric of several Communist parties operating within the democracies of Western Europe. It has been particularly associated with the Communist parties of France, Italy, and Spain. Eurocommunism consists of two basic political policies. The first is the assertion of the independence of the parties involved from the influence of the Communist Party of the Soviet Union. Second, these parties have said publicly that they are willing to function within the existing parliamentary systems. The latter policy has been taken to mean a renunciation of revolution as a path to political power and the acceptance of existing constitutional arrangements. That is, these Communist parties have said that if they lose an election while in office, they will then surrender office to the victorious party. We have already noted these ideas in contemporary Italy.

Eurocommunism has developed primarily since 1968. The Soviet invasion of Czechoslovakia, the well-publicized persecution of Soviet dissidents, and the general absence of human rights in the Soviet Union made the Russian experience a rather unattractive model for young Europeans of the post-World War II generation. The West European Communist parties could hardly expect to win elections so long as they remained intimately aligned with the Soviet Union. Moreover, the postwar prosperity of Western Europe that has contrasted so markedly with the life of Eastern Europe also meant that western Communist parties felt the need to modify their tactics. The "historic compromise" of the Italian Communist Party and the cooperation of the French Communist Party with the French Socialists from 1972 to 1977 were examples of these new tactics. In Spain, under the leadership of Santiago Carillo the Communist Party has even attempted to introduce democratic procedures within the party itself. This latter policy has not been followed in France or Italy.

In 1977 the Soviet Union formally condemned Eurocommunism. The Soviet Union seems to have feared that too much independence on the part of West European Communist parties might lead to further unrest in Eastern Europe.

Although no European Communist Party advocating the policy of Eurocommunism has come to power, the phenomenon of Eurocommunism has made a large impression in the United States. European voters, on the other hand, and most particularly the large democratic socialist parties, have remained quite sceptical. There are several reasons for scepticism. First, Communist calls for independence from Moscow are not new. West European Communist parties have always displayed some independence of the Soviet Union and have insisted that the special conditions in their own nations must be taken into account in formulating policy. Second, from time to time in the past, most notably in the Popular Front governments of the 1930s and the immediate postwar cabinets of several countries, the Communists have participated. Neither of those previous developments changed the goal of the Communist parties from the pursuit of a monopoly of power in the state. On the whole European voters have not fully believed the Communist pledge to give up power upon the loss of future elections. Europeans of conservative, liberal, and democratic-socialist persuasion have seen the Communist parties change tactics and policies in the past. They remain uncertain about the sincerity and the permanence of the policies of Eurocommunism. They are not certain that once in power or in the cabinets the Communists would not revert to their former goals.

Finally, Europeans, unlike many American observers, have not equated the Eurocommunist call for independence from Moscow with democratic politics. With the exception of the Spanish Communist Party, the West European Communist parties have remained very centrally organized. They have not permitted any significant internal democracy or internal criticism. So long as this rigid organization is retained, European voters may remain wary of the democratic protestations of the Communists.

Nonetheless, Eurocommunism remains one of the most significant political phenomena of the present day in Europe. One major question is whether any of these parties will be able to enter a government. The Italian Communist Party is the one more likely to do so within the near future. But another question is whether the advance of Communist parties under the name of Eurocommunism will provoke a major conservative or right-wing political backlash. Such has often been the case with the political advance of the left in Europe, and it might again be the case in the future.

The Soviet Union and Eastern Europe
The Soviet Union Since the Death of Stalin (1953)

Many Russians had hoped that the end of the war would signal a lessening of Stalinism. No other nation had suffered greater losses or more deprivation than the Soviet Union. Its people anticipated some immediate reward for their sacrifice and heroism. They desired a reduction in the scope of the police state and a redirection of the economy away from heavy industry to consumer products. They were disappointed. Stalin did little or nothing to modify the character of the regime he had created. The police remained ever-present. The cult of personal-

ity expanded, and the central bureaucracy continued to grow. Heavy industry was still favored over production for consumers. Agriculture continued to be troubled. Stalin's personal authority over the party and the nation remained unchallenged. In foreign policy Stalin moved to solidify Soviet control over Eastern Europe for the purposes of both Communist expansion and Soviet national security. He attempted to impose the Soviet model on those nations. The Cold War stance of the United States simply served to confirm Stalin in his ways.

By late 1952 and early 1953 it appeared that Stalin might be ready to unloose a new series of purges. In January 1953 a group of Jewish physicians was arrested and charged with plotting the deaths of important leaders. Charges of extensive conspiracy appeared in the press. All of these developments were similar to the events that had preceded the purges of the thirties. Then quite suddenly in the midst of this new furor, on March 6, 1953, Stalin died. There have remained unconfirmed suspicions that his sudden death may have been related to the impending purges.

For a time no single leader replaced Stalin. Rather the Presidium (the renamed Politburo) pursued a policy of collective leadership. A considerable amount of reshuffling occurred among the top party leaders. Lavrenti Beria (1899–1953), the dreaded director of the secret police, was removed from his post and eventually executed. Georgi Malenkov (b. 1902) became premier, a position he held for about two years. Gradually, however, power and influence began to devolve on Nikita Khrushchev (1894–1971), who in 1953 had been named party secretary. By 1955 he had edged out Malenkov and had successfully urged the appointment of Nikolai Bulganin (1895–1975) in his place. Three years later Khrushchev himself became premier. His rise constituted the end of collective leadership, but at no time did he enjoy the extraordinary powers of Stalin.

The Khrushchev era, which lasted until the autumn of 1964, witnessed a marked retreat from Stalinism though not from extreme authoritarianism. Indeed, the political

Khrushchev Denounces the Crimes of Stalin: The Secret Speech

In 1956 Khrushchev denounced Stalin in a secret speech to the Party Congress. The *New York Times* published a text smuggled from Russia.

STALIN *acted not through persuasion, explanation, and patient cooperation with people, but by imposing his concepts and demanding absolute submission to his opinion. Whoever opposed this concept or tried to prove his viewpoint and the correctness of his position was doomed to removal from the leading collective [group] and to subsequent moral and physical annihilation. . . .*

Stalin originated the concept "enemy of the people." This term automatically rendered it unnecessary that the ideological errors of a man or men engaged in a controversy be proved; this term made possible the usage of the most cruel repression violating all norms of revolutionary legality, against anyone who in any way disagreed with Stalin, against those who were only suspected of hostile intent, against those who had bad reputations.

This concept "enemy of the people" actually eliminated the possibility of any kind of ideological fight or the making of one's views known on this or that issue, even those of a practical character. In the main, and in actuality, the only proof of guilt used, against all norms of current legal science, was the "confession" of the accused himself; and, as subsequent probing proved, "confessions" were acquired through physical pressures against the accused. . . .

Lenin used severe methods only in the most necessary cases, when the exploiting classes were still in existence and were vigorously opposing the revolution, when the struggle for survival was decidedly assuming the sharpest forms, even including civil war.

Stalin, on the other hand, used extreme methods and mass repressions at a time when the revolution was already victorious, when the Soviet State was strengthened, when the exploiting classes were already liquidated and Socialist relations were rooted solidly in all phases of national economy, when our party was politically consolidated and had strengthened itself both numerically and ideologically. It is clear that here Stalin showed in a whole series of cases his intolerance, his brutality and his abuse of power. Instead of proving his political correctness and mobilizing the masses, he often chose the path of repression and physical annihilation, not only against actual enemies, but also against individuals who had not committed any crimes against the party and the Soviet Government. . . .

The New York Times, June 5, 1956, pp. 13–16.

repression of Stalin had been so extensive that there was considerable room for relaxation of surveillance within the limits of tyranny. Politically the demise of Stalinism meant shifts in leadership and party structure by means other than purges. In 1956, at the Twentieth Congress of the Communist Party, Khrushchev made a secret speech (later published outside the Soviet Union) in which he denounced Stalin and his crimes against socialist justice during the purges of the thirties. The speech caused shock and consternation in party circles and opened the way for limited, but genuine, internal criticism of the Soviet government. Gradually the strongest supporters of Stalinist policies were removed from the Presidium. By 1958 all of Stalin's former supporters were gone, but none had been executed.

Soviet Premier Nikita Khrushchev attacked the policies of Stalin in a long secret speech before the 1956 Communist Party Congress in Moscow. Subsequently his own adventuresome foreign policy and unsuccessful agricultural policy led to his downfall in 1964. [United Press International Photo.]

Under Khrushchev, intellectuals were somewhat more able to express their opinions. This so-called thaw in the cultural life of the country was closely related to the premier's interest in the opinions of experts on problems of industry and agriculture. He often went outside the usual bureaucratic channels in search of information and new ideas. Novels such as Alexander Solzhenitsyn's (b. 1918) *One Day in the Life of Ivan Denisovich* (1963) could be published. However, Boris Pasternak (1890–1960), the author of *Dr. Zhivago*, was not permitted to accept the Nobel Prize for literature in 1958. The intellectual liberalization of Soviet life during this period should not be overestimated. It looked favorable only in comparison with what had preceded it and has continued to seem so because of the decline of such freedom of expression since Khrushchev's fall.

The economic policy also somewhat departed from the strict Stalinist mode. By 1953 the economy had recovered from the strains and destruction of the war. Consumer goods and housing still remained in very short supply. The problem of an adequate food supply also continued. Malenkov had favored improvements in meeting the demand for consumer goods; Khrushchev also favored such a departure. The latter also moved in a moderate fashion to decentralize economic planning and execution. During the late fifties Khrushchev often boasted that Soviet production of consumer goods would overtake that of the West. Steel, oil, and electric-power production continued to grow, but the consumer sector improved only marginally. The ever-growing defense budget and the space program that successfully launched the first man-made satellite of the earth, *Sputnik*, in 1957 made major demands on the nation's productive resources. Economically Khrushchev was attempting to move the country in too many directions at once.

Khrushchev strongly redirected Stalin's agricultural policy. He recognized that in spite of the collectivization of the thirties the Soviet Union had not produced an agricultural system capable of feeding its own people. Administratively Khrushchev removed many of the most restrictive regulations on private cultivation. The machine tractor stations were abandoned. Existing collective farms were further amalgamated. The government undertook an extensive "virgin lands" program to extend wheat cultivation by hundreds of thousands of acres. This policy initially increased grain production to new records. However, in a very few years the new lands became subject to erosion. The farming techniques applied had been inappropriate for the soil. The agricultural problem has simply continued to grow. Currently the Soviet Union imports vast quantities of grain from the United States and other countries. United States grain imports have constituted a major facet of the policy of detente.

Adventuresomeness also characterized Khrushchev's foreign policy. In 1956 the Soviet Union adopted the phrase "peaceful coexistence" in regard to its relationship to the United States. The policy implied no less competition with the capitalist world but suggested that war might not be the best way to pursue Communist expansion. The previous year Khrushchev had participated in the Geneva summit meeting alongside Bulganin. Thereafter followed visits around the world, culminating with one to the United States in 1959. By the early sixties it had become clear that Khrushchev had made few inroads on Western policy. He was under increasing domestic pressure and also pressure from the Chinese. The militancy of the denunciation of the U-2 flight, the aborting of the Paris summit meeting, the Berlin Wall, and the Cuban missile crisis were all responses to those pressures. The last of these adventures brought a clear Soviet retreat.

By 1964 numerous high Russian leaders and many people lower in the party had concluded that Khrushchev had tried to do too much too soon and had done it too poorly. On October 16, 1964, after defeat in the Central Committee of the Communist Party, Khrushchev resigned. He was replaced by Alexei Kosgygin (b. 1904) as Premier and Leonid Brezhnev (b. 1906) as party secretary. The latter eventually emerged as the dominant figure. In 1977 the constitution of the Soviet Union was

Anatoly Shcharansky represents the emergence of an open movement of dissent within the Soviet Union, just as his imprisonment shows the continuing official repression accompanying the movement. The fate of Shcharansky and others commanded international attention in 1978. [United Press International Photo.]

changed to combine the offices of president and party secretary. Brezhnev became president, and thus head of the state as well as of the party. He holds more personal power than any Soviet leader since Stalin.

Domestically the Soviet government has become markedly more repressive since 1964. All intellectuals have enjoyed less and less freedom and little direct access to the government leadership. In 1974 the government expelled Solzhenitsyn. Perhaps most important among recent developments, Jewish citizens of the Soviet Union have become subject to harassment. Major bureaucratic obstacles have been placed in the way of the emigration of Soviet Jews to Israel. These policies suggest a return to the limitations of the Stalinist period.

The internal repression has given rise to a dissident movement. Certain Soviet citizens have dared to criticize the regime in public and to carry out small demonstrations against the government. They have accused the Soviet government of violating the human rights provisions of the Helsinki agreements. The dissidents have included a number of prominent citizens such as the Nobel Prize physicist Andrei Sakharov. The response of the Soviet government to the dissident movement has been further repression. Prominent dissidents, such as Anatoly Shcharansky, Aleksandr Ginzburg, and Vladimir Slepak, have been arrested, tried on clearly trumped-up charges, and sentenced to long periods of imprisonment or internal exile in Siberia. The Soviet government obviously feels it cannot tolerate the dissident movement. The questions that now arise and cannot be answered have to do with how much internal opposition to the government exists in the Soviet Union and what, if any, possibility the opposition has of making its thought and will known.

In foreign policy the Brezhnev years have witnessed attempts to reach accommodation with the United States while continuing to press for expanded Soviet influence and further attempts to maintain Soviet leadership of the Communist movement. During the Vietnam war the Soviet Union pursued a policy of restrained support for North Vietnam. Under President Richard Nixon the United States pursued a policy of *détente* based on arms limitation and trade agreements. Nonetheless, Soviet spending on defense, and particularly on naval expansion, has continued to grow. During the Ford and Carter administrations in the United States, Soviet involvement in African affairs has been troubling. Soviet-African activities, as well as violation of the human rights of Russian dissidents, have brought a cooling of relations between the two superpowers. As with so many other aspects of contemporary Europe, the future direction of the Soviet Union remains unclear. Certainly in domestic policy authoritarianism will continue and may intensify. In foreign affairs divisions among the Communist nations and parties may determine the course of future policy.

Polycentrism in the Communist World

Throughout the Cold War observers in the West concentrated their attention on the tensions between the Soviet Union and the United States. But beyond its continuing confrontation of and rivalry with America, the Soviet government also had to deal with growing tension and division within the world communist movement. During most of the Stalin era the Soviet Union was the center of world communism. Stalin hoped to impose his model on other parties. Immediately after the war the Soviets attempted to construct governments in the people's democracies of Eastern Europe in the Stalinist mold. Since the late forties the unity of world communism, which was always more frail than Cold War rhetoric suggested, became strained and finally shattered. As early as 1948 Yugoslavia began to construct its own model for socialism independent of Moscow. From 1956 onward the governments of eastern Europe began to seek a freer hand in internal affairs. By the late fifties the monumental split between the Soviet Union and the People's Republic of China had developed. The communist world has come to have many centers—thus the descriptive term *polycentrism*—and the Soviet Union has had to compete for leadership.

There have been three stages in postwar relations

between the Soviet Union and eastern Europe. They were the years of Stalinism, then of revolt, and finally of socialist polycentrism. The stages closely paralleled internal developments in the Soviet Union itself.

Prior to the death of Stalin in 1953 the so-called peoples' democracies were brought steadily into line with Soviet policy. By 1948 single-party communist governments had been established in Bulgaria, Romania, Hungary, Yugoslavia, Albania, Czechoslovakia, Poland, and East Germany. Yugoslavia, headed by Marshal Tito (b. 1891), pursued an independent course of action and was bitterly denounced by Stalin. Elsewhere, however, Soviet troops and Stalinist party leaders prevailed. The economies of those states were made to conform to the requirements of Soviet economic recovery and growth. The Soviet Union paid low prices for its imports from Eastern Europe and demanded high prices for its exports. In this fashion and through outright reparations it drained the resources of the region for its own uses. The Soviet Union prevented the eastern European nations from participating in the Marshall Plan and responded with its own Council for Economic Mutual Assistance in 1949. In 1955 it organized the Warsaw Pact to confront NATO.

The Stalinist system of control was bound to generate discontent. This first manifested itself shortly after Stalin's death in 1953, when a brief revolt occurred in East Berlin. It was immediately crushed. Talk in the early Eisenhower administration in America about the "liberation" of eastern Europe may have contributed to this disturbance by raising hopes of some form of United States support. Khrushchev's speech of 1956 in which he denounced Stalin sent reverberations throughout eastern Europe as well as the Soviet Union. It was no accident that following the speech came the Polish October Revolution and the Hungarian Revolution of 1956. In the short run the bids for independence had the most limited kind of success; however, in retrospect they can be seen as marking the close of the Stalinist period and as paving the way for the emergence of polycentrism.

During the early years of the Cold War it was com-mon in the West to regard the communist movement as a single monolithic structure. There was a failure to take into account the role of nationalism in eastern Europe and the potential for division between the Soviet Union and China. The events of 1956 delineated the limits of acceptable independence for the Soviet-dominated successor states. Those nations of eastern Europe must remain members of the Warsaw Pact, and their leaders had to be willing to consult and cooperate with the Soviet Union. They might trade with Western Europe and the United States and even establish cultural contacts, but their chief political and economic orientation must remain with the Soviet Union.

Since 1956, within these limits considerable diversity has appeared in eastern Europe. In Poland Wladyslaw Gomulka (b. 1905) and his successors have made peace with the Roman Catholic Church, halted land collectivization, established trade with the West, and participated in cultural exchange programs. However, Poland has experienced persistent shortages in food and consumer goods. Such discontent led to Gomulka's departure in 1970 and has remained a pervasive undercurrent in Polish affairs ever since. In Hungary the Janos Kadar (b. 1912) government, which was installed by Soviet troops, pursued a program of economic growth and consumer satisfaction. Hungary is now probably the most prosperous and stable country in the area. East Germany and Bulgaria retained the closest relationships to the Soviet Union. Only after the Berlin Wall crisis of 1961 and the subsequent halt in the outflow of refugees did the East German government begin to achieve anything resembling economic prosperity. Romania has witnessed a resurgence of limited nationalism. Under the leadership of President Nicolae Ceauşescu (b. 1918), it has maintained ties with both the Soviet Union and China. Moreover, it has cultivated friendly relations with the United States, as witnessed by President Nixon's visit in 1969 and President Ceauşescu's visit to America in 1977. However, in all of these countries the independence achieved still exists within the confines of one-party gov-

In the early summer of 1968, before the invasion of Czechoslovakia by the Soviet Union and others, the leaders of the Warsaw Pact nations met in Bratislava, Czechoslovakia. The front row of their striking group photograph is an all-star cast of East European Communist figures of the mid-1960s: (left to right) Janos Kadar, Hungary; Nikolai Podgorny and Alexei Kosygin, Soviet Union; Todor Zhivkov, Bulgaria; Ludvik Svoboda, Czechoslovakia; Leonid Brezhnev, Soviet Union; Wladyslav Gomulka, Poland; Walter Ulbricht, East Germany; Alexander Dubcek, Czechoslovakia; Mikhail Suslov, Soviet Union. [Camera Press.]

ernment, authoritarianism, and absence of the traditional civil liberties.

In 1968 the Soviet Union moved to crush an experiment in developing a socialist model independent of Soviet domination. In that year the nations of the Warsaw Pact invaded Czechoslovakia to halt the political experimentation of the Alexander Dubcek government. It was quite clear that the Soviet Union felt that it could

In the summer of 1968 troops of the Soviet Union and other Warsaw Pact nations invaded Czechoslovakia to bring to an end the Czech experiment in a more liberal version of communism. Unlike Budapest twelve years earlier, Prague offered little or no violent resistance by the Czechs to the invasion, as this scene reveals. [United Press International Photo.]

not tolerate so·liberal a communist regime on its own borders. Dubcek was permitting in Czechoslovakia the very kind of intellectual freedom and discussion that was simultaneously being suppressed within Russia itself. At the time of the invasion Soviet Party Chairman Brezhnev declared the right of the Soviet Union to interfere in the domestic politics of other communist countries. Such interference has nevertheless not occurred since 1968. Moreover, at a conference of communist parties held in East Berlin in 1976 the Soviet Union accepted a declaration stating that there could be several paths to socialism. The main proponents of this policy were the communist parties of Western Europe. As the Communist Party of Italy in particular, as well as that of France, has seen election to full or shared power as a genuine possibility, it has attempted to put distance between itself and the Soviet Union. However, to date none of these declarations and acknowledgements of socialist independence from Soviet domination has been put to a meaningful test. A time of considerable trial and error probably lies ahead.

SUGGESTED READINGS

S. H. BEER, *British Politics in the Collectivist Age* (1965). The best discussion of twentieth-century political structures in Britain.

C. E. BLACK, *The Dynamics of Modernization: A Study in Comparative History* (1966). A useful study with implications for both European and non-European history.

Z. BRZEZINSKI, *The Soviet Block: Unity and Conflict* (1967). A discussion of Eastern Europe.

R. EMERSON, *From Empire to Nation: The Rise to Self-Assertion of Asian and African Peoples* (1960). An important discussion of the origins of decolonization.

B. B. FALL, *The Two Vietnams: A Political and Military Analysis*, rev. ed. (1967). A discussion by a journalist who spent many years on the scene.

R. HISCOCKS, *The Adenauer Era* (1966). A treatment of postwar German political development.

S. HOFFMAN (Ed.), *In Search of France* (1963). A useful collection of essays on the problems of postwar France.

W. W. Kulski, *De Gaulle and the World: The Foreign Policy of the Fifth French Republic* (1968). A straightforward treatment of De Gaulle's drive toward French and European autonomy.

Walter Laqueur, *Europe Since Hitler* (1970). A well-balanced and comprehensive account of postwar developments.

W. Leonhard, *The Kremlin Since Stalin* (1962). A brief but informative discussion of the post-Stalin power struggles.

W. Leonhard, *Three Faces of Communism* (1974). An analysis of the ideological divisions within the Communist world.

D. MacRae, Jr., *Parliament, Politics, and Society in France, 1946–1958* (1967). A close analysis of the turmoil of the Fourth Republic.

R. Mayne, *The Recovery of Europe, 1945–1973* (1973). A sound treatment emphasizing the movement toward economic integration.

G. Myrdal, *Asian Drama: An Inquiry into the Poverty of Nations*, 3 vols. (1968). A significant discussion of the economic and social problems of the postcolonial world by a thoughtful economist.

M. M. Postan, *An Economic History of Western Europe, 1945–1964* (1967). A basic survey.

A. Sampson, *The New Anatomy of Britain* (1973). A critical discussion of the British political and economic elite.

L. Schapiro, *The Communist Party of the Soviet Union* (1960). An important analysis of the most important institution of Soviet Russia.

J. J. Servan-Schreiber, *The American Challenge* (trans., 1968). A French journalist's analysis of American economic influence in France.

R. Shaplen, *The Lost Revolution: The U.S. in Vietnam* (1965). A clear analysis of the problems that confronted the United States.

Adam Ullam, *Expansion and Coexistence: The History of Soviet Foreign Policy, 1917–1967* (1968). The best one-volume treatment.

H. C. Wallich, *Mainsprings of the German Revival* (1955). A discussion of the origins of the German economic miracle.

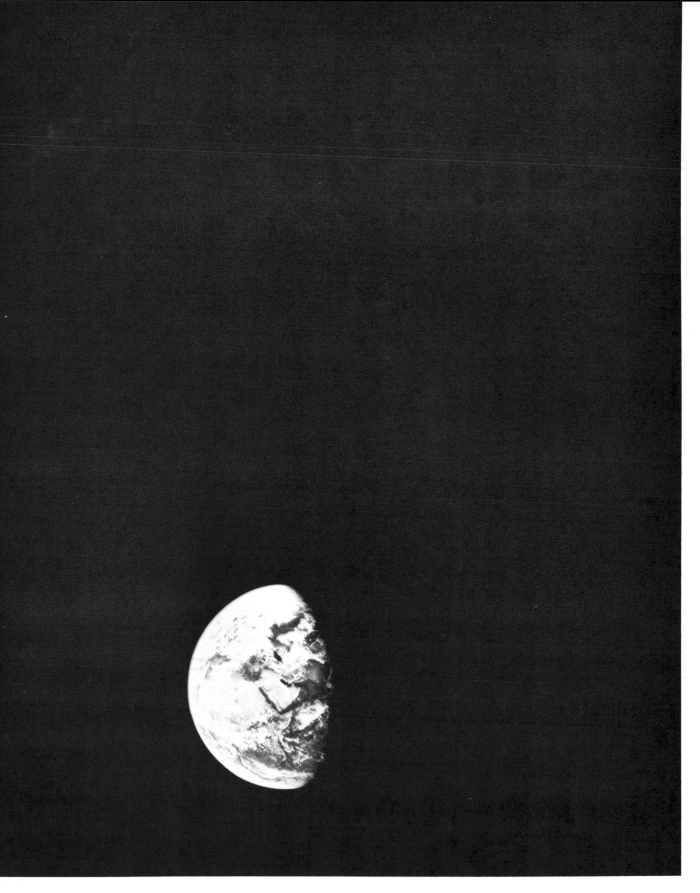

35
Twentieth-Century States of Mind

THE PLURAL form of the word *state* in the title of this chapter is quite intentional. No single characteristic has so marked the thought of twentieth-century Europe as the absence of unity and shared values. As discussed in Chapter 29, many of the traditional religious and intellectual certainties dissolved during the fifty years prior to 1914. Already philosophers, theologians, writers, and social thinkers had found themselves compelled to look for new paths of thought and new intellectual signposts. The crises that flowed from the two world wars, the Great Depression, the conflict of political ideologies, and the shadow of atomic warfare have in turn created problems more rapidly, perhaps, than solutions can be formulated. The pressure of events, as well as the absence of intellectual certainty, has caused major thinkers to go in more different directions than ever before in the European experience. Anxiety, fear, and even desperation have been the chief features of that search for new values.

The intellectual life of this century has taken place amidst the most extreme social and political conditions. The world wars confirmed the power of human beings not simply to do great harm to each other but actually to destroy the species. From the opening months of World War I onward, Europeans have known that they could kill scores of thousands of each other between a single rising and setting of the sun. Since 1945 the entire world has been aware of the devastating potential of atomic weapons. Within individual nation-states, people have experienced the most extreme forms of political repres-

sion in the history of the West, and that repression has occurred under both right-wing and left-wing governments. In sheer magnitude the racial atrocities of the Nazis and the peasant slaughters under Stalin's agricultural policy were unprecedented. The economic unrest of the 1920s and 1930s brought uncertainty and in many cases extreme suffering to millions of people. Throughout the colonial world the onetime subject nations began to rebel and to condemn the major values of Western civilization. The attempts by Western nations to maintain colonial dominance and influence gave rise to widespread internal criticism. During all of these developments the technology that had brought Europe and the West to its pinnacle of world domination seemed to be turning against its creator, first in the destructiveness of war and then as a danger to the environment.

Such a time of turmoil was not entirely new to the Western experience. The third and fourth centuries saw a variety of differing attempts to come to grips with the social and political disintegration of the Roman Empire. The problems of the late empire brought about major political reorganization and the conversion to Christianity. Many twentieth-century intellectuals have regarded themselves as living in no less a tumultuous period.

Extreme social and political conditions have encouraged extreme intellectual solutions. Between the wars distinguished writers and philosophers in considerable numbers supported either fascism or communism. Other writers began to identify with the aspirations of the restive colonial peoples. These intellectuals condemned both colonialism and the civilization that fostered it. A major segment of the intellectual community rejected rationalism, reason, and science as the primary guides to a better and more humane life. Equally significant, most of the intellectual movements addressing themselves to modern problems have been very short-lived. Whereas one can see the Enlightenment as extending over most of the eighteenth century, the chief intellectual developments of this century have often sustained themselves for only a decade.

This picture of the earth, taken on May 20, 1969 from 100,000 miles in space during the first American flight to the moon, has come to illustrate both the technological accomplishment of the twentieth century and the sense that human beings must devote more care to the limited resources of their relatively small planet. [National Aeronautics and Space Administration.]

Head, by Amedeo Modigliani (1884–1920), an Italian painter and sculptor of the early twentieth century, displays the impact of nonwestern art on Europe. Its portrayal of a traditional subject of sculpture in a nontraditional manner illustrates the way in which various strains of European thought and art became transformed in the late nineteenth and early twentieth centuries. [The Tate Galley, London.]

Torso, by Antoine Pevsner (1886–1962), was completed in 1926. By depicting the traditional theme of the human form through use of new materials from the present, it illustrates a sense of disjunction between present and past cultures and of the artist's alienation from contemporary technology. The torso, with few recognizable features, has become what almost amounts to a plastic skeleton. To some, it suggests that technology has too radically reshaped human life. [Construction in plastic and copper: $29\frac{1}{2}''$ x $11\frac{5}{8}''$. Collection, The Museum of Modern Art, New York; Katherine S. Dreier Bequest.]

The Jodrell Bank radio telescope in Great Britain came into operation in 1957. It is an example of the vast new interest in space that commenced in the 1950s and of the many complex technologies, like that of radio astronomy, required to support that interest. [British Tourist Authority, New York.]

Although writers have been testing new solutions for the new problems of this century, there has also been considerable continuity with the past. New departures have not meant total separation. For example, although rationalism and the prestige of science have been challenged, science, medicine, and rational business and government practices have touched the realities of everyday life as never before. Through World War II the most extreme modes of nationalism flourished in Europe, but since 1945 the kind of international cooperation that the *philosophes* of the eighteenth century desired has made unprecedented progress. This century has been one of ever-growing secularism, but Christian theologians and religious institutions have demonstrated considerable vitality. Finally, in its very self-criticism the civilization of twentieth-century Europe has displayed its links with the past. For it has been the capacity of the West to nurture internal criticism that has permitted it to adapt itself to new problems and conditions.

The Diffusion of Knowledge and Culture

The twentieth century has witnessed unparalleled changes in the pursuit and diffusion of knowledge. The invention and institutionalization of radio, television, and computers have created an informational revolution. The communications revolution has made the world smaller and has led to a wider uniformity of culture. The daily events of politics are reported instantaneously. Different nations can share the same programing, and the same products can be advertised. Through computer science more information of all kinds can be gathered and stored. There has also been a continuation of the vast explosion of printed matter that began about the middle of the nineteenth century. In the face of radio and television, Europeans have not ceased to read and write books. This century has seen more books of every kind printed than ever before; storage is now a problem for libraries. However, the printed word has become only one mode of public communication. The sheer quantity of information now available on practically every subject has in and of itself contributed to the fragmentation of public opinion and intellectual endeavor.

The increase in the quantity of information has been accompanied by a growing number of Europeans' receiving some form of university education. At the turn of the century in every major European country only a few thousand people were enrolled in the universities. By the 1970s that figure had risen to hundreds of thousands. More people from more different kinds of social and economic backgrounds were receiving higher education. Equally important, for the first time large numbers of women were receiving such training. This expansion in the student and educated populations has been closely related to the intense self-criticism of Europeans. Millions of citizens have become equipped with those critical intellectual skills that in previous centuries were usually the possession of very small literate elites.

The "student experience"—that is, leaving home and settling for several years in a community composed primarily of late adolescents—has come to be widely shared. Previously only a relatively few privileged persons had known this experience. Since World War II it has become one of the major features of European and Western society. One of its most striking results was the student rebellion of the late sixties. Students at the Sorbonne in Paris were the leading instigators of the events in France, which in May 1968 shook the foundations of the Gaullist government. About the same time German students forced the entire restructuring of the university system. Students were also in the forefront of the socialist experiment in Czechoslovakia, which was suppressed by the Soviet invasion in 1968. Student disturbances occurred in several of the British universities, and Italian students have been no less active. The growth in the number of students and their political activities in part accounted for the disunity of intellectual life. As more different kinds of people came to participate in university and intellectual life, there was bound to be less unity.

The expansion in the number of students has also meant a general increase in the numbers of university teachers. As a result, there have been more scientists, historians, economists, literary critics, and other professional intellectuals during the last seventy-five years than in all previous human history. Moreover, not since the early years of the Reformation have university intellectuals exerted such widespread influence. The major intellectual developments of the seventeenth, eighteenth, and nineteenth centuries took place primarily, though not entirely, outside the university. In the twentieth century the university has become the most likely home for the intellectual. And the symbol of success on the part of a writer in almost any field has been the inclusion of his work in the university curriculum.

All of these factors, in addition to the difficult political and social events of the century, have meant that the former unity of Western thought has become shattered. Some observers have considered this development as opening the possibility for new creativity. For one highly significant group of twentieth-century writers the disruption of intellectual unity and the disappearance of former spiritual guideposts spawned a situation of extreme anxiety.

Existentialism

The single intellectual movement that perhaps best characterizes the predicament and mood of twentieth-century European culture is existentialism. It is symptomatic that most of the philosophers associated with this movement disagree with each other on major issues. Existentialism, which has been termed the philosophy of Europe in the twentieth century, like the modern Western mind in general, has been badly divided. The movement represents in part a continuation of the revolt against reason that commenced in the nineteenth century.

Friedrich Nietzsche, whose thought was considered in

Chapter 29, was one of the major forerunners of existentialism. Another was the Danish writer Sören Kierkegaard (1813–1855), who wrote during the second quarter of the nineteenth century but received little attention until after World War I. He was a rebel against Hegelian philosophy and Christianity as he found it in Denmark. In works such as *Fear and Trembling* (1843), *Either/Or* (1843), and *Concluding Unscientific Postscript* (1846), he urged that the truth of Christianity could not be contained in creeds, doctrines, and church organizations. It could be grasped only in the living experience of those who faced extreme human situations. This emphasis on lived experience as the true test of the validity of philosophy and religion has characterized most twentieth-century existential writers. Kierkegaard also criticized Hegelian philosophy and, by implication, all modes of academic rational philosophy. Its failure, he felt, was the attempt to contain all of life and human experience within abstract categories. Kierkegaard spurned this faith in the power of mere reason. "The conclusions of passion," he once declared, "are the only reliable ones." [1]

The intellectual and ethical crisis of World War I brought Kierkegaard's thought to the fore and also created new interest in Nietzsche's critique of reason. The human sacrifice and the destruction of property made many people doubt whether human beings were actually in control of their own destiny. The conflict stood as an affront to the concept of human improvement and the view of human beings as creatures of rationality. The war itself had been fought with the instruments developed through rational technology. The pride in rational human achievement that had characterized much nineteenth-century European civilization lay in ruins. The sunny faith in rational human development and advancement had not been able to withstand the extreme experiences of war.

Existential thought came to thrive in this climate and received further encouragement by the trauma of World War II. The major existential writers included the Germans Martin Heidegger (1889–1976) and Karl Jaspers (1883–1969) and the Frenchmen Jean-Paul Sartre (b. 1905) and Albert Camus (1913–1960). Their books were often very difficult and in some cases simply obscure, and the writers frequently disagreed with each other. Yet all of them in one way or another questioned the primacy of reason and scientific understanding as ways of coming to grips with the human situation. Heidegger went so far as to argue, "Thinking only begins at the point where we have come to know that Reason, glorified for centuries, is the most obstinate adversary of thinking." [2] The tradition of the Enlightenment suggested that analysis or the separation of human experience into its component parts was the proper path to understanding. Existential writers

1 Quoted in Walter Kaufmann (Ed.), *Existentialism from Dostoevsky to Sartre* (Cleveland: The World Publishing Company, 1962), p. 18.

2 Quoted in William Barrett, *Irrational Man* (Garden City, N.Y.: Doubleday, 1962), p. 20.

Sartre Discusses the Character of His Existentialism

Jean-Paul Sartre, dramatist and philosopher, is the most important French contemporary existentialist. He is widely read in European and American universities. In the first paragraph of this 1946 statement Sartre asserts that all human beings must experience a sense of anguish or the most extreme anxiety when undertaking a major commitment. That anguish arises because consciously or unconsciously they are deciding whether all human beings should make the same decision. In the second paragraph he argues that the existence or non-existence of God would make no difference for human affairs. What humankind must do is to discover the character of its own situation by itself.

THE *existentialist frankly states that man is in anguish. His meaning is as follows—When a man commits himself to anything, fully realizing that he is not only choosing what he will be, but is thereby at the same time a legislator deciding for the whole of mankind—in such a moment a man cannot escape from the sense of complete and profound responsibility. There are many, indeed, who show no such anxiety. But we affirm that they are merely disguising their anguish or are in flight from it. Certainly, many people think that in what they are doing they commit no one but themselves to anything: and if you ask them, "What would happen if everyone did so?" they shrug their shoulders and reply, "Everyone does not do so." But in truth, one ought always to ask oneself what would happen if everyone did as one is doing; nor can one escape from that disturbing thought except by a kind of self-deception. The man who lies in self-excuse, by saying "Everyone will not do it" must be ill at ease in his conscience, for the act of lying implies the universal value which it denies. By its very disguise his anguish reveals itself.*

. . . .

Existentialism is nothing else but an attempt to draw the full conclusions from a consistently atheistic position. Its intention is not in the least that of plunging men into despair. And if by despair one means—as the Christians do—any attitude of unbelief, the despair of the existentialist is something different. Existentialism is not atheist in the sense that it would exhaust itself in demonstration of the non-existence of God. It declares, rather, that even if God existed that would make no difference from its point of view. Not that we believe God does exist, but we think that the real problem is not that of His existence; what man needs is to find himself again and to understand that nothing can save him from himself, not even a valid proof of the existence of God. In this sense existen-

Jean-Paul Sartre and Simone de Beauvoir (born 1908) have been two leading French intellectuals of the mid-century. His is a major voice of the existentialist movement, and she has written extensively on the social position, experience, and psychology of women, as well as on other social and philosophical issues. [United Press International Photo.]

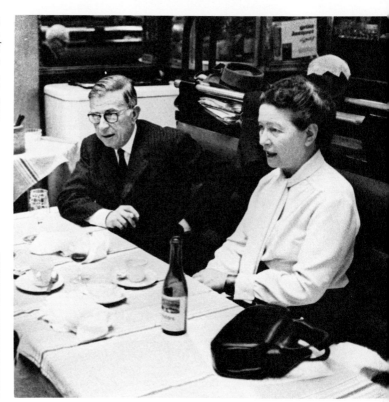

tialism is optimistic. It is a doctrine of action, and it is only by self-deception, by confusing their own despair with ours that Christians can describe us as without hope.

Jean-Paul Sartre, *Existentialism and Humanism*, trans. by Philip Mairet (London: Methuen, 1960), in Walter Kaufman, ed., *Existentialism from Dostoevsky to Sartre* (New York: Meridian Books, Inc., 1956), pp. 292, 310–311.

rejected this approach. They argued that the human condition was greater than the sum of its parts and must be grasped as a whole.

The Romantic writers of the early nineteenth century had also questioned the primacy of reason, but they did so in a much less radical manner than the existentialists. The Romantics emphasized the imagination and intuition, but the existentialists tended to dwell primarily on the extremes of human experience. Death, dread, fear, and anxiety provided their themes. The titles of their works illustrate their sense of forboding and alienation: *Existence and Time* (1962) by Heidegger; *Nausea* (1938) and *Being and Nothingness* (1943) by Sartre; *The Plague* (1947) and *The Stranger* (1942) by Camus. The touchstone of philosophic truth became the experience of individual human beings under such extreme situations. The existentialists saw human beings as compelled to formulate their own ethical values rather than being able to find ethical guidance from traditional religion, rational philosophy, intuition, or social customs. This opportunity and necessity to lay down values for oneself became the dreadful freedom of existentialist philosophy.

In large measure the existentialists were protesting against a world in which reason, technology, and the rational policies of war and genocide had produced unreasonable results. Their thought reflected the uncertainty of social institutions and ethical values that existed during the era of the two world wars. However, since the

sixties their thought has become the subject of study in universities throughout the world. They will probably continue to be subjects of philosophy and literature classes, but it seems unlikely that they will again achieve their former popularity. In that respect their demise reflects the relative prosperity and material comfort achieved by a growing majority of Europeans during the last quarter century. The new generation of Europeans born after World War II has not known the experiences that gave rise to existential philosophy. Existentialism was the philosophy of the political and social crisis of Europe in the first half of the twentieth century. As the perceived crisis passed, so also has the immediate influence of existentialism.

Intellectuals and Politics

After World War I writers, philosophers, critics, and artists throughout Europe believed that a new course had to be set for their culture. Many of them thought that the political values and institutions of liberal democracy had failed. Liberalism had neither prevented the war nor achieved a minimum standard of decent living for the general population. Conservative intellectuals saw liberalism as fostering social and political unrest and undermining national greatness. Consequently considerable numbers of intellectuals during the twenties and the thirties felt that they must align themselves with either

The Unknown Political Prisoner, by the Italian sculptor Luciano Minguzzi, is an expressionist work that takes up the theme of hopeless entrapment. Its title identifies it socially with the experience of millions of Europeans under authoritarian regimes. [The Tate Gallery, London.]

fascism or communism. Political ideology had become the order of the day. Art, literature, and philosophy were subordinated to political ends.

Hitler and Mussolini attracted numerous intellectuals and university teachers to support their policies. Some of these writers were little more than paid literary hacks, but others were persons of considerable standing in the university community. However, the most important political movement to attract the allegiance of twentieth-century European intellectuals was communism. It seemed to provide a very direct manner of dealing with the social question and a vehicle for opposing the spread of fascism.

As the liberal democracies floundered in depression and as right-wing regimes spread across the continent, communism seemed to many people at the time a way to protect humane values. Throughout Europe students in the universities affiliated with the Communist Party. They and older intellectuals visited the Soviet Union and praised Stalin's achievements. Some of these writers did not know of Stalin's terror; others simply closed their eyes to it, somehow believing that humane ends might come from inhumane methods. During the late twenties and the thirties communism became little less than a substitute religion. One group of former Communists, writing after World War II, described their attraction and later disillusionment with communism in a book entitled *The God That Failed* (1949).

The Russian Revolution and its later developments led both to the attraction of intellectuals to communism and eventually to their later rejection of the ideology. In Russia the revolution had seemed to construct a new social order in the name and on the behalf of the proletariat. Under Lenin there had occurred a brief period of literary and artistic experimentation. Later the Soviet Union had also taken a lead in opposing fascism. However, the revolution had also split the ranks of socialists between communists and "democratic" socialists. Many writers and philosophers of left-wing orientation had chosen communism because of its discipline and because of its proved success in Russia. But as the brutal nature of Stalinism became known, numerous intellectuals attempted to set distance between themselves and the Soviet experiment.

Four events proved crucial to the disillusionment of the intellectuals. These were the great public purge trials of 1936 and later, the Spanish Civil War (1936–1939), the Nazi–Soviet Pact of 1939, and the Soviet invasion of Hungary in 1956. Arthur Koestler's *Darkness at Noon* (1940) recorded a former communist's view of the purges. George Orwell, who had never been a communist but who had sympathized, presented the disappointment with Stalin's policy in Spain in *Homage to Catalonia* (1938). The Nazi–Soviet Pact removed the image of Stalin as an opponent of fascism. Jean-Paul Sartre long put faith in the Soviet Union, but the Hungarian invasion cooled his ardor.

Yet disillusionment with the Soviet Union or with Stalin did not in all cases mean disillusionment with Marxism or with a radical socialist critique of European society. Some writers and social critics looked to the establishment of alternative communist governments based on non-Soviet modes. During the decade after World War II Yugoslavia provided such a different model. Since the late fifties radical students and intellectuals have looked for inspiration to the Chinese Revolution. Still other groups have hoped for the development of a European Marxist system. Among the more important

Karl Barth was the Swiss theologian whose books, appearing shortly after World War I, were part of a Protestant theological revival. [United Press International Photo.]

contributors to this non-Soviet tradition was the Italian communist Antonio Gramsci (1891–1937) and his work *Letters from Prison* (published posthumously in 1947). The thought of such non-Soviet communists has become very important to West European communist parties, such as that of Italy, which hope to gain office democratically.

Another mode of Marxist accommodation within mid-twentieth-century European thought has been a redefinition of the basic message of Marx himself. During the 1930s a considerable body of previously unprinted essays by Marx was published. These books and articles are quite abstract and philosophical and were written by Marx before *The Communist Manifesto* of 1848. They make the "young Marx" appear to belong more nearly to the humanist rather than to the revolutionary tradition of European thought. Since World War II these works, including *Philosophic Manuscripts of 1844* and *German Ideology*, have been widely read. Today many people are more familiar with them than with the *Manifesto* or *Capital*. The writings of young Marx have allowed many people to consider themselves sympathetic to Marxism without also seeing themselves as revolutionaries or supporters of the Soviet Union.

In effect, by the last quarter of this century Marxism and even communism have become fragmented. Politically their supporters stand divided in loyalty to the differing models of the Soviet Union, China, Yugoslavia, and others in the non-European world. Ideologically there are divisions among Soviet ideologues, Maoists, and the more independent thinkers of Western Europe. Yet in its various forms Marxism still remains probably the single most influential tradition of political thought in Europe today. Even for people who may not wish a communist state, Marxism has come to provide a vehicle for the criticism of contemporary European society. Moreover the impact of various modes of Marxist thought in the non-European world may now constitute the most important Western influence in the postcolonial age.

The Christian Heritage

In most ways Christianity has continued to be hard-pressed during the twentieth century. Material prosperity and political ideologies have replaced the faith as the dominant factors in many people's lives. However, despite their loss of much popular support and former legal privileges, the Christian churches still exercise considerable social and political influence. In Germany the Protestant churches were one of the few major institutions not wholly conquered by the Nazis. Lutheran clergymen, such as Martin Niemoller and Dietrich Bonhoffer, were leaders of the opposition to Hitler. After the war, in Poland and elsewhere in eastern Europe the Roman Catholic Church actively opposed the influence of communism. In western Europe religious affiliation provided much of the initial basis for the Christian Democratic parties. Across the continent the churches have raised critical questions about colonialism, nuclear weapons, human rights, and other moral issues. Consequently, in the most secular of all ages the Church has affected numerous issues of state.

A theological revival also took place during the first half of the century. Nineteenth-century theologians had frequently softened the concept of sin and had tended to portray human nature as not too far removed from the divine. The horror of World War I destroyed that optimistic faith. Many Europeans felt that evil had stalked the continent.

The most important Christian response to this experience was the theology of Karl Barth (1886–1968). In 1919 this Swiss pastor published *A Commentary on the Epistle to the Romans*, which reemphasized the transcendence of God and the dependence of humankind upon the divine. Barth portrayed God as wholly other than, and different from, humankind. In a sense Barth was returning to the Reformation theology of Luther, but the work of Kierkegaard had profoundly influenced his reading of the reformer. Barth, like the Danish writer,

[*Text continued on page 984*]

Two approaches to contemporary architecture are seen in these contrasting churches, where modern design is in service of age-old modes of Christian worship. [BELOW] The interior of the Church of Notre Dame at Le Raincy near Paris (1922) was designed by Auguste Perret (1874–1954). It is a high point in the new technology of architectural use of reinforced concrete. [OPPOSITE] The Church of the Holy Family in Barcelona is a major work of Spanish architect Antonio Gaudi (1852–1926). Rounded, growing forms characterize this structure, and it is still far from complete. [BELOW: French Cultural Services, New York. OPPOSITE: Spanish National Tourist Office, New York.]

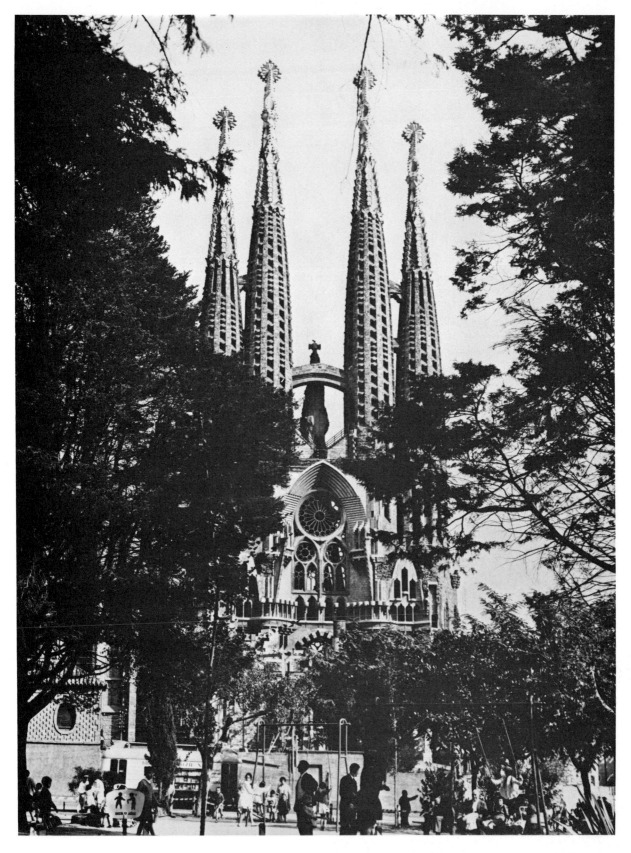

regarded the lived experience of men and women as the best testimony to the truth of his theology. Those extreme moments of life described by Kierkegaard provided the basis for a real knowledge of humankind's need for God. This view totally challenged much nineteenth-century writing about human nature. Barth's theology, which became known as *neo-orthodoxy*, proved to be very influential throughout the West in the wake of new political disasters and human suffering.

Liberal theology, however, was not swept away by neo-orthodoxy. The German–American Paul Tillich (1886–1965) was the most important liberal theologian. He looked to a theology of culture and tended to regard religion as a human rather than a divine phenomenon. Whereas Barth saw God as dwelling outside humankind, Tillich believed that evidence of the divine had to be sought from within human nature and human culture. Other liberal theologians, such as Rudolf Bultmann (1884–1919), continued to work out the problems of naturalism and supernaturalism that had plagued earlier writers. His major writing took place prior to World War II but was popularized thereafter in Anglican Bishop John Robinson's *Honest to God* (1963). Another liberal Christian writer from Britain, C. S. Lewis (1878–1963), attracted millions of readers during and after World War II. He was a layman and his books were often in the form of letters or short stories. His most famous work is *The Screwtape Letters* (1942).

Perhaps the most significant postwar religious departures occurred within the Roman Catholic Church. Pope John XXIII (1958–1963) undertook the most extensive changes to occur in Catholicism for over a century and some would say since the Council of Trent in the sixteenth century. In 1959 Pope John summoned the twenty-first ecumenical council of the church to be called since the series started under the emperor Constantine in the fourth century. It was known as Vatican II. He died before it had completed its work; but his successor, Pope Paul VI, continued the council, which met between 1962 and 1965. Among the numerous changes in liturgy, the

mass became celebrated in the vernacular. Free relations were established with other Christian denominations. More power was shared with bishops. Pope Paul also appointed a number of cardinals from nations of the former colonial world. For a brief time it seemed that Catholicism might experience a genuine revival. However, after having taken these very liberal moves, the pope firmly upheld the celibacy of priests and maintained the church's prohibition on contraception. The former position caused many men and women to leave the priesthood and religious orders. Many of the laity have deeply resented the policy on family planning. Today,

---

Hans Küng Expresses His Hopes for Vatican II

Küng (born 1928) is one of the most important post–World War II liberal Roman Catholic theologians. In a book written in 1961, shortly before Vatican II, this Swiss theologian spoke of the opportunity for Christian renewal that the calling of the Council presented.

INSOFAR *as the Church is constantly, repeatedly deformed, she has to be constantly, repeatedly reformed. . . .*

But reform is necessary not only because of deformation. Fundamentally, it is not just a negative matter of house-cleaning and repairs, but a vast positive task of constructive building. It is not only because there are mistaken developments and mistaken attitudes in the Church that she has this task. Even if there were none (there always will be) the Church would still have the great task of renewal. For the mustard seed must grow. The Church . . . is in the stream of time: she has to keep adopting new forms, new embodiments. She has to keep giving herself a new form, a new shape in history; she is never simply finished and complete. She must go into all the world and preach the good news to every creature . . . , to all nations, to all cultures, to all ages, until Christ comes again. Such is her incomparably happy mission. Hence she is forever faced afresh with the task of renewing herself. Hence, again, this renewal is not just something which she stringently must *do, but which she joyously* may *do; a joyful service to the Kingdom of God, looking toward him who will make all* things new, *a new heaven and a new earth. The Pope's summons to renew the Church is, most solemnly and truly, a joyful summons.*

Hans Küng, *The Council, Reform, and Reunion*, trans. by Cecily Hastings (New York: Sheed and Ward, 1961), p. 36.

Pope Paul VI (1963–1978) at the altar of Saint Peter's in Rome presides over a session of the Second Vatican Council. The gathering initiated more changes in the Roman Catholic Church than had any development since the Council of Trent in the sixteenth century. [Archivio Fotografico, Musei Vaticani.]

John Paul II became pope October 17, 1978 after the brief thirty-four-day reign of John Paul I. In more than one way the choice of the new pope is epoch-making. At 58 he is the youngest pontiff since Pius IX. More important, he is the first non-Italian to hold the position since the sixteenth century; and, being Polish, he brings personal experience with the eastern, communist-dominated areas of Europe to the papacy for the first time. [United Press International Photo.]

after having made numerous important accommodations, the Roman Catholic Church still remains at odds with much of the spirit of modernity.

Toward the Twenty-first Century

A century ago a book like this one might have concluded with a statement of the superiority of Western over all other cultures. In that hundred years the position of Europe in power politics has changed. The century has seen vast destruction and inhumanity. Consequently this volume must conclude with a statement of the continuity of Western culture with its past, its potential for new creativity, and its capacity for new interaction with other cultures.

Europeans have not outgrown their history. Many of the formative influences traced in this volume continue to hold sway. For some observers technology may appear to be an enemy and a threat to the environment, but science touches in a positive manner the lives of more people than even fifty years ago might have been imagined. And it will be from scientific understanding that the problems of the environment and of resource shortages will be solved. Although many intellectuals have praised the irrational,

BELOW: Recumbent Figure, by the English sculptor Henry Moore (born 1898), uses basic shapes and materials in a traditional manner, but it exemplifies the twentieth-century search for new perspectives on human nature and on physical nature. Although the statue is clearly modern, its "eroded" form suggests less separation from past culture than do many contemporary works. [The Tate Gallery, London.]

rationalism in the processes of everyday life has never been more present, and the use of reason still promises the best hope of humankind. Since World War II the problems of constitutional order and human rights have continued to be major concerns of political life and discussion. Within both communist and noncommunist Europe the spirit of criticism still thrives, though in very different ways.

These persistent features of European life have not assured that its civilization, as well as the results flowing from it, will be morally good, but they have meant that it has possessed in itself the possibility of correcting itself and of raising the questions of what are the good life and the good society. The possibility of asking those questions is necessary before the desired improvement and reform can be attained. Perhaps the chief carriers of Western culture today are those within its midst who most criticize it and demand that it justify itself.

SUGGESTED READINGS

W. M. Abbott (Ed.), *The Documents of Vatican II* (1966). A useful way of looking at the changes in contemporary Catholicism.

R. Aron, *The Opium of the Intellectuals* (1957). A critical discussion of Communism and the intellectual community.

B. Barber, *Science and the Social Order* (1952). A good introduction to the institutional impact of science in this century.

W. Barrett, *Irrational Man* (1958). A sound treatment of existentialism in its broader intellectual context.

F. L. Baumer, *Modern European Thought: Continuity and Change in Ideas, 1600–1950* (1977). Excellent chapters on this century.

R. Crossman (Ed.), *The God That Failed* (1949). Essays from former Communist intellectuals.

W. P. Dizard, *Television: A World Review* (1966). A useful discussion of an important topic.

D. Fleming and B. Bailyn (Eds.), *The Intellectual Migration: Europe and America, 1930–1960* (1969). An important collection of essays on the migration of European intellectuals to the United States largely due to the political situation in twentieth-century Europe.

E. Fromm (Ed.), *Socialist Humanism: An International Symposium* (1965). Essays dealing with humanistic approaches to Marxism.

H. S. Hughes, *The Obstructed Path: French Social Thought in the Years of Desperation, 1930–1960* (1968). A book that well illustrates the fragmentation of twentieth-century thought.

M. Jay, *The Dialectical Imagination* (1973). An important work on the development of Marxist thought among German intellectuals.

W. Kaufmann (Ed.), *Existentialism from Dostoevsky to Sartre* (1956). An excellent introduction to this movement of thought.

J. Passmore, *A Hundred Years of Philosophy* (1968). An exceptionally fine one-volume history.

S. P. Schilling, *Contemporary Continental Theologians* (1966). A basic survey of modern theology.

R. N. Stromberg, *After Everything: Western Intellectual History Since 1945* (1975). A lively and thoughtful account of a very difficult subject.

W. Wagar (Ed.), *European Intellectual History Since Darwin and Marx* (1966). A collection of high-quality essays.

W. Wagar (Ed.), *Science, Faith, and Man: European Thought Since 1914* (1968). A collection of documents with good introductions.

Appendix
SOME PRINCIPAL EMPERORS, KINGS, AND POPES

ROMAN EMPIRE

Augustus	27 B.C.–A.D. 14
Tiberius	14– 37
Caligula	37– 41
Claudius	41– 54
Nero	54– 68
Vespasian	69– 79
Titus	79– 81
Domitian	81– 96
Trajan	98–117
Hadrian	117–138
Antoninus Pius	138–161
Marcus Aurelius	161–180
Commodus	180–193
Septimius Severus	193–211
Caracalla	211–217
Elagabalus	218–222
Severus Alexander	222–235
Philip the Arab	244–249
Decius	249–251
Valerian	253–260
Gallienus	260–268
Aurelian	270–275
Diocletian	284–286

WEST		EAST	
Maximian	286–305	Diocletian	284–305
Constantius	305–306	Galerius	305–311
		Maximius	308–313
		Licinius	308–324
Constantine	308–337	Constantine	324–337
Maxentius	307–312		
Constantine II	337–340		
Constans	337–350		
Constantius II	351–361	Constantius II	337–361
Julian	360–363	Julian	361–363
Jovian	363–364	Jovian	363–364
Valentinian	364–375	Valens	364–378
Gratian	375–383		
Valentinian II	383–392		
Theodosius	394–395	Theodosius	379–395

CAROLINGIAN KINGDOM

Pepin, Mayor of the Palace	680–714
Charles Martel, Mayor of the Palace	715–741
Pepin the Short, Mayor of the Palace	741–751
Pepin the Short, King	751–768
Charlemagne and Carloman, Joint Kings	768–771
Charlemagne, King	771–814
Charlemagne, Emperor	800–814
Louis the Pious, Emperor	814–840

WEST FRANKS	LOTHARINGIA	EAST FRANKS
Charles the Bald 840–877	Lothar 840–855	Louis the German
Louis II the Stammerer 877–879	Louis II 855–875	840–876
	Charles 855–863	Carloman 876–880
	Lothar II 855–869	
Louis III 879–882		Louis 876–882
Carloman 879–884		Charles the Fat 884–887

WEST		EAST	
Honorius	395–423	Arcadius	393–408
		Theodosius II	408–450
Valentinian III	425–455	Marcian	450–457
		Leo	457–474
Romulus	475–476	Zeno	474–491
		Anastasius	491–518
		Justin	518–527
		Justinian	527–565

i

HOLY ROMAN EMPIRE

SAXONS

Henry the Fowler	
	919– 936
Otto I	962– 973
Otto II	973– 983
Otto III	983–1002

SALIANS

Conrad II	1024–1039
Henry III	1039–1056
Henry IV	1056–1106
Henry V	1106–1125
Lothar II	1125–1137

HOHENSTAUFENS

Frederick I Barbarossa	
	1152–1190
Henry VI	1190–1197
Philip of Swabia	
	1198–1208
Otto IV (*Welf*)	
	1198–1215
Frederick II	1215–1250
Conrad IV	1250–1254

LUXEMBURG, HAPSBURG, AND OTHER DYNASTIES

Rudolf of Hapsburg	
	1273–1291
Adolph of Nassau	
	1292–1298
Albert of Austria	
	1298–1308
Henry VII of Luxemburg	1308–1313
Ludwig IV of Bavaria	
	1314–1347
Charles IV	1347–1378
Wenceslas	1378–1400
Rupert	1400–1410
Sigismund	1410–1437

HAPSBURGS

Frederick III	1440–1493
Maximilian I	1493–1519
Charles V	1519–1556
Ferdinand I	1556–1564
Maximilian II	1564–1576
Rudolf II	1576–1612
Matthias	1612–1619
Ferdinand II	1619–1637
Ferdinand III	1637–1657
Leopold I	1658–1705
Joseph I	1705–1711
Charles VI	1711–1740
Charles VII	1742–1745
Francis I	1745–1765
Joseph II	1765–1790
Leopold II	1790–1792
Francis II	1792–1806

THE PAPACY

Leo I	440– 461
Gregory I	590– 604
Nicholas I	858– 867
Silvester II	999–1003
Leo IX	1049–1054
Nicholas II	1058–1061
Gregory VII	1073–1085
Urban II	1088–1099
Paschal II	1099–1118
Alexander III	1159–1181
Innocent III	1198–1216
Gregory IX	1227–1241
Boniface VIII	1294–1303
John XXII	1316–1334
Gregory XI	1370–1378
Martin V	1417–1431
Eugenius IV	1431–1447
Nicholas V	1447–1455
Pius II	1458–1464
Alexander VI	1492–1503
Julius II	1503–1513
Leo X	1513–1521
Adrian VI	1522–1523
Clement VII	1523–1534
Paul III	1534–1549
Paul IV	1555–1559
Pius V	1566–1572
Gregory XIII	1572–1585
Pius VII	1800–1823
Gregory XVI	1831–1846
Pius IX	1846–1878
Leo XIII	1878–1903
Pius X	1903–1914
Benedict XV	1914–1922
Pius XI	1922–1939
Pius XII	1939–1958
John XXIII	1958–1963
Paul VI	1963–1978
John Paul I	1978
John Paul II	1978–

Appendix: Some Principal Emperors, Kings, and Popes

ENGLAND

ANGLO-SAXONS

Alfred the Great
             871– 900
Ethelred the Unready
            978–1016
Canute (*Danish*)
           1016–1035
Harold I   1035–1040
Hardicanute 1040–1042
Edward the Confessor
           1042–1066
Harold II   1066

NORMANS

William the Conqueror
           1066–1087
William II   1087–1100
Henry I   1100–1135
Stephen   1135–1154

ANGEVINS

Henry II   1154–1189
Richard I   1189–1199
John   1199–1216
Henry III   1216–1272
Edward I   1272–1307
Edward II   1307–1327
Edward III   1327–1377
Richard II   1377–1399

HOUSES OF LANCASTER AND YORK

Henry IV   1399–1413
Henry V   1413–1422
Henry VI   1422–1461
Edward IV   1461–1483
Edward V   1483
Richard III 1483–1485

TUDORS

Henry VII   1485–1509
Henry VIII 1509–1547
Edward VI   1547–1553
Mary I   1553–1558
Elizabeth I 1558–1603

STUARTS

James I   1603–1625
Charles I   1625–1649
Charles II   1660–1685
James II   1685–1688
William III and Mary II
           1689–1694
William III alone
           1694–1702
Anne   1702–1714

HANOVERIANS (from 1917, WINDSORS)

George I   1714–1727
George II   1727–1760
George III   1760–1820
George IV   1820–1830
William IV 1830–1837
Victoria   1837–1901
Edward VII 1901–1910
George V   1910–1936
Edward VIII   1936
George VI   1936–1952
Elizabeth II 1952–

FRANCE

CAPETIANS

Hugh Capet 987– 996
Robert II the Pious
            996–1031
Henry I   1031–1060
Philip I   1060–1108
Louis VI   1108–1137
Louis VII   1137–1180
Philip II Augustus
           1180–1223
Louis VIII 1223–1226
Louis IX   1226–1270
Philip III   1270–1285
Philip IV   1285–1314
Louis X   1314–1316
Philip V   1316–1322
Charles IV 1322–1328

VALOIS

Philip VI   1328–1350
John   1350–1364
Charles V   1364–1380
Charles VI 1380–1422
Charles VII 1422–1461
Louis XI   1461–1483
Charles VIII 1483–1498
Louis XII   1498–1515
Francis I   1515–1547
Henry II   1547–1559
Francis II   1559–1560
Charles IX 1560–1574
Henry III   1574–1589

BOURBONS

Henry IV   1589–1610
Louis XIII 1610–1643
Louis XIV 1643–1715
Louis XV   1715–1774
Louis XVI 1774–1792

POST 1792

Napoleon I, Emperor
           1804–1814
Louis XVIII (*Bourbon*)
           1814–1824
Charles X (*Bourbon*)
           1824–1830
Louis Philippe (*Bourbon-Orléans*) 1830–1848
Napoleon III, Emperor
           1851–1870

Appendix: Some Principal Emperors, Kings, and Popes   **iii**

SPAIN

Ferdinand and	1479–1516
Isabella	1479–1504

HAPSBURGS

Philip I	1504–1506
Charles I (Holy Roman Emperor as Charles V)	1506–1556
Philip II	1556–1598
Philip III	1598–1621
Philip IV	1621–1665
Charles II	1665–1700

BOURBONS

Philip V	1700–1746
Ferdinand VI	1746–1759
Charles III	1759–1788
Charles IV	1788–1808
Ferdinand VII	1808
Joseph Bonaparte	1808–1813
Ferdinand VII (restored)	1814–1833
Isabella II	1833–1868
Amadeo	1870–1873
Alfonso XII	1874–1885
Alfonso XIII	1886–1931
Juan Carlos I	1975–

AUSTRIA AND AUSTRIA-HUNGARY

(Until 1806 all except Maria Theresa were also Holy Roman Emperors.)

Maximilian I, Archduke	1493–1519
Charles I (Emperor as Charles V)	1519–1556
Ferdinand I	1556–1564
Maximilian II	1564–1576
Rudolf II	1576–1612
Matthias	1612–1619
Ferdinand II	1619–1637
Ferdinand III	1637–1657
Leopold I	1658–1705
Joseph I	1705–1711
Charles VI	1711–1740
Maria Theresa	1740–1780
Joseph II	1780–1790
Leopold II	1790–1792
Francis II	1792–1835
Ferdinand I	1835–1848
Francis Joseph	1848–1916
Charles I	1916–1918

PRUSSIA AND GERMANY

HOHENZOLLERNS

Frederick William the Great Elector	1640–1688
Frederick I	1701–1713
Frederick William I	1713–1740
Frederick II the Great	1740–1786
Frederick William II	1786–1797
Frederick William III	1797–1840
Frederick William IV	1840–1861
William I	1861–1888
Frederick III	1888
William II	1888–1918

RUSSIA

Ivan III	1462–1505
Basil III	1505–1533
Ivan IV the Terrible	1533–1584
Theodore I	1584–1598
Boris Godunov	1598–1605
Theodore II	1605
Basil IV	1606–1610

ROMANOVS

Michael	1613–1645
Alexius	1645–1676
Theodore III	1676–1682
Ivan IV and Peter I	1682–1689
Peter I the Great alone	1689–1725
Catherine I	1725–1727
Peter II	1727–1730
Anna	1730–1740
Ivan VI	1740–1741
Elizabeth	1741–1762
Peter III	1762
Catherine II the Great	1762–1796
Paul	1796–1801
Alexander I	1801–1825
Nicholas I	1825–1855
Alexander II	1855–1881
Alexander III	1881–1894
Nicholas II	1894–1917

ITALY

Victor Emmanuel II	1861–1878
Humbert I	1878–1900
Victor Emmanuel III	1900–1946
Humbert II	1946

Index

Entries relating to the color album are preceded by the letter C.

Lenin Nikolai (Vladimir Ilich Ulyanov), 688, 762, 763, 796, 827–829, 832, 861–864
Leningrad, 512, 908
Leo I, Pope, 237–238
Leo III, Pope, 239, 243, 306
Leo III the Isaurian, 234, 239
Leo IX, Pope, 239, 261
Leo X, Pope, 373, 390
Leo XIII, Pope, 776–777, 779
Leonardo da Vinci, 346, 347, 356
Leonidas, 69
Leopold I of Austria, 457, 458, 503
Leopold II of Austria, 586, 605
Leopold of Hohenzollen-Sigmaringen, 713
Leopold of Saxe-Coburg, 668
Leotychidas, 71
Lepanto, battle of (1571), 409, 415, 417, 424, 474, C15
Le Petit Journal, 770
Lepidus, M. Aemilius, 160, 162
Leptis Magna, 209
Lesbos, 62, 77
Lessing, Gotthold, 572, 576, 628
Letters from Prison, 981
Letters on the English, 569
Leucippus, 94, 114
Leuctra, 84, 85
Leuger, Karl, 792, 852
Levée en masse, 611, 616
Lewis, C. S., 984
Lexington, 560
Liaotung peninsula, 803
Liberal arts, 246, 268–269, 284, 340–341
  and Protestant educational reform, 399
Liberalism, defined, 660–662
Liberia, 798
Liberum veto, 503, 610
Libri Carolini, 243
Libya, 136, 907, 816
Licentia docendi, 268
Licinian-Sextian laws, 132
Liebknecht, Wilhelm, 759
Liège, 675
Liege lord, 254
Life of Jesus, 774
Ligurians, 125
Lille, 461, 675
Limbourg, Pol de, 291, C11
Linacre, Thomas, 366
Linear B script, 38
Linke, Lilo, 850
Lisbon, 361
Literacy, 246, 368, 769–770
Lithuania, 835, 904
Little Entente, 841–842
Liverpool, England, 549, 677
Liverpool, Lord, 653, 669
Livingston, David, 799
Livy, 123, 134, 142, 165, 166, 170, 218, 391
Lloyd George, David, 755, 831–833, 843

Locarno Pact, 839, 855, 897
Locke, John, 445, 484–486, 558, 561, 568, 581, 639
Lodi, Treaty of (1454–1455), 354
Logri, 269, 271
Loiseleur, Nicolas, 318
Lollardy, 369–370, 390
Lombard, Peter, 269, 399
Lombards, 225, 232, 235, 238, 239, 241, 242, 244
Lombardy, 298, 300
London, 287, 532, 740, 906
  Tower of, 335
  Treaty of, 659
London Conference (1913), 820
London Corresponding Society, 609
London Working Men's Association, 682
Longbow, 34
Longhi, Pietro, C19
Lordship, 247, 281, 289
Lorenzo the Magnificent, 340
Lorraine, 457, 714, 821
Lothar I, 249, 250
Lothar II, 250
Lotharingia, 250, 257
Louis II, son of Othar, 250
Louis IV, emperor, 315, 326, 327, 368, 370
Louis VI of France, 296
Louis VII of France, 264, 294, 296
Louis VIII of France, 307, 310
Louis IX of France, Saint, 278, 291, 300, 309–310, 322 323, 324
Louis XI of France, 333
Louis XII of France, 355
Louis XIII of France, 447, 448, 454
Louis XIV of France, 414, 434, 443, 444, 447, 448–461, 489, 569, 620, 906
Louis XV of France, 491–494, 593–594
Louis XVI of France, 593–595, 597–600, 602, 606–607, 608, 649
Louis XVIII of France, 657, 665
Louis Napoleon. *See* Napoleon III
Louis Philippe, 666–668, 684, 694
Louis of Nassau, 409, 419
Louis the German, 249, 250
Louis the Pious, 248–250, 253
Louis, prince of Condé, 408, 409
Louisberg, 555
Louvois, François Michel Le Tellier, marquis of, 456
Lovejoy, Arthur O., 638
Lovett, William, 682
Low, David, 904, 906
Low Countries, 810
Lublin, 924
Lucan, 183
Lucaria, 136
Lucerne, 376
Lucinde, 643
Lucretius, 168, 169

Ludendorff, General Erich, 823, 829, 853
Luder, Peter, 366
Ludwig II of Bavaria, C25
Luftwaffe, 907
Luneville, Treaty of, 621
Lusitania, 825
Luther, Martin, 343, 366, 367, 371–374, 387, 393, 395, 400, 410, 662, 981
  Catechism of, 398
Lutheranism, 393, 403, 410, 427–428
Lützen, battle of (1632), 432
Luxembourg, 820, 904, 930
Lyceum (Peripatos), 103, 114
Lycurgus, 51, 52
Lydia, 63, 66
Lyell, Charles, 771, 775
Lyons, 333, 668, 675
  Council of (1274), 322
Lyrical Ballads, 641
Lysander, 83, 84
Lysippus of Sicyon, 99
Lytton Report, 896

M

MacArthur, General Douglas, 940–941
Macaulay, Thomas B., 670
MacDonald, Ramsay, 843, 874–875
Macedon (Macedonia), 45, 75, 82, 85, 103, 107–114, 116, 142, 144, 160, 816
Macedonian dynasty of Byzantine emperors, 234
Macedonian Wars, 142–143
Machiavelli, Niccoló, 340, 343, 356
Mack, Ernst, 780
MacMahon, Marshal Marie Edwé, 719–720
Macmillan, Harold, 951–952
Madagascar, 910
Madame Bovary, 773, 783
Madrid, 899
  population of, 740
Maecenas, 162, 169, 170
Magdeburg, 382
Magellan, Ferdinand, 363
Magenta, 709
Maginot Line, 898, 902, 904, 905
Magna Carta (1215), 265, 295, 296, 300, 316
Magna Graecia, 45
Magnesia, 142
Magyar, 251, 552, 699, 722–724, 835
Mainz, 361
  archbishopric of, 335
Maison Carée at Nimes, 178
Malaya, 802, 911, 913
Malenkov, Georgi, 964, 966
Malleus Maleficarum (1485–1486), 285
Mallus, 245
Malplaquet, battle of (1709), 460
Malta, 136, 939
Malthus, Thomas, 683–684, 771
Mamertines, 136